THE ROUGH GUIDE TO

Provence
& the Côte d'Azur

written and researched by

Neville Walker and Greg Ward

ROUGH GUIDES

roughguides.com

Contents

Introduction to

Provence
& the Côte d'Azur

The ancient Provençal version of Genesis maintains that prior to introducing Adam to the world, the Creator realized that he had several materials left over; large expanses of celestial blue; rocks of all kinds, shapes and colours; rich soil that was bursting with seeds; and a full spectrum of as-yet unused tastes and smells that ranged from the most subtle and delicate to the most powerful. "Well," He thought, "why don't I make a beautiful résumé of my world, my own special paradise?" And so it was that Provence came into being.

This paradise encompasses the snow-peaked lower Alps and their foothills, which in the east descend right to the sea, and to the west extend almost to the Rhône. In central Provence, the wild, high plateaux are cut by the deepest gorge in all Europe – the Grand Canyon du Verdon. The coastal hinterland is made up of range after range of steep, forested hills, while the shore is an ever-changing series of geometric bays giving way to chaotic outcrops of glimmering rock and deep, narrow inlets, like miniature fjords – the *calanques*. All these elements would count for nothing, however, were it not for the magical Mediterranean light. At its best in spring and autumn, it is both soft and brightly theatrical, as if some expert had rigged the lighting for each landscape for maximum colour and definition with minimum glare.

Food and wine are the other great pleasures of Provence. Local-grown produce – olives and garlic, asparagus and courgettes, grapes, melons and strawberries, *cèpe* and *morille* mushrooms, almonds and sweet chestnuts, basil and wild thyme – forms an integral part of the region's simple, healthy cuisine, while Provençal wines range from the dry, light rosés of the Côtes de Provence and Bandol to the deep and delicate reds of the Côtes du Rhône and Châteauneuf-du-Pape.

Such earthly pleasures, however, have been both a blessing and a curse. Successive waves of invaders and visitors have found the paradise they sought in Provence, and at the height of summer on the Riviera finding an unoccupied strip of beach can seem a far-fetched dream.

ABOVE ROUSSILLON **OPPOSITE** LAVENDER FIELD IN HAUTE PROVENCE

Where to go

This is a large region, and a diverse one, whose contrasting landscapes encompass the rural fields and villages of inland Provence, the remote mountainous regions of the Alpes-Maritime in the east and north, and the high-rise developments and autoroutes of the Riviera in the south. The capital of the Riviera, **Nice** – a vibrant and intriguing blend of Italianate influence, faded *Belle Époque* splendour and first-class art – makes a perfect base, with wonderful food, affordable accommodation and lively nightlife. North of the city, densely wooded alpine foothills are home to a series of exquisite **villages-perchés** (medieval hilltop villages), while to the east, the lower Corniche links the picturesque seafront towns of **Villefranche**, **St-Jean-Cap-Ferrat** and **Beaulieu**; the higher roads offer some of the most spectacular coastal driving in Europe, en route to the perched village of **Èze** and the tiny principality of **Monaco**. The Riviera's western half claims its best beaches – at jazzy **Juan-les-Pins** and at **Cannes**, a glitzy centre of designer shopping and film.

The Riviera also boasts heavyweight cultural attractions, with highlights including the Picasso museum in **Antibes**, Renoir's house at **Cagnes-sur-Mer** and the superb **Fondation Maeght** and **Fernand Léger** museums in the attractive perched villages of **St-Paul-de-Vence** and **Biot** respectively. The world's perfume capital, **Grasse**, and the ancient town of **Vence**, home to a wonderful chapel that stands as Matisse's final masterpiece, both shelter in the hills behind the busy coastal resorts, while for a real escape from the bustle of the coast, the tranquil **Îles des Lérins** lie just a few kilometres offshore from Cannes.

West of the ancient Massif of the **Esterel**, beyond the Roman towns of **Fréjus** and **St Raphaël**, loom the dark wooded hills of the **Massif des Maures**. Here, the coast is

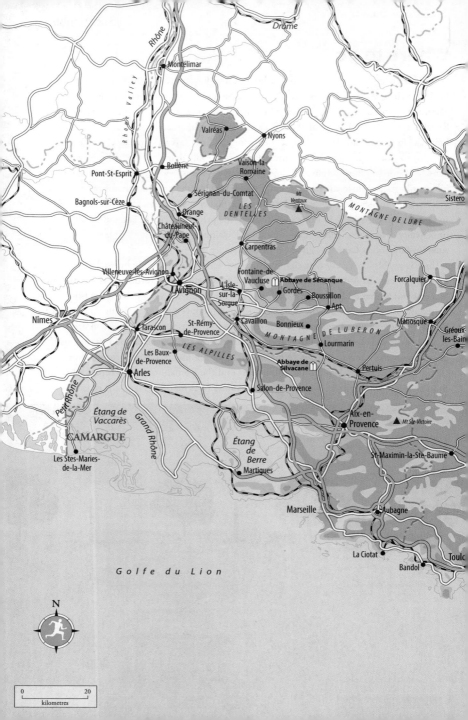

THE ART OF PROVENCE

Since the late nineteenth century, Provence and the Côte d'Azur have been home and inspiration to some of the greatest names of modern art – **Van Gogh**, **Cézanne**, **Renoir**, **Matisse** and **Picasso** among them. The brilliant **southern light** was one of the most influential factors in their work here, with Matisse remarking that, had he gone on painting in the north, "there would have been cloudiness, greys, colours shading off into the distance…". Instead, during his time in Nice he produced some of his most famous, colourful works, such as *Interior with Egyptian Curtains* (*Le Rideau égyptien*) and *Icarus* (*Icare*). It was in Provence too, in Arles and St-Rémy, that Van Gogh fully developed his distinct style of bright, contrasting colours. His landscapes of olive trees, cypresses and harvest scenes, such as *La Sieste* and *Champ de Blé et Cyprès* (*Wheat Field With Cypresses*), all pay tribute to the intensity of the **Provençal sun**. The painters in turn had a major impact on the region. Hand-in-hand with the writers and socialites who flocked to the Côte d'Azur during the interwar years, their artistic, and touristic, legacy helped to shape the Provence that exists today.

home to the fabled hot spots of **Ste-Maxime** and **St-Tropez**, still a byword for glamour and excess over fifty years after Brigitte Bardot put it firmly on the jetsetters' map. In dramatic contrast, the **Corniche des Maures** stretches to the west, its low-key resorts interspersed with blissfully unspoiled strips of Mediterranean coastline. Beyond lies the original Côte d'Azur resort of **Hyères** with its elegant villas, fascinating old town, and offshore **Îles d'Hyères**, popular with nature lovers, naturists and divers.

Further west, past the great natural harbour of **Toulon** and the superb wine country of the **Bandol** AOP, lies the buzzing metropolis of **Marseille**. The region's largest city, this tough port has overcome its former sleazy reputation to become a lively, cosmopolitan and very likeable spot. On its eastern edge lie the **calanques**, a series of beautiful rocky coves recently declared a national park. In their midst lies the picture-postcard village of **Cassis**, linked to the working port of La Ciotat to the east by the spectacular **Corniche des Crêtes**. North of Marseille is the elegant city of **Aix**, with its handsome stone houses, café-lined boulevards and some of the finest markets in Provence. Cézanne lived and painted here, taking his inspiration from the countryside around the nearby **Mont Ste-Victoire**.

Beyond Aix, the Lower Rhône Valley is home to some of the most ancient cities in Provence. Both romantic **Arles** and tiny **Orange** still boast spectacular Roman structures, while **Avignon**, city of the popes and for centuries one of the great artistic centres of France, remains focused around its immaculately preserved medieval core. The Rhône runs past the vineyards of **Châteauneuf-du-Pape** and the impressive fortifications of **Villeneuve-lès-Avignon**, before meeting the sea at the lagoon-studded marshlands of the **Camargue**, with its rich wildlife including bulls, horses and flamingos.

The **Luberon** region, inland from Marseille, is a fertile rural hinterland whose attractive old villages are now dominated by second-homeowners. Nearby lie the great medieval monasteries of **Silvacane** and

Sénanque. Beyond the plateau de Vaucluse, the mighty **Mont Ventoux** dominates the horizon; a legendary challenge on the Tour de France, it attracts thousands of dedicated amateur cyclists each summer. Immediately west, celebrated wine-producing villages nestle amid the jagged pinnacles of the **Dentelles de Montmirail**.

East of the Luberon, in the Provençal heartland, an archetypal landscape of lavender fields dotted with old stone villages stretches north towards the dramatic **Grand Canyon du Verdon**. Beyond the canyon, narrow **clues**, or gorges, open onto a secret landscape perfect for adventurous activities of all kinds, with the fortified towns of **Entrevaux** and **Colmars** defining the former frontier between France and Savoy. A third fortress town, **Sisteron**, on the Durance, marks the gateway to the mountains and the **Alps** proper, where the delightful town of **Barçelonette** provides skiing in winter and kayaking and hiking in the summer. Stretching south from here towards the **Roya valley** and the border with Italy is the **Parc National du Mercantour**, a genuine wilderness, whose only permanent inhabitants are its wildlife: ibex, chamois, wolves and golden eagles.

When to go

Beware **the coast** at the height of summer. The heat and humidity can be overpowering and the crowds, the exhaust fumes and the costs overwhelming. For **swimming**, the best months are from June to mid-October, while sunbathing can be done any time from **February through to October**. February in particular is a great month on the Côte d'Azur – museums, hotels and restaurants are mostly open, the mimosa is in blossom, and the contrast with northern Europe's climate is at its most delicious.

Much the same applies to inland Provence. The lower Alps are usually under snow from late November to early April. October can erupt in storms that quickly clear, and in May, too, weather can be erratic. In **summer**, the vegetation is at its most barren save for high up in the mountains, though the lavender season tends to last from late June into early August. Wild bilberries and raspberries, purple gentians and leaves turning red to gold are the rewards of **autumn** walks. **Springtime** brings such a profusion of wild flowers you hardly dare to walk. In March, a thousand almond orchards blossom.

| **AVERAGE DAYTIME TEMPERATURES (°C)** | | | | | | | | | | | |
Jan	Feb	Mar	Apr	May	Jun	Jul	Aug	Sep	Oct	Nov	Dec
RHÔNE VALLEY											
7.4	6.7	10.8	15.8	17.3	25.6	27.6	27.6	23.5	16.5	10.4	7.8
RIVIERA/CÔTE D'AZUR											
12.2	11.9	14.2	18.5	20.8	26.6	28.1	28.4	25.2	22.2	16.8	14.1

| **AVERAGE SEA TEMPERATURES (°C)** | | | | | |
May	Jun	Jul	Aug	Sep	Oct
MONTPELLIER TO TOULON					
15	19	19	20	20	17
ÎLE DU LEVANT TO MENTON					
17	19	20	22	22	19

Author picks

Our authors have explored every corner of the region over several decades and here share some of their top tips, favourite sights, hidden gems and quintessential Provençal experiences.

Rural markets Arriving in a charming market town such as Aups (p.208) or Fayence (p.215), to find its streets and squares filled with stalls overflowing with fresh local produce and seasonal delicacies, ranks among the greatest delights of exploring rural Provence.

Provence wildlife Away from the cities, Provence remains (almost) as wild as ever. The mysterious marshlands of the Camargue (p.103) are still home to wild horses and flocks of flamingoes, while mouflon and eagles inhabit the mountainous Parc Nacional du Mercantour (p.225).

Favourite new museum Hilltop Mougins, just outside Cannes, is more famous for cooking than culture, but its fabulous new Musée d'Art Classique (p.314) may change that. As well as Classically inspired modern works, it holds a wonderful collection of ancient armour and weapons, including helmets worn by the foot soldiers of ancient Mesopotamia and Alexander the Great.

Sanary-sur-Mer Fishing boats take pride of place in the perfect little harbour of Sanary-sur-Mer (p.255), a reminder that not everywhere on the coast is geared to the whims of the super-rich. Sanary's strongest associations are with literature, not money.

The Côte d'Azur out of season May can be magical; June and September a treat. Avoid peak season and discover a kinder, gentler Côte d'Azur, where the queues are shorter and the prices generally lower – from St Tropez without tears (p.276) to Nice when it's nice (p.342).

Bandol rosé Rosé is the characteristic wine of the coast, perfect on a warm summer's night with seafood and a seat on the terrace. Head for Bandol (p.252) to discover sublime rosé with a sea view.

> Our author recommendations don't end here. We've flagged up our favourite places – a perfectly sited hotel, an atmospheric café, a special restaurant – throughout the guide, highlighted with the ★ symbol.

FROM TOP MARKET NEAR MONT VENTOUX; FLAMINGOS IN THE CAMARGUE; BANDOL AOP ROSÉ

20
things not to miss

It's not possible to see everything Provence has to offer in one trip – and we don't suggest you try. What follows is a selective taste of the region's highlights: outstanding beaches and ancient sites, natural wonders and colourful festivals. All highlights have a page reference to take you straight into the Guide, where you can find out more. Coloured numbers refer to chapters in the Guide.

1 THE CALANQUES
Page 73
Take a boat trip to these hidden inlets east of Marseille, where the shimmering white rock shelters crystal-clear waters.

2 THE PERCHED VILLAGE OF SIMIANE LA ROTONDE
Page 183
One of the loveliest of the region's *villages-perchés* – medieval villages originally built for defence and now much admired for their maze of streets, mellow stone houses and spectacular settings.

3 ARLES
Page 82
Stroll the same streets as Van Gogh in this romantic, Rhône-side and above all Roman city.

4 WILDLIFE IN THE CAMARGUE
Page 103
Saddle up one of the white Camargue horses and explore this watery marshland on horseback.

9

5 FONDATION MAEGHT
Page 338

Don't miss this highly original art museum, whose building and setting are as impressive as its modern sculptures and paintings.

6 DINING ALFRESCO IN VIEUX NICE
Page 357

Sit outside a Vieux Nice café watching the vibrant street life, and tuck into salade niçoise, *pissaladière* or a slice of *socca* straight from the pan.

7 MARSEILLE
Page 44

Don't let its former reputation put you off visiting this earthy, multi-ethnic Mediterranean metropolis with good food, great bars, excellent football and culture in abundance.

8 VINEYARDS OF CHATEAUNEUF-DU-PAPE
Page 129

Sample a glass of Provence's world-famous wine at the *domaine* where it was made.

9 ABBAYE DE SENANQUE
Page 191

The beauty of the twelfth-century Cistercian abbey of Sénanque is enhanced by its position, surrounded by lavender fields.

10 THE GYPSY PILGRIMAGE, STES-MARIES-DE-LA-MER
Page 106

An annual spectacle of music, dancing and religious ritual, dating from the sixteenth century.

10

16 RIVIERA BEACHES
Page 302

From lobster and champagne on an elegant hotel beach to celebrity-spotting during the Cannes film festival, the Riviera has a beach culture all its own.

17 MONT STE-VICTOIRE
Page 165

Walk up to the top of the mountain that inspired so much of Cézanne's work.

18 LES BAUX
Page 92

The eleventh-century citadel and picture-perfect *village perché* of Les Baux offer incredible views south over La Grande Crau to the sea.

19 AVIGNON'S PALAIS DES PAPES
Page 114

This vast medieval building was home to successive popes – and anti-popes – during Avignon's fourteenth-century heyday.

20 SCENIC THRILLS ON THE RIVIERA'S CORNICHES
Page 365

Soak up the grand coastal views along one of the world's most scintillating drives.

Itineraries

You could never hope to see all the wonders of Provence on a single trip. We've therefore handpicked the following itineraries to help visitors with specific interests, ranging from the Roman relics of Arles to the vineyards of the Dentelles.

ANCIENT PROVENCE

Exploring Provence's impressive ancient sites, dating back even beyond the Romans and the Greeks, will take at least a week.

❶ **Vaison-la-Romaine** Walk actual Roman residential streets, complete with mosaic-floored houses, theatre and baths. **See p.135**

❷ **Orange** Arguably the best preserved Roman theatre in the world is still in use for summer concerts. **See p.130**

❸ **St-Rémy** Just outside the modern town lie the remains of ancient Glanum, settled first by Greeks and later by Romans. **See p.94**

❹ **Arles** This lovely city still holds an all-but-intact amphitheatre, plus a theatre, baths, necropolis, intriguing underground vaults, and a superb archeology museum. **See p.82**

❺ **Marseille** Used in turn by Phoenician, Greek and Roman sailors, Marseille's Vieux Port is artfully evoked by the city's museums. **See p.44**

❻ **Fréjus** Set just back from the Med, and smaller now than in Roman times, Fréjus preserves the full Roman complement: theatre, amphitheatre and aqueduct. **See p.291**

❼ **Antibes** Founded by the Greeks, Antibes has a good museum of Classical treasures. **See p.319**

❽ **Tende** A fascinating museum interprets the mysterious prehistoric carvings of the nearby, high-mountain Vallée des Merveilles. **See p.240**

SCENIC SPLENDOURS

You'll need a good two weeks to admire the full range of landscapes that Provence has to offer.

❶ **Les Calanques** Best seen on a boat tour, or from the Corniches des Crêtes coastal road between Cassis and La Ciotat, the dramatic rocky shoreline east of Marseille is an unforgettable spectacle. **See p.73**

❷ **Haut Var** The rocky cliffs and pinnacles of the Haut Var are peppered with picturesque medieval villages, including gorgeous Cotignac. **See p.196**

❸ **Grand Canyon du Verdon** You could devote days on end to exploring the continent's deepest canyon, from its turquoise waters to its towering peaks. **See p.216**

❹ **Col de la Bonette** What's said to be the highest paved road in Europe crosses this stark summit, high above the head of the verdant Tinée Valley. **See p.234**

❺ **The Luberon** With its wooded slopes, buttercup-filled meadows, fields of lavender and hilltop villages, the Luberon ridge rewards endless wandering. **See p.184**

❻ **Mont Ventoux** While it's a notoriously gruelling circuit for Tour-de-France cyclists, the loop around Mont Ventoux makes a wonderful scenic drive. **See p.139**

ABOVE GRAND CANYON DU VERDON; ROMAN AMPHITHEATRE, ORANGE

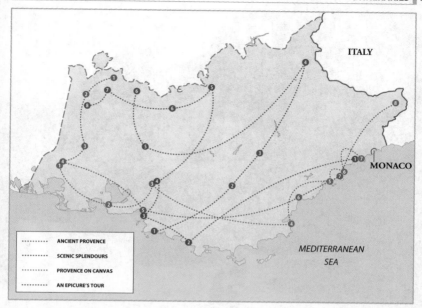

ITALY

MONACO

MEDITERRANEAN
SEA

- - - - - - - - - ANCIENT PROVENCE
- - - - - - - - - SCENIC SPLENDOURS
- - - - - - - - - PROVENCE ON CANVAS
- - - - - - - - - AN EPICURE'S TOUR

PROVENCE ON CANVAS

See Provence as the artists of the nineteenth and twentieth centuries saw it on this ten-day trail.

❶ Arles Van Gogh was enchanted by this ancient city, where he painted sunflowers and the Café de Nuit. **See p.82**

❷ Martigues Corot captured Martigues' Miroir aux Oiseaux on canvas; Picabia depicted the Etang de Berre's choppy waters. **See p.67**

❸ Aix-en-Provence Reminders of Cézanne are everywhere here, from the artist's childhood home, to his studio and the mountain he painted obsessively. **See p.155**

❹ St-Tropez Before it was a VIP haunt, St-Tropez attracted a who's who of artists, from Signac to Matisse; the superb Musée de l'Annonciade is their legacy. **See p.276**

❺ Le Cannet This unassuming Cannes suburb was home to Pierre Bonnard and now hosts the first museum dedicated to his work. **See p.308**

❻ Antibes An exuberant phase of Picasso's career is remembered at Antibes' seafront Château. **See p.319**

❼ Nice Matisse was attracted by Nice's cosmopolitan life, but Dufy's canvasses in the Musée des Beaux Arts immortalize it. **See p.342**

AN EPICURE'S TOUR

Allow a week for a leisurely culinary meander through the best of Provence's food and wine.

❶ Nice From *socca* to salade niçoise, Nice has a culinary heritage all its own. **See p.357**

❷ Bandol The coast's best wines, with the mysterious mourvèdre grape working its magic in dark, intense reds and pale, crisp rosé. **See p.252**

❸ Marseille Provence's great port city is celebrated for bouillabaisse, the fishermen's stew that is now a gourmet treat. **See p.44**

❹ Aix-en-Provence Wonderful street markets, a restaurant on every corner and sweet calissons to take home as souvenirs – Provence's loveliest major city is foodie heaven. **See p.155**

❺ Sisteron The lamb from the rugged countryside around Sisteron is renowned. **See p.175**

❻ Banon Remote, timeless Banon is home to the goats' cheese of the same name – pungent, leaf-wrapped and very, very good. **See p.182**

❼ The Dentelles Beaumes de Venise, Gigondas, Vacqueyras: the villages of this limestone region are a roll-call of winemaking renown. **See p.137**

❽ Châteauneuf-du-Pape Rich, ruby-red wines have carried the fame of this village to the far corners of the world. **See p.129**

THE CORNICHE DE L'ESTEREL

Basics

Getting there

The quickest and cheapest way to get to Provence from the UK or Ireland is usually to fly. The region has two of France's largest provincial airports, at Nice and Marseille, as well as lesser airports at Toulon-Hyères and Avignon. There are few direct intercontinental flights, though, so travellers from outside Europe are more likely to fly into Paris or London, then transfer flights or complete the journey by train. Eurostar rail services through the Channel Tunnel link to the fast TGV system, making rail a viable alternative, although you'll normally need to change at Paris or Lille. It's possible to reach Marseille or Nice by car from the UK, too, though it's a long drive, most comfortably accomplished with an overnight stop somewhere halfway.

Flights from the UK and Ireland

Several **budget airlines** fly between the UK, Ireland and southern France. **Tickets** are priced for each specific flight, and vary from moment to moment. Book as early as possible for the cheapest seats: budget airline fares have risen in recent years in reaction to soaring fuel costs, but if you're flexible about when you fly you may still pick up a bargain. Assorted surcharges – including fees for baggage or to pay with a credit card – can easily add £30 or more each way.

Routes can change so it's always worth checking the airline websites, but as this book went to press **Ryanair** (Ⓦ ryanair.com) flies to Marseille from Stansted, East Midlands and Edinburgh; to Toulon from Stansted; and to Nice from Dublin and Manchester. **EasyJet** (Ⓦ easyjet.com) connects Nice with Belfast, Bristol, Edinburgh, Liverpool, Newcastle and three London airports; and Marseille with Bristol and Gatwick. **Flybe** (Ⓦ flybe.com) links

Avignon with Southampton, and Nice with Exeter and Southampton; and **Jet2** (Ⓦ jet2.com) operates between Nice and East Midlands, Leeds and Manchester. Ryanair also serves Nîmes and easyJet flies to Montpellier – both of which are a short way west of the area covered in this book.

It's also worth checking out the **major national airlines**, like Air France (Ⓦ airfrance.com), British Airways (Ⓦ ba.com) and Aer Lingus (Ⓦ aerlingus.com), which have been forced to cut their fares to match the budget carriers. Note however that as they're more orientated towards business travellers, it's not always cheaper to fly midweek. **British Airways** flies daily from London Heathrow and London Gatwick to **Nice**, and from Heathrow to **Marseille**; low-season return fares start around £100 to Nice and £120 to Marseille including taxes. **Aer Lingus** fly from Dublin to Nice year-round, with return fares dropping to around €125 in low season and rising to more than €200 in summer; they also fly from Cork to Nice between April and October, and from Dublin to Marseille between May and September only, at slightly lower prices than the equivalent fares to Nice.

Flights from the US and Canada

Very few **direct flights** connect the US and Canada with southern France. From April to September **Delta Airlines** (Ⓦ delta.com) flies non-stop from JFK in **New York** to Nice for around $1100–2000 return. Additionally, Canadian charter carrier **Air Transat** (Ⓦ airtransat.com) links **Montréal** with Nice and Marseille in summer (roughly May–Oct), with a few flights to Marseille from **Quebec**; fares start around Can$900 return in May, rising to around Can$1350 in July and August.

These direct flights aside, most journeys to Provence from North America will involve a **transfer**, either using an internal North American flight to hook up with the Delta or Air Transat flights or flying direct to Paris or some other major European hub, with onward connections by air or train.

Several major airlines have **scheduled flights to Paris** from the US and Canada. Transatlantic **fares** to France have risen sharply of late, reflecting high fuel costs. An off-season midweek direct return flight to Paris can be US$940 before taxes from New York, US$1070 from Los Angeles or Houston. From Canada, prices to Paris start at around Can$930 from Montréal or Toronto.

Air France (Ⓦairfrance.com) operates the most frequent service to Paris, with good onward connections to Provence, including frequent services to Nice, Marseille and Toulon-Hyères. Many internal Air France flights depart from Paris Orly Airport, which requires a cross-town transfer from Charles de Gaulle, but there are also internal flights to Marseille and Nice from Charles de Gaulle, which is the main portal for intercontinental flights. Another option is to fly with a European carrier – such as British Airways (Ⓦba.com), Iberia (Ⓦiberia .com) or Lufthansa (Ⓦlufthansa.com) – to its European hub and then continue on to Paris or a regional French airport.

Flights from Australia, New Zealand and South Africa

There are **no direct flights** to Provence from Australia, New Zealand or South Africa. Most travellers from **Australia and New Zealand** choose to fly to France via London, although the majority of airlines can add a Paris leg to an Australia/New Zealand–Europe ticket. Flights via Asia or the Gulf States, with a transfer or overnight stop at the airline's home port, are generally the cheapest option; those routed through the US tend to be slightly pricier. Return **fares** start at around Aus$1900 from Sydney, Aus$1870 from Perth, Aus$1890 from Melbourne and NZ$2725 from Auckland.

From **South Africa**, Johannesburg is the best place to start, with Air France (Ⓦairfrance.com) flying direct to Paris from around R8000 return; from Cape Town, they fly via Johannesburg or Amsterdam and are more expensive, starting at around R9000. British Airways (Ⓦba.com), flying via London, costs upwards of R9000 from Johannesburg or R10,000 from Cape Town. South African Airways (Ⓦflysaa .com) operates a codeshare with Lufthansa, routing via Frankfurt or Munich to Paris for around R9700.

By train

For visitors arriving by air in Paris, fast **TGV trains** link Charles de Gaulle airport with Marseille in a little under four hours, with one-way fares from as little as €45; direct trains from Charles de Gaulle to Nice take around six and a half hours, with one-way fares from around €70.

The channel tunnel provides a direct train link from England. **Eurostar** trains from London St Pancras International, which carry foot passengers only, take two hours fifteen minutes to reach **Paris** Gare du Nord. In May and June, there are Eurostar services via Lyon to **Avignon** and **Aix**, while from mid-July to early Sept there are weekly direct trains from London to Avignon (Sat; 5hr 30min); standard non-flexible return fares to Avignon start at £109. All year, travellers heading for Avignon and other stations on the TGV line to **Marseille** can change at **Lille**, one hour twenty minutes out from London; the fastest journey to Marseille takes around five and a half hours, with non-flexible fares starting at £119 return. **Nice**-bound travellers have to change at Paris; the journey time is around nine hours and fares start at £119. **Tickets** can be bought online or by phone from Eurostar, as well as through travel agents and websites like Ⓦlastminute.com.

Tickets can be bought online, at major stations or by phone from Eurostar, as well as through travel agents and websites like Ⓦlastminute.com. InterRail and Eurail **passes** (see p.26) entitle you to discounts on Eurostar trains. Bicycles can be carried free of charge in the carriage provided that they can fold; if not, you'll have to reserve a space and pay a £30 fee, or send it as registered baggage to Paris or Lille for £25 – it won't necessarily travel on the same train as you, but will be ready for collection within 24 hours.

By car

Getting to Provence **by car from the UK** is relatively straightforward, with ferries from England operating to seven French ports. The easiest way to access the French autoroute network is to take either a ferry from Dover or Folkestone to Calais or Dunkerque or the Channel Tunnel to **Calais**. From there, the best route follows the E17 to the east of Paris via Troyes and Dijon, then the E15 from Beaune via Lyon to Provence. For much of the way, **traffic** is light; as a rule, congestion is only a problem south of Lyon.

The entrance to the **Channel Tunnel** is less than two hours' drive from London, off the M20 at Junction 11A, just outside Folkestone. Once there, you drive your car onto a two-tier train, which takes 35 minutes to reach Coquelles, just outside Calais. There are up to four departures per hour (one every 1hr 30min from midnight to 6am). You can turn up and buy your ticket at the check-in booths, but you'll pay a premium and at busy times booking is strongly recommended; if you have a booking, you must arrive at least thirty minutes before departure. Note that Eurotunnel does not transport cars fitted with LPG or CNG tanks.

Standard non-flexible **fares** start at £60 one-way if you book far enough ahead and/or travel off-peak, rising to £157 for peak travel. Fully refundable and changeable FlexiPlus fares cost £149 each way for a short stay (up to 5 days) and £199 for longer periods. There's room for only six **bicycles** on any departure, so book ahead in high season – a standard return costs £32 for a bike plus rider.

If you're travelling by **ferry**, note that Dover–Calais is the shortest crossing. At the time of writing the very cheapest fares, which start at less than £30 one-way, are on DFDS sailings from Dover to Calais and Dunkerque. Some ferry companies (but not DFDS) also offer fares for **foot passengers**, typically £40–50 return on cross-Channel routes; accompanying **bicycles** can usually be carried free.

From Ireland, putting the car on the ferry from Cork (14hr) or Rosslare (17hr 30) to Roscoff in Brittany, or Rosslare to Cherbourg (19hr) in Normandy, cuts out the drive across Britain to the Channel. One-way fares from Ireland kick off at around €119 for a car and two adults.

AGENTS AND OPERATORS

GENERAL

Abercrombie & Kent US ☎ 1800 554 7016, ⊛ abercrombiekent .com. Deluxe tailored tours: 4 days Provence from $3415; 4 days Côte d'Azur $4295.

Allez France UK ⊛ allezfrance.com. UK tour operator offering accommodation as well as short breaks and other holiday packages throughout France.

Arblaster & Clarke UK ☎ 01730 263 111, ⊛ winetours.co.uk. Wine-themed tours to all the great wine regions, including Bandol and Gigondas.

France Vacations US ☎ 1800 539 7098, ⊛ francevacations.net. Flight/hotel and fly-drive packages, including nine-day trips to Paris, Provence and the Riviera for $1579 and up, and nine-day cooking courses.

The French Experience US ☎ 1800 283 7262, ⊛ frenchexperience.com. Flexible escorted and self-drive tours, plus day-trips from Avignon, Nice and Marseille.

French Travel Connection Aus ☎ 02 9966 1177, ⊛ frenchtravel.com.au. Australian company offering everything to do with travel to and around France: accommodation, car hire, tours and even cooking classes.

Infohub ⊛ infohub.com. Web portal with a huge range of escorted and self-guided cultural, gastronomy and activity holidays in France.

Martin Randall Travel ☎ 020 8742 3355, ⊛ martinrandall.com.

Cultural tours on specialist themes including art, archeology and gastronomy. Eight-day "Modern Art on the Côte d'Azur" tour £2360.

North South Travel UK ☎ 01245 608 291, ⊛ northsouthtravel .co.uk. Friendly, competitive travel agency, offering discounted fares worldwide. Profits are used to support projects in the developing world, especially the promotion of sustainable tourism.

Peregrine Adventures UK ☎ 0845 863 9667, Australia ☎ +61 38601 4444; ⊛ peregrineadventures.com. Small-group active and cultural tours. Eight-day "Hidden Villages of Provence" tour £1790.

Viking River Cruises UK ☎ 0808 163 7097 ⊛ vikingrivercruises .com. French river cruises, including an eight-day trip to Avignon along the Saône and the Rhône, starting at £1495 in low season.

ACCOMMODATION

Canvas Holidays UK ☎ 0845 268 8027, ⊛ canvasholidays.co.uk. Camping holidays on the Côte d'Azur.

CIT Holidays Aus ☎ 1300 380 992, ⊛ cit.com.au. Australian operator offering mid-priced hotels in major resorts on the Riviera, and in Aix, Avignon and Marseille.

Dominique's Villas UK ☎ 020 7738 8772, ⊛ dominiquesvillas .co.uk. Upmarket agency with a diverse range of tempting properties, mostly for larger groups.

Eurocamp UK ☎ 0844 406 0402, ⊛ eurocamp.co.uk. Camping at or near the coast and at Castellane.

Holiday in France ☎ 01225 310 822, ⊛ holidayinfrance.co.uk. Upmarket villas and houses to rent, including some very large properties.

Gîtes de France ☎ gites-de-france.fr. Comprehensive list of houses, cottages and chalets throughout France that can be booked online.

Keycamp Holidays UK ☎ 0844 406 0200, Republic of Ireland ☎ 021 425 2300; ⊛ keycamp.com. Caravan and camping holidays on the Côte d'Azur.

Lagrange Holidays ☎ 020 7371 6111, ⊛ lagrange-vacances .com. Self-catering and hotel-based holidays on the Côte d'Azur.

ACTIVITY HOLIDAYS

Adventure Center US ☎ 1800 228 8747, ⊛ adventurecenter.com. Small-group hiking or cycling tours. Six-day Provence Cycling Weekend from $1118.

The Alternative Travel Group UK ☎ 01865 315 678, ⊛ atg-oxford.co.uk. Five- and seven-day walking tours in the Luberon from £745.

Austin-Lehman Adventures US ☎ 1-800-575-1540, ⊛ austinlehman.com. Good range of bike and walking tours all over France; seven-day Provence cycling tour from $3498.

Backroads US ☎ 1800 462 2848, ⊛ backroads.com. Trendy bike-tour company offering six-day Provence cycling or hiking trips from $4298.

Belle France UK ☎ 01580 214 010, ⊛ bellefrance.co.uk. Cycling, walking and boating holidays in and around Arles, St Rémy, the Luberon and the Riviera.

Butterfield & Robinson US & Canada ☎ 1866 551 9090, ⊛ butterfield.com. Six-day Provençal biking or walking tours from Can$3995.

Cycling for Softies UK ☎ 0161 248 8282, ⊛ cycling-for-softies.co.uk.

Easy-going cycle holiday operator to rural France, including the Luberon.

Inntravel UK ☎ 01653 617 001, ✉ inntravel.co.uk. Award-winning operator offering walking, riding and cycling holidays. Four-night "The Best of Roman Provence" walking tour from £860.

Mountain Travel Sobek US & Canada ☎ 1888 831 7526, ⓦ mtsobek.com. Hiking trips in Provence; fourteen days hiking the GR5 from the Alps to the sea $4995.

Walkabout Gourmet Adventures Aus ☎ 02 98715526, ⓦ walkaboutgourmet.com. Walking tours with an emphasis on cooking and good food. Seven-day "Pagnol's Provence" costs Aus$3625.

World Expeditions Can ☎ 1866 606 1721, UK ☎ 020 8545 9030, Aus ☎ 020 8270 8400, ⓦ worldexpeditions.com. Self-guided and escorted cycling and trekking holidays, including eight-day cycling trips in Provence.

RAIL CONTACTS

Eurail ⓦ eurail.com
European Rail UK ☎ 020 7619 1083, ⓦ europeanrail.com
Eurostar UK ☎ 0843 218 6186, ⓦ eurostar.com
International Rail UK ☎ 0871 231 0790, ⓦ international-rail.com
Rail Europe (SNCF French Railways) UK ☎ 0844 848 4064;
US ☎ 1-800-622-8600, Canada ☎ 1-800-361-7245,
ⓦ raileurope.com
Rail Plus Australia ☎ 1300 555 003, New Zealand ☎ 09 377 5415;
ⓦ railplus.com.au
Trainseurope UK ☎ 0871 700 7722, ⓦ trainseurope.co.uk
World Travel South Africa ☎ 011 628 2319, ⓦ worldtravel.co.za

FERRY CONTACTS

Brittany Ferries UK ☎ 0871 244 0744, ⓦ brittany-ferries.co.uk;
Republic of Ireland ☎ 021 4277 801, ⓦ brittanyferries.ie
Condor Ferries UK ☎ 0845 609 1024, ⓦ condorferries.co.uk
DFDS UK ☎ 0871 574 7235, ⓦ dfdsseaways.co.uk
Direct Ferries UK ☎ 0871 890 0900, ⓦ directferries.co.uk
EuroDrive UK ☎ 0844 371 8021, ⓦ eurodrive.co.uk
Ferry Savers UK ☎ 0844 371 8021, ⓦ ferrysavers.com.
Irish Ferries Republic of Ireland ☎ 0818 300 400, ⓦ irishferries.com
LD Lines UK ☎ 0844 576 8836, ⓦ ldlines.com
MyFerryLink UK ☎ 0844 248 2100, ⓦ myferrylink.com
P&O Ferries UK ☎ 0871 664 2121, ⓦ poferries.com

CHANNEL TUNNEL

Eurotunnel UK ☎ 0844 335 3535, ⓦ eurotunnel.com.

Getting around

Travelling by train is the most reliable and economical means of visiting Provence's main cities. Once you reach your destination you can use the local bus networks to get around, both in the town and out into the surrounding areas. Away from the major towns, however, it's best to have your own transport: the rail network is sparse, and bus services infrequent and often extremely slow.

By train

SNCF (☎ 36 35, €0.34/min; ⓦ voyages-sncf.com) is the national rail network, responsible for the vast majority of rail services in Provence. Pride of the network is the high-speed **TGV** (*train à grande vitesse*), which is capable of speeds of over 300kph and links the region with Paris and the rest of France, with stations at Orange, Avignon, Aix and Marseille, before continuing via Toulon, Hyères and Les Arcs-Draguignan to serve major Riviera resorts, including St-Raphaël, Cannes, Nice and Monaco.

Once in Provence you'll find **TER** (Transport Express Régional) services more useful. These trains are often still impressively modern and comfortable, and stop at more intermediate stations. Outside peak hours (7–9am & 4.30–6.30pm) you can carry a **bicycle** free of charge on these trains, stowing it either in the baggage car or in the bicycle spaces provided. In addition to the principle lines along the Rhône valley and the coast, a second major line heads north from Marseille through Aix and along the Durance to Manosque, Sisteron and beyond, towards Gap and Grenoble; another line heads north from Nice towards the Italian border at Tende, linking many of the communities of the *pays-arrière niçois* with the coast.

Tickets can be bought through the website ⓦ voyages-sncf.com, which has an English-language option, or at stations, and must be validated in the orange *compostage de billets* machines prior to boarding the train (this doesn't apply to passes or e-tickets you've printed off at home).

Timetables are divided into cheaper blue (off-peak) and white (peak) periods. From June to September a one-day **Pass Isabelle** (€14) allows unlimited travel on TER trains between Fréjus and the Italian border and inland to Grasse and Tende. If you're travelling in a family group you can buy a Pass **Isabelle Famille**, which gives one (€35) or three (€80) days' unlimited travel; like the Pass Isabelle, it's not valid on TGV trains. If you're planning a longer stay in the region it may be worth considering a ZOU! annual regional travel card. Some of these are open only to Provence residents, but the **ZOU! 50–75% card** does not have a residence qualification and – as its name implies – offers reductions of between 50 and 75 percent on ticket purchases for trains and LER rail replacement buses. The card costs €15 if you're under 26 and €30 If you're over 26.

Provence's other rail network is the narrow-gauge **Chemin de Fer de Provence** (Ⓦtrainprovence .com; see box, p.355), a wonderfully scenic (if slow), meandering ride from Nice to Digne.

By bus

Along the coast and between the major towns, Provence is well served by **buses**, with the best and most frequent routes being the fast Aix–Marseille and Marseille–Aubagne shuttles, and the services that link Nice with the other principal resorts along the Riviera. Elsewhere bus services are much less satisfactory, being geared to the needs of school-children and shoppers visiting local markets, and usually both slow and infrequent – even more so in school holidays.

SNCF buses (Ⓦinfo-ler.fr) are useful for getting to places on the rail network no longer served by passenger trains, such as intermediate stops on the Manosque–Sisteron line and the entire Château Arnoux–Digne line. **Inter-urban buses** are otherwise coordinated on a departmental basis, with **timetables** and other information often available online: Ⓦlepilote.com for Marseille and surroundings; Ⓦvarlib.fr for the Var, Ⓦvaucluse.fr for Avignon, the Vaucluse and around; Ⓦcg06.fr for Nice and the Riviera, and for the Alpes de Haute-Provence. Most towns have a central **gare-** (or **halte-) routière** (bus station), frequently – though not invariably – close to the *gare SNCF*.

By car

Away from the big cities, Provence is a superb, scenic place to get behind the wheel. Driving allows you to explore the more remote villages and the most dramatic landscapes, which are otherwise inaccessible. In the **cities**, driving is much less enjoyable – the old historic parts of many towns are all but inaccessible, car crime is a problem and traffic and parking can be nightmarish, particularly in Nice and Marseille.

Unleaded (95 and 98 octane), diesel (*gazole*) and LPG **fuel** are all readily available. In common with other European countries, fuel **costs** are higher than North American drivers will be used to. Most places accept credit cards, though in rural areas, filling stations are scarce, pumps are often automated out of hours and foreign credit cards are invariably not accepted. It's therefore a good idea to keep your tank topped up, especially if touring in remote parts of Provence. Outside the travel-to-work area of Marseille, **tolls** apply on the autoroutes: you pick up a ticket at the entrance to a toll section and pay in cash or by credit card when you leave the toll area. UK motorists can now use the Liber-T automatic tolling lanes if their cars are fitted with the relevant transponder; to register in advance for a transponder and for more information see Ⓦwww.saneftolling.co.uk. In contrast to the rest of France, autoroutes in Provence are often congested.

Car rental agencies cluster around the airports and at major rail stations, with most well-known international brands represented. Prepaying via a website usually produces the best deals. **Rates** for the smallest cars (Citroën C1 or similar) start at around €180 for a week in low season, though it's worth shopping around.

The French **drive on the right**. Most people used to driving on the left find it easy to adjust; the biggest problem in a right-hand-drive car tends to be visibility when you want to overtake. The law of *priorité à droite* – which means you have to give way to traffic coming from your right, even when it's coming from a minor road – still sometimes applies in built-up areas, so be vigilant at junctions. A sign showing a yellow diamond on a white background indicates that you have **right of way**,

---

TOP 5 DRIVES

Corniche des Crêtes Regular belvederes provide breathtaking coastal views from this route along Provence's highest sea cliffs. See p.77

Grand Canyon du Verdon You'll struggle to keep your eye on the wheel circling Europe's most spectacular gorge on the route des Crêtes and Corniche Sublime. See p.216

Col de Turini Twisting, challenging mountain driving in the Riviera's hinterland, as driven by TV's *Top Gear* team in their search for the world's greatest road. See p.238

Corniche de l'Esterel Rust-red rocks and deep blue sea make a lasting impression on this lovely coastal drive. See p.298

Moyenne Corniche Pop on your shades and follow the tracks of a thousand car commercials on the Riviera's most glamorous drive. See p.370

ROAD INFORMATION

Up-to-the-minute information regarding traffic jams and road works throughout France can be obtained from the Bison Futé free-dial recorded information service (☎0800 100 200; French only) or their website ⓦbison-fute.equipement.gouv.fr. For information regarding autoroutes, you can also consult the bilingual website ⓦautoroutes.fr. Once on the autoroute, tune in to the national 107.7FM information station for 24-hour music and updates on traffic conditions.

---

while the same sign with an oblique black slash warns you that vehicles emerging from the right have priority. **Stop signs** mean stop completely; *Cédez le passage* means "Give way". Other signs warning of potential dangers include *déviation* (diversion), *gravillons* (loose chippings) and *chaussée déformée* (uneven surface).

Speed limits are 50kph in towns (with 30kph common in villages and historic towns), 90kph outside built-up areas and 110kph on dual carriageways, with a limit of 130kph on autoroutes in fine weather, reduced to 110kph in the rain. Speed limits are also lower on autoroutes that pass through urban areas, including the stretch of the A8 that runs along the Riviera. Radar and speed camera detectors are illegal.

Drivers of right-hand-drive cars must adjust their **headlights** to dip to the right. This is most easily done by sticking on glare deflectors, which can be bought at most motor accessory shops, at the Channel ferry ports or the Eurostar terminal and on the ferries. It's more complicated if your car is fitted with High-Intensity Discharge (HID) or halogen-type lights; check with your dealer about how to adjust these well in advance. Dipped headlights must be used in poor daytime visibility.

All non-French vehicles must display their **national identification letters** (GB, etc) either on the number plate or by means of a sticker, and all vehicles must carry a red **warning triangle**, a reflective **safety jacket** and (since 2012) a single-use **breathalyser**. You are also strongly advised to carry a spare set of bulbs, a fire extinguisher and a first-aid kit. **Seat belts** are compulsory and children under 10 years must travel in an approved child seat, harness or booster appropriate to their age and size.

CAR-RENTAL AGENCIES

Avis ⓦ avis.com
Argus Car Hire ⓦ arguscarhire.com
Auto Europe ⓦ autoeurope.com
Europcar ⓦ europcar.com
Europe by Car ⓦ europebycarblog.com
Hertz ⓦ hertz.com
Holiday Autos ⓦ holidayautos.com

By scooter and motorbike

Scooters are ideal for pottering around locally. They're easy to rent – places offering bicycles often also rent out scooters. Expect to pay in the region of €35 and up a day for a 50cc machine. If you were born before 1 January 1988 you don't need a licence for a 50cc moped – just passport/ID – but otherwise you'll need a driving licence.

For anything from 50cc to 125cc you'll need to have held a driving licence for at least two years regardless of your age, and for anything over 125cc you need a full **motorbike** licence. Rental **prices** are around €60–70 a day for a 125cc bike; expect to leave a hefty deposit by cash or credit card – over €1000 is the norm – which you may lose in the event of damage or theft. Crash helmets are compulsory on all bikes, and the headlight must be switched on at all times. For bikes over 125cc it is compulsory to wear reflective clothing. It is recommended to carry a first-aid kit and a set of spare bulbs.

By bike

As the proliferation of specialist biking tours demonstrates, **cycling** on backroads of rural Provence can be delightful, if strenuous due to the often rugged terrain. Cycles can easily be **hired**, particularly down on the coast where many towns have a branch of the Holiday Bikes chain (ⓦholidaybikes.fr), which also rents out motorcycles and scooters. Marseille and Nice also have Paris-style credit-card-operated public bike rental stations.

Accommodation

Finding accommodation on the spot in the larger towns and cities of Provence is only likely to prove difficult during high season, July and August. On the Riviera,

however, things get booked up earlier in the year: in May, the Cannes Film Festival makes it extremely difficult to find reasonably priced accommodation on the western Riviera, while the Monaco Grand Prix creates the same problem along the coast east of Nice. In any case, booking a couple of nights in advance is reassuring at any time of year.

Hotels

Hotels in Provence, as in the rest of France, are **graded** zero to five **stars**. The price more or less corresponds to the number of stars, though the system is a little haphazard, having more to do with ratios of bathrooms per guest than genuine quality; ungraded and single-star hotels are often very good. North American visitors accustomed to staying in rooms equipped with coffee-makers, safes and refrigerators should not automatically expect the same facilities in French hotels, even the more expensive ones – and hotels don't invariably have lifts, either. Genuine **single rooms** are rare. On the other hand, most hotels willingly equip rooms with extra beds, at a good discount.

Prices in the swankier **resorts** such as Cannes or St-Tropez tend to be higher than in the rest of the region – though Nice has a good supply of cheap accommodation throughout most of the year – and in high season (July–Aug), rates soar in the Côte d'Azur resorts.

Outlets of the various **budget motel chains** proliferate alongside motorway exits and on major through-routes on the outskirts of larger towns. While characterless, these are generally inexpensive, and can make a good alternative option for motorists, especially late at night. They have prompted their family-run rivals to sharpen themselves up, with more en-suite rooms, brighter decor, and cable or satellite TV. In the very cheapest hotels, rooms may lack private bath, shower or WC, but will usually have a washbasin (*lavabo*); it's also not uncommon to

have a shower but no WC. More expensive hotels usually have private facilities; you'll get more for your money outside the popular resorts, in small towns or in working cities like Toulon and Marseille.

Many **family-run hotels close** for two or three weeks a year in low season. In smaller towns and villages they may also shut up shop for one or two nights a week, usually Sunday or Monday. Details are given where relevant throughout the book, but as dates change from year to year and as some places may decide to close for a few days in low season if they have no bookings, it's always wise to call ahead to check.

Breakfast, which is never included in the quoted price, will add anything between €6 and €30 per person to a bill – though there is no obligation to take it. In high season some hotels – particularly in popular tourist destinations – insist on half board (*demi-pension*).

There are a number of nationwide **hotel federations** in France. The biggest and most useful is **Logis de France** (✆01 45 84 70 00, ⊕logishotels .com), which produces a free annual guide, available in French tourist offices, from *Logis de France* itself and from member hotels. Two other, more upmarket federations worth mentioning are **Châteaux & Hôtels de France** (✆01 72 72 92 02, ⊕chateauxhotels.com) and the **Relais du Silence** (✆01 70 23 81 63, ⊕relaisdusilence.com), both of which offer high-class accommodation in beautiful older properties, often in rural locations.

HOTEL GROUPS

Châteaux & Hôtels de France ✆ 01 72 72 92 02, ⊕ chateauxhotels.com. High-class accommodation in beautiful older properties, often in rural locations.

Logis de France ✆ 01 45 84 70 00, ⊕ logishotels.com. The biggest and most useful hotel federation in France. It produces a free annual guide, available in French tourist offices, from *Logis de France* itself and from member hotels.

Relais du Silence ✆ 01 70 23 81 63, ⊕ relaisdusilence.com. Similar to *Châteaux & Hôtels de France*, offering upmarket accommodation in characterful, luxurious properties.

ACCOMMODATION PRICES

Throughout this book we give a headline price for every accommodation reviewed. This indicates the **lowest rack rate price for a double/twin room during high season** (usually July and August). Single rooms, where available, usually cost between 60 and 80 percent of a double or twin; in many budget chain hotels in particular there is no discount for single occupancy of a double or triple-bed room. At **hostels**, we give the price for a dorm bed and, where applicable, a double room, and at **campsites**, the cost of two people and a tent pitch.

BUDGET CHAIN MOTELS

The following motel chains are listed in approximately ascending order of price and comfort.

F1 ⓦ hotelf1.com

B&B ⓦ hotel-bb.com

Première Classe ⓦ premiereclasse.fr

Ibis ⓦ ibis.com

Campanile ⓦ campanile.com

Bed and breakfast and self-catering

In country areas, in addition to standard hotels, you will come across **chambres d'hôtes** – bed-and-breakfast accommodation in someone's house, château or farm. Though the quality varies, on the whole standards are high, offering more character and greater value than an equivalent hotel. Prices generally range between €50 and €120 for two including breakfast; payment is usually expected in cash. Some offer meals on request (*tables d'hôtes*), usually evenings only.

If you're planning to stay a week or more in any one place it's worth considering renting **self-catering accommodation**. This will generally consist of self-contained country cottages known as **gîtes**. "Gîtes Panda" are *gîtes* located in a national park or other protected area and are run on environmentally friendly lines.

You can get lists of both *gîtes* and *chambres d'hôtes* from the government-funded agency Gîtes de France (☎ 01 49 70 75 75, ⓦ gites-de -france.com), or search on their website for accommodation by location or theme (for example, *gîtes* near fishing or riding opportunities). In addition, every year the organization publishes a number of national guides, such as *Nouveaux Gîtes* (listing new addresses); these guides are available to buy online or from departmental offices of Gîtes de France, as well as from bookstores and tourist offices. Tourist offices will also have lists of places in their area which are not affiliated to Gîtes de France.

Hostels

At around €12–26 per night for a **dormitory bed**, usually with breakfast thrown in, youth hostels – *auberges de jeunesse* – are invaluable for single travellers of any age on a budget. Some now offer rooms, occasionally en suite, but they don't necessarily work out cheaper than hotels – particularly if you've had to pay a taxi fare to reach them. However, many allow you to cut costs by eating in the hostels' cheap canteens, while in a few you can prepare your own meals in the communal kitchens.

In addition to those belonging to the two French hostelling associations listed below, there are now also several independent hostels, particularly in Nice and Marseille.

Youth hostel associations

There are two **French hostelling associations** – the Fédération Unie des Auberges de Jeunesse (FUAJ: ☎ 01 44 89 87 27, ⓦ fuaj.org) and the smaller Ligue Française (LFAJ: ☎ 01 44 16 78 78, ⓦ auberges-de -jeunesse.com). In either case, you normally have to show a current Hostelling International (HI) **membership card**. It's usually cheaper and easier to join before you leave home, provided your national youth hostel association is a full member of HI. Alternatively, you can purchase an HI card in certain French hostels (€7 HI Welcome tariff for foreign visitors at FUAJ hostels, €11/16 under/over 26 at LFAJ hostels).

Gîtes d'étape and refuges

In the countryside, another hostel-style option exists in the form of **gîtes d'étape**. Aimed at hikers and long-distance bikers, *gîtes d'étape* provide bunks and primitive kitchen and washing facilities for around €15–25 per person. They are marked on the large-scale IGN walkers' maps and listed in the Topo guides. Mountain areas are well supplied with **refuges**, mostly run by the Fédération Français des Clubs Alpins et de Montagne (FFCAM; ☎ 01 53 72 87 00, ⓦ ffcam.fr). Generally only staffed in summer, these offer dorm accommodation and meals, and are the only available shelter once you are above the villages. Costs are around €17–26 for the night, or half of this if you're a member of a climbing organization affiliated to FFCAM, plus around €20–25 for breakfast and dinner. Outside the summer season, some offer very limited, basic shelter at reduced cost.

More information can be found online at ⓦ gites-refuges.com, where you can download four printable regional *Gîtes d'Étape et Réfuges* guides for €5 per region.

Camping

Most villages and towns in Provence have at least one **campsite** (notable exceptions being Marseille and Nice). Camping is extremely popular with the French and, especially for those from the north,

Provence is a favourite destination. The cheapest sites – from around €12 – are often the **camping municipaux** run by the local authority in small communes in rural Provence. Another countryside option – usually with minimal facilities – is camping **à la ferme** – on private **farmland**. Local tourist offices will usually have lists of such sites.

On the Côte d'Azur, **commercial sites** can be vast, with hundreds of pitches and elaborate facilities including swimming pools and restaurants; reckon on paying up to €45 per night for a car, tent and two people in high season on the coast. Sites are graded according to quality from one to four stars; the more stars, the better the facilities – and the higher the price.

You can search for a site by *département* on the Camping France website (W campingfrance.com) and Gîtes de France (W gites-de-france.fr), or search local tourist board sites. **Camping Qualité** (W campingqualite.com) lists campsites with particularly high standards of hygiene, service and privacy, while the **Clef Verte** (W laclefverte.org) label is awarded to sites (plus hostels and hotels) run along environmentally friendly lines.

Camping rough (*camping sauvage*) is strongly discouraged in summer due to the high risk of forest fires; in any case, you should never camp rough without first asking the landowner's permission, as farmers have been known to shoot first and ask questions later. Camping on the **beach** is not permitted in major resorts.

Food and drink

Food is as good a reason as any for going to Provence. The region boasts one of France's most distinctive and exceptional regional cuisines, as well as some very fine wines.

Provence has a considerable number of top gourmet **restaurants**, particularly in the cities and along the Côte d'Azur where – if your budget can stretch to perhaps €100 or more – you can enjoy the creations of some of France's most celebrated kitchens. Further down the price scale mediocre or even bad meals are not unknown in tourist areas, but if you choose carefully, you should be able to eat well without spending a fortune.

The **markets** of Provence are a sensual treat as well as a lively social event; the best ones are listed in the text. For a **glossary** of food and drink terms, see pp.411–418.

Breakfast

Depending on the class of hotel or hostel, **breakfast** may be a simple affair of coffee and freshly baked baguette with jam and butter, or a much more elaborate spread involving croissants or a hot and cold buffet – though the splendour of the breakfast buffet will be reflected in the **bill**: a breakfast buffet in even a mid-range hotel might set you back €12 per day, whereas a simpler

REGIONAL DELICACIES

Bouillabaisse This fishermen's stew from Marseille is the most famous of all Provençal seafood dishes – at its best it's pricey but memorable.

Ravioles Ravioli is a classic niçois dish, often stuffed with *blette* – Swiss chard – and daube, served with a splash of meaty daube sauce.

Pieds et paquets Sheep's trotters and stomachs may be an acquired taste, but they're characteristic of Marseille.

Socca Best eaten hot and fresh from the pan, this Niçois chickpea pancake is perfect street food – simple, wholesome and tasty.

Farcis Stuffed vegetables are a delicious speciality of the coast, but vegetarians beware – the stuffing is usually meat or sausage.

Chèvre de Banon Pungent and good, this goat's cheese from the remote village of Banon comes wrapped in chestnut leaves.

Calissons A speciality of Aix-en-Provence, these lozenge-shaped sweetmeats are made from almonds and candied lemon and are perfect with a strong espresso.

Tapenade Capers, anchovies and black olives give this famous Provençal spread its distinctively pungent, salty flavour.

Oursins Sea urchins washed down with local white wine are the classic flavour combination if you're dining on Cassis's pretty harbour.

Daube de Boeuf Provence's winter warmer is a beef stew enriched with red wine and seasoned with juniper, orange peel and chopped bacon.

bread-and-coffee affair in a cheaper hotel might be half that. If you're sure that you're going to be staying in town it can be cheaper to opt out and go to a local café for a croissant, *pain au chocolat* (a chocolate-filled croissant) or a sandwich, washed down with coffee or hot chocolate – though if you decide to do this, be sure your hotel understands you do not require breakfast so it is not added to your bill.

Lunch and dinner

At lunchtime, and sometimes in the evening, you'll find that many restaurants and cafés offer good-value **plats du jour** (chef's specials) at prices below the **à la carte** menu prices. You'll also come across lunchtime **formules** – a menu of limited or no choice, including perhaps a main course and a drink. Most restaurants also have one or more elaborate **prix-fixe** (set-price) *menus*, which usually offer a limited selection of the dishes available on the full à la carte menu at a reduced price. The usual accompaniment to a full meal is wine; stick to the house wine – often served in 25 or 50cl *pichets* – if you want to keep the bill down.

If you want to experience the full glory of **Provençal cooking** you really need to eat in a **restaurant**. It's still possible to eat well for €30 or less in a small, family-run place where you'll enjoy hearty, home-cooked dishes such as *daube de boeuf* or *pieds et paquets*, though the real gems are not as easy to find as they were.

One very appealing and affordable alternative to Provençal cuisine – particularly in Marseille – is **North African** food; other inexpensive ethnic options include the numerous **Asian** fast-food buffets, though the quality of Asian cooking in Provence is very variable, even in the more upmarket restaurants, and some visitors may find the food bland, as spicing tends to be toned down to suit less adventurous French palates.

For vegetarians in particular, the numerous **pizzerias** can be a godsend; they usually advertise pizza cooked *au feu de bois* – in a wood-fired oven – and served with a drizzle of oil. Fresh **pasta**, a speciality of Nice, is affordable and often very good – and another safe option for veggies.

Brasseries and **cafés** vary widely in price and style, from those that are merely large bars serving a restricted food menu to very grand (and expensive) affairs resembling the celebrated Parisian eateries of the Left Bank; generally speaking, brasseries serve **quick meals** at any time of the day, including salads and lighter options. **Crêperies** and **salons de thé** are also a good bet for light meals.

Snacks and street food

Provence – and especially Nice – is a wonderful place to eat on the hoof. Colourful **markets** are an excellent source of fresh produce, meats and cheeses, while **patisseries** often sell the delicious savoury *pain fougasse*, a finger-shaped bread that may contain olives, anchovies, sausage, cheese or bacon. Along the Riviera the **sandwich** of choice is the *pan bagnat*, a delicious mix of tuna, hard-boiled egg and bitter mesclun salad leaves drizzled with oil, usually available for less than €5; **Niçois street food** includes the simple onion tart *pissaladière*, *farcis* (vegetables stuffed with a meat mixture) and hot wedges of *socca* – a pancake made with chickpea flour. In **Marseille** in particular, other options include Tunisian snacks such as *brik à l'oeuf* (a delicious filo pastry snack stuffed with soft-set egg), spicy merguez sausages and falafel.

Drinks

Coffee is the beverage of choice, served long and milky as a *café au lait* at breakfast time and drunk short and strong as an *express* (espresso) later in the day – ask for *une crème* or *une grande crème* if you want a coffee with milk in a café. Ordinary **tea** is usually Lipton's, served in the cup with a tea bag; ask for *un peu de lait frais* if you want it with milk, English-style. Herb or fruit teas – known as infusions or *tisanes* – are also widely available.

Draught **beer** – usually Kronenbourg – is one of the cheaper alcoholic drinks you can buy; you'll also see French and Belgian bottled beers and, in larger towns and cities, a big international selection in Dutch- or Irish-style pubs. Provençal **wines** include the very grand vintages of Châteauneuf-du-Pape, the renowned wines of Vacqueyras, Gigondas and Bandol, and the famous dessert wines of Beaumes de Venise; prices for these nobler wines can be high, but there's plenty of inexpensive Côtes de Luberon or Côtes de Provence to enjoy too.

Those in search of something stronger should note that the region is the homeland of **pastis**, the aniseed-flavoured spirit traditionally served with a bowl of olives before meals, and there's also an abundance of cognac, armagnac and various flavours of *eaux de vie*, of which the most delicious is Poire Williams; *marc* is a spirit distilled from grape pulp. Cocktails are served at most late-night bars and discos.

The media

Anyone who can read French, or understand it when spoken, will find that the print and electronic media in France match any in the world. Otherwise, English-language newspapers are usually available, many hotels offer English-language TV, and BBC radio can easily be picked up.

Newspapers and magazines

Getting hold of **international editions** of British and north American **newspapers** and magazines in Provence is relatively easy. Newsstands at airports and railway stations, and at branches of Virgin in the major cities invariably stock the major publications, though such is the influx of English-speaking expatriates that these days you may just as easily find the latest edition of the **Wall Street Journal** or **Financial Times** on sale in some idyllic village in the Luberon.

As for the **French press**, Le Monde (Ⓦlemonde.fr) is the most intellectual and respected national daily, though it can be a bit tedious; Libération (Libé for short; Ⓦliberation.fr;) is moderately left-wing, independent and more colloquial; L'Humanité (Ⓦhumanite.fr) is communist; and Le Figaro (Ⓦlefigaro.fr) is the most respected of the right-leaning newspapers. That said, you're more likely as a visitor to find the major regional newspapers such as Marseille's La Provence (Ⓦlaprovence.com) or Nice's Nice Matin (Ⓦnicematin.com) useful, more for their listings than their indifferent news coverage.

Weekly publications, on the Newsweek/Time model, include the left-leaning Le Nouvel Observateur (Ⓦnouvelobs.com), its right-wing counterpart L'Express (Ⓦlexpress.fr), and Marianne (Ⓦmarianne2.fr), the centrist with bite. The best, and funniest, investigative journalism is in the satirical Canard Enchaîné (Ⓦlecanardenchaine.fr), but it's almost incomprehensible to non-native speakers.

Although it's aimed more at expats than visitors, the **English-language magazine** Riviera Reporter (Ⓦriviera-reporter.com), which you can pick up free at English bookshops and occasionally at tourist offices, often contains articles of interest. Riviera Times (Ⓦrivieratimes.com) is similar, but published in newspaper format.

Radio

Riviera Radio (106 5FM in France, 106 3FM in Monaco, Ⓦrivieraradio.mc) broadcasts out of Monaco and faithfully reflects its British expat audience with a homespun local-radio mix of suburban chat and middle-of-the-road hits; it's also worth listening to if you're on the Côte d'Azur, thanks to its news and events coverage.

Radio France (Ⓦradiofrance.fr) operates eight stations. These include France Culture for arts, France Info for news and France Musique for classical music. Other major stations include **Europe 1** (Ⓦeurope1.fr) for news, debate and sport. **Radio France International** (RFI; Ⓦrfi.fr) broadcasts in French and various foreign languages, including English; you can listen on the website or through your mobile phone.

Television

French **terrestrial TV** has six channels: three public (France 2, France 3 and Arte/France 5); one subscription (Canal Plus – with some unencrypted programmes); and two commercial (TF1 and M6). Of these, TF1 (Ⓦtf1.fr) and France 2 (Ⓦfrance2.fr) are the most popular channels, showing a broad mix of programmes.

In addition there are any number of **cable and satellite channels**, including CNN, BBC World, Euronews, Eurosport, Planète (which specializes in documentaries) and Jimmy (Friends and the like in French). The main French-run music channel is MCM.

Festivals

Provence is home to some of France's most celebrated festivals. The real cultural heavyweights are the Avignon and Aix festivals, which use the historic settings of the two cities to stunning effect as a backdrop for high culture in the early summer. But many smaller towns and villages have their own events too, from traditional folk festivals to events celebrating jazz or film.

Arles and Les-Stes-Maries-de-la-Mer still have Spanish-style férias or **bullfights**. The principality of Monaco makes up for its modest size with a packed programme of events of its own – including, most famously, the **Grand Prix** in May (see box, p.380; Ⓦacm.mc).

JANUARY TO APRIL

International Circus Festival, Monaco Mid- to late January.
Fête du Citron, Menton Feb. Floats decorated entirely with lemons form part of this annual celebration. Ⓦfeteducitron.com
Nice Carnival Feb–March. Massive fifteen-day carnival featuring

colourful flower parades and night-time processions.
W nicecarnaval.com

Violet festival, Tourrettes-sur-Loup First or second Sun in March. Floats decorated with thousands of violets parade through the village.

Printemps des Arts, Monaco March & April Classical and contemporary dance festival.

MAY

Festival de Cannes Second half of May. World-famous international film festival (see box, p.305). W www .festival-cannes.com

Fête de Ste Sarah, Les Stes-Maries-de-la-Mer May 24–25. Romany festival celebrating Sarah, their patron saint (see box, p.108).

La Féria de Nîmes Pentecost, seven weeks after Easter. Bullfights.

Fête de Transhumance, St-Rémy Whit Monday, May/June. Traditional Provence festival that sees a flock of four thousand sheep parade through town.

JUNE

Festival du Premier Film, La Ciotat Early June. Annual film festival in the town where cinema first started (see box, p.78). W berceau-cinema.com

Nuit de Petit St-Jean, Valréas June 23 and 24. Night-time procession and show.

Tarasque Festival, Tarascon Last full weekend of June. Bull and equestrian events, fireworks and a parade of the mythical Tarasque monster through the streets (see box, p.101).

Festival International d'Art Lyrique, Aix-en-Provence June & July. Classical music and opera. W festival-aix.com

JULY AND AUGUST

Festival des Jazz, St-Raphaël Early July. International jazz festival.

Les Suds à Arles, Arles Mid-July. Festival of world music. W suds-arles.com

Festival d'Avignon July. Three-week cultural festival of theatre, contemporary dance, classical music and exhibitions (see box, p.118). The fringe festival is known as the Festival Off. W festival-avignon.com W avignonleoff.com

Jazz à Juan, Juan-les-Pins Two weeks in mid-July. International jazz festival (see box, p.318). W jazzajuan.com

Jazz Festival, Nice Late July. W nicejazzfestival.fr

Chorégies d'Orange, Orange July. Choral festival (see box, p.131). W choregies.asso.fr

Vaison Danse, Vaison-la-Romaine Mid to late July. Contemporary dance festival. W vaison-danses.com

Musique à l'Emperi, Salon-de-Provence July & Aug. Classical music festival in the château. W festival-salon.com

International Fireworks, Monaco July & Aug.

Festival de Musique, Menton Late July–early Aug. Classical music concerts by the quayside. W musique-menton.fr

Rencontres d'Arles, Arles July–Sept. Europe's most prestigious annual photography festival (see box, p.85). W www .rencontres-arles.com

Fête des Vins de l'Enclave, Valréas First Sun in Aug. Wine festival.

Festival of Jewish Music, Carpentras Early Aug.

Carreto Ramado, St Remy Aug 15. Harvest thanksgiving procession.

SEPTEMBER

Festival International de Gastronomie, Mougins Sept. Foodie festival in this little village famed for its gastronomy. W lesetoilesdemougins.com

OCTOBER

Fiesta des Suds, Marseille Oct. World music and arts festival in the industrial setting of the city's docklands. W dock-des-suds.org

Sports and outdoor activities

The benign Provençal climate encourages outdoor activities of all kinds, from swimming, sailing and diving in clear coastal waters to adventure sports for adrenaline junkies in the Grand Canyon du Verdon.

Spectator sports

Football is the most popular spectator sport in Provence, especially in Marseille, home of Olympique de Marseille (W om.net), one of the top French teams. Motor racing takes precedence in Monaco, while enthusiasm for **cycle racing** is as great as anywhere in France, and the annual **Tour de France** generally has a stage in Provence, most notoriously on Mont Ventoux. In and around the Camargue, the number one spectator sport is **bullfighting** (see box, p.87); though not to everyone's taste, it is, at least, less gruesome than the variety practised in Spain. The world-famous **Formula One Grand Prix** (see box, p.380) takes place in Monaco in May, while some of Provence's remote inland routes make perfect terrain for **rallying**. Monaco also hosts an international **Tennis Open** championship, the Monte Carlo Rolex Masters.

The characteristic Provençal sporting pastime is **pétanque**, the region's version of *boules*, which you'll see played in practically every town or village square, in parks and sometimes in purpose-built arenas. The principle is the same as in bowls, but the terrain is rough, never grass, and the area of play much smaller.

Sailing and watersports

There can scarcely be a coast anywhere in the world with as many **yachting facilities** as the Côte d'Azur, and most coastal resorts have at least one marina, often more. Of the **regattas**, Hyères hosts the Semaine Olympic des Voiles in the spring, a major sailing event that national teams often use to select their Olympic teams. In September, the attraction of St-Tropez's Les Voiles is as much glamour as sport, while Marseille's Septembre en Mer offers all manner of nautical activities, from sunset sea-kayak trips along the coast to voyages on a historic barque.

The chief problem for **watersports** enthusiasts on the Côte d'Azur is simple congestion, with the thousands of yachts dodging jet skis, motorboats and windsurfers and adding up to a traffic headache. Nonetheless, the sea is warm and placid and there are plenty of opportunities to hire equipment.

Elsewhere, there are opportunities for **diving** in the clear waters around Cassis, Bandol and Sanary, along the Corniche des Maures and at Saint Raphaël. **Swimming** is most enjoyable in the *calanques* of Marseille or around the quieter and more remote beaches away from the big cities; purpose-built **water parks** on the coast offer extensive facilities in exchange for their rather steep entry prices.

Outdoor and adventure activities

Provence makes a superb venue for **outdoor sports** and **adventure pursuits**. The beautiful alpine scenery is wonderful for walking, particularly around the Grand Canyon du Verdon (see p.217) and in the Parc National du Mercantour (see p.225). The former is also popular for **hiking**, **rafting**, **canyoning**, **kayaking**, **rock climbing**, **hang-gliding**, **mountain biking** and **horse-riding**: Castellane and La Palud Sur Verdon are the two main centres for active sports in the gorge; nearby St-André-les-Alpes is popular for **paragliding** and hang-gliding. Gentler airborne pursuits include **hot-air ballooning** in the Pays de Forcalquier. The Camargue is Provence's most famous centre for **horseriding**; information on holidays on horseback is included in "Agents and operators" on p.25.

Cycling is popular almost everywhere, with public bike hire schemes in Marseille and Nice and bicycle rental available in most other towns, and there are numerous organized cycling **tours** available (see p.25). **Bike rental** information is given throughout this book. Cycle tourism is particularly well supported in the Luberon and Pays de Forcalquier, where you can even arrange to have your luggage transported ahead of you to your next hotel. Bikes are by no means confined to paved roads: in the alpine districts of the Alpes Maritime and Parc du Mercantour there are signposted and mapped VTT (*vélo tout terrain*) trails for mountain-biking enthusiasts.

Skiing and snowboarding

Thanks to the unique topography of the region, it's possible to **ski** remarkably close to the coast – the closest resort to the Côte d'Azur being Gréolières-les-Neiges, a short distance from Grasse. More reliable snow and more extensive facilities are, however, found inland: at Valberg, Isola 2000, La Foux d'Allos, Auron and in the resorts around Barçelonette.

SKI RESORTS

Auron ⓦ auron.com. Resort with 135km of pistes, mostly blue or red (easy to intermediate).

La Foux d'Allos ⓦ valdallos.com. Purpose-built, high-altitude ski resort in the Val d'Allos, which has 180km of pistes – the most extensive network in the southern Alps.

Isola 2000 ⓦ isola2000.com. At an altitude of 2000m on the fringe of the Parc National du Mercantour, with 120km of pistes.

Valberg ⓦ valberg.com. Resort claiming the best snow record in the region, with 90km of downhill pistes and a preponderance of red runs.

La Vallée de l'Ubaye ⓦ ubaye.com. The region around Barçelonette harbours several skiing resorts, including Le Sauze Super Sauze, Sainte Anne la Condamine, and Pra Loup, whose pistes link up with those of La Foux d'Allos.

TOP 10 BEACHES

Plage du Prado, Marseille See p.58

Les Sablettes, La-Seyne-sur-Mer See p.260

Plage Notre Dame, Porquerolles See p.269

Silver sands of the Corniche des Maures See p.271

Plage du Gigaro, La Croix Valmer See p.276

Plage de Pampelonne, St-Tropez See p.282

Plage de la Croisette, Cannes See p.305

Juan-les-Pins See p.317

Plage de la Salis, Antibes See p.321

Plage Mala, Cap d'Ail See p.370

Travel essentials

Costs

Provence is one of the most **expensive** French regions to visit: prices in some of the chic hotspots on the Côte d'Azur can rival those in the more prestigious *arrondissements* of Paris, and costs for accommodation on the coast soar during the July and August peak season when foreign visitors have to compete with the French for scarce hotel rooms.

For a reasonably comfortable stay, you need to allow a **budget** of around €100 (£80/$130) a day, assuming two people sharing a mid-priced room. By counting the pennies – staying at youth hostels or camping and being strong-willed about extra cups of coffee and doses of culture – you could probably manage on €60 (£48/$75) a day. Costs vary a lot, with the Riviera more expensive than the rest of the Provence – St-Tropez and Monaco considerably so – and accommodation at its most expensive during the July-August high season.

As in other European Union countries, you'll routinely find that **Value Added Tax** (*TVA*) makes up part of your hotel, restaurant or shopping bill; prices are usually quoted inclusive of the tax. At restaurants you only need to leave an additional cash **tip** if you have received exceptional service, since restaurant prices include a service charge.

Crime and personal safety

Though certain sections of **Marseille**, **Toulon** and **Nice** have a distinctly dodgy feel, violent crime against tourists is pretty rare. **Petty theft**, however, is endemic along the Côte d'Azur and also a problem in the more crowded parts of the big cities, while occasional serious crimes contribute to the region's somewhat lurid reputation.

A recent trend is the targeting at night of foreign drivers on unlit sections of autoroute by **fake police** equipped with uniforms and flashing blue lights. Having stopped the drivers for some "offence", they make off with their documentation and a considerable "fine". Violence has sometimes been involved.

It obviously makes sense to take the normal **precautions**: don't flash wads of notes around; carry your bag or wallet securely and be especially careful in crowds; never leave valuables lying in view; and park your car overnight in a monitored parking garage or, at the very least, on a busy and well-lit street. Be wary of unmanned *aires* (rest areas) on the autoroute at night. It's also wise to keep a separate record of cheque and credit card numbers and the phone numbers for cancelling them. Finally, make sure you have a good insurance policy (see p.37).

Note that although there are two main types of **police** in France – the Police Nationale and the Gendarmerie Nationale – for all practical purposes they are indistinguishable.

Take care when **crossing roads** – inattentiveness is a problem, with many French drivers paying little heed to pedestrian crossings or lights. Do not step onto a crossing assuming that traffic will stop.

Drug use is just as prevalent in Provence as anywhere else in Europe – and just as risky; the authorities make no distinction between soft or hard drugs. People caught smuggling or possessing drugs, even just a few grams of marijuana, are liable to find themselves in jail.

As a long-standing stronghold of the extreme right, Provence has a regrettable reputation for **racism**, directed mainly against the Arab community. Anti-Semitic violence has had a high profile in France since the torture and murder of a young Jewish man, Ilan Halimi, in a Paris *banlieue* in 2006; an attack on a school in Toulouse in March 2012 left four dead. If you suffer a **racial assault**, contact the police, your consulate or one of the local anti-racism organizations (though they may not have English-speakers): SOS Racism (Ⓦsos-racisme.org) and Mouvement contre le Racisme et pour l'Amitié entre les Peuples (MRAP; Ⓦmrap.fr) have offices in most regions of France. Alternatively, you could contact the **English-speaking helpline** SOS Help (daily 3–11pm; ☎01 46 21 46 46, Ⓦsoshelpline.org); the service is staffed by trained volunteers who not only provide a confidential listening service, but also offer practical information for foreigners facing problems in France.

EMERGENCY NUMBERS

Police ☎17
Medical emergencies/ambulance (SAMU) ☎15
Fire brigade/paramedics ☎18
Emergency calls from a mobile phone ☎112
Rape crisis (Viols Femmes Informations) ☎0800 05 95 95
SOS Homophobie ☎0810 108 135
All emergency numbers are toll-free.

Electricity

Voltage is officially 230V, using **plugs** with two round pins. If you need an adapter, it's best to buy one before leaving home, though you can find them in big department stores.

Entry requirements

Citizens of **EU countries** can enter France freely on a valid passport or national ID card, while those from many **non-EU countries**, including Australia, Canada, New Zealand and the United States, do not need a visa for stays of **up to ninety days**. South African citizens require a short-stay visa, which should be applied for in advance, and costs €60.

Non-EU citizens wishing to remain **longer than ninety days** must apply for a long-stay visa, for which you'll have to show proof of income (or sufficient funds to support yourself) and medical insurance. Regulations can change, so it's advisable to check with your nearest French embassy or consulate before departure. For further information consult the Ministry of Foreign Affairs website: ⓦ diplomatie.gouv.fr.

Visa requirements for **Monaco** (an independent principality) are identical to those of France; there are no border controls between the two.

Gay and lesbian travellers

The prevalence of conservative attitudes tradition-ally meant that **lesbian and gay** life in Provence was rather discreet, but in the cities that has changed: both **Nice** and **Marseille** have annual gay pride celebrations, and while Marseille's bar scene is rather low-key, Nice has an increasingly high-profile gay scene, notably in the emerging "Petit Marais" district close to the port.

Attitudes are relaxed in the smaller, chic resorts such as **Cannes** and **St-Tropez**, where the gay presence is long-established and relatively integrated into the mainstream. Away from the coast, both **Aix** and **Avignon** have small-scale but lively bar scenes.

Addresses of local gay and/or lesbian establish-ments are listed in this book. Also useful is the Têtu website (ⓦ tetu.com), and the *France Gay et Lesbien* guide published by Petit Futé (ⓦ petitfute.com).

Health

Visitors to Provence have little to worry about as far as health is concerned. No vaccinations are required, there are no nasty diseases and tap water is safe to drink. If you do need treatment, however, you'll be in good hands: France's health-care system is one of the world's best.

Under the French health system, all services incur an upfront charge. **EU citizens** are entitled to a refund (usually 70 percent) of medical and dental expenses, provided the doctor is government-regis-tered (*un médecin conventionné*) and you have a **European Health Insurance Card** (EHIC; *Carte Européenne d'Assurance Maladie*). Present your EHIC card to avoid upfront charges; if you're admitted to hospital you'll generally only have to pay a 20 percent co-payment for treatment there. Everyone in the family, including children, must have their own EHIC card, which is free. In the UK, you can apply for them online (ⓦ ehic.org.uk), by phone (☎ 0845 606 2030) or by post – forms are available at post offices. Even with the EHIC card, you might want to take out additional insurance to cover the shortfall. **Non-EU visitors** require adequate medical insurance cover.

For minor complaints go to a **pharmacie**, signalled by an illuminated green cross. You'll find one in every small town and even in some villages. They keep shop hours (roughly 9am–noon & 3–6pm), though some stay open late and in larger towns at least one (known as the *pharmacie de garde*) is open overnight according to a rota; details are displayed in pharmacy windows. Local police will also have information.

Condoms (*préservatifs*) are available in pharma-cies, supermarkets and coin-operated vending machines. The pill (*la pilule*) is available only on prescription but emergency contraception (*la pilule du lendemain*) can be obtained at pharmacies.

For anything more serious you can get the name of a **doctor** from a pharmacy, local police station, tourist office or your hotel. Alternatively, look under "Médecins" in the Yellow Pages of the phone directory. The consultation fee is in the region of €23 to €25; some practitioners charge an additional fee on top of the official rate. You'll be given a *Feuille de Soins* (Statement of Treatment) for later insurance claims. Any prescriptions will be fulfilled by the pharmacy and must be paid for; little price stickers (*vignettes*) from each medicine will be stuck on the *Feuille de Soins*.

In serious **emergencies** you will be admitted to the nearest general hospital (*centre hospitalier*). Phone numbers and addresses of hospitals in the main cities are given where relevant.

Insurance

Even though EU citizens are entitled to health-care privileges in France, they would do well to take out an **insurance policy** before travelling in order to cover against theft, loss, illness or injury. Before paying for a new policy, however, it's worth checking whether you are already covered: some all-risks home insurance policies may cover your possessions when overseas, and many private medical schemes include cover when abroad.

After investigating these possibilities, you might want to contact a **specialist travel insurance** company. A typical travel insurance policy usually provides cover for the loss of baggage, tickets and – up to a certain limit – cash or cheques, as well as cancellation or curtailment of your journey. Most exclude so-called **dangerous sports** unless an extra premium is paid.

Internet

Wireless internet (**wi-fi**) is increasingly the norm in even the cheapest hotels and is often – though not invariably – free. Many hotels also have a computer terminal in a public area for those who do not have laptops or smartphones. **Internet cafés** are less common than they were but can still be found in the cities, sometimes also offering cheap international calls or other services such as photocopying. They usually have French, rather than English QWERTY keyboards.

Laundry

Inexpensive self-service **laundries** or *laveries automatiques* are commonplace in Provençal towns, and are listed in the guide for larger destinations such as Nice. They are often unattended, so come armed with small change. The alternative *blanchisserie* or pressing services are more expensive, as are hotel laundry services. Most hotels forbid doing laundry in your room, though you should get away with just one or two items.

Living in Provence

EU citizens are free to work in France on the same basis as a French citizen. This means you no longer have to apply for a residence or work permit except in very rare cases. You will, however, need to apply for a Carte du Séjour from a police station within three months of your arrival – contact your nearest French consulate for further information. **Non-EU citizens** are not allowed to work in France unless their prospective employer has obtained an *autorisation de travail* from the Ministry of Labour before their arrival. Under the "Compétences et Talents" scheme, a three-year renewable work permit may be issued to individuals with specific skills. Students who have completed one academic year in France can work on renewable three-month work permits under strict conditions, subject to obtaining prior permission from the Ministry of Labour. Au pair visas must also be obtained before travelling to France. Contact your nearest French consulate for more information on what rules apply in your particular situation.

When **looking for a job**, a good starting point is *Live & Work in France* published by Crimson (Ⓦcrimsonbooks.co.uk). You can search for jobs online at Monster (Ⓦmonster.fr) and Job Etudiant (Ⓦjobetudiant.net), which focuses on jobs for students. In France, try the youth information agency CIDJ (Ⓦcidj.com), or CIJ (Centre d'Information Jeunesse) offices in cities, which have information about temporary jobs and working in France.

A degree and a TEFL (Teaching English as a Foreign Language) or similar qualification are normally required for **English-language teaching** posts. The online *EL Gazette newsletter* (Ⓦwww.elgazette.com) is a useful source of information; so too is *Teaching English Abroad* published by Vacation Work and the TEFL website (Ⓦwww.tefl.com).

The Riviera has a large expat Anglophone community, and there is consequently demand for **English-language services** of various kinds, from domestic staff to *immobiliers* and experienced crew members on yachts. Riviera Radio (see p.33) often carries job ads, though these usually require fluent French. It may also be worth checking the business section of the *Riviera Times* (Ⓦ rivieratimes.com) or the classified sections of *Anglo Info* (Ⓦ riviera .angloinfo.com; Ⓦ provence.angloinfo.com).

STUDY AND WORK PROGRAMMES

AFS Intercultural Programs Ⓦ afs.org. Intercultural exchange organization with programmes in over fifty countries.
American Institute for Foreign Study Ⓦ aifsabroad.com. Language and culture courses in Cannes over a summer, a semester or a year.

Mail

As a rule, **post offices** (*bureaux de poste* or PTTs) are open from around 8.30/9am to 6/7pm Monday to Friday, and from 8.30am to noon on Saturday; look for bright yellow *La Poste* signs. Smaller branches usually close for lunch.

For **sending mail**, standard letters (20g or less) and postcards in France and beyond cost €0.57; to other European Union countries a charge of €0.05 per 10g is added to the basic fee for heavier letters and of €0.11 per 10g to all other countries. You can also buy stamps from *tabacs* and newsagents. In order to post your letter on the street, look for the bright yellow postboxes.

Maps

In addition to the maps in this guide and the various free town plans and regional maps you'll be offered along the way, the one extra map you might want is a good, up-to-date **road map** of France. The best are those produced by Michelin (1:200,000; Ⓦ viamichelin.fr) and the Institut Géographique National (IGN; 1:250,000; Ⓦ ign.fr), either as individual sheets or in one large spiral-bound *atlas routier*. If **walking**, it's worth investing in the more detailed (1:25,000) IGN maps. **Free town maps** handed out by tourist offices are often surprisingly good; the quality of those covering rural areas is more variable and they tend to be geared more towards inspiring you than providing practical information.

Money

France's currency, the **euro**, is divided into 100 cents (often still referred to as *centimes*). There are seven **notes** – in denominations of 5, 10, 20, 50, 100, 200 and 500 euros – and eight different **coins** – 1, 2, 5, 10, 20 and 50 cents, and 1 and 2 euros. In practice, you'll rarely see 200 or 500 euro notes, and shopkeepers are not keen to accept them.

By far the easiest way to access your money in France is to use your credit or debit card to withdraw cash from an **ATM** (known as a *distributeur* or *point argent*); machines are every bit as ubiquitous as in Britain or North America, and most give instructions in several languages. Check with your bank before you leave home if you're in any doubt, and note that there is often a transaction fee, so it's more efficient to take out a sizeable sum each time rather than making lots of small withdrawals.

Similarly, all major **credit cards** are almost always accepted in hotels, restaurants and shops, although some smaller establishments don't accept cards, or only for sums above a certain threshold. Visa – called Carte Bleue in France – is almost universally recognized, followed by MasterCard (also known as EuroCard). American Express ranks a bit lower.

Opening hours and public holidays

Basic **hours of business** are Monday to Saturday 9am until noon, and 2pm to 6pm. In big city centres, shops and other businesses stay open throughout the day, while in July and August most tourist offices and museums are open without interruption. Otherwise almost everything – shops, museums, tourist offices, most banks – closes for a couple of hours at midday. Small food shops may not reopen till halfway through the afternoon, closing around 7.30 or 8pm, just before the evening meal. The standard **closing day** is Sunday, even in larger towns and cities, though some food shops and newsagents are open in the morning. Some shops and businesses, particularly in rural areas, also close on Mondays.

Museums tend to open at around 10am, close for lunch at noon until 2pm (sometimes 3pm) and then run through until only 5 or 6pm; summer opening hours often differ, with a longer lunch break or later closing. Closing days are usually Monday or Tuesday, sometimes both.

Phones

Payphones (*cabines*) are increasingly rare due to the proliferation of mobile phones. You can make and receive calls – look for the number in the top right-hand corner of the information panel. The vast majority of public phones require a prepaid phonecard (*télécarte*) available from *tabacs* and newsagents; they come in units of 50 and 120 (€7.50 and €15 respectively). Alternatively, a more flexible option is to get one of the many prepaid phonecards which operate with a unique code (*tickets téléphoniques*). these are on sale at Orange outlets, post offices, *tabacs*, newsagents, and can be used from both private and public phones. Orange's Ticket France Europe, for example, for domestic and European calls, is available in €5 and €10 denominations, while the prices for the Ticket International are €7.50 and €15. The €15 card buys up to 1000 minutes to landlines in the US and Canada. You can also use credit cards in many call boxes.

Calling within France

For calls within France – local or long distance – simply dial all ten digits of the number. Numbers beginning ☎0800 and ☎0805 are free-dial numbers; those beginning ☎081 are charged as a local call; numbers beginning ☎086 cost €0.1 for the first minute and €0.02 per minute thereafter. Note that some of these ☎08 numbers cannot be accessed from abroad. Numbers starting ☎06 and 07 are mobile numbers and are therefore more expensive to call.

Mobile phones

If you want to use your **mobile/cell phone**, contact your phone provider to check whether it will work in France and what the call charges are – they tend to be pretty exorbitant, and remember you're likely to be charged extra for receiving calls. French mobile phones operate on the GSM standard; if you're travelling from the US your cell phone may not work if it is not tri-band or from a supplier that has switched to GSM.

If you are going to be in France for any length of time it may be worth buying a pay-as-you-go **French SIM card** from any of the big mobile providers (Orange, SFR and Bouygues Telecom), all

---

CALLING ABROAD FROM FRANCE

Note that the initial zero is omitted from the area code when dialling from abroad.
Australia 0061 + area code + number
New Zealand 0064 + area code + number
Republic of Ireland 00353 + area code + number
UK 0044 + area code + number
US and Canada 001 + area code + number
South Africa 0027 + area code + number

---

of which have high-street outlets. SFR does a SIM-only deal for around €20 including a limited amount of call time and texts, while Bouygues and Orange both do very low cost SIM cards; you can then decide how much prepaid time to buy. Remember you'll need either a plug adapter for your phone charger or a charger compatible with French power sockets – phone shops stock the most popular models. One other option – if your hotel has free wi-fi – is to use your Skype account.

Shopping

Provence offers a rich variety of local **crafts** and **produce** to buy as souvenirs, with everything from *santons* in Aubagne or Marseille to high-quality glassware in Biot and fine art and handicrafts in every chic village along the Côte d'Azur.

Food can be a particular joy, from soft nougat and farmhouse honey to olive oil and fine wine, *marrons glacés* from Collobrières and *calissons* from Aix. One of the pleasures of shopping in Provence is the opportunity to taste oils and wines as you go; another is the region's many excellent markets.

Most larger towns have considerable shopping facilities in the centre, including perhaps a **department store** as well as the usual range of **fashion** and **footwear** chains; most Provençal towns of any size also have sizeable edge-of-town **retail parks** which include not only mammoth supermarkets but also discount shoe and clothing retailers. Some of the Côte d'Azur resorts – in particular St-Tropez, Cannes, Nice and Monte Carlo – also have a considerable selection of luxury stores, with all the usual international **designer** names.

Smoking

Smoking is **banned** in all public places, including public transport, museums, cafés and restaurants.

PUBLIC HOLIDAYS

January 1 New Year's Day
Easter Monday
Ascension Day (forty days after Easter)
Whit Monday (seventh Monday after Easter)
May 1 Labour Day
May 8 Victory in Europe (VE) Day 1945
July 14 Bastille Day
August 15 Assumption of the Virgin Mary
November 1 All Saints' Day
November 11 Armistice Day
December 25 Christmas Day

Time

France is in the **Central European Time Zone** (GMT+1). This means it is one hour ahead of the UK, six hours ahead of Eastern Standard Time and nine hours ahead of Pacific Standard Time. **Daylight Saving Time** (GMT+2) in France lasts from the last Sunday of March to the last Sunday of October.

Tourist information

The **French Government Tourist Office** (Maison de la France) has offices throughout the world, each with its own website holding general countrywide information. For practical details on a specific location, contact the relevant regional or departmental tourist offices; contact details are listed below and can also be found online at ⓦ fncrt.com and ⓦ fncdt.net respectively.

In France itself, practically every town (and many a village) has a tourist office – usually an **Office du Tourisme** (OT) but sometimes a **Syndicat d'Initiative** (SI). These provide local information, including hotel and restaurant listings, leisure activities, car and bike rental, bus times, laundries and countless other things; many can also book accommodation for you. Most can provide a town plan, and sell maps and local walking guides.

REGIONAL TOURIST WEBSITES

Alpes de Haute Provence ⓦ alpes-haute-provence.com
Bouches du Rhône ⓦ visitprovence.com
Côte d'Azur ⓦ cotedazur-tourisme.com
Var ⓦ visitvar.fr
Vaucluse ⓦ provenceguide.com

FRENCH GOVERNMENT TOURIST OFFICES ABROAD

Australia and New Zealand ⓦ au.franceguide.com
Canada ⓦ ca-en.franceguide.com
Ireland ⓦ ie.franceguide.com.
South Africa ⓦ za.franceguide.com
UK ⓦ uk.franceguide.com
USA ⓦ us.franceguide.com

Travellers with disabilities

Travellers with **disabilities**, and particularly those using wheelchairs, will find haphazard parking habits, stepped village streets and cobbled paving among the challenges of a visit to Provence – but the situation is improving. All hotels are required to adapt at least one room to be wheelchair accessible and a growing number of *chambres d'hôtes*

are doing likewise. Hotels, sights and other facilities are inspected under the nationwide "Tourisme & Handicap" scheme and, if they fulfil certain criteria, issued with a certificate and logo. A supplementary scheme, "Destination pour tous" was rolled out in 2011 to recognize communities that promote disabled access to tourism. Museums, stations and other sites are gradually being adapted with **ramps** or other forms of access, though provision varies. The **public transport** situation is improving as networks are modernized: Nice's Tramway, for instance, has been designed to be fully accessible.

The national association **APF** (Association des Paralysées de France) is a useful source of information and has representatives in each *département*.

AFP (ASSOCIATION DES PARALYSÉES DE FRANCE) CONTACTS

ⓦ apf.asso.fr (in French)
Avignon ☏ 04 90 16 47 40
La Garde (Var) ☏ 04 98 01 30 50
Manosque ☏ 04 92 71 74 50
Marseille ☏ 04 91 79 99 99
Nice ☏ 04 92 07 98 00

Travelling with children

Children and babies are generally welcome everywhere, including most bars and restaurants. Hotels charge by the room, and many either have a few large **family rooms**, or charge a small supplement for an additional bed or cot. Family-run places will often **babysit** or offer a listening service while you eat or go out. Especially in seaside towns, most restaurants have **children's menus** or cook simpler food on request.

Most tourist offices have details of specific **activities** for children. Children under 4 years travel free on **public transport**, while those between 4 and 11 pay half-fare. **Museums** and the like are generally free to under-12s and half-price or free up to the age of 18.

Travelling with pets from the UK

If you wish to take your dog (or cat) to France, the **Pet Travel Scheme** (PETS) enables you to avoid putting it in quarantine when re-entering the UK as long as certain conditions are met. Current regulations are available on the Department for Environment, Food and Rural Affairs (DEFRA) website (ⓦ www.defra.gov.uk/wildlife-pets/pets/travel/index.htm) or through the PETS Helpline (☏ 0870 241 1710).

Marseille
and around

CALANQUE EN VAU

1

Marseille and around

The Marseille conurbation is by far the most populated and industrialized part of Provence, and indeed of southern France. After Lyon and Paris it is France's third-largest urban region, an area where tourism takes a back seat to other industries: to shipping in Marseille city; and petrochemicals around the Étang de Berre. Yet the area also has vast tracts of deserted mountainous countryside and a shoreline of high cliffs, jagged inlets and sand beaches with stretches still untouched by the holiday industry. For visitors, the great attraction is Marseille itself, a vital commercial port for more than two millennia. France's second city is, for all its notorious reputation, a wonderful place with a distinctive, unconventional character that never ceases to surprise.

The first foreigners to settle in Provence, the ancient **Greeks** from Phocaea and their less amiable successors from **Rome**, left evidence of their presence in Marseille, where museums guard reminders of the indigenous peoples whose civilization they destroyed. The wider region has strong military connections. **Salon-de-Provence** holds a training school for French air-force pilots but also preserves reminders of Nostradamus; **Aubagne** is home to the French Foreign Legion but also to the characters of **Pagnol**.

There are great seaside attractions here too: the pine-covered rocks and beaches of the **Côte Bleue**; the *calanques* (rocky inlets) between Marseille and **Cassis**; the sand beaches of **La Ciotat** bay; and the dizzying, dramatic heights from which to view the coast on the **route des Crêtes**. The area also has great **wines** at Cassis, and great **seafood**, particularly in Marseille, home of the famous fish stew, bouillabaisse.

Marseille

In recent years **MARSEILLE** has undergone a marked **renaissance**, shaking off much of its old reputation for sleaze to attract a wider range of visitors. The TGV has made it accessible to northerners, the rejuvenated docks have become a magnet for cruise ships and the shops in the streets south of La Canebière are increasingly trendy or elegant. In 2008, a Marseille restaurant was awarded three Michelin stars for the first time; in 2013, the city will be European Capital of Culture. The forward march of progress is not, however, relentless. All too often, last year's prestige civic project becomes this year's broken, bottle-strewn fountain, while Marseille's easy tolerance of graffiti means it sometimes *looks* like the toughest city in France. In short, it's a rough diamond.

See past the grit, and chances are you'll warm to this down-to-earth, vital metropolis. It has a powerful magnetism as a true Mediterranean city, surrounded by mountains

ROOF TERRACE AT L'UNITÉ D'HABITATION, MARSEILLE

Highlights

❶ The Vieux Port, Marseille An intoxicating blend of food, history, water and sunlight at the very heart of France's great Mediterranean metropolis. **See p.47**

❷ L'Unité d'Habitation, Marseille Le Corbusier's highly sculptural concrete masterpiece is a truly ground-breaking piece of modernist architecture. **See p.56**

❸ Château d'If The most compelling of Marseille's islands was the sinister setting for Dumas' *The Count of Monte Cristo*. **See p.58**

❹ Bouillabaisse Marseille's very own fish stew is the true taste of the south of France – and an unmissable Marseille experience. **See p.61**

❺ Calanques Whether you walk, swim or simply take a boat trip, don't miss the blinding white rocks, crystal-clear waters and fjord-like inlets of the coastal national park between Marseille and Cassis. **See p.73**

❻ Corniche des Crêtes Don't get blown away by the spectacular scenery (or high winds) on this scenic drive from Cassis to La Ciotat. **See p.77**

HIGHLIGHTS ARE MARKED ON THE MAP ON P.46

1

and graced with hidden corners that have the unexpected air of fishing villages. Built (for the most part handsomely) of warm stone, it has its triumphal architecture, too, as well as the cosmopolitan atmosphere of a major port. Perhaps the most appealing quality, however, is the down-to-earth nature of its gregarious, talkative inhabitants.

Some history

Marseille has been a **trading city** for over two and a half thousand years, ever since ancient Greeks from Ionia discovered shelter in the Lacydon inlet, today the Vieux Port, and came to an agreement with the local Ligurian tribe. The story goes that the locals, noticing the exotic cargo of the strangers' boats, sent them off to the king's castle where the princess's wedding preparations were in full swing. The Ligurian royal custom at the time was that the king's daughter could choose her husband from among her father's guests. As the leader of the Greek party walked through the castle gate, he was handed a drink by a woman and discovered that she was the princess and that he was the bridegroom. The king gave the couple the hill on the north side of the Lacydon, and Massalia came into being.

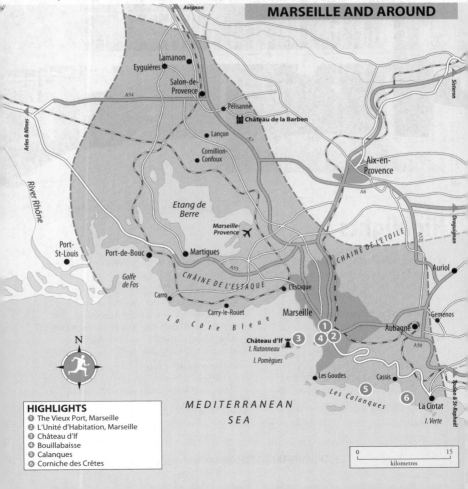

MARSEILLE AND AROUND

HIGHLIGHTS
❶ The Vieux Port, Marseille
❷ L'Unité d'Habitation, Marseille
❸ Château d'If
❹ Bouillabaisse
❺ Calanques
❻ Corniche des Crêtes

1

MARSEILLE ORIENTATION

Marseille is divided into sixteen arrondissements that spiral out from the **Vieux Port**. Due north lies **Le Panier**, the old town and site of the original Greek settlement of Massalia; further north still **Les Docks** are the focus for Marseille's ambitious inner-city regeneration programmes. **La Canebière**, the wide boulevard starting at quai des Belges at the head of the Vieux Port, is the central east–west axis of the town, with the **Centre Bourse** shopping centre and the little streets of **quartier Belsunce** to the north, and the main shopping streets to the south. The main north–south axis is **rue d'Aix**, becoming **cours Belsunce** then **cours St-Louis**, **rue de Rome**, **avenue du Prado** and **boulevard Michelet**. The trendy quarter around **place Jean-Jaurès** and **cours Julien** lies to the east of rue de Rome. On the headland west of the Vieux Port are the village-like *quartiers* of **Les Catalans** and **Malmousque** from where the **Corniche** heads south past the city's most favoured residential districts towards the beaches, bars and restaurants of the **Plage du Prado**.

Since then, Marseille has both prospered and been ransacked over the centuries. It has lost its privileges to sundry French kings and foreign armies, refound its fortunes, suffered plagues, religious bigotry, republican and royalist fervour and had its own Commune and Bastille-storming. It was the epic march of revolutionaries from Marseille to Paris in 1792 which gave the name to the Hymn of the Army of the Rhine that became the **national anthem** – La Marseillaise.

The Vieux Port

The **Vieux Port** is, more or less, the ancient harbour basin, and the original inlet that the ancient Greeks sailed into, though nowadays its historic resonances are overlaid by the hubbub of sunglass-wearing idlers on the port-side café terraces. The morning **fish market** on the quai des Belges provides some natural Marseillais theatre; and the seafood restaurants on the **pedestrianized streets** between the southern quay and cours Estienne d'Orves ensure that the Vieux Port stays busy well into the evening. The best view of the Vieux Port is from the **Palais du Pharo**, built on the headland at the harbour mouth by Emperor Napoléon III for his wife and now used as a conference centre. Its surrounding park (8am–9pm) hides an underground *mediathèque* and exhibition space.

Notre-Dame-de-la-Garde

Rue Fort du Sanctuaire • Daily: summer 7am–7.15pm; winter 7am–6.15pm • ☎ 04 91 13 40 80, ⓦ notredamedelagarde.com • Bus #60 or tourist train from Vieux Port

For a sweeping view of the port, islands and Marseille's littoral, head up to the city's highest point, **Notre-Dame-de-la-Garde**, on boulevard André-Aune, which tops the hill south of the harbour. Crowned by a monumental gold Madonna and Child and dating from the Second Empire, the church is a monstrous riot of neo-Byzantine design and the most distinctive of Marseille's landmarks. Inside, model ships hang from the rafters while the paintings and drawings displayed are by turns kitsch, unintentionally comic and deeply moving, as they depict the shipwrecks, house fires and car crashes from which the virgin has supposedly rescued grateful believers. A World War I soldier's helmet pierced by a bullet hole is a prominent exhibit.

THE MARSEILLE CITY PASS

If you intend visiting several of Marseille's museums it's worth considering the **Marseille City Pass**, which for €22 (one day) or €29 (two days) includes free admission to municipal museums, Le Panier guided tours (see p.59), entry to the Château d'If and free travel on métros and buses.

1

AVENUE DU MERLAN
13e
AV. DE VALDONNE
BD. JEAN PAUL SARTRE
AVENUE DE MONTOLIVET
BD. LOUIS GILLET
MZAOUHER
PLACE CAIRE
12e
AV. DE ST-JULIEN
R. ALPH. DAUDET
AV. DE ST-BARNABE
AV. DE MONTAIGNE

AV. SALVADOR ALLENDE
AV. PROS. MERIMEE
BD. L.
Hôtel du Département
Creuset des Arts
BD. MAL. JUIN
BD. FRANÇOISE DUPARC
BD. SAKAKINI
BD. JEANNE D'ARC
BD.

14e
VILLECROZE
Le Dôme
AV. ALEX. FLEMING
4e
Palais de Longchamp
BD. DU CAMAS
BOULEVARD CHAVE
RUE FERRARI
5e

AVENUE DE STE-MARTHE
La Friche la Belle de Mai/ Théâtre Massalia
Musée Grobet-Labadi
R. DES BONS ENFANTS

AUTOROUTE NORD
BD. DE PLOMBIÈRES
3e
BOULEVARD NATIONAL
Gare SNCF
PL. JEAN JAURES
R. ST-SAVOURNIN

RUE DE LYON
15e
Marché aux Puces
AVENUE ROGER SALENGRO
RUE DE RUFFIN
1er
COURS BELSUNCE
RUE DE ROME
6e

BOULEVARD DE DUNKERQUE
Gare Maritime
Le Silo d'Arenc
Les Docks
PL. DE LA JOLIETTE
RUE DE LA RÉPUBLIQUE
2e
LE PANIER
QUAI DE LA JOLIETTE
BD. NOTRE DAME
BD. CORDERIE

Alhambra
DU LITTORAL
AUTOROUTE
QUAI DU PORT
BD. CHARLES LIVON
AV. DE LA COURSE
7e

Digue du Largo

Rade de Marseille

SEE "MARSEILLE: LE VIEUX PORT" MAP

Plage des Catalans

Vallon des Auffes

Rochers de Pendus

CORNICHE PRÉSIDENT J.

● BARS	
Au Petit Nice	4
Aux 3G	3
Le Greenwich	6
Le Red Lion	7
Sports Beach Café	5
Trash	1

● CAFÉ	
Plauchut	2

● RESTAURANTS	
Chez Fonfon	8
La Grotte	10
Petit Nice-Passédat	9

■ LIVE MUSIC & CLUBS	
L'Affranchi	1
Bazar	3
Les Docks des Suds	6
L'Intermédiare	5
New Cancan	4
Le Poste à Galène	2

■ ACCOMMODATION	
Auberge de Jeunesse Bonneveine	4
Le Corbusier	2
Edmond Rostand	3
Mama Shelter	1
Le Richelieu	5

N

Abbaye St-Victor

3 rue de l'Abbaye • Daily: 9am–7pm • Crypt €2 • ☎ 0496112260, ⓦ saintvictor.net

Above the Bassin de Carénage and the slip road for the Vieux Port's tunnel is
Marseille's oldest church, the **Abbaye St-Victor**. Originally part of a monastery
founded in the fifth century on the burial site of various martyrs, the church was
built, enlarged and fortified – a vital requirement given its position outside the city

1

CHAÎNE DE SAINT CYR

MARSEILLE

RUE ST-PIERRE

11e

BD. DE PONT DE VIVAUX

AUTOROUTE EST

RUE ROMAIN ROLLAND

AVENUE DE LA CAPELETTE

10e

BOULEVARD DU REDON

9e

BOULEVARD DE SAINTE MARGUERITE

JEAN MOULIN

RUE RABATAU

AVENUE MARÉCHAL DE LATTRE DE TASSIGNY

❶

RUE ROGER BRUN

BD. SCHLOESING

Palais des Sports

AVENUE JULES CANTINI

RUE RABATAU

❸

Stade Vélodrome/
Olympique
de Marseille

AVENUE DE PRADO

Rond-Point du Prado Ⓜ

BOULEVARD MICHELET

RUE E. ROSTAND

RUE PARADIS

AVENUE DE PRADO

Unité d'Habitation
❷ Le Corbusier

AVENUE DE MAZARGUES

CH. DU LANCIER

CH. DE ROI
D'ESPAGNE

AV. DE RAÏFA

MAC

AV. ANDRÉ ZENATTI

8e

AVENUE DU PRADO

AVENUE CLOT BEY

Ballet National
de Marseille

Parc
Borély

Château
Borély

BD. DU SABLIER

❹

Notre Dame
de la Garde

AV. JOSEPH VIDAL

PROMENADE
POMPIDOU

AVENUE PIERRE

❺

MENDÈS-FRANCE

❻

AV. DES GOUMIERS

❼

Plage du Prado

AV. DE MONTREDON

MONTAGNE DE MARSEILLEVEYRE

Jardin
Valmer

F. KENNEDY

Musée de
la Faïence

❾

MALMOUSQUE

Rade d'Endoume

Port de Plaisance
de la Pte. Rouge

MADRAGUE DE MONTREDON

Les Goudes & the calanques **❿**

Îles d'Endoume

LA MADRAGUE

0		1

kilometre

walls – over a period of two hundred years from the middle of the tenth century. With the walls of the choir almost 3m thick, it certainly looks and feels more like a fortress, and it's no conventional ecclesiastical beauty. Nevertheless the **crypt**, in particular, is fascinating: a crumbling warren of rounded and propped-up arches, small side chapels and secretive passageways, its proportions are more impressive than the church above and it contains a number of sarcophagi.

1

■ **ACCOMMODATION**

Alizé	5
Bellevue	4
Hermès	3
Ibis Budget Vieux Port	8
Lutétia	2
Du Palais	10
Radisson Blu	6
St Ferréol	7
Vertigo	1
Vertigo Vieux Port	9

0   200
metres

■ **LIVE MUSIC & CLUBS**

Cité de la Musique	1
Machine à Coudre	4
Pelle Mêle	3
Trolleybus	2

N

Hospice de la Vieille Charité

Cathédrale de la Major

AVENUE ROBERT SCHUMAN

R. DE CHABITE

RUE DES P. PUITS

RUE DU THIER

ESPLANADE DE LA TOURETTE

Cathédrale Vieille Major

RUE DE L'EVECHE

RUE DE LA BUSSE

PL. DES MOULINS

AV. VAUDOYER

PLACE DE LA MAJOR

LE PANIER

Musée Regards de Provence

RUE TERRASSON

RUE DES MOULINS

AVENUE DE LA TOURETTE

PLACE DE LENCHE

MONTÉE DES ACCOULES

MuCEM

RUE ST-LAURENT

RUE CAISSERIE

Théâtre de Lenche

PLACE DAVIEL

Fort St Jean

AV. ST-JEAN

Maison Diamantée

PLACE VIVAUX

Eglise St-Laurent

RUE DE LA LOGE

Musée des Docks Romains

QUAI DU PORT

Palais du Pharo

ESPLANADE DU PHARO

Jardin du Pharo

Anse de la Reserve

Vieux Port

BOULEVARD CHARLES LIVON

Fort St-Nicolas

QUAI DE RIVE NEUVE

RUE CHARRAS

AVENUE PASTEUR

RUE ROBER

Théâtre de la Criée

RUE NVE. STE-CATHERINE

● **BARS**

O'Malley's	12
Bar de la Marine	11

RAMPE SAINT-MAURICE

RUE SAINTE

PLACE ST-VICTOR

RUE D'ENDOUME

Musée du Santon

RUE SAINTE

RUE DU PETIT CHANTIER

RUE DE LA CROIX

RUE DES TYRANS

RUE RIGORD

● **CAFÉS**

Le Carthage	9
Cup of Tea	2
L'Equitable	17
Torrefaction Noailles	7

St-Victor

AVENUE DE LA COURSE

BOULEVARD DE LA CORDERIE

RUE JOEL RECHER

RUE FRANÇOIS TADDEI

RUE DU RAMPART

Jardin Puget

● **RESTAURANTS**

Les Arcenaulx	16
Chez Sauveur	10
La Garbure	14
La Kahena	5
Le Marseillois	6
La Part des Anges	18
La Passarelle	13
Sur le Pouce	1
Toinou Coquillages	8
La Trilogie des Cépages	15
Une Table, au Sud	4
La Virgule	3

RUE SAUVEUR TOBELEM

RUE CANDOLLE

MONTÉE DE L'ORATOIRE

BOULEVARD ANDRÉ AUNE

● **SHOPS**

La Compagnie de Provence	2/4
Four des Navettes	5
La Maison du Pastis	3
Place aux Huiles	1
Virgin	6

RUE D'ENDOUME

BOULEVARD TELLENE

Musée du Santon

47–49 rue Neuve Sainte-Catherine • Jan–Nov Tues–Sat 10am–12.30pm & 2–6.30pm; Dec Mon–Sat Tues–Sat 10am–12.30pm & 2–6.30pm • Free • ☎ 04 91 54 26 58, ⓦ santonsmarcelcarbonel.com

Close to the Abbaye St Victor, the **Musée du Santon** is dedicated to *santons* – the little Christmas figurines characteristic of the region – and has examples from the time of the Revolution to the present day, by some of the greatest *santon* makers. Alongside the

MARSEILLE: LE VIEUX PORT

Map labels:

- BOULEVARD DES DAMES
- Gare Routiére
- PLACE VICTOR HUGO
- Jules Guesde
- BOULEVARD C. NEDELEC
- RUE TRIGANCE
- R. DE LORETTE
- RUE JEAN TRINQUET
- RUE B. DU BOIS
- Gare St-Charles
- Porte d'Aix
- RUE DE LA FABE
- St-Charles
- RUE ST-ANTOINE
- R. DES BELLES ECUELLES
- R. FR. DE PRESSENSE
- R. DES PETITES MARIES
- PL. SADI CARNOT
- Colbert
- RUE D'AIX
- RUE DE L'ETOILE
- BOULEVARD D'ATHENES
- RUE LAFAYETTE
- RUE PUVIS DE CHAVANNES
- Hôtel Dieu
- RUE DES CAPUCINS
- RUE DES DOMINICAINES
- RUE COLBERT
- QUARTIER BELSUNCE
- R. CONVALESCENTS
- GRANDE RUE
- RUE CH. ROZE
- RUE MERY
- RUE BARBUSSE
- COURS BELSUNCE
- Bibliothèque Alcazar
- RUE DU PL. ST. JEAN
- R. NATIONALE
- BOULEVARD D'ATHENES
- RUE DE JEMMAPES
- Hôtel de Cabre
- RUE BONETERIE
- Jardin des Vestiges
- RUE LONGUE DES CAPUCINS
- RUE TAPIS VERT
- A.L. GAMBETTA
- Hôtel de Ville
- RUE DE LA COUTELLERIE
- Centre Bourse
- RUE THUBANEAU
- Mémorial de la Marseillaise
- BD. DUGOMMIER
- RUE BIR HAKEIM
- RUE REINE ELIZABETH
- RTM
- RUE DES FABRES
- RUE VINCENT SCOTTO
- Les Variétés
- Odéon
- RUE MAZAGRAN
- R.G. MOCQUET
- Bourse/Musée de la Marine et de l'economic
- LA CANEBIERE
- BD. GARTHALDI
- Lycée Thiers
- Vieux Port-Hôtel de Ville
- QUAI DES BELGES
- PLACE DU G. DE GAULLE
- RUE DU MARCHE DES CAPUCINS
- RUE DU MUSEE
- Noailles
- Palais des Arts
- RUE PAVILLON
- COURS ST-LOUIS
- RUE BEAUVAU
- RUE DE VACON
- RUE L'ACADEMIE
- RUE DES 3 MAGES
- PLACE THIERS
- ST-SAENS
- RUE ST-SAENS
- RUE HAXO
- RUE ST-FERREOL
- RUE D'AUBAGNE
- Espace Julien
- PLACE AUX HUILES
- RUE FORT NOTRE-DAME
- PLACE J. BALLARD
- RUE PARADIS
- J. JEAN ROQUE
- COURS JULIEN
- COURS D'ESTIENNE D'ORVES
- Opéra
- RUE LULLI
- RUE SAINTE
- RUE VENTURE
- Maison de l'Artisanat et des Métiers d'Art
- RUE SAINTE
- RUE DE LA PAIX MARCEL PAUL
- RUE GRIGNAN
- RUE ESTELLE
- COURS LIEUTAUD
- M. D. du Mont Cours Julien
- PLACE DE LA CORDERIE
- RUE EMILE POLLAK
- RUE GRIGNAN
- Musée Cantini
- RUE DE ROME
- RUE BRETEUIL
- RUE MONTGRAND
- RUE DIEUDE
- PL. P. CEZANNE
- COURS PIERRE PUGET
- RUE ROUX DE BRIGNOLES
- RUE LAFON
- RUE FONGATE
- RUE DE LODI
- BOULEVARD NOTRE-DAME
- Estrangin-Préfecture
- RUE ARMENY
- PLACE DE PREFECTURE
- PLACE DE ROME
- BD. L. SALVATOR
- RUE DES BERGERS
- Préfecture
- Police
- RUE SYLVABELLE
- RUE ST-JACQUES

museum is **Carbonel atelier**, the workshop of Marcel Carbonel, one of the most renowned producers of *santons*; the Carbonel atelier was the first to fire them – they'd hitherto been made of unfired clay.

Maison de l'Artisanat et des Métiers d'Art

21 cours d'Estienne d'Orves • Tues–Fri 10am–noon & 1–6pm, Sat 1–6pm • Free • ☎ 04 91 54 80 54, ⓦ maisonde.lartisanat.org

1

Occupying a beautiful, wood-beamed eighteenth-century premises on the site of Louis XIV's arsenal, the **Maison de l'Artisanat et des Métiers d'Art** hosts excellent temporary exhibitions of applied arts and crafts, providing a showcase for the region's own applied artists as well as hosting touring exhibitions of applied art from elsewhere in Europe and overseas.

Musée des Civilisations d'Europe et de la Méditerranée (MuCEM)

Fort St-Jean • Due to open in 2013; check website for opening hours and admission prices • ⓦ mucem.org

One of two fortresses guarding the harbour entrance, medieval **Fort St-Jean** is undergoing conversion and the addition of a modernist annexe by Algerian-born Provençal architect Rudy Ricciotti to create the new national **Musée des Civilisations d'Europe et de la Méditerranée (MuCEM)**, scheduled to open in 2013. The new building will house exhibitions tracing the important phases of Mediterranean civilization and focusing on its cities, people and societies, while the fort will house an exhibition on the festivals and spectacles of Mediterranean civilization. There will also be a roof garden on the battlements of the fort.

The fortress dates from the Middle Ages when Marseille was an independent republic; its enlargement in 1660, and the construction of **Fort St-Nicolas** on the south side of the port, represented the city's final defeat as a separate entity. Louis XIV ordered the new fort to keep an eye on Marseille after he had sent in an army, suppressed the city's council, fined it, arrested all opposition and, in an early example of rate-capping, set ludicrously low limits on Marseille's subsequent expenditure and borrowing. Fort St-Nicolas is still a military installation today.

Cathédrale de la Major and the waterfront

1 avenue Robert Schuman • Tues–Sat: summer 10am–7pm; winter 10am–6pm • ☎ 04 91 90 53 57, ⓦ marseille.catholique.fr/-La-Major-cathedrale-de-Marseille

The **Cathédrale de la Major**, on the north side of the Vieux Port overlooking the modern docks, is an imposing nineteenth-century structure whose striped, neo-Byzantine bulk completely overshadows what remains of its forlorn predecessor, the Romanesque **Vieille Major**, which stands alongside, closed, shuttered and structurally undermined by the road tunnel beneath it. The construction of a tree-lined waterfront promenade as part of the **Euroméditerranée** docklands regeneration is currently transforming the cathedral's hitherto rather marginalized and neglected surroundings.

Musée Regards de Provence

Avenue Vaudoyer • Daily 10am–6pm • Due to open in 2013; check website for opening hours and admission prices • ⓦ museeregardsdeprovence.com

Occupying a long, low modernist structure wedged between the cathedral and the Fort St-Jean, the new **Musée Regards de Provence** opens in 2013 to display works from the Fondation Regards de Provence's 850-strong collection of art from and about Provence, including works by Ziem, Dufy and Monticelli among others.

Le Panier

Rising above the north side of the Vieux Port, **Le Panier** is the oldest part of Marseille. This is where the ancient Greeks built their Massalia, and where, up until World War II, tiny streets, steep steps and a jumble of houses formed a Vieille Ville typical of this coast. Much of the old quarter was destroyed during World War II (see box opposite) and replaced afterwards by solid apartment blocks in a vaguely Art Deco style. Amongst all this are the landmark structures that the Nazis spared: the seventeenth-century **Hôtel de Ville** on the quay; the half-Gothic, half-Renaissance **Hôtel de Cabre** on the corner of rue Bonneterie and Grande rue; and the **Maison Diamantée** of 1620, so-called for the pointed shape of its facade stonework, on rue de la Prison.

> **THE DESTRUCTION OF OLD LE PANIER**
>
> In 1943, Marseille was under **German occupation** and Le Panier represented everything the Nazis feared and hated, an uncontrollable warren providing shelter for *Untermenschen* of every sort, including Resistance leaders, Communists and Jews. They gave the twenty thousand inhabitants one day's notice to leave. While the curé of St-Laurent pealed the bells in protest, squads of SS moved in; they cleared the area and packed the people, including the curé, off to Fréjus, where concentration camp victims were selected. Out of seven hundred children, only 68 returned. Dynamite was laid, carefully sparing three old buildings that appealed to the Fascist aesthetic, and everything in the lower part of the quarter, from the waterside to rue Caisserie and Grande rue, was blown sky high.

Musée des Docks Romains

10 Place Vivaux • Tues–Sun 10am–6pm • €3 • ☎ 04 91 91 24 62, ⓦ musee-des-docks-romains.marseille.fr

After World War II, archeologists reaped some benefits from Le Panier's destruction in the discovery of the remains of a warehouse from the first-century AD Roman docks, now displayed in situ at the **Musée des Docks Romains**. You can see vast food-storage jars for oil, grain and spices in their original positions, and part of the original jetty, along with models, mock-ups and a video to complete the picture.

Above Rue Casserie

Above rue Caisserie, the old street patterns and architectural styles of Le Panier survive. Overlooking the small **place Daviel** is an impressive eighteenth-century bell tower, all that remains of the Église des Accoules, destroyed in 1794 because it had served as a meeting place for counter-revolutionaries after the French Revolution. To the north of here is the vast nineteenth-century **Hôtel Dieu**, now undergoing conversion into a five-star hotel. At the junction of rue de la Prison and rue Caisserie, the steps of montée des Accoules lead up and across to **place de Lenche**, site of the Greek agora and today a good café stop.

Hospice de la Vieille Charité

2 rue de la Charité • **Musée d'Archéologie Méditerranéenne** Tues–Sun 10am–6pm • €3 • ☎ 04 91 14 58 59, ⓦ musee-archeologie-mediterraneenne.marseille.fr **Musée des Arts Africains, Océaniens et Amérindiens** Tues–Sun 10am–6pm • €3 • ☎ 04 91 14 58 38, ⓦ maaoa.marseille.fr

Climb rue du Réfuge and you'll find yourself in a modern piazza, with new buildings in traditional styles, and an uninterrupted view of the refined **Hospice de la Vieille Charité** at the far end. This seventeenth-century workhouse, with a gorgeous Baroque chapel surrounded by handsome columned arcades in pink stone, is now a cultural centre, hosting some excellent temporary exhibitions and two museums, a café and a bookshop.

The **Musée d'Archéologie Méditerranéenne** contains some very beautiful fourth- and fifth-century BC pottery and glass, an Egyptian collection with mummies and their accompanying boxes for internal organs, plus a mummified crocodile. It also displays fascinating finds from a Celto-Légurian settlement at Roquepertuse, between Marseille and Aix, including a double-headed statue.

The other permanent collection at the Vieille Charité is the **Musée des Arts Africains, Océaniens et Amérindiens**, that has beautiful *objets* from as far afield as Mali and Vanuatu, and rooms devoted to Mexico, Africa, Oceania and the Americas.

Euroméditerranée and Les Docks

A five-square-kilometre swathe of Marseille's north side – wedged between the sea and the Gare St-Charles and formerly dominated by harbour-related activities – has since 1995 been rechristened **Euroméditerranée** and is the focus of ambitious, long-term

1

regeneration plans. Gateway to the area is the hitherto run-down **Rue de la République**, a nineteenth-century boulevard that runs north–west from the Vieux Port to place de la Joliette. Buildings along its entire length are gradually being refurbished and their fine stone facades cleaned; in the wake of this, there's a wave of retail-based gentrification, with smart boutiques at the Vieux Port end. The obvious focus of Euroméditerranée is the magnificent restored warehouse building known as **Les Docks**, fronting place de la Joliette. North of it is a cluster of new tower blocks by star architects, including Zaha Hadid's sleek 33-storey **Tour French Line**.

Les Docks
10 place de la Joliette • ☎ 04 91 90 04 69, ⓦ les-docks.fr

The sheer scale of Les Docks makes the old warehouse's conversion into an office complex impressive, with one long central corridor lined with restaurants and shops. Most animated at its southern end close to place de la Joliette, the building's internal mall is – unusually for Marseille – a little sterile in its further reaches; nevertheless, it's worth continuing as far as the **Centre d'Informations** (Mon–Fri 11.30am–6.30pm) to see what else is planned for this part of the city.

La Canebière and around
La Canebière, the grandiose (if dilapidated) boulevard that runs for about 1km east from the port, is Marseille's main street. Named after the hemp (*canabè*) that once grew here and provided the raw materials for the town's thriving rope-making trade, it was originally modelled on the Champs-Élysées, though it's no pavement-café hotspot and its shops are – with one or two exceptions – fairly lacklustre nowadays. It is also home, at the port end, to one museum.

Immediately north of La Canebière is the ugly **Centre Bourse** shopping centre and the **Jardin des Vestiges**, where the ancient port extended, curving northwards from the present quai des Belges. Excavations have revealed a stretch of the Greek port and bits of the city wall with the base of three square towers and a gateway, dated to the second or third century BC.

Musée de la Marine et de l'Economie
Palais de la Bourse, La Canebière • Daily 10am–6pm • €2 • ☎ 04 91 39 33 21

The evocative **Musée de la Marine et de l'Economie**, on the ground floor of the Neoclassical stock exchange, is devoted to the theme of Marseille's maritime history and contains a superb collection of model ships, including the legendary 1930s transatlantic liner *Normandie* and Marseille's very own prewar queen of the seas, the *Providence*.

Musée d'Histoire de Marseille
Square Belsunce, Centre Bourse • Due to reopen in 2013; check website for opening hours and admission prices • ⓦ musee-histoire-de-marseille.marseille.fr

The **Musée d'Histoire de Marseille**, inside the Centre Bourse shopping centre, shows the main finds of Marseillaise excavations, of which the most dramatic is a third-century AD wreck of a Roman trading vessel. There are models of the city, reconstructed boats, everyday items such as shoes and baskets, and a beautiful Roman mosaic of a dolphin, plus a great deal of information on text panels and a video about the Roman, Greek and pre-Greek settlements. Laws that were posted up in Greek Massalia are cited, forbidding women to drink wine and allowing would-be suicides to take hemlock if the 600-strong parliament agreed. Refurbishment and extension of the museum will double the previous exhibition space.

Porte d'Aix and the quartier Belsunce
The **Bibliothèque Alcazar** on cours Belsunce is another of the regeneration projects

MARSEILLE'S COMMUNE

Within the space of four years from its completion in 1867, the Marseille **Préfecture** had flown the imperial flag, the red flag and the tricolour. The red flag was flying in 1871, during Marseille's Commune. The counter-revolutionary forces advanced from Aubagne, encountering little resistance, and took the heights of Notre-Dame-de-la-Garde from where they directed their cannons down onto the Préfecture. The defeat was swifter but no less bloody than the fate of the Parisian Communards. One of the Marseillaise leaders, Gaston Crémieux, a young idealistic bourgeois with great charisma, escaped the initial carnage but was subsequently caught. Despite clemency pleas from all quarters of the city, Thiers, president of the newly formed Third Republic and a native of Marseille, would not relent and Crémieux was shot by a firing squad near the Palais du Pharo in November 1871.

gradually supplanting the dilapidated tenements north of La Canebière, its slick modernity softened by a Beaux-Arts portal that recalls the old Alcazar music hall which once occupied the site and where the likes of Tino Rossi and Yves Montand performed. The continuation of cours Belsunce, rue d'Aix, stretches to **Porte d'Aix**, Marseille's Arc de Triomphe, modelled on the ancient Roman arch at Orange. This was part of the city's grandiose mid-nineteenth-century expansion which included the Cathédrale de la Major and the Joliette docks, paid for with the profits of military enterprise, most significantly the conquest of Algeria in 1830. Today it's a popular meeting place for north African men, as are the narrow streets of the **quartier Belsunce** to the east, stretching between cours Belsunce/rue d'Aix, boulevard d'Athènes and the Gare St-Charles.

Mémorial de la Marseillaise

25 rue Thubaneau • Mid-June to mid-Sept daily 10am–6pm; Feb to mid-June & mid-Sept to Dec Tues–Sun 2–6pm • €7; free English audioguide • ☎ 04 91 91 91 97, ⓦ memorial-marseillaise.com

The main reason for visiting the quartier Belsunce is to visit the **Mémorial de la Marseillaise**, which presents the story of France's national anthem with some panache in the old real tennis court in which it was first performed in Marseille. You can listen to various versions of Rouget de Lisle's 1792 anthem – which was actually composed in Strasbourg – and discover more about the Marseille volunteers and their epic march on Paris (see p.396).

South of La Canebière

The prime shopping quarter of Marseille centres around three streets running south from La Canebière: rue de Rome, rue Paradis and rue St-Ferréol, which terminates at the pseudo-Renaissance **Préfecture**, where demonstrations in the city traditionally converge. The streets are lined with chic designer boutiques, and there's a scattering of cafés and patisseries.

Musée Cantini

19 rue Grignan • Due to reopen after refurbishment in 2013; check website for admission prices • Tues–Sun 10am–6pm • ☎ 04 91 54 77 75, ⓦ musee-cantini.marseille.fr

Between rue St-Ferréol and rue Paradis, on rue Grignan, is the city's most important art museum, the **Musée Cantini**, paintings and sculptures dating from the end of the nineteenth century up to the 1950s. The Fauvists and Surrealists are well represented, works by Matisse, Léger, Picasso, Ernst, Le Corbusier, Miró and Giacometti.

Cours Julien and around

East of rue de Rome, the streets around **cours Julien** are full of bars and music shops, and the *cours* itself, with its pools, fountains, restaurant tables and enticing boutiques, is populated by Marseille's bohemian crowd and its diverse immigrant community. By day this is one of the most pleasant places to idle in the city, though almost every surface is buried under graffiti; the atmosphere at night can be a little edgy, particularly around the métro station. There are small, one-off couturiers, bookshops and art galleries to browse in and engrossing markets to enliven the street scene (see p.64).

Palais de Longchamp and around

Musée des Beaux-Arts Closed for refurbishment at time of writing; check website for opening hours and admission price • ⓦ musee-des-beaux-arts.marseille.fr **Musée d'Histoire Naturelle** Tues–Sun 10am–6pm • €5 • ☎ 04 91 14 59 50, ⓦ museum-marseille.org • Mᵒ Longchamp-Cinq-Avenues or tram #2 same stop

Now home to two museums, the **Palais de Longchamp** was completed in 1869, the year the Suez Canal opened, bringing a new boom for Marseillaise trade. It was built as the grandiose conclusion of an aqueduct at Roquefavour (no longer in use) bringing water from the Durance to the city. Water is still pumped into the centre of the colonnade connecting the two palatial wings of the building. Below, an enormous statue looks as if it's honouring some great feminist victory: three well-muscled women stand above four bulls wallowing in a pool from which a cascade drops the four or five storeys to ground level.

The palace's north wing holds the city's **Musée des Beaux-Arts** (closed for renovation at the time of writing), which has a fair share of delights, including works by Rubens, Jordaens, Corot and Signac and a room devoted to the nineteenth-century artist and caricaturist from Marseille, Honoré Daumier.

The palace's southeastern wing is occupied by the **Musée d'Histoire Naturelle**, and its collection of stuffed animals and fossils. The oldest parts of the collection date back to the eighteenth century, and there are some 200,000 botanical specimens alone.

Musée Grobet-Labadié

140 bd Longchamp • Tues–Sun 10am–6pm • €3 • ⓦ musee-grobet-labadie.marseille.fr • Mᵒ Longchamp–Cinq-Avenues or or tram #2 same stop

Opposite the palace is the **Musée Grobet-Labadié** an elegant late nineteenth-century townhouse filled with exquisite *objets d'art* representing the tastes of a typical family from Marseille's affluent merchant class at its zenith. It also stages temporary exhibitions.

South of the centre

Avenue du Prado, the continuation of rue de Rome, is an eight-lane highway, with impressive fountains and one of the city's biggest **daily markets** between métros Castellane and Périer. At the *rond point* du Prado, the avenue turns west to meet the corniche road.

Parc Chanot

The city's north–south axis continues as boulevard Michelet past **Parc Chanot**, the site of Olympique de Marseille's ground, the Stade Vélodrome. OM's reputation for occasional brilliance means that home matches are almost always sold out, but tickets can be bought online from the team's website (ⓦom.net). At the far side of the stadium on rue Raymond-Teisseire, the vast **Palais des Sports** hosts boxing matches, tennis, showjumping and other spectacles.

Unité d'Habitation

280 boulevard Michelet • Open access • Guided tours (French only; €7) on Fridays; book via tourist office • Bus #21 from Mᵒ Rd-Pt-du-Prado to "Le Corbusier"

Set back from the west side of the boulevard Michelet on the way south out of the city, Le Corbusier's **Unité d'Habitation**, designed in 1946 and completed in 1952, is a mould-breaking piece of architecture. A seventeen-storey housing complex on stilts, the Unité was the prototype for thousands of apartment buildings the world over, though close up the difference in quality between this – the *couture* original – and the industrially produced imitations becomes apparent. Confounding expectations, this concrete modernist structure is extremely complex, with 23 different apartment layouts, to suit single people and varying sized families: the larger apartments are split across two floors with balconies on both sides of the building, giving unhindered views of mountains and sea. It's a remarkably happy place; many of the original tenants are still in residence, and people chat and smile in the lobby. At ground level the building is decorated with Corbusier's famous human figure, the Modulor, while on the third floor is a **restaurant** with a terrace and superlative Mediterranean views, and a **hotel** (see p.60). The iconic, sculptural **rooftop** recreational area is probably the highlight, because it's here that Le Corbusier's infatuation with ocean liners seems most obvious.

MAC

69 av d'Haïfa • Tues–Sun 10am–6pm • €3 • Ⓦ mac.marseille.fr • Bus #23 from M° Rd-Pt-du-Prado, stop "Ste-Anne-Haïfa" or bus #45 from M° Rd-Pt-du-Prado, stop "Haïfa Marie-Louise"

The southern suburbs are the setting for Marseille's contemporary art museum, **MAC**. The permanent collection, displayed in perfect, pure-white surroundings, is the continuation of the Cantini collection (see p.55) with works from the 1960s to the present. The artists include the Marseillais César and Ben, along with Buren, Christo, Klein, Niki de Saint Phalle, Tinguely and Warhol.

Parc Borély

Av du Park-Borély, just off av du Prado **Park** Daily 6am–9pm • Free • **Botanical garden** Daily: March–Oct 10am–noon & 1–6pm; Nov–Feb 10am–12.30pm & 1.30–4.30pm • €3 • **Museum** Due to open in 2013 – check with tourist office for opening hours and admission prices • Bus #19 or 83 from M° Rd-Pt-du-Prado or #83 from Vieux Port

The city's best green space, the **Parc Borély**, lies between avenue d'Haïfa and the sea, and comes with a boating lake, rose gardens, palm trees and a **botanical garden**. The eighteenth-century **Château Borély** itself is scheduled to reopen in June 2013 as a museum of decorative arts to house collections hitherto scattered in various locations across the city, including fashion and eighteenth- and nineteenth-century ceramics from the Marseille area.

The corniche and south to Les Goudes

While the waterfront north of the Vieux Port is largely devoted to docks, the corniche that winds south from it is where Marseille lets its hair down. The most popular stretch of sand close to the city centre is the small Plage des Catalans, a few blocks south of the Palais du Pharo. This marks the beginning of Marseille's **corniche Président J.F. Kennedy**, initiated and partly built after the 1848 revolution. Despite its inland bypass of the Malmousque peninsula, it's a corniche as good as any on the Riviera, with *belle époque* villas on the slopes above, the Îles d'Endoume and the Château d'If in the distance, cliffs below and high bridge piers for the road to cross the inlets of La Fausse-Monnaie and the Vallon des Auffes.

Vallon des Auffes

Prior to the construction of the corniche, Malmousque and the **Vallon des Auffes** were inaccessible from the town unless you followed the "customs men's path" over the rocks or took a boat. There was nothing on Malmousque, but the Vallon des Auffes had a freshwater source and a small community of fishermen and rope-makers. Amazingly, it is not much different today, with fishing boats pulled up around the rocks, tiny jumbled houses, and restaurants serving the catch (see p.61). Only one road, rue du Vallon-des-Auffes, leads out; otherwise it's the long flights of steps up to the corniche.

1

Malmousque

Malmousque is now a very desirable residential district, favoured by the champagne-socialist set, and home to Marseille's most distinguished hotel-restaurant, *Le Petit Nice-Passédat* (see p.62). Behind La Fausse-Monnaie inlet, a path leads to the Théâtre Silvain, an open-air theatre set in a wilderness of trees and flowers and the setting in summer for concerts of opera, classical music and jazz. There's more greenery, of a formal nature, a short way further along the corniche at no. 271 in the **Jardin Valmer** (daily: May–Aug 8am–8pm; March, April, Sept & Oct 8am–7pm; Nov–Feb 8am–5.30pm; free; bus #83, stop "Corniche J-Martin"), and you can explore the tiny streets that lead up into this prime district of mansions with high-walled gardens.

The Plage du Prado and Montredon

The corniche J.F. Kennedy ends at the **Plage du Prado**, the city's main sand beach backed by a wide strip of lawns and overlooked by the Ecale Borély complex of bars and restaurants, best visited at night when it is one of the liveliest night spots in town (see p.62). The promenade continues – lined intermittently with café and bar terraces – to the coastal suburb of **Montredon**, where the road curves inland just before the harbour of **Point Rouge**, served by ferries from the Vieux Port in summer, and an access point for the Parc national des Calanques, which stretches from here to Cassis and beyond (see p.73).

The Château d'If and the Îles de Frioul

Mid-May to mid-Sept daily 9.30am–6.10pm; mid-Sept to March Tues–Sun 9.30am–4.45pm; April to mid-May daily 9.30am–4.45pm • €5.50 • ⓦ if.monuments-nationaux.fr • Boats depart quai des Belges on the Vieux Port (subject to weather conditions) every 35–55min daily; 25min to Île d'If, 40min to Îles de Frioul; €10.10 to Île d'If, €15.20 to Îles de Frioul; ⓦ www.frioul-if-express.com

Blacker than the sea, blacker than the sky, rose like a phantom the giant of granite, whose projecting crags seemed like arms extended to seize their prey.

The Count of Monte Cristo, by Alexandre Dumas

So the **Château d'If** appears to Edmond Dantès, hero of Alexandre Dumas' *The Count of Monte Cristo*, having made his watery escape after five years of incarceration as the innocent victim of treachery. In reality, most prisoners of this island fortress died before they reached the end of their sentences – unless they were nobles living in the less fetid upper-storey cells, such as a certain de Niozelles who was given six years for failing to take his hat off in the presence of Louis XIV; and Mirabeau, who had run up massive debts with shops in Aix. More often, the crimes were political. After the revocation of the Edict of Nantes in 1685, thousands of Marseillais Protestants, who refused to accept the new law, were sent to the galleys and their leaders entombed in the Château d'If. Revolutionaries of 1848 drew their last breath here, too.

Apart from the castle, there's not much else to the Île d'If; it's little more than a rock. Dumas fans will love it, others may raise an eyebrow at the cell marked "Dantès" in the same fashion as non-fictional inmates' names. However you it, it's a horribly well-preserved sixteenth-century edifice and the views back towards Marseille are wonderful. Note that if the Mistral is blowing, access to the Île can be impossible as the ferries don't run.

Îles de Frioul

You can combine a trip to the Château d'If with a round trip taking in the other two islands of the Frioul archipelago, **Pomègues** and **Ratonneau**, which are linked by the same ferry service as the Île d'If and joined by a causeway enclosing a yachting harbour. In days gone by these islands were used as a quarantine station, most ineffectually in the early 1720s when a ship carrying the plague was given the go-ahead to dock in the city, resulting in the decimation of the population. Ratonneau has a brace of small beaches.

ARRIVAL AND DEPARTURE

By plane The city's airport, the Aéroport Marseille-Provence (☎04 42 14 14 14, ⓦmarseille-airport.com), is 20km northwest of the city, linked to the *gare SNCF* by bus (every 15–20min 5.10am–12.10am; 25min; €8).

Destinations Bristol (3 weekly; 1hr 50min); Dublin (3 weekly; 2hr 5min); Edinburgh (2 weekly; 2hr 30min); London Gatwick (5 daily; 1hr 50min); London Stansted (daily; 2hr 5min); Montreal (4 weekly; 8hr 55min); Paris CDG (7 daily; 1 hr 30min); Quebec (1 weekly; 8hr).

By train The *gare SNCF St-Charles* (☎3635) is on the northern edge of the 1er arrondissement on square Narvik. From the station, a staircase leads down to bd d'Athènes and on to La Canebière, Marseille's main street.

Destinations Aix-en-Provence (every 30–40min; 35–45min); Aix-en-Provence TGV (every 20min–1hr; 12min); Arles (every 30min–1hr; 42min–1hr); Aubagne (up to 4 per hr; 15min); Avignon (every 30min–1hr; 30–35min); Cannes (every 30min–1hr; 2hr 5min); Carry le Rouet (14 daily; 30min); Cassis (every 30min–1hr; 25min); Fréjus (1 daily; 1hr 36min); La Ciotat (every 20min–1hr; 30–35min); Les Arcs for Draguignon (12 daily; 1hr 20min); L'Estaque (up to 4 per hr; 12–14min); Lyon Part Dieu (every 30min–1hr; 1hr 40min); Martigues (14 daily; 46–50min); Nice (every 30min–1hr; 2hr 30min); Paris Gare de Lyon (hourly; 3hr 17min); St Raphaël (every 30min–1hr; 1hr 37min–1hr 47min); Salon (hourly; 53min); Sisteron (6 daily; 1hr 50min–2hr 10min).

By bus The *gare routière* is alongside the train station on place Victor Hugo (☎0810 000).

Destinations Aix-en-Provence (every 20min; 30min); Aubagne (every 20min; 15min); Barçelonnette (via Gap: 1–2 daily; 5hr 40min–6hr); Cassis (10 daily; 40–50min); Grenoble (1 daily; 4hr 35min); La Ciotat (approx. hourly; 55min); Manosque (3 daily; 1hr 40min); Martigues (every 40–50min; 50min); Sisteron (3 daily; 2hr 45min).

By car Arriving by car, you'll descend into Marseille from the surrounding heights of one of three mountain ranges. Follow signs for the Vieux Port to reach the city centre.

By ferry SNCM, 61 bd des Dames (☎32 60, ⓦsncm.fr), runs ferries to Corsica, Tunisia and Algeria.

INFORMATION

Tourist office 4 La Canebière, down by the Vieux Port (Mon–Sat 9am–7pm, Sun & public hols 10am–5pm; ☎0826 500 500, ⓦwww.marseille-tourisme.com). The office organizes guided tours of the city on various themes, though most are in French; the exception is the bilingual Le Panier tour (Sat at 2pm in English and French); see the tourist office website for details.

GETTING AROUND

BY PUBLIC TRANSPORT

Bus, tram and metro Marseille has an efficient public transport network (☎rtm.fr). The métro runs from 5am until 10.30pm on weekdays and until after midnight at weekends; trams run from 5am to after midnight.

Information You can get a plan of the transport system from most métro stations' *points d'accueil* (daily 6.50am–7.40pm) or at the RTM office at the Centre Bourse (6 rue des Fabres; Mon–Fri 8.30am–6pm).

Tickets and passes Flat-fee tickets for buses, trams and the métro can be used for journeys combining all three as long as they take less than 1hr. You can buy individual tickets (€1.50) from bus and tram drivers, and from métro ticket offices or machines on métro stations and tram stops. Two-journey *Tickets 2 Voyages* (€3) and ten-journey *Cartes 10 Voyages* (€12.80) can be bought from métro stations, RTM kiosks and shops displaying the RTM sign. Consider also the good-value one-day *Pass Journée* (€5) and three-day *Pass 3 Jours* (€10.50), available from the same outlets. Tickets must be punched in the machines on the bus, on tramway platforms or at métro gates.

Ferry RTM runs a ferry between the Vieux Port and Pointe Rouge in the south of the city for easier access to the beaches and *calanques* (daily: March to mid-May 7am–7pm; mid-May to mid-Sept 7am–10pm; hourly; €2.50).

BY BIKE

Bike rental Blue bicycles belonging to Le Vélo scheme (ⓦlevelo-mpm.fr) can be rented from the 130 self-service rental points throughout the city using a bank card (€1 for 7-day membership, after which first 30min is free, €1 for each additional 30min). Mountain bikes can be rented from Tandem, 16 av du Parc Borély (☎04 91 22 64 80).

BY CAR

Car parks cours Estienne-d'Orves, 1er; rue Breteuil, 6e; Centre Bourse, 1er; place Géneral-de-Gaulle, 1er; place Jean-Jaurès 5er.

Car rental Avis, Gare St-Charles (☎04 86 82 01 17, ⓦavis.com); National Citer, 31 bd Voltaire 1er (☎04 91 05 90 86, ⓦciter.fr); Europcar, 31 bd Voltaire 1er (☎0825 825 680, ⓦeuropcar.com); Hertz, 31 bd Voltaire, 1er (☎04 91 05 51 20, ⓦhertz.com). All also have offices at the airport.

BY TAXI

Taxis Taxi Radio Marseille (☎04 91 02 20 20); Taxi Marseillais (☎04 91 92 92 92).

1

ACCOMMODATION

Demand for accommodation in Marseille isn't as tied to the tourist season as in the coastal resorts, and finding a room in August is no more difficult than in November. **Hotels** are plentiful, with lots of reasonable two- and three-star options around the Vieux Port and on the streets running south from it; real budget bargains are rarer, while of late the number of more luxurious options has risen considerably. The simplest way to **reserve a room** is through the tourist office website.

HOTELS

Alizé 35 quai des Belges, 1er ☎ 04 91 33 66 97, ⓦ alize-hotel.com; map pp.50–51. Comfortable, attractive two-star hotel on the Vieux Port. Public areas are a little gloomy but rooms are modern, soundproofed and a/c, the more expensive ones look out onto the Vieux Port. €109

Bellevue 34 quai du Port, 2e ☎ 04 96 17 05 40, ⓦ hotelbellevuemarseille.com; map pp.50–51. Boutique-style hotel on the port above a famous old bar, with good views, chic modern decor, a/c, games consoles and wi-fi, but no lift, so rooms on upper floors are for the fit only. €125

Le Corbusier Unité d'Habitation, 280 bd Michelet, 8e ☎ 04 91 16 78 00, ⓦ hotellecorbusier.com; map pp.48–49. Landmark hotel on the third floor of this renowned architect's iconic high-rise, with fabulous views and a variety of room styles, from simple studios to elegant mini suites with access to a large eighth-floor balcony. €70

Edmond-Rostand 31 rue Dragon, 6e ☎ 04 91 37 74 95, ⓦ hoteledmondrostand.com; map pp.48–49. Friendly *Logis de France*-affiliated two-star centrally located in the antiques district, a short walk uphill from the Vieux Port. Simple but comfortable, smallish a/c rooms with contemporary furnishings, en-suite bath and free wi-fi. €86

Hermes 2 rue Bonneterie, 2e ☎ 04 96 11 63 63, ⓦ hotelmarseille.com; map pp.50–51. Two-star in a superb position just off the Vieux Port, with plain but comfortable rooms with free wi-fi and flatscreen TV. Some have terraces and views and there's a roof terrace with fabulous views over the Vieux Port. €90

Ibis Budget Vieux Port 46 rue Sainte, 1er ☎ 0892 680 582, ⓦ etaphotel.com; map pp.50–51. This budget chain hotel is worth a stay for its location alone, close to the Vieux Port. Situated in a historic building, some of the rooms have timber beams – it's incredibly popular, so book ahead. €63

Lutétia 38 allée Léon-Gambetta, 1er ☎ 04 91 50 81 78, ⓦ hotelmarseille.com; map pp.50–51 Pleasant two-star just off La Canebière, with soundproofed and air-conditioned rooms with flatscreen TV. Cheaper rooms have showers; some superior rooms have larger beds and there are two singles. €72

★ **Mama Shelter** 64 rue de la Loubière, 6e ☎ 04 84 35 20 00, ⓦ mamashelter.com; map pp.48–49. Eagerly awaited Marseille sister of the hip Paris original, combining stylish design and boutique hotel comforts – including iMacs for TV, internet and free on-demand movies – with budget prices. There's a restaurant and bar, and on-site parking. €79

Du Palais 26 rue Breteuil, 6e ☎ 04 91 37 78 86, ⓦ hoteldupalaismarseille.com; map pp.50–51. Nicely appointed three-star hotel in a good location a short walk from the Vieux Port. The standard rooms are a little small, but all are soundproofed and a/c, with bathrooms and wi-fi. €95

Radisson Blu 38–40 quai de Rive Neuve, 7e ☎ 04 88 92 19 50; ⓦ radissonblu.com/hotel-marseille; map pp.50–51. Stylish, primarily business-oriented modern luxury hotel with a great port-side location and an open-air pool with spectacular views. €158

Le Richelieu 52 corniche J.F Kennedy, 7e ☎ 04 91 31 01 92, ⓦ hotel-richelieu-marseille.com; map pp.48–49. Simple, friendly two-star place, and one of the more affordable of the corniche hotels, right by the sea overlooking the plage des Catalans, with bold, funky colours in the cheaper rooms. €75

St Ferréol 19 rue Pisançon, corner rue St-Ferréol, 1er ☎ 04 91 33 12 21, ⓦ hotelsaintferreol.com; map pp.50–51. Three-star comforts including understated modern decor, free high-speed internet, a/c and soundproofing, plus a very central location in the main pedestrianized shopping area. €97

HOSTELS

Auberge de Jeunesse Bonneveine Impasse Bonfils, av J.-Vidal, 8e ☎ 04 91 17 63 30, ⓦ fuaj.org; map pp.48–49. Attractive modern hostel just 200m from the plage du Prado. Facilities include internet access, restaurant and bar. Rates include breakfast. Reception 6am–1am. Closed mid-Dec to mid-Jan. Mo Rd-Pt-du-Prado, then bus #44 (direction "Floralia Rimet", stop "Place Bonnefon") or night bus #583 from Vieux Port. €21

★ **Vertigo** 42 rue des Petites Maries, 1er ☎ 04 91 91 07 11, ⓦ hotelvertigo.fr; map pp.50–51. Funky backpacker hotel and hostel near the train and bus stations, with simple, stylish rooms and dorms, youthful staff, and a bar in the lobby. En-suite double rooms fill up fast, so book those in advance. Dorms €25.40; doubles €60

★ **Vertigo Vieux Port** 38 rue Fort Notre Dame, 7e ☎ 04 91 54 42 95, ⓦ hotelvertigo.fr; map pp.50–51. This sister hostel to *Vertigo* (see above) has a similarly cool atmosphere, with accommodation in simple twin rooms or small mixed or all-female dorms, all en suite. Rates include breakfast. Dorms €25; twins €60

EATING AND DRINKING

Fish and seafood are the main ingredients of the Marseillais diet, and the superstar of dishes is the city's own invention, **bouillabaisse**, a saffron- and garlic-flavoured fish soup with croûtons and *rouille* to throw in. There are conflicting theories about which fish should be included and where and how they must be caught, though it's generally agreed that rascasse is essential. The other city speciality is *pieds et paquets*, mutton or lamb belly and trotters. The best, and most expensive, restaurants are close to the **corniche**, though for international choice the trendy **cours Julien** is the place to head, while **rue Sainte** is good for smart and fashionable dining close to the opera and Vieux Port. The pedestrian precinct behind the south quay of the **Vieux Port** is more tourist-oriented and fishy, while **Le Panier** has a few tiny, inexpensive bistros.

CAFÉS

Le Carthage 8 rue d'Aubagne, 1ᵉ ☎ 04 91 54 72 85; map pp.50–51. This traditional *salon de thé* close to the marché des Capucins sells Tunisian sandwiches from €4, but it's the tempting piles of sticky North African pastries (from €1.30) that draw the eye. Mon–Sat 7am–8pm, Sun 7am–noon.

Cup of Tea 1 rue Caisserie, 2ᵉ ☎ 04 91 90 84 02; map pp.50–51. A gorgeous Le Panier bookshop and *salon de thé* strategically located midway up the climb from the Vieux Port to the Vieille Charité. Huge selection of teas, including green tea or rooibos from €3.50; coffee from €1.60. Mon–Sat 8.30am–7pm.

L'Équitable 54 cours Julien, 6ᵉ ☎ 04 91 47 34 48; map pp.50–51. Groovy, community-focused organic café/bar in Marseille's bohemian quarter, serving artisan beers, organic wines, teas and herbal infusions and with a wide variety of debates and events. Annual membership is compulsory, but free. Tues–Thurs 3–11pm, Fri 3pm–midnight, Sat 3pm–1am; closed Aug.

★ **Plauchut** 168 La Canebière, 1ᵉ ☎ 04 91 48 06 67, ⓦ plauchut.com; map pp.48–49. Beautiful old *patissier-chocolatier-glacier* and *salon de thé*, established in 1820, selling delicious home-made ice cream, croissants, *calissons* and *macarons*, plus *pogne* (a type of brioche) and traditional *navettes* – a hard orange-scented biscuit – from €1. Tues–Sun 8am–8pm.

Torrefaction Noailles 56 la Canebière, 1ᵉʳ ☎ 04 91 55 60 66; map pp.50–51. Celebrated confectioner and café, with high stools, a wonderful aroma of fresh ground coffee and plenty of nougat, *calissons*, candied fruits and caramels to take away afterwards. Tea and hot chocolate €3; coffee from €1.30. Mon–Sat 7am–7pm, Sun 9.30am–7pm.

RESTAURANTS

★ **Les Arcenaulx** 25 cours d'Estienne-d'Orves, 1ᵉʳ ☎ 04 91 59 80 30, ⓦ les-arcenaulx.com; map pp.50–51. This classy place has an atmospheric and intellectual vibe, as it's also a bookshop; there's a €20 lunch *menu* and a six-course *menu découverte* for €59; otherwise, expect to pay around €17 for the likes of *tartare de boeuf* with *frites* and mesclun. Mon–Sat noon–11pm.

Chez Sauveur 10 rue d'Aubagne, 1ᵉʳ ☎ 04 91 54 33 96, ⓦ chezsauveur.fr; map pp.50–51. Established in 1943, this modest Sicilian restaurant close to the marché des Capucins is renowned locally for its excellent wood-fired pizzas, including a few made with *brousse*, a type of goat's cheese. Prices from around €9.50. Tues–Sat 11am–2pm & 7–10.30pm.

Chez Fonfon 140 Vallon des Auffes, 7ᵉ ☎ 04 91 52 14 38; ⓦ chez-fonfon.com; map pp.48–49. There's no debate about the quality of the bouillabaisse (€47) here, for this chic restaurant overlooking a small fishing harbour is one of an elite band guarding the true recipe of the dish. Mon 7.15–9.45pm, Tues–Sat noon–1.45pm & 7.15–9.45pm.

La Garbure 9 cours Julien, 6ᵉ ☎ 04 91 47 18 01, ⓦ restaurant-marseille-lagarbure.com; map pp.50–51. Rich specialities from southwest France, including duck *cassoulet* or duck *confit* with ceps in this wonderfully romantic and stylish restaurant. Three-course *menu* at €15; otherwise main courses cost around €15 and up. Booking advised. Mon–Fri 12.30–2.30pm & 7.30–11pm, Sat 7.30–11pm.

La Kahena 2 rue de la République, 2ᵉ ☎ 04 91 90 61 93; map pp.50–51. Great Tunisian restaurant just off the Vieux Port, with a bright interior, elaborate patterned tiles, couscous from €10 and *brochettes* with salad and *frites* from €12. There are a few North African bottles on the wine list. Daily noon–2.30pm & 7.30–10.30pm.

Le Marseillois Quai du Port, 2ᵉ ☎ 04 91 90 72 52, ⓦ lemarseillois.com; map pp.50–51. Set on board an old sailing vessel moored in the Vieux Port, with lots of fish and seafood on the €27 *prix-fixe* evening menu; a three-course lunch costs €25. Mon 7.30–10.30pm, Tues–Sat noon–2pm & 7.30–10.30pm.

★ **La Part des Anges** 33 rue Sainte, 1ᵉʳ ☎ 04 91 33 55 70, ⓦ lapartdesanges.com; map pp.50–51. Wonderful *cave à vins* serving hearty food and cheese platters from a chalked-up daily menu to mop up the classy wines; *plats* from around €13.50. Wines are listed by region and the selection changes daily. Mon–Sat 9am–2am, Sun 9am–1pm & 6pm–2am.

La Passarelle 52 rue Plan Fourmiguier, 7ᵉ ☎ 04 91 33 03 27, ⓦ restaurantlapassarelle.fr, map pp.50–51. Relaxed and informal restaurant tucked behind La Criée theatre, with a short, daily changing seasonal menu featuring the likes of baked *daurade*, courgette flower *beignets* and lamb chops. Main courses around €18. The garden terrace is one of the prettiest (and most peaceful) in the city. Daily noon–2pm & 6–10.30pm.

Petit Nice-Passédat Anse de Maldormé, Corniche J.F. Kennedy, 7ᵉ ☎ 04 91 59 25 92, ⓦ passedat.fr; map pp.48–49. Gerald Passédat's gorgeous hotel-restaurant on the Corniche is the undisputed pinnacle of fine dining in Marseille, with three Michelin stars and highly inventive, seafood-based menus from €85 to €280. There's also simpler (and cheaper) fare available at the bar. Tues–Sat noon–2pm & 7–10pm.

Sur le Pouce 2 rue des Convalescents, 1er ☎ 04 91 56 13 28; map pp.50–51 Inexpensive Tunisian restaurant in the *quartier* Belsunce, with a huge range of couscous from €5.50 to €10, plus grills, Merguez sausages and *brochettes* from around €6. Daily noon–3pm & 5–11pm.

Toinou Coquillages 3 cours Saint-Louis, 1er ☎ 08 11 45 45 45, ⓦ toinou.com; map pp.50–51. Popular with locals and visitors alike for the choice of more than forty types of shellfish, served in the restaurant and sold fresh from the counter at the front. Lunchtime *moules-frites formule* €14.90; oysters from €8.40 for six. Mon, Tues & Sun 11.30am–10.30pm, Wed & Thurs 11.30am–11pm, Fri & Sat 11.30am–midnight.

★ **La Trilogie des Cépages** 35 rue de la Paix Marcel Paul, 1er ☎ 04 91 33 96 03, ⓦ trilogiedescepages.com; map pp.50–51. A truly vast selection of wines accompanies the *cuisine gastronomique* at this popular, classy restaurant close to the Vieux Port. Meat & fish main courses cost around €35, lunch menu €25, *ménu symphonie* €57. Mon & Tues & Sat 8–9.30pm, Wed–Fri noon–1.30pm & 8–9.30pm.

Une Table, au Sud 2 quai du Port, 2ᵉ ☎ 04 91 90 63 53, ⓦ www.unetableausud.com; map pp.50–51. Stylish, Michelin-starred gastronomic restaurant overlooking the Vieux Port. Chef Lionel Lévy's contemporary take on Provençal cooking includes his signature dish, bouillabaisse milkshake (€18). The two-course daily changing lunch menu costs €29, otherwise *menus* start at €71. Tues–Thurs noon–2.30pm & 7–10pm, Fri & Sat noon–2.30pm & 7pm–midnight.

La Virgule 27 rue de la Loge, 2ᵉ ☎ 04 91 90 91 11, ⓦ lavirgule.marseille.free.fr; map pp.50–51. Funky but affordable modern bistro just off the Vieux Port, offering the likes of grilled fish with a tian of Provençal vegetables, *faux filet* or *andouillette*. Three courses with risotto cost €27; otherwise three courses €36. Tues–Sat noon–2pm & 7.30–10pm, Sun noon–2pm.

BARS

Au Petit Nice 28 place Jean-Jaurès, 1er ☎ 04 91 48 43 04; map pp.48–49. A Marseille institution in the most bohemian quarter of the city. The terrace is the place to head for on Saturday during the market, with a great selection of reasonably priced beers (from €2.30 *pression*, €3 in bottles). Tues–Fri 11am–2am, Sat & Sun 8am–2am.

Aux 3G 3 rue St-Pierre, 5ᵉ ☎ 04 91 48 76 36, ⓦ aux3g. site-forums.com; map pp.48–49. Marseille's only lesbian bar, close to La Plaine market and regularly packed for its weekend DJ nights, when they spin anything from dance music to 80s hits. Gay men are also welcome. Thurs 7pm–midnight, Fri & Sat 7pm–2am.

Le Greenwich 142 av Pierre-Mendès-France, 8ᵉ ☎ 04 91 22 67 92, ⓦ legreenwich.com; map pp.48–49. Spacious brasserie and cocktail bar by the sea in the Escale Borely complex, with a big terrace on which to enjoy ice creams (€12), cocktails (from around €9) and a full restaurant menu inside, plus Olympique de Marseille matches on TV and a house DJ. Daily 8am–2am.

O'Malley's 9 quai de Rive-Neuve, 1er ☎ 04 91 33 65 50; map pp.50–51. Classic expat-friendly Irish pub on the Vieux Port, with the familiar Celtic trappings plus live music every Thursday at 9.30pm and daily happy hour (5–9pm), when pints are €4.50. Mon, Tues & Sun 4pm–2am, Wed & Thurs 4pm–3am, Fri & Sat 4pm–4am.

Bar de la Marine 15 quai de Rive-Neuve, 1er ☎ 04 91 54 95 42, ⓦ facebook.com/bardela.marine.3; map pp.50–51. A favourite bar for Vieux Port lounging, and inspiration for Pagnol's celebrated Marseille trilogy. It's open from breakfast: at lunchtime you might tuck into a €10 *salade niçoise* or €12 *plat du jour*; in the evening tapas anchor down the mojitos and wine. Daily 7am–2am.

Le Red Lion 231 av Pierre-Mendès-France, 8ᵉ ☎ 04 91 25 17 17, ⓦ pub-redlion.com; map pp.48–49. Large British-style pub close to the beach with a big selection of beers including Kronenbourg, Grimbergen and Guinness; draught beer from €5.50. The interior is dark and cavernous, though when the sun shines everyone crowds onto the narrow terrace at the front. Mon–Fri 4pm–2am, Sat & Sun 4pm–4am.

Sports Beach Café 138 av Pierre-Mendès-France, 8ᵉ ☎ 04 91 76 12 35, ⓦ sportsbeachcafe.fr; map pp.48–49. Open-air bar, terrace and restaurant in the Escale Borély complex by the sea, with a swimming pool and DJs spinning everything from salsa to reggae and rock. Three-course lunch €19; otherwise three courses €36. Daily: summer 10am–2am; winter Mon–Sat 10am–2am, Sun 10am–6pm.

Trash 28 rue du Berceau, 5ᵉ ☎ 04 91 25 52 16, ⓦ letrashbar.com; map pp.48–49. Slick, cruisy gay men's bar with DJs and live entertainment at weekends and a more raunchy ambiance during the week, when there are various themed nights, for which there are sometimes entry charges. Mon, Wed & Thurs 9pm–2am, Fri & Sat 10pm–late.

NIGHTLIFE AND ENTERTAINMENT

Marseille's nightlife has something for everyone. Of the various free **local arts newspapers** the free fortnightly *Ventilo* and *Sortir* are the most useful; pick them up from tourist offices, museums and cultural centres, from the Virgin Megastore at 75 rue St-Ferréol, or FNAC in the Centre Bourse: these stores – and the tourist office's ticket bureau – are the best places for **tickets and information**.

LIVE MUSIC AND CLUBS

L'Affranchi 212 bd de St Marcel, 11ᵉʳ ☏ 04 91 35 09 19, ⓦ www.facebook.com.LAffranchiMarseille; map pp.48–49. Concert venue in the eastern suburbs with a varied programme of clubs and live gigs, with a particular emphasis on hip-hop.

Bazar 90 bd Rabatau, 8ᵉ ☏ 06 58 52 15 15, ⓦ bazariceclub.com; map pp.48–49. Big, expensive mainstream disco playing house and occasionally hosting big-name international DJs, with outdoor dancing under the palms from May to Oct plus a Grey Goose ice bar at a chilly -20°C. Open Thurs–Sat from midnight.

Cité de la Musique 4 rue Bernard du Bois, 1ᵉʳ ☏ 04 91 39 28 28, ⓦ citemusique-marseille.com; map pp.50–51. Music school and live venue close to Porte d'Aix, with an intimate cellar venue and a larger auditorium staging jazz, classical & contemporary concerts.

Les Docks des Suds 12 rue Urbain V, 2ᵉ ☏ 04 91 99 00 00, ⓦ dock-des-suds.org; map pp.48–49. Vast warehouse that hosts Marseille's annual Fiesta des Suds world-music festival (Oct) and is a regular live venue for hip-hop, electro and world music.

L'Intermédiare 63 place Jean-Jaurès, 6ᵉ ☏ 06 20 72 86 24, ⓦ www.facebook.com/Intermediare.live; map pp.48–49. Loud, hip club and bar with regular live bands and DJs and a highly eclectic music policy, ranging from rock to electro, hip house, dance hall, reggae and world music.

Machine à Coudre 6 rue Jean-Roque, 1ᵉʳ ⓦ lamachineacoudre.com; map pp.50–51. Music café hosting alternative rock, pop and punk acts. €4–7 entry charge depending on act. Open on concert nights only from 9 or 10pm, depending on the event.

New Cancan 3–7 rue Sénac, 1ᵉʳ ☏ 04 91 48 59 76, ⓦ newcancan.com; map pp.48–49. It's pretty cheesy, but the *New Cancan* is nevertheless Marseille's only gay disco and something of a local institution, with regular Sunday cabaret nights. Entry with *conso* Fri & Sun €10, Sat €16–18. Fri–Sun midnight–dawn & Thurs in Aug.

Pelle Mêle 8 place aux Huiles, 1ᵉʳ; map pp.50–51. Intimate and lively jazz club and piano bar just off the Vieux Port, with frequent live sets. Drinks prices are – by Marseille standards – a little on the high side, with a big range of whiskies from €9. Mon–Sat 6pm–2am.

Le Poste à Galène 103 rue Ferrari, 5ᵉ ☏ 04 91 47 57 99, ⓦ leposteagalene.com; map pp.48–49. Intimate and popular venue with regular live pop, folk, jazz, rock and electro, plus 80s and 90s DJ nights (Sat at 11pm; €6) and a bar.

Trolleybus 24 quai de Rive-Neuve, 7ᵉ ☏ 04 91 54 30 45, ⓦ letrolley.com; map pp.50–51. Atmospheric bar and club in a series of vaulted seventeenth-century catacombs that once housed an arsenal; DJ nights have an emphasis on electro but there are also regular live gigs. Free on Thurs & Fri, €10 on Sat with *conso*. Thurs–Sat midnight–6am.

FILM, OPERA, THEATRE AND CONCERTS

Alhambra 2 rue du Cinéma, 16ᵉ ☏ 04 91 03 84 66, ⓦ alhambracine.com; map pp.48–49 Art-house cinema in the north of the city with an emphasis on world cinema, occasionally showing undubbed English-language films (*v.o.*). Tickets €5.

Ballet National de Marseille 20 bd Gabès, 8ᵉ ☏ 04 91 32 72 72, ⓦ ballet-de-marseille.com; map pp.48–49. The home venue of the famous dance company, founded in 1972 by Roland Petit. Now under the direction of Fréderic Flamand, the company also performs at the Opéra and at La Criée theatre, as well as touring worldwide.

Château de la Buzine 56 traverse de la Buzine, 11ᵉ ☏ 04 91 43 91 23, ⓦ chateaudelabuzine.com; bus #50 from Castellane to La Valentine, then bus #51; map pp.48–49. It's a long trek from the centre, but the villa that Pagnol dreamed of turning into a *cinematheque* is now exactly that – and a fantastic place to see his films. Matinées and evening screenings; tickets €6.90.

Creuset des Arts 21 rue Pagliano, 4ᵉ ☏ 04 91 06 57 02, ⓦ www.creusetdesarts.com; map pp.48–49. Comedy and live music venue, featuring traditional French chanson and drama from established and up-and-coming performers. Tickets €17; performances generally start at 4pm.

Le Dôme 48 av de St-Just, 4ᵉ ☏ 04 91 12 21 21, ⓦ le-dome.com; map pp.48–49. Marseille's large-capacity live venue, hosting big-name and tame middle-of-the-road acts, plus children's shows, comedy, boxing and other spectacles.

Espace Julien 39 cours Julien, 6ᵉ ☏ 04 91 24 34 10, ⓦ espace-julien.com; map pp.50–51. Vibrant, municipally run arts centre staging everything from live comedy to jazz, electro and rock bands. There's a large main auditorium and a second, more intimate venue, the *Café Julien*.

La Friche la Belle de Mai 41 rue Jobin, 3ᵉ ☏ 04 95 04 95 04, ⓦ lafriche.org; map pp.48–49. Interdisciplinary arts complex occupying a former industrial site in the north of the city, hosting theatre, dance, live music, circus, puppetry and art exhibitions.

Odéon 162 La Canebière, 1ᵉʳ ☏ 04 96 12 52 70, ⓦ odeon .marseille.fr; map pp.50–51. Marseille's municipal theatre, with a wide repertoire that embraces serious drama and classic operetta as well as light classical concerts. Performances generally start at 2.30pm or 8.30pm.

Opéra 2 rue Moliére, 1ᵉʳ ☏ 04 91 55 11 10, ⓦ opera .marseille.fr; map pp.50–51. High opera and symphony concerts by the Orchestre Philharmonique de Marseille take place in this magnificent setting, part Neoclassical, part Art Deco. There are good last-minute deals on unsold tickets.

1

Le Silo d'Arenc 35 quai Lazaret, 2ᵉ ☎ 04 91 90 00 00, ⓦ silo-marseille.fr; map pp.48–49. 1920s-built former dockside grain silo converted into a 2000-seat multi-purpose concert venue, hosting everything from ballet to rock, swing and jazz-funk.

Théâtre de Lenche 4 place de Lenche, 2ᵉ ☎ 04 91 91 52 22, ⓦ theatredelenche.info; map pp.50–51. Dance, cabaret and drama is showcased at this Le Panier theatre, where the resident company's repertoire ranges from Molière to Chekhov and contemporary drama.

Théâtre Massalia La Friche la Belle de Mai, 41 rue Jobin 3ᵉ ☎ 04 95 04 95 70, ⓦ theatremassalia.com; map pp.48–49. Lively puppet theatre with changing programme of inventive shows, with both evening and matinee shows aimed primarily at a family audience.

Théâtre National la Criée 30 quai de Rive-Neuve, 7ᵉ ☎ 04 91 54 70 54, ⓦ theatre-lacriee.com; map pp.50–51. Marseille's most prestigious stage for drama, home base of the Théâtre National de Marseille and occasional venue for ballet.

Les Variétés 37 rue Vincent Scotto, 1ᵉʳ ☎ 0892 68 95 97; map pp.50–51. Five-screen art-house cinema just off La Canebière that frequently shows undubbed (*v.o*) English-language and other foreign films. There's also a bar and exhibition area. Tickets €8.

SHOPPING

The city's copious **street markets** provide a feast of fruit and veg, olives, cheeses, sausages and spit-roast chickens – everything you'd need for a picnic except for wine, which is most economically bought at supermarkets. The markets are also good for cheap clothes. La Plaine and avenue du Prado are the biggest; the Capucins the oldest. Marseille's Sunday flea market, **Marché aux Puces**, is a brilliant spectacle and good for serious haggling. There's a relaxed atmosphere, plenty of cafés, and everything and anything for sale.

MARKETS

Capucins Place des Capucins, 1ᵉʳ; Mᵒ Noailles. Fruit and veg. Mon–Sat 8am–7pm.

Cours Julien 6ᵉ; Mᵒ N.D. du Mont Cours Julien. Food Mon–Sat 8am–1pm; stamps Sun 8am–1pm; antiquarian books second Sat of month 8am–1pm; organic produce Wed 8am–1pm; secondhand goods third Sun of the month 8am–1pm.

Marché aux Puces Av du Cap-Pinède, 15ᵉ; bus #35 from Mᵒ Joliette (stop "Cap-Pinède") or bus #36 from Mᵒ Bougainville (stop "Lyon-Cap Pinède"). Food Tues–Sun 8am–6pm; bric-a-brac Sat 8am–1pm; flea market Sun 6am–1pm.

La Plaine Place Jean-Jaurès, 5ᵉ; Mᵒ N.D. du Mont Cours Julien. Food Mon–Sat 7.30am–1.30pm; bric-a-brac Tues, Thurs & Sat 7.30am–1.30pm; flowers Wed 7.30am–1.30pm.

Prado Av du Prado, 6ᵉ; Mᵒ Castellane and Périer. Fruit, veg, fish and general food produce daily 7am–1.30pm; flowers Fri 7.30am–1.30pm.

Quai des Belges Vieux Port, 1ᵉʳ; Mᵒ Vieux Port. Fish sold straight off the boats. Daily 8am–1pm.

SHOPS

La Compagnie de Provence 18 rue Francis Davso, 1ᵉʳ ☎ 04 91 33 04 17; 1 rue Caisserie, 2ᵉ ☎ 04 91 56 20 94; ⓦ compagniedeprovence.com; map pp.50–51. Authentic Marseille soaps and upmarket toiletries that make excellent gifts. Mon–Fri 10am–1pm & 2–7pm, Sat 10am–7pm.

Four des Navettes 136 rue Sainte, 7ᵉ ☎ 04 91 33 32 12, ⓦ fourdesnavettes.com; map pp.50–51. Marseille's oldest bakery is famous for its delicious, subtly orange-scented *navette* biscuits which they sell by the dozen (€9) or two dozen (€18). Mon–Sat 7am–8pm, Sun 9am–1pm & 3–7.30pm.

La Maison du Pastis 108 quai du Port, 2ᵉ ☎ 04 91 90 86 77, ⓦ lamaiondupastis.com; map pp.50–51. There are 95 varieties of *pastis* and absinthe on sale in this alcoholic Aladdin's cave of a shop, right on the Vieux Port. Mon–Sat 10am–7pm, Sun 10am–6pm.

Place aux Huiles 2 place Daviel 2ᵉ ☎ 04 91 90 05 55, ⓦ placeauxhuiles.com; map pp.50–51. Taste the oils before you buy them at this Le Panier shop, which is a treasure trove for lovers of olive oil, tapenade, *anchoïade* and other edible treats. Mon–Sat 10.30am–1pm & 2–7pm, Sun 10am–6pm.

DIRECTORY

Bookshops Virgin, 75 rue St-Ferréol, 1ᵉʳ, and FNAC in the Centre Bourse, have English books sections.

Consulates UK, 24 av du Prado, 6e (☎ 04 91 15 72 10); USA, place Varian Fry, 6ᵉ (☎ 04 91 54 92 00).

Health Ambulance ☎ 15; doctor ☎ 3624; 24hr casualty department at Hôpital de la Conception, 147 bd Baille, 5ᵉ (☎ 04 91 38 00 00); medical emergencies for travellers at SOS Voyageurs, Gare St-Charles, 3ᵉ (☎ 04 91 62 12 80);

bilingual pharmacy at Pharmacie de la République, 7 rue de la République, 2ᵉ (Mon–Fri 9am–7.30pm, Sat 9.30am–7pm; ☎ 04 91 90 32 27).

Lost property 41 bd de Briançon, 3ᵉ (☎ 04 91 14 68 97).

Police Commissariat Central, 2 rue Antoine-Becker, 2ᵉ (24hr; ☎ 04 91 39 80 00).

Post office 25 rue Colbert, 1ᵉʳ.

1

L'Estaque and the Côte Bleue

Marseille's docks finally end at the one-time fishing village of **L'Estaque**, now a suburb of the city. Between here and Carry-le-Rouet, the hills of the **Chaîne de l'Estaque** come right down to the coast to form the first, wildest part of the coast known as the Côte Bleue: a gorgeous wilderness of white rock, pines and brilliant yellow scented broom. The shore is studded with picturesque little *calanques* where the real estate is desirable and the water exceptionally clean; you can look across the roadstead of Marseille to the islands and the entrance of the Vieux Port. At weekends in summer, road access to these *calanques* is strictly limited and you may have to park some distance from the sea.

L'Estaque and around

The erstwhile fishing village of **L'ESTAQUE**, an easy fifteen-minute train ride from the city centre, was much loved by painters in the nineteenth century, though it was no rural paradise even in 1867, as a gouache by Cézanne of the factory chimneys of L'Estaque shows (the painting, originally given to Madame Zola, is now exhibited in Cézanne's studio in Aix). Yet it still has fishing boats moored alongside yachts, lovely old villas and a short but engrossing walk along an **art-themed trail** marked with bilingual plaques – there's a clear map of it in the Marseille tourist office's free city guide and it's also downloadable from their website. The very pleasant artificial **beaches** to the west ensure that L'Estaque remains a popular escape from the city.

From L'Estaque, the train tunnels its way westwards above the shore while the main road, the D568, then D5, takes an inland route through **La Rove** and **Ensues-la-Redonne**, with smaller roads looping down to the fishing villages and summer holiday homes of **Niolon**, **Méjean** and **La Redonne**.

Musée Monticelli

Fortin de Corbières, route du Rove, L'Estaque • Wed–Sun 10am–5pm • €5 • ☎ 04 91 03 49 46, ⓦ fondationmonticelli.com

On the northern edge of L'Estaque, a nineteenth-century coastal fort, the **Musée Monticelli**, has been beautifully restored to exhibit paintings by Adolphe Monticelli (1824–66), a Marseille-born artist whose work was an influence on the young Cézanne. It also stages temporary exhibitions of work by other Provençal painters.

Carry-le-Rouet and around

The peace and intimate scale of this coast end at the small but bustling resort of **CARRY-LE-ROUET**, its port overshadowed by a rather unfortunate 1960s tower block. Carry is popular for diving – there's a marine reserve just offshore – and modestly swanky, with a brasserie-lined marina and a casino. It was the home of the jazz singer Nina Simone towards the end of her life, and it was here that she died in 2003.

The Côte Bleue is flatter and less rocky west of Carry towards Martigues. The town merges into its western neighbour Sausset-les-Pins, where the beaches are stony and artificial, without any break in the seaside houses and apartment buildings. For **beaches** it's best to head beyond Tamaris where there are long, sandy beaches around the pleasantly downmarket family resorts of **Carro** and **La Couronne**, though you may be put off by the proximity of the petrochemical plants on the southern shore of the Étang de Berre.

INFORMATION   **L'ESTAQUE AND THE CÔTE BLEUE**

CARRY LE ROUET
Tourist office In the Espace Nautique Roger Grange, Carry Le Rouet (July & Aug Mon–Sat 10am–noon & 2–6pm, Sun 10am–noon; Sept–June Tues–Sat 10am–noon & 2–5pm; ☎ 04 42 13 20 36, ⓦ carry-lerouet.com).

From the train station, turn right out of the *gare SNCF* onto avenue Pierre Semard, which becomes av Aristide Briand and continues to the port; follow the left side of the port to reach the tourist office.

ACCOMMODATION

Lou Cigalon Chemin de Tamaris, La Couronne ☎ 04 42 49 61 71, ⊛ loucigalon.com. Three-star campsite west of Carry on the tiny, relatively peaceful sandy cove, with a restaurant, bar, pizzeria, pool and Jacuzzi and wi-fi. Closed Oct–March. €20

Hôtel La Tuilière 34 av Draïo de la Mar, Carry le Rouet ☎ 04 42 44 79 79, ⊛ hotel-tuiliere.com. Two-star comforts 50m from the sea, west of Carry's port on the road to Sausset, with a pool, restaurant and a/c. €82

EATING

L'ESTAQUE

Le Cabanon Route du Rove, L'Estaque, 16ᵉ ☎ 04 91 03 18 12. Grilled fish and seafood in chic portside surroundings at the far end of L'Estaque's waterfront, with a shaded terrace and *plats du jour* from around €17. If you simply want a snack, the local *chichis* (hot, doughnut-like confections) from the kiosks alongside L'Estaque's main road delicious. Wed–Sun noon–2pm & 8–10pm.

MÉJEAN

Le Mange Tout 8 chemin du Tire-Cul, Méjean ☎ 04 42 45 91 68. Simple meals of grilled fish and *petites fritures*

(around €20–35) are served overlooking the tiny port on the *calanque* of Méjean. Daily 10.30am–4pm & 7–9.30pm; closed Mon & Tues evenings in winter.

CARRY LE ROUET

La Brise Quai Vayssière, Carry le Rouet ☎ 04 42 45 30 55, ⊛ restaurant-labrise.com. A little old-fashioned but nevertheless a cut above the portside brasseries, with an open terrace overlooking the harbour and plenty of lamb and fish on its €33 and €43 *menus*. Tues–Sat 12.15–1.30pm & 7.30–9.30pm, Mon & Sun 7.30–9.30pm; closed Sun eve in winter.

Martigues

MARTIGUES straddles both sides of the Caronte Canal and an island in the middle, at the southwest corner of the Étang de Berre – a 22km long and 15km wide lagoon ringed by oil refineries and petrochemical industries, to which the town is the maritime gateway. In the sixteenth century when the union of three separate villages – Jonquières to the south, Ferrières to the north and the island, known simply as l'Île – created Martigues, there were many more canals than the three that remain today. But Martigues has joined the long list of places with waterways to be dubbed the "Venice" of the region, and it deserves the compliment, however fatuous the comparison.

In the centre of l'Île, in front of the sumptuous facade of the airy Église de la Madeleine, a low bridge spans the Canal St-Sébastien where fishing boats moor and houses in ochre, pink and blue look straight down onto the water. This appealing spot is known as the **Miroir aux Oiseaux** and was painted by Corot, Ziem and others at the turn of the twentieth century.

Musée Ziem

Boulevard du 14 Juillet, Ferrières • July & Aug Mon & Wed–Sun 10am–noon & 2.30–6.30pm; Sept–June Wed–Sun 2.30–6.30pm • Free • ☎ 04 42 41 39 60

Works by some of the artists who painted in Martigues, including Ziem's *Vieux Port de Marseille*, can be seen in the wonderful **Musée Ziem**. The collection includes works by Dérain, Dufy and Signac, while François Picabia's 1905 *Étang de Berre* shows the lagoon to be every bit as choppy as it is today. The upper floor contains local archeological and ethnological displays.

Galerie de l'Histoire de Martigues

Rond Point de l'Hôtel de Ville, Ferrières • July–early Sept Wed–Sun 10am–12.30pm & 3–7pm; early Sept–June Wed–Fri 9am–noon & 1.30–6.30pm, Sat & Sun 2.30–6.30pm • Free • ☎ 04 42 44 34 02

Martigue's well-presented local history museum, the **Galerie de l'Histoire de Martigues**, charts the town's development from prehistoric times with lavish use of old maps and

1

visual material. The section dealing with medieval and early modern Martigues is particularly engrossing, though the second half of the exhibition – which brings the story up to date – is a little heavy on the town hall's preferred political line.

ARRIVAL AND INFORMATION   MARTIGUES

By bus Buses from Marseille stop at the Hôtel de Police, next to the tourist office.

Destinations Aix-en-Provence (every 1–2hr; 2hr) Marseille (hourly; 34 min); Salon (every 1–2hr; 1hr 10min)

By train From the *gare SNCF* take bus #23 (direction "L. Degut") to the centre.

Destinations Carry-le-Rouet (12 daily; 15min); Marseille (12 daily; 48min); Salon (2 daily; 36 min).

By car There's plentiful off-street parking close to the tourist office in Ferrières.

Tourist office Rond Point de l'Hôtel de Ville, Ferrières (June & Sept Mon–Fri 9am–6pm, Sat 9am–12.30pm & 2.30–5.45pm, Sun 9am–1pm; July & Aug Mon–Fri 9am–6.30pm, Sat 9am–12.30pm & 2.30–5.45pm, Sun 9am–1pm; Oct–May Mon–Sat 9am–noon & 2–5.30pm, Sun 10am–12.30pm; ☎ 04 42 42 31 10, ⊛ martigues-tourisme.com).

ACCOMMODATION

St-Roch Avenue Georges-Braque, Ferrières ☎ 04 42 42 36 36, ⊛ hotelsaintroch.com. Martigues' fanciest hotel is a three-star affair a short distance from the tourist office, with a pool, restaurant and 61 spacious non-smoking rooms; rates include breakfast. **€116**

Le 5 37 boulevard du 14 Juillet, Ferrières ☎ 04 42 80 49 16, ⊛ martigues-hotel.fr. Despite the noisy location this smartly renovated, a/c hotel is a good budget choice, with simple but tastefully decorated modern rooms with en-suite bath, flatscreen TV and wi-fi. **€60**

EATING

July and August see the spectacle of the **Sardinades**, when thousands of plates of grilled sardines are sold cheaply each evening along the quays near the *mediathèque* in the Quartier de l'Île. Aside from these, the **food** to look out for is *poutargue*, a paste made from salted mullet, and *melets*, seasoned fish-fry fermented in olive oil.

Le Miroir 4 rue Marcel Galdy ☎ 04 42 80 50 45. Classy restaurant in a pretty waterside position in L'Île, with a two-course lunch *menu* at €19.50; otherwise three courses cost €26.50 or €39. Daily noon–2pm & 7.30–10pm; closed Wed & Sun evenings & all-day Mon out of season.

Quai du Trou du Mât 15 quai Toulmond ☎ 04 42 80 63 92. Quayside restaurant on l'Île, with fish-focused €20 and €35 *menus* matched with Coteaux d'Aix, Bandol & Côtes de Provence wines. Tues–Sat 10am–2pm & 7–11pm, Sun 10am–2pm.

Salon-de-Provence and around

Jets scream through the air above **SALON-DE-PROVENCE,** a reminder that the town's principal activities include teaching air-force pilots to fly – indeed, legendary 1930s singer Charles Trenet was just one of thousands to undertake their military service here. Salon's more enduring claims to fame are its olives and the famous predictions of **Nostradamus** which were composed here, though the museum dedicated to him is less appealing than the mementoes of Napoléon in Salon's castle, the **Château de l'Empéri**. The château rises above a **Vieille Ville** that was the subject of misguided modernization

---

SALON'S BLACK GOLD

In medieval times, Salon's economy was dependent on its tanneries, a saffron crop and flocks of sheep reputed for the quality of their mutton. True prosperity arrived in the shape of the small black olives that produced an oil, **olivo selourenco**, of great gastronomic renown. By the end of the nineteenth century the Salonais were making soap from their oil, a highly profitable commodity manufactured in appalling conditions in subterranean mills. Those to whom the dividends accrued built themselves opulent *belle époque* **villas**, the grandest of which are in the streets between the town centre and the *gare SNCF* to the west, and though most have long since been given over to other uses or divided into apartments, they give the town a quiet, surprising grace.

from the 1960s on, though of late boutiques and restaurants have recolonized it, lending it some of the pleasingly animated air of the rest of the town centre – particularly on market days, when Salon bustles. A good time to visit is in July and August for the annual **classical music festival** (ⓦfestival-salon.fr) in the château.

The countryside **around Salon** affords glimpses of the traditional agriculture of the arid Crau region, as well as a remarkable cave-village at Lamanon and a child-friendly castle and zoo at La Barben.

Château de l'Empéri

Montée de Puech • Mid-April to Sept & school holidays Tues–Sun 9.30am–noon & 2–6pm; Oct to mid-April Tues–Sun 1.30–6pm • €4.70, or €7.20 combined ticket with one other museum • ☎ 04 90 44 72 80

The centrepiece of the Vieille Ville is the massive **Château de l'Empéri**, a proper medieval fortress built to suit the worldliness of its former proprietors, the archbishops of Arles. It now houses the **Musée de l'Empéri**, whose collections of military uniforms cover the period from Louis XIV to World War I; the sections devoted to the Revolution and Napoleon are particularly fascinating. Also included in the admission price is entry to the **Salle Théodore Jourdan**, whose exhibition of paintings and drawings by the eponymous local artist is a precursor to a planned new museum of Salon and La Crau.

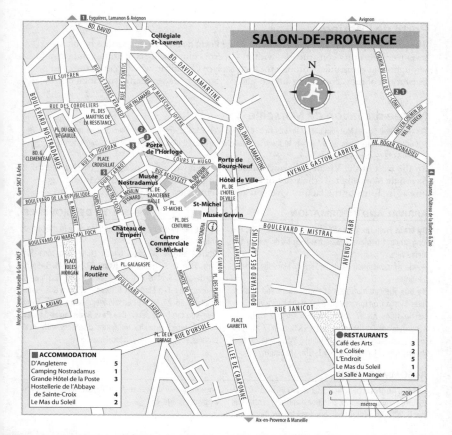

1

Musée Grévin de la Provence

Place des Centuries • Mon–Fri 9am–noon & 2–6pm, Sat & Sun 2–6pm • €4.70, or €7.20 combined ticket with one other museum •
☎ 04 90 56 36 30

The focus of the Vieille Ville is place des Centuries, a wide-open space fringed by café terraces and the **Musée Grévin de la Provence**, a series of waxwork scenes illustrating episodes from the legends and history of Provence with taped commentaries available in several different languages.

Museé Nostradamus

Rue Nostradamus • Mon–Fri 9am–noon & 2–6pm, Sat & Sun 2–6pm • €4.70, or €7.20 combined ticket with one other museum; English audioguide • ☎ 04 90 56 64 31

Just north of the place des Centuries stands the **Museé Nostradamus**, the home, until his death, of the soothsayer. Nostradamus (see p.94), arrived in Salon in 1547 – already famous for his aromatic plague cure, administered in Aix and Lyon – and married a rich widow. After some fairly long Italian travels, he returned to Salon and settled down to study the stars, the weather, cosmetics and the future of the world. The museum tells his multifaceted life story in a series of tableaux, and also stages temporary exhibitions.

Nostradamus died in Salon in 1566 and his tomb is in the Gothic **Collégiale St-Laurent**, at the top of rue du Maréchal-Joffre, north of the Vieille Ville.

Porte de l'Horloge

The principle gateway to the Vieille Ville is the **Porte de l'Horloge**, a serious bit of seventeenth-century construction, with its Grecian columns, coats of arms, gargoyles and wrought-iron campanile. Through the arch is place Crousillat, which centres on a vast mushroom of moss concealing a three-statued fountain – a wonderful spot for a café break.

Musée du Savon de Marseille

148 avenue Paul-Bourret **Museum** July & Aug Mon–Fri 8.30am–noon & 2–5.30pm; Sept–June Mon–Thurs 8.30am–noon & 2–5pm, Fri 8.30am–4pm **Factory tours** July & Aug daily 10.30am; Sept–June Mon & Thurs 10.30am • €2.50, or €3.50 including factory tour • ☎ 04 90 53 82 75, ⓦ marius-fabre.fr

To the west of the Vieille Ville and located within a working *savonnerie*, the **Musée du Savon de Marseille** tells the story of soap-making in Provence from the Middle Ages onwards. Tours of the factory give you a first-hand view of the industry.

ARRIVAL AND INFORMATION   SALON-DE-PROVENCE

By train From the *gare SNCF* on avenue Émile-Zola, the long straight boulevard Maréchal-Foch leads you to the Vieille Ville.
Destinations Avignon (10 daily; 55min); Marseille (8 daily; 53min).

By bus The *halt routière* is at the southern end of place Jules-Morgan, on the western edge of the Vieille Ville.
Destinations Aix (7 daily; 45min); Arles (7 daily, 1hr 47min); Eyguières (hourly; 15min); La Barben (7 daily; 22 min); Lamanon (4 daily; 35min); Marignane Airport (hourly; 1hr); Martigues (every 1–2hr; 1hr 5min).

By car There's secure off-street parking close to the tourist office.
Tourist office 56 cours Gimon (June–Aug Mon–Sat 9am–1pm & 3–7pm, Sun 10am–12.30pm & 3–5pm; March–May, Sept & Oct Mon–Sat 9.30am–12.30pm & 2–6pm; Nov–Feb Mon–Sat 9.30am–12.15pm & 2–5pm; ☎ 04 90 56 27 60, ⓦ visitsalondeprovence.com). From here, you can buy a seven-day **Pass Avantages Séjour** for €10, which provides numerous discounts with local businesses plus free entry to local museums.

ACCOMMODATION

Hôtel d'Angleterre 98 cours Carnot ☎ 04 90 56 01 10, ⓦ hotel-angleterre.biz. Traditional and very central two star hotel, with refurbished, soundproofed a/c rooms with en-suite bath or shower, wi-fi and flatscreen TV. There's also a private garage. **€57**

Grand Hôtel de la Poste 1 rue des Frères John et Robert Kennedy ☎ 04 90 56 01 94, ⓦ ghpsalon.com. Overlooking place Crousillat's mossy fountains and the town's prime café terraces, with a/c rooms, all with TV and wi-fi; there are also some three- and four-bed rooms. No lift. **€50**

Hostellerie de l'Abbaye de Sainte Croix Route du Val de Cuech ☎ 04 90 56 24 55, ⓦ hotels-provence.com. Luxury in the atmospheric surroundings of an ancient abbey, 3km from Salon on the D16, with a/c rooms occupying the old monks' cells, each bearing the name of a saint. **€215**

Le Mas du Soleil 38 chemin Saint-Côme ☎ 04 90 56 06 53, ⓦ lemasdusoleil.com. In a quiet location a short distance from the town centre, with ten comfortable and individually styled a/c rooms, some with terrace. There's a pool and a renowned restaurant (see below). **€195**

CAMPING

Camping Nostradamus Route d'Ayguières ☎ 04 90 56 08 36, ⓦ camping-nostradamus.com. Three-star campsite just off the D17 towards Eyguières, with an outdoor pool, restaurant, wi-fi and games facilities. It also has some mobile homes. Closed Dec–Feb. Mobile homes **€110**; camping **€22.50**

EATING AND DRINKING

Though some of its best restaurants are out of town, central Salon is full of reasonably priced places to eat and drink, with the smarter bars and brasseries clustering at the north end of the Vieille Ville. Salon's famous olive oil can be bought at the busy Wednesday **market** on place Morgan (6.30am–1pm), the Saturday morning organic market in the town centre, or the Sunday market on place de-Gaulle, along with wonderful ingredients for a picnic, from olives or cheeses to fresh fruit and vegetables.

Café des Arts 20 place Crousillat ☎ 04 90 56 00 07, ⓦ cafedesarts-restaurant.fr. Prettily old-fashioned, and more restaurant than café, with the hearty likes of *andouillettes* or lamb *brochettes* from a chalked-up selection; two courses €16, three courses €25. Noon–2pm & 7–10pm; closed Wed eve & Sun in winter.

Le Colisée 1 place Crousillat ☎ 04 90 50 07 47. Big brasserie taking up the entire north side of place Crousillat, with a large terrace for cocktail sipping (from €7), burgers and salads from €11 and a two-course *prix fixe* lunch for €17. Daily 7am–1am.

L'Endroit 20 montée André Viallat ☎ 04 42 85 85 32, ⓦ lendroit13300.fr. Provençal flavours meet international influences at this restaurant with a terrace in the shadow of the château; there's carpaccio of beef and bavette with shallot sauce on a €28 *menu*. Mon–Sat noon–2.30pm & 7.30–10.30pm.

Le Mas du Soleil 38 chemin Saint-Côme ☎ 04 90 56 06 53, ⓦ lemasdusoleil.com. *Maitre cuisinier* Francis Robin creates refined Provençal dishes at this intimate hotel-restaurant close to the town centre, with roast sea bream with tian of aubergine and baby marrow on the €35 weekday-only *menu terroir*; otherwise *menus* from €43. Tues–Sat noon–2pm & 7.30–9.30pm, Sun noon–2pm.

La Salle à Manger 6 rue du Maréchal-Joffre ☎ 04 90 56 28 01. The most romantic of central Salon's restaurants, with softly lit Italianate interior, excellent Provençal cooking and a sheltered courtyard garden at the back. Two courses €29. Tues–Sat noon–1.30pm & 7–9.30pm.

Around Salon

Ten kilometres north of Salon, the main road and highway pass through a narrow gap in the hills by **Lamanon**, a village which was never much more than a stopover on the transhumance routes (used for the moving of flocks, and still followed by the Crau shepherds every June), though it does have a château. The countryside west of Lamanon is typical of the dry Crau region: around **Eyguières** you may see llamas grazing along with goats and horses. Llamas are excellent at keeping forest firebreaks

JEAN MOULIN

The northern exit from the Autoroute du Soleil to Salon-de-Provence takes you past a memorial to **Jean Moulin**, the Resistance leader who was parachuted into the nearby Alpilles range in order to coordinate the different *maquis* groupings in Vichy France. He was caught near Lyon on June 21, 1943, tortured horribly and interrogated by Klaus Barbie; he subsequently died of his injuries while on a train to Germany. In death Moulin has become the most revered of all Resistance figures, his portrait – in fedora and scarf – familiar throughout France. The bronze **sculpture**, by Marcel Courbier, is of a lithe figure landing from the sky like some latter-day Greek god, very beautiful though somewhat perplexing if you're not aware of the invisible parachute.

1

trim – so, too, are goats, but the latter are forbidden from running loose in the forests, thanks to an unrevoked Napoleonic law.

Grottes de Cales
Lamanon • Open access

Above Lamanon, hidden amongst rocks and trees, is a remarkable troglodyte village, the **Grottes de Cales**, which was inhabited from Neolithic times until the nineteenth century. Stairs lead down into grottoes, part natural, part constructed, with hooks and gutters carved into the rock; at the centre is a sacrificial temple. Access is free, though some parts of the complex are fenced off for safety reasons: follow the Montée de Cales which ascends from opposite Lamanon's tourist office. The *grottes* themselves are on the GR6 footpath.

Château de la Barben and Zoo
Route du Château, La Barben, 12km east of Salon, just beyond Pélissanne • **Château** Hourly tours April–Nov daily 11am–6pm; Feb to early March & weekends during March daily 2–6pm • €8, or €13 including dungeons • ☎ 04 90 55 25 41, ⓦ chateaudelabarben.fr **Zoo** Daily: July & Aug 9.30am–7pm; Sept–Nov & Feb–June 10am–6pm; Dec & Jan 10am–5.30pm • €14.50 • ☎ 04 90 55 19 12, ⓦ zoolabarben.com

Bears, elephants, big cats, hippos and a host of other non-native mammals and birds are on show at the **La Barben Zoo**, which also has plenty of child-friendly entertainment such as miniature train rides. The **Château de la Barben** itself was lived in for a while by Napoleon's sister, Pauline Borghese, and her apartments are still decorated in imperial style, while the rest retains a feeling of seventeenth-century luxury.

Aubagne

Marseille's suburbs extend relentlessly east along the autoroute and D8N corridor to **AUBAGNE**, set between rugged mountain ranges. With a triangle of autoroutes around it and dismal postwar developments encroaching on its historic core there's little reason to stay. Yet Aubagne is not without interest; it's the headquarters of the French Foreign Legion and a major centre for the production of *santons*, the traditional Provençal Christmas figures. Its main claim to fame, however, is as the birthplace of writer and film-maker **Marcel Pagnol** (1895–1974) and the now much-altered setting for his tales.

Maison Natale
16 cours Barthelémy • April–Oct daily 10am–1pm & 2–6pm; Nov–March Tues–Sun 2–5.30pm • €3 • ☎ 04 42 03 49 98

Marcel Pagnol's birthplace is now the **Maison Natale**, which houses plenty of displays on the writer and film-maker, as well as a fascinating fifteen-minute film (in French only). Enquire at the tourist office (see opposite) about **walks** into the surrounding countryside to visit the locations of Pagnol's films, though access to the hills around the town is subject to restrictions from June to September due to the fire risk (see p.75).

JEAN DE FLORETTE AND MANON DES SOURCES

Marcel Pagnol was an early convert to film; Alexander Korda's French-language version of *Marius* was an international hit as early as 1931. But it was the huge popularity in the 1980s of Claude Berri's films of Pagnol's *Jean de Florette* and *Manon des Sources*, starring Gérard Depardieu and Emmanuelle Béart, that really widened Pagnol's international appeal. In *Jean de Florette*, an outsider inherits a property on the arid slopes of the Garlaban mountain, whose rocky crest rears north of Aubagne like a stegosaurus's back. The local peasants who have blocked its spring watch him die from the struggle of fetching water, delighted that his new scientific methods won't upset their market share.

> **THE FRENCH FOREIGN LEGION**
>
> The tradition of foreigners serving in France's armies dates back to 1346, but the **Legion** as it exists today was created by King Louis Philippe in 1831. It received its baptism of fire in **Algeria** in 1832, and was closely associated with North Africa for much of its history, founding the garrison at Sidi Bel Abbès in 1843. The town grew to be a modern city of 100,000 and remained the Legion's home until France withdrew from Algeria in 1962. How sudden that withdrawal was is demonstrated by the fact that just a year previously the Legion had opened a Salle d'Honneur in Sidi Bel Abbès – the immediate predecessor to the one that can now be visited in Aubagne.

Petit Monde de Marcel Pagnol

Esplanade Charles de Gaulle • Daily: Jan–March & Sept–Nov 10am–12.30pm & 2–5.30pm; April–June & Dec 9am–12.30pm & 2.30–6pm; July & Aug 10am–1pm & 2–7pm • Free • ☎ 04 42 03 49 98

The fertile soil around Aubagne makes excellent pottery, hence the town's renown for *santons* – traditional Christmas figures – and ceramics. The most impressive display of *santons* is to be found at **Le Petit Monde de Marcel Pagnol**, where two hundred finely detailed figures of Pagnol characters (including Pagnol himself) play out their parts on a model of the district, complete with farms and villages.

From mid-July to the end of August and in December, a huge daily **market of ceramics** and **santons** takes place on the central street of cours Maréchal-Foch. At any time of the year you can visit the potters' workshops that are dotted all over town – pick up a leaflet from the tourist office.

Musée de la Légion Étrangère

Route de la Thuilière (D44A), quartier Vienot • Tues, Wed & Fri–Sun 10am–noon & 3–6pm • Free • ⓦ samle.legion-etrangere.com

Aubagne's claim to fame as headquarters of the French Foreign Legion (see box above) is commemorated by the **Musée de la Légion Étrangère**, inside the barracks in the *quartier* Vienot on the far side of the A50 autoroute from the town. Here, a sombre Salle d'Honneur commemorates the legion's founders and its dead, and evocative displays catalogue the Legion's campaigns. Exhibits include the white *képis* familiar from cinematic depictions of Beau Geste.

ARRIVAL AND INFORMATION   AUBAGNE

By train From the *gare SNCF* it's a five-minute walk along avenue Jeanne d'Arc to cours Foch and on to cours Barthelémy, where you'll find the tourist office.
Destinations Bandol (every 30min–1hr; 30min); Cassis (every 30min–1hr; 8min); La Ciotat (every 30min–1hr; 15min); Marseille (up to 6 per hr at peak times; 18min); Toulon (every 30min–1hr; 37–42 min).
By bus Buses arrive at the *pôle d'échanges* alongside the gare SNCF.
Destinations Aix (approx. hourly; 50min); Gémenos (every 20min–1hr Mon–Sat; 17min); La Ciotat (7 daily; 33min);

Marseille (every 8 min at peak times; 15min).
By car There's off-street parking in the centre of Aubagne; on-street spaces can be rather scarce.
Tourist office 8 cours Barthelémy (July & Aug Mon–Sat 9am–1pm & 2–7pm, Sun 10am–12.30pm; April–June, Sept & Oct Mon–Sat 9am–noon & 2–6pm; Nov–March Mon–Fri 9am–noon & 2–6pm, Sat 9am–12.30pm; ☎04 42 03 49 98, ⓦtourisme-paysdaubagne.fr). The office can provide information on Pagnol itineraries and local potteries and *santon*-makers.

The calanques

One of the most delightful paradoxes of Provence is that its most pristine stretch of coast abuts its largest city. For more than 20km – from **Les Goudes** on the southern fringe of Marseille to the chic little resort of **Cassis** – the coast is a wilderness of white limestone and crystal-clear turquoise water in long, fjord-like rocky inlets known as *calanques,* accessible for the most part only on foot or by sea.

1

THE COSQUER CAVE

In 1991, **Henri Cosquer**, a diver from Cassis, discovered paintings and engravings of animals, painted handprints and finger tracings in a cave between Marseille and Cassis, whose sole entrance is a long, sloping tunnel that starts 37m under the sea. The cave would have been accessible from dry land no later than the end of the last ice age, and carbon dating has shown that the oldest work of art here was created around 27,000 years ago. Over a hundred animals have been identified, including seals, auks, horses, ibex, bisons, chamois, red deer and a giant deer known only from fossils. Fish are also featured along with sea creatures that might be jellyfish. Most of the finger tracings are done in charcoal and have fingertips missing, possibly to convey bent fingers and therefore some sort of sign language. For safety reasons it's not possible to visit the cave, though diving schools in Cassis organize dives in the bay and the *calanques*.

The flora of the *calanques* is exceptionally rich, while rare Bonelli's eagles are among the 67 protected bird species found here, alongside 13 species of bats and nocturnal geckos. No wonder this entire stretch of coast – plus a further section between Cassis and La Ciotat, along the Corniche des Crêtes (see opposite) – was in 2012 declared a **national park** (Ⓦwww.calanques-parcnational.fr). The park extends offshore to protect the marine environment, which is home to coral and turtles, sea horses and sea urchins – as well as a remarkable submerged archeological site, the **Cosquer Cave** (see box above), in the Calanque de la Triperie between Sormiou and Morgiou.

Visiting the calanques

Easiest of all the *calanques* to reach are the little inlets that face west into the setting sun between La Madrague and Les Goudes, on Marseille's coastal fringe – ideal for evening swims and supper picnics. But the full majesty of the landscape begins just 2km or so to the east at the fishing settlement of Callelongue, where the road peters out and the **GR98 footpath** winds its way through the rocky wilderness to Cassis (see opposite). Just two of the more distant *calanques* – **Sormiou** and **Morgiou** – are at all accessible by car, and even then only outside the summer season; each has a small port and tiny settlement. If you're walking from Cassis, you set off along the **GR98 footpath** from port-Miou on the western side of the town; it's about a ninety-minute walk to the **Calanque en Vau**, where you can climb down rocks to the shore. Intrepid pine trees find root-holds, and sunbathers find ledges on the chaotic white cliffs. The water is deep blue and swimming between the vertical cliffs is an experience not to be missed. Whether you start in Callelongue or Cassis, to walk the whole route is a long, arduous day's work and for most of the way there are no refreshment stops, so take water.

If the full hike is too much, take the bus to the Luminy university campus and then hike the 45 minutes overland to the **Calanque de Sugiton**, roughly midway between Les Goudes and Cassis, or take a bus to Baumettes for a similar hike to Morgiou. Boat excursions offer a less arduous – if also potentially less rewarding – alternative.

ARRIVAL AND INFORMATION   THE CALANQUES

BY BUS

Bus #19 links Mᵒ Rd-Pt-du-Prado in Marseille with La Madrague de Montredon, from where bus #20 continues to Les Goudes; bus #21 serves Luminy from Canebière/Bourse in Marseille; and #22 serves Baumettes from Mᵒ Rd-Pt-du-Prado.

BY BOAT

From Cassis Various companies offer boat trips to the

calanques from Cassis for around €15; check whether they let you off or just tour in and out, and be prepared for rough seas. You can also hire boats with or without a skipper in Cassis from Loca' Bato, impasse du Grand Carnot, on the port (☎ 04 42 01 27 04, Ⓦ loca-bato-cassis.com).

From Marseille Croisières Marseille Calanques runs daily two-hour (€22) and three-hour (€28) trips to the *calanques* from the Vieux Port (☎ 04 91 58 50 58, Ⓦ croisieres-marseille -calanques.com). In July and August it also runs a cruise to

Sugiton with a scheduled stop for swimming (€28). Icard Maritime (☏ 04 91 33 03 29, ⊛ visite-des-calanques.com) offers more or less identical itineraries for the same prices.

From La Ciotat Catamaran Le Citharista runs trips to the *calanques*, sometimes in a glass-bottomed boat (late March to end Oct except during bad weather; up to 8 daily

in high season; €16–28; ☏ 06 09 35 25

INFORMATION

Tourist offices in Marseille (see p.59) and Cassis (se[...]
are useful sources of information; Marseille's tourist of[...]
sells IGN maps that cover the GR98 route in detail.

ACCOMMODATION

La Fontasse 12km west of Cassis ☏ 04 42 01 02 72, ⊛ fuaj.org. Solar-powered eco-friendly hostel in the hills above the *calanques*. It's pretty basic: there are no showers, you'll need to bring your own food and will be expected to help with chores. You can hike here along the GR98. Not bookable online. Reception 8–10am & 5–9pm. Closed Dec to mid-March. **€12.50**

Le Joli Bois Route de la Gineste ☏ 04 42 01 02 68, ⊛ hotel-du-joli-bois.com. Simple one-star hotel in the heart of the national park and massif, between Marseille and Cassis on the D559, with nineteen rooms and private parking for cars and bicycles. Popular with hikers. **€44.50**

EATING AND DRINKING

Le Château Route du feu de la Calanque de Sormio ☏ 04 91 25 08 69. Fish and bouillabaisse (order in advance) in glorious surroundings on the *calanque* of Sormiou; expect to pay around €40 for three courses. If you book, you can also drive here – the road is otherwise closed to non-residents in summer. Daily noon–3pm & 8–11pm; closed Oct–March.

La Grotte 1 av des Pebrons, Calellongue ☏ 04 91 73 17 79, ⊛ lagrotte-13.com; map ; map pp.48–49. Popular and surprisingly refined restaurant on the tiny port at

Callelongue, serving the likes of grilled fish and *pieds et paquets* from around €17. Daily 10am–1pm & 7.30–10.30pm.

Nautic Bar Calanque de Morgiou ☏ 04 91 40 06 37. On the portside at Morgiou, the *Nautic* specializes in *friture* – fried fish or girelle crab – for around €13.50 and bouillabaisse (€42). If you book here, you can drive here – the road is otherwise closed to visitors in summer. March to mid-Nov Tues–Sat noon–2pm & 7pm–midnight, Sun noon–2pm only.

Cassis and around

It's hard to imagine the chic little fishing port of **CASSIS**, on the main coast road south from Marseille, as a busy industrial harbour in the mid-nineteenth century, trading with Spain, Italy and Algeria. Its fortunes had declined by the time Dérain, Dufy and other Fauvist artists started visiting at the turn of the twentieth century. In the 1920s Virginia Woolf stayed while working on *To the Lighthouse*, and later Winston Churchill came here to paint. These days it's scarcely an undiscovered secret, as one glance at property prices or the crowds in the portside restaurants will tell you. The place bustles with activity: stalls sell handicrafts, guitarists busk round the port and day-trippers circle the one-way system trying to find a parking space. But many people still rate Cassis the best resort this side of St-Tropez, its residents most of all.

The cliffs hemming it in and the value of its vineyards on the slopes above have prevented Cassis becoming a relentless sprawl, and the little modern development that exists is small-scale. Portside posing, eating *oursins* (sea urchins) and drinking

le modest beach and look up at
the counts of Les Baux and
: authoritarian boss of the family
ids. If you're feeling more active
couple of diving outfits.

et Traditions Populaires

ıy 10am–12.30pm & 2.30–5.30pm • Free •

éditerranéen d'Art et Traditions
resbytery just inland from the port.
tings and photographs of Cassis and
phorae.

CASSIS AND AROUND

ose to the port; failing that, there's a free park-and-
ar park – parking relais des Gorguettes – on the
ırts, connected to the port by a shuttle bus (€1).

By train The *gare SNCF* is 3.5km from town, connected by
bus (7.15am–8.25pm; every 35min–1hr; 20min).
Destinations Bandol (every 30min–1hr; 18min); La Ciotat
(every 30min–1hr; 6min); Marseille (every 20min–1hr;
25–30min); St Cyr/Les Lecques (every 30min–1hr; 12min).
By car Parking in Cassis can be difficult even in low season;
the multistorey car park in avenue de la Viguerie is the best

iist office Quai des Moulins (March, April & Oct Mon–
Sat 9am–12.30pm & 2–6pm, Sun 10am–12.30pm; May,
June & Sept Mon–Sat 9am–6.30pm, Sun 9.30am–12.30pm
& 3–6pm; July & Aug Mon–Sat 9am–7pm, Sun
9.30am–12.30pm & 3–6pm; Nov–Feb Mon–Sat
9.30am–12.30pm & 2–5pm, Sun 10am–12.30pm;
☎ 08 92 25 98 92, ⓦ www.ot-cassis.com).

ACCOMMODATION

Le Cassiden 7 av Victor-Hugo ☎ 04 42 01 72 13,
ⓦ hotel-le-cassiden.fr. Just back from the port, this
newly renovated hotel has ten small, attractive modern
rooms with simple decor, en-suite shower rooms plus free
wi-fi. Rooms are double glazed and a/c. Good value for the
standard. **€70**
Château de Cassis Traverse du Château ☎ 04 42 01 63
20, ⓦ chateaudecassis.com. Luxurious suites and double
rooms in the spectacular setting of Cassis' clifftop castle,
complete with views, stunning architectural features, a
swimming pool and private parking. **€290**
Le Clos de Arômes 10 rue Abbé Paul-Mouton ☎ 04 42
01 71 84, ⓦ le-clos-des-aromes.com. Charming, quiet
hotel a short way inland from the bustle of the port, with
14 rooms, a lovely garden restaurant and one room that
sleeps four. **€69**
Le Commerce 12 rue St-Clair ☎ 04 42 01 09 10,
ⓦ hotel-lecommerce.fr. A handy budget option just
uphill from the quayside, offering basic en-suite comforts
with rooms sleeping one to four; some rooms have sea

views. There is also a cottage, which sleeps up to 19 people.
Closed Dec to mid-Feb. **€50**
Le Golfe 3 place du Grand Carnot ☎ 04 42 01 00 21,
ⓦ legolfe-cassis.fr. In the middle of all the action, with
some rooms overlooking the port, and with a brasserie, bar
and glacier. Rooms have en-suite bath or shower, TV and
a/c. Closed Nov–March. **€90**
Les Roches Blanches Av des Calanques ☎ 04 42 01 09
30, ⓦ roches-blanches-cassis.com. Cassis' best hotel is in
an idyllic setting amid pines on the Presqu'île, west of the
port. Rooms have contemporary decor, bathrooms and a/c
and many have either a balcony or terrace. There's a pool,
plus direct access to the sea. **€150**

CAMPING

Les Cigales Inland just off the D559 on the edge of the
village ☎ 04 42 01 07 34, ⓦ campingcassis.com. Cassis'
only campsite is a two-star affair, and a 15min walk from
the port, with free wi-fi and 250 pitches. Closed mid-Nov to
mid-March. **€19**

EATING AND DRINKING

Sea urchins – **oursins** - accompanied by the delicious, crisp Cassis white **wine** are the speciality here. Restaurant tables
are abundant along the portside on quai des Baux, quai Calandal and quai Barthélemy; prices vary but the best bet is to
follow your nose, and seek out the most enticing fish smells. For picnic food, head for the **market**, held around place
Baragnon east of the port on Wednesday and Friday mornings.

> **CASSIS WINES**
>
> Cassis **wines**, from grapes grown on the slopes above the D559, are very special. Mistral described the white as "shining like a limpid diamond, tasting of the rosemary, heather and myrtle that covers our hills". It's best to call ahead before visiting **local vineyards**; the tourist office can supply a list. Alternatively, there's the **Maison des Vins** (☎ 04 42 01 15 61, ⓦ maisondesvinscassis.com) on the outskirts of the village on the D559 route de Marseille.

Chez Gilbert 19 quai des Baux ☎ 04 42 01 71 36. Renowned portside restaurant and member of the Charte de la Bouillabaisse, which guards the authentic recipe of bouillabaisse – that aside, there's freshly grilled fish priced according to weight. *Menus* €32 and €40. Mon, Tues & Thurs–Sun noon–2pm & 7–10pm.

Le Chaudron 4 rue Adolphe Thiers ☎ 04 42 01 74 18, ⓦ resto-lechaudron.skyrock.com. Esteemed, old family-run bistro in the streets behind the port, with modern decor, pasta from €13 and duck breast with honey and lavender on the *carte*. *Menus* €25 and €34. Mon & Wed–Sun from 7.15pm.

Le Clos des Arômes 10 rue Abbé P. Mouton ☎ 04 42 01 71 84, ⓦ le-clos-des-aromes.com. Classic Provençal cooking in a simple, rustic dining room or in a pretty garden, with dishes like *daube à l'ancienne, pieds et paquets* and *pissaladière*. *Menus* €21 or €38. Mon, Tues, Fri & Sat noon–1.30pm & 7.15–9.30pm, Wed, Thurs & Sun 7.15–9.30pm; closed Jan.

Bar de la Marine 5 quai des Baux ☎ 04 42 01 76 09. The most animated of the portside café terraces, great for people-watching or merely soaking up the sun over a glass of wine. Breakfasts from €4.50, coffee €1.50 and draught beer from €2. Daily 7am–2am; closed Tues in winter.

La Presqu'Île Quartier Port Miou ☎ 04 42 01 03 77, ⓦ restaurant-la-presquile.fr. Beautifully situated by the sea to the west of the port, with accomplished cooking and a heavy emphasis on fish and seafood. *Menus* €38 or €52. Booking essential. Tues–Sat noon–2pm & 7.30pm–9.30/10pm, Sun noon–2pm.

The Corniche des Crêtes

For those with a car or motorbike – or a bicycle and prodigious fitness – the spectacular **Corniche des Crêtes** road south from Cassis to La Ciotat (the D141) is definitely a ride not to be missed. From Cassis the chemin St-Joseph turns off avenue de Provence, climbs at a maximum gradient to the Pas de la Colle, then follows the inland slopes of the Mont de la Canaille. Much of the landscape is often blackened by fire, but once in a while the road loops round a break in the chain to give you dramatic views over the sea. You can **walk** the route as well, in about three and a half hours: the path, beginning from Pas de la Colle, takes a precipitous straighter line, passing the road at each outer loop. Note that the corniche is closed in high winds.

La Ciotat and around

Cranes still loom incongruously over the old shipbuilding town of **LA CIOTAT**, where 300,000-tonne oil and gas tankers were built as recently as 1989. Today, the town's economy relies on property development, tourism and mooring and repairing yachts, yet it remains a pleasantly unpretentious place, with a golden Vieille Ville above the bustling quayside, affordable hotels and restaurants, and attractive beaches stretching northeast from the port.

The Vieille Ville

The Vieille Ville's seventeenth-century church, **Notre-Dame-de l'Assomption**, has a Baroque facade and inside there's a striking early seventeenth-century painting by André Gaudion of the *Descent of the Cross* alongside modern works of art; note that it's usually locked except when mass is on. The streets behind the church are uneventful and still a bit run-down in places, though the proliferation of estate agents suggests that is set to change.

FILM IN LA CIOTAT

In 1895 **Auguste** and **Louis Lumière** filmed the first ever moving pictures in La Ciotat and in 1904 went on to develop the first colour photographs. La Ciotat's train station has a commemorative plaque to the film **L'Arrivée d'un train en gare de La Ciotat**, which was one of a dozen or so films, including *Le déjeuner de bébé* and the comedy *L'Arroseur arrosé*, shown in the family's Château Lumière in September 1895. The audience jumped out of their seats as the image of the steam train hurtled towards them. Three months later the reels were taken to Paris for the capital's citizens to witness cinema for the first time.

There's a solid 1950s **monument** to Auguste and Louis Lumière at plage Lumière. Nearby, at the top of allée Lumière, lies the **Château Lumière** where some of their seminal films were shot, though the house is private property and not open to the public. The brothers appear again in a mural on the covered market halls which house the modern **cinema** on place Evariste-Gras, visible as you walk up rue Réynier from boulevard Guérin north of the port. La Ciotat's crumbly **Eden Theatre**, on the corner of bd A.-France and bd Jean-Jaurès, is the world's oldest movie house, opened in 1889 ; it's currently closed but is the subject of a €5 million restoration project to coincide with Marseille's stint as European Capital of Culture in 2013.

THE FILM FESTIVAL

La Ciotat celebrates its relatively unknown status as the cradle of cinema with an annual **film festival**, the Festival du Premier Film (🖰 berceau-cinema.com), in early June, screening a limited selection of films before an invited jury, which awards the *Lumières d'Honneur* prize. Tickets for screenings – which are free – can be obtained from La Ciotat's tourist office shortly before the festival begins.

Musée du Vieux Ciotat

1 quai Ganteaume • July & Aug Wed–Mon 4–7pm; Sept–June 3–6pm • €3.20 • 🕿 04 42 71 40 99

The dignified nineteenth-century former *mairie* at the end of quai Ganteaume now houses the **Musée du Vieux Ciotat** fifteen rooms charting the history of the town back to its foundation by the ancient Greeks of Marseille, when local shipbuilding began. The museum also includes sections on the birth of cinema and on *pétanque*.

Parc du Mugel

Daily: April–Sept 8am–8pm; Oct–March 9am–6pm • Free • Bus #30 from port, stop "Mugel"

South of the port La Ciotat's lovely botanical garden – the **Parc du Mugel** – curves around the cove of Anse du Petit Mugel, in the shadow of a strikingly odd-shaped promontory – the so-called "Bec d'Aigle" or Eagle's Beak. From the southern end of the park a path leads up through luxuriant vegetation to a narrow belvedere overlooking the sea.

Immediately to the west (fifteen minutes or so on foot from the port, or take bus #30 to Figuerolles) you can reach the **Anse de Figuerolles** *calanque* down the avenue of the same name, and its neighbour, the **Gameou**. Both have pebbly beaches and a different, darker rock colour from the blinding white *calanques* of Cassis and Marseille.

ARRIVAL AND INFORMATION

LA CIOTAT

By train The *gare SNCF* is 5km from the town, connected to the Vieux Port by bus #40 (frequent at peak times; 20min). Destinations Cassis (every 20min–1hr; 6min); St Cyr-Les Lecques (every 30min–1hr; 5min); Bandol (every 30min–1hr; 10–21 min); Marseille (every 20min–1hr; 33min).

By car There's parking on the seafront behind the tourist office.
Tourist office Bd Anatole-France (June–Sept Mon–Sat 9am–8pm, Sun 10am–1pm; Oct–May Mon–Sat 9am–noon & 2–6pm; 🕿 04 42 08 61 32, 🖰 tourisme-laciotat.com).

ACCOMMODATION

La Marine 1 av Fernand Gassion 🕿 04 42 08 35 11, 🖰 hotellamarine.free.fr. About the cheapest you'll get in La Ciotat, nothing fancy but close to the port and cheerful enough for the price. Some rooms sleep three or four; cheaper options don't have shower or toilet. **€36**

BOAT TRIPS FROM LA CIOTAT

For a blissful afternoon offshore, Île Verte Navette makes the crossing to the islet of **Île Verte** (daily: May–June & Sept hourly 10am–noon & 3–5pm; July & Aug hourly 9am–7pm; April & Oct enquire at Vieux Port or call; €11 return; ☎06 63 59 16 35, ✆laciotat-ileverte.com); the lotus-eating pleasures of its rocks, woods and *calanques* aside, there's also a restaurant, *Chez Louisette* (☎06 75 50 74 98) .

For details of Catamaran Le Citharista's trips to the **calanques of Cassis and Marseille** see p.75.

Miramar 3 bd Beaurivage, La Ciotat-Plage ☎04 42 83 33 79, ✆miramarlaciotat.com. Comfortable family-run hotel in the beach suburb of La Ciotat-Plage, right on the palm-fringed seafront, with a/c en-suite rooms, some with balconies, plus free wi-fi. There's also a restaurant. **€105**

La Rotonde 44 bd de la République ☎04 42 08 67 50, ✆hotel-larotonde-ciotat.fr. Good-value non-smoking two-star 200m from the port. Standard rooms have private bath and flatscreen TV, the cheapest share toilets, and around half the 31 rooms have balconies. **€48**

Vieux Port 258 quai F Mitterrand ☎04 42 04 00 00, ✆bestwestern-laciotat. Smart, contemporary three-star hotel right on the port, with a restaurant/bar and underground parking. Soundproofed and a/c rooms include some with balconies facing the sea. **€105**

CAMPING

Le Soleil 751 av Emile Bodin ☎04 42 71 55 32, ✆camping-dusoleil.com. The most central of La Ciotat's three campsites, around 1.5km from the beach and harbour, this two-star has an on-site restaurant and takeaway. Mobile homes (per week) **€460**; bungalows (per week) **€480**; camping **€20**

EATING, DRINKING AND ENTERTAINMENT

La Ciotat's restaurants are not gastronomically renowned, though there is plenty of choice along the port. There's a Sunday **market** on the quay; **rue des Poilus** in the Vieille Ville is a good hunting ground for bakers, fish and fresh fruit and vegetables. La Ciotat has an animated **cultural scene**, focused on the Théâtre du Golfe on the seafront at boulevard Anatole-France (☎04 42 08 92 87). Away from the port on place E-Gras, the Atelier Convergences (☎04 42 71 81 25) is a live **jazz** venue.

RESTAURANTS AND CAFÉS

Le Golfe 14 bd Anatole-France ☎04 42 08 42 59. Unpretentious choice close to the tourist office, with a fish-heavy menu that includes bouillabaisse for €42, grilled fish mains for around €15 plus pizza and pasta for under €10. Daily in season 11am–11pm.

L'Office'In 18 rue des Combattants ☎04 42 36 86 25. The Vieille Ville's trendiest culinary offering, with a pretty interior and a terrace overlooking the port, plus the likes of soba noodles with yakitori sauce or grilled entrecôte with *frites* on its eclectic *carte*. *Menus* from €24. May–Sept Tues–Sun noon–3pm & 7–11pm; Oct–April Tues–Thurs & Sun noon–3pm, Fri & Sat noon–3pm & 7–11pm.

O'Kylian's 1 quai François Mitterrn and ☎04 42 62 08 41. Grungy but popular all-day Irish pub on the portside, with cheap breakfasts (€1.90 or €3.60) and ice creams (from €1.80) alongside the Guinness, fruit-flavoured beers and draught Stella. Daily 7.30am–2/3am.

Roche Belle Corniche du Liouquet ☎04 42 71 47 60, ✆www.roche-belle.fr. In an idyllic setting near the sea between La Ciotat and Les Lecques, with a shady terrace and dishes like fillet of beef with morel sauce and potato *galette*. There's a three-course *menu* at €35 and they serve Bandol wines. Main courses from around €22. July & Aug Mon & Tues 7.30–9.30pm, Wed–Sat noon–1.30pm & 7.30–9.30pm; Sept–June Mon–Sat noon–1.30pm & 7.30–9.30pm.

De la Vigne a l'Olivier 44 quai François Mitterrn and ☎04 86 33 27 02. Classy restaurant/café and wine bar at the far side of the port, with seafood salads from €10 and wines by the glass from €3. There's a lunchtime *formule* of pasta and wine for €12. Tues–Sat 9am–7.30pm, Sun 9am–1.30pm.

Arles and the Camargue

FLAMINGOS IN THE CAMARGUE

Arles and the Camargue

The stretch of the River Rhône that flows south from Avignon to the sea has always been a vital trading route, bringing wealth and fame to the towns that line its banks. The great riverside castles at Tarascon and Beaucaire are testament to the Rhône's strategic importance, while further south, at the point where the river divides into separate channels as the Petit and Grand Rhône, is Arles, once the centre of Roman Provincia – which extended from the Pyrenees to the Alps – and later, towards the end of the Roman era, the capital of Gaul. Arles' great amphitheatre still seats thousands for summer entertainments, while further evidence of Roman occupation is apparent at Glanum, outside St-Rémy-de-Provence, where you can see the overlaid remains of Greek and Roman towns.

South of Arles, spreading across the Rhône delta, the strange watery land of the **Camargue** has its own unique natural history and way of life. The wet expanses sustain flocks of flamingos and other birds, while black bulls and wild white horses graze along the edges of the marshes and lagoons. The Camargue also provides a sanctuary for unique social traditions – every May, **gypsies** from all around the Mediterranean come to the seaside resort of **Les Stes-Maries-de-la-Mer** to celebrate their patron saint.

The modest plains north and east of Arles, enclosed by the River Durance and the Rhône and separated by the abrupt ridge of the **Alpilles**, are known as **La Petite Crau** and **La Grande Crau**. The villages and small towns here have retained a nineteenth-century charm, living out the traditions revived by the great Provençal poet **Frédéric Mistral**. This is the countryside that **Van Gogh** painted when he spent a year at Arles and then sought refuge in St-Rémy. Both towns celebrate his tragic brilliance.

Arles

With its sun-kissed golden stone, small-town feel and splendid setting on the east bank of the Rhône, **ARLES** is one of the loveliest cities in southern France. It's also among the oldest, with the extraordinarily well-preserved Roman amphitheatre at its heart, **Les Arènes**, being simply the most famous of several magnificent monuments.

Originally a Celtic settlement, it later became the Roman capital of Gaul, Britain and Spain, and survived the collapse of the Roman Empire as a base for the counts of Provence before unification with France. For centuries, the port of Arles prospered by way of the inland trade route up the Rhône, profiting especially whenever France's enemies blockaded its eternal rival, Marseille. Decline set in with the arrival of the railways, however, and the town where **Van Gogh** spent a lonely

LES ARÈNES, ARLES

Highlights

❶ Les Arènes For its sheer size, Arles' ancient Roman amphitheatre is one of Provence's most impressive Roman remains. **See p.85**

❷ Les Baux-de-Provence Scramble over the hillsides to explore this extraordinary citadel, carved into the bleached rocks atop the Alpilles range. **See p.92**

❸ Carrières de Lumières A fascinating audiovisual extravaganza, projected into the cavernous interior of a former quarry in the Valley of Hell. **See p.93**

❹ St-Paul-de-Mausole Home for a year to Vincent van Gogh, this psychiatric hospital in picturesque St-Rémy offers an emotive insight into the artist's suffering. **See p.94**

❺ Château du Roi René Tarascon's colossal riverside castle is impressive in its own right, and also plays host to fascinating annual exhibitions on the life and lore of medieval Provence. **See p.101**

❻ The Camargue The expansive marshland of the Rhône delta is home to pink flamingos, white horses and unearthly, watery landscapes, as well as the colourful gypsy festival in Les Stes-Maries-de-la-Mer. **See p.103**

HIGHLIGHTS ARE MARKED ON THE MAP ON P.84

and miserable – but highly prolific – period in the late nineteenth century was itself inward-looking and depressed.

Arles today is pleasantly laidback – at its liveliest on Saturdays, when farmers from the Camargue and La Crau come in for the weekly market – and a delightful place simply to stroll around. Its compact central core, tucked into a ninety-degree curve in the river, is small enough to cross on foot in a few minutes, and holds all the major sights except the **Musée Départemental Arles Antique** to the southwest, and **Les Alyscamps** necropolis to the southeast. While ancient ruins are scattered everywhere, the heart of the Roman city, the **place du Forum**, remains the hub of popular life. Medieval Arles, on the other hand, centred on what's now the place de la République,

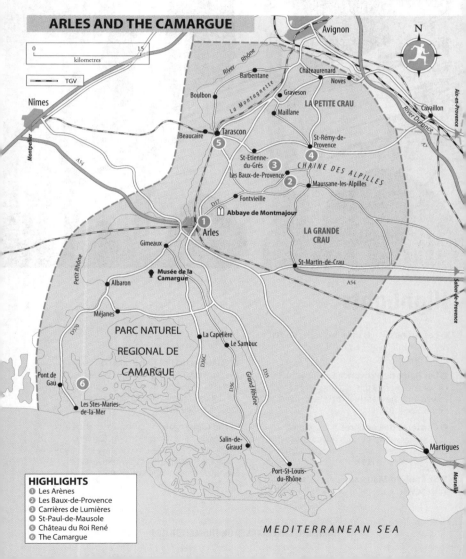

ARLES AND THE CAMARGUE

0   15
kilometres

━━━ TGV

Avignon

N

Nîmes

River – Rhône

Barbentane

Châteaurenard

Noves

Cavaillon

Aix-en-Provence

La Montagnette

Boulbon

Graveson

LA PETITE CRAU

River Durance

Maillane

A7

Montpellier

Beaucaire

Tarascon

⑤

St-Rémy-de-Provence

④

A54

St-Etienne-du-Grès

③

CHAINE DES ALPILLES

Les Baux-de-Provence

②

Maussane-les-Alpilles

D17

Fontvieille

① Abbaye de Montmajour

LA GRANDE CRAU

① Arles

Gimeaux

St-Martin-de-Crau

A54

Salon-de-Provence

Petit Rhône

Albaron

Musée de la Camargue

Méjanes

PARC NATUREL

D570

La Capelière

Le Sambuc

REGIONAL DE

D36C

Grand Rhône

D35

CAMARGUE

Pont de Gau

⑥

D36

Les Stes-Maries-de-la-Mer

Salin-de-Giraud

Martigues

Marseille

Port-St-Louis-du-Rhône

MEDITERRANEAN SEA

HIGHLIGHTS
❶ Les Arènes
❷ Les Baux-de-Provence
❸ Carrières de Lumières
❹ St-Paul-de-Mausole
❺ Château du Roi René
❻ The Camargue

> ### THE RENCONTRES D'ARLES
>
> The **Rencontres d'Arles** (ⓦ www.rencontres-arles.com), widely acknowledged to be Europe's most prestigious annual **photography festival**, takes over more than a dozen venues throughout the city between July and late September. Visitors can either pay €3.50–11 for admission to a single exhibition, or buy passes – €27 for one day, €35 for the whole festival – from ticket offices in the place de la République and elsewhere.

the pedestrianized site of both the **Cathédrale St-Trophime** and the Hôtel de Ville. The one area where the city's former **walls** have survived lies to the east, in a quiet and attractive little corner. Sadly, the **riverfront**, once teeming with bars and bistros, was heavily damaged during World War II.

Roman Arles

To this day, Arles remains recognizable as the **Roman** city that was first thrust to greatness when Julius Caesar built an entire fleet here in less than a month. After using the ships to win control of Rome, he devastated Marseille for its support of his enemy Pompey, and Arles became a major port. The Mediterranean was a little closer to the city at that time, while the extensive wheat fields of the Camargue were known as the "granary of Rome".

Having reached its apogee as a world trading centre during the fifth century, Arles' relative isolation after the empire crumbled allowed its heritage to be preserved. The site of its Roman forum, the **place du Forum**, still holds the pillars of an ancient archway and the first two steps of a monumental stairway, now embedded in the corner of the *Nord-Pinus* hotel.

Les Arènes

Daily: March, April & Oct 9am–6pm; May–Sept 9am–7pm; Nov–Feb 10am–5pm • €6 with Théâtre Antique • ☎ 04 90 49 36 74, ⓦ www.arenes-arles.com

Constructed at the end of the first century AD, Arles' most dramatic monument, the amphitheatre known as **Les Arènes**, was the largest Roman building in all Gaul. Looming above the city centre, it measures 136m long by 107m wide; its two tiers of sixty arches each (the lower Doric, the upper Corinthian) were originally topped by a third, and thirty thousand spectators would cram beneath its canvas roof to watch gladiator battles and other spectacles. During the Middle Ages, it became a fortress (and effectively a miniature town), sheltering over two hundred dwellings and three churches. Since this medieval quarter was cleared away in 1830, the Arènes has once more been used for entertainment. While it's impressive from the outside, it's only worth paying for admission when a performance, such as a bullfight (see box, p.87) or concert, is taking place; it makes an absolutely stunning venue.

Théâtre Antique

Entrance on rue du Cloître • Daily: March, April & Oct 9am–noon & 2–6pm; May–Sept 9am–7pm; Nov–Feb 10am–noon & 2–5pm • €6 with Les Arènes • ☎ 04 90 18 41 20

The **Théâtre Antique** is nowhere near as well preserved as the amphitheatre immediately to the north. Only one pair of columns is still standing, all the statuary has been removed, and the sides of the stage are littered with broken chunks of stone. Built a hundred years before Les Arènes, it was quarried to build churches not long after the Roman empire collapsed, and later became part of the city's fortifications – one wing was turned into the **Tour Roland**, whose height gives an idea where the top seats would have been. While there's little to see on an ordinary day, it's an atmospheric venue for performances and festivals year-round.

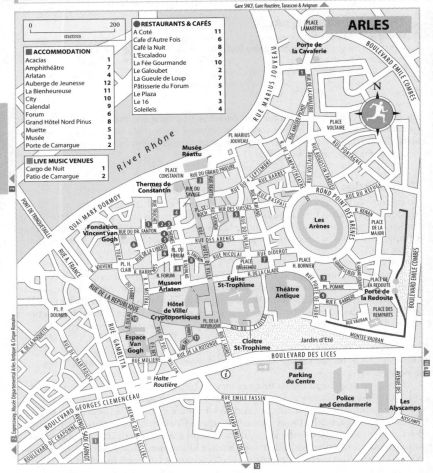

Gare SNCF, Gare Routière, Tarascon & Avignon

ARLES

ACCOMMODATION	
Acacias	1
Amphithéâtre	7
Arlatan	4
Auberge de Jeunesse	12
La Bienheureuse	11
City	10
Calendal	9
Forum	6
Grand Hôtel Nord Pinus	8
Muette	5
Musée	3
Porte de Camargue	2

RESTAURANTS & CAFÉS	
A Coté	11
Cafe d'Autre Fois	6
Café la Nuit	8
L'Escaladou	9
La Fée Gourmande	10
Le Galoubet	2
La Gueule de Loup	7
Pâtisserie du Forum	5
Le Plaza	1
Le 16	3
Soleileïs	4

LIVE MUSIC VENUES	
Cargo de Nuit	1
Patio de Camargue	2

Thermes de Constantin

Rue du Grand-Prieuré • Daily: March, April & Oct 9am–noon & 2–6pm; May–Sept 9am–noon & 2–7pm; Nov–Feb 1–5pm • €3 • ☎ 04 90 49 36 74

The ruins of the **Thermes de Constantin**, which may well have been the biggest Roman baths in Provence, are all that remain of the emperor's palace that extended along the Rhône waterfront. You can see the heating system below a thick Roman concrete floor and the divisions between the different areas, but there's nothing to help you imagine the original. The most striking feature, the high and rather elegant wall of an apse that sheltered one of the baths, in alternating stripes of orange brick and grey masonry, is best viewed from outside on place Constantin.

Cryptoportiques

Accessed via Hôtel de Ville, place de la République • Daily: March, April & Oct 9am–noon & 2–6pm; May–Sept 9am–noon & 2–7pm; Nov–Feb 10am–noon & 2–5pm • €3.50

Arles' most unusual – and spookiest – Roman remains, the **Cryptoportiques**, are reached via stairs that lead down from inside the Hôtel de Ville (see p.89). No one

BULLFIGHTS IN THE ARENA

Bullfighting, or more properly *tauromachie* (roughly, "the art of the bull"), comes in two styles in Arles and the Camargue. In the local **courses camarguaises**, held at *fêtes* from late spring to early autumn (the most prestigious of which is Arles' Cocarde d'Or, on the first Monday in July), *razeteurs* run at the bulls in an effort to pluck ribbons and cockades tied to the bulls' horns, cutting them free with special barbed gloves. The drama and grace is in the stylish way the men leap over the barrier away from the bull, and in the competition for prize money. In this gentler bullfight, people are rarely injured and the bulls are not killed.

More popular, however, are the brutal Spanish-style **corridas**, consisting of a strict ritual leading up to the all-but-inevitable death of the bull. After its entry into the ring, the bull is subjected to the *bandilleros* who stick decorated barbs in its back, the *picadors*, who lance it from horseback, and finally, the *torero*, who endeavour to lead the bull through as graceful a series of movements as possible before killing it with a single sword stroke to the heart. In one *corrida* six bulls are killed by three *toreros*, for whom injuries (sometimes fatal) are not uncommon.

While outsiders may disapprove, *tauromachie* has a long history here, and offers a rare opportunity to join in local life. It's also a great way to experience Arles' Roman arena in use. Assorted bullfighting events are staged at Les Arènes between Easter and September each year, including non-fatal *courses camarguaises* at 5.30pm each Wednesday & Friday from early July until late August; and Spanish-style corridas in late April, early July and September.

Tickets, sold at the arena, cost from €10 for the *courses camarguaises* up to €97 for a prime spot at a corrida (**W** www.arenes-arles.com).

knows quite what these huge, dark and dank underground galleries were for, but they may have been built simply to prop up one side of the town's level open forum, which stood above, and then used as a food store, or a barracks for public slaves. They're empty now, but gloriously atmospheric for a fifteen-minute subterranean stroll.

Musée Départemental Arles Antique

Av 1ere Division France Libre, 15min walk southwest of place du Forum • Daily except Tues 10am–6pm • €6, free 1st Sun of each month • **T** 04 13 31 51 03, **W** www.arles-antique.cg13.fr

The superb modern **Musée Départemental Arles Antique**, the best place to get an overall sense of Roman Arles, stands immediately southwest of the city centre on a spit of land between the Rhône and the Canal de l'Ecluse. Open-plan, flooded with natural light and immensely spacious, it starts with regional prehistory, then leads through the Roman era. The story of Arles is traced from Julius Caesar's legionnaire base and its development under Augustus, via its fourth-century status as the Christian emperor Constantine's capital of Gaul, to the height of its importance as a trading centre during the fifth century. At that time, Emperor Honorius could say "the town's position, its communications and its crowd of visitors is such that there is no place in the world better suited to spreading, in every sense, the products of the earth". Excellent models show the changing layout of the city and the sheer size of its monuments, while thematic displays explore such topics as medicine, industry and agriculture, and the use of water power. Overhead walkways enable visitors to admire some fabulous mosaics, while sculptures on the sarcophagi salvaged from Les Alyscamps (see p.87) depict everything from music and lovers to gladiators and Christian miracles. A planned **expansion** of the museum, likely to be completed during the lifetime of this book, will focus especially on the story of Arles' Roman port.

The museum is positioned on the axis of the second-century **Cirque Romaine**, an enormous chariot racetrack that stretched back 450m and seated twenty thousand spectators. Little is now discernible on the ground, however.

Les Alyscamps

Av des Alyscamps • Daily: March, April & Oct 9am–noon & 2–6pm; May–Sept 9am–7pm; Nov–Feb 10am–noon & 2–5pm • €3.50 • **T** 04 90 49 36 74

The Roman necropolis of Arles, known as **Les Alyscamps**, lies just southeast of the city centre, a few minutes' walk south of boulevard des Lices. Originally much larger, it was regarded as the most hallowed Christian burial ground in all Europe long after the Roman era had ended; until the twelfth century, mourners far upstream would launch sumptuous coffins to float down the Rhône, for collection at Arles. Only one of its many alleyways now survives, and even that is foreshortened by a rail line, while the finest of its sarcophagi and statues have long since disappeared. Nonetheless, ancient tombs still line the shaded walk, as painted by Van Gogh (who rendered the tree trunks azure blue), and the tranquil 400-metre stroll ends at the twelfth-century Romanesque church of **St-Honorat**, which is wonderfully simple, and cool on a hot day.

VAN GOGH IN ARLES

On February 21, 1888, **Vincent van Gogh** arrived in Arles from Paris, to be greeted by snow and a bitter Mistral wind. He started painting immediately, and within the year produced such celebrated canvases as *The Sunflowers, Van Gogh's Chair, The Red Vines* and *The Sower*. He always lived near the station, staying first at the *Hotel Carrel*, 30 rue de la Cavalarie, and then the *Café de la Gare*, until the so-called "Yellow House", at 2 place Lamartine, had been rendered fit for use as a home as well as a studio.

From the daily letters he wrote to his brother Théo, it's clear that Van Gogh found few kindred souls in Arles. He finally managed to persuade **Paul Gauguin** to join him in late October. Although the two were to influence each other substantially in the following weeks, their relationship quickly soured as the increasingly bad November weather forced them to spend more time together indoors.

Precisely what transpired on the night of December 23, 1888, will probably never be known. According to Gauguin, Van Gogh, feeling threatened by his friend's possible departure, finally succumbed to a fit of psychosis and attacked first Gauguin and then himself. He cut off the lower part of his **left ear**, wrapped it in newspaper, and handed it to a prostitute. An alternative version of the story emerged in 2009, with allegations that it was in fact an infuriated Gauguin who'd lopped off the offending lobe with a sword, and that the two artists had concocted a cover story to protect Gauguin from the law.

In any event, Gauguin left Arles, and although Vincent's wound soon healed, his mental health swiftly deteriorated. In response to a petition from thirty of his alarmed neighbours, he was packed off to the **Hôtel-Dieu** hospital, where he had the good fortune to be treated by a young and sympathetic doctor, Félix Rey. Van Gogh painted Rey's portrait while in the hospital, as well as the hospital itself, whose inmates are clearly suffering not from violent frenzy, but from an unhappiness only Van Gogh could express. Upon leaving hospital, Van Gogh also left Arles, moving voluntarily to St-Rémy (see p.94).

IN THE FOOTSTEPS OF VAN GOGH

None of Van Gogh's paintings remains in Arles, and the Yellow House was destroyed by bombing during World War II. Vestiges of the city that he knew still survive, however. Behind the Réattu museum, lanterns line the river wall where Van Gogh used to wander, wearing candles on his hat, watching the night-time light: *Starry Night over the Rhône* shows the Rhône at Arles. The café he painted in *Café Terrace at Night* is still open for business in place du Forum, while the distinctive Pont Langlois drawbridge, which he painted in March 1888, survives on the southern edge of town. The Hôtel-Dieu hospital itself, on rue du Président-Wilson, has become the **Espace Van Gogh**, which houses a *mediathèque* and university departments, and has a bookshop and a *salon de thé* in the arcades, and flowerbeds in the courtyard that re-create the garden that Van Gogh both painted and described.

As this book was being researched, the **Fondation Vincent van Gogh**, which for many years ran a small gallery near the amphitheatre, was expecting to open a much larger exhibition and research facility in the newly converted Hôtel Léautaud de Donines on rue du Dr-Fanton. As well as displaying its own collection of contemporary works inspired by Van Gogh, it hopes to arrange temporary loans of paintings by the artist himself. For the latest details on the project, visit ⓦfondation-vincentvangogh-arles.org.

Place de la République

The dominant feature of the old town's central, pedestrianized **place de la République** is an obelisk of Egyptian granite. It may originally have stood in the middle of the Cirque Romaine, but was placed here by Louis XIV, who fancied himself as a latter-day Augustus.

Also on place de la République is the palatial seventeenth-century **Hôtel de Ville**, which was inspired by the Palace of Versailles. A staircase inside leads down to the Roman **Cryptoportiques** (see p.86); in fact, the flattened vaulted roof of its entrance hall was expressly designed to minimize stress on the galleries below.

2

Église St-Trophime

Place de la République • Cathedral mid-April to June Mon–Sat 8am–noon & 2–6pm, Sun 9am–1pm & 3–7pm; July–Sept Mon–Sat 8am–noon & 3–7pm, Sun 9am–1pm & 3–7pm; Oct to mid-April daily 8am–noon & 2–6pm • Free Cloisters Daily: March, April & Oct 9am–noon & 2–6pm; May–Sept 9am–7pm; Nov–Feb 10am–noon & 2–5pm • €3.50

Unusually, Arles' **Église St-Trophime** does not stand alone, but instead is simply one relatively inconspicuous facade among many on place de la République. Superb twelfth-century Provençal stone carving around its doorway depicts the Last Judgement, trumpeted by angels playing with the enthusiasm of jazz musicians; as the damned are led naked and chained down to hell, the blessed – all female and draped in long robes – process upwards. Work on the cathedral itself started in the ninth century, on the spot where, in 597 AD, Saint Augustine was consecrated as the first bishop of the English. The high nave is now decorated with d'Aubusson tapestries, while there's more Romanesque and Gothic stone carving, including an image of Saint Martha leading away the tamed Tarasque (see p.101), in the extraordinarily beautiful **Cloître St-Trophime**, reached by a separate entrance to the right.

Musée Réattu

10 rue du Grand-Prieuré • Tues–Sun: July–Sept 10am–7pm; Oct–June 10am–12.30pm & 2–6.30pm • €7 • ☎ 04 90 49 37 58, ⓦ museereattu.arles.fr

The must-see **Musée Réattu** stands beside the river and opposite the Roman baths, in a beautiful fifteenth-century priory. It centres on 57 ink and crayon sketches, made between December 1970 and February 1971, donated by **Pablo Picasso** in appreciation of the many bullfights he'd seen in Arles. Among the split faces, clowns and hilarious Tarasque (see box, p.101), there's a beautifully simple portrait of Picasso's mother, painted from life in 1923. Other twentieth-century pieces dotted about the landings, corridors and courtyard niches include Mario Prassinos' black-and-white studies of the Alpilles, and *Odalisque*, Zadkine's polychromed sculpture of a woman playing a violin. The museum also hosts very good temporary exhibitions.

ARRIVAL AND INFORMATION

ARLES

By train Arles' *gare SNCF* is on av Pauline Talabot, a few blocks north of the Arènes.

Destinations Avignon (17 daily; 20min); Avignon TGV (2 daily; 20min); Lyon (7–9 daily; 2hr 30min); Marseille (hourly; 45min–1hr); Nîmes (7 daily; 30min); Paris (2 daily; 4hr); Tarascon (4 daily; 10min).

By bus Most buses arrive at the unstaffed *gare routière* alongside the *gare SNCF* on av Pauline Talabot, but all local services stop on bd Georges Clemenceau, just east of rue Gambetta.

Destinations Aix (7 daily; 1hr 30min); Avignon (7 daily; 1hr); Avignon TGV (10 daily; 55min); Les Baux (5 daily; 40min); Nîmes (11 daily; 1hr 5min); Les Stes-Maries-de-la-Mer

(9 daily; 50min); St-Rémy (8 daily; 50min); Tarascon (10 daily; 20min).

By car In summer, drivers are better off parking on the periphery, such as in the Centre car park on boulevard des Lices, rather than venturing into the central maze of narrow one-way streets. There's free street parking a little further out, for example on place Lamartine and near Les Alyscamps.

Tourist office Bd des Lices (Easter–June & Sept daily 9am–6.45pm; July & Aug daily 9am–7.45pm; Oct–Easter Mon–Sat 9am–4.45pm, Sun 10am–1pm; ☎ 04 90 18 41 20, ⓦ arlestourisme.com).

Bike rental Europbike, 5 rue Marius Jouveau (daily 8am–6pm; ☎ 06 38 14 49 50, ⓦ europbike-provence.net).

ACCOMMODATION

Acacias 2 rue de la Cavalerie ☎ 04 90 96 37 88, ⓦ hotel-acacias.com. Modern, simple but cheerfully decorated – and soundproofed – rooms in a friendly hotel, not far from the train station. Closed late Oct to March. **€76**

★ **Amphithéâtre** 5–7 rue Diderot ☎ 04 90 96 10 30, ⓦ hotelamphitheatre.fr. Very central hotel, where the spacious and beautifully decorated a/c rooms feature lots of warm colours, tiles and wrought ironwork, and large well-equipped bathrooms; the four-person rooms and suites are also good value. **€67**

Arlatan 26 rue du Sauvage ☎ 04 90 93 56 66, ⓦ hotel-arlatan.fr. Set in a beautiful antique-decorated fifteenth-century mansion, this hotel has plenty of character, plus a heated swimming pool and its own (€12.50) garage, but some rooms are rather small. Closed Jan. **€85**

Auberge de Jeunesse 20 av du Maréchal-Foch ☎ 04 90 96 18 25, ⓦ fuaj.org/arles. Old-style hostel, 500m south of the centre – from the *gare SNCF*, take bus #3 to stop "Clemenceau" – with rock-hard beds in large dorms, and spartan facilities. Bike hire available. Reception 7–10am & 5–11pm (midnight in summer). Closed mid-Dec to mid-Feb. Rates include breakfast. Dorms **€18.50**

Calendal 5 rue Porte-de-Laure ☎ 04 90 96 11 89, ⓦ lecalendal.com. Welcoming hotel, overlooking the Théâtre Antique and glowing at sunset, with bright a/c rooms overlooking a pleasant shaded garden; rates include access to the indoor spa. **€119**

Forum 10 place du Forum ☎ 04 90 93 48 95, ⓦ hotelduforum.com. Run by the same family for almost a century, this venerable hotel, in Arles' most appealing little square, offers plain but tasteful and reasonably spacious rooms, plus a tiny pool and a bar that's barely changed since Picasso hung out here fifty years ago. **€80**

Grand Hôtel Nord Pinus 14 place du Forum ☎ 04 90 93 44 44, ⓦ nord-pinus.com. Chic, luxurious rooms in a grand mansion dominating the pretty place du Forum in the heart of the old town. Much favoured by the vedettes of the bullring, it's decorated with assorted trophies and evocative photos. **€175**

★ **Muette** 15 rue des Suisses ☎ 04 90 96 15 39, ⓦ hotel-muette.com. Charming old stone hotel, close to Les Arènes, where the tasteful, tranquil rooms are decked out in beiges and creams, with rough-hewn terracotta-tiled floors and lots of Van Gogh touches, down to the (artificial) sunflowers on the tables. Nice buffet breakfast, and friendly management. Closed Jan & Feb. **€84**

Musée 11 rue du Grand-Prieuré ☎ 04 90 93 88 88, ⓦ hoteldumusee.com. Small, good-value, family-run place, set in a seventeenth-century mansion in a quiet spot opposite Musée Réattu, with a pretty, flower-filled terrace, and its own art gallery. Closed Jan & first 2 weeks of March & Dec. **€65**

Porte de Camargue 15 rue Noguier ☎ 04 90 96 17 32, ⓦ portecamargue.com. Attractive, very peaceful hotel, with light, simple rooms, and a rooftop terrace, just across the Pont du Trinquetaille from the centre – parking is much easier this side of the river. Closed late Oct to early March. **€65**

CAMPING

La Bienheureuse N453, Raphèle-lès-Arles ☎ 04 90 98 48 06, ⓦ labienheureuse.com. Well-shaded three-star site, 7km southeast on the Aix bus route, that's the best of Arles' half-dozen campsites, with two pools and a Provençal-styled restaurant. Open all year. **€17**

City 67 rte de Crau ☎ 04 90 93 08 86, ⓦ camping-city.com. The closest campsite to town, 1.5km southeast on the Crau bus route, this three-star is not very attractive, but there's a certain amount of shade, and a pool. Closed Oct–March. **€19**

EATING AND DRINKING

Arles has a good range of **restaurants** – many excellent, many cheap, and a fair number both – while the place du Forum is the centre of **café** life. Most of Arles, however, packs up for the night around 10.30pm. Saturday's **market** extends the length of boulevard Georges-Clemenceau, boulevard des Lices and boulevard Émile-Combes and many of the adjoining streets. A smaller food market is held every Wednesday in place Lamartine, with bric-a-brac stalls spreading down boulevard Émile-Combes.

RESTAURANTS

A Coté 21 rue des Carmes ☎ 04 90 47 61 13, ⓦ bistro-acote.com. The most affordable of three all-but-adjoining restaurants belonging to acclaimed chef *Jean-Luc Rabanel*, along a tiny but very central alleyway, this informal bistro has pleasant outdoor seating. Open from breakfast onwards, it serves full menus from €29, but also mouthwatering tapas such as aubergine caviar from around €8, and varying *plats*

from €18. Daily 9am–midnight.

L'Escaladou 23 rue Porte-de-Laure ☎ 04 90 96 70 43. Behind its old-fashioned facade, near the upper side of the Théâtre Antique, this local favourite holds three substantial dining rooms, all often sufficiently packed for some to dismiss it as a tourist trap. It may be noisy and not exactly romantic, and the service perfunctory at times, but the honest local food is delicious. *Menus* from €19; magnificently garlicky fish specials include a sumptuous

€28 Arlesian bouillabaisse. Mon, Tues & Fri–Sun noon–1.30pm & 7.30–9.30pm, Thurs 7.30–9.30pm.

La Fee Gourmande 39 rue Dulau ☎ 04 90 18 26 57. Great-value home cooking in a friendly, slightly kitsch environment, with *menus* and *plats* from just €13. The house speciality is melt-in-your-mouth slow-cooked lamb. Wed–Sun noon–1.30pm & 7.30–9.30pm.

Le Galoubet 18 rue de Dr-Fanton ☎ 04 90 93 18 11. Classy central bistro, offering al fresco streetside dining beneath a canopy of trees. The very welcoming young owners offer Provençal classics, like cold minestrone soup with foie gras, on *menus* costing €18 at lunchtime, €29 at dinner. Tues–Sat noon–1.30pm & 7.30–9.30pm.

★ **La Gueule de Loup** 39 rue des Arènes ☎ 04 90 96 96 69. Cosy stone-walled restaurant, squeezed into a venerable townhouse, with the open kitchen plus four tables downstairs, and the main dining room upstairs. Elaborate and delicate Provençal dishes include a courgette-blossom mousse and turbot on a bed of puréed aubergine. *Menus* from €13 lunch, €25 dinner; reservations recommended. Mon 7.30–9.30pm, Tues–Sat noon–1.45pm & 7.30–9.30pm.

Le Plaza 28 rue du Dr-Fanton ☎ 04 90 96 33 15. Smart but very friendly place, also known as *La Paillote*, with a good €21 *menu* full of Provençal starters and main courses such as *papillote de taureau* (bull), as well as a €33 *menu* of house specialities, with no choice. Reserve for outdoor seating. Mon & Thurs–Sun noon–1.20pm & 7–9.30pm, Tues 7–9.30pm, Wed noon–1.20pm.

Le 16 16 rue du Dr-Fanton ☎ 04 90 93 77 36, ⓦ le16restaurant.com. Friendly little indoor, air-conditioned traditional bistro, just off the place du Forum. The lunch *formule* costs just €14, while for dinner you can get a two-course *menu* for €19, three courses for €24, or simply order a *plat*, such as the €13 *gardianne de taureau*. Mon–Fri noon–1.45pm & 7–9.30pm, Sat noon–1.45pm.

CAFÉS, BARS AND ICE CREAM

Café d'Autre Fois 22 rue de la Liberté ☎ 06 09 24 39 59, ⓦ cafedautrefois.com. Alternative coffee bar, close to the heart of things but with a laidback atmosphere that makes its outdoor terrace a welcome escape. Organic espressos and pricey but refreshing all-fruit smoothies (75cl €6.70), plus breakfast for €4.40 and salads or *plats* for around €8. Daily 7.30am–7pm.

Café la Nuit 11 place du Forum ☎ 04 90 96 44 56. Immortalized in Van Gogh's *Café Terrace at Night* – though it's not the same café depicted in The *Night Café*, which was near the station – this long-established café remains *the* place to enjoy Arles' pretty central square. Have a drink on the terrace and you'll find yourself in quite a few holiday snaps; don't eat here though, the food is very poor. Daily 8am–11pm.

Pâtisserie du Forum 4 rue de la Liberté ☎ 04 90 96 03 72. *Salon de thé* with a whole patisserie full of goodies to go with the Earl Grey, plus ice cream and hot chocolate. Mon–Sat 8am–6pm.

Soleileïs 9 rue du Dr-Fanton ☎ 04 90 93 30 76. Delicious home-made ice cream with all-natural ingredients, from €1.50 per scoop, plus fresh squeezed juices. Daily 2–6.30pm & 8.30–10.30pm.

LIVE MUSIC

Cargo de Nuit 7 av Sadi-Carnot ☎ 04 90 49 55 99, ⓦ cargodenuit.com. This lively venue puts on an excellent and eclectic line-up of live jazz, electronic and world music concerts, and also comedy. It's only open when an event is scheduled, when the bar section also serves tapas. Schedule varies, but especially likely to be open Fri & Sat; bar opens 8pm, concerts start 9.30pm.

Patio de Camargue 51bis Chemin Barriol ☎ 04 90 49 51 76, ⓦ chico.fr. Arles was the original base for the world-conquering *Gipsy Kings* group. Founder-member Chico now runs this riverfront restaurant-cum-music venue, roughly 1km southwest of the centre, which puts on regular dinner concerts; they're typically on Saturday nights, and cost upwards of €50; check website for current schedules.

La Grande Crau

The region known as **La Grande Crau** (or just La Crau) stretches east from Arles and the Rhône delta for around 30km, as far as Salon. A very long time ago, this was the bed of the Rhône and the Durance. Its name derives from a Greek word meaning "stony", and even though several areas are now irrigated and planted with fruit trees, protected by windbreaks of cypresses and poplars, much of it is still rock-strewn desert, unbearably hot and shadeless in summer.

Only as the Grande Crau approaches the western end of the **Alpilles**, the chain of hills that defines its north edge – its peaks resemble the crest of a wave about to engulf the plain – does the countryside become more amenable, offering potentially interesting stop-offs at the **Abbaye de Montmajour** and the village of **Fontvieille**.

Abbaye de Montmajour

D17, 3km north of Arles • April–June daily 9.30am–6pm; July–Sept daily 10am–6.30pm; Oct–March Tues–Sun 10am–5pm; last admission 45min before closing • €7.50, under-18s free • ☎ 04 90 54 64 17, ⓦ montmajour.monuments-nationaux.fr

The Romanesque ruins of the **Abbaye de Montmajour** climb the side of a small hill, next to the D17 as it sets off towards Les Baux. Take heed when you climb the 124 steps of the fortified watchtower, as your arrival will undoubtedly startle dozens of pigeons; the view from the top, of La Grande Crau, the Rhône and the Alpilles, is stunning. Below, in the **cloisters**, a menacing stone menagerie of beasts and devils enlivens the bases of the vaulting. Throughout the year, the abbey hosts photographic exhibitions, in association with the Rencontres d'Arles (see box, p.85).

The eleventh-century funerary chapel of **Ste-Croix**, with its perfect proportions and frieze of palm fronds, is set in a farmyard 200m east, amid tombs cut out of the rock.

Fontvieille

Little **FONTVIEILLE**, 5km northeast of Montmajour, is a site of literary pilgrimage for the French, as the setting for Alphonse Daudet's nineteenth-century *Lettres de Mon Moulin*, a much-loved collection of short stories that focus especially on rural Provençal life. Daudet never lived in the eponymous windmill, just south of town, but now, as the **Moulin de Daudet**, it's a small museum (daily: Feb & March 10am–noon & 2–6pm; April–June 9am–6pm; July–Sept 9am–7pm; Oct–Dec 10am–noon & 2–6pm; €3.50).

A couple of kilometres south of the windmill, the crossroads where the D33 meets the D82 is dominated by the remains of two Roman **aqueducts** that formerly served Arles. Slightly further south still, a left turning, signposted "Meunerie Romain", leads to the dramatic excavation of the sixteen-wheel **Barbegal mill**. Powered by water from one of the aqueducts, it's thought to have produced up to three tonnes of flour a day.

Les Baux-de-Provence

The distinctly unreal fortified village of **LES BAUX-DE-PROVENCE** perches atop the Alpilles ridge, 15km northeast of Arles: unreal partly because the ruins of its eleventh-century **castle** merge almost imperceptibly into the plateau, whose rock is both foundation and part of the structure. And unreal, too, because this Ville Morte (Dead City) and a vast area of the plateau around it are accessible only via a turnstile from the living village below.

When the medieval lords of Les Baux, who owed allegiance to none, died out at the end of the fourteenth century, the town passed to the counts of Provence and then to the kings of France who, in 1632, razed the feudal citadel to the ground and fined the population into penury. For the next two hundred years, both citadel and village were inhabited almost exclusively by bats and crows. The subsequent discovery of the mineral bauxite (whose name derives from "Les Baux") in the neighbouring hills brought back some life, and tourism has more recently transformed the place. Today the population stays steady at around 400, augmented by more than 1.5 million visitors each year. Even the former bauxite quarries, cut from the jagged rocks of the **Val d'Enfer**, are now tourist attractions, as home to the imaginative gallery known as the **Carrières de Lumières**.

The great majority of Les Baux's visitors are day-trippers, who tend to be thinning out by 5pm or so. To avoid the crowds, especially in summer, it's well worth turning up later in the day.

The château

Daily: March–June 9am–7.15pm; July & Aug 9am–8.15pm; Sept–Nov 9.30am–6pm; Dec–Feb 10am–5pm; last entry 1hr before closing • April–Sept €9, Oct–March €7; free audioguide in English available • ☎ 04 90 54 55 56, ⓦ chateau-baux-provence.com

Although universally known as a château, the enormous and extraordinary **castle** at Les

Baux is in truth more of a large citadel. The only gate to the complex is at the far end of the main village street. That leads first to open ground below the walls, scattered with replica siege engines and catapults that perform assorted re-enactments through the day in summer, and then to a network of footpaths over and through assorted buildings which include the ruins of the feudal castle demolished on Richelieu's orders, the partially restored **Chapelle Castrale** and the **Tour Sarrasine**. The higher you climb, the more spectacular the views become.

The village

The actual **village** of Les Baux, straggling over the hilltop just below the château, is a too-good-to-be-true collection of sixteenth- and seventeenth-century churches, chapels and mansions. Several of its most beautiful buildings are given over to museums.

In the Hôtel des Porcelets, the **Musée Yves Brayer** (mid-Feb to March & Oct–Dec daily except Tues 10am–12.30pm & 2–5.30pm; April–Sept daily 10am–12.30pm & 2–6.30pm; €4) shows the paintings (and hats) of the twentieth-century figurative artist whose work also adorns the seventeenth-century **Chapelle des Pénitents Blancs** on place de l'Église. Changing exhibitions by contemporary Provençal artists are displayed in the **Hôtel de Manville** (hours vary; free), while the **Musée des Santons** in the old Hôtel de Ville (daily 9am–7pm; free) displays traditional Provençal nativity figures.

The Carrières de Lumières

D27, 500m north of Les Baux • Daily: April–Sept 10am–6pm; Oct–March 10am–5pm • €8.50 • ☏ 04 90 54 47 37, ⓦ carrieres-lumieres.com

It's said that Dante took his inspiration for the nine circles of the *Inferno* from a trip he made to the valley known as the **Val d'Enfer** (Valley of Hell), immediately north of Les Baux, while staying at Arles. Jean Cocteau used its contorted rocks and bauxite quarries as a location for his 1959 film, *Le Testament d'Orphée*.

More recently, those same quarries have been turned into an audiovisual experience called the **Carrières de Lumières**. Projection is continuous, so you don't have to wait to go in. The effect is similar to entering an Egyptian temple that has been carved from the rock, but here you're surrounded by images projected over the floor, ceilings and walls of the vast rectangular caverns, accompanied by music that resonates strangely in the captured space. The precise content changes yearly, though it's often devoted to a particular artist or school of painting. Really, though, it makes little difference; the sensation is just mind-blowing, as you wander on and through the changing shapes and colours.

ARRIVAL AND INFORMATION

By car Les Baux village is pedestrianized. Parking costs €5 close to the gate, €3 a little lower down, and nothing at the Carrières de Lumières, so if you plan to walk there and back anyway you might as well park there in the first place.

LES BAUX-DE-PROVENCE

Tourist office Maison du Roy, rue Porte Mage, at the start of Grande-Rue (daily: May–Sept Mon–Fri 9am–6pm, Sat & Sun 10am–5.30pm; Oct–April Mon–Fri 9.30am–5pm, Sat & Sun 10am–5.30pm; ☏ 04 90 54 34 03, ⓦ lesbauxdeprovence.com).

ACCOMMODATION AND EATING

Hostellerie de la Reine Jeanne ☏ 04 90 54 32 06, ⓦ la-reinejeanne.com. The only moderately priced hotel in the village, near the tourist office. Very friendly staff, simple rooms with views of the citadel, and good *menus* starting at €27. Closed mid-Jan to mid-Feb. **€56**

Oustau de Baumanière ☏ 04 90 54 33 07, ⓦ oustaudebaumaniere.com. Among the many

luxurious options in the countryside near Les Baux, this spectacularly situated mansion, just west towards the Val d'Enfer, ranks very high indeed. Past guests have included Queen Elizabeth II. *Menus* in its renowned restaurant start at €99 for lunch, €158 for dinner. Closed Nov–Feb, except Xmas. **€250**

Le Prince Noir Rue de l'Orme ☏ 04 90 54 39 57,

2

NOSTRADAMUS IN ST-RÉMY

Were famed astrologer **Michel de Nostradamus** somehow to return to St-Remy, he would of course not be the slightest bit surprised to find that the house on rue Hoche where he was born on December 14, 1503, is still standing, though it's not open to visitors. Educated as a physician, Nostradamus first received recognition for his innovative treatment of plague victims. Only in the latter part of his life did his interest in astrology and the occult lead to the publication of **The Prophecies of Michel Nostradamus**, a collection of 942 prophetic quatrains. Fearing persecution should the authorities fully understand his predictions, he deliberately wrote in an obscure and cryptic style. The end result was some extremely ambiguous French verse, which has since been the subject of numerous forgeries, urban legends and off-the-wall interpretations. Events he's been credited as predicting include the rise of Napoleon and Hitler, the Great Fire of London, and the 9/11 attacks. While Nostradamus may or may not have been able to accurately foresee the future, his success as a writer remains undisputed: the collection of prophecies, now known as *Centuries*, has been in print continuously since its first publication in 1551. Neither was Nostradamus himself persecuted; by the time he died in 1566, he had become Physician-in-Ordinary to King Charles IX.

ⓦ leprincenoir.com. An eccentric B&B in the home of an artist, in the uppermost house in the village. Choose between the one comfortable bedroom or the two luxurious suites; two-night minimum stay. **€95**

Les Variétés 29 rue du Trencat ☎ 04 90 54 55 88. The village's best-value restaurant has a lovely interior courtyard and sells good salads and pasta dishes for around €10. **Daily noon–2pm & 7–9pm; closed Oct–Feb.**

St-Rémy-de-Provence

The dreamy, little-changed community of **ST-RÉMY-DE-PROVENCE**, where Van Gogh sought psychiatric help and painted some of his most lyrical works, nestles against the northern base of the Alpilles, 30km from either Arles or Avignon. St-Rémy is a beautiful spot, centring on a charmingly low-key old town, the **Vieille Ville**, an enchanting tangle of narrow lanes and ancient alleyways, lined with stately residences and interspersed with peaceful little squares. While it only takes a few minutes to walk from one side to the other along its main east–west axis, **rue Carnot**, it's worth exploring every nook and cranny. Despite the presence of several boutiques and restaurants, it's all surprisingly sleepy. There's not even a café where you can sit and watch the world go by; instead virtually all the town's commercial life takes place on the four busy boulevards that ring the entire ensemble.

Several exceptional sites and attractions lie within walking distance to the south: Van Gogh's hospital of **St-Paul-de-Mausole**, a **Roman arch** and the ruins of the ancient city of **Glanum**.

Musée des Alpilles

Place Favier • June–Sept Tues–Sun 10am–6pm; Oct–May Tues–Sat 1–5.30pm • €3.10 • ☎ 04 90 92 68 24

Housed in the Renaissance Hôtel Mistral de Mondragon, halfway along rue Carnot in the old town, the **Musée des Alpilles** offers a thorough overview of St-Rémy and the surrounding region. Interesting sections on folklore, festivities and traditional crafts include an exhibit on cicadas, a symbol of Provence associated with author Frédéric Mistral.

St-Paul-de-Mausole

Av Vincent-van-Gogh, just under 2km 1600m south of central St-Rémy • Daily: April–Oct 9.30am–7pm; Nov–March 10.15am–4.45pm • €4 • ☎ 04 90 92 77 00, ⓦ cloitresaintpaul-valetudo.com

The former monastery of **St-Paul-de-Mausole**, where **Vincent van Gogh** was a voluntary psychiatric patient between May 8, 1889 and May 16, 1890, is a twenty-minute walk from St-Rémy's old town. It's only 100m east of the main road south, across from Les Antiques (see below), though for a more peaceful walk you may prefer to follow avenues Pierre-Barbier and Marie-Gasquet. Placards along this route, marked out as the "Promenade dans l'Univers de Van Gogh", show where he painted some of the 150 canvases he produced during the year, including *La Route aux Cyprès* and *Les Blés Verts*, though sadly it's characterized by suburban villas rather than sweeping vistas these days.

Visiting St-Paul-de-Mausole itself is a profoundly moving experience. Amazingly enough, it's still a psychiatric hospital, and although tourists are kept well clear of the active area, you get a real sense of its ongoing work. Displays in the church and cloisters contrast Van Gogh's diagnosis and treatment with modern-day practices, and you can see a mock-up of his former room and walk in the glorious gardens, planted with lavender and poppies. Far from being kept under lock and key, Vincent was allowed to wander around the town and Alpilles, so long as he stayed within an hour's walk of the hospital. Art therapy forms a major component of current treatment here, and patients' work is on sale in the on-site shop.

Les Antiques

Rte des Baux-de-Provence, 1500m south of central St-Rémy • Free access 24hr, car parking €2.50

Beside the main road south from St-Rémy, across from St-Paul-de-Mausole, an open patch of ground holds two Roman monuments, jointly known as **Les Antiques**, which originally marked the entrance to the town of Glanum. One is a triumphal arch celebrating the Roman conquest of Marseille, the other a well-preserved mausoleum thought to commemorate two grandsons of Augustus. Both display intricate patterning and a typically Roman sense of proportion.

Glanum

Rte des Baux-de-Provence, 1600m south of central St-Rémy • April–Aug daily 10am–6.30pm; Sept Tues–Sun 10am–6.30pm; Oct–March Tues–Sun 10am–5pm • €7.50, car parking €2.50 • ⓦ glanum.monuments-nationaux.fr

The impressive ancient settlement of **GLANUM** was dug from the alluvial deposits at the foot of the Alpilles. This site originally held a Neolithic homestead, before the Gallo-Greeks, probably from Massalia (Marseille), built a city here between the second and first centuries BC. Then the Gallo-Romans constructed yet another town, which lasted until the third century AD.

A footpath drops from the site entrance to run through the centre of the ruins. While plenty of maps and captions line the way, getting to grips with Glanum is far from easy. Not only were the later buildings moulded on to the earlier ones, but there was also a fashion, around the time of Christ, for an archaic Hellenistic style. Greek levels can be most readily distinguished from the Roman by the stones: the earlier civilization used massive hewn rocks, as opposed to the smaller, more accurately shaped stones preferred by the Romans.

THE FESTIVALS OF ST-RÉMY

The ideal time to visit St-Rémy is for one of Provence's most vibrant traditional festivals, the **Fête de Transhumance** on Whit Monday, when a flock of four thousand sheep, accompanied by goats, rams and donkeys, makes a tour of the town before being packed off to the Alps for the summer. Other events in the busy local calendar include the **Carreto Ramado** on August 15, a harvest thanksgiving procession in which the religious or secular symbolism of the floats reveals the political colour of the various village councils; and a pagan rather than workers' **Mayday** celebration, with donkey-drawn floral floats on which people play fifes and tambourines. On July 14, August 15 and the fourth Sunday in September, the intrepid local youth attempt to set loose six **bulls** that are herded round the town by their mounted chaperones.

2

At the site's southern end, where it narrows into a ravine, a Greek edifice stands around the **spring** that made this location so desirable. Steps lead down to a pool, with a slab above for the libations of those too sick to descend. An inscription records that Agrippa restored it in 27 BC, and dedicated it to Valetudo, the Roman goddess of health. **Altars** to Hercules remain in evidence, however, while traces of a prehistoric settlement that also depended on this spring survive up the hill to the west. The Gallo-Romans directed the water through canals to heat houses and, of course, to the **baths** that lie near the site entrance. There are superb sculptures on the Roman **Temples Geminées** (twin temples), as well as fragments of mosaics, fountains of both periods and first-storey walls and columns.

ARRIVAL AND INFORMATION ST-RÉMY-DE-PROVENCE

By bus The main bus stop is in place de la République, on the eastern edge of the old town.
Destinations Arles (8 daily; 50min); Avignon (8 daily; 40min); Les Baux (4 daily; 15min); Cavaillon (3 daily; 35min).
Tourist office Place Jean-Jaurès, just south of the old town (mid-March to June & Sept to mid-Oct Mon–Sat

9am–12.30pm & 2–6.30pm, Sun 10am–12.30pm; July & Aug Mon–Sat 9am–12.30pm & 2–7pm, Sun 10am–12.30pm & 2.30–5pm; mid-Oct to mid-March Mon–Sat 9am–12.30pm & 2–5.30pm; ☏ 04 90 92 05 22, ⓦ saintremy-de-provence.com).
Bike rental Telecycles will deliver anywhere in the area (☏ 04 90 92 83 15, ⓦ telecycles-location.com).

ACCOMMODATION

Canto Cigalo 8a chemin de Canto Cigalo ☏ 04 90 92 14 28, ⓦ cantocigalo.com. Very nice, peaceful country-villa hotel beside the canal, a 20min walk southeast of the old town, with good-sized rooms, some with a/c, and cricket-themed decor (as in the insect, not the sport), plus a pool and plenty of outdoor space on the terrace and in the large gardens. **€69**
Le Castelet des Alpilles 6 place Mireille ☏ 04 90 92 07 21, ⓦ castelet-alpilles.com. Pleasant, good-sized traditional rooms, 300m south of the centre on the road towards Glanum; those with south-facing balconies have great views, and there are pleasant gardens. Closed early Nov to late March. **€79**
Gounod 18 place de la République ☏ 04 90 92 06 14, ⓦ hotel-gounod.com. Luxurious central hotel, where the ornately decorated rooms couple antique furnishings with bright modern linens; there's also a swimming pool and garden. Rates include breakfast. Closed Feb & March. **€148**
★ **Le Soleil** 35 av Pasteur ☏ 04 90 92 00 63, ⓦ www .hotelsoleil.com. Very welcoming hotel, set back from the main road a short walk south of the centre, with a pool and private parking. Nice, simple rooms; three self-contained apartments; and a bar but no restaurant. Closed early Nov to late March. **€70**; apartments **€130**

★ **Sous les Figuiers** 3 av Taillandier ☏ 04 32 60 15 40, ⓦ hotel-charme-provence.com. Gorgeous place just north of the old town, run by a creative team of photographer and painter. Of the fourteen well-appointed rooms, the best eleven cost extra, and have their own private garden terraces; there are no TVs, but there's a swimming pool and an on-site artist's studio (art classes available). Closed mid-Jan to mid-March. **€92**

CAMPING

Mas de Nicolas Av Plaisance du Touch ☏ 04 90 92 27 05, ⓦ camping-masdenicolas.com. Spacious, well-shaded four-star municipal site with its own pool, 800m from the centre on a turning off the route de Mollèges. Closed Nov to mid-March. **€25**
Monplaisir Chemin Monplaisir ☏ 04 90 92 22 70, ⓦ camping-monplaisir.fr. Family-run, five-acre, two-star campsite, 1km northwest of town along the rte de Maillane, with a pool and snack facilities. Closed Nov to early March. **€31.80**
Pegomas 3 av Jean-Moulin ☏ 04 90 92 01 21, ⓦ campingpegomas.com. The nearest site to the town centre, this three-star option, 1km east towards Cavaillon, has a pool, a bar and a small shop. Closed late Oct to mid-March. **€25.50**

EATING AND DRINKING

Brasseries and **restaurants** abound in St-Rémy, both within the Vieille Ville (along rue Carnot in particular), and along the surrounding boulevards; take a leisurely evening stroll, and something will undoubtedly catch your eye. It's also a great place to shop for picnic food and deli items, with **markets** on Wednesday morning in the old town, and on Saturday in place de la Mairie. The liveliest **bars** line the peripheral boulevards, especially boulevard Gambetta.

L'Aile ou la Cuisse 5 rue de la Commune ☏ 04 32 62 00 25. Very romantic, upscale restaurant in the old town, with a pricey à la carte menu of main dishes at €26–35, as well

as a deli selling posh picnic items and delectable jams and olive oils. Tues–Sun noon–1.30pm & 7.30–9.30pm.
La Cassolette 53 rue Carnot ☏ 04 90 92 40 50. Inexpensive

but high-quality little French restaurant in the old town. The prize seats are out on the pavement of this tiny street; inside things are a bit more formal. Lunch costs from €13; in the evening, the €18 *menu* includes *taureau*, while the €23 *menu* is a definite step up, featuring a *grand aioli*. No credit cards. Daily noon–1.30pm & 7.30–9.30pm.

Cinecitta 4bis rue Estrine ☎04 90 92 82 20, ⦿www .artemoda-cinecitta.fr. Enter this restaurant via rue Estrine, a small alleyway, and you might not realize what a strange combination it is; the other entrance, on rue du Château, takes you through a stylish Italian fashion boutique, ArteModa, with tables set out among the clothes racks. The main dining area is in a pleasant enclosed courtyard, where you can enjoy a very flexible selection of Italian and Mediterranean specialities. Portions on the set *menus* are enormous; the €16 *Cinema* is great value, the €29 *Gourmand* consistently delicious. April–Sept daily noon–3pm & 7pm–midnight; Oct–March Wed, Thurs & Sun noon–3pm & 7pm–midnight, Fri & Sat noon–3pm & 7pm–midnight.

Grain de Sel 25 bd Mirabeau ☎04 90 92 00 89, ⦿graindesel-resto.com. Inside, this place looks like a glitzy big-city jazz lounge; outside, it's a pavement bistro like most of its neighbours. As a restaurant the concept is a little confusing: either order à la carte – in which case conventional French starters cost around €15, *plats* more like €25 – or for around €28 get a *Grande Assiette*, which is a very big plate filled with individual hot and cold dishes, to eat in whatever order you fancy. The food itself, though, is excellent, ranging from salmon tartare with a wasabi mousse to duck in pastry parcels. Mon–Sat noon–1.30pm & 7.30–9.30pm, Sun noon–1.30pm.

Taberna Romana Site of Glanum, Av van-Gogh, 1500m south of central St-Rémy ☎04 90 92 65 97, ⦿taberna-romana.com. This self-styled Roman restaurant, serving authentic Roman dishes, makes a very nice open-air lunch spot, overlooking the ruins of Glanum from a well-shaded terrace; you don't have to pay to go in, and in fact you can see the ruins pretty well from here for free. The food itself is fun, zestful and a bit different, with a large mixed plate of, say, *samsa* (spicy olives), *cicerona* (chick peas) and goat's cheese for €18, or a *matza*, which closely resembles a chicken wrap, for €9. They also serve "Roman beer". Tues–Sun 10am–6.30pm, closed Nov–March.

La Petite Crau

The plain known as **La Petite Crau**, stretching north from the Alpilles to the confluence of the Rhône and the Durance, is today richly cultivated, with cherries and peaches as its main crops. Once, however, it was a swampy wasteland, the only extensive bit of solid ground being the rocky outcrop of **La Montagnette**, which runs parallel to the Rhône for 10km. Villages are few and far between, built on the scattered bases of rock and often retaining their medieval elements of fortified walls and churches and tangled narrow streets. This is the Provence that inspired **Frédéric Mistral** and Vincent van Gogh. Although La Montagnette is lovely **walking** country, fire risk precludes access between July and mid-September.

Châteaurenard

Halfway between St-Rémy and Avignon, the main town in La Petite Crau, **CHÂTEAURENARD**, is dominated by the two remaining towers of its Romanesque and Gothic medieval **castle** (May–Sept Tues–Sat 10am–noon & 2.30–6.30pm, Sun 2.30–6.30pm; Oct–April daily except Fri 3–5pm; €4), described by Frédéric Mistral as "twin horns on the forehead of a hill". The castle's **Tour du Griffon** offers fabulous views across La Petite Crau to the Alpilles and La Montagnette.

MARKETS IN LA PETITE CRAU

If you're in La Petite Crau on a Friday, the **Marché Paysan** on the place du Marché in **Graveson** (May–Oct, Fri 4–8pm; ⦿lemarchepaysan.com), is not to be missed, with *paysans* from La Grande and La Petite Crau, the Camargue and from across the Durance selling their goat's cheeses, olives, flowers, and fruit and vegetables picked the same morning.

Ordinary morning markets in La Petite Crau take place on Sunday in **Châteaurenard**; Tuesday in **Rognonas**, the village just across the Durance from Avignon; Wednesday in **Barbentane**; Thursday in **Maillane** and **Noves**; and on Friday in **Graveson** itself.

2

The town is packed out every Sunday, when it hosts a massive wholesale fruit and vegetable **market**.

Maillane

The poet **Frédéric Mistral** was born in **MAILLANE**, 7km northwest of St-Rémy, in 1830 and buried there in 1914. Primarily responsible for the early twentieth-century revival of all things Provençal, he won the Nobel Prize for Literature in 1904, a feat no other writer of a minority language has ever achieved. The house where he lived from 1876 onwards has been preserved intact as the **Museon Mistral**, 11 rue Lamartine (Tues–Sun: April–Sept 9.30–11.30am & 2.30–6.30pm; Oct–March 10–11.30am & 2–4.30pm, call in advance on weekdays; €4; ☎04 90 95 84 19). La Petite Crau was Mistral's "sacred triangle", and its customs and legends were a great source of inspiration to him.

Boulbon

A strategic site overlooking the Rhône, **BOULBON** was heavily fortified in the Middle Ages, and today the ruins of its enormous fortress, built half within and half above a rocky escarpment, look like some picture-book crusader castle. Celebrated on the last Sunday of August, Boulbon's **Fête de Saint-Éloi** involves chariots drawn by teams of horses in Saracen harness doing the rounds of the village, and much drinking by all the villagers.

It's possible to reach Boulbon by following a **footpath** 5km west from St-Michel-de-Frigolet, which leads over the Montagnette ridge.

Barbentane

In **BARBENTANE**, 8km northeast of Boulbon at the northern edge of La Montagnette, the fourteenth-century **Tour Anglica** keeps watch on the confluence of the Rhône and Durance. The town has two medieval gateways and a beautifully arcaded Renaissance building, the **Maison des Chevaliers**, plus a much more recent **château** (Easter–June & Oct daily except Wed 10am–noon & 2–6pm; July–Sept daily 10am–noon & 2–6pm; €7.50; ☎04 90 95 51 07), designed for grandeur rather than defence. Accessible on French-language 45min guided tours only, this seventeenth-century ducal residence has gorgeous grey and white Tuscan marble floors, and all the painted ceilings, chandeliers and antique furniture that you'd expect of a house still owned by the same aristocratic family. The Italianate gardens are the highlight.

INFORMATION   LA PETITE CRAU

Tourist office 11 cours Carnot, Châteaurenard (June & Sept Mon–Sat 9am–noon & 2–5.45pm; July & Aug Mon–Sat 9am–noon & 2–5.45pm, Sun 10am–noon; Oct–May Mon–Sat 10am–noon & 2–5.45pm; ☎04 90 24 25 50, ⓦ ot.chateaurenard.com).

ACCOMMODATION AND EATING

Auberge de Noves Rte de Châteaurenard, Noves, 5km east of Châteaurenard ☎04 90 24 28 28, ⓦ aubergedenoves.com. Set in huge gardens, west of Noves towards Châteaurenard, this beautiful farmhouse hotel boasts huge rooms, many with outdoor patios, sumptuous if somewhat dated 1980s-style fixtures and fittings, and impeccable service. Its restaurant (closed Mon & Tues Oct–May) serves such delicacies as foie gras, snails, truffles and lobster, coupled with fine wines (weekday lunch *menu* €50; dinner *menu* from €68). **€240**

Castel Mouisson Quartier Castel Mouisson, Barbentane ☎04 90 95 51 17, ⓦ hotel-castelmouisson .com. Peaceful, slightly faded family-run hotel, a 15-min walk south of the centre, with a pleasant garden and pool, but no restaurant. The cheapest rooms are very small. Closed mid-Oct to mid-March. **€49**

Le Central 27 cours Carnot, Châteaurenard

CLOCKWISE FROM TOP LES BAUX-DE-PROVENCE (P.92); CARRIÈRES DE LUMIÈRES (P.93); ST-PAUL-DE-MAUSOLE (P.94) >

📞 04 90 94 10 90, 🌐 hotel-lecentral.com. Thirteen simple en-suite rooms above a pavement brasserie. While not a place to base yourself for any length of time, it makes an inexpensive overnight stop. *Menus* at €13 and €23; restaurant closed Sun. **€40**

CAMPING

Le Pilon d'Agel Rte de Mollégès, 3km southwest of Noves 📞 04 90 95 16 23, 🌐 pilondagel.com. Good-value campsite with a pool, restaurant, kids' playground, and access for people with disabilities. Closed Oct–April. **€21**

Tarascon and around

Dozing gently beside the Rhône, roughly halfway between Arles and Avignon, the two-thousand-year-old city of **TARASCON** feels far removed from the tourist mainstream of Provence. Despite its imposing castle, the old town centre is, apart from the arcaded rue des Halles and a couple of busy commercial alleyways running off it, not only largely residential but also quite faded and run-down. That makes Tarascon a relaxing, atmospheric place to spend a day or two. Just don't expect much drama or excitement, unless you're here for one of its annual festivals, such as June's spectacular carnival in honour of the city's namesake, the amphibious monster known as the Tarasque (see box opposite).

TARASCON

RESTAURANTS
Bistrot des Anges	2
Lilie La Fourmi	1
Méo Bistro	3

■ ACCOMMODATION
Camping St-Gabriel	6
Camping Tartarin	1
Échevins	2
Provençal	4
Provence	5
Rue du Chateau	3

Château du Roi René

Daily: Feb–May & Oct 9.30am–5.30pm; June–Sept 9.30am–6.30pm; Nov–Jan 9.30am–5pm • €7 • ☎ 04 90 91 01 93,
Ⓦ chateau.tarascon.fr

A vast and impregnable mass of stone, Tarascon's riverfront **Château du Roi René** has
been beautifully restored to its defensive fifteenth-century stance. Those of its towers
that face the enemy across the Rhône are square, while those at the back are round.
Nowhere on the exterior is there any hint of softness.

Inside, however, is another matter. Work on the castle began in 1400, and from 1447
onwards it was remodelled as a residence for King René of Provence, with all the luxury
that the period permitted. The mullioned windows and vaulted ceilings of the royal
apartments and the spiral staircase that overlook the **cour d'honneur** all have graceful
Gothic lines, and assorted wooden ceilings are painted with monsters and similar
medieval motifs.

The rooms themselves lack historic furnishing these days; instead they're used for what
are usually very entertaining annual exhibitions, in which artists explore various aspects of
medieval life, and some also hold explanatory panels. In several places, as with the carvings
of boats in the **Salles des Gallères**, graffiti testify to the castle's long use as a prison.

Visits end with a climb up to the **roof**, from which revolutionaries and counter-
revolutionaries alike were thrown in the 1790s. It's now an extensive open platform,
offering wonderful views in all directions.

Collégiale Royale Sainte-Marthe

Place de la Concorde • Daily 8am–6pm • Free • ☎ 04 90 91 09 50

The crypt of the **Collégiale Royale Sainte-Marthe**, across the street from the castle,
contains the tomb of Martha, the saint who saved the town from the Tarasque monster.
St Martha also appears in the paintings by Nicolas Mignard and Vien that decorate its
Gothic interior, along with works by Pierre Parrocel and Van Loo.

Cloître des Cordeliers

Place Frédéric-Mistral • Mon–Fri 10am–12.30pm & 2–6pm, Sat 1.30–6pm • Free • ☎ 04 90 91 38 71

The sixteenth-century **Cloître des Cordeliers**, in the heart of the old town, has had its three
aisles of light cream stone beautifully restored. As well as holding displays on Tartarin du
Tarascon, the hero of three nineteenth-century adventure novels by Alphonse Daudet, it's
used for exhibitions, sometimes of contemporary paintings, and often by young artists.

THE TARASQUE AND TARTARIN

On the last full weekend of June, the **Tarasque**, a mythical 6m-long creature with glaring eyes
and shark-sized teeth, storms the streets of Tarascon in the fashion of a Chinese dragon, its tail
swishing back and forth to the screaming delight of children. The monster is said to have been
tamed by Saint Martha after a long history of clambering out of the Rhône, gobbling people
and destroying the ditches and dams of the Camargue with its long crocodile-like tail. It serves
as a reminder of natural catastrophe, in particular floods, kept at bay here by the sometimes
unreliable drainage ditches and walls. The weekend-long festivities involve public balls, bull
and equestrian events, and a firework and music finale.

Another larger-than-life character – **Tartarin**, the nineteenth-century literary creation of
Alphonse Daudet – is celebrated at the same time, even though his antics have left Tarascon
synonymous with foolishness in French eyes. Making himself out to be a great adventurer, Tartarin
scales Mont Blanc, hunts leopards in Algeria, and brings back exotic trees for his garden at 55bis
boulevard Itam. The address is real, though not currently open to the public. During the Tarasque
procession, a local man, chosen for his fat-bellied figure, strolls through the town as Tartarin.

Musée Souleïado

39 rue Charles Deméry • mid-June to mid-Oct Mon–Sat 10am–7pm • €7 • ☎ 04 90 91 08 80, ⊕ souleiado-lemusee.com

The **Musée Souleïado**, on a quiet backstreet, pays tribute to the family business that revived Tarascon's 200-year-old **textile** tradition of making brightly coloured, patterned, printed fabrics, now sold all over Provence. As well as eighteenth-century wood blocks from which many of the patterns are still made, it tastefully displays such products as a table setting dedicated to the bulls of the Camargue.

ARRIVAL AND INFORMATION

TARASCON

By train Trains from Arles (4 daily; 10min) and Avignon (20 daily; 12min) arrive at Tarascon's *gare SNCF* on bd Gustave-Desplaces , immediately south of the centre.
By bus Buses run from Arles (10 daily; 20min), Barbentane (5 daily; 25min) and Boulbon (5 daily; 10min).
Tourist office Av de la République, facing the château

and the road bridge across to Beaucaire (June & Sept Mon–Sat 9am–12.30pm & 2–6pm; July & Aug Mon–Sat 9am–12.30pm & 2–6pm, Sun 9.30am–12.30pm; Oct–May Mon–Sat 9am–12.30pm & 2–5.30pm; ☎ 04 90 91 03 52, ⊕ tarascon.org).

ACCOMMODATION

Échevins 26 bd Itam ☎ 04 90 91 01 70, ⊕ hotel-echevins.com. Handsome old townhouse, where the large but ageing bedrooms don't quite live up to the promise of the public spaces. Attractive terrace restaurant. Closed Nov–Easter. **€78**
Provençal 12 cours A-Briand ☎ 04 90 91 11 41, ⊕ leprovencal-tarascon.com. Family-run budget hotel close to the station, offering twenty plain en-suite rooms with paper-thin walls, plus free parking but no restaurant. **€51**
★ **Hotel de Provence** 7 bd Victor-Hugo ☎ 04 90 91 06 43, ⊕ hotel-provence-tarascon.com. Rather lovely little hotel, run by enthusiastic new managers. Half of the large, comfortably furnished rooms open on to a garden courtyard, the rest to a sleepy backstreet. Air-conditioning; no restaurant. **€69**
Rue du Chateau 24 rue du Château ☎ 04 90 91 09 99,

⊕ chambres-hotes.com. This delightful red-ochre house near the castle, with a lovely interior courtyard, offers five crisp, simple but very comfortable en-suite B&B rooms. Two-night minimum stay in summer. Closed mid-Nov to Easter. **€85**

CAMPING

Camping St-Gabriel Mas Ginoux, rte de Fontvieille ☎ 04 90 91 19 83, ⊕ campingsaintgabriel.com. Small, verdant two-star site with a pool, focused around an old coaching inn 5km southeast of town off the Arles road. Closed Dec to mid-Jan. **€19**
Camping Tartarin Rte de Vallabrègues ☎ 04 90 91 01 46, ⊕ campingtartarin.fr. Well-shaded two-star site right beside the river, just north of the castle, with its own bar, restaurant, pool and even mini-golf. Closed Nov–March. **€19**

EATING AND DRINKING

Bistrot des Anges 20 place du Marché ☎ 04 90 91 05 11. Tarascon's best lunch spot serves alluring Provençal dishes such as *carpaccio de taureau* and seafood tart, with *plats* from €9 and an €18 *menu*. Mon–Sat noon–3pm.
Lilie La Fourmi 14 bd Itam ☎ 06 62 25 55 93. This attractive little lunch-only restaurant, best entered on rue du Château, prepares good *plats* centring on each day's fresh produce, and also offers a €16 *menu*. Mon–Fri noon–2.30pm.

Méo Bistro 1 place Colonel Berrurier ☎ 04 90 91 47 74, ⊕ meo-tarascon.fr. Trendy lounge-style restaurant-cum-bar, by the *gare SNCF*, which serves contemporary dinner *menus*, themed around the elements Earth, Air, Fire and Water, costing from €27 to €65. It's also open between and beyond meal times, and is by far the best place for a drink in town. Wed–Sun noon–10.30pm; food served noon–2pm & 7.30–9.30pm.

Beaucaire

Facing Tarascon from the west bank of the Rhône, over in Languedoc, the rival town of **BEAUCAIRE** boasts a better-preserved maze of medieval streets, and is a more pleasant town to simply stroll around, though it has even fewer facilities and the only real sight is its ruined **castle**. Although it's just 1km away, few would want to walk across the busy river bridge in the heat of summer. Look out for the sculpture of Drac, a protective dragon that's Beaucaire's equivalent of the Tarasque, in the old town's most characterful square, the **place de la République** immediately below the castle.

Château Royale de Beaucaire

Gardens April–Oct daily except Tues 10am–6pm • Free • **Musée Auguste-Jacquet** Daily except Tues: April–Oct 10am–12.30pm & 2–6pm; Nov–March 10am–noon & 2–5pm • €5 • ☎ 04 66 59 90 07

To reach the **Château Royale de Beaucaire**, thread your way north through the old town to the hill at the far end, atop which its one surviving tower far surmounts those of Tarascon across the river. While visitors are no longer permitted to ramble freely around the ruins, the castle **gardens** remain open. A modern building here houses the **Musée Auguste-Jacquet**, which has a small but interesting collection of Roman remains, and displays documents relating to Beaucaire's medieval fair, once one of the largest in Europe.

2

INFORMATION   BEAUCAIRE

Tourist office 24 cours Gambetta, 300m straight on from the bridge, beside a canal (April–June, Aug & Sept Mon–Fri 8.30am–12.15pm & 1.30–6pm, Sat 9.30am–12.30pm & 3–6pm; July Mon–Fri 8.30am–12.15pm & 1.30–6pm, Sat 9.30am–12.30pm & 3–6pm, Sun 9.30am–12.30pm; Oct–March Mon–Fri 8.30am–12.15pm & 1.30–6pm; ☎ 04 66 59 26 57, 🖥 ot-beaucaire.fr).

ACCOMMODATION AND EATING

Napoléon 4 place Frédéric-Mistral ☎ 04 66 59 05 17. Pretty, pastel-yellow budget hotel, beside the river in the old town, with some very cheap single rooms, and a restaurant serving *menus* from €18. **€50**

Le Soleil 30 quai du Général-de-Gaulle ☎ 04 66 59 28 52. The pick of several café-restaurants lined up facing the canal not far from the bridge, with a good-value €11 lunch *menu* and an €18 dinner *menu* featuring *tellines* (tiny shellfish) from the Camargue. Daily 7.30am–1am.

The Camargue

Spreading across the Rhône delta, defined by the Petit Rhône to the west, the Grand Rhône to the east, and the Mediterranean to the south, the drained, ditched and now protected land known as the **CAMARGUE** is utterly distinct from the rest of Provence.

BULLS, BIRDS AND BEAVERS: CAMARGUAIS WILDLIFE

The Camargue is a treasure trove of bird and animal species, both wild and domestic, with its most famous denizens being the **bulls** and the **white horses** ridden by the region's **gardians** (herdsmen). Neither beast is truly wild, though both run in semi-liberty. A distinct breed of unknown origin, the Camargue horse is born dark brown or black, and turns white around its fourth year. It is never stabled, surviving the humid heat of summer and the wind-racked winter cold outdoors.

The *gardians*, likewise, are a hardy community. Still conforming, to some extent, to the popular cowboy myth, they play a major role in preserving Camarguais traditions. Their traditional homes, or *cabanes*, are thatched, windowless one-storey structures, with bulls' horns over the door to ward off evil spirits. Throughout the summer, the *gardians* are kept busy, with spectacles involving bulls and horses in every village arena; winter is a good deal harder. Although ever fewer Camarguais property owners can afford the extravagant use of land required to rear bulls, an estimated 2500 *gardians* remain active, of whom around ten percent are women.

Camargue **wildlife** ranges from wild boars, beavers and badgers; tree frogs, water snakes and pond turtles; to marsh and seabirds, waterfowl and birds of prey. The best time for **birdwatching** is the mating season, from April to June. Of the region's fifty thousand or so **flamingos**, ten thousand remain during the winter (Oct–March) when the rest migrate to north Africa. They're born grey, incidentally, then turn pink aged between four and seven. Their tendency to trample young rice shoots in the paddy fields is an ongoing problem for park managers.

The rich **flora** of the park includes reeds, wild irises, tamarisk, wild rosemary and juniper trees. Growing to a height of 6m, the junipers form the Bois des Rièges on the islands between the Étang du Vaccarès and the sea, part of the central **National Reserve** to which access is restricted to those with professional research credentials.

2

THE CAMARGUE

N

Salon-de-Provence & Aix-en-Provence

Martigues

St-Martin-de-Crau

A54

Tarascon & Avignon

Arles

Nîmes & Montpellier

N113/E80

Gimeaux

Musée de la Camargue

D570

Saliers

Albaron

D37

Petit Rhône

St-Gilles

N572

Aigues-Mortes

Montpellier

Pont de Sylvéréal

Sylvéréal

PONT DE SYLVÉRÉAL

D85

Pin Fourcat

PETITE CAMARGUE

Pont de Gau

Parc Ornithologique

D38

D38A

Étang de Ginès

Ploch-Badet

D570

D38B

D85A

Étang de Consecanière

Digue De Gabriel

Étang de Malagroy

Cacharel

RÉSERVE DES IMPÉRIAUX

Étang de Ginès (l'Imperial)

Stes-Maries-de-la-Mer

Digue A La Mer

BOIS DES RIÈGES

RÉSERVE NATIONALE DE CAMARGUE

Étang du Lion

Étang du Vaccarès

PARC NATUREL RÉGIONAL DE CAMARGUE

Méjanes

Gageron

D37

D36

Villeneuve

D570

Grand Rhône

D35

D35

D37

La Capelière

Le Sambuc

N568

Eta du Fournelet

Vieux Rhône

Salin-de-Giraud

D36C

D36

Étang de Galabert

Étang du Fangassier

Étang du Gr. Rascaillon

Beauduc Lighthouse

Étang du Vaisseau du Beauduc

Etang du Galabert

Ferry

Saltworks

Port-St-Louis-du-Rhône

They de la Gracieuse

Domaine de la Palissade

Étg. de Grande Palun

Plage Napoléon

Etang de Faraman

Plage de Piemanson

MEDITERRANEAN SEA

Scale

0   5
kilometres

- - - - Footpaths
········ Dykes
━━━━ Border of Parc Naturel
.... Régional de Camargue

With land, lagoon and sea sharing the same horizontal plain, its shimmering horizons appear infinite, its boundaries not apparent until you come upon them.

The whole of the Camargue is a Parc Naturel Régional, which sets out to maintain an equilibrium between tourism, agriculture, industry and hunting on the one hand, and the indigenous ecosystems on the other. When the Romans arrived, the northern part of the Camargue was a forest; they felled the trees to build ships, then grew wheat. These days, especially since the northern marshes were drained and re-irrigated with fresh water after World War II, the main crop is **rice**. There's still some wheat, though, along with **vines** – which, because their stems were underwater, survived the nineteenth-century phylloxera infestation that devastated every other wine-producing region in France – as well as fruit orchards and the ubiquitous rapeseed.

The Camargue is effectively split into two separate sections by the large **Étang du Vaccarès** at its heart, a lagoon that, along with its various islands, is out of bounds to tourists. Most visitors focus their attention on the western half of the region, which is home to the Provençal Camargue's one sizeable town, lively **Stes-Maries-de-la-Mer**, and also most of its commercial attractions, such as wildlife parks and activity operators. For drivers who don't mind scurrying, though, it is possible to take a quick look at both the western and eastern halves of the Camargue within a single day-trip.

There's no **ideal season** to visit. The Camargue's notorious **mosquitoes** can make the months from March to November unbearable; they're less prevalent beside the sea, but elsewhere you'll need serious chemical weaponry. Biting flies are also a problem, as are the strong autumn and winter **winds**, which make cycling hard despite the flat terrain. And finally, in summer, the weather can be so hot and humid that the slightest movement is an effort.

The western Camargue: the road to Stes-Maries

The **western** side of the Camargue is busy all summer with tourists, who flock down its main artery, the D570, towards **Stes-Maries-de-la-Mer**. For a true sense of what makes the region special, take the time to explore the marshes and dunes en route, or follow the waterfront nature trails.

TOURS AND ACTIVITIES IN THE CAMARGUE

Many visitors explore the Camargue entirely by car, simply admiring the view through their windows as they drive to and from Les Stes-Maries. You'll get a much better sense of the region, however, by signing up for one of the many activities on offer, which range from boat and jeep tours to cycling and horse riding.

River trips The paddle steamer Le Tiki III offers 90min trips from the mouth of the Petit Rhône, 2.5km west of Les Stes-Maries-de-la-Mer (mid-March to Oct 1–5 daily; €12; ☎ 04 90 97 81 68, ⊛ tiki3.fr), and so too does the Camargue from the port in Stes-Maries, just west of the tourist office (mid-March to mid-Oct 1–4 daily; €12; ☎ 04 90 97 84 72, ⊛ bateau-camargue.com).

Horseriding Around thirty Camargue farms offer horseriding, costing from €16/hr up to €85/day. Recommended options include the Domaine Paul Ricard in Méjanes (☎ 04 90 97 10 62, ⊛ www.mejanes .camargue.fr); you can find full lists at ⊛ saintesmaries .com, ⊛ promenades-a-cheval.com and ⊛ camargue .fr.

Cycling Bikes can be rented in Les Stes-Maries-de-la-Mer from Le Vélociste, back from the sea on place Mireille (☎ 04 90 97 83 26, ⊛ www.levelociste.fr), and Le Vélo Saintois, 19 rue de la République (☎ 04 90 97 74 56, ⊛ www.levelosaintois.camargue.fr), and in Salin-de-Giraud from Mas St Bertrand (☎ 04 42 48 80 69, ⊛ mas-saint-bertrand.fr).

Canoeing and kayaking Canoes and kayaks are available from Kayak Vert in Sylvéréal, beside the Petit-Rhône on the D38C, 17km northwest of Les Stes-Maries-de-la-Mer (☎ 04 66 73 57 17, ⊛ kayakvert-camargue.fr) and cost from €10 for 1hr.

Jeep safaris Camargue Safari (☎ 04 90 93 60 31, ⊛ www.safari-4x4-gallon.camargue.fr) offer jeep safaris, starting from Arles or Stes-Maries, for €36 for 3hr and upwards.

Musée de la Camargue

D570, 10km southwest of Arles • Feb, March & Oct–Dec daily except Tues 10am–12.30pm & 1–5pm; April–Sept daily 9am–12.30pm & 1–6pm; closed Jan • €4.50, under-18s free • ☎ 04 90 97 10 82, ⓦ parc-camargue.fr

The main **information centre** for the Camargue lies in a working roadside farm, 10km out of Arles towards Stes-Maries. The adjoining **Musée de la Camargue** documents the history, traditions and livelihoods of the Camarguais people, with particular emphasis on rice, wine and bulls. Overall, the displays are excellent, though not very accessible if you don't read French, and include an audiovisual presentation on the museum building's former life as a sheep barn. A 3.5-kilometre **trail** loops through the adjacent farmland, giving the opportunity to see how the traditional Provençal farmhouse (mas) related to the land around it. An observation tower at the end gives an overview of the mingled marsh and farmlands.

Draille de Cacharel

The best **hiking trail** in the western Camargue follows a drover's path, 9-kilometre **Draille de Cacharel**, between Cacharel, 4km north of Ste-Maries, and the D37 just north of Méjanes. Running initially along the narrow strip that separates two lesser lagoons, the Étang de Consecanière and the Étang de l'Impérial, it then skirts the western shoreline of the Étang du Vaccarès.

Parc Ornithologique de Pont de Gau

Pont de Gau, 4km north of Stes-Maries • Daily: April–Sept 9am–sunset; Oct–March 10am–sunset • €7.50 • ☎ 04 90 97 82 62, ⓦ parcornithologique.com

For anyone interested in seeing the birdlife of the Camargue, the engrossing **Parc Ornithologique de Pont de Gau** makes a great stop before you reach Stes-Maries. Clearly marked paths lead around and over three separate lagoons in a thirty-acre marsh, making birdwatching easy. Much of it is closer to the main road than you might prefer, but that doesn't seem to bother the abundant flamingos, and for that matter you may well see horses wading knee-deep in water too. Signs and information are plentiful, while some of the less easily spotted species, such as owls and vultures, are kept in aviaries. In a rather cruel twist, wild cranes choose to nest on the roofs above their caged *confrères*.

Les Stes-Maries-de-la-Mer

Although most visitors to the Camargue head straight to **LES STES-MARIES-DE-LA-MER**, 37km southwest of Arles, in essence this commercialized seaside village has much more in common with France's other Mediterranean beach resorts than with the wild and empty land that surrounds it.

That said, Stes-Maries is an attractive little town that's most famous for its annual **gypsy festival** on May 24–25, when Romanies celebrate **Sarah**, their patron saint. A line of **beaches**, sculpted into successive little crescents by stone breakwaters and busy with bathers and windsurfers throughout the summer, stretches away west from its central core of white-painted, orange-tiled houses, while the pleasure **port** to the east offers boat trips to the lagoons and fishing expeditions. With its seafront *arène*, between the port and the tourist office, staging bullfights, cavalcades and other entertainment (events are posted on a board outside), and musicians playing in the street, a stay of a night or two can be very good fun.

Église des Stes-Maries

Place Jean XXIII • Rooftop Daily: July & Aug Mon–Sat 10am–sunset, Sun 1pm–sunset; March–June & Sept to mid-Nov Mon–Sat 10am–12.30pm & 2pm–sunset, Sun 2pm–sunset • €2.20

The spiders-web tangle of streets and alleyways at the heart of old Stes-Maries, filled with everything from supermarkets and delis to bucket-and-spade shops and art galleries, opens out into a sequence of spacious squares on all sides of the grey-gold Romanesque **Église des Stes-Maries**. Fortified in the fourteenth century in response to frequent attacks by pirates, the church has beautifully pure lines and fabulous acoustics.

During the era of Saracen raids, the high, barrel-vaulted interior provided shelter for all the villagers; it even holds its own freshwater well.

At the far end, steps lead up to the altar or down to the low **crypt**, where the tinselled, sequined and dark-skinned statue of Sarah (see box, p.108) is surrounded by candles, while two bones are displayed in a tabernacle nearby. The naïve ex-voto paintings behind glass upstairs were dedicated in thanks for blessings and cures.

Although you can't climb to the top of the tower, you can pay to scramble onto and over the church **roof**, for great views over the town.

2

Musée Baroncelli
Rue Victor-Hugo • April to mid-Oct daily except Tues 10am–noon & 2–5.30pm • €2

The **Musée Baroncelli** is named after the man who, in 1935, was responsible (along with various *gardians*) for initiating the gypsies' annual procession down to the sea with the statue of Sarah. This was motivated by a desire to give a special place in the pilgrimage to the Romanies. Displays cover this event, as well as other Camarguais traditions and local fauna and flora

ARRIVAL AND INFORMATION
LES STES-MARIES-DE-LA-MER

By bus Buses from Arles (9 daily; 50min) arrive at the north end of place Mireille, 400m short of the sea.

By car In summer the paid parking spots along the seafront tend to fill up early; there's usually more space in the free car parks that face the lagoon inland, not far west.

Tourist office 5 av Van-Gogh, on the seafront (daily: Jan, Feb, Nov & Dec 9am–5pm; March & Oct 9am–6pm; April–June & Sept 9am–7pm; July & Aug 9am–8pm; ☎ 04 90 97 82 55, ⓦ www.saintesmaries.com).

ACCOMMODATION

At any time between April and October, and especially during the Romany festival, it's necessary to book **accommodation** well in advance. Don't worry too much if you can't find a room in Stes-Maries itself; appealing options are scattered through the marshlands nearby.

STES-MARIES

Bleu Marine 15 av du Dr-Cambon ☎ 04 90 97 77 00, ⓦ hotel-bleu-marine.com. Friendly, peaceful retreat at the western end of town, with simple but immaculate rooms, a nice pool and easy parking. **€70**

Le Dauphin Bleu/La Brise de Mer 31 av G-Leroy ☎ 04 90 97 80 21, ⓦ www.hotel-dauphin-bleu .camargue.fr. Good-value white-painted hotel-restaurant, on the seafront a few hundred metres from the centre at the east end of the beach road. The nicest of the rather austere rooms have balconies overlooking the sea. **€60**

★ **Mangio Fango** Rte d'Arles ☎ 04 90 97 80 56, ⓦ hotelmangiofango.com. Tranquil farmhouse, overlooking the Étang des Launes 600m north of central Stes-Maries, with a Mediterranean twist. Stylish, comfortable rooms (get one at the back, with a balcony, if possible), pricey restaurant, and a pool surrounded by lush green foliage. Closed Dec–March, except Christmas & New Year. **€135**

★ **Mediterranée** 4 av F-Mistral ☎ 04 90 97 82 09. Decked out in jolly flowers, this welcoming hotel has pretty Provençal-style rooms and is in the heart of the town on the main restaurant street, seconds from the sea. The cheapest rooms share toilets, and there are some well-priced 4-person options. **€45**

OUT OF TOWN

Cacharel Rte de Cacharel ☎ 04 90 97 95 44, ⓦ hotel-cacharel.com. Sixteen luxurious rooms in one of the Camargue's oldest farms, 4km north of Stes-Maries on the D85A, with open fires to warm you in winter, a pool to cool off in summer, and horseriding available year-round, but no restaurant. **€131**

Flamant Rose D37, Albaron ☎ 04 90 97 10 18, ⓦ leflamantrose13.com. Pleasant, inexpensive roadside hotel-restaurant, 23km north of Stes-Maries and 14km southwest of Arles, where the actual rooms are brightly decorated but the common areas plain and rather charmless. **€45**

Hostellerie du Pont de Gau Rte d'Arles, Pont de Gau ☎ 04 90 97 81 53, ⓦ www.pontdegau.camargue.fr. Old-fashioned Camarguais decor and a really excellent restaurant, 4km north of Stes-Maries near the Parc Ornithologique. Rates include breakfast. Closed Jan to mid-Feb. **€70**

Lou Mas Doù Juge Rte du Bac-du-Sauvage, Pin Fourcat ☎ 04 66 73 51 45, ⓦ loumasdoujuge.com. Lovely B&B on a working farm out in the countryside beside the Petit Rhône, 10km northwest of Stes-Maries; evening meal and horseriding available if requested in advance. **€95**

Mas de Pioch Pioch-Badet ☎ 04 90 97 50 06,

2

THE LEGEND OF SARAH AND THE GYPSY FESTIVALS

According to legend, **Mary Jacobé**, the aunt of Jesus, and **Mary Salomé**, mother of two of the Apostles, along with Mary Magdalene and various other New Testament characters, were driven out of Palestine by the Jews and put on a boat without sails and oars.

The boat subsequently drifted effortlessly to an island in the mouth of the Rhône where the Egyptian god Ra was worshipped. Here Mary Jacobé, Mary Salomé and **Sarah**, their servant, set about spreading the Gospel, while the rest headed off for other parts of Provence. Sarah, who was herself Egyptian, was according to some accounts the former wife of Pontius Pilate, repudiated for becoming a Christian.

In 1448 the women's relics were "discovered" in the fortress **church** of Stes-Maries on the former island, around the time that the Romanies were migrating into the area from the Balkans and from Spain. It's thought the two strands may have been reunited in Provence.

The gypsies adopted Sarah as their patron saint – the French word for gypsies, *gitans*, originated as a corruption of "Egyptian" – and have been making their **pilgrimage** to Stes-Maries since the sixteenth century. It's a time for weddings and baptisms as well as music, dancing and fervent religious activities. On May 24, after Mass, the shrines of the saints are lowered from the high chapel to an altar where the faithful stretch out their arms to touch them. Then the statue of Sarah is carried by the gypsies to the sea. On the following day the statues of Mary Jacobé and Mary Salomé, sitting in a wooden boat, follow the same route, accompanied by mounted *gardians* in full Camargue dress, Arlesians in traditional costume, and all and sundry present. The sea, the Camargue, the pilgrims and the gypsies are blessed by the bishop from a fishing boat, before the procession returns to the church with much bell-ringing, guitar-playing, tambourine-bashing and singing. Another ceremony in the afternoon sees the shrines lifted back up to their chapel.

A separate pilgrimage takes place on the Sunday closest to October 22, dedicated solely to Mary Jacobé and Mary Salomé and without the participation of the gypsies.

Ⓦ masdepioch.com. Great-value B&B in a converted nineteenth-century hunting inn just off the main road 10km north of Stes-Maries. Large rooms and a pool. Book well in advance. **€51**

CAMPING

Camping La Brise Rue Marcel-Carrière ☎ 04 90 97 84 67, Ⓦ camping-labrise.fr. Very large three-star site, very close to the sea on the east side of Stes-Maries, 800m from the centre with a pool, snack bar, shop and laundry facilities, and a full programme of summer *animations*. Tents, mobile homes or bungalows available for rent. Closed mid-Nov to mid-Dec. **€22.40**

Camping Le Clos du Rhône Rte d'Aigues-Mortes ☎ 04 90 97 85 99, Ⓦ camping-leclos.fr. Busy four-star site at the mouth of the Petit Rhône, 800m west of central Stes-Maries along an easy seaside path, with a pool, laundry and shop. Closed early Nov to April. **€25.50**

EATING AND DRINKING

Of a summer evening, Stes-Maries gets very lively indeed, with the *terrasses* of its **restaurants** and bars sprawling out across the streets and squares, and flamenco or gypsy-jazz guitarists and buskers everywhere. Camarguais **specialities** include *tellines*, tiny shiny shellfish served with garlic mayonnaise; *gardianne de taureau*, bull's meat cooked in wine, vegetables and Provençal herbs; eels from the Vaccarès; rice, asparagus and wild duck; and *poutargue des Stes-Maries*, a mullet roe dish. The town **market** takes place on place des Gitans every Monday and Friday.

La Bouvine 1 place Esprit Pioch ☎ 04 90 97 87 09. Very large restaurant on Stes-Maries' main dining street, with lots of outdoor seating and a choice of pretty much any French or Spanish dish you care to mention, from paella (€12) to bouillabaisse (€54 for two), plus a €15 *menu* featuring *gardianne de taureau*. Daily except Thurs noon–2pm & 7–10pm.

Brûleur de Loups Av Léon Gambetta ☎ 04 90 97 83 31. Smart, all-round Provençal restaurant, facing the beach; its terrace is among the very few places in Stes-Maries where you get a sea view while you eat. *Menus* €18–40. Mon & Thurs–Sun noon–2pm & 7.30–9.30pm, Tues noon–2pm; closed mid-Nov to mid-Dec.

Casa Romana 6 rue Joseph-Roumanille ☎ 04 90 97 83 33. Friendly Provençal restaurant, with outdoor seating on a side street near the church. Two daily €12.50 *plats du jour* at lunchtime, such as mussels or *taureau*, also feature on an €18.50 *menu*; the evening *menu* is €22. Tues 5.30–10pm, Wed–Sun noon–2pm & 7–10pm; closed Jan.

The eastern Camargue

Cut through by the final canalized stretch of the Grand Rhône, the **eastern** side of the Camargue is much less visited than its counterpart to the west. While less agricultural and more industrial, it holds its own share of wildlife reserves and tranquil refuges, as well as the quiet little village of **Salin-de-Giraud**.

The chief business here is the production of **salt**. Evaporation was originally undertaken by the Romans in the first century AD, and the Camargue now holds one of the biggest saltworks in the world. Saltpans and pyramids add an extra-terrestrial feel to the landscape.

Although the D35 and D36, are the principal access routes, paralleling the east and west banks of the Grand Rhône all the way from Arles, the **D36B** respectively along the eastern edge of the Étang du Vaccarès allows you to enjoy the best of the scenery.

La Capelière

D36B, 23km south of Arles and 19km northwest of Salin-de-Giraud • April–Sept daily 9am–1pm & 2–6pm; Oct–March daily except Tues 9am–1pm & 2–5pm • €3 • ☎ 04 90 97 00 97, ⓦ reserve-camargue.org

La Capelière, the main information centre for the eastern half of the Camargue, holds rather faded displays on Camargue wildlife and how best to see it. Outside, a short but excellent 1.5-kilometre initiation trail circles a small lagoon, with superb **birdwatching** opportunities along the way from camouflaged hides equipped with telescopes (strict silence is observed).

Salin-de-Giraud

In contrast to Stes-Maries, **SALIN-DE-GIRAUD**, just west of the Grand Rhône in the southeastern corner of the Camargue, is an industrial village, based on the saltworks company and its related chemical factory; its tall, terraced workers' houses were built on a strict grid pattern during the Second Empire.

There's nothing really to see in Salin, nor even a town centre for that matter. If you'd like a look at the lunar landscape of the **salt piles** – the saltworks here cover 110 square kilometres and produce a million tonnes a year for domestic use and export – visit the viewing point with information panels a short way south, just off the D36d. A regular **ferry**, the *bac de Barcarin*, crosses the Grand Rhône from Salin (daily every 15min; vehicles €5); at **Port-St-Louis-du-Rhône**, just downstream, the rice and salt of the Camargue are loaded onto ships, and a small fishing fleet is still active.

A good **hiking trail** starts 5km west of Salin-de-Giraud. A prime observation point for **flamingos**, it follows the dyke between the Étangs du Fangassier and Galabert.

Domaine de la Palissade

Just off the D36D, 7km southeast of Salin-de-Giraud • Daily 9am–5pm • €3 • ☎ 04 42 86 81 28, ⓦ conservatoire-du-littoral.fr

Beside the Grand Rhône just short of the sea is the **Domaine de la Palissade**, a natural sanctuary that's devoted to preserving the fauna and flora of its neighbouring lagoons. As well as a small and rather dull exhibition, housed in its visitor centre, it holds a good nine-kilometre **trail** past duck and flamingo nesting grounds, as well as a shorter 1.5-kilometre path. In summer, one- or two-hour guided **horseback** tours, by advance reservation only, cost €15 and €25 per person respectively.

ACCOMMODATION	THE EASTERN CAMARGUE
Mas de Peint Le Sambuc ☎ 04 90 97 20 62, ⓦ masdepeint.com. The most luxurious accommodation in the eastern Camargue, 13km north of Salin-de-Giraud on the D36. Centred on a seventeenth-century farmhouse, this rural getaway offers opulent rooms and a gourmet restaurant. €235	**Saladelles** 4 rue des Arènes, Salin-de-Giraud ☎ 04 42 86 83 87. Nice little family-run hotel, with simple but bargain-priced rooms, and a popular restaurant on its shaded terrace that serves *menus* from €13.50. €32

Avignon and the Vaucluse

FORT ST-ANDRE, VILLENEUVE-LÈS-AVIGNON

Avignon and the Vaucluse

Above its confluence with the Durance, the Rhône served for many centuries as the frontier between Provence and France. Avignon on the Provençal side, the magnificent city of the popes, squared off against heavily fortified Villeneuve-lès-Avignon across the river on the French side. Otherwise, the best-known attractions in what's now the Vaucluse *département* are the smaller towns of Orange and Vaison-la-Romaine, with their remarkable Roman remains. Away from the monuments, museums and ruins, the villages and countryside also hold great appeal. Just north of Avignon, the vineyards of Châteauneuf-du-Pape adorn a rich green sweep of wine-producing country that stretches northeast past the jagged hills of the Dentelles to the bare, imposing slopes of Mont Ventoux. Gorgeous little hill towns and rural communities that make wonderful overnight stops include Séguret, Pernes-les-Fontaines, and the mysterious source of the River Sorgue to the south at Fontaine-de-Vaucluse.

As an area with a distinct identity, the Vaucluse dates back only as far as the Revolution. It was created to tidy up assorted bits and pieces: the Papal Enclave of the Comtat Venaisson that became part of France in 1791, the principality of Orange won by Louis XIV in 1713, and sundry parts of Provence that didn't fit happily into the initial three *départements* drawn up in 1791. That said, its boundaries are basically natural – the River Rhône to the west, Mont Ventoux to the east, the northern boundary of the huge Vaucluse plateau to the north, and the River Durance to the south.

Avignon

Capital of the Catholic Church during the early Middle Ages and for centuries one of the major artistic centres of France, **AVIGNON** remains an utterly unmissable destination. During the **Festival d'Avignon** in July, it becomes *the* place to be in Provence.

Central Avignon is still ringed by low medieval **walls**, which encircle the old town as it nestles up against a ninety-degree bend in the Rhône river. With the gates and towers all restored, the ramparts give cohesion and unity to the historic core, dramatically marking it off from the formless sprawl of the modern city beyond. Despite their menacing crenellations, however, the walls were never a formidable defence, even when sections were girded by a now-vanished moat. The major monuments occupy a compact quarter up against the river, just beyond the principal **place de l'Horloge**, which itself stands at the northern end of rue de la République, the chief axis of the old town.

SOURCE OF THE RIVER SORGUE, FONTAINE-DE-VAUCLUSE

Highlights

❶ Palais des Papes Avignon's most spectacular monument makes a superb backdrop for the Festival d'Avignon, held each July. **See p.114**

❷ Villeneuve-lès-Avignon More laidback than its bigger cousin across the river, Villeneuve has no shortage of impressive sights. **See p.126**

❸ Châteauneuf-du-Pape The rich red wines of Châteauneuf rank among the most famous – and delicious – in the world. **See p.129**

❹ Vaison's Haute Ville Across the river from the Roman ruins of Vaison's town centre, visitors can climb through quiet medieval streets to reach a ruined clifftop castle. **See p.136**

❺ Les Dentelles This region of jagged limestone pinnacles is home to some exceptional and varied wines, as well as plenty of good hiking trails. **See p.137**

❻ Mont Ventoux Western Provence's highest summit, a fabled target for amateur and professional cyclists alike, offers unrivalled panoramas. **See p.139**

❼ Fontaine-de-Vaucluse Enjoy a ravishing riverside stroll to reach the dramatic and intriguing source of the River Sorgue. **See p.146**

HIGHLIGHTS ARE MARKED ON THE MAP ON P.114

Yes, Avignon can be dauntingly crowded, and stiflingly hot, in summer. But it's worth persevering, not simply for the colossal **Palais des Papes** – home to the medieval popes – and the fine crop of museums and ancient churches, but also for the sheer sense of life and energy that throbs through the city's vibrant lanes and alleyways.

The Palais des Papes

Daily: first half of March 9am–6.30pm; mid-March to June & mid-Sept to Oct 9am–7pm; July & first half of Sept 9am–8pm; Aug 9am–9pm; Nov–Feb 9.30am–5.45pm; last ticket 1hr before closing • €10.50, or €13 with Pont St-Bénézet; €8.50/10 with Avignon Passion pass (see box opposite) • ☎ 04 32 74 32 74, ⓦ www.palais-des-papes.com

Perched at the north end of the walled city, overlooking the curving Rhône, Avignon's vast **Palais des Papes** soars above the cobbled place du Palais. Although the palace was built primarily as a fortress, and equipped with massive stone vaults, battlements and sluices for pouring hot oil on attackers, the two pointed towers that hover above its

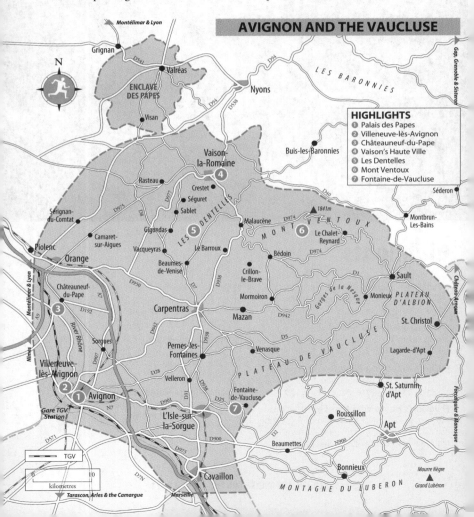

AVIGNON AND THE VAUCLUSE

HIGHLIGHTS
1. Palais des Papes
2. Villeneuve-lès-Avignon
3. Châteauneuf-du-Pape
4. Vaison's Haute Ville
5. Les Dentelles
6. Mont Ventoux
7. Fontaine-de-Vaucluse

POPES AND ANTIPOPES – THE INTRIGUING HISTORY OF AVIGNON

The first **pope** to come to Avignon, **Clement V**, was invited over by the astute King Philippe le Bel ("the Good") in 1309, ostensibly to protect him from impending anarchy in Rome. In reality, Philip saw a chance to extend his power by keeping the pope in Provence, during what came to be known as the Church's "Babylonian captivity". Clement's successor, **Jean XXII**, had previously been bishop of Avignon, so he re-installed himself quite happily in the episcopal palace. The next Supreme Pontiff, **Benedict XII**, acceded in 1334; accepting the impossibility of returning to Rome, he demolished the bishop's palace to replace it with an austere fortress, now known as the **Vieux Palais**.

Though Gregory XI finally moved the Holy See back to Rome in 1378, this didn't mark the end of the papacy here. After Gregory's death in Rome, dissident local cardinals elected their own pope in Avignon, provoking the Western Schism, a ruthless struggle for the control of the Church's wealth. That lasted until **Benedict XIII** – officially considered now to have been an **antipope** – fled into self-exile near Valencia in 1409. It was Benedict who built Avignon's still-surviving walls in 1403, when under siege by French forces loyal to Rome. Avignon itself remained papal property right up until the Revolution.

As home to one of the richest courts in Europe, fourteenth-century Avignon attracted princes, dignitaries, poets and raiders, who arrived to beg from, rob, extort and entertain the popes. According to Petrarch, the overcrowded, plague-ridden papal entourage was "a sewer where all the filth of the universe has gathered".

3

gate are incongruously graceful. Inside, so little remains of its original decoration and furnishings that one could easily suppose that all the popes and their retinues were as pious and austere as the last official occupant, Benedict XIII. The denuded interior leaves hardly a whiff of the corruption and decadence of fat, feuding cardinals and their mistresses; the thronging purveyors of jewels, velvet and furs; the musicians, chefs and painters competing for patronage; and the riotous banquets and corridor schemings.

The Vieux Palais

Steered by fancy multimedia audioguides, visits to the Palais des Papes follow a linear course. They begin in the original **Vieux Palais**, constructed from 1335 onwards, during the papacy of Benedict XII. The first building you enter, the **Pope's Tower**, is also known as the Tower of Angels. It's accessed via the vaulted **Treasury**, where the Church's deeds and finances were handled. Four large holes in the floor of the smaller downstairs room, originally concealed but now covered by glass, held the papal gold and jewels. The same cunning storage device was used in the **Chambre du Camérier** or Chamberlain's Quarters, off the Jesus Hall upstairs.

In the adjoining **Papal Vestiary**, the pope had a small library and would dress before receiving sovereigns and ambassadors in the **Consistoire** of the Vieux Palais, on the other side of the Jesus Hall.

On the floor above, the **kitchen** offers powerful testimony to the scale of papal gluttony, with its square walls becoming an octagonal chimney piece for a vast central cooking fire. Major feasts were held in the **Grand Tinel**, or dining room, where only the pope was allowed to wield a knife. During the conclave in which they elected a new pope, the cardinals were locked into this room, adjourning to conspire and scheme in additional chambers to the south and west.

AVIGNON PASSION PASSPORTS

The tourist offices in Avignon and Villeneuve-lès-Avignon distribute free **Avignon Passion passports**. After paying the full admission price for the first museum you visit, you and your family receive discounts of 10–50 percent on the entrance fees of all subsequent museums in Avignon. The pass also gives discounts on tourist transport (such as riverboats and bus tours), and is valid for fifteen days after its first use.

3

AVIGNON

N

ÎLE DE LA BARTHELASSE

Swimming Pool

Pont St-Bénézet

Boat to Île de la Barthelasse

BOULEVARD DE LA LIGNE

Porte du Rocher

Rocher des Doms

Musée du Petit Palais

Cathédrale Notre-Dame-des-Doms

Cinéma Utopia

CHEMIN DE BAGATELLE

Villeneuve-lès-Avignon

Free Parking

Nîmes

PONT DALADIER

CHEMIN DE L'ÎLE PIOT

BOULEVARD DU RHÔNE

BOULEVARD DU RHÔNE

RUE REMPART DU RHÔNE

RUE LIMAS

RUE GRANDE FUSTERIE

RUE FERRUCE

RUE LIMASSET

RUE DES GROTTES

RUE CHIRON

RUE DE LA BALANCE

PLACE DU PALAIS

River Rhône

Cruises Mireio

ALLÉE DE L'OULLE

Porte de l'Oulle

PLACE CRILLON

R. BARONCELLI

RUE DE LA PLAISANCE

RUE DU MAIL

RUE ST-ÉTIENNE

RUE PETITE FUSTERIE

RUE RACINE

RUE MOLIÈRE

RUE CORNEILLE

Conservatoire de Musique

Opéra

RUE VILAR

RUE DE MONS

Palais des Papes

Maison Jean Vilar

PLACE CHÂTAIGNES

BOULEVARD DE L'OULLE

RUE JOSEPH-VERNET

PASSAGE DE L'ORATOIRE

RUE SAINT-THOMAS D'AQUIN

RUE ST-ANDRÉ

RUE FÉLIX GRAS

St-Agricol

Hôtel de Ville

PLACE DE L'HORLOGE

RUE ST-AGRICOL

Palais du Roure

PLACE DE LA PRINCIPALE

PLACE DU CHANGE

St-Pierre

PLACE CARNOT

RUE DES MARCHANDS

RUE DU VIEUX-

RUE DE LA RÉPUBLIQUE

RUE VICTOR HUGO

RUE PTE. CALADE

RUE VIALA

RUE DE LA BOULQUERIE

Musée Calvet

Musée Vouland

RUE D'ANNANELLE

RUE SAINT-ANDRÉ

RUE LANTERNE

Musée Requien

RUE HORACE VERNET

RUE BASILE

RUE BOISSERIN

St-Didier

PLACE ST-DIDIER

RUE DU ROI RENÉ

Porte St-Dominique

BOULEVARD ST-DOMINIQUE

RUE VELOUTERIE

RUE ST-CHARLES

RUE JOSEPH-VERNET

Musée Lapidaire

RUE F. MISTRAL

Musée Angladon

RUE DES 3 FAUCONS

RUE DES ÉTUDES

RUE DES LICES

Collection Lambert

BOULEVARD RASPAIL

BOULEVARD RASPAIL

RUE ST-CHARLES

RUE VIOLETTE

RUE DE L'OBSERVANCE

Agricole Perdiguier

RUE AGRICOL PERDIGUIER

TCRA Office

RUE DE LA BOURSE

AVENUE L. DE TASSIGNY

PLACE DES CORPS SAINTS

RUE ST-MICHEL

Anc. Couvent des Célestins

Porte St-Roch

RUE PAUL-MÉRINDOL

AVENUE EISENHOWER

RUE DU REMPART SAINT-ROCH

BOULEVARD ST-ROCH

Porte St-Charles

COURS PRÉS KENNEDY

COURS JEAN-JAURÈS

Porte de la République

BOULEVARD ST-ROCH

AVENUE DE BLANCHISSAGE

PLACE DE LA RÉPUBLIQUE

Gare SNCF

AVENUE MONCLAR-NORD

Gare Routière

Gare TGV

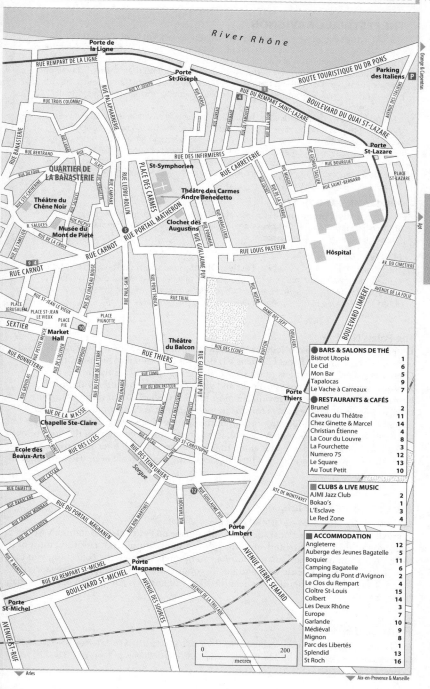

River Rhône

Porte de
la Ligne

RUE REMPART DE LA LIGNE

Porte
St-Joseph

ROUTE TOURISTIQUE DU DR PONS

Parking
des Italiens

RUE ST-JOSEPH

RUE DU REMPART SAINT-LAZARE

BOULEVARD DU QUAI ST-LAZARE

RUE TROIS COLOMBES

RUE BANASTERIE

RUE BERTRAND

QUARTIER DE
LA BANASTERIE

Théâtre du
Chêne Noir

St-Symphorien

RUE DES INFIRMIERES

RUE CARRETERIE

Porte
St-Lazare

PLACE
ST-LAZARE

RUE BOURGUET

RUE SAINT-BERNARD

PLACE DES CARMES

Théâtre des Carmes
André Benedetto

Musée du
Mont de Piété

Clocher des
Augustins

RUE LOUIS PASTEUR

Hôpital

RUE CARNOT

RUE CARNOT

AV. DU CIMETIERE

AVENUE DE LA FOLIE

BOULEVARD LIMBERT

PLACE
JERUSALEM / PLACE ST-JEAN
LE VIEUX

SEXTIER

PLACE
PIE

Market
Hall

Théâtre
du Balcon

RUE THIERS

RUE BONNETERIE

RUE DE LA MASSE

Porte
Thiers

Chapelle Ste-Claire

RUE DES LICES

Ecole des
Beaux-Arts

Sorgue

RUE DAMETTE

RUE BARACANE

RUE DU PORTAIL MAGNANEN

Porte
Limbert

RTE DE MONTFAVET

Porte
Magnanen

AVENUE PIERRE SEMARD

RUE DU REMPART ST-MICHEL

BOULEVARD ST-MICHEL

Porte
St-Michel

AVENUE ST-RUF

Arles

Aix-en-Provence & Marseille

Orange & Carpentras

Apt

3

● **BARS & SALONS DE THÉ**

Bistrot Utopia	1
Le Cid	6
Mon Bar	5
Tapalocas	9
Le Vache à Carreaux	7

● **RESTAURANTS & CAFÉS**

Brunel	2
Caveau du Théâtre	11
Chez Ginette & Marcel	14
Christian Étienne	4
La Cour du Louvre	8
La Fourchette	3
Numero 75	12
Le Square	13
Au Tout Petit	10

■ **CLUBS & LIVE MUSIC**

AJMI Jazz Club	2
Bokao's	1
L'Esclave	3
Le Red Zone	4

■ **ACCOMMODATION**

Angleterre	12
Auberge des Jeunes Bagatelle	5
Boquier	11
Camping Bagatelle	6
Camping du Pont d'Avignon	2
Le Clos du Rempart	4
Cloitre St-Louis	15
Colbert	14
Les Deux Rhône	3
Europe	7
Garlande	10
Médiéval	9
Mignon	8
Parc des Libertés	1
Splendid	13
St Roch	16

0   200

metrès

3

THE FESTIVAL OF AVIGNON

Starting in the second week in July, the annual, three-week **Festival d'Avignon** focuses especially on theatre, while also featuring classical music, dance, lectures and exhibitions. The city's great buildings make a spectacular backdrop to the performances, while the streets throng with bright-eyed performers eagerly promoting their shows. Everywhere stays open late, and everything from accommodation to obscure fringe events gets booked up very quickly; getting around or doing anything normal becomes virtually impossible.

Founded in 1947 by actor-director **Jean Vilar**, the festival has included, over the years, theatrical interpretations as diverse as Euripides, Molière and Chekhov, performed by companies from across Europe. Each year, one or two "associate artists" from other countries curate performances of contemporary works from their land of origin. While big-name directors draw the largest crowds to the main venue, the Cour d'Honneur in the Palais des Papes, lesser-known troupes and directors also stage new works, and the festival spotlights a different culture each year.

PROGRAMME AND TICKETS

The main **festival programme** is usually available from the second week in May on ⓦfestival-avignon.com, while **tickets** go on sale around mid-June, and remain available until three hours before each performance.

FESTIVAL OFF

The fringe contingent known as the **Festival Off** (ⓦavignonleoff.com) adds an additional element of craziness and magic, with a programme of innovative, obscure and bizarre performances taking place in more than a hundred venues as well as in the streets. A *Carte Public Adhérent* for €16 gives you thirty percent off all fringe shows.

The Palais Neuf

Despite its name, the **Palais Neuf** is only a few years newer than the Vieux Palais – it was erected by the very next Pope, Clement VI. Both his bedroom and his study, the **Chambre du Cerf**, bear witness to his secular concerns. The walls in the former are adorned with wonderful entwined oak- and vine-leaf motifs, the latter with superb hunting and fishing scenes. Providing almost the first dash of colour during the tour, these rooms can get unbearably crowded in high summer. As you continue, austerity resumes in the cathedral-like proportions of the **Grande Chapelle**, or **Chapelle Clementine**, and in the **Grande Audience**, its twin in terms of volume, on the floor below.

The circuit also includes a walk along the roof terraces, which offer such tremendous views that it's worth heading up a little higher to the rooftop café even when the signs insist it's closed.

Musée du Petit Palais

Daily except Tues 10am–1pm & 2–6pm • €6 • ☎ 04 90 86 44 58, ⓦ petit-palais.org

Immediately north of the Palais de Papes, the **Musée du Petit Palais** contains a vast collection of first-rate thirteenth- to fifteenth-century painting and sculpture, most of it by masters from northern Italian cities. As you progress through the collection, you can watch as the masters wrestle with and finally conquer the representation of perspective - a revolution from medieval art, where the size of figures was a reflection of their social importance.

Pont St-Bénézet

Daily: first half of March 9am–6.30pm; mid-March to June & mid-Sept to Oct 9am–7pm; July & first half of Sept 9am–8pm; Aug 9am–9pm; Nov–Feb 9.30am–5.45pm; last ticket 1hr before closing • €4.50, or €13 with Palais des Papes • ☎ 04 32 74 32 74, ⓦ www.palais-des-papes.com

Now merely jutting halfway out to the Île de Barthelasse, the twelfth-century **Pont St-Bénézet** originally reached all the way to Villeneuve, and was the only bridge to cross the Rhône between Lyon and the Mediterranean. A picturesque ruin since a flood in 1668, with just four of its 22 arches surviving, the bridge is famous not for its truncated state, but because it's the **Pont d'Avignon** immortalized in the famous song *Sur le pont d'Avignon* ("... *l'on y danse, l'on y danse* ..."). The song has existed in various forms for five centuries, but both words and tune as we know them today come from popular nineteenth-century French operettas. It's generally agreed that the lyrics should really say "*Sous le pont*" (under the bridge) rather than "*Sur le pont*" (on the bridge), and that they referred either to the dancing of the general populace on the Île de Barthelasse on feast days, or to the thief and trickster clientele of a tavern there dancing with glee at the arrival of more potential victims.

The narrow bridge itself is open for visits. Displays beneath its landward end explain the history of both bridge – which may have been erected on the site of a larger Roman bridge by the eponymous Bénézet, who later became the patron saint of architects – and song, with assorted celebrity recordings. After that, you're free to walk to the end and back, and dance upon it too for that matter.

Rocher des Doms

Commanding lovely views from its high hilltop position north of the Palais des Papes, down to the Pont St-Bénézet and across the river to Villeneuve, the peaceful **Rocher des Doms** park is the best place in the city for a picnic. Whether you approach from the west, via the Musée du Petit Palais, or from the tangle of alleyways to the east, the steep climb up is rewarded with relaxing lawns, fountains and ducks, as well as a little café.

The **Cathédrale Notre-Dame-des-Doms** (daily: July & Aug 7am–7pm; Sept–June 8am–6pm) immediately south is topped by an enormous gilded Virgin on its belfry. It might once have been a luminous Romanesque structure; sadly, though, its interior has had a bad attack of Baroque and the result is a stifling clutter.

Place de l'Horloge

Frenetically busy year-round, the café-lined **place de l'Horloge** holds Avignon's imposing **Hôtel de Ville** and **clock tower**, as well as the **Opéra**. Around the square, on rues de Mons, Molière and Corneille, famous faces appear in windows painted on the buildings. Many of these figures depict historical visitors to the city, who described the powerful impact of hearing over a hundred bells ring at once. On Sunday mornings – traffic lulls permitting – you can still hear myriad different peals from churches, convents and chapels in close proximity.

Palais du Roure

3 rue Collège du Roure • Guided tours Tues 3pm • €4.60 • ☎ 04 90 80 80 88

A centre for Provençal culture, the beautiful fifteenth-century **Palais du Roure**, south of the Place de l'Horloge, often hosts art exhibitions. Its gateway and courtyard are always worth a look, but visitors can only access the interior on Tuesday afternoons, when tours ramble through the attics to see Provençal costumes, publications and presses, photographs of the Camargue in the 1900s and an old stagecoach.

Maison Jean Vilar

8 rue de Mons • July daily 10.30am–6.30pm; Sept–June Tues & Fri 1.30–5pm, Wed & Thurs 9am–noon & 1.30–5pm, Sat 10am–5pm; closed Aug • Free • ☎ 04 90 86 59 64, ⊕ maisonjeanvilar.org

The seventeenth-century Hôtel de Crochans, east of the Place de l'Horloge, is home to the **Maison Jean Vilar**. Named after the theatre director who set up the "Week of Dramatic Art" in 1947 – the forerunner of the Festival d'Avignon – it houses festival memorabilia, an excellent library dedicated to the performing arts, and recordings of everything from Stanislavski to last year's street theatre.

Quartier de la Banasterie

The **quartier de la Banasterie**, immediately east of the Palais des Papes and north of place Pie, dates almost entirely from the seventeenth and eighteenth centuries. With tourism largely kept in check, this remains an atmospheric and beautiful district, particularly at night. Its heavy wooden doors, with their highly sculptured lintels, today bear the nameplates of lawyers, psychiatrists and doctors. Between Banasterie and **place des Carmes** lies a tangle of tiny streets where you're almost certain to get lost. Pedestrians have priority over cars on many of them, and there are plenty of tempting café and restaurant stops.

3

Place Pie and around

Avignon's main **pedestrianized area** stretches between the chain store blandness of rue de la République and the jaw-dropping (some might say, hideous) modern **market hall** on **place Pie**, active every morning except Monday. To the northwest is the Renaissance **church of St-Pierre** on place St-Pierre (Mon–Wed & Sun 10am–1pm; Thurs–Sat 10am–1pm & 2–6pm), with superb doors sculpted in 1551, and an altarpiece dating from the same period.

South of place Pie, the **Chapelle Ste-Claire** is where the poet Petrarch first saw and fell in love with Laura, during the Good Friday service in 1327, as recorded in a note on the pages of his copy of Virgil. A little way east is the atmospheric **rue des Teinturiers**, a centre for calico printing during the eighteenth and nineteenth centuries. The cloth was washed in the Sorgue canal, which still runs alongside, though the four of its mighty watermills that survive no longer turn.

Musée Angladon

5 rue Labourer • Mid-April to mid-Nov Tues–Sun 1–6pm; mid-Nov to mid-April Wed–Sun 1–6pm • €6 • ☎ 04 90 82 29 03, ⓦ angladon.com

The **Musée Angladon** displays what remains of the private collection of Parisian *couturier* Jacques Doucet. Apart from Antonio Forbera's extraordinary *Le Chavalet du Peintre*, a trompe l'oeil painting from 1686 depicting the artist's easel, complete with sketches and palette as well as work in progress, the older works are largely unexceptional, but Doucet's contemporary collection alone is worth the admission price. It includes Modigliani's *The Pink Blouse*, various Picassos, including a self-portrait from 1904, and Van Gogh's *The Railroad Cars*, his only Provençal painting on permanent display in the region.

Musée Calvet

65 rue Joseph-Vernet • Daily except Tues 10am–1pm & 2–6pm • €6, or €7 with Musée Lapidaire • ☎ 04 90 86 33 84, ⓦ musee-calvet-avignon.com

The excellent, airy **Musée Calvet** is housed in a lovely eighteenth-century palace. Highlights include a wonderful gallery of languorous nineteenth-century marble sculptures, among them Bosio's *Young Indian*; the Puech collection of silverware and Italian and Dutch paintings; and works by Soutine, Manet and Joseph Vernet, as well as Jacques-Louis David's subtle, moving *Death of Joseph Barra*. It also holds some much

PALAIS DES PAPES, AVIGNON (P.114) >

more ancient artefacts, like enigmatic stelae from the fourth-century BC, carved with half-discernible faces, and Bronze Age axes.

Musée Lapidaire

27 rue de la République • Daily except Mon 10am–1pm & 2–6pm • €2, or €7 with Musée Calvet • ☎ 04 90 84 75 38, Ⓦ musee-calvet-avignon.com

The **Musée Lapidaire**, a former Baroque chapel, is home to larger pieces from the archeological collection of its sister museum, the Musée Calvet (see p.120). Besides Egyptian statues and Etruscan urns, it abounds in Roman and Gallo-Roman sarcophagi, and early renditions of the mythical Tarasque (see box, p.101).

Musée Requien

67 rue Joseph-Vernet • Tues–Sat 10am–1pm & 2–6pm • Free • ☎ 04 90 82 43 51, Ⓦ museum-requien.org

Founded in the nineteenth century, and centring on an old-school collection of stuffed and fossilized natural-history specimens, the **Musée Requien** can be thoroughly inspected in the space of quarter of an hour. Its oldest exhibits, such as ancient trilobites, a huge tyrannosaurus skull and assorted Neanderthal bones, fit more comfortably with modern visitors than do its more recent stuffed gorilla and tiger.

Musée Vouland

17 rue Victor-Hugo • Tues–Sun: Jan, March–June & Oct–Dec 2–6pm; July–Sept noon–6pm; closed Feb • €6 • ☎ 04 90 86 03 79, Ⓦ vouland.com

Near Porte St-Dominique on the west side of the walled city, the **Musée Vouland** is filled to bursting point with the fittings, fixtures and furnishings enjoyed by French aristocrats both before and after the Revolution. It's laid out like a still-occupied house, with most of the contents barely labelled or railed off, and there's a certain pleasure in the playful juxtaposition of items from different eras.

Collection Lambert

5 rue Violette • July & Aug daily 11am–7pm; Sept–June Tues–Sun 11am–6pm • €7 • ☎ 04 90 16 56 20, Ⓦ collectionlambert.com

Avignon's major contemporary art gallery, the thoughtfully curated **Collection Lambert**, has gone through a considerable expansion since collector Yvon Lambert committed to donate his lovingly amassed artworks to the city in perpetuity, in 2011. The superb space is used both to house large-scale temporary exhibitions, one of which each year is usually devoted to a specific contemporary artist, and to show off the results of previous such shows. The permanent display includes pieces created by Jean-Michel Basquiat for Lambert's Paris gallery in 1988, as well as works by Cy Twombly, Anselm Keifer and Roni Horn.

ARRIVAL AND DEPARTURE

By car Driving into Avignon involves negotiating a nightmare of junctions and one-way roads. The cheapest and easiest parking options for day-trippers are two free, guarded car parks, connected with the town centre by free electric shuttle buses: **Île Piot** (Mon–Fri 7.30am–8.30pm, Sat 1.30–8.30pm), which is actually part of the Île de la Barthelasse between Avignon and Villeneuve, and **Parking des Italiens** (Mon–Sat 7.30am–8.30pm), beside the river immediately northeast of the old town. Both are primarily intended for commuters; neither stays open late, and only Île Piot is ever open on Sundays or public holidays, and even then only in high summer. Otherwise, the oversubscribed parking spaces inside the city walls are expensive, starting at around €2 per hour; check whether your hotel offers free or discounted parking.

By train Avignon's *gare SNCF* is just outside the walls south of the old city. Do not confuse it with the separate **TGV** station, 2km south, and linked by shuttle buses to and from cours Président-Kennedy, by the Porte de la République at the southern end of the city (daily, 2–4

hourly; departures from station 6.22am–11.27pm, from town 5.46am–11.14pm; €3; ⓦtcra.fr); a taxi into town (call ☎04 90 82 20 20) can cost €15 or more.

Destinations (*gare SNCF*) Arles (hourly; 20–45min); Cavaillon (9–14 daily; 35min); Lyon (12 daily; 2hr 30min); Marseille (14 daily; 1hr 5min); Orange (17 daily; 15min); Tarascon (20 daily; 12min); Valence (12 daily; 1hr 20min).

Destinations (*gare TGV*) Aix-en-Provence TGV (22 daily; 20min); Lille-Europe (5 daily; 4hr 30min); London St Pancras (summer 1 on Sat only; 5hr 53min); Lyon (14 daily; 1hr 10min); Marseille (every 30min; 30min); Paris (17 daily; 2hr 40min); Paris CDG Airport (5 daily; 3hr 30min); Valence TGV (9 daily; 30–40min).

By bus Avignon's *gare routière* is alongside the *gare SNCF*, just outside the walls south of the old city.

Destinations Aix (6 daily; 1hr 15min); Arles (7 daily; 1hr); Carpentras (frequent; 35–45min); Cavaillon (9 daily; 35min); Digne (3–4 daily; 3hr–3hr 30min); Fontaine-de-Vaucluse (4 daily; 55min); L'Isle-sur-la-Sorgue (10 daily; 40min); Orange (every 30–45min; 50min); St-Rémy (8 daily; 40min); Vaison (3 daily; 1hr 25min).

By plane Avignon-Caumont Airport, 8km southeast of the centre (☎04 90 81 51 51, ⓦavignon.aeroport.fr), is connected with Birmingham, Exeter and Southampton on Flybe (ⓦflybe.com), and with London City Airport on Cityjet (ⓦcityjet.com). It's connected to the town centre and *gare TGV* on bus #22 (€1.70).

GETTING AROUND

By bus The main TCRA local bus stops are on cours Président-Kennedy and outside Porte de l'Oulle facing the river (tickets €1.20 each; book of 10 tickets €10; one-day pass €3.60; ⓦtcra.fr).

By boat A free boat service crosses the river from east of Pont St-Bénézet to the Île de la Barthelasse, site of the city's campsites (March & Oct Wed 2–5.30pm, Sat & Sun

10am–noon & 2–5.30pm; April–June & Sept daily 10am–12.30pm & 2–6.30pm; July & Aug daily 11am–9pm).

By bike Provence Bike, immediately east of the *gare SNCF* at 7 av St-Ruf (☎04 90 27 92 61, ⓦprovence-bike.com), rents bicycles, scooters and motorbikes.

By taxi There is a taxi rank on place Pie (☎04 90 82 20 20, ⓦtaxis-avignon.fr).

INFORMATION AND TOURS

Tourist office 41 cours Jean-Jaurès, at the southern end of the city (April–June & Aug–Oct Mon–Sat 9am–6pm, Sun 9.45am–5pm; July Mon–Sat 9am–7pm, Sun 10am–5pm; Nov–March Mon–Fri 9am–6pm, Sat 9am–5pm, Sun 10am–noon; ☎04 32 74 32 74, ⓦavignon-tourisme.com).

Boat trips In summer, from a base just south of place

Crillon, Cruises Mireio (☎04 90 85 62 25, ⓦmireio.net) offer 45-minute river trips on the Rhône (April–June & Sept daily 2pm, 3pm & 4.15pm; July & Aug daily 2pm, 3pm, 4pm, 5pm & 6pm; €8), as well as dinner cruises upstream towards Châteauneuf-du-Pape and downstream to Arles (€35.50–68, meal included).

ACCOMMODATION

Even outside festival time, finding a **room** in Avignon can be a problem: cheap hotels fill fast, so book in advance. Villeneuve-lès-Avignon, just across the river, may have rooms when its larger neighbour is full. Between the two, the Île de la Barthelasse is an idyllic spot for **camping**. The tourist office keeps track of which hotels have vacancies.

Angleterre 29 bd Raspail ☎04 90 86 34 31, ⓦhoteldangleterre.fr. Located in a quiet neighbourhood in the southwest corner of the old city, well away from night-time noise, this is a traditional hotel with plain, low-priced rooms, many of them very small but equipped with reasonable bathrooms. **€75**

★ **Boquier** 6 rue du Portail Boquier ☎04 90 82 34 43, ⓦhotel-boquier.com. Extremely welcoming little hotel near the tourist office, with funkily decorated, widely differing, and consistently inexpensive en-suite rooms, some very small, some sleeping three or four. **€60**

Cloître St-Louis 20 rue du Portail Boquier ☎04 90 27 55 55, ⓦcloitre-saint-louis.com. A large but personable and good-value hotel, with elegant modern decor in the seventeenth-century setting of a former Jesuit school. Some of the a/c rooms have attractive wood-beamed ceilings, and there's a rooftop pool. **€210**

★ **Le Clos du Rempart** 35 rue Crémade ☎04 90 86 39 14, ⓦclosdurempart.com. Delightful B&B in a pretty nineteenth-century house in the northeast corner of the city with two large, luxurious and very peaceful en-suite rooms; there's a wonderful wisteria-covered breakfast terrace and a hammock to doze in on sunny afternoons. **€160**

Colbert 7 rue Agricol Perdiguier ☎04 90 86 20 20, ⓦavignon-hotel-colbert.com. At the south end of town and handy for local trains and buses, this hotel has warmly and imaginatively decorated rooms, mostly large and all a/c, plus a pleasant central courtyard complete with fountain. The helpful owners are always ready with suggestions. Rates drop significantly in low season. Closed Nov to mid-March. **€100**

Europe 12 place Crillon ☎04 90 14 76 76, ⓦheurope .com. Very comfortable upscale hotel, in a sixteenth-century townhouse. Unpretentiously classy, it's set back in a shaded courtyard, with bright, modern, soundproofed rooms, home-made breakfasts and an excellent restaurant. **€209**

Garlande 20 rue Galante ☎04 90 80 08 85, ⓦhoteldegarlande.com. Stylish little family-run hotel, in a pedestrian street near the Palais des Papes. Each of the eleven generally spacious rooms has its own colour scheme and Provençal touches, as well as a decent bathroom. **€92**

Médiéval 15 rue Petite Saunerie ☎04 90 86 11 06, ⓦhotelmedieval.com. Very central hotel in a fine seventeenth-century townhouse, with very reasonable rates and a lovely garden courtyard, but rather plain, dated rooms of widely varying sizes. **€72**

Mignon 12 rue Joseph-Vernet ☎04 90 82 17 30, ⓦhotel-mignon.com. The decor may be a little fussy for some tastes, but this small hotel is amazing value for money considering its spotless little rooms and fantastic location on a chic street. Closed Jan. **€71**

Splendid 17 rue Agricol Perdiguier ☎04 90 86 14 46, ⓦavignon-splendid-hotel.com. Very decent one-star in a great location just off the main drag; there's a steep narrow staircase to reach the upper floors. Fresh bathrooms and friendly management. The six rooms with a/c cost €20 extra. Closed mid-Nov to mid-Dec. **€95**

St Roch 9 Paul Merindol ☎04 90 16 50 00, ⓦhotelstroch-avignon.com. Thirty-room budget hotel, in an old building outside the city walls not far from the *gare SNCF*. Recently restored, it offers plain but acceptable rooms, many overlooking a pleasant garden. **€70**

CAMPING

Camping Bagatelle 25 allées Antoine-Pinay, Île de la Barthelasse ☎04 90 86 30 39, ⓦcampingbagatelle.com. Well wooded three-star campsite, with laundry facilities, a shop and café. It's the closest to the city centre, visible as you cross the Daladier bridge from Avignon; bus #20 from the post office, or a 15min walk from place de l'Horloge. The campsite also offers basic hostel facilities, with beds in two-, four- or six-person dorms, plus private rooms sleeping from two to four, with and without en-suite facilities; all hostel rates include breakfast. Open all year. Dorms **€19**; rooms **€51**; camping **€22**

Camping du Pont d'Avignon 10 chemin de la Barthelasse ☎04 90 80 63 50, ⓦaquadis-loisirs.com. Well-shaded four-star site, with a lovely pool, on the island directly facing Pont St-Bénézet across the river, a fair walk from the centre but accessible on bus route #20. Closed late Nov to early March. **€24.50**

Les Deux Rhône chemin de Bellegarde, Île de la Barthelasse ☎04 90 85 49 70, ⓦcamping2rhone.com. Avignon's smallest campsite, around 3km from the city centre on the north side of the island, and equipped with pool and restaurant; bus #20 ("Gravière" stop). Open all year. **€15**

Parc des Libertés 4682 rte de l'Islon, Île de la Barthelasse ☎04 90 85 17 73, ⓦparcdeslibertes.fr. This summer-only campsite, 5km out from the centre, is the cheapest of Avignon's four sites; no laundry. Closed mid-Sept to mid-April. **€11.10**

EATING AND DRINKING

Avignon has an enormous number of **restaurants**, ranging from expensive gastronomic rendezvous to cheap snack places and takeaways. The large café-brasseries on the terraces of place de l'Horloge and rue de la République all serve quick, if not necessarily memorable, meals; place des Corps Saints holds elbow-to-elbow tables beneath the plane trees in summer; and the old pedestrian lanes are packed with atmospheric possibilities. Note that many restaurants open every day during the July festival.

RESTAURANTS AND CAFÉS

★ **Au Tout Petit** 4 rue d'Amphoux ☎04 90 82 38 86, ⓦautoutpetit.fr. Popular acclaim has ensured that this market-area restaurant, specializing in what it calls "*cuisine re-créative*", is no longer as "*petit*" as the name suggests. Served indoors only, the food remains imaginative, fresh and unbeatable; the service brisk and efficient; and the owner extremely friendly. Two-course lunch *formule* for €12, dinner *menus* from €17. Tues–Sat noon–2pm & 6.30–10pm.

Brunel 46 rue de la Balance ☎04 90 85 24 83. This cheerful restaurant, with a flowery terrace near the Palais des Papes, serves superb regional dishes, including *bourride*, with a *plat du jour* for €12.50 and dinner *menus* from €32.50. Tues–Sat noon–1.30pm & 7.30–9pm.

Caveau du Théâtre 16 rue des Trois Faucons ☎04 90 82 60 91, ⓦcaveaudutheatre.com. Friendly bistro, with pretty painted walls, jolly red tables out on the street, and occasional live jazz, serving delicious dishes like market-fresh fish baked with liquorice (€14.50) or huge mixed salads (€15). Lunch *menu* €14, dinner *menus* €19 and €23. Mon–Fri noon–2.30pm & 7pm–midnight, Sat 7pm–midnight; closed 2nd half of Aug.

Chez Ginette & Marcel 27 place des Corps-Saints ☎04 90 85 58 70. The most attractive of several restaurants on this lively, youthful little square; if you sit outside, be sure to have a peek into the restaurant itself – it's a fun evocation of a 1950s French grocery, filled with funky bric-a-brac. €5 *tartines* and salads are the speciality; you can get a substantial meal for well under €10, while breakfast, including a *tartine* of course, is just €6. Mon–Sat 9am–midnight.

★ **Christian Étienne** 10 rue de Mons ☎04 90 86 16 50, ⓦchristian-etienne.fr. Avignon's best-known gourmet restaurant, housed in a twelfth-century mansion, with a terrace overlooking the place du Palais. Mouthwatering Provençal delights might include a whole *menu* devoted to tomatoes, or lobster with ginger, asparagus and sesame seeds followed by orange and carrot macaroons with almond sorbet. Dinner *menus* range from €70 to €115 – the latter being the *menu confiance*, in which you trust the chef to bring whatever takes his fancy that day – but you can sample the restaurant's pleasures on a €31 lunch *menu*. Tues–Sat noon–1.30pm & 7–9.15pm.

La Cour du Louvre 23 rue St-Agricol ☎04 90 27 12 66, ⓦlacourdulouvre.com. Hidden peacefully away from the old-town bustle in a delightful interior courtyard at the end of a *cour*, with a romantic atmosphere and good Mediterranean cooking. *Menus* from €26 for lunch – when there's also a €13.50 *plat du jour* – and €36 for dinner. Mon–Sat noon–2.15pm & 7–10pm.

La Fourchette 17 rue Racine ☎04 90 85 20 93. Bright, busy yet refined restaurant serving up classic and sophisticated fish and meat dishes – try the tasty sardines marinated in coriander – on €32 and €42 dinner *menus*. Mon–Fri 12.15–1.45pm & 7.15–9.45pm; closed first 3 weeks in Aug.

Numero 75 75 rue Guillaume Puy ☎04 90 27 16 00, ⓦnumero75.com. Housed in a beautiful nineteenth-century mansion – the former home of Jules Pernod, who invented his namesake drink here in 1870 – this smart restaurant has indoor and garden seating, and serves Provençal dinner *menus* from €32.50, but offers a €14.50 lunchtime *plat du jour*. Mon–Sat noon–1.45pm & 7.30–9.30pm.

Le Square Square Agricol Perdiguier ☎04 06 21 86 71 94. There's nothing very exceptional about the food in this outdoor café/brasserie, that's set in a spacious park behind the tourist office, but it makes a great spot for a summer-morning coffee, or a simple lunchtime salad or *plat* for under €10. Daily 8am– sunset.

BARS AND SALONS DE THÉ

Bistrot Utopia La Manutention, 4 rue Escaliers Ste-Anne ☎06 37 57 52 31. In the shadow of the Palais des Papes, around the back, this café has changing exhibitions adorning the walls, live jazz some nights, and adjoins a good cinema (see below). Mon–Fri noon–1am, Sat & Sun 2pm–1am.

Le Cid 11 place de l'Horloge ☎04 90 82 30 38, ⓦlecidcafe.com. Trendy mixed gay/straight bar and terrace that opens up at the crack of dawn, and keeps going long after the rest of place de l'Horloge has closed for the night. Daily 6.30am–1pm.

Mon Bar 17 rue Portail Matheron. Pleasantly old-fashioned café, 400m east of the place du Palais and steeped in the lore of Avignon, with a laidback atmosphere. Mon–Sat 7am–8pm, Sun 1–8pm.

Tapalocas 15 rue Galante ☎04 90 82 56 84, ⓦtapalocas-avignon.com. Tapas at under €3 each, plus Spanish music, sometimes live, in a large, atmospheric bar with contemporary stylings and outdoor seating. Daily 11.45am–1am.

Le Vache à Carreaux 14 rue Peyrollerie ☎04 90 80 09 05, ⓦvache-carreaux.com. This intimate, homely wine bar styles itself a "restaurant de fromage et vins", and cheese is indeed prominent on the food menu, which features €12 baked half-camemberts alongside large €9 salads. Mon–Fri noon–2pm & 7–10.30pm, Sat 7–11.30pm, Sun noon–2pm & 7–11.30pm.

NIGHTLIFE AND ENTERTAINMENT

Though Avignon saves a lot of its energy for the festival, the city is busy with **nightlife** and **cultural events** all year round, particularly café-theatre, and plenty of **classical concerts** are performed in churches, usually for free.

LIVE MUSIC AND CLUBS

AJMI Jazz Club La Manutention, 4 rue Escalier Ste-Anne ☎04 90 86 08 61, ⓦwww.jazzalajmi.com. This popular club, above *Bistrot Utopia* (see above), hosts a year-round programme of major acts and some adventurous new jazz and improvised music; check the website for the latest schedule. Hours vary.

Bokao's 9bis bd du Quai St-Lazare ☎04 90 82 47 95, ⓦbokaos.fr. Mainstream, youth-oriented club, in a converted barn with outdoor space, across from the river just outside the walls, playing an eclectic mix of music styles. Thurs–Sat 10pm–5am.

L'Esclave 12 rue du Limas ☎04 90 85 14 91, ⓦesclavebar .com. Avignon's gay and lesbian bar, with regular DJs, drag shows and karaoke nights at ground level, and more secluded areas upstairs. Tues–Sun 11pm until dawn.

Le Red Zone 25 rue Carnot ☎04 90 27 02 44, ⓦredzonebar.com. Sweaty, very crimson club where DJs play anything from salsa to electro according to the night. Mon & Sun 10pm–3am, Tues–Sat 9pm–3am.

THEATRE AND CINEMA

Cinéma Utopia La Manutention, 4 rue Escalier Ste-Anne ☎04 90 82 65 36, ⓦwww.cinemas-utopia.org. Part of a hip converted warehouse complex that also includes the *Bistrot Utopia* and *AJMI Jazz Club* (see above), this wildly popular venue shows a busy repertory programme of films from all over the world, many in *version originale* (undubbed).

Opéra Place de l'Horloge ☎04 90 82 81 40, ⓦoperatheatredavignon.fr. Avignon's most prestigious venue for classical opera and ballet, with a season running from October to June.

Théâtre du Balcon 38 rue Guillaume-Puy ☎ 04 90 85 00 80, ⊚ theatredubalcon.org. Venue staging everything from African music and twentieth-century classics to contemporary theatre.

Théâtre des Carmes André Benedetto 6 place des Carmes ☎ 04 90 82 20 47, ⊚ theatredescarmes.com.

Set up by, and now named after, one of the founders of Festival Off, this theatre specializes in avant-garde performances.

Théâtre du Chêne Noir 8bis rue Ste-Catherine ☎ 04 90 86 58 11, ⊚ chenenoir.fr. Programmes at this eclectic theatre range anywhere from mime or musicals to Molière.

DIRECTORY

Emergencies Doctor/ambulance ☎ 15; Hospital, Centre Hospitalier H. Duffaut, 305 rue Raoul-Follereau (☎ 04 32 75 33 33, ⊚ www.ch-avignon.fr); Night chemist, ☎ 3237, ⊚ www.3237.fr.

Laundry 9 rue du Chapeau-Rouge (with wi-fi; ⊚ www .savom.fr); 24 rue Lanterne.

Markets Flea market: place des Carmes (Sun morning). Flowers: place des Carmes (Sat morning). Food: in the

covered halls on place Pie (Tues–Fri until 1.30pm; Sat & Sun until 2pm).

Police Municipale 13 quai St-Lazare ☎ 08 00 00 84 00 or 04 90 85 13 13.

Post office Cours Président-Kennedy (Mon & Wed–Fri 8.30am–6pm, Tues 8.30am–8pm, Sat 9am–4pm).

Swimming pool Piscine Jean Clement, Chemin de la Martelle ☎ 04 90 31 38 73.

Villeneuve-lès-Avignon

Pretty and prosperous, though little more than a village at its core, **VILLENEUVE-LÈS-AVIGNON** (also spelled Villeneuve-lez-Avignon) rises up a rocky escarpment above the west bank of the Rhône, looking down across the river upon its older and larger neighbour from behind far more convincing fortifications. Despite ongoing rivalry, Villeneuve has effectively been a suburb of Avignon for most of its history, holding

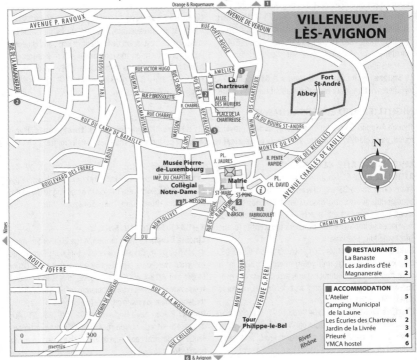

palatial residences constructed by the cardinals and a great monastery founded by Pope Innocent VI.

To this day, Villeneuve is technically a part of Languedoc and not Provence. It might well be better known were it further from Avignon, whose monuments it can almost match for colossal scale. It is, however, a very different – and really rather sleepy – kind of place, where daily activity centres around the lovely little place Jean-Jaurès. As such, it retains a repose and a sense of timelessness that bustling Avignon inevitably lacks. In summer it provides venues for the Avignon Festival as well as alternatives for accommodation overspill, but whatever time of year you visit it's certainly worth a day spent exploring.

Market days in Villeneuve's Place Charles-David are Thursday, for food, and Saturday for bric-a-brac.

Fort St-Andre

Fort St-Andre Daily: April to mid-May & last 2 weeks of Sept 10am–1pm & 2–5.30pm; mid-May to mid-Sept 10am–1pm & 2–6pm; Oct–March 10am–1pm & 2–5pm • €5.50, €4.50 with Avignon Passion passport (see p.115) • ☎ 04 90 25 45 35, Ⓦ fort-saint-andre. monuments-nationaux.fr **Abbey** Tues–Sun: April–Sept 10am–12.30pm & 2–6pm; Oct–March 10am–12.30pm & 2–5pm • €5/€4 with passport ☎ 06 71 42 16 90, Ⓦ abbaye-saint-andre.com

Originally, Villeneuve-lès-Avignon was enclosed within the walls of its mighty castle, the enormous **Fort St-André**, on a rise to the east. Then, in 1770, the Rhône shifted its course roughly 1km to the south, and the fort lost its strategic importance. Now basically a hollow shell, it can be reached by climbing either the montée du Fort from place Jean-Jaurès, or the "rapid slope" of rue Pente Rapide, a cobbled street of tiny houses that leads off rue des Recollets on the north side of place Charles-David.

Once inside the bulbous, double-towered gateway that penetrates the fort's vast white walls, you find yourself on what used to be the narrow main street of the town. Buying a ticket for the fort itself allows you to continue up the street, passing assorted tumbledown ruins, and then walk along the parapets, where a cliff-face terrace offers tremendous views of both modern Villeneuve and Avignon across the river. You can also pay separately to visit its former **abbey**, now privately owned, which offers more magnificent views, as well as gardens of olive trees, ruined chapels, lily ponds and dovecotes.

La Chartreuse du Val du Bénédiction

58 rue de la République • April–June daily 9.30am–6.30pm; July & Sept daily 9am–6.30pm; Aug daily 9am–7.30pm; Oct–March Mon–Fri 9.30am–5pm, Sat & Sun 10am–5pm • €7.70, €6.10 with Avignon Passion pass (see p.115) • ☎ 04 90 15 24 24, Ⓦ chartreuse.org

La Chartreuse du Val du Bénédiction, one of the largest Carthusian monasteries in France, spreads below the Fort St-André. Founded by the sixth of the Avignon popes, Innocent VI, it was sold off after the Revolution. Gradually restored last century, the buildings are totally unembellished, and except for the Giovanetti frescoes in the chapel beside the refectory, all the artworks have been dispersed. Visitors are free to wander around unguided, through the three cloisters, the church, chapels, cells and communal spaces, which have little to see but plenty of atmosphere to absorb. It's one of the best venues of the Festival of Avignon (see p.118).

Musée Pierre-de-Luxembourg

3 rue de la République • Tues–Sun: Feb, March & Oct–Dec 10am–noon & 2–5pm; April–Sept 10am–12.30pm & 2–6.30pm; closed Jan • €3.20, €2.20 with Avignon Passion passport (see p.115) • ☎ 04 90 27 49 66

The **Musée Pierre-de-Luxembourg**, just off the central place Jean-Jaurès, holds treasures from the fourteenth-century **Église Collègiale Notre-Dame** nearby, including a rare fourteenth-century smiling Madonna and Child carved from a single tusk of ivory. The collection also features several paintings taken from the Chartreuse, including the stunning *Coronation of the Virgin*, painted in 1453 by Enguerrand Quarton.

Tour Philippe-le-Bel

Tues–Sun: Feb, March, & Oct 2–5pm; April–Sept 10am–12.30pm & 2.30–6.30pm; closed Nov–Jan • €2.20, €1.70 with Avignon Passion passport (see p.115) • ☏ 04 32 70 08 57

The stout **Tour Philippe-le-Bel**, south of the centre alongside the main road from Avignon, was built to guard the western end of Avignon's Pont St-Bénézet. The rather tricky climb to the top is rewarded with one last overview of Villeneuve and Avignon.

ARRIVAL AND INFORMATION
VILLENEUVE-LÈS-AVIGNON

By bus The #11 bus (every 30min) takes ten minutes to ply between Villeneuve's unprepossessing place Charles-David and the cours Président-Kennedy in Avignon; it also stops halfway along at Avignon's Porte de l'Oulle.

Tourist office Place Charles-David (April–June, Sept &

Oct Mon–Sat 9am–12.30pm & 2–6pm; July Mon–Fri 10am–7pm, Sat & Sun 10am–1pm & 2.30–7pm; Aug daily 9am–12.30pm & 2–6pm; Nov–March Mon–Sat 9.30am–12.30pm & 2–5pm; ☏ 04 90 25 61 33, ⓦ tourisme-villeneuvelezavignon.fr),

ACCOMMODATION

In terms of **accommodation**, Villeneuve is more a boutique destination than a mere alternative to Avignon, with a handful of charming, good-value **hotels** and **B&Bs**. Rates rise especially during July's festival.

★ **L'Atelier** 5 rue de la Foire ☏ 04 90 25 01 84, ⓦ hoteldelatelier.com. Very tasteful rooms in a charming sixteenth-century house with a central stone staircase bathed in light, plus huge open fireplaces and a delightful well-shaded courtyard garden with terraces. Closed Jan. **€89**

Les Écuries des Chartreux 66 rue de la République ☏ 04 90 25 79 93, ⓦ ecuries-des-chartreux.com. Three self-catering units in a light and airy rustic house, formerly part of the stables for the monastery, with exposed stone walls and antique furniture; all have kitchenettes, one sleeps four. **€75**

Jardin de la Livrée 4bis rue Camp de Bataille ☏ 04 90 26 05 05, ⓦ www.la-livree.fr. Clean, comfortable B&B rooms in an old house in the centre of the village, with a swimming pool, and an appealing Mediterranean restaurant (closed Mon), which serves an €18 lunch *menu* and a €26 dinner *menu*. The one drawback is the noise of passing trains. **€92**

Prieuré 7 place du Chapitre ☏ 04 90 15 90 15, ⓦ leprieure.com. If you fancy being surrounded by tapestries, finely carved doors, old oak ceilings and other

baronial trappings, this old priory surrounded by a peaceful flower-filled garden is indisputably the first choice. The restaurant serves Provençal cuisine with a gourmet twist. Closed Jan to mid-Feb & Nov. **€242**

YMCA hostel 7bis chemin de la Justice ☏ 04 90 25 46 20, ⓦ ymca-avignon.com. Beautifully situated hostel, overlooking the river by Pont du Royaume (the extension of Pont Daladier). Balconied rooms for one to four people, with and without en-suite facilities, and available both as dorms and as private rooms, plus an open-air swimming pool. Stop "Pont d'Avignon" on buses heading from Avignon to Villeneuve, "Gabriel Péri" in the other direction. Dorms **€23**, doubles **€32**

CAMPING

Camping Municipal de la Laune Chemin St-Honoré ☏ 04 90 25 76 06, ⓦ camping-villeneuvelezavignon .com. A spacious, well-shaded three-star site off the D980, north of both town and fort near the sports stadium and municipal swimming pool. Closed mid-Oct to March. **€15.75**

EATING AND DRINKING

Most of Villeneuve's **restaurants** are special-treat places for day-trippers from Avignon, though there are a handful of pleasant little cafés on place Jean-Jaurès where you can enjoy a simple snack with your drink.

La Banaste 28 rue de la République ☏ 04 90 25 64 20. Bountiful Provençal and Languedocien *terroir* meals, with *menus* from €24 (two courses) or €30 (three). It's more pleasant indoors than on the cramped roadside terrace. July to mid-Aug daily noon–2pm & 7–9.30pm; mid-Aug to June daily except Thurs noon–2pm.

★ **Les Jardins d'Été de la Chartreuse** Cloître St-Jean, La Chartreuse ☏ 04 90 15 24 23, ⓦ chartreuse.org. A truly memorable experience; in summer only, you can thread your way through the labyrinthine old monastery to find this open-air restaurant in a secluded courtyard. Some tables have lovely sunset views. Friendly service and *menus* of substantial Provençal cuisine from €19 for lunch, €28 for dinner, plus early-evening drinks and snacks. June–Aug daily noon–2.30pm & 6–9.30pm.

Magnaneraie 37 rue du Camp de Bataille ☎04 90 25 11 11, ⓦhostellerie-la-magnaneraie.com. Excellent, upmarket restaurant 5min walk west of the centre, serving delicacies such as foie gras marinated in peach wine. There's an evening *menu* at €35; going à la carte will cost more. May to mid-Oct Mon–Fri & Sun noon–1.30pm & 7.30–9.30pm, Sat noon–1.30pm; mid-Oct to April Mon, Tues, Thurs & Fri noon–1.30pm & 7.30–9.30pm, Sat & Sun noon–1.30pm.

Châteauneuf-du-Pape

The large village of **CHÂTEAUNEUF-DU-PAPE**, halfway along the back road between Avignon and Orange, takes its name from the summer palace of the Avignon popes. However, its fame derives neither from the views down the Rhône valley from its ruined fourteenth-century château, nor from its photogenic medieval streets. Instead, of course, it's the local **vineyards** that produce the magic, with the grapes warmed at night by large pebbles that cover the ground and soak up the sun's heat by day. Their rich ruby-red wine ranks among the most renowned in France, though the lesser-known white, too, is exquisite.

As in so many Provençal villages, commercial activity in Châteauneuf is largely confined to the main road that loops around the base of its small central hill. Walk up from the busy little **place du Portail**, and as soon as you step off the pedestrian route towards the castle, you're in a delightful tangle of sleepy, verdant alleyways. As for the **château** itself, which can also be reached by car, a couple of deceptively intact walls still crown the top of the hill, but they simply define a hollow shell, which is freely accessible at all times.

Musée du Vin Brotte

Bd Pierre-de-Luxembourg • Daily: May to mid-Oct 9am–1pm & 2–7pm; mid-Oct to April 9am–noon & 2–6pm • ☎04 90 83 70 07 • Free

Despite being run by one specific wine-producing firm to promote its own products, the best place to learn about the local wines in Châteauneuf-du-Pape is the **Musée du Vin Brotte**, southwest of the centre on the road towards Avignon. As well as providing a good historical overview of the wine industry, covering the geology of the region and the nineteenth-century phylloxera epidemic that devastated all French wines, it illustrates traditional tools and techniques, offers free tasting, and, of course, sells Brotte wines.

INFORMATION	CHÂTEAUNEUF-DU-PAPE

Tourist office Place du Portail (June–Sept Mon–Sat 9.30am–6pm; Oct–May Mon, Tues & Thurs–Sat 9.30am–12.30pm & 2–6pm; ☎04 90 83 71 08, ⓦccpro .fr/tourisme).

SAMPLING THE WINES OF CHÂTEAUNEUF-DU-PAPE

During the first full weekend of August, the **Fête de la Véraison** celebrates the ripening of the grapes, with free *dégustation* (tasting) stalls throughout the village, as well as parades, dances, equestrian contests, folklore floats and so forth. As well as wine, a good deal of grape liqueur (*marc*) is imbibed.

At other times, free **tastings** are available all over the village. The tourist office maintains up-to-date listings of which local estates currently offer tastings, which offer English-language tours, and so on. No single outlet sells all the Châteauneuf-du-Pape wines; the best selection under one roof is at **La Maison des Vins**, 8 rue du Maréchal Foch (daily: mid-June to mid-Sept 10am–7pm; mid-Sept to mid-June 10.30am–noon & 2–6.30pm; ☎04 90 83 70 69, ⓦwww .vinadea.com).

ACCOMMODATION AND EATING

Garbure 3 rue Joseph-Ducos ☎ 04 90 83 75 08, ⓦ la-garbure.com. Cosy, very central village hotel, with eight cheerful rooms and an excellent restaurant, with dinner *menus* from €28 and terrace seating across the street. Garage parking for €12. Restaurant closed Sun & Mon, hotel closed 3 weeks in Nov. €76

Mère Germaine Av Cdt-Lemaître ☎ 04 90 22 78 34, ⓦ lameregermaine.fr. Lively and very pleasant small hotel-restaurant, in the heart of the village, with seven welcoming rooms. Well-crafted Provençal cuisine on *menus* from €23 for lunch, €37 for dinner; lunch daily, dinner Tues–Sat only. €75

Sommellerie 2268 route de Roquemaure ☎ 04 90 83 50 00, ⓦ la-sommellerie.fr. This charming, renovated country house, 3km north of the village, has fourteen modern pastel-painted rooms, two larger suites, a pool and a restaurant (daily in summer; closed Sat lunch, Sun dinner & all Mon Oct–March) producing superb dishes such as grilled lamb with garlic, rosemary and tapenade, on *menus* starting at €31 for lunch, €48 for dinner. Closed Jan. €112

Le Verger des Papes 4 montée du Château ☎ 04 90 83 50 40, ⓦ vergerdespapes.com. This utterly delightful restaurant, well away from the traffic near the château at the top of the hill, serves traditional food on a peaceful panoramic terrace with *menus* at €19 for lunch, €30 for dinner. July & Aug Mon–Sat noon–2pm & 7.30–9.30pm, Sun noon–2pm; Sept–June Tues–Sat noon–2pm & 7.30–9.30pm, Sun noon–2pm.

Orange

Thanks to its spectacular **Roman theatre**, the small town of **ORANGE**, well west of the Rhône 20km north of Avignon, is famous out of all proportion to its size. Now home to fewer than thirty thousand citizens, it was founded as Aurisio in 35 BC; only much later did its name become conflated with the fruit and colour. In the eighth-century, Charlemagne made it the seat of the counts of Orange, a title that passed to the Dutch crown in the sixteenth century. The family's best-known member was Prince William, who ascended the English throne with his consort Mary in the 1688 "Glorious Revolution", and whose supporters in Ireland established the Protestant Orange Order.

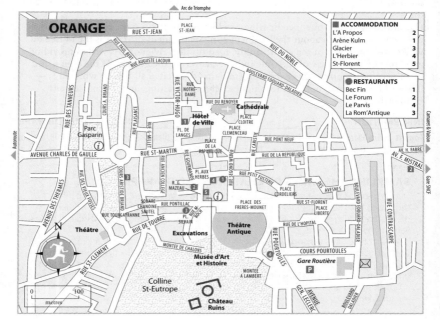

The Roman theatre, now known as the Théâtre Antique, is the city's one must-see attraction, at its best and busiest during the Chorégies **opera festival** in July (see box below). Otherwise, with its medieval street plan, fountained squares, houses with ancient porticoes and courtyards, and Thursday-morning market, Orange is an attractive enough place to stroll around, but the only reason to stay more than a day or two is to use it as a quiet base for exploring the region.

Théâtre Antique

Daily: March & Oct 9.30am–5.30pm; April, May & Sept 9am–6pm; June–Aug 9am–7pm; Nov–Feb 9.30am–4.30pm • €8.50 including Musée d'Art et Histoire; €7.50 for last hour of each day • ☎ 04 90 50 17 60, ⓦ theatre-antique.com

The enormous wall of the **Théâtre Antique**, at the southern end of Orange's medieval centre, with the hill of St-Eutrope rising behind, dominates the entire town. Said to be the world's best-preserved Roman theatre, it's the only one with its stage wall still standing. Around 55 AD, audiences of ten thousand could spend their days off watching farce, clownish improvisations, song and dance and, perhaps, for the sake of a visiting dignitary, a bit of Greek tragedy in Latin. Having survived periods as a fortification, slum and prison before its careful reconstruction in the nineteenth century, the Théâtre still hosts musical performances in summer (see box below), and is also open to visitors as an archeological site.

Spreading a colossal 36m high by 103m wide, the Théâtre's outer face resembles a monstrous prison wall, despite the ground-level archways leading into the backstage areas. Inside, an excellent audioguide paints an evocative picture of its history and architecture. The enormous **stage**, originally sheltered by a mighty awning, could accommodate vast numbers of performers, while the acoustics allowed a full audience to hear every word. Though missing most of its original decoration, the inner side of the wall above the stage is extremely impressive. Below columned niches, now empty of their statues, a larger-than-life statue of Augustus, raising his arm in imperious fashion, looks down centre stage. Seating was allocated strictly by rank; an inscription "EQ Gradus III" (third row for knights) remains visible near the orchestra pit. Arches along the uppermost internal passageway now hold audiovisual displays, including footage of rock festivals held here during the 1970s.

Spectators who grew bored during the day-long performances could slip out of the west door to a semicircular complex cut into the rock. Some archeologists suggest this held baths, a stage for combats and a gymnasium equipped with three 180-metre running tracks; others say it was the forum, or even a circus.

The best **viewpoint** over the entire theatre, on St-Eutrope hill, can be accessed without paying from both east and west. As you look down towards the stage, the ruins at your feet are those of the short-lived seventeenth-century castle of the princes of Orange. Louis XIV had it destroyed in 1673, and the principality of Orange was officially annexed to France forty years later.

Musée d'Art et Histoire

Rue Madeleine Roch • Daily: March & Oct 9.45am–12.30pm & 1.30–5.30pm; April, May & Sept 9.15am–6pm; June–Aug 9.15am–7pm; Nov–Feb 9.45am–12.30pm & 1.30–4.30pm • €5.50, or €8.50 with Théâtre • ☎ 04 90 50 17 60, ⓦ theatre-antique.com

---

THE CHORÉGIES

When Orange's **choral festival**, known as the **Chorégies** (☎ 04 90 34 24 24, ⓦ www .choregies.asso.fr), began in 1879, it marked the first performance at the Théâtre Antique in 350 years. The festival these days consists of one or two performances per week all through July, with a varied programme of opera, oratorios and orchestral concerts. Tickets cost from €23 to €263, and go on sale in October of the preceding year. Check the Théâtre's own website (ⓦ theatre-antique.com) for details of other events and exhibitions throughout the year.

Orange's **Musée d'Art et Histoire**, across from the Théâtre, covers local history from the Romans onwards, and also hosts temporary exhibitions. Artefacts taken from the Théâtre complex include the largest known Roman land-survey maps, carved on marble (though these were badly damaged when the museum itself collapsed in 1962), along with a couple of sphinxes and a mosaic floor. The two upper levels, dedicated to the Gasparin family who promoted the safeguarding of Roman Orange, are filled with family portraits, mementoes and a reconstructed *salon*.

Arc de Triomphe

Av de l'Arc de Triomphe • 24hr access

The second major Roman monument in Orange, the impressive, triple-bayed **Arc de Triomphe**, occupies a lozenge-shaped traffic island 400m north from the city centre. Built around 20 BC, its intricate friezes and reliefs celebrate the victories of the Roman Second Legion against the Gauls, who are depicted naked and chained.

ARRIVAL AND INFORMATION   ORANGE

By train The *gare SNCF* is on av Frédéric-Mistral, 800m east of the centre.

Destinations Avignon (17 daily; 15min); Paris (2 daily; 2hr 30min).

By bus The *gare routière* is on bd Edouard-Daladier, 250m east of the theatre.

Destinations Carpentras (3 daily; 40–45min); Châteauneuf-du-Pape (3 daily; 25min); Séguret (10 daily; 40min); Sérignan (7 daily; 15min); Vaison (10 daily; 40–50min).

By car There's very limited parking in the city centre; for short stays (of less than 2hr 16min, to be precise), use the metered parking along cours Aristide Briand; for overnight stays use the underground car park east of the theatre near the bus station, entered from bd Edouard-Daladier.

Tourist office 5 cours Aristide Briand (April–June & Sept Mon–Sat 9am–6.30pm, Sun 10am–1pm & 2–6.30pm; July & Aug Mon–Sat 9am–7.30pm, Sun 10am–1pm & 2–7pm; Oct–March Mon–Sat 10am–1pm & 2–5pm; ☎ 04 90 34 70 88, ⊛ otorange.fr).

ACCOMMODATION

L'A Propos 15 av Frédéric-Mistral ☎ 04 90 34 54 91, ⊛ lapropos.com. Luxury B&B, set in spacious gardens on the edge of the centre towards the train station, with a pool, spa facilities and tapas bar. As well as four lavish modern suites (€240), there's one slightly smaller room with its own terrace. **€160**

Arène Kulm 8 place de Langes ☎ 04 90 11 40 40, ⊛ hotel-arene.fr. Very presentable hotel, with spacious rooms, a pool and an Italian restaurant, on a quiet, pedestrianized (though not especially attractive) square. The cheapest rooms are in a separate annex. **€70**

Glacier 46 cours Aristide Briand ☎ 04 90 34 02 01, ⊛ le-glacier.com. Comfortable, cosy Provençal-style rooms in yellows and blues with pretty quilts and floral curtains. All en-suite and a/c, they vary widely in size and

amenities; the two smallest (€50) are tiny. Good breakfasts are available in the little pavement café downstairs. Nov–Feb closed Fri–Sun. **€60**

L'Herbier 8 place aux Herbes ☎ 04 90 34 09 23, ⊛ lherbierdorange.com. A good budget option, set in a seventeenth-century house overlooking a pretty square very near the Théâtre Antique. Rooms are simple and clean; all have at least showers, and there are some good-value family rooms. Note that the parking they offer is a public car park 500m away. **€59**

St-Florent 4 rue du Mazeau ☎ 04 90 34 18 53, ⊛ hotel-orange-saintflorent.com. Very central, inexpensive hotel, with appealingly kitsch decor and a wide range of rooms; some have four-poster beds, all are en-suite, and there are some extremely cheap singles. **€57**

EATING AND DRINKING

Bec Fin rue Segond Weber ☎ 04 90 34 05 10. Large restaurant, with tables both indoors and sprawled along a narrow alley with slender views of the Théâtre Antique. Hearty salads and tasty pizzas for around €12, plus a good €28 dinner *menu*, featuring gazpacho, slow-cooked bream and a delicious dessert. Mon–Sat noon–2pm & 7.30–10pm.

Le Forum 3 rue du Mazeau ☎ 04 90 34 01 09. Small, intimate restaurant near the Théâtre. *Menus* (from €29)

revolve around seasonal ingredients; in January, truffles feature heavily, while in May, it's asparagus. Often booked up, so reserve ahead. Mon & Tues 7.30–9.30pm, Thurs–Sun noon–2pm & 7.30–9.30pm.

Le Parvis 55 cours Pourtoules ☎ 04 90 34 82 00. The best Provençal food in Orange, though the service can be very slow. Straight from the market, ingredients are whipped up into tempting, good-value dishes such as pikeperch with asparagus *millefeuille*. Lunch *menus* from €14.50, dinner from €28 for three courses. Tues–Sat noon–1.30pm & 7.30–9.15pm; closed last 3 weeks in Nov & last 3 weeks in Jan.

La Rom'Antique 5 place Silvain, rue Madeleine Roch ☎04 90 51 67 06, ⊕la-romantique.com. This stylish modern restaurant is a slightly incongruous presence immediately east of the Roman theatre (hence the punning name), but the food is good, with a €22 *menu* that features a delicious chickpea gazpacho. A few outdoor tables complement the cool, crisp a/c indoor dining room. June–Sept Tues–Fri & Sun noon–2pm & 7.30–9.30pm, Sat 7.30–9.30pm; Oct–May Tues–Fri noon–2pm & 7.30–9.30pm, Sat 7.30–9.30pm, Sun noon–2pm.

Sérignan-du-Comtat

The pretty little village of **SÉRIGNAN-DU-COMTAT**, 8km northeast of Orange, is noteworthy only as the former home of a remarkable pioneering entomologist, **Jean Henri Fabre** (1823–1915). A statue of Fabre stands beside the red-shuttered *mairie*, while the home where he spent the last 36 years of his life, known as the **Harmas**, is open to visitors. A newer attraction alongside, the **Naturoptère**, also honours his work.

Harmas Jean Henri Fabre

Route d'Orange · April–June & Sept Mon, Tues, Thurs & Fri 10am–12.30pm & 2.30–6pm, Sat & Sun 2.30–6pm; July & Aug Mon–Fri 10am–12.30pm & 3.30–7pm, Sat & Sun 3.30–7pm; Oct Mon, Tues, Thurs & Fri 10am–12.30pm & 2–5pm, Sat & Sun 2–5pm · €5, or €8 with Naturoptère, or €11.50 with Théâtre Antique in Orange · ☎04 90 30 57 62, ⊕ museum-paca.org

A remarkable self-taught scientist, Jean Henri Fabre is famous primarily for his insect studies, but he also composed poetry, wrote songs and painted his specimens with artistic brilliance. In his forties, with seven children to support, he was forced to resign from his teaching post at Avignon because parents and priests considered his lectures on the fertilization of flowering plants licentious, if not downright pornographic. His friend John Stuart Mill eventually bailed him out with a loan, allowing him to settle in Orange, and he subsequently moved on to Sérignan. His house, which he named the **Harmas** – Latin for fallow land – is on the western edge of the village.

Inside, you can look round Fabre's study, with its various specimens of insects and other invertebrates and his complete classification of the herbs of France and Corsica. The room gives a strong sense of a person in love with the world he researched, an impression echoed in Fabre's extraordinary **watercolours** of the fungi of the Vaucluse, displayed on video screens on the ground floor. The stunning colours and almost hallucinogenic detail make these pictures seem more like holograms. After visiting the house you're free to wander round the **garden**, where over a thousand species grow in wild disorder, exactly as the scientist wanted it.

Naturoptère

Chemin du Grés · July & Aug Mon, Tues, Thurs & Fri 9am–12.30pm & 1.30–6pm, Wed, Sat & Sun 1.30–6pm; Sept–June Mon, Tues, Thurs & Fri 9am–12.30pm & 1.30–5pm, Wed, Sat & Sun 1.30–6pm · €5, or €8 with Harmas · ☎04 90 30 33 20, ⊕ naturoptere.fr

Constructed according to the latest eco-conscious specifications, and topped by a roof of soil and grass, the **Naturoptère** stands across a small lane from the Harmas. It hosts changing exhibitions each year, which honour the legacy of Jean Henri Fabre by examining such themes as the role of insects, or carnivorous plants, and are generally aimed at school students.

The Enclave des Papes

The **Enclave des Papes**, north of Orange and centred on the town of **Valréas**, is not part of the Drôme *département* that surrounds it, but part of Vaucluse. That anomaly dates back to 1317 when the land was bought by Pope Jean XXII as part of his policy of expanding the papal states around his Holy See at Avignon. When the Vaucluse *département* was drawn up, the enclave was allowed to keep its old links and hence remains part of Provence. Both **Grignan**, immediately outside the western edge of the enclave, and Valréas have luxurious **châteaux** and **vineyards**.

Valréas

VALRÉAS, at the heart of the Enclave des Papes, lies 35km northeast of Orange. The former Château de Simiane, a mainly eighteenth-century mansion whose arcades, windows and balustrades would look more at home in Paris, now serves as the **Hôtel de Ville**. The **market** is held on Wednesday on place Cardinal-Maury; local truffles figure prominently between November and March. The main local **festivals** are the **Nuit de Petit St-Jean** on June 23 and 24, when there's a night-time procession and show, and the **Fête des Vins de l'Enclave** on the first Sunday in August.

At other times, most visitors are here to buy **wine**. As well as the Côtes du Rhône *appellation*, there's also Valréas Villages and Visan Villages, distinctive enclave wines, with flavours of violet, red fruits and pepper; such wines supposedly persuaded Pope Jean XXII to buy this area in the first place. The **Cave Coopérative** is at the Caveau St-Jean, avenue de l'Enclave des Papes (☎04 90 35 00 66, ⊛cavelagaillarde.com).

Musée du Cartonnage et de l'Imprimerie

3 av Maréchal Foch • April–Oct Mon & Wed–Sat 10am–noon & 3–6pm; Sun 3–6pm; Nov–March Mon & Wed–Sat 10am–noon & 2–5pm, Sun 2–5pm • €3.50 • ☎04 90 35 58 75

The surprisingly intriguing **Musée du Cartonnage et de l'Imprimerie**, in a warehouse just outside town on the road west to Orange, honours Valréas' role as a centre for cardboard production. Displays, some of which change yearly, delve into every aspect of boxes and cartons, from manufacture to typography.

INFORMATION	VALRÉAS

Tourist office Av Maréchal Leclerc (March–June, Sept & Oct Mon–Sat 9.15am–12.15pm & 2–6pm; July & Aug Mon–Sat 9am–12.30pm & 2.30–6.30pm, Sun 9am–12.30pm; Nov–Feb Mon–Fri 9.15am–12.15pm & 2–5pm, Sat 9.15am–12.15pm; ☎04 90 35 04 71, ⊛ot-valreas.fr).

ACCOMMODATION AND EATING

Café de la Paix 26 rue de l'Hôtel de Ville ☎04 90 46 88 25. This beautiful café, opposite the *Grand Hôtel*, makes a great spot to sample the local wines, and serves *menus* at €19 and €25. Mon–Sat 10am–4pm & 7–11pm.

Le Mas des Sorcières Route d'Orange ☎04 90 35 69 61, ⊛gite-de-provence.com. Five delightful B&B rooms, set in a tastefully restored fourteenth-century farmhouse with pool, 3km southwest of the centre. The friendly and helpful owners serve an evening meal for €26. Rates include breakfast, and reduce for stays of two nights or more. **€95**

Château de Grignan

Grignan, 10km west of Valréas • April–June, Sept & Oct daily 10am–12.30pm & 2–6pm; July & Aug daily 10am–6pm; Nov–March Mon & Wed–Sun 10am–12.30pm & 2–6pm • €4.50 • ☎04 75 91 83 55, ⊛chateaux.ladrome.fr

The enormous **Château de Grignan**, 10km west of Valréas, dominates the little town of Grignan below, rising above the heavy towers and walls of St-Saveur's church and the medieval houses below the southern facade. Though eleventh-century in origin, the château was transformed in the sixteenth century into a Renaissance palace, with tiers of huge windows facing the south and statues lining the roof; the older parts lie to the north. It hosts a **jazz festival** in November.

The château's most famous resident, the writer **Madame de Sévigné**, came here for long periods to visit her daughter, the countess of Grignan. You can see the comforts and craftsmanship of the contemporary furnishings, plus eighteenth-century additions, in the tour of the *salons*, galleries and grand stairways, Mme de Sévigné's bedroom and the count's apartments.

Vaison-la-Romaine

The charming old town of **VAISON-LA-ROMAINE**, 27km northeast of Orange, is divided into two very distinct halves, either side of the deep gorge cut by the River Ouvèze and connected by a single-arched Roman bridge. Throughout its history, the town centre has shifted from one side to the other, depending on whether its inhabitants needed the defensive position offered by the steep, forbidding hill south of the river. Now known as the **Haute Ville**, and topped by a ruined twelfth-century castle, this was the site of the original Celtic settlement. The **Romans**, however, built their homes on the flatter land north of the river, and that's where all the activity of the modern town is centred. As a result, the medieval Haute Ville remains a self-contained and largely unspoiled village; while its lanes attract throngs of day-trippers, it holds just a handful of restaurants and hotels, and no shops.

Roman ruins

Av Général-de-Gaulle • Daily: Feb, Nov & Dec 10am–noon & 2–5pm; March & Oct 10am–12.30pm & 2–5.30pm; April & May 9.30am–6pm; June–Sept 9.30am–6.30pm; closed Jan • €8 with cathedral cloisters

Vaison's two excavated Roman residential districts, known as the **Vestiges de Puymin** and the **Vestiges de la Villasse**, lie either side of the main road through the town centre. While you can peek through the railings for free, you'll get a much better sense of the style and luxury of the era if you pay for admission, which includes a brief but succinct audio tour as well as the excellent museum.

Vestiges de Puymin

The eastern portion of Vaison's Roman archeological district, the **Vestiges de Puymin**, stretches up a gentle hillside. The ground plans of several mansions and houses are discernible in the foreground, along with a colonnade known as the *portique de Pompée*, while slightly higher up is the **museum**, which holds all sorts of detail and decoration unearthed from the ruins. Everyday artefacts include mirrors of silvered bronze, lead water pipes, weights and measures, taps shaped as griffins' feet and dolphin doorknobs, and there are also some impressive statues and stelae. A rather thrilling tunnel through the hillside leads to an ancient Roman **theatre**, which still seats seven thousand people during the July **dance festival** (ⓦvaison-danses.com).

Vestiges de la Villasse

Vaison's smaller, western Roman ruins, the **Vestiges de la Villasse**, reveal a clear picture of the layout of a comfortable, well-serviced town of the Roman ruling class. As well as a row of arcaded shops, they include patrician houses (some with mosaics still intact), a basilica and the baths.

Cathédrale Notre-Dame

Cours Talignan, west of Roman ruins • Daily: Feb, Nov & Dec 10–11.45am & 2–4.45pm; March & Oct 10am–12.15pm & 2–5.15pm; April & May 9.30am–5.45pm; June–Sept 9.30am–6.15pm; closed Jan • Cathedral free, cloisters €8 with Roman ruins

The apse of the former **Cathédrale Notre-Dame** is a confusing overlay of sixth-, tenth- and thirteenth-century construction, some of it using pieces quarried from the Roman ruins. Its **cloisters** are fairly typical of early medieval workmanship, pretty enough but not wildly exciting.

Haute Ville

From the south side of the **Pont Romain**, the sturdy ancient bridge across the River Ouvèze, a cobbled lane climbs upwards towards place du Poids and the fourteenth-century gateway to the medieval **Haute Ville**. More steep zigzags take you past the Gothic gate and overhanging portcullis of the belfry and into the heart of this sedately quiet, largely uncommercialized *quartier*. There are pretty fountains and flowers in all the squares, and right at the top, from the ruined twelfth- to sixteenth-century **castle**, you'll have a great view of Mont Ventoux. Every Tuesday in summer, Vaison's **market** spreads up into the Haute Ville.

ARRIVAL AND INFORMATION

VAISON-LA-ROMAINE

By bus The *gare routière* is on avenue des Choralies, 500m east of the centre.

Destinations Avignon (3 daily; 1hr 25min), Orange (10 daily; 40–50min).

By car Parking is free throughout Vaison; if there's no room to park on the central place du Chanoine-Sautel, there should be spaces on quai Pasteur down by the river.

Tourist office Place du Chanoine-Sautel, between the two Roman sites (mid-May to June Mon–Fri 9.30am–1pm & 2–5.45pm, Sat 9.30am–noon & 2–5.45pm, Sun 9.30am–noon; July & Aug Mon–Fri 9.30am–6.45pm, Sat & Sun 9.30am–12.30pm & 2–6.45pm; Sept to mid-May Mon–Sat 9.30am–noon & 2–5.45pm, Sun 9.30am–noon & 2–5.45pm; ☎04 90 36 02 11, ⍟vaison-la-romaine .com). The office has free wi-fi.

ACCOMMODATION

★ **Le Beffroi** Rue de l'Évêché ☎04 90 36 04 71, ⍟le-beffroi.com. Beautiful, luxurious rooms in a sixteenth-century residence in a lovely setting in the Haute Ville, with a pool, and a great restaurant where the terrace enjoys unsurpassable views over the valley. Hotel closed Feb–March; restaurant closed Tues, and all Nov–March. **€115**

Burrhus 1 place Montfort ☎04 90 36 00 11, ⍟burrhus .com. Large, modern if somewhat characterless bedrooms in the heart of town, with tiled floors and very comfortable beds. It can be noisy at weekends, but the sunny breakfast balcony is a real plus. **€65**

★ **L'Évêche** 14 rue de l'Évêché ☎04 90 36 13 46, ⍟eveche.free.fr. Lovely B&B in the Haute Ville, with comfortable modern rooms and a homely atmosphere. Enjoy coffee and croissants on the little terrace at the back. **€84**

La Fête en Provence Place du Vieux Marché ☎04 90 36 36 43, ⍟hotellafete-provence.com. Gorgeous,

comfortable rooms and apartments, surrounding a pool and flower-decked patio, in the Haute Ville. **€75**

Les Tilleuls d'Élisée 1 av Jules-Mazen, chemin du Bon-Ange ☎04 90 35 63 04, ⍟vaisonchambres.info. Five pretty, peaceful and great-value B&B rooms in a family home, a short walk west of the Vestiges de la Villasse; breakfast in the garden is a delight in the summer. **€72**

CAMPING

Camping du Théâtre Romain Chemin du Brusquet, off av des Choralies, quartier des Arts 04 90 28 78 66, ⍟camping-theatre.com. Small, four-star campsite, 500m northeast of the centre and 150m from the Roman theatre, with good facilities and an emphasis on peaceful family fun. Reserve well ahead in summer. Closed early Nov to mid-March. **€22.50**

EATING AND DRINKING

Vaison has a large number of good **restaurants**, on both sides of the river. For a more local feel, stick to the modern town, particularly around place de Montfort and cours Taulignan, but the places in the Haute Ville – including *Le Beffroi* on Rue de l Évêché (see above) – cannot be beaten for their lovely views. The **cafés** on place Montfort are the best place to head for drinks.

L'Auberge de la Bartavelle 12 place Sus-Auze ☎04 90 36 02 16. A lively place in an otherwise drab square in the modern town, immediately south of place Montfort, with decent and affordable specialities from southwest France – rabbit ravioli, *confit de canard* and the like – on *menus* costing from €16 lunch, €22 at dinner. Fun black-and-white photos honour the author Marcel Pagnol. Tues–Thurs, Sat & Sun noon–1.30pm & 7.30–9.30pm, Fri 7.30–9.30pm; closed Jan.

Le Brin d'Olivier 4 rue de Ventoux ☎04 90 28 74 79. Welcoming Provençal restaurant, serving lunch *menus* from €18 and dinner from €29 that's down towards the river, though its pretty courtyard has no views. Mon, Tues, Thurs, Fri & Sun noon–1.30pm & 7.30–9.30pm, Wed & Sat 7.30–9.30pm; closed Wed Oct–June.

La Lyriste 45 cours Taulignan ☎04 90 36 04 67. Of several restaurants spreading across the broad pavements of this quiet boulevard, just north of place

Montfort, the *Lyriste* stands out for its changing, high-quality *menus*, based around themes like cheese, exotic fruits or scallops. The simple €19 *menu découverte* is great value. Tues & Thurs–Sun noon–1.30pm & 7.30–9.30pm, Wed 7.30–9.30pm.

The Dentelles

Running northeast to southwest between Vaison and Carpentras, the jagged hilly backdrop of the **DENTELLES DE MONTMIRAIL** is best appreciated from the contrasting landscape of level fields, orchards and vineyards lying to their south and west. Although the connection with "teeth" (*dents*) might seem appropriate, the range is in fact named after lace (*dentelles*), as its pinnacles slant and converge like the contorted pins on a lace-making board. To geologists, the Dentelles are Jurassic limestone folds, forced upright and then eroded by the wind and rain.

On the western and southern slopes lie the **wine-producing villages** of **Gigondas**, **Beaumes-de-Venise**, **Séguret**, **Vacqueyras** and, across the River Ouzère, **Rasteau**. The Dentelles are also good for long **walks**, happening upon mysterious ruins or photogenic panoramas of Mont Ventoux and the Rhône Valley, and for **rock climbing**; local tourist offices can provide full information on both. The Col de Cayron pinnacle is prized by serious climbers, while the Dent du Turc needs only decent shoes and a head for heights to give a thrill.

Musée du Vigneron

10km west of Vaison on the Rte de Roaix, Rasteau • Mon & Wed–Sat: April–June & Sept 2–6pm; July & Aug 11am–6pm; • €2 • ☎ 04 90 83 71 79, Ⓦ beaurenard.fr

The **Musée du Vigneron**, on the D975 just east of the tiny, ivy-covered village of **RASTEAU**, offers a good introduction to the art and science of winemaking. For the serious wine enthusiast, the collection of old bottles, nineteenth-century agricultural implements, pickers' baskets and root injectors for fighting phylloxera is less interesting than the instructive displays on geology, soil, vine types, parasites and wine growing throughout the world. Visits end with a free tasting (no obligation to buy).

Séguret

The most immediately attractive of all the Dentelles villages, **SÉGURET**, is an alluring spot that blends into the side of a rocky cliff, with a ruined castle soaring high above. With its steep cobbled streets, vine-covered houses and medieval structures, including an old stone laundry and a belfry with a one-handed clock, it embodies the charms of Provence.

Gigondas

Known as "Jocunditas" (light-hearted joy) in Roman times, the village of **GIGONDAS** sits at the base of a hill. The **église Ste-Catherine** higher up offers superb views over limestone pinnacles emerging from the vineyards below. A separate eminence in the upper reaches of the village holds the vestiges of the old fortifications and château.

Gigondas' wine has the highest reputation of all the Dentelles *appellations*; reputation of all the Dentelles appellations; almost always red, and quite strong, it has a back taste of spice or nuts and is best aged at least four or five years. Sampling the varieties could not be easier; the **Syndicat des Vins** runs a *caveau des vignerons* (daily 10am–noon & 2–6pm) in place de la Mairie where you can taste and ask advice about the produce from forty different *domaines*. Bottles cost the same here as at the vineyards.

Vacqueyras

Three kilometres south of Gigondas, the village of **VACQUEYRAS** is best known as the birthplace of a troubadour poet called **Raimbaud**, who wrote love poems to Beatrice in Provençal and died in the Crusades in 1207. Another Dentelles village with its own *appellation*, Vacqueyras is home to an annual **wine festival** (on July 13 & 14) and a wine-tasting competition on the first weekend of June.

Beaumes-de-Venise

The picturesque village of **BEAUMES-DE-VENISE**, on the southern flank of the Dentelles, is home to the region's most distinctive wine, a sweet muscat. Topped by a Romanesque bell tower, the village's twelfth-century church, **Notre-Dame-d'Aubune**, reflects the key local concern in the trailing vines and classical wine containers sculpted over the door.

Cave Balma Venitia

228 rte de Carpentras • Daily: May–Sept 8.30am–12.30pm & 2–7pm; Oct–April 8.30am–noon & 2–6pm • ☎ 04 90 12 41 00, 🌐 beaumes-de-venise.com

The best place to buy the sweet Beaumes-de-Venise muscat is the **Cave Balma Venitia**, set in a huge low building beside the D7, 1km west of the centre. Pale amber in colour, with a hint of roses and lemon, it can usually convince the driest palates of its virtue; if you remain resistant, the *cave* also sells red, rosé and white Côtes du Rhône Villages, and the light Côtes du Ventoux.

Le Barroux

To the east of the Dentelles, on the Vaison–Malaucène road, the largely untouristy **LE BARROUX** is a perfect *village perché*, with narrow, twisting streets leading up to its château at the top. Dating from the twelfth to the eighteenth century, the **château** (daily: June–Sept 10am–7pm; April–May & Oct 2–6pm; €4) was restored just before World War II, only to be set on fire by the Nazis in 1944 – the blaze burned for ten days – before being restored again from 1960 to 1990.

INFORMATION	THE DENTELLES

GIGONDAS
Tourist office Rue du Portail (April–June, Sept & Oct Mon–Sat 10am–12.30pm & 2.30–6pm; July & Aug Mon–Sat 10am–12.30pm & 2.30–6.30pm, Sun 10am–1pm; Nov–March Mon–Sat 10am–noon & 2–5pm; ☎ 04 90 65 85 46, 🌐 gigondas-dm.fr).

BEAUMES-DE-VENISE
Tourist office Maison des Dentelles, 11 place du Marché (Mon–Sat: June–Sept 9am–noon & 2.30–6.30pm; Oct–May 9am–noon & 2–6pm; ☎ 04 90 62 94 39, 🌐 ot-beaumesdevenise.com).

ACCOMMODATION AND EATING

SÉGURET
★ **Bastide Bleue** Rte de Sablet ☎ 04 90 46 83 43, 🌐 bastidebleue.com. This delightful rural villa, at the foot of the hill below Séguret, offers simple but attractive en-suite rooms, plus a pool. Its rustic dining room, closed Tues & Wed in low season, serves *menus* from €27 in the evening. Rates include breakfast. €85
La Table du Comtat ☎ 04 90 46 91 49. Pleasant hotel, perched near the top of the village and commanding fabulous views, with comfortable, peaceful rooms, and a small deck pool. Zestful Provençal food is served on a delightful shaded terrace, with dinner *menus* from €29. €99

GIGONDAS
Les Florets Rte des Dentelles ☎ 04 90 65 85 01, 🌐 hotel-lesflorets.com. Charming hotel, 2km north of Gigondas towards Séguret, with elegant and very comfortable rooms and an excellent restaurant (closed Wed) that serves *menus* from €25 lunch, €32 dinner. Closed Jan to mid-March. €110
Gîte d'Etape des Dentelles Le village ☎ 04 90 65 80 85, 🌐 gite-dentelles.com. This simple, inexpensive gîte, at the entrance to the village, offers two large shared dorms, ten very plain double rooms, and one triple, none of them en suite. Closed Jan & Feb. Dorms €15, doubles €34
L'Oustalet Place du Village ☎ 04 90 65 85 30,

ⓦrestaurant-oustalet.fr. Thanks to a dynamic young chef, this modern restaurant, with seating indoors and out on a pleasant shaded terrace, offers the best dining in the village centre. Full dinner *menus* start at €39. Tues–Sat noon–1.30pm & 7.30–9.15pm; also Sun noon–1.30pm in summer.

VACQUEYRAS

Montmirail ⓣ 04 90 65 84 01, ⓦ hotelmontmirail.com. Upmarket hotel, in spacious grounds just south of the centre, with a good Provençal restaurant, serving lunch *menus* from €24, dinner from €35. Closed Nov to mid-April. €72

BEAUMES-DE-VENISE

Amerigo Vespucci 210 av Jules-Ferry ⓣ 04 90 62 95 27,

ⓦlerelaisdesdentelles.fr. Just south of the village centre, across the river, the old Relais des Dentelles is no longer a hotel, but it's still open as a restaurant, serving good quality Provençal food. *Menus* range from a simple €17.50 option up to €37.50. Daily noon–1.30pm & 7.30–9.30pm.

LE BARROUX

Les Géraniums Place de la Croix ⓣ 04 90 62 41 08, ⓦ hotel-lesgeraniums.com. Small, very peaceful, comfortable and unpretentious hotel in the heart of the village, with spacious rooms and views of the Dentelles. Its popular *terrasse* restaurant serves decent food on lunch and dinner *menus* for €18 and €30 respectively. Closed Dec–Feb. €75

3

Mont Ventoux and around

Visible from the valleys of the Rhône, Luberon and Durance, the 1912-metre summit of **MONT VENTOUX** looms high on the horizon east of the Dentelles. White with snow, black with storm-cloud shadow or reflecting myriad shades of blue, the barren pebbles of its topmost 300m are like a coloured weather vane for all of western Provence. From a distance the mountain looks distinctly alluring; indeed, the fourteenth-century Italian poet Petrarch climbed the heights simply for the experience, although the local guides he chartered for the two-and-a-half-day hike considered him completely crazy. Small wonder – weather conditions at the top can be ferocious. The northern Mistral accelerates across Ventoux at up to 250km per hour, and wind, rain, snow and fearsome sub-zero temperatures are constant threats.

These days, for drivers at any rate, the expedition to the summit is straightforward, thanks to a zigzagging 42-kilometre road that loops up and back at typical gradients of around nine percent. It starts and ends at two little towns, just 13km apart on the mountain's western flanks: **Malaucène**, southeast of Vaison-la-Romaine; and prettier **Bédoin**, northeast of Carpentras. Both towns make good bases.

Mont Ventoux is most famous, however, for the challenge it presents to **cyclists**. Countless amateurs flock to emulate the legendary athletes of the Tour de France by completing the gruelling counter-clockwise ascent from Bédoin.

Malaucéne

Unless you happen to coincide with its Wednesday-morning market, there's no great reason to stop in the small town of **MALAUCÈNE**, 10km southeast of Vaison-la-Romaine, other than to use it as a base for seeing Mont Ventoux. At its southern end, the narrow main road curves west to avoid the massive bulk of a medieval church. It meets the D974, the access road to Mont Ventoux, in the town centre just beyond, where you'll find several pavement cafés and small hotels.

Bédoin

BÉDOIN, 15km northeast of Carpentras and 13km southwest of Malaucène, is a large and rather pretty village that's bustling for most of the year with cyclists, walkers and day-trippers heading to and from Mont Ventoux. Commercial activity is concentrated along a plane-tree-lined boulevard that doubles as the D974, where assorted bars, cafés, hotels and restaurants jostle in amiable competition.

The road to the summit

Whether you start the ascent from Bédoin – the route traditionally followed by cyclists – Malaucéne, or indeed from Sault to the east, the defining moment on any climb up Mont Ventoux comes when you pass from the well-shaded woodlands lower down to the pitiless exposed pebblescape that lies above the tree line.

The deforestation of Mont Ventoux dates from Roman times, and by the nineteenth century it had got so bad that the entire mountain appeared shaved. Oaks, pines, boxwood, fir and beech have since been replanted and the owls and eagles have returned, but the greenery is unlikely ever to reach the summit again. As a result, the final 6km of the road up the eastern side of the mountain, from the Chalet Reynard way station, is utterly unforgiving for cyclists. A poignant shrine 1km short of the top commemorates the great British cyclist **Tom Simpson**, who died here from heart failure in 1967 on one of the hottest days ever recorded in the Tour de France. Popular legend has it that his last words were "Put me back on the bloody bike."

Surrounded by hardy scientific and metereological observatories, the **summit** itself offers one of the most wonderful panoramas, not just in France, but in all Europe. Note that between November and May, the road is covered by snow and impassable, with only the tops of the black and yellow poles beside the road still visible.

Sault

At **SAULT**, 26km southeast of the summit of Mont Ventoux, the steep forested rocks give way to fields of lavender, cereals and grazing sheep. Wild products of the woods – *lactaire* and *grisel* mushrooms, truffles and game, as well as honey and lavender products – are bought and sold at its Wednesday **market**; autumn is the best time for these local specialities.

Gorges de la Nesque

The spectacular **GORGES DE LA NESQUE** lies south of Ventoux, stretching for 20km beside and beneath the D942, between Carpentras and Sault. This magnificent, little-known canyon was carved by the River Nesque, although the river itself is seldom visible from the road that clings to the rocks high above, and burrows repeatedly through cliff-edge tunnels.

The 200-metre-high **Rocher du Cire** on the canyon's southern side, 5km southwest of the village of Monieux, is coated in wax from the hives of wild bees. Men from the village are said in days gone by to have abseiled down the rock to gather honey.

INFORMATION AND TOURS

MONT VENTOUX AND AROUND

MALAUCÈNE

Tourist office Place de la Marie (Mon–Sat: April–Sept 9.30am–noon & 2.30–6pm; Oct–March 9.30am–noon & 2.30–5.30pm; ☎ 04 90 65 22 59, ⓦ www.malaucene.fr).

BÉDOIN

Tourist office Espace M.-L.-Gravier (late June to Aug Tues–Fri 9am–12.30pm & 2–6pm, Sat 9.30am–12.30pm & 3–6pm, Sun 9.30am–12.30pm; Sept to mid-June

Tues–Fri 9am–12.30pm & 2–6pm, Sat 9.30am–12.30pm; ☎ 04 90 65 63 95, ⓦ www.bedoin.org). In summer, it organizes a weekly night-time ascent, to camp near the summit and await the sunrise (July & Aug, Wed & Fri 11.30pm; €15).

Bike rental Bédoin Location, chemin de la Feraille (☎ 04 90 65 94 53, ⓦ bedoin-location.fr) rents out bikes and can arrange for van transportation to the summit, from where you cycle back down.

ACCOMMODATION AND EATING

MALAUCÈNE

Camping Municipal de Grozeau Rte de Grozeau ☎ 04 90 65 20 17. Malaucène's charming municipal

campsite, 1.5km southeast of the village, is tucked into the final curve of the D974 just before it starts to ascend Mont Ventoux, and feels more like a park, with no set

boundaries between the pitches and only basic facilities. Closed Nov–March. **€9**

Le Domaine des Tilleuls Rte du Mont Ventoux ☎ 04 90 65 22 31, ⊛ hotel-domainedestilleuls.com. Country-house hotel, set in wooded grounds just outside the village at the foot of Mont Ventoux, with twenty rustic, slightly faded but spacious and comfortable rooms, but no restaurant. Closed mid-Nov to mid-March. **€85**

BÉDOIN

Camping Pastory Rte de Malaucène ☎ 04 90 12 85 83, ⊛ camping-pastory.com. Pleasant, simple little two-star campsite, in a peaceful rural setting 1km northwest of the village on the D19. Closed Oct–March. **€13.50**

L'Escapade Place Portail l'Olivier ☎ 04 90 65 60 21, ⊛ lescapade.eu. Plain, good-value hotel on Bédoin's main square, with free parking opposite and a decent restaurant downstairs (closed all day Thurs & Fri lunch). **€65**

Le Grillon Rue Barral des Beaux ☎ 04 90 65 66 89. Centring on a wood-burning grill, this cosy central restaurant offers pavement tables beneath an enormous plane tree. A huge Provençal burger costs €9.50 at lunchtime, while the €18.50 *menu* includes a tasty cod cassolette. Daily noon–2.30pm & 7–9.30pm.

SAULT

Le Louvre Place du Marché ☎ 04 90 64 08 88, ⊛ louvre-provence.com. This very appealing little pastel-painted hotel offers sixteen tasteful en-suite rooms, and opens onto a peaceful square behind the main drag that's almost entirely filled with tables from its restaurant, which serves traditional Provençal food on *menus* costing €15 and up. **€75**

Carpentras

With a population of around 30,000, **CARPENTRAS** is a substantial city for this part of the world. It's also a very old one, its known history commencing in 5 BC as the capital of a Celtic tribe. The Greeks who founded Marseille came to Carpentras to buy honey, wheat, goats and skins, and the Romans had a base here. For a brief period in the fourteenth century, it became the papal headquarters and gave protection to Jews expelled from France. Today, Carpentras is a somewhat faded provincial town, where immaculately restored squares and fountains alternate with gently decayed streets of seventeenth- and eighteenth-century houses, some forming arcades over the pavement. To experience it at its liveliest, come during the last fortnight in July for the **Estivales**, a series of music, theatre and dance performances staged in front of the cathedral.

A bird's-eye view of Carpentras clearly shows its ancient perimeter line (rues Vigne, des Halles, Raspail, du Collège and Moricelly), encircled in turn, further out, by the ring of broader boulevards that follow the line of the medieval town wall. Of this, only the massive, crenellated **Porte d'Orange** and the odd rampart remain.

Palais de Justice

Place Charles-de-Gaulle • Guided tours April–Oct; contact tourist office on ☎ 04 90 63 00 78

The **Palais de Justice** at the heart of Carpentras was built as an episcopal palace to indulge the dreams – or more likely the unrealized desires – of a seventeenth-century cardinal of Carpentras. Nicolas Mignard was commissioned to fresco the walls with sexual scenes of satyrs and nymphs, but a later incumbent had all the erotic details effaced.

CARPENTRAS MARKET

Friday is the major **market** day in Carpentras, with the local **fruit and vegetables** that appear so early in the lowlands of Vaucluse available all round the town. **Flowers and plants** are sold on avenue Jean-Jaurès; **antiques and bric-a-brac** on rue Porte-de-Monteux and place Colonel-Mouret; and from the annual St-Siffrein fair (November 24–27) to the beginning of March, place Aristide-Briand and place du 25 Août 1944 are given over to the selling of **truffles** – the fungi, not the chocolate kind.

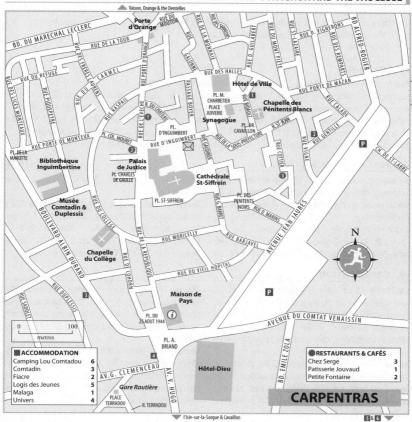

CARPENTRAS

■ ACCOMMODATION	
Camping Lou Comtadou	6
Comtadin	3
Fiacre	2
Logis des Jeunes	5
Malaga	1
Univers	4

● RESTAURANTS & CAFÉS	
Chez Serge	3
Patisserie Jouvaud	1
Petite Fontaine	2

Jewish Carpentras

The **Synagogue du Carpentras**, near the Hôtel de Ville on Place Juiverie (Mon–Thurs 10am–noon & 3–5pm, Fri 10am–noon & 3–4pm; closed Jewish holidays; free; ☎04 90 63 39 97), is a seventeenth-century construction on fourteenth-century foundations, making it the oldest surviving place of Jewish worship in France. The **Porte Juif**, on the southern side of the fifteenth-century Cathédrale St-Siffrein nearby, is so named because Jews used to pass through it to enter the cathedral in chains. Inside, whether coerced, bribed or otherwise persuaded, they would be unshackled as converted Christians. The door itself bears strange symbolism of rats encircling and devouring a globe. Carpentras hosts a **Festival of Jewish Music** at the start of each August.

Musée Comtadin et Duplessis

Bd Albin-Durand • April–Sept daily except Tues 10am–noon & 2–6pm • €2

The **Musée Comtadin-Duplessis** occupies two floors of a rather decrepit old house on the western edge of central Carpentras. The Comtadin collection, downstairs, consists of assorted keys, guns, *santons*, seals, papal bulls, bells and bonnets, plus some naïve ex-voto paintings celebrating divine intervention in various domestic incidents, and more accomplished French canvases from the eighteenth and nineteenth centuries.

Upstairs, the Duplessis holds a few Roman and Egyptian artefacts and, in a *trompe-l'oeil* Renaissance study, a handful of miniatures.

Hotel Dieu

Place Aristide-Briand • Guided tours April–Oct; contact tourist office on ☎ 04 90 63 00 78

Carpentras's huge **Hôtel Dieu**, built as a hospice in the eighteenth century, is due to be converted into a museum and cultural centre. Its opulent original **pharmacy** still holds gorgeously decorated vials and boxes containing cat's foot extract, Saturn salt, deer antler shavings and dragon blood; the painted lower cupboards tell a very "Age of Reason" moral tale of wild and happy monkeys ending up as tame and dutiful labourers.

ARRIVAL AND INFORMATION   CARPENTRAS

By bus Buses arrive either at the *gare routière* on place Terradou (from Avignon, Vaison and other points north and west), or on av Victor-Hugo (from Marseille, Aix and Cavaillon).

Destinations Avignon (frequent; 35–45min); Cavaillon (2–5 daily; 45min); Gigondas (1–3 daily; 30min); L'Isle-sur-la-Sorgue (5 daily; 20min); Marseille (3 daily; 1hr 15min–2hr 5min); Orange (3 daily; 40–45min); Vaison (4 daily; 45min).

Tourist office 97 place du 25 aout 1944, on the south side of the old town (July & Aug Mon–Sat 9am–1pm & 2–7pm, Sun 9.30am–1pm; Sept–June Mon & Wed–Sat 9.30am–12.30pm & 2–6pm, Tues 9.30am–12.30pm & 3–6pm; ☎ 04 90 63 00 78, ⍾ carpentras-ventoux.com).

ACCOMMODATION

Comtadin 65 bd Albin-Durand ☎ 04 90 67 75 00, ⍾ le-comtadin.com. Nicely restored traditional hotel, a very short walk west of the tourist office on the peripheral boulevard. Affiliated to *Best Western*, it offers light, double-glazed rooms and a sunny breakfast patio. **€90**

Fiacre 153 rue Vigne ☎ 04 90 63 03 15, ⍾ hotel-du-fiacre.com. Grand eighteenth-century townhouse, with a central courtyard and nicely decorated rooms, two with terraces. The friendly owners can help plan walking and cycling tours. **€72**

Logis des Jeunes du Comtat Venaissin 200 rue Robert-Lacoste ☎ 04 90 67 13 95, ⍾ carpentras-ventoux. com. Hostel offering simple accommodation in 4- or 5-bed dorms, 2km southeast of the centre near the Pierre de Coubertin sports centre. Amenities include a pool, table tennis and a cafeteria. Dorms **€14.50**

Malaga 37 place Maurice-Charretier ☎ 04 90 60 57 96, ⍾ lemalaga@orange.fr. Eight clean en-suite rooms, rather kitsch but perfectly satisfactory for budget travellers, centrally located and above a decent pavement brasserie. **€40**

Univers 110 place A-Briand ☎ 04 90 63 00 05, ⍾ hotel-univers.com. The actual bedrooms inside this imposing old building, near the tourist office, are large but rather drab, but there's no quarrelling with the low prices, especially for the four-person rooms. **€51**

CAMPING

Lou Comtadou Route St-Didier, 881 av Pierre-de-Coubertin ☎ 04 90 67 03 16, ⍾ campingloucomtadou .com. Very pleasant, well-equipped four-star campsite, in shaded rural surroundings 1km south of the centre. Closed Nov–Feb. **€24**

EATING AND DRINKING

The winding streets of Carpentras' ancient core hold plenty of small **restaurants**, while brasseries spread across the larger squares to the south. The local sweet speciality is the **berlingot**: you'll see these small, striped fruit *bonbons* on signs, in shops, and at the end of your meal as an accompaniment to your bill – the mint flavour is the most famous, but the coffee one is absolutely delicious.

Chez Serge 90 rue Cottier ☎ 04 90 63 21 24, ⍾ chez-serge.com. Sleek bistro serving changing daily *plats* on its tree-shaded terrace. The lunch *menu* is €15, dinner *menus* start at €34, with a major emphasis on truffles; by way of contrast, there's also a wide selection of pizzas for around €10. Daily noon–2pm & 7.30–10pm.

Patisserie Jouvaud 40 rue de l'Evêche ☎ 04 90 63 15 38. This cosy tearoom and patisserie, which also has

three tables on the pedestrian street outside, makes a fabulous stop-off for tea and cakes. Daily 10am–8pm.

Petite Fontaine 13/17 place du Colonel Mouret ☎ 04 90 60 77 83, ⍾ lapetitefontaine84.fr. Cheery restaurant, situated as the name suggests beside a little fountain, and serving delicious fresh food, with a €25 *menu*. Mon, Tues & Thurs–Sat noon–1.30pm & 7.30–9.30pm.

Pernes-les-Fontaines

The delightful small town of **PERNES-LES-FONTAINES** lies 6km south of Carpentras. Everything in Pernes – from the 36 fountains for which it's named to the ramparts, gateways, towers, covered market hall, Renaissance streets and half a dozen chapels – seems to blend into a single complex structure, and the passages between its squares feel more like corridors between rooms.

Of Pernes' fourteenth-century ramparts, only three gates now remain. The most impressive, the sixteenth-century **Porte Notre-Dame**, serves as the entrance to the north side of the walled town. Accessed via a narrow medieval stone bridge that crosses a surviving section of the town's ancient moat, it leads to an elegant **cormorant fountain** and seventeenth-century market hall.

Up to the right, the massive twelfth-century keep of the castle of the counts of Toulouse, now known as the **Tour Ferrande**, has been turned into a clock tower by the simple expedient of sticking two big clocks onto it halfway up. Inside, immaculately preserved fourteenth-century **frescoes** portray scenes from the legend of William of Orange and the life of Charles of Anjou.

Continue west along rue Gambetta to reach **Porte Villeneuve**, which is flanked by two imposing round towers, and opens off the main road through town, av Jean-Jaurès. Alternatively, head south from Porte Notre-Dame on rue Raspail, and you'll come to the other remaining gate, **Porte St-Gilles**.

3

INFORMATION   PERNES-LES-FONTAINES

Tourist office 72 cours Frizet (July & Aug Mon–Fri 9am–1pm & 2–6.30pm, Sat 9am–1pm & 2–5pm, Sun 9.30am–12.30pm; Sept–June Mon–Fri 9am–noon & 2–5.30pm, Sat 9am–12.30pm; ☎04 90 61 31 04, 🌐 tourisme-pernes.fr).

ACCOMMODATION AND EATING

Au Fil de Temps 51 place Louis-Giraud ☎04 90 30 09 48. Delightful restaurant in the old town, serving creative Provençal cuisine on *menus* starting at €25 for lunch, and ranging from €29 to €49 for dinner. There's a focus on unusual ingredients, such as rare tomato varieties. Wed–Sun noon–2pm & 7.30–9.30pm.

★ **La Margelle** 56 place Louis-Giraud ☎04 90 40 18 54, 🌐 la-margelle.net. This stylish, good-value hotel, stretching back from Pernes' southern boulevard ring to a sleepy old square, holds six smart upgraded rooms plus a luxury apartment. A high-class garden restaurant (closed Sun & Mon) serves lunch *menus* at €16, dinner from €32. **€95**

Venasque

The gorgeous, perfectly contained village of **VENASQUE** perches atop a spur of rock 9km east of Pernes, just before the road starts to wind over the Plateau de Vaucluse towards Apt. Oddly, only its upper end needed to be fortified, and it remains screened off by a curtain wall punctuated by three round towers. Like so many Provençal villages, it swings between its sleepy winter state and being a tourist honeypot in summer. The best time to visit is in May and June, before the main season begins, and when the daily **market** sells succulent local cherries.

Baptistère de l'Église Notre-Dame

Place du Presbytère • Daily: early Jan–March & Oct to early Dec 9.15am–1pm & 2–5pm; April–Sept 9am–1pm & 2–6.30pm • €3 • ☎04 90 66 62 01

The remarkable **Baptistère** (baptistery) that adjoins the Église Notre-Dame at the lower end of Venasque ranks among the oldest religious buildings in France. Erected on the site of a Roman temple dedicated to Venus, surviving vestiges of which include a sarcophagus from 420 AD, it's thought to have been Christianized later in the fifth century.

INFORMATION

Tourist office Grande Rue (April–June & Sept–Oct Mon & Sun 2–6pm, Tues–Sat 10am–noon & 2–6pm; July & Aug

ACCOMMODATION AND EATING

La Fontaine Place de la Fontaine ☎04 90 60 64 05, ⓦmaisondecharme-venasque.com. Venasque's finest accommodation option holds four smart split-level apartments, impeccably furnished to match a minimalist modern aesthetic. Closed Nov, Feb & March. **€135**
Remparts Rue Haute ☎04 90 66 02 79,

VENASQUE

Tues–Sat 10am–12.30pm & 3–7pm, Mon & Sun 3–7pm; ☎04 90 66 11 66, ⓦwww.tourisme-venasque.com).

ⓦhotellesremparts.com. Set into the ramparts at the top of the main street, its ivy-covered walls rippling in the wind, this inexpensive hotel offers eight pretty rooms, and superb views from its panoramic dining room, where lunch *menus* start at €20, dinner at €26. Closed mid-Nov to mid-March. **€65**

L'Isle-sur-la-Sorgue

Halfway between Carpentras and Cavaillon to the south, and 23km east of Avignon, **L'ISLE-SUR-LA-SORGUE** straddles five branches of the River Sorgue, with little canals and waterways running through and around the centre. Once filled with otters and beavers, eels, trout and crayfish, the river powered **medieval industries** including tanneries and dyeing works. It still holds huge water wheels, but these days they turn for show only, and L'Isle has become a popular day-trip destination. It's at its most cheerful on Sundays, when an **antiques market** spills out across town.

While there are few sights to head for, the central **place de l'Église** and **place de la Liberté** do provide reminders of past prosperity, most obviously in the Baroque seventeenth-century **church** (Tues–Sat: July & Aug 10am–noon & 3–6pm, Sun 3–6pm; Sept–June 10am–noon & 3–5pm), by far the richest religious edifice for many kilometres around. Each column in the nave supports a sculpted Virtue: whips and turtledoves are Chastity's props, a unicorn accompanies Virginity, and medallions and inscriptions carry the adornment down to the floor.

ARRIVAL AND INFORMATION

By train The *gare SNCF* is a short walk southwest of the centre.
Destinations Cavaillon (20 daily; 8min).
By bus Buses arrive by pont Gambetta, on the southeast edge of the old centre.

ISLE-SUR-LA-SORGUE

Destinations Cavaillon (7 daily; 15min); Fontaine-de-Vaucluse (5 daily; 15min).
Tourist office Place de l'Église (Mon–Sat 9am–12.30pm & 2.30–6pm, Sun 9am–12.30pm; ☎04 90 38 04 78, ⓦoti-delasorgue.fr).

ACCOMMODATION AND EATING

★ **La Prévôté** 4 rue J.J. Rousseau ☎04 90 38 57 29, ⓦla-prevote.fr. Charming hotel, arrayed around a quiet courtyard behind the church in the heart of the old town. The five rooms are decked out in beautiful terracotta tiles, wooden beams and Provençal quilts; a small, superb restaurant, downstairs in the old sacristy (closed Mon lunch, Wed lunch & all Tues), serves top-quality *menus* from €39. **€160**
La Sorguette 41 Les Grandes Sorgues ☎04 90 38 05 71, ⓦcamping-sorguette.com. The three-star municipal

campsite enjoys a lovely riverside location, 1km east of the centre on the Apt road, and offers teepees and yurts as well as tent pitches. Closed mid-Oct to mid-March. **€22.30**
Vivier 800 cours Fernande Peyre ☎04 90 38 52 80, ⓦlevivier-restaurant.com. For a true feast, you can't do better than this delightful restaurant, 1km northeast of the centre, where *menus* start at €30 lunch, €50 dinner. Tues–Thurs noon–1.30pm & 7.30–9.15pm, Fri & Sat 7.30–9.30pm, Sun noon–2pm.

Fontaine-de-Vaucluse

The ancient riverside village of **FONTAINE-DE-VAUCLUSE**, 7km east of L'Isle-sur-la-Sorgue, provides the only access to the spectacular source of the Sorgue River, a short but beautiful walk beyond. As a result, it's all but overwhelmed by summer day-trippers. While the source itself is well worth seeing, and it would be too harsh to say the village has been ruined by commercialization, Fontaine-de-Vaucluse is too much of a tourist trap to make it worth staying very long. Arrive in the evening, though, after the crowds have gone, and it makes a pleasant overnight stop.

At the centre of the village, a mossy water wheel stands alongside a bridge that spans the already broad Sorgue. On the northern bank, around the circular place de Colonne, six enormous plane streets spread to form a canopy over the eponymous column in the middle. Visitors can only follow the Sorgue upstream from here on foot.

The source of the Sorgue

Thanks to a geological anomaly, all the rainwater that falls on the vast chalk plateau atop the hills east of Fontaine-de-Vaucluse is funnelled into a single channel, to create what's said to be the most powerful natural springs in Europe. Measured at 630 million cubic metres per year, that flow emerges from a mysterious tapering fissure at the foot of towering 230-metre cliffs, to become the Sorgue River.

To reach the **source of the Sorgue**, follow a gentle 500-metre footpath, known as the chemin de la Fontaine, along the north bank from Fontaine-de-Vaucluse. Even with the usual crowds, it's a lovely walk, climbing through a narrowing gorge, with the glorious green river cascading beneath thickly wooded slopes to your right.

Most visitors continue beyond the safety barriers at the path's far end, stepping gingerly down the rubble-strewn slopes to get close-up views of the limpid pool of azure-blue water that wells up from an otherworldly cavern – in technical parlance, a **sinkhole**. Don't even dream of entering the abyss; scuba divers have reached the astonishing depth of 205 metres below the surface, while remote-controlled camera have descended over 300 metres without reaching the bottom.

Ecomusée du Gouffre

Chemin de la Fontaine • Feb to mid-Nov daily 9.30am–12.30pm & 2–6pm; last admission 1hr before closing; hourly tours in French only • €5.50 • ☏ 04 90 20 34 13

To learn more about the source of the Sorgue, stop off at the **Ecomusée du Gouffre** on the riverside path, best suited to French speakers. Volunteers eager to communicate their passion for crawling about in the bowels of the earth lead forty-minute tours through mock-up caves and passages, while displays document the intriguing history of the exploration of the spring. The museum winds up with a collection of subterranean concretions, ranging from huge, jewellery-like crystals to pieces resembling fibre optics.

Moulin à Papier Vallis Clausa

Chemin de la Fontaine • Daily: Jan & Dec 10am–12.30pm & 2–5.30pm; Feb, March & Oct 10am–12.30pm & 2–6pm; April 9.30am–12.30pm & 2–6.30pm; May, June & Sept 10am–12.30pm & 2–7pm; July & Aug 9am–7.30pm • Free • ☏ 04 90 20 34 14, ⓦ moulin-vallisclausa.com

The waters of the Sorgue have long turned the wheels of manufacturing. Fontaine's first paper mill was built in 1522, while the last ceased operations in 1968. The medieval method of pulping rags to paper has been re-created in the **Moulin à Papier Vallis Clausa**, where flowers are added to the pulp and the resulting paper is printed with drawings, poems and prose, ranging from Martin Luther King's "I Have A Dream" to cloying homilies and delightful etchings.

The south bank of the Sorgue

It's possible to escape the crowds in Fontaine-de-Vaucluse by walking on the south bank of the river. There's no access to the source, but follow signs to Petrarch's house, and you'll swiftly find yourself in a lovely shaded park. The ruined thirteenth-century **castle** perched on the outcrop above originally belonged to the bishops of Cavaillon. There's no formal path to the top, but with good shoes you can scramble up the rough hillside to reach what's now just a hollow shell, with great views over the village. Make sure you stay well clear of the dangerous, unprotected drop-offs.

Musée de Pétrarque

Daily except Tues: April, May & first half of Oct 10am–noon & 2–6pm; June–Sept 10am–12.30pm & 1.30–6pm; second half of Oct 10am–noon & 2–5pm • €3.50 • ☎ 04 90 20 37 20

Seven centuries ago, the poet Petrarch spent sixteen unrequited years pining in Fontaine-de-Vaucluse, then as now a rustic backwater, for his beloved Laura. To learn a little more about Petrarch and his significance to early Renaissance culture, drop into the **Musée de Pétrarque**, just across the bridge south of the river.

ARRIVAL AND INFORMATION
FONTAINE-DE-VAUCLUSE

By car Parking can be hard to find; the largest car park is a short walk south of the river.

Tourist office Chemin de la Fontaine (May–Sept daily 10am–1pm & 2–6pm; Oct–April Mon–Sat 9.30am–12.30pm & 1.30–5.30pm, Sun 1.30–5.30pm; ☎ 04 90 20 32 22, ⓦ oti-delasorgue.fr).

Canoe rental In summer, Kayak Vert (☎ 04 90 20 35 44) rents canoes either for short paddles, or for a fairly effortless 8km trip down to L'Isle-sur-la-Sorgue.

ACCOMMODATION AND EATING

★ **Auberge La Figuière** ☎ 04 90 20 37 41, ⓦ la-figuiere.fr. Simple but attractive B&B rooms in the heart of the village, with terracotta tiles, tasteful Provençal furnishings and excellent walk-in showers. With tables spread across a pleasant flowery courtyard, the restaurant downstairs serves a great-value €23 *menu*. Closed Oct to mid-Feb. No credit cards for rooms. **€65**

Restaurant Philip Chemin de la Fontaine ☎ 04 90 20 31 81. This gorgeous riverside spot is sure to catch your eye as you walk up to the spring. At the very least, it's worth

enjoying a quick drink on the bar section of its long, peaceful terrace, but the food is a lot better than you might expect, with full *menus* starting at €27. Easter–Sept daily noon–9pm.

L'Hotel du Poète ☎ 04 90 20 34 05, ⓦ hoteldupoete.com. Despite its uninspiring exterior, this former water mill, just outside the village below the main D25 on the river's north bank, offers luxurious accommodation, with large, comfortable rooms and a pool, but no restaurant. Closed Dec to mid-March. **€95**

Cavaillon

Approaches to **CAVAILLON**, directly south of L'Isle-sur-la-Sorgue and 25km southeast of Avignon, pass through fields of fruit and vegetables, watered by the Durance and Coulon rivers. Market gardening is a major business, and Cavaillon, its Roman origins notwithstanding, is known simply as a **melon** town. The melon in question – the Charentais, a small pale-green ball with dark green stripes and brilliant orange flesh – is honoured by a **melon festival** in mid-July. Cavaillon itself, however, is not wildly alluring, and there's no great reason to linger long. All that remains of Roman Cavaillon is the **Arc de Triomphe** on place du Clos, which on Mondays is surrounded by the weekly **market**.

Cathédrale St-Véran

Mon–Sat: April–Sept 8.30am–noon & 2–6pm; Oct–March 9am–noon & 2–5pm

On the south side of Cavaillon's archaic-looking, thirteenth-century **Cathédrale St-Véran**, God appears above a sundial looking like a winged and battered Neptune. Inside, in the St-Véran chapel above the altar, there's a painting of Saint Véran hauling off a slithery reptile known as Couloubre, who terrorized the locality in 6 AD.

ARRIVAL AND INFORMATION

CAVAILLON

By train The *gare SNCF* is on av P-Semard, 250m east of the centre.
Destinations L'Isle-sur-la-Sorgue (20 daily; 8min).
By bus Alongside the *gare SNCF* on av P-Semard.
Destinations L'Isle-sur-la-Sorgue (7 daily; 15min); Pernes-les-Fontaines (7 daily; 35min).

Tourist office Place François-Tourel – marked by a giant melon (Mon–Sat 9am–12.30pm & 2–6.30pm; ☏ 04 90 71 32 01, ⓦ cavaillon-luberon.com).

ACCOMMODATION AND EATING

Le Parc 183 place François-Tourel ☏ 04 90 71 57 78, ⓦ hotelduparccavaillon.com. Elegant, agreeable former *maison bourgeoise*, beside the tourist office; its flamboyant decor suits the building, though the rooms themselves are more subdued. Breakfast is served in a pleasant courtyard. €72
Le Prevot 353 av de Verdon ☏ 04 90 71 32 43, ⓦ restaurant-prevot.com. The best local dining, 1km

southeast of the tourist office. Lunch *menus* start at €25, while dinner *menus*, organized around seasonal themes or ingredients such as melons or mushrooms, vary from €38 to €55. Tues–Sat noon–1.30pm & 7.30–9pm.
Toppin 70 cours Gambetta ☏ 04 90 71 30 42, ⓦ hotel-toppin.com. This appealing, central *Logis de France* offers large, warmly decorated and comfortable rooms, but no restaurant. €65

3

Aix-en-Provence, the Durance and the Luberon

SENTIER DES OCRES, ROUSSILLON

Aix-en-Provence, the Durance and the Luberon

A wide, rushing torrent in winter that reduces to a dribble in summer, the Durance is one of the great alpine rivers of France, slashing 320km southwest from its source near Briançon to its confluence with the Rhône near Avignon. Four *départements* converge where the Durance meets the Verdon, a few kilometres northeast of the Pont Mirabeau. Three of the four – the Alpes de Haute Provence, the Vaucluse and the Bouches du Rhône – are at their most atypical here. The portion of the Alpes de Haute Provence west of the Durance lacks the genuine alpine grandeur of the area to the east; the Luberon's history of dissent during the Wars of Religion distinguishes it from the papal tradition of the Vaucluse as a whole; and the pastoral charms of the Coteaux d'Aix and grandeur of the Mont Ste-Victoire contrast strongly with the metropolitan feel of the Marseille conurbation. Unrepresentative of their *départements*, together these regions offer a distillation of all that, for visitors, seems most typically Provençal – of lavender and honey, crumbling hilltop villages and ancient abbeys, lively markets and excellent cuisine rooted in the *terroir*.

The charms of **Aix-en-Provence** – the region's only real city – are commonly sung. With a historic core as perfect as any in France, it glories in the medieval period of independent Provence, the riches of its seventeenth- and eighteenth-century growth and the memory of its most famous sons, Zola and Cézanne.

To the north of Aix, the transition between Mediterranean and Alpine France becomes clear along the valley of the Durance. Downstream, the fruitful countryside between sleepy **Cadenet** and bustling **Pertuis** is classically Provençal, but east of Pertuis, the landscape becomes wilder, the valley narrowing to a rocky gorge at the Défilé de Mirabeau. To the north, **Manosque** offers a rare taste of urban life, while dramatic **Sisteron** acts as a gateway to the Alps and as the northern point of departure from Provence. West of the Durance, the delights of the **Pays de Forcalquier** include the venerable town of **Forcalquier** itself and the remote and beautiful hilltop village of **Simiane-la-Rotonde**.

Sweeping further to the west, the great green surge of the **Luberon** massif is as lauded as any landscape in France, not least in the books of Peter Mayle, and its beautiful

Highlights

❶ **Cézanne's Aix** Visit his atelier, tour his childhood home then explore a living Cézanne landscape in the country around the Mont Ste-Victoire. **See p.160, p.159 & p.164**

❷ **Forcalquier** Discover this once grand, now slumbering, historic town, and its beautiful, unspoilt pays. **See p.179**

❸ **Ochre in the Luberon** Brilliant colour enfolds the friendly villages of Rustrel and Roussillon, and enlivens the extraordinary mine of Bruoux. **See p.189**

❹ **Medieval hilltop villages** Though Gordes is the best known, Lacoste, Saignon and

Simiane-la-Rotonde are equally picturesque and much less busy. **See p.190, p.193, p.185 & p.183**

❺ **Abbaye de Sénanque** The ancient Cistercian monastery is as much a symbol of Provence as the lavender fields surrounding it. **See p.191**

❻ **Abandoned hilltop ruins** Quiet and crumbling, Oppède-le-Vieux and the Fort de Buoux provide an atmospheric insight into life in the medieval *villages perchés*. **See p.192 & p.186**

HIGHLIGHTS ARE MARKED ON THE MAP ON P.154

villages are nowadays distinctly chic. Its principal centre, **Apt**, is a lively market town slowly evolving in the face of the influx of wealthy Parisians and foreigners that has transformed the surrounding districts. The attractions of the countryside are diverse: the multi-hued ochre mines of **Bruoux**, **Rustrel** and **Roussillon**, the abandoned villages at **Buoux** and **Oppède-le-Vieux**, the immaculate village of **Gordes** and the twelfth-century Cistercian monasteries at **Sénanque** and **Silvacane**.

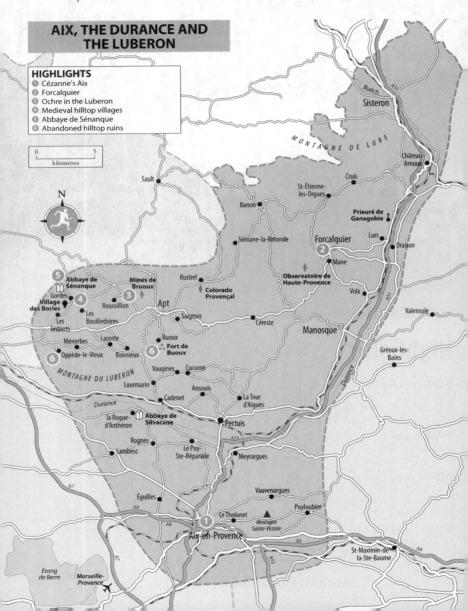

AIX, THE DURANCE AND THE LUBERON

HIGHLIGHTS
1. Cézanne's Aix
2. Forcalquier
3. Ochre in the Luberon
4. Medieval hilltop villages
5. Abbaye de Sénanque
6. Abandoned hilltop ruins

Aix-en-Provence and around

With its colourful markets, splashing fountains, pavement cafés and general air of civilized ease, **AIX-EN-PROVENCE** measures up to the popular fantasies of the Provençal good life better than any city in the region. It's a stunningly beautiful place, its riches based on landowning and the liberal professions. Hundreds of foreign students, particularly Americans, study in Aix, reinforcing the city's youthful feel; the humanities and arts faculties of the university Aix shares with Marseille are based here, where the original university was founded in 1409. In the nineteenth century Aix was home to two of France's greatest contributors to painting and literature, Paul Cézanne and his close friend Émile Zola. A series of brass studs set into the pavements now allows visitors to follow a Cézanne trail through the heart of the city.

The old city, **Vieil Aix**, defined by its ring of boulevards and the majestic **cours Mirabeau**, is in its entirety the great monument here, far more compelling than any single attraction within it. With so many streets alive with people, so many tempting restaurants, cafés and shops, plus the best markets in Provence, it's easy to pass a day or two wandering around without any itinerary or destination. Beyond Vieil Aix, there are a few museums in the **quartier Mazarin** south of cours Mirabeau and, further out, the **Vaserely Foundation**, **Cézanne's studio** and the Cézanne family home, **Jas de Bouffan**. Aix also makes an ideal base for **excursions** into the beautiful surrounding countryside, a landscape made famous by Cézanne.

Some history

Aix began life as Aquae Sextiae, a Roman settlement based around its **hot springs** – there's still a thermal establishment on the site of the Roman baths in the northwest corner of the Vieille Ville. From the twelfth century until the Revolution Aix was the capital of Provence. In its days as an independent fiefdom, its most beloved ruler, **King René of Anjou** (1409–80), held a brilliant court renowned for its popular festivities and patronage of the arts. René introduced the muscat grape to the region, and today he stands in stone in picture-book medieval fashion, a bunch of grapes in his left hand, looking down the majestic seventeenth-century replacement to the old southern fortifications, the cours Mirabeau.

Cours Mirabeau

As a preliminary introduction to life in Aix, take a stroll beneath the gigantic plane trees of **cours Mirabeau**, stopping off along the way at one of the many cafés along its sunny north side. In contrast, the shady south side is decidedly businesslike, lined with banks and offices lodged in seventeenth- to eighteenth-century mansions. These have a uniform hue of weathered stone, with ornate wrought-iron balconies and Baroque decorations, at their heaviest in the tired old musclemen holding up the porch of the *Hôtel d'Espargnet* at no. 38.

Opposite the hotel is Aix's most famous café, *Les Deux Garçons* (see p.162) with a reputation dating back to World War II of serving intellectuals, artists and their entourage; earlier still, Cézanne was a customer. The interior is all mirrors with darkening gilt panels and reading lights that might have come off the old *Orient Express*.

Vieil Aix

To explore the heart of Aix, wander north from cours Mirabeau and then anywhere within the ring of cours and boulevards. The layout of **Vieil Aix** is not designed to assist your sense of direction, but it hardly matters when there's a fountained square to rest at every 50m and a continuous architectural backdrop of treats from the sixteenth and seventeenth centuries.

4

Manosque & Sisteron

Vauvenargues

Le Fontaine d'Argent

Pertuis, Manosque & Sisteron

Avignon & Puyricard

Atelier Cézanne, Terrain des Peintres & Oppidum d'Entremont

Avignon

AIX-EN-PROVENCE

■ ACCOMMODATION

Auberge de Jeunesse	10
Augustins	3
Camping Arc en Ciel	4
Camping Chantecler	5
La Caravelle	9
Cardinal	6
Grand Hôtel Nègre Coste	2
Paul	1
Le Pigonnet	11
Quatre Dauphins	8
St-Christophe	7

BOULEVARD F. & E. ZOLA

COURS ST-LOUIS

RUE CHASTEL

RUE LISSE ST-LOUIS

RUE SUFFREN

RUE SUFFREN

RUE PORTALIS

RUE CHASTEL

RUE MANUEL

RUE LACÉPÈDE

RUE ÉMÉRIC-DAVID

RUE THIERS

PETIT RUE ST JEAN

Église de la Madeleine

PL DE LA MADELEINE

PLACE DES PRÊCHEURS

PLACE DE VERDUN

PLACE D'ALBERTAS

RUE MIGNET

RUE CONSTANTIN

RUE PEYRESC

RUE MONCLAR

RUE MARIUS-REINAUD

Palais de Justice

RUE RIFLE RAFLE

BOULEVARD A. BRIAND

RUE LOUBET

RUE DU PUITS NEUF

RUE BOUGON

RUE MATHERON

RUE LOUBON

RUE CHAUDRONNIERS

Musée d'Histoire Naturelle

RUE P. & M. CURIE

RUE GRIFFON

RUE CAMPRA

RUE GIBELIN

RUE PAUL-BERT

RUE GRANET

Ancienne Halle aux Grains

RUE AUDE

Ancien Archevêché

PLACE DES MARTYRS DE LA RÉSISTANCE

PLACE RICHELME

RUE MAL-FOCH

PLACE DE L'HÔTEL DE VILLE

Cathédrale St-Sauveur

RUE G. DE SAPORTA

Musée du Vieil Aix

Hôtel de Ville

RUE DE LA VERRERIE

PLACE RAMUS

RUE J. DE LAROQUE

RUE VENEL

RUE DES CORDELIERS

RUE F.-GAUT

RUE DES MAGNANS

AV. PASTEUR

RUE DES GUERRIERS

RUE CANCEL

PLACE DES CARDEURS

RUE DU BON PASTEUR

RUE MÉRINDOL

RUE LIEUTAUD

RUE D'ENTRECASTEAUX

RUE FERMÉE

RUE DE LA TREILLE

RUE LISSE DES CORDELIERS

COURS SEXTIUS

Thermes Sextius

RUE VAN LOO

RUE CÉLONY

Pavillon de Vendôme

Jardin de Vendôme

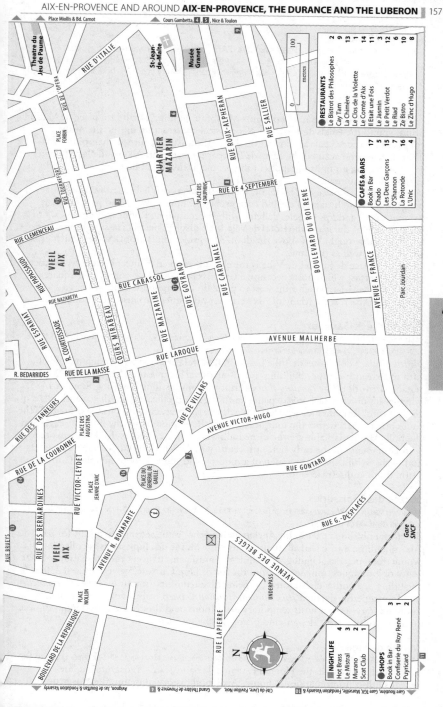

Place Miollis & Bd. Carnot

Cours Gambetta, 4, 5, Nice & Toulon

Théâtre du Jeu de Paume

RUE D'ITALIE

RUE DE L'OPERA

PLACE FORBIN

RUE TOURNEFORT

St-Jean-de-Malte

Musée Granet

RUE ROUX-ALPHERAN

RUE SALLIER

QUARTIER MAZARIN

RUE DE 4 SEPTEMBRE

PLACE DES 4 DAUPHINS

BOULEVARD DU ROI RENE

RUE CLEMENCEAU

VIEIL AIX

RUE PASSADOU

RUE NAZARETH

RUE CABASSOL

RUE MAZARINE

RUE GOYRAND

RUE CARDINALE

AVENUE A. FRANCE

Parc Jourdan

RUE ESPARIAT

R. COURTEISSADE

COURS MIRABEAU

RUE LAROQUE

AVENUE MALHERBE

R. BEDARRIDES

RUE DE LA MASSE

RUE DE VILLARS

AVENUE VICTOR-HUGO

RUE DES TANNEURS

PLACE DES AUGUSTINS

RUE GONTARD

RUE DE LA COURONNE

RUE VICTOR-LEYDET

PLACE JEANNE D'ARC

PLACE DU GENERAL DE GAULLE

RUE G.-DESPLACES

Gare SNCF

RUE BUEUYS

RUE DES BERNARDINES

VIEIL AIX

AVENUE N. BONAPARTE

AVENUE DES BELGES

UNDERPASS

PLACE NIOLLON

BOULEVARD DE LA REPUBLIQUE

RUE LAPIERRE

N

RESTAURANTS

Le Bistrot des Philosophes	2
Cay Tam	9
La Chimère	13
Le Clos de la Violette	1
Le Comte d'Aix	14
Il Était une Fois	11
Le Jasmin	3
Le Petit Verdot	12
Le Riad	6
Ze Bistro	10
Le Zinc d'Hugo	8

CAFÉS & BARS

Book in Bar	17
Chado	5
Les Deux Garçons	15
O'Shannon	7
La Rotonde	16
L'Unic	4

NIGHTLIFE

Hot Brass	4
Le Mistral	3
Murano	2
Scat Club	1

SHOPS

Book in Bar	3
Confiserie du Roy René	1
Puyricard	2

0   100   metres

4

AIX FOR LESS

Offering excellent value, the **Pass Aix Pays d'Aix** (€2) gives discounted admission to the principal museums, plus half-price guided tours and reduced rates at wineries. Alternatively, a **Pass Cézanne** (€15; available April–Oct) is worth considering if you're visiting all of the sites related to the artist.

Starting from the eastern end of cours Mirabeau, heading north into place de Verdun brings you to the **Palais de Justice**, a Neoclassical construction on the site of the old counts of Provence's palace. Count Mirabeau, the aristocrat turned champion of the Third Estate, who accused the États de Provence, meeting in Aix for the last time in 1789, of having no right to represent the people, is honoured here by a statue and allegorical monument.

Further west, in place de l'Hôtel de Ville at the heart of Vieil Aix, a massive foot hangs over the architrave of the old corn exchange, now a library and post office. It belongs to the goddess Cybele, dallying with the masculine Rhône and Durance. On the west side of the *place*, the **Hôtel de Ville** itself displays perfect classical proportions and filigreed wrought iron above the door. Alongside stands a **clock tower** which gives the season as well as the time.

South of place de l'Hôtel de Ville is the elegant, cobbled eighteenth-century Rococo **place d'Albertas**, which hosts occasional concerts on summer evenings. The square is just off rue Espariat, which runs west to place du Général-de-Gaulle and has a distinctly Parisian style. Many of Aix's classiest boutiques are clustered in this area.

Cathédrale St-Sauveur

34 place des Martyrs de la Résistance • Daily 8am–noon & 2–6pm; free tours of cloisters at 9.30am then every 30min 10.30–11.30am & 2.30–5.30pm • ☎ 04 42 23 45 65, ⓦ cathedrale-aixenprovence-monument.fr

North of place de l'Hôtel de Ville lies the **Cathédrale St-Sauveur**, a conglomerate of fifth to sixteenth-century buildings full of medieval art treasures. The cathedral's most notable artwork is *The Burning Bush*, a triptych commissioned by King René in 1475; whether it's on view or not is dependent on the liturgical calendar. The carved pillars of the beautiful Romanesque **cloisters** are perhaps the best sculptures in the cathedral. The four corner pillars depict the four beasts of the Revelation: man, the lion, the eagle and the bull. Also remarkable are the cathedral's west doors, carved by Toulon carpenter Jean Guiramand in the early sixteenth century to depict four Old Testament prophets and twelve sybils, the wise women of antiquity who supposedly prophesied Christ's birth, death and resurrection.

Musée des Tapisseries

28 place des Martyrs de la Résistance • Daily except Tues: mid-April to mid-Oct 10am–12.30pm & 1.30–6pm; mid-Oct to mid-April 1.30–5pm • €3.30 • ☎ 04 42 23 09 91

The former bishop's palace, the **Ancien Archevêché**, is the setting, each July, for part of Aix's grandiose music festival. It also houses the **Musée des Tapisseries**, a collection of wonderful tapestries. Highlights include the musicians, dancers and animals in a 1689 series of grotesques; nine scenes from the life of Don Quixote, woven in the 1730s, including one with a club-footed cat being divested of its armour by various *demoiselles*; and four superbly detailed *Jeux Russiens* (*Russian Games*) from a few decades later. A contemporary section hosts temporary exhibitions, and there's also a section given over to the costumes, stage designs and history of the music festival.

Musée de Vieil Aix

17 rue Gaston de Saporta • Daily except Tues: mid-April to mid-Oct 10am–6pm; mid-Oct to mid-April 1.30–5pm • Free • ☎ 04 42 21 43 55

Close to the cathedral, the Hôtel d'Estienne de Saint Jean – a magnificent late seventeenth-century mansion – houses Aix's local history museum, the **Musée de Vieil**

Aix. Its collections encompass furniture, costume, *santons* and faïence and include a section on the Fête-Dieu (Corpus Christi); this late spring religious festival was highly popular in Aix until the start of the twentieth century and was celebrated with a procession, feasts and plays.

Musée de l'Histoire Naturelle

6 rue Espariat • Daily 10am–noon & 1–5pm • €3.30 • ☎ 04 42 27 91 27, ⓦ museum-aix-en-provence.org

The impressive seventeenth-century Hôtel Boyer d'Eguilles houses the **Musée de l'Histoire Naturelle**, where the cherubs and garlands decorating the ceilings are slightly at odds with the stuffed birds and beetles, ammonites and dinosaur eggs below. Nonetheless, it makes for a good rainy-day refuge, and the dinosaur remains – including those of a rhabdodon found close to Marseille airport in 2007 – should please younger visitors.

Quartier Mazarin

Taking rue Clemenceau south over cours Mirabeau brings you into the heart of the **quartier Mazarin**, built in five years in the mid-seventeenth century by the archbishop brother of the cardinal who ran France when Louis XIV was a baby. It's a very dignified district, and very quiet, centred on the beautiful place des Quatre Dauphins with its four-dolphin fountain.

Musée Granet

Place St Jean de Malte • Tues–Sun: June–Sept 10am–7pm; Oct–May noon–6pm • €4, higher during summer exhibition • ☎ 04 42 52 88 32, ⓦ www.museegranet-aixenprovence.fr

The former priory of the Knights of Malta, east of the place des Quatre Dauphins, is home to the most substantial of Aix's museums, the **Musée Granet**. Covering art and archeology, the museum exhibits finds from the Oppidum d'Entremont (see p.164), a Celto-Légurian township 3km north of Aix, along with the remains of the Romans who routed them in 124 BC. Its paintings are a mixed bag, from Italian, Dutch and French art of the seventeenth- to nineteenth-century to works by Cézanne, who studied on the ground floor of the building, and modernist pieces by Giacometti, Picasso and others. Rather overshadowing the permanent collection is the excellent annual **summer exhibition**, which began in 2006 with a hugely successful show marking the centenary of Cézanne's death.

Jas de Bouffan

17 rte de Galice • Guided tours, pre-booked through tourist office (see p.160): Jan–March Wed & Sat at 10am; April, May & Oct Tues, Thurs & Sat at 10.30am, noon & 3.30, English tour at 2pm; June–Sept daily at 10.30am, noon & 3.30, English tour at 2pm • €5.50

The man who came to be regarded as the father of modern painting cut a lonely figure for much of his life, spurned by the Parisian art establishment and happier away from the capital in his beloved Aix. **Paul Cézanne** was born in Vieil Aix at 28 rue de l'Opéra, the son of a hatter of Italian descent turned prosperous banker, but he grew up in a grand eighteenth-century house west of the city – long since subsumed into its suburbs. The house, known as **Jas de Bouffan**, can be seen only on a pre-booked tour from the tourist office; during the visit you'll also get to see the vantage points in the lovely garden from which Cézanne painted pictures including *Le Bassin du Jas de Bouffan en hiver*.

Fondation Vasarely

1 av Marcel-Pagnol • Tues–Sun 10am–1pm & 2–6pm • €9 • ☎ 04 42 20 01 09, ⓦ fondationvasarely.org • Bus #2 (direction "CC Bouffan", stop "Vasarely")

The hill of the Jas de Bouffan area is dominated by the **Fondation Vasarely**, a bold modernist building in black and white geometric shapes created by the

Hungarian-born artist Victor Vasarely in 1976. The seven hexagonal spaces of the ground floor are hung with 44 of Vasarely's monumental kinetic tapestries and paintings, while the rest of the museum hosts large-scale temporary exhibitions.

The Atelier Paul Cézanne

9 av Paul-Cézanne • Daily: April–June & Sept 10am–noon & 2–6pm, tour in English at 5pm; July & Aug 10am–6pm, tour in English at 5pm; Oct–March 10am–noon & 2–5pm, tour in English at 4pm • €5.50 • ☏ 04 42 21 06 53, ⊛ atelier-cezanne.com • Bus #5 (direction "parc relais Brunet", stop "Atelier Cézanne") or #18 (direction "Puyricard", stop "Atelier Cézanne"), or a ten-minute walk uphill from the north end of the Vieille Ville

Cézanne used many studios in and around Aix, but at the turn of the twentieth century, four years before his death, he had a house built for the purpose at what is now 9 av Paul-Cézanne, overlooking Aix from the north. By this stage in his life Cézanne had achieved both financial security and the recognition that had so long eluded him. It was here that he painted the *Grandes Baigneuses*, the *Jardinier Vallier* and some of his greatest still lifes. The **Atelier Paul Cézanne** has been left exactly as it was at the time of his death in 1906: coat, hat, wine glass and easel, the objects he liked to paint, his pipe, a few letters and drawings – everything save the man himself, who would probably have been horrified at the thought of it being public. The guides are true enthusiasts, and provided the atelier isn't too busy a visit is a real joy. Admission is by timed entry, with a film show while you wait.

The Terrain des Peintres

Chemin de Marguerite • Free access • Bus #12 (direction "Couteron", stop "Les Peintres")

Two kilometres north of the Atelier Cézanne up the hill of Les Lauves is the **Terrain des Peintres**, an informal Mediterranean garden on the spot where, towards the end of his life, Cézanne painted **Mont Ste-Victoire** over and over again. Despite the suburban development that has covered Les Lauves since Cézanne's day, the view is intact, and this is still the highest vantage point in Aix from which to view the mountain. At the top of the garden plaques depict several of the Mont Ste-Victoire canvases, though they're scarcely necessary, as it would be impossible to imagine this now as anything other than Cézanne's landscape.

ARRIVAL AND DEPARTURE

AIX-EN-PROVENCE

By train Aix's *gare TGV* lies 8km southwest of the town, and is connected to town by bus (every 30min; €3.80). Local trains, including those from Marseille, arrive about 500m from here at the old *gare SNCF* on rue Gustave-Desplaces.

Destinations Marseille (every 20min at peak times; 35–45min); Manosque/Gréoux Bains (2 daily; 50min); Pertuis (9 daily; 30min); Sisteron (5 daily; 1hr 30min); Paris TV (13 daily; 3hr).

By bus Aix's *gare routière* (☏ 0810 00 13 26) is on av de l'Europe, southwest of place du Général-de-Gaulle along av des Belges.

Destinations Aix (every 30min; 15min); Apt (2 daily; 1hr 50min); Arles (6 daily; 1hr 20min); Aubagne (19 daily; 40min–1hr); Cavaillon (3–5 daily; 1hr 15min); La Ciotat (7 daily; 1hr 35min); Éguilles (every 30min–1hr; 20min); Manosque (10 daily; 50min–1hr 15min); Marseille (every 5min at peak times; 30–50min); Marseille-Provence Airport (every 30min–1hr; 25–30min); Martigues (hourly; 1hr 20min); Nice (5 daily; 2hr 20min–4hr 5min); Pertuis (every 20–40min; 45min); Puyloubier (up to 11 daily; 50min); Salon (every 10–40min; 35–50min); Sisteron (5 daily; 1hr 55min–2hr 5min); Vauvenargues (up to 12 daily; 35min).

INFORMATION

Tourist office 300 av Guiseppe Verdi, in the allées Provençales shopping mall just west of cours Mirabeau (June–Sept Mon–Sat 8.30am–8pm, Sun 10am–1pm & 2–6pm; Oct–May Mon–Sat 8.30am–7pm, Sun 10am–1pm & 2–6pm; ☏ 04 42 16 11 61, ⊛ aixenprovencetourism.com). There's plenty of information on touch-screen panels, and you can pick up information on the Cézanne trail in and around Aix.

GETTING AROUND

By bus Local bus services are provided by Aix en Bus (☎0970 80 90 13, ⊛aixenbus.fr); a single ticket costs €1, a three-day "Ticket Trois Jours" €5.

By taxi Taxi Radio Aixois (24hr) ☎04 42 27 71 11, ⊛taxisradioaixois.com; Taxi Mirabeau ☎04 42 21 61 61.

Car rental AGL Thrifty, 34 rue Irma-Moreau ☎04 42 64 64

64; Avis, 14 rue Gustave Desplace ☎0820 61 16 37, Europcar, 55 bd de la République ☎0825 89 69 76.

Bike rental Aix'Prit Vélo, 20 rue Fernand Dol ☎04 42 21 24 05, ⊛aixpritvelo.com; Holiday Bikes, 27 bd de la République ☎04 42 26 72 70.

ACCOMMODATION

If you're planning to visit in the summer, particularly during the June and July festivals, it's worth reserving accommodation well in advance. You can **book** accommodation through the tourist office's website or by calling Résaix on ☎04 42 16 11 85/84.

Auberge de Jeunesse 3 av Marcel-Pagnol, 2km west of the centre next to the Fondation Vasarely ☎04 42 20 15 99, ⊛auberge-jeunesse-aix.fr; bus #2 from the *gare routière* or rotonde Bonaparte to stop "Vasarely". Facilities include dining room, bar, laundry facilities, wi-fi and parking. Accommodation is in four- or five-bed dorms, with a few doubles for couples or families; reception 7am–2pm & 4.30pm–midnight (1am in summer). Closed mid-Dec to early Jan. **€21.10**

Hôtel des Augustins 3 rue de la Masse ☎04 42 27 28 59, ⊛hotel-augustins.com. Smart three-star hotel in a converted medieval monastery just off the cours Mirabeau. Very central and atmospheric, with gothic stone vaulting and modern comforts. **€99**

La Caravelle 29 bd Roi-René ☎04 42 21 53 05, ⊛lacaravelle-hotel.com. Well-maintained, friendly and soundproofed hotel set back slightly from the boulevards ringing Vieil Aix. The more expensive rooms overlook courtyard gardens; some, but not all, have a/c. **€60**

Hôtel Cardinal 24 rue Cardinale ☎04 42 38 32 30, ⊛hotel-cardinal-aix.com. A clean, peaceful and welcoming small hotel in the *quartier* Mazarin, with a/c and 29 rooms furnished in period style, including a few suites with kitchenette. **€75**

Grand Hôtel Nègre Coste 33 cours Mirabeau ☎04 42 27 74 22, ⊛hotelnegrecoste.com. Splendidly situated, rather traditional hotel in a handsome eighteenth-century house with a/c, wi-fi, refurbished bathrooms and comfortable, soundproofed, high-ceilinged rooms, plus private parking. **€90**

Hôtel Paul 10 av Pasteur ☎04 42 23 23 89, ✉hotel. paul@wanadoo.fr. A rare one-star cheapie in the centre of Aix, though on a busy road. It's nothing fancy, but all rooms

have shower and WC and the more expensive ones face the leafy garden at the back. There's public parking nearby. **€51.30**

Hotel le Pigonnet 5 av du Pigonnet ☎04 42 59 02 90, ⊛hotelpigonnet.com. Five-star luxury in the beautiful setting of an eighteenth-century *bastide* surrounded by lush gardens, 10min on foot from the *quartier* Mazarin and with a fancy restaurant, *Le Riviera*. **€315**

Hôtel des Quatre Dauphins 54 rue Roux-Alphéran ☎04 42 38 16 39, ⊛lesquatredauphins.fr. Small hotel with plenty of warm, old-world charm in the peaceful *quartier* Mazarin, with a/c, wi-fi and small, prettily furnished en-suite rooms in traditional Provençal style. **€70**

St-Christophe 2 av Victor-Hugo ☎04 42 26 01 24, ⊛hotel-saintcristophe.com. Comfortable three-star hotel above a smart brasserie close to the tourist office and cours Mirabeau, with touches of Art Deco and a/c, soundproofed rooms. **€97**

CAMPING

Camping Arc-en-Ciel Pont des Trois Sautets, 50 av Henri Malacrida ☎04 42 26 14 28, ⊛campingarcenciel .com; bus #13 (direction "Le Tholonet", stop "les Trois Sautets"). Close to Chantecler on Aix's southeastern outskirts, this is another four-star site; it's not particularly big, but it has a pool, *pétanque* and barbecue facilities. Open April–Sept. **€19.50**

Camping Chantecler 41 av du Val St-André ☎04 42 26 12 98, ⊛campingchantecler.com; bus #4 from *gare SNCF* (stop Val St-André). Four-star site 3km southeast of town. The facilities are excellent and include a pool, volleyball court and restaurant. Open year-round. **€20.90**

EATING

Aix is stuffed full of places to eat. **Place des Cardeurs**, west of the Hôtel de Ville, is nothing but restaurant, brasserie and café terraces; **rue de la Couronne** on the western fringe of Vieil Aix has several worthwhile options, and the elegant café-brasseries lining **cours Mirabeau**, though occasionally pricey, are tempting. That said, Aix's restaurant scene repays careful exploration, as some of the best places are away from these hotspots. As for **drinking**, Aix's preferred style is to lounge on a café or brasserie terrace rather than cram into a noisy bar; there are plenty of the former and a (lively) handful of the latter.

CAFÉS AND BARS

Book in Bar 4 rue Cabassol ☎ 04 42 26 60 07, ⊛ www
.bookinbar.com. Charming café and *salon de thé* in Aix's
English bookshop, with extra seating upstairs, scones and
cakes from €2.50, tea from €2.10 and espresso for €1.30.
Mon–Sat 9am–7pm.

Cha do 46 cours Sextius ☎ 04 42 27 70 63, ⊛ chado.fr.
Trendy gay bar and café on the western fringe of Vieil Aix,
with a full lunch menu of salads (€10), pasta (from €9) and
a few meaty main courses; there's tapas from 6pm to soak
up evening drinks. Tues–Sat 11am–2am.

★ **Les Deux Garçons** 53 cours Mirabeau ☎ 04 42 26
00 51, ⊛ les2garcons.fr. Albert Camus' old haunt
undoubtedly trades on past glories but has a lovely period
interior and good – if not cheap – brasserie food: salads are
€15 or up and there's a €25 *menu*. The terrace is Aix's best
for people-watching over a €10 cocktail or €3.20 *pression*.
Daily 7am–2am.

O'Shannon 30 rue de la Verrerie ☎ 04 42 23 31 63.
Boisterous Irish pub that's just about the liveliest spot for
serious drinking in Aix, with Guinness for €6, Leffe or Stella
at €3–5, plus shots. Mon–Sat 10am–2am.

La Rotonde 2 place Jeanne d'Arc ☎ 04 42 91 61 70,
⊛ larotonde-aix.com. Trendy brasserie on a prime site at
the western end of cours Mirabeau next to the taxi rank,
with a wide terrace, clubby ambience and DJs nightly. Lunch
formule €13, cocktails from €10.50. Daily 8am–2am.

L'Unic 40 rue Vauvenargues ☎ 04 42 96 38 28. One of
the nicest of the bar/cafés facing onto lively place Richelme,
with a terrace that's animated at any hour of the day,
serving beer (from €3) and cocktails (from €5). There's free
tapas from 6pm until 9pm. Daily 7am–1am.

RESTAURANTS

Le Bistrot des Philosophes 20 place des Cardeurs ☎ 04
42 21 64 35. One of the classier offerings on tourist-
oriented place des Cardeurs, with hearty *plats* and a
spacious outdoor terrace. Pasta from €16; grilled tuna with
confit aubergine €17, duck breast with ceps, potato gratin
and lardons €19. Daily noon–2.30/3pm & 7–10.30/11pm.

Cay Tam 29–31 rue de la Verrerie ☎ 04 42 27 28 11,
⊛ caytam.com. Well-regarded Asian restaurant offering
Chinese, Thai, Vietnamese and Japanese cooking in
upmarket surroundings, with *menus* at €16.50 and €21.50.
Mon–Thurs 7.30–11pm, Fri–Sun noon–2pm & 7.30–
11pm; Sept–June closed Mon.

La Chimère 15 rue Bruyès ☎ 04 42 38 30 00,
⊛ lachimerecafe.com. Fun, distinctive restaurant with
over-the-top Baroque decor, red plush, tapas at the bar

(from €7) and plenty of choice on the eclectic menu: €31 for
two courses, €35 for three. Daily 7.30–11.30pm.

Le Clos de la Violette 10 av de la Violette ☎ 04 42 23
30 71, ⊛ closdelaviolette.com. Brigitte and Jean-Marc
Banzo's renowned gastronomic temple offers the likes of
roast sea bream with aubergine cannelloni, *pain napolitain*
and cherry tomatoes, or duck foie gras nougat with
chickpea salad. *Menus* at €50, €90 and €130. In summer
2013 the restaurant is due to move to the new *Renaissance
Hotel* on av Wolfgang Amadeus Mozart, close to the
Pavillon Noir. Tues–Sat noon–1pm & 7.30–9.30pm.

★ **Le Comte d'Aix** 17 rue de la Couronne ☎ 04 42 26
79 26. Cheap, cheerful place serving fish with basil crumble
or minute steak in anchovy butter on an excellent-value
€15 *menu*; the waiter sometimes has to run to keep up with
demand. Mon 7.15–10.30pm, Tues–Sat noon–2pm &
7.15–10.30pm.

Il Etait une Fois 4 rue Lieutaud ☎ 04 42 58 78 56.
Stylish but simple modern dining room, where the €23 and
€37 *menus* include dishes like roast scallops with courgettes
stuffed with *chèvre*, lemon & basil. Daily noon–2.30pm &
7–10.30pm.

Le Jasmin 6 rue de la Fonderie ☎ 04 42 38 05 89,
⊛ lejasmin.net. Charming little Iranian restaurant on the
old town's eastern fringe, with €26 and €32 *menus* and
cocktails from €7.50. Mon–Fri noon–3pm & 7–11pm,
Sat 7–11pm.

★ **Petit Verdot** 7 rue Entrecasteaux ☎ 04 42 27 30
12, ⊛ lepetitverdot.fr. Booking is advised at this amiable
restaurant, where an interior decorated with recycled wine
boxes sets the scene for dishes like braised leg of lamb with
thyme (€20), *pieds et paquets* (€15) or sole with *pistou*,
rocket and lemon (€24). Mon–Fri 7pm–midnight, Sat
noon–2.30pm & 7pm–midnight.

Le Riad 21 rue Lieutaud ☎ 04 42 26 15 79, ⊛ leriad
.com. Upmarket Moroccan restaurant with plush ambiance
and a pretty garden at the back, serving couscous from €14
and with a €35 *menu*. Daily noon–2pm, 7.30–10pm.

Ze Bistro 31 bis rue Manuel ☎ 04 42 39 81 88,
⊛ zebistro.com. Inventive, informal bistro on the eastern
side of Vieil Aix, with a contemporary setting, seasonal
produce and inventive cooking from chef Olivier Scola.
Menus €29 and €39. Tues–Sat noon–2pm &
7.30pm–midnight.

★ **Le Zinc de Hugo** 22 rue Lieutaud ☎ 04 42 27 69 69,
⊛ zinc-hugo.com. Funky, rustic modern bistro and wine
bar with hearty portions of beautifully presented food; the
€26 three-course *menu* is great value. Tues–Sat noon–
2.30pm & 7pm–midnight.

NIGHTLIFE AND ENTERTAINMENT

For **what's on information** check out *Agenda Culturel* available free from the tourist office (see p.160), where you can
also book tickets for events in Aix and elsewhere. Aix nightlife is at its best during the summer **festivals**, when much of
the entertainment happens in the streets.

AIX-EN-PROVENCE FESTIVALS

Aix hosts a wide variety of festivals and events, encompassing everything from cartoons to comedy, and from Hispanic cinema to a half marathon (in May: ⓦsemi-marathon-aix.fr). The undoubted highlight of the festival calendar is the **Festival International d'Art Lyrique** (ⓦfestival-aix.com), dedicated to opera and classical concerts and with an international reputation. It's held in July; ticket prices for major events can really scale the heights – as much as €240 or as little as €20, though you won't necessarily have an unrestricted view if you opt for the cheapest. Tickets can be purchased from mid-February through the festival website, from the box office on place de l'Archevêché (ⓣ0820 922 923), or at FNAC stores.

CLUBS AND LIVE MUSIC VENUES

Hot Brass 1857 chemin d'Eguilles ⓣ04 42 23 13 12, ⓦhotbrassaix.com. Famous former jazz club, recently revamped but still attracting live acts including some star performers, though these days it's more of a disco for the over-25 crowd; smart dress is expected. Entry €26. Fri & Sat 10.30pm–6am.

Le Mistral 3 rue Frédéric Mistral ⓣ04 42 38 16 49, ⓦfacebook.com/mistralclub. Central Aix's liveliest disco, with regular guest DJs and a music policy that spans hip-hop, electro, techno and house. Entry €20, though it's occasionally free for women. Tues–Sun midnight–6am.

Le Murano 24 rue de la Verrerie ⓣ06 06 56 21 97. Buzzy small disco and live venue, handily located on Vieil Aix's main late-night strip and with a variety of themed nights and no cover charge. Tues–Sat midnight–6am.

Le Scat Club 11 rue de la Verrerie ⓣ04 42 23 00 23, ⓦfacebook.com/ScatClub. All kinds of rock, funk and R&B – the best live-music venue in Vieil Aix. Tues–Sat 11pm–dawn; live music Wed, Thurs & Fri.

CINEMA, THEATRE AND DANCE

Institut de l'Image Cité du Livre 8–10 rue des Allumettes ⓣ04 42 26 81 82, ⓦinstitut-image.org. Aix's main art-house cinema, in a former match factory turned arts centre next to the Pavillon Noir, with programmes that include retrospectives of big-name

international directors. Performance times vary.

La Fontaine d'Argent 5 rue de La Fontaine-d'Argent ⓣ04 42 38 43 80, ⓦlafontainedargent.com. Café-theatre with a diverse programme and an emphasis on comedy and children's theatre. Ticket and performance times vary.

Grand Théâtre de Provence 380 av Max Juvénal ⓣ0820 13 20 13, ⓦlestheatres.net. Aix's main stage presents the international stars of classical music and dance, in suitably imposing, modern surroundings opposite the Pavillon Noir. Performances generally start at 8.30pm.

Le Pavillon Noir 530 av Wolfgang Amadeus Mozart ⓣ0811 020 111, ⓦpreljocaj.org. Architecturally impressive modernist performance base for the internationally renowned Ballet Preljocaj, designed by Algerian-born Provençal architect Rudy Ricciotti. The venue also hosts touring productions. Performances times vary, but generally start between 6.30pm and 8.30pm.

Le Renoir 24 cours Mirabeau ⓣ0892 68 72 70, ⓦlescinemasaixois.com. Mainstream multi-screen cinema occasionally showing foreign films in their original language; its sister cinemas are the Cézanne on rue Marcel Guillaume, and the Mazarin on rue Laroque.

Théâtre du Jeu de Paume 17–21 rue de l'Opéra ⓣ0820 13 20 13, ⓦlestheatres.net. Aix's "second stage" is an intimate yet grand 493-seat venue for mainstream and musical theatre, in eighteenth-century Rococo surroundings. Performances generally start at 8.30pm.

SHOPPING

Book in Bar 4 rue Cabassol ⓣ04 42 26 60 07, ⓦwww .bookinbar.com. Aix's English-language bookshop is a charming place to browse, with a café (see opposite). It also

organizes twice-monthly readings. Mon–Sat 9am–7pm.

Confiserie du Roy René 13 rue Gaston de Saporta ⓣ04 42 26 67 86, ⓦcalisson.com. The place to go for

AIX-EN-PROVENCE MARKETS

Aix's markets – possibly the best in all Provence – are not to be missed. On Tuesdays, Thursdays and Saturdays the whole of Vieil Aix is taken up with **markets**. Fruit, vegetables and regional specialities are sold on **place des Prêcheurs** and **place Richelme** (8am–1pm); **Place de l'Hôtel de Ville** is filled with lilies, roses and carnations (8am–12.30pm), the flower market takes place on other days on place des Prêcheurs. Beyond the Palais de Justice, **place de Verdun** hosts the flea market (8am–1pm). Clothes are sold on **cours Mirabeau** on Tuesdays (8.30am–2pm) and Thursdays (8am–2.30pm), and on Saturdays around the Palais de Justice (8am–1pm).

Aix's speciality almond and melon sweets, *calissons*. A lozenge-shaped 160g gift box costs €9.30. Mon–Sat 9.30am–1pm & 2–6.30pm, Sun 10am–4pm.
Puyricard 7–9 rue Rifle-Rafle ☎ 04 42 21 13 26,

ⓦ puyricard.fr. Chocolates of the highest quality, manufactured in the village of the same name just north of Aix. They're not cheap: they cost around €49 for a 400g assorted box. Mon–Sat 9am–7pm.

DIRECTORY

Health SAMU ☎ 15; Centre Hospitalier, av des Tamaris ☎ 04 42 33 50 00; SOS Médecins ☎ 04 42 26 24 00.
Laundry 60 rue Boulégon; 11 rue des Bernardines; 5 rue de la Fontaine.
Money exchange L'Agence, 15 cours Mirabeau

☎ 04 42 26 84 77.
Police Av de l'Europe ☎ 04 42 93 97 00; emergency ☎ 17.
Post office Place de l'Hôtel de Ville (Mon–Wed & Fri 9am–6pm, Thurs 9am–12.15pm & 1.30–6pm, Sat 9am–12.30pm).

Around Aix

There is gorgeous countryside to be explored around Aix, particularly to the east, where you'll find **Cézanne**'s favourite local subject, the **Montagne Ste-Victoire**. In addition, there is the ancient site at **Oppidum d'Entremont** and Picasso's château in **Vauvenargues**. North of the city, the vineyards of the **Coteaux d'Aix** stretch towards the **Abbaye de Silvacane** and the river Durance.

Oppidum d'Entremont

D14 route de Puyricard • Daily except Tues: May–Aug 9am–noon & 2–6pm; Sept–April 9am–noon & 2–5pm; closed first & last Mon of month • Free • Bus #11 (direction "Puyricard", stop "Entremont")

On the northern outskirts of Aix behind impressive ramparts is the Celto-Ligurian archeological site of **Oppidum d'Entremont**, for a brief period the chief settlement of one of the strongest confederations of indigenous people in Provence. Built around 175 BC, it was divided into two parts: the upper town, where the warriors are thought to have lived; and the larger lower town for artisans and traders. Though much of the site remains unexcavated the distinction is still clear, with the latter the more interesting to explore, and there's helpful explanatory signage in English. The site lay on an important trade crossroads from Marseille to the Durance Valley and from Fréjus to the Rhône. Marseille merchants finally persuaded the Romans to dispose of this irritant to their expanding business. The elevated site ensures sweeping views across Aix towards the Montagne Ste-Victoire.

The Montagne Ste-Victoire circuit

The sixty-kilometre circuit of the Montagne Ste-Victoire makes a scenically rewarding day-trip from Aix. Leaving the city, the D10 road east to Vauvenargues passes the quarry of **Bibémus**, painted by Cézanne (guided walks April–May & Oct Mon, Wed, Fri & Sun at 10.30am & 3.30pm; June–Sept daily at 9.45am; Nov–March Wed & Sat at 3pm; €5.50; book through Aix tourist office – see p.160), and the lake and barrage of Bimont.

Vauvenargues

At **VAUVENARGUES**, 14km from Aix, the weatherbeaten, red-shuttered fourteenth-century **château** bought by Picasso in 1958 overlooks the village with nothing between it and the slopes of the mountain. **Picasso** lived there till his death in 1973, and is buried in the gardens, his grave adorned with his sculpture *Woman with a Vase*. The château is kept as Picasso knew it; ask at Aix's tourist office about the possibility of booking a visit (June–Sept only).

Puyloubier

East of Vauvenargues, the D10 splits, with the right fork eventually leading to **PUYLOUBIER**. Here you can visit the French Foreign Legion's **Pensioners' Château**, which sits in a magnificent landscape surrounded by vineyards 1.5km from the

---

CLIMBING THE MONTAGNE STE-VICTOIRE

Though the daunting appearance of its sheer, 500m southern face suggests otherwise, it is perfectly possible to **climb** the **Montagne Ste-Victoire**. Just about the quickest way up is from the Puits d'Auzon car park at Col des Portes on the north side; the ascent to the summit – the 1011m **Pic des Mouches** – takes an hour and you'll need forty minutes for the return leg. From Puyloubier the route is longer and more difficult, the ascent taking two hours with an hour and a half to return. The GR9 footpath runs the length of the crest, following some breathtakingly vertiginous cliff faces; continuing along it you'll reach a pilgrimage chapel and the monumental **Cross of Provence**. Several routes ascend to the cross from the northwestern side of the mountain.

Whatever route you take it's a reasonably serious hike, requiring stamina, sun cream, a hat and at least a couple of litres of water per person. Access to the entire massif is controlled in summer according to the same traffic-light system used in the *calanques* (see box, p.75), and at times of particularly high **fire risk** there may be no access at all; call ☎0811 20 13 13 before setting off to find out what the day's risk level is. For more **information** and a clear map showing the various routes and parking areas (€5), visit the **Maison Sainte Victoire** (April–June, Sept & Oct Mon–Fri 9.30am–6pm, Sat & Sun 10.15am–7pm; July & Aug Mon–Fri 10am–6.30pm, Sat & Sun 10.15am–7pm; Nov–March daily 9.30am–6pm; ☎04 13 31 94 70), on the D17 in the hamlet of Saint Antonin sur Bayon on the south side of the mountain. The Maison Sainte Victoire also has a restaurant.

---

crossroads in Puyloubier at the end of the chemin de la Pallière. Its small **museum** (Tues–Sun 10am–noon & 2–5pm; free, but donation requested) is one for the military buffs, its extensive collection of uniforms including an intriguing series of handkerchiefs printed with instructions on everything from hygiene to boot care and how to assemble a revolver. A shop sells Legion sweatshirts, books and souvenirs.

Le Tholonet

From Puyloubier, the D17 skirts the spectacular southern side of Mont Ste-Victoire to **LE THOLONET**, with its Italianate seventeenth-century château (closed to the public). On the east side of the village, an old windmill, the **Moulin de Cézanne** (hours vary according to exhibitions; call ☎04 42 66 76 28 for information), serves as an exhibition space for art and sculpture, with a bronze relief of Cézanne himself on a stele outside.

The Le Tholonet region also has its own tiny AOC, the **Vins de Palette**, comprising just 23 hectares and a handful of producers: Château Crémade, rte de Langesse (☎04 42 66 76 80, ⓦchateaucremade.com); Château Henri Bonnaud, 945 chemin de la Poudrière (☎04 42 66 86 28, ⓦchateau-henri-bonnaud.fr); and Château Simone, chemin de la Simone (☎04 42 66 92 58, ⓦchateau-simone.fr).

EATING

LE THOLONET

Chez Thomé La Plantation, Le Tholonet ☎04 42 66 90 43, ⓦchezthome.fr. Popular restaurant set back from the main crossroads in Le Tholonet, with tables under the trees, classic *plats du jour* like confit duck, *pieds et paquets* or *andouillette*, and a *menu* at €28. Tues–Sun lunch only.

The Route des Vins

To the north and west of Aix, the vineyards of the **Coteaux d'Aix** fan out across a broad belt of countryside between the city and the river Durance. At 35 square kilometres, this is the second-largest AOC in Provence after the Côtes de Provence itself, and one which is still forging its reputation. The soil is particularly suited to the production of great red wines, with Grenache, Syrah, Cabernet Sauvignon and Vermentino the main grape varieties grown. The rosés are rich and fruity and go well with Provençal dishes like *bourride*; white wines are much less common, but are fresh and fragrant.

A signposted **Route des Vins** follows a circuit through the heart of the AOC, beginning and ending in the village of **ÉGUILLES,** 9.5km west of Aix on the D17; along the circuit the opportunities to stop and try the wines are fairly frequent. Some of the vineyards produce *vin cuit*, a Provençal curiosity that is heated during maturation.

Alongside its winery, **Château Lacoste** at Le Puy Ste Réparade, 20km north of Éguilles, close to the Durance, has an impressive contemporary **art centre** by Japanese architect Tadao Ando (daily 10am–7pm; €12; ⓦchateau-la-coste.com), and an art and architecture walk with sculptures by Louise Bourgeois, Alexander Calder and others.

INFORMATION	THE ROUTE DES VINS

Tourist office Place Gabriel Payeur, Éguilles (Mon–Fri 10am–noon & 2–6pm; in July & Aug also Sat 10am–noon ☎04 42 92 49 15, ⓦmairie-eguilles.fr). Éguilles' tourist office can supply a list of wine producers with opening times and a map of the Route des Vins.

The Abbaye de Silvacane

D561 La Roque d'Anthéron • June–Sept daily 10am–6pm; Oct–May Tues–Sun 10am–1pm & 2–5pm • €7.50 • ☎04 42 50 41 69, ⓦabbaye-silvacane.com

Just off the D561 a little to the east of the village of La Roque d'Anthéron stands the **Abbaye de Silvacane**, built by the same order and in the same period as the abbeys of Sénanque (see p.191) and du Thoronet (see p.205), although the "wood of rushes" from which the name Silvacane derives had already been cleared by Benedictine monks before the Cistercians arrived in 1144. As at the other two great monasteries, the architecture of Silvacane reflects the no-nonsense rule of Saint Benedict (Benoît) in which manual work, intellectual work and worship comprised the three equal elements of the day.

The stark, pale-stoned church and its surrounding buildings and cloisters look pretty much as they did seven hundred years ago, with the exception of the refectory, rebuilt in 1423 and given Gothic ornamentation that the earlier monks would never have tolerated. The windows in the church would not have had stained glass either. The only heated room would have been the *salle des monies* where the work of copying manuscripts was carried out, and the only areas where conversation would have been allowed were the *salle capitulaire*, where the daily reading of "the Rule" and the hearing of confessions took place, and the *parloir* (literally, a room for talking in).

Along the Durance

Twenty-six kilometres from Aix, the D543 from Éguilles reaches the broad River Durance at the **Pont de Cadenet**, an incongruously impressive structure – particularly in summer, when the mighty alpine river it crosses is often reduced to a pathetic dribble. The countryside on the river's north bank shelters below the massifs of the Grand and Petit Luberon and is Mediterranean in climate – hot and dry, fragrant with pines and wild thyme, ablaze with yellow and gold honeysuckle and immortelle, and alive with the quick movements of sun-basking lizards. The Durance Valley is highly fertile and yields the region's classic crops, including all the ingredients for ratatouille, while the lower slopes of the Luberon massifs are dotted with cherry trees and vines, grown both for wine and grapes. Because of the importance of agriculture, the villages here are still very Provençal in character, with fewer Parisians and other foreigners than in the northern Luberon.

As a touring base **Cadenet** has its charms, while the market town of **Pertuis** has the best transport links in the area. The beautiful villages of **Lourmarin**, **Vaugines** and **Cucuron** sit amidst vineyards and the unspoilt countryside of the Grand Luberon foothills, while **La Tour d'Aigues** and **Ansouis** boast elegant châteaux.

BANON
MASCARÉ
SÉCHON
CENDRÉ

East of the dramatically narrow Défilé de Mirabeau and north of its confluence with the Verdon, the Durance has a somewhat different character. The Alps are close here, the river itself is exploited for electricity generation and the valley is busier and more urbanized. The major centres are **Manosque**, a bustling market town, and **Sisteron**, dominated by its splendid citadel. Between the two, the A51 Marseille–Grenoble autoroute speeds along the River Durance, bypassing the industrial town of **St-Auban** and its older neighbour **Château-Arnoux**, renowned for its superb restaurant, *La Bonne Étape*. The views from the fashionable little village of **Lurs** and the ancient **Prieuré de Ganagobie** have not been affected, nor has their isolation. **Volx** is the site of an impressive museum devoted to the olive.

Cadenet

The main road heading north to Lourmarin detours round **CADENET**, lending the place a sleepy charm with few of the chichi airs of the villages to the north. The central place du Tambour d'Arcole holds a statue of a manic drummer-boy, hair and coat-tails flying as he runs. The monument commemorates André Étienne for his inspired one-man diversion that confused the Austrians and allowed Napoleon's army to cross the River Durance in 1796.

Chateau de Cadenet

Off chemin des Rougettes • Free access

An energetic walk or short drive via cours Voltaire and chemin des Rougettes brings you to the crumbly remains of Cadenet's **château**, which was destroyed with pickaxes during the Revolution; most of what remains dates from the sixteenth and eighteenth centuries. It's a bit of a scramble to explore it properly but it's an intriguing ruin, with hidden stairwells and chambers built into the rock face. It's much more extensive than it first appears, and there are wonderful views – over the village's huddled rooftops and the valley of the Durance beyond. On a hot day you'll most likely have it to yourself, with only the deafening noise of the *cigales* for company.

INFORMATION	CADENET
Tourist office 11 place du Tambour d'Arcole (Mon–Sat: July & Aug 9.30am–12.30pm & 2–7pm; Sept–June	9.30am–12.30pm & 1.30–5.30pm; ☎04 90 68 38 21, ⓦ ot-cadenet.com).

ACCOMMODATION AND EATING

L'Ardoise 2 place du Tambour d'Arcole ☎04 90 68 35 35. Centrally located restaurant and crêperie serving salads, savoury *galettes* and a few meat or fish mains as well as sweet crêpes, with a €24 three-course *menu*. Daily noon–2pm & 7–10pm.

L'Auberge de la Fenière Rte de Lourmarin ☎04 90 68 11 79, ⓦ reinesammut.com. Chic *restaurant gastronomique* midway between Cadenet and Lourmarin, using absolutely fresh ingredients to create seriously gourmet concoctions on its €65–125 *menus*. There's also a bistro serving simpler fare on a €35 *menu*. Tues–Sat noon–1.30pm & 7.30–9.30pm.

Camping Val de Durance Les Routes ☎04 90 68 37 75, ⓦ camping-levaldedurance.com. Four-star lakeside campsite between Cadenet village and the Durance, with sports facilities, a pool and children's club. Mobile homes (per week) €490; camping €29

Lourmarin

LOURMARIN stands at the bottom of a *combe* or narrow valley 4km north of Cadenet, its Renaissance **château** lording it over the village from a small rise to the west. The most famous literary figure associated with Lourmarin is the writer **Albert Camus**, who spent the last years of his life here and is buried in the cemetery. Nowadays the village is extremely chic, and often overrun with visitors in summer.

Château de Lourmarin

Jan Sat & Sun 2.30–4pm; Feb, Nov & Dec daily 10.30–11.30am & 2.30–4pm; March, April & Oct daily 10.30–11.30am & 2.30–4.30pm;
May & Sept daily 10–11.30am & 2.30–5.30pm; June–Aug daily 10am–6pm • €6.50 • ☏ 04 90 68 15 23, ⓦ chateau-de-lourmarin.com

A fortress once defended this strategic vantage point but the current **château** dates from
the sixteenth century when comfort was beginning to outplay defence – hence the
generous windows. Since 1929 the château has belonged to the University of Aix, who
use it to give summer sabbaticals to artists and intellectuals. Many have left behind
works of art, which you can see as you stroll through vast rooms with intricate wooden
ceilings, massive fireplaces and beautifully tiled floors where the favoured cultural
workers socialize. **Concerts** are held from June to October and art **exhibitions** of all
sorts are staged.

INFORMATION   LOURMARIN

Tourist office Place H. Barthelemy (Mon–Sat   ⓦ lourmarin.com). Can organize Camus-themed literary
10am–12.30pm & 3–6pm; ☏ 04 90 68 10 77,   walks.

ACCOMMODATION AND EATING

Le Four à Chaux Rte d'Apt ☏ 04 90 68 24 28, ⓦ le-four   secluded hotel set in spacious grounds just outside the
-a-chaux.com. Simple *gîte d'étape* 300m from the village   village off the D943 to Apt. **€96**
on the road to Apt, with two dormitories and one double   **Moulin de Lourmarin** Rue du Temple ☏ 04 90 68 06
room, plus private parking. Dorms **€15**; doubles **€40**   69, ⓦ moulindelourmarin.com. The luxury place to stay
Les Hautes Prairies Rte de Vaugines ☏ 04 90 68 02 89,   in the heart of the village, this eighteenth-century former
ⓦ campinghauteprairies.com. Three-star campsite with   oil mill has nineteen rooms and one suite, stylish Provençal
a pool, food store and a choice of pitches, chalets or mobile   decor and a restaurant. **€150**
homes to rent. Mobile homes (per week) **€469**; chalets   **La Récréation** 15 rue Philippe de Girard ☏ 04 90 68 23
€65; camping **€18.30**   73. Restaurant and *salon de thé* which serves everything
Hostellerie Le Paradou Rte d'Apt ☏ 04 90 68 04 05,   from omelettes and salads to meat and fish mains on a
ⓦ hotelparadou.com. Thai-style decor and a Thai   pretty shaded terrace, with *menus* at €27.50 and €34. Daily
restaurant are the distinguishing features of this small,   noon–2pm & 7–9.15.

Cucuron

East of Lourmarin on the D27, **CUCURON** is large but extremely fetching, with
some of its ancient ramparts and gateways still standing and a bell tower with a
delicate campanile on the central place de l'Horloge. Cucuron had a glimpse of
fame when it was taken over by the film industry for the shooting of Rappeneau's
1995 movie *The Horseman on the Roof*, based on a Giono novel and, at the time, the
most expensive French film ever made; the village has been revisited by film location
crews many times since.

Cucuron's main business, however, is olive oil; there's a twelfth-century **mill** in a
hollow of the rock face on rue Moulin à l'Huile that is still used to press olives. At the

---

THE WARS OF RELIGION IN THE LUBERON

During five days in April 1545 a great swathe of the Petit Luberon, between **Lourmarin** and
Mérindol, was burnt and put to the sword; three thousand people were massacred and six
hundred sent to the galleys. Their crime was having Protestant tendencies in the years leading
up to the devastating **Wars of Religion**. Despite the complicity of King Henri II, the ensuing
scandal forced him to order an enquiry which then absolved those responsible – the Catholic
aristocrats from Aix.

Lourmarin itself suffered minor damage but the castle in Mérindol was violently dismantled,
along with every single house. Mérindol's remains, on the hill above the current village on the
south side of the Petit Luberon, are a visible monument to those events, and to this day the
south face of the Petit Luberon remains sparsely populated.

top of the rock a scrubby open **park** surrounds the surviving *donjon* of the citadel; the journey up to the castle above the Tour de l'Horloge takes you through the oldest and most beautiful parts of the village.

At the other end of Cucuron is the **Église Notre-Dame-de-Beaulieu**, which contains a seventeenth-century altarpiece in coloured marble originally commissioned for the Chapelle de la Visitation in Aix. From the end of May to the middle of August a huge felled poplar leans against the church, a tradition dating back to 1720 when Cucuron was spared the plague. On rue de l'Église, a short way from the church, is a small **museum** (Mon & Wed–Sun 10.30am–noon & 2–5.30pm, Tues 2–5.30pm; ring the bell in the hallway to gain entry; free) on local traditions and early history, with a collection of daguerreotypes.

INFORMATION CUCURON

Tourist office Cours Pourrieres (April–June & Sept Mon–Sat 9.15am–12.15pm & 2.30–5.30pm; July & Aug Mon–Sat 9.30am–12.30pm & 3–6pm, Sun 9.30am–12.30pm; Oct–March Mon–Sat 9am–noon; ☎ 04 90 77 28 37, ⓦ cucuron-luberon.com).

ACCOMMODATION AND EATING

Hôtel de L'Étang Place de l'Étang ☎ 04 90 77 21 25, ⓦ hoteldeletang.com. *Logis de France*-affiliated hotel-restaurant on the north side of the village, by the *Étang* – a pond shaded by plane trees – with a/c double rooms and a restaurant that's open daily for lunch and dinner, with *menus* from €22. **€80**

Lou Badaréu Rte de l'Étang de la Bonde ☎ 04 90 77 21 46, ⓦ loubadareu.com. Two-star campsite 800m east of the village off the D27, with an organic grocery store, *boules* and volleyball courts and table tennis. **€11.10**

La Petite Maison Place de l'Étang ☎ 04 90 68 21 99, ⓦ lapetitemaisondecucuron.com. In the shade of plane trees by the side of the *Étang*, this Michelin-starred restaurant serves seasonal Provençal dishes with luxurious cosmopolitan touches like wagyu beef or *pata negra*, with *menus* at €46, €68 and €90. Wed–Sun 12.30–3pm & 8–11.30pm.

Ansouis

Halfway between Cucuron and Pertuis, the immaculate hilltop village of **ANSOUIS** is crowned by a superb **château** (guided tours April–Aug daily except Tues at 2.30pm, 3.30pm & 4.30pm; €8; ☎ 06 84 62 64 34, ⓦ chateauansouis.fr), which was lived in by the same family from the twelfth century until it was sold at auction in 2008; a millennium old, it owes its present appearance to its gradual transformation from fortress to noble residence during the seventeenth century. The town's austere thirteenth-century **church**, dedicated to St Martin, abuts against the château's outer defences. At the foot of the village on rue du Vieux Moulin is the **Musée Extraordinaire de Georges Mazoyer** (daily 2–6pm; €3.50; ☎ 04 90 09 82 64), is an eccentric miscellany of Luberon fossils, Provençal furniture, paintings by the artist Georges Mazoyer and a blue coral grotto.

Musée des Arts et des Métiers du Vin

Rte de Pertuis, 5km from Ansouis on the D56 • June & July daily 9.30am–noon & 2.30–6pm; Aug–May Mon 2.30–6pm, Tues & Thurs–Sat 9.30am–noon & 2.30–6pm • €5 • ☎ 04 90 09 83 33, ⓦ chateau-turcan.com

A working *domaine* is the setting for the **Musée des Arts et des Métiers du Vin**, a spacious museum devoted to the wine industry and its associated trades, just east of Ansouis. Among the exhibits are an eighteenth-century wine press, bottles and glassware and a section on the craft of cooperage. Afterwards, there's a free tasting of the estate's wines.

EATING ANSOUIS

La Closerie Bd Platanes ☎ 04 90 09 90 54, ⓦ lacloserieansouis.com. Strategically located midway between Ansouis' tourist car park and the château, this classy restaurant serves roast Provençal lamb or veal kidneys in veal *jus*, with a €25 lunchtime *formule* and a €38 *menu gourmand*. Mon, Tues, Fri & Sat lunch & dinner, Sun lunch only.

Pertuis

The one sizeable town this side of the Durance is **PERTUIS**, likeable enough but of interest primarily as a transport hub and as an inexpensive touring base. Like so many towns in the area, it only really comes to life on **market** day, Friday in this case. In August there's a big-band festival (ⓦfestival-bigband-pertuis.com). The town centres around place Parmentier, rue Colbert – the main clothes shopping street leading up to place Jean-Jaurès – and the more historic place Mirabeau just to the north.

Château Val Joanis

West of Pertuis, just off the D973 to Cadenet • April–June & Sept daily 10am–1pm & 2–7pm; July & Aug daily 10am–7pm; Oct daily 10am–1pm & 2–6pm; Nov–March Fri–Sun 10am–1pm & 2–5pm • Winery free, gardens €4.50 • ☎04 90 79 29 77, ⓦval-joanis.com

On the western fringes of Pertuis, the gardens and winery of **Val Joanis** surround the sixteenth-century *bastide* of the same name. Re-established in 1978 by Cécile Chancel and awarded the title French Garden of the Year in 2008, the gardens are an attempt to re-create an eighteenth-century garden with both ornamental and productive elements, including a traditional kitchen garden and a beautiful long arbour planted with rambling roses. The vineyard produces increasingly respected Côtes du Luberon wines, and there are opportunities to taste these – the reserve rosé is particularly fine – and the estate's olive oil.

ARRIVAL AND DEPARTURE   PERTUIS

By train Pertuis is served by the TER (regional train network) from Marseille and Aix. The *gare SNCF* is 1km to the south of town.

Destinations Aix-en-Provence (8 daily; 30min); Marseille (8 daily; 1hr).

By bus The *halte routière* is on place Garcin, within easy

walking distance of the centre; buses from Aix are more frequent than trains.

Destinations Aix (every 25–35min; 55min); Ansouis (up to 3 daily; 15min); Apt (3 daily; 1hr 20min); Cadenet (up to 7 daily; 20min); Cucuron (up to 3 daily; 20min); La Tour d'Aigues (up to 10 daily; 11–23min); Lourmarin (up to 8 daily; 40min).

INFORMATION

Tourist office Le Donjon, place Mirabeau (April–June, Sept & Oct Mon 10am–noon & 2–6pm, Tues–Fri 9am–noon & 2–6pm, Sat 9.30am–noon & 2.30–6pm; July & Aug Mon 10am–12.30pm & 2–6.30pm, Tues–Fri 9am–12.30pm & 2–6.30pm, Sat 9.30am–12.30pm & 2.30–6.30pm; Nov–March Tues–Fri 9am–noon &

2–6pm, Sat 9.30am–noon; ☎04 90 79 15 56, ⓦtourismepertuis.fr).

Bike rental Bikes, including mountain bikes (VTT) and electric bikes, can be rented at Vélo Luberon, impasse François Gernelle, ZAC Saint-Martin ☎04 90 09 17 33.

ACCOMMODATION AND EATING

Le Boulevard 50 bd J. Baptiste Pécout ☎04 90 09 69 31, ⓦrestaurant-leboulevard.com. Pretty, a/c upstairs dining room just south of the town centre, serving the likes of saddle of rabbit with herbs, tian of lamb or stuffed courgette flowers, with a €19 lunch *menu* and a €28 *menu Durance*. Mon & Thurs–Sat noon–1.30pm & from 7.30–9.30pm, Tues & Sun noon–1.30pm.

Hôtel du Cours 100 place Jean-Jaurès ☎04 90 79 00 68, ⓦhotelducours.com. The only option in the centre of town is this small, family-run hotel, with twenty renovated rooms with en-suite bath or shower, plus private parking;

cheapest rooms have showers but share WC facilities. €39

Les Pinèdes Av Pierre Augier ☎04 90 79 10 98, ⓦfranceloc.fr. Three-star campsite in a pine forest east of the town centre, with a pool, paddling pool and activities for children and adults. Closed mid-Oct to mid-March. Mobile homes (per week) €322; camping €26

Le Village Provençal ZAC Saint-Martin rue B. Franklin ☎04 90 09 70 18, ⓦhotel-levillageprovencal.com. Modern hotel in an industrial zone to the south of the town, with a/c rooms, an outdoor pool, restaurant and bowling alley. €66

Château de la Tour d'Aigues

April–June, Sept & Oct Tues–Sat 10am–12.30pm & 2–6pm, Mon & Sun 2–6pm; July & Aug Tues–Sat 10am–1pm & 3–6pm, Mon & Sun 3–6pm; Nov–March Tues–Sat 10am–12.30pm & 2–5pm, Mon & Sun 2–5pm • €5 • ☎04 90 07 50 33, ⓦchateaulatourdaigues.com

Heading northeast from Pertuis towards Grambois brings you to **LA TOUR D'AIGUES**, where the vast shell of the **Château de la Tour d'Aigues** dominates the village centre. It was half destroyed during the Revolution but the most finely detailed Renaissance decoration, based on classical designs including Grecian helmets, angels, bows and arrows and Olympic torches, has survived on the gateway arch. You can admire most of the ruins' glories from the outside, but there's also a **Musée de Faïence** and a small exhibit on the rural habitat of the area inside, covering local archeological finds, the development of traditional rural homes (*mas*) in the area, plus temporary exhibitions. The château is also a popular venue for year-round music and dance concerts.

ACCOMMODATION AND EATING	LA TOUR D'AIGUES
Auberge de la Tour 5a, rue Antoine de Trets ☏ 04 90 07 34 64. Pretty stone-vaulted restaurant opposite the church, with a €12.50 three-course lunch (Wed–Fri); otherwise *menus* at €19 and €25. Noon–2pm & 7–9.30pm; closed Mon & Tues lunch in July & August; closed Mon & Tues Sept–June.	**Le Petit Mas de Marie** Le Revol ☏ 04 90 07 48 22, ⓦ lepetitmasdemarie.com. Three-star hotel a little to the west of the village on the road to Pertuis, with a pool and garden. Closed mid-Oct to early Nov and Jan to mid-March. **€85**

Manosque and around

MANOSQUE, 36km northeast of Pertuis, is an ancient town, strategically positioned just above the right bank of the River Durance. Its small old quarter is surrounded by nondescript blocks, and beyond them by ever-spreading industrial units and superstores. It is a major population centre in the *département* of Alpes de Haute Provence, profiting from the new corridor of affluence that follows the autoroute north.

Manosque is home of the phenomenally successful soap and oil retailer **L'Occitane en Provence**, founded in 1976 by Olivier Baussan, and thus is as responsible as anywhere for propagating the idyllic image of Provence internationally. For the French, however, it is most famous as the home town of the author **Jean Giono**. As well as mementoes of the writer, the town contains an extraordinary work of art on the theme of the Apocalypse by the Armenian-born painter **Jean Carzou**.

Vieux Manosque

Barely half a kilometre wide, **Vieux Manosque** is entered through either of its two remaining medieval gates: Porte Saunerie in the south, or Porte Soubeyran in the north, which sports a tiny bell suspended within the iron outline of an onion dome. Once through the gates it's a little dull, the streets lined with practical but unexciting country-town shops (and quite a few empty premises in the quieter streets); **rue Grande** is much the most enticing, with a fishmonger, a couple of *chocolatiers*, shops selling chèvre de Banon cheese and wine, and a branch of L'Occitane en Provence. Things get livelier for the weekly **market** on Saturday (8am–12.30pm).

Midway between the two gates, on rue Grand, a more intricate bell tower graces the **Église de St-Sauveur**. Neither this nor the **Église de Notre-Dame-de-Romigier**, further up the same street, is a particularly stunning church, though the walls of both bow outwards with the weight of the centuries, and the latter's Black Virgin (black due to the effect of gold leaf on wood) boasts a lengthy resumé of miracles.

At the heart of old Manosque, the **Place de l'Hôtel de Ville** is a pleasant place to linger awhile at a pavement café, though the seventeenth-century town hall itself has suffered from bland modernization.

Centre Jean Giono

3 bd Élémir Bourges • April–June & Sept Tues–Fri 9.30am–12.30pm & 2–6pm, Sat 9.30am–noon & 2–6pm; July & Aug Tues–Fri 9.30am–12.30pm & 2–6pm, Sat & Sun 9.30am–noon & 2–6pm; Oct–March Tues–Sat 2–6pm • €4 • ☏ 04 92 70 54 54, ⓦ centrejeangiono.com

The attractive eighteenth-century house that is now the **Centre Jean Giono**, by Porte

> ## JEAN GIONO
>
> Born in Manosque, the novelist **Jean Giono** (1895–1970) set many of his books in his native Provence. He was imprisoned at the start of World War II for his pacifism, and again after liberation because the Vichy government had promoted his belief in the superiority of nature and peasant life over culture and urban civilization as supporting the Nazi cause. In truth, far from being a fascist, Giono was a passionate ecologist, and the countryside around Manosque plays as strong a part in his novels as do the characters. World War II embittered him, and his later novels are less idealistic. Giono – who detested cities, above all Paris – never left Manosque and died here in 1970.

Saunerie, was the first house built outside the town walls. As well as manuscripts, photos, letters and a library of translations of Giono's work, the centre has an extensive video collection of films based on his novels, as well as interviews and documentaries. Giono himself did not live here, but at **Lou Paraïs**, off montée des Vrais Richesses, 1.5km north of the Vieille Ville (free guided tours Fri & Sat 2.30–4.30pm by arrangement only; call ☎04 92 87 73 03).

Fondation Carzou
7–9 bd Élémir Bourges • Mon–Sat 9am–noon & 2–6pm • Free • ☎ 04 92 87 40 49 ⓦ fondationcarzou.fr

The French-Armenian painter **Jean Carzou**, a contemporary of Jean Giono, confronts the issues of war, technology, dehumanization and the environmental destruction of the planet head on in his extraordinary, monumental **L'Apocalypse**. The work is composed of painted panels and stained-glass windows in the former church of the Couvent de la Présentation, now the **Fondation Carzou**, just up from the Centre Jean Giono. Everything from the French Revolution to Pol Pot's massacres is portrayed here, in nightmarish detail.

L'Occitane en Provence factory
ZI Saint Maurice • **Museum and shop** Mon–Sat 10am–7pm • Free • **Factory** Free 1hr guided tours Mon–Fri by arrangement with Manosque tourist office (see p.174) • ☎ 04 92 72 16 00, ⓦ loccitane.com

On the far side of the A51 autoroute in the industrial quarter of Saint-Maurice is the **L'Occitane en Provence** factory, free guided tours of which include a film and a workshop on the ingredients used in the products. There's also an interactive museum and the marque's largest French store.

Maison de la Biodiversité
Chemin de la Thomassine • July–Sept Tues–Sat 10.30am–1pm & 3–6.30pm; Oct–June Wed 10am–12.30pm & 2–4.30pm • €4 • ☎ 04 92 87 74 40

To the northwest of Manosque, the Parc Naturel Régional du Luberon runs the **Maison de la Biodiversité**, which explains the domestication of fruits and other crops by man, aided by a series of terraced gardens in the shade of a traditional Provençal *bastide*. There's everything from palms to roses, figs and willows, plus a section devoted to old varieties of food crops.

The Écomusée l'Olivier at Volx
Ancienne route de Forcalquier, Volx, signposted off the D4096 • Mon–Fri 10am–12.30pm & 2–6.30pm, Sat & Sun 2–6.30pm; Sept–June closed Sun • €4 • ☎ 04 92 72 66 91, ⓦ ecomusee-olivier.com

Just over 8km north of Manosque in the village of **VOLX**, the **Écomusée l'Olivier** tells, with the help of attractively laid out interactive exhibits and audiovisual displays, the story of the olive – the "gift of the Mediterranean" – and the cultures that have nurtured it, from Provence to the eastern Mediterranean. You can taste and buy Provençal oils of exceptional quality here, and there's also a café.

4

ARRIVAL AND DEPARTURE

By train The *gare SNCF* is 1.5km south of the centre along av Jean Giono and av Lattre de Tassigny, linked by free bus #4 (every 30min) to the *gare routière*.
Destinations Aix-en-Provence (6 daily; 45min); Marseille (6 daily; 1hr 15min); Sisteron (6 daily; 37min).
By bus The *gare routière* is a short walk south of Vieux

MANOSQUE AND AROUND

Manosque on bd Charles-de-Gaulle.
Destinations Aix-en-Provence (every 20min–1hr 10min; 50min–1hr 10min); Forcalquier (7 daily; 30min); Mane (7 daily; 25min); Marseille (every 20min–1hr 10min; 1hr 20min–1hr 50min); Sisteron (3 daily; 45min–1hr); Volx (7 daily; 10min).

INFORMATION

Tourist office 16 place du Dr-Joubert (March to mid-June & Oct Mon–Sat 9am–12.15pm & 1.30–6pm; mid-June to end June & Sept Mon–Sat 9am–12.15pm & 1.30–6pm, Sun 10am–noon; July & Aug Mon–Sat

9am–12.30pm & 2–6.30pm, Sun 10am–noon; Nov–Feb Mon–Fri 9am–12.15pm & 1.30–6pm, Sat 9am–12.15pm; ☎04 92 72 16 00, ⓦmanosque-tourisme.com).

ACCOMMODATION

François 1er 18 rue Guilhempierre ☎04 92 72 07 99, ⓔhotel-francois1er@orange.fr. Reasonably priced two-star hotel in Vieux Manosque; rooms have flatscreen TV and there's free parking for bikes and motorbikes, plus wi-fi. Cheaper rooms share facilities. **€35**
Hôtellerie de La Fuste La Fuste ☎04 92 72 05 95, ⓦlafuste.com. Four-star country hotel across the Durance and 1km along the D4 towards Oraison, in a leafy setting at the foot of the plateau de Valensole, with fourteen individually styled rooms and a restaurant. **€130**

Le Pré St Michel 435 Montée de la Mort d'Imbert ☎04 92 72 14 27, ⓦpresaintmichel.com. Pleasant three-star hotel on the heights overlooking Manosque, with pretty, a/c rooms decorated in Provençal style, plus a restaurant and pool. **€90**
Les Ubacs Av de la Repasse ☎04 92 72 28 08, ⓦville-manosque.fr. One-star municipal campsite on a shady, four-hectare site with 110 pitches, two pools, a children's play area, *boules* pitch and a snack bar/takeaway. Closed Oct–March. **€12.30**

EATING AND DRINKING

La Barbotine Place de l'Hôtel de Ville ☎04 92 72 57 15. Prettily situated in the heart of the old town, with a shady terrace and a chalked-up selection of dishes like veal escalope milanaise or fresh pasta with *pistou*; menu €26. Mon–Sat 8am–1am.

Le Petit Lauragais 6 place du Terreau ☎04 92 72 13 00. Modest place serving cuisine from the southwest, with roast duck with hazelnut *pistou*, sea bass with avocado, basil and pepper oil and a €24.50 *menu*. Mon, Tues, Thurs & Fri noon–2pm & 7–10pm, Wed & Sat 7–10pm.

Lurs and around

Perched on a narrow ridge above the west bank of the Durance some 20km north of Manosque, **LURS** is a *village de caractère*, undeniably charming yet extremely conscious of its picturesque status. Immaculately restored houses stand amid immaculately maintained ruins; there's a tiny, Roman-style theatre, but little commerce. From the top of the village, you can see across the wide, multi-branching river to the abrupt step up to the Plateau de Valensole, with the snowy peaks beyond; to the south the land drops before rising again in another high ridge along the river; while to the west and north the views are just as extensive, from the rolling hills around Forcalquier to the Montagne de Lure. The best way to appreciate this geography is to follow the

THE DRUMMOND MYSTERY

By the late 1940s Lurs was deserted save for the odd passing bandit, but it gained international notoriety in 1952 when the British scientist **Sir Jack Drummond** and his family were murdered while camping alongside the Durance below the village. The case was never satisfactorily solved: the man convicted of the murder was spared execution and ultimately released from custody, and in recent years it has been suggested that Sir Jack was a victim of the Cold War, assassinated because he was a British spy.

Promenade des Evêques – marked by fifteen small oratories – to the small chapel of **Notre-Dame-de-Vie** along the narrowing escarpment.

The village has latterly become a centre for **graphic artists** and **printers**, including the author of the universal nomenclature for typefaces, and their presence has brought life back to Lurs. There's even an annual conference here, the Rencontres Internationales de Lure, which draws in practitioners of the graphic arts, from calligraphers to computer-aided-design consultants, over the last week in August.

The Prieuré de Ganagobie

Signposted off the D4096 south of Ganagobie village • Tues–Sun 3–5pm, closed one week in mid-January • Free • ☎ 04 92 68 00 04, ⓦ ndganagobie.com

About 7km north of Lurs, at the twelfth-century **Prieuré de Ganagobie**, the floor of the priory church is covered with mosaics composed of red, black and white tiles: they depict fabulous beasts whose tails loop through their bodies, and the four elements represented by an elephant (earth), a fish (water), a griffon (air) and a lion (fire). Interlocking and repeating patterns show a strong Byzantine influence, and there's a dragon slain by a St George in Crusader armour. These decorations and the splendidly monumental west portal aside, the church has an almost fortress-like austerity.

Afterwards, you can stroll for a couple of minutes through the oaks and pines along the allée des Moines to reach the edge of the **Plateau de Ganagobie**, 350m above the Durance, and with excellent views.

ACCOMMODATION	LURS

Le Séminaire Place de la Fontaine ☎ 04 92 72 25 57, ⓦ balneotherapie-remise-en-forme.com. *Gîte* and *chambres d'hôte* housed in the old summer residence of the bishops of Sisteron; a/c rooms have wi-fi and en-suite bath or shower, and spa treatments are available. **€65**

The Pénitents des Mées and Château-Arnoux

North of Ganagobie, the impending confluence of the Durance and Bléone is announced by the **Pénitents des Mées**, a remarkable long line of pointed rocks on the east bank, said to be the remains of cowled monks, literally petrified for desiring the women slaves a local lord brought back from the Crusades. By the time you reach **CHÂTEAU-ARNOUX**, hills once more close in and the river takes on a smoother, more majestic prospect, with a barrage just east of the town creating a 7km-long artificial lake. Dominating the centre of the town – pounding traffic aside – is an imposing Renaissance **castle** (closed to the public), with five towers and multicoloured roof tiles. The main reason to stop, however, is to eat at *La Bonne Étape*, renowned as one of the best **restaurants** in Provence (see below).

ACCOMMODATION AND EATING	CHÂTEAU-ARNOUX

La Bonne Étape Chemin du Lac ☎ 04 92 64 00 09, ⓦ bonneetape.com. One of Provence's best restaurants, *La Bonne Étape*'s cooking celebrates the produce of the region without trendy foreign influences on *menus* ranging from €73 to €110. There's also a cheaper bistro, *Au Gout du Jour*, and you can stay here in four-star comfort (€215). Daily noon–1.30pm & 7.30–9.30pm; Oct–June closed Mon & Tues.

Sisteron and around

The last Provençal stretch of the Route Napoléon (see box, p.319) runs from Château-Arnoux to **SISTERON**, the first sight of which reveals its strategic significance as the major mountain gateway to Provence. The town, fortified since ancient times, was half-destroyed by the Anglo-American bombardment of 1944, but its **citadel** still stands as a fearsome sentinel over the city and the solitary bridge across the river. After heavy rains the Durance, the colour of *café au lait*, becomes a raging torrent pushing through the narrow Sisteron

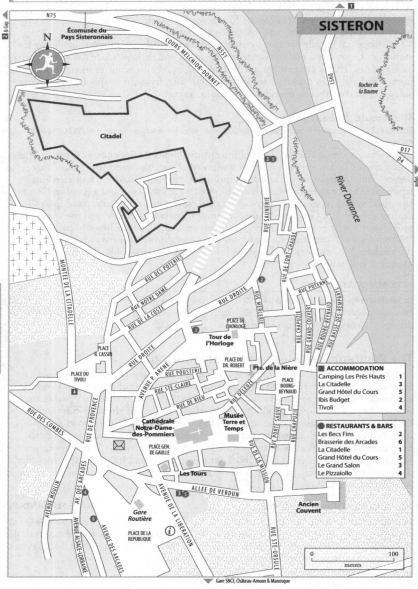

gap. Sisteron today is a lively place, its prosperity based as much on the extensive industrial zone that has grown up to the north along the D4075 as it is on tourism.

The citadel

Daily: April & Oct to mid-Nov 9am–6pm; May 9am–6.30pm; June & Sept 9am–7pm; July & Aug 9am–7.30pm • €6.10 • ☎ 04 92 61 27 57, ⓦ citadelledesisteron.fr

To do justice to the **citadel**, you could easily spend half a day scrambling from the

NAPOLEON IN SISTERON

Sisteron gave **Napoleon** something of a headache. Its mayor and the majority of its population were royalist, and given the fortifications and geography of the town, it was impossible for him to pass undetected. However, luck was still with the Corsican in those days, as the military commander of the *département* was a sympathizer and removed all ammunition from Sisteron's arsenal. Contemporary accounts say Napoleon sat nonchalantly on the bridge, contemplating the citadel above and the tumultuous waters below, while his men reassembled and the town's notables, ordered to keep their pistols under wraps, looked on impotently. Eventually Napoleon entered the city, took some refreshment at a tavern and received a tricolour from a courageous peasant woman before rejoining his band and taking leave of Provence.

highest ramparts to the lowest subterranean passage. There is a leaflet in English but no guides, just tape recordings in French and English attempting to re-create historic moments, such as Napoleon's march (see box above) and the imprisonment in 1639 of Jan Kazimierz, the future king of Poland. Most of the extant defences were constructed after the Wars of Religion, and added to a century later by Vauban when Sisteron was a frontline fort against neighbouring Savoy. No traces remain of the first Ligurian fortification nor of its Roman successor, and the eleventh-century castle was destroyed in the mid-thirteenth century during a pogrom against the local Jewish population.

As you climb up to the fortress, there seems no end to the gateways, courtyards and other defences. The outcrop on which the fortress sits abruptly stops at the lookout post, **Guérite du Diable**, 500m above the narrow passage of the Durance, and affording the best views. On the other side of the ravine, the vertical folds of the **Rocher de la Baume** provide a favourite training ground for local mountaineers.

In the fortress grounds, a **festival** known as *Nuits de la Citadelle* takes place in late July and early August, with open-air concerts and performances of opera, drama and dance. There is also a **museum** with a room dedicated to Napoleon, and an exhibition on Vauban and his predecessors. The vertiginous late medieval chapel, **Notre-Dame-du-Château**, was restored to its Gothic glory and given very beautiful subdued stained-glass windows in the 1970s.

The old town

Outside the citadel, perhaps the most striking features of Sisteron are the three huge **towers** which belonged to the ramparts, built around the expanding town in 1370. Though one still has its spiralling staircase, only ravens use them now.

You can follow a signposted route through Sisteron's **lower town**, along narrow passages with steep steps that interconnect through vaulted archways, known here as *andrônes*. Houses on the downslope side of rue Saunerie, overlooking the river, often descend at the back a further three or four storeys to the lanes below. In the troubled days of 1568, during the Wars of Religion, sixty lanterns were put in place to light the alleyways and deter conspiracies and plots; there's no such luxury today, and Old Sisteron can take on a spooky aspect at night. In the **upper town**, on the other side of rue Saunerie and rue Droite, the houses, like the citadel, follow the curves of the rock.

Cathédrale Notre-Dame-des-Pommiers

Place du Général-de-Gaulle • Mid-April to mid-Sept Tues–Sat 9am–noon & 2–6pm, Mon & Sun 3–6pm; mid-Sept to end Oct Tues–Sat 10am–noon & 2–3pm, Mon & Sun 3–6pm

The twelfth-century former **Cathédrale Notre-Dame-des-Pommiers** has a strictly rectangular interior that contrasts with its riot of stepped roofs and an octagonal gallery adjoining a square belfry topped by a pyramidal spire. The altarpiece incorporates a Mignard painting; other seventeenth-century works adorn the chapels.

Musée Terre et Temps

Place du Général-de-Gaulle • Feb–Nov Tues–Sat 9am–noon & 2–6pm • Free • ☎ 04 92 61 61 30

At the rear of the cathedral, a former convent of the Visitandine order houses the **Musée Terre et Temps**, which charts the measurement of time from ancient sundials through calendars to the latest atomic clocks, in parallel with the measurement of geological time, though after the thrills of the citadel it's all a bit sedate.

Écomusée du Pays Sisteronnais

Cours Melchior-Donnet • Mid-June to early July & early Sept to mid-Sept Mon 2–6pm & Wed–Sun 9–11am & 2–6pm; early July to early Sept Mon 3–7pm & Wed–Sun 10am–noon & 3–7pm • Free • ☎ 04 92 32 48 75

Occupying a striking modern structure on the north side of the Citadelle and with a fine view of the confluence of the Büech and Durance rivers, the small **Écomusée du Pays Sisteronnais** documents the rural life and customs of the Sisteron region, with exhibits of agricultural implements and traditional local crafts.

ARRIVAL AND DEPARTURE   SISTERON

By train Sisteron's *gare SNCF* is on av de la Libération, a short walk south of the central place de la République.

Destinations Aix-en-Provence (up to 6 daily; 1hr 20min); Château-Arnoux (up to 6 daily; 14min); Manosque (up to 6 daily; 42min); Marseille (up to 6 daily; 1hr 53min).

By bus Sisteron's *gare routière* is on place de la Republique near the tourist office.

Destinations Aix (up to 5 daily; 1hr 40min–2hr); Château-Arnoux (up to 12 daily; 15min); Digne (up to 9 daily; 50min–1hr 5min); Manosque (up to 4 daily; 50min–1hr); Marseille (up to 5 daily; 2hr 10min–2hr 35min).

INFORMATION

Tourist office 1 place de la République (July & Aug Mon–Sat 9am–7pm, Sun 10am–5pm; Sept–June Mon–Sat 9am–noon & 2–6pm; ☎ 04 92 61 36 50, ⊛ sisteron.fr). It sells walking and cycling guides and you can pick up a free map of cycling itineraries in the region, including one which crosses the summit of the Montagne de Lure.

ACCOMMODATION

La Citadelle 126 rue Saunerie ☎ 04 92 61 13 52, ⊛ hotel-lacitadelle.com. Inexpensive and central option overlooking the river, with a restaurant, bar and wi-fi. All rooms have TV; cheaper ones share bathroom facilities and they have a family room that sleeps four. **€30**

Ibis Budget 1 allée des Tilleuls, parc d'activités Sisteron-Nord ☎ 0892 680 755, ⊛ ibis.com. Modern, well-equipped budget chain hotel, by the exit from the A51 autoroute 4km north of town, with simple en-suite rooms, free wi-fi and parking. There's a plusher *Ibis* next door **€59**

Grand Hôtel du Cours Allée de Verdun ☎ 04 92 61 04 51, ⊛ hotel-lecours.com. Sisteron's best – and snootiest

– option is family-run, right in the centre of town, with three-star comforts, fifty a/c en-suite rooms, a good restaurant and private parking. **€80**

Les Prés-Hauts 44 chemin des Prés Hauts ☎ 04 92 61 19 69, ⊛ camping-sisteron.com. Well-equipped four-star municipal campsite 3km north of Sisteron off the D951, with a pool, *boules* pitch, children's playround, grocery store, wi-fi and TV room. Closed Oct–March. **€21**

Tivoli 21 place René Cassin ☎ 06 51 36 17 75, ⊛ tourisme.sisteron.fr/acvs/hotels.php Decent two-star hotel just off place de la République. Cheerful and good value, with revamped decor, parking and a terrace with views towards the citadel. **€50**

EATING AND DRINKING

Les Becs Fins 16 rue Saunerie ☎ 04 92 61 12 04, ⊛ becsfins.free.fr. A good bet in the old town, with *pieds et paquets* Sisteron-style on a €16 three-course lunch *menu* or roast duck breast with pepper sauce on a €21.90 *menu*. Daily 11.30am–2.15pm & 6.30–9pm.

Brasserie des Arcades 4 av des Arcades ☎ 04 92 61 02 52. Pleasant, modern bar/brasserie that is Sisteron's best spot for relaxed drinking, with a wide terrace, a light menu of ice creams, salads and sandwiches, draught beer from around €3 and *pichets* of wine for €4. Daily 6.30am–1am.

La Citadelle 126 rue Saunerie ☎ 04 92 61 13 52, ⊛ hotel-lacitadelle.com. Informal brasserie and bar with views over the Durance and a versatile *carte* offering big salads from €12, pizza from €9 and Sisteron-style *pieds et paquets* for €14. There's also a €28 *menu*. Daily noon–1.45pm & 7–9pm.

Grand Hôtel du Cours Allée de Verdun ☎ 04 92 61 04 51. Copious meals in comfortable surroundings, including the renowned *côtes d'agneau de Sisteron* (€20); there's also a €19 *sisteronnais gourmand* platter with lamb and

> **SISTERON MARKET**
>
> **Place de l'Horloge**, at the other end of rue Deleuze from the cathedral, is the site for the Wednesday and Saturday **market**, where stalls congregate to sell sweet and savoury *fougasse*, lavender honey, nougat and almond-paste *calissons* that rival those from Aix. On the second Saturday of every month the market becomes a **fair**, spilling over the much larger space around the Hôtel de Ville. There are likely to be flocks of sheep and lambs, and cages of pigeons as well as stalls selling clothes and bric-a-brac.

andouillette, and a €25 *menu*. Daily noon–2pm & 7–9pm.

Le Grand Salon 33 place Paul-Arène ☎ 04 92 61 15 79. Centrally located café and *confiserie* overlooking the market, with good nougat and *calissons*, sandwiches from €3.40, pasta from €5.20 and a chalked-up selection of *plats du jour* from around €9. Open daily; lunch served noon–2.30pm.

Le Pizzaiollo 2 av des Arcades ☎ 04 92 62 62 60. Friendly and informal, with big portions of pizza and salad plus a few local specialities, including *pieds et paquets Sisteronnais*; pizzas from €8.50, lunchtime *formule* €10. Daily noon–3pm & 7–10pm; closed Sun lunch out of season.

From the Durance to the Luberon

Bounded in the east by the valley of the Durance, to the north by the **Montagne de Lure** and shading to the south and west into the **Parc Naturel Régional du Luberon** (see box, p.187), the **Pays de Forcalquier** is a beguiling mix of agrarian plenty and scenic beauty, with honey, fruit aperitifs, olive oil and cheese to savour and clear skies and pure air to enjoy. It's a region far removed from urban centres, and even the venerable capital, **Forcalquier**, has a sleepy, rural feel to it. The countryside, gentle enough around Forcalquier and the neighbouring village of **Mane**, becomes progressively wilder towards the Plateau d'Albion in the west. Here, remote villages such as **Simiane-la-Rotonde** and **Banon** have a particular charm, not yet as smart as the villages of the Luberon but easily their equal for beauty and history. It's in the more northerly villages of the Pays de Forcalquier, including Banon, that you're likely to hear Provençal being spoken and see aspects of rural life that have hardly changed over centuries. It was here too, in a tiny place called Le Contadour on the Lure foothills due north of Banon, that Jean Giono (see box, p.173) set up his summer commune in the 1930s to expostulate the themes of peace, ecology and the return to nature. But it's not all bucolic and timeless, for the pristine atmospheric conditions have also attracted the attentions of astronomers, whose **Observatoire de Haute-Provence** sits in splendid isolation close to the village of **St-Michel-l'Observatoire**.

Forcalquier

Mellow **FORCALQUIER**, 11km west of the Durance on the D12, dominates the surrounding countryside, its distinctive hilly outline visible for many kilometres around. Close up, the glories of the little town's history are there for all to see, and consequently Forcalquier is as appealing as anything in the gentle, hilly countryside that surrounds it. The town is at its most animated on Mondays when the main **market** takes place.

Some history

Despite its slumbering air, Forcalquier was once a place of some significance, as its public buildings and the elaborate architectural details of its Vieille Ville betray. In the twelfth century the **counts of Forcalquier** rivalled those of Provence, with dominions spreading south and east to the Durance and north to the Drôme. Gap, Embrun, Sisteron, Manosque and Apt were all ruled from the **citadel** of Forcalquier, which even

---

CYCLING IN THE PAYS DE FORCALQUIER

With its beautiful landscapes and relatively quiet roads, the **Pays de Forcalquier** is wonderful territory for cycling holidays. There's a 78-kilometre signposted circuit of the region which takes in Forcalquier, Lurs, Cruis and St Étienne-les-Orgues. For the supremely fit the most tempting route is the 18-kilometre, 1000-metre ascent of the Montagne de Lure, which you can tackle as a self-timed challenge using your smartphone; see ⓦchallenge-lure.com for more details.

For more **information** on cycling in the region see ⓦveloloisirluberon.com; tourist offices sell a mountain biking map of the Pays de Forcalquier (€2) and you can hire bikes in Forcalquier from Cycles Bachelas, 5 bd de la République (☏04 92 75 12 47).

---

minted its own currency. When this separate power base came to an end, Forcalquier was still renowned as the **Cité des Quatre Reines**, since the four daughters of Raimond Béranger V, who united Forcalquier and Provence, all married kings. One of them, Eleanor, married Henry III of England, a fact commemorated by a modern plaque on the Gothic fountain of place du Bourguet.

The Vieille Ville

Looming over the central place du Bourguet, the twelfth-century former **Cathédrale Notre-Dame** has an asymmetric and defensive exterior, a finely wrought Gothic porch and a Romanesque nave. Behind it are the huddled houses of the **Vieille Ville** which date from the thirteenth to the eighteenth century. Bearing right along rue Plauchud from the cathedral you'll reach place St-Michel, where the fountain – a twentieth-century copy of the sixteenth-century Renaissance original – bears decorative figures engaged in bawdy activities.

East of place Vieille off rue des Lices, the house that was supposedly Forcalquier's medieval **synagogue** marks the site of the former Jewish quarter; nearby on rue des Cordeliers is the one remaining gateway to the Vieille Ville, the **Porte des Cordeliers**.

Couvent des Cordeliers

Université Européene des Senteurs & Saveurs ☏ 04 92 72 50 68, ⓦ couventdescordeliers.com

The superior power of the Roman Catholic Church is represented by the **Couvent des Cordeliers**, just off boulevard des Martyrs beyond the Porte des Cordeliers. Built between the twelfth and fourteenth centuries, it bears the scars of wars and revolutions but preserves a beautifully vaulted scriptorium and a library with its original wooden ceiling. Nowadays the complex is the **Université Européene des Senteurs & Saveurs** (☏04 92 72 50 68, ⓦcouventdescordeliers.com), which offers workshops on wine tasting, aromatherapy and olfactory skills. You can wander in the beautiful restored cloister and lovely gardens.

Distillerie et Domaines de Provence

9 av St-Promasse • Mon–Fri 9am–7pm, Sat 9am–1pm & 3–7pm, Sun 9am–1pm • ☏ 04 92 75 15 41, ⓦ distilleries-provence.com.

Just down from place Bourguet, the **Distillerie et Domaines de Provence**, which has been going since 1898, is well worth a visit for its Henri Bardoun pastis and wide range of *eaux de vie*, aperitifs and *absente*, an absinthe liqueur.

The Citadel

Not much actually survives of the ancient fortress of the counts of Forcalquier which once crowned the wooded hill that dominates the town, though the superb 360-degree view of the surrounding countryside is reason enough to make the steep ascent up rue St-Mary from the Vieille Ville. Beside the ruins of a tower and the half-buried walls of the original cathedral of St-Mary there's a neo-Byzantine nineteenth-century chapel, **Notre-Dame-de-Provence**, its distinctive profile visible for many kilometres around.

ARRIVAL AND INFORMATION

FORCALQUIER

By bus Buses generally drop you off at place Martial Sicard, one block back from the main place du Bourguet, except on market days when they stop at place du Bourguet.

Destinations Aix-en-Provence (4 daily; 1hr 40min); Apt (up to 5 daily; 42min); Banon (2–3 daily; 35min); Mane (8 daily; 5min); Manosque (8 daily; 30min); Marseille (4 daily;

2hr 20min); St-Michel-l'Observatoire (up to 5 daily; 8min); Volx (8 daily; 20min).

Tourist office 13 place du Bourguet (July & Aug Mon 9am–1.30pm & 3–4.15pm, Tues–Sat 9am–12.30pm & 3–6.15pm, Sun 10am–noon; Sept–June Mon–Sat 9am–noon & 2–6pm; ☎04 92 75 10 02, ⊛forcalquier.com).

ACCOMMODATION

Auberge Charembeau Rte de Niozelles ☎04 92 70 91 70, ⊛charembeau.com. Three-star hotel in a restored eighteenth-century farmhouse, 2km out of town at the end of a long drive signed off the road to Niozelles. Closed mid-Nov to Feb. **€75**

La Bastide St Georges Rte de Banon ☎04 92 75 72 80, ⊛bastidesaintgeorges.com. Stylish four-star hotel 2km from the centre of Forcalquier, with a restaurant, heated

outdoor pool and spa. A/c rooms have terraces and there are two family rooms that sleep 4–5. **€150**

Camping Indigo ☎04 92 75 27 94, ⊛camping-indigo .com. Three-star campsite on a modest 3-hectare site, 500m out of town on the road to Sigonce, past the cemetery; it also rents out mobile homes, for which there's a two-night minimum stay. Closed early Oct to late April. Mobile homes **€110**; camping **€22.50**

EATING AND DRINKING

L'Aïgo Blanco 5 place Vieille ☎04 92 75 27 23. Classy restaurant and *salon de thé* in the Vieille Ville, with a wonderfully shady terrace and a €17 lunch *menu* including salmon crumble with rosemary cream or *pieds et paquets*; otherwise main courses from €17. Daily noon–2pm & 7–10pm.

Café le Bourguet 7 place du Bourguet ☎04 92 75 00 23. With a broad terrace fronting the central square, this is

about the classiest place for a coffee, drink or snack, with sandwiches from €3.50 and *pression* beer from €2.30. Daily 6am–10pm.

Café du Commerce 4 place du Bourguet ☎04 92 75 00 08. Bustling place on the main square, with main course salads for €12, meat or fish main courses around €17 and a €15 three-course *menu*. Daily: 7.30am–midnight in summer; 7.30am–9pm in winter.

4

Mane and around

The village of **MANE**, 4km south of Forcalquier at the junction of the roads from Apt and Manosque, still has its feudal citadel – now a private residence and closed to the public – and Renaissance churches, chapels and mansions remarkably intact.

Notre-Dame-de-Salagon

Feb–April & Oct to mid-Dec daily except Tues 10am–6pm; May & Sept daily 10am–7pm; June–Aug daily 10am–8pm • €7 with audioguide May–Sept, €5 in winter • ☎04 92 75 70 50, ⊛musee-de-salagon.com

Mane's most impressive building is a former Benedictine priory, **Notre-Dame-de-Salagon**, half a kilometre out of the village off the Apt road. The fortified twelfth-century Romanesque church shows traces of fourteenth-century frescoes and sculpted scenes of rural life. Archeological digs in the choir have revealed the remnants of an earlier, sixth-century church. In addition to the church, the complex comprises fifteenth-century monks' quarters, seventeenth-century stables and a smithy, which is used to display traditional farm tools; there's also an exhibition about lavender. The five **gardens** include one of aromatic plants, a medieval one with medicinal, floral and vegetable sections, a traditional Provençal garden and another which traces the geographical origins of common modern plants. The priory is also the venue for various exhibitions, seminars and discussions.

Château de Sauvan

2.5km south of Mane along the D4100 Apt road • Guided tours at 3.30pm: Feb & March Sun; April–June & Sept to mid-Nov Mon & Thurs–Sun; July & Aug daily • €7.50 • ☎04 92 75 05 64, ⊛chateaudesauvan.com

A few kilometres south of Mane, past a medieval bridge over the River Laye, you come to a palatial residence that has been called the Petit Trianon of Provence. The pure eighteenth-century ease and luxury of the **Château de Sauvan** come as a surprise in this harsh territory, leagues from any courtly city. Though there are hundreds of mansions like it around Paris and along the Loire, the residences of the rich and powerful in Haute Provence tend towards the moat and dungeon, not to French windows giving onto lawns and lake. The furnishings are grand and the hall and stairway would take some beating for light and spaciousness, but what's best is the setting: the swans and geese on the square lake, the peacocks strutting by the drive and the views back to the aristocratic house itself. The gardens are slowly being restored to their historic form, with help from the ministry of culture and the *département* of Alpes de Haute Provence. Work to date has included the planting of 50,000 lavender plants.

Observatoire de Haute Provence

Observatoire de Haute Provence Tours: mid-April to June & Sept to mid-Nov Wed at 2.15pm, 3pm & 4pm; July & Aug Tues, Wed & Thurs 2–5pm • €4.50 • ☎ 04 92 70 64 00, ⓦ obs-hp.fr • Access by shuttle bus from village of St-Michel-l'Observatoire **Centre d'Astronomie** Plateau du Moulin à Vent • Star-gazing vigils July–Sept Mon–Thurs & Sat at 9.30pm, plus monthly vigils on Fri & Sat in winter • €11 • ⓦ centre-astro.fr

The tourist literature promoting the pure air of Haute Provence is not just hype. Proof of the fact is the National Centre for Scientific Research **observatory** on the wooded slopes 2.5km north of the village of **ST-MICHEL-L'OBSERVATOIRE**, southwest of Mane, sited here because it has the fewest clouds, the least fog and the lowest industrial pollution in all France. Visible from many kilometres around, it presents a peculiar picture of domes of gleaming white mega-mushrooms pushing up between the oaks. It's open for **guided tours** during which you get to see some telescopes and blank monitors, and the mechanism that opens up the domes and aims the lens. More exciting, however, are the night-time sky-watching vigils at the associated **Centre d'Astronomie** just east of the village.

Banon

The houses of the tiny Haute Ville of **BANON**, 25km northwest of Forcalquier on the D950, form a guarding wall. Within the impressive fourteenth-century fortified gate, the **Portail à Machicoulis**, the bustle of the modern village below disappears and all is peaceful and immaculate; the houses of the rue des Arcades arch across the roadway and the village peters out just beyond the former chapel of the château at the top of the slope, with only a few stretches of ruined masonry beyond. As lovely as its old quarter is, however, Banon is chiefly famous for the chestnut-wrapped **chèvre cheese** that bears the village's name (see box below).

CHÈVRE DE BANON

Banon is famous above all for its **cheese**. The *plateau des fromages* of any half-decent Provence restaurant will include a round goat's cheese marinated in brandy and wrapped in sweet chestnut leaves, but there's nothing like tasting different ages of the untravelled cheese, sliced off for you by the *fromager* at a **market** stall on place de la République (Tues & Fri mornings). As well as ensuring that you taste the very young and the well-matured varieties, they may give you an accompaniment in the form of a sprig of *savory*, an aromatic local plant of the mint family.

If you want to know more about how *chèvre de Banon* is made, visit the **Écomusée Chèvre de Banon** at the factory on route de Carniol (April–June, Sept & Oct Mon–Fri 2.30–5.30pm; July & Aug Mon–Sat 2.30–5.30pm; €4.50; ☎ 04 92 73 25 03, ⓦ fromagerie-banon.fr).

La Bastide des Mûriers Les Coustoullies ☎ 06 65 67 38 80, ✉ claudetteju04@gmail.com. Two/three bed *chambres d'hôte* in a restored seventeenth-century *bastide* just outside Banon, with private bath, fridge and microwave and access to a pool in summer. €70

L'Épi Bleu Les Gravières ☎ 04 92 73 30 30, ⓦ campingepibleu.com. Well-equipped three-star campsite just outside the village with a restaurant, barbecue, pool and organized children's activities. Mobile homes (per week) €550; camping €19

Les Voyageurs Rue de la Bourgade ☎ 04 92 73 21 02. Lively café/restaurant with a shaded terrace fronting Banon's main square, with a €15 two-course lunch and a €26.80 *menu*. Daily 6am–11pm; closes 8pm in winter.

The Montagne de Lure

Roads north of Banon peter out at the lower slopes of the **Montagne de Lure**. To reach the summit of the Lure, by road or the GR6, you have to head east to **St-Étienne-les-Orgues**, 12km north of Forcalquier. The footpath from St-Étienne avoids the snaking D113 and D53 roads for most of the way, but you're walking through relentless pine plantation and it's a long way without a change of scenery (about 15km). Just below the summit you'll see the **ski lifts**. The mountain is the oldest skiing area in the southern French Alps, and offers green runs for beginners as well as Nordic skiing. You can hire equipment during the ski season (☎ 06 98 29 70 31).

When the forests stop you find yourself on a stony peak, softened only by alpine pastures and a few stunted trees. The 1826-metre **summit** itself is an enclosed mass of telecommunications aerials and dishes. That said, the point of the climb is that the Lure has no close neighbours, giving you near-360-degree **views**, as if you were airborne; the vistas take in the valley of the Durance and, far to the west, Mont Ventoux. The view of the distant snowy peaks to the north is the best; those with excessive stamina can keep walking towards them along the GR6 to Sisteron. The ascent (and descent) of the Montagne de Lure is also popular with cyclists (see box, p.180).

★ **Auberge de l'Abbaye** Cruis ☎ 04 92 77 01 93, ⓦ auberge-abbaye-cruis-monsite-orange.fr. Excellent small hotel in the charming village of Cruis, 5km northeast of St-Étienne-les-Orgues, with simple but pretty rooms in Provençal style and a well-regarded restaurant serving refined creations using local produce on its €47 *menu*. Restaurant open Mon–Thurs 7.45–8.45pm, Fri–Sun

12.15–1.30pm & 7.45–8.45pm. €55

Gîte d'Étape des Crêtes de Lure St Étienne les Orgues ☎ 04 92 73 19 14, ⓦ gitecretesdelure.com. Simple, modern *gîte d'étape* just below the summit of the Montagne de Lure, close to the ski runs and GR6 and with a restaurant, *La Sauvagine*, nearby. Accommodation is in 3- to 7-bed dorms. Dorms €28

Simiane-la-Rotonde

The spiralling cone of **SIMIANE-LA-ROTONDE**, 9.5km southwest of Banon on the D51, marks the horizon with an emphasis greater than its size would warrant. However many *villages de caractère* (Simiane's official classification) you may have seen, this is one to re-seduce you, though it is gradually acquiring the same patina of metropolitan chic as the Luberon villages to the west.

The modern village and much of the commerce – what there is of it – lies in the plain by the D51, cleanly separated from the old village's winding streets of honey-coloured stone in which each house is part of the medieval defensive system. As you ascend through the village you pass all sorts of eye-catching architectural details: heavy carved doors with stone lintels in exact proportion, wrought-iron street lamps, the scrolling on the dark wooden shutters of the building opposite the covered hall of the **old market**, Simiane's most stunning building. With its columns framing open sky, the hall almost overhangs the hillside on the steepest section of the village; no longer used as a marketplace, it's now occupied by café tables.

The Rotonde

March, April & Sept to early Nov Wed–Mon 1.30–6pm; May–Aug daily 10.30am–1pm & 1.30–7pm • €4.50

Simiane's zigzagging streets end at the **Rotonde**, a large domed building that was once the chapel of the castle but looks more like a keep. Nineteenth-century restoration work added smooth limestone to its rough-hewn fortress stones, but the peculiar feature is the asymmetry between its interior and exterior, being hexagonal on the outside and irregularly dodecagonal on the inside. The set of the stones on the domes is wonderfully wonky and no one knows what once hung from or covered the hole at the top. In August the Rotonde is a venue for the annual international **festival of ancient music** (w festival-simiane.com).

INFORMATION   SIMIANE-LA-ROTONDE

Tourist office In the Rotonde (March, April & Sept to early Nov Wed–Mon 1.30–6pm; May–Aug daily 10.30am–1pm & 1.30–7pm; ☎ 04 92 73 11 34, w simiane-la-rotonde.fr). It can supply information on *gîtes* and *chambres d'hôte* in the area.

ACCOMMODATION

Camping de Valsaintes Simiane-la-Rotonde ☎ 04 92 75 91 46, w valsaintes.com. Small two-star *camping à la ferme* southeast of Simiane close to Carniol, with a pool. Closed mid-Oct to March. Bungalows (per week) €460; camping €12.60

Gîte de Chaloux Simiane-la-Rotonde ☎ 04 92 75 99 13, w gite-chaloux.com. *Gîte d'étape* and *chambres d'hôte* off the D51 about 3km south of the village, at the junction of the GR4 and GR6 footpaths. Dorms €17; doubles €59

EATING AND DRINKING

Aux Plaisir des Yeux Haut Village ☎ 04 92 75 94 65, w auxplaisirdesyeux.fr. Restaurant and *salon de thé* serving a €10 two-course lunchtime *formule*; on Thursdays there's a four-course *menu* for €20. You can also buy honey, liqueurs and *crème de marrons*. Mon, Wed & Fri–Sun

10am–7pm, Thurs 10am–10pm.
La Palette Salle Couvert, Haut Village ☎ 04 92 75 95 43. *Saladerie* and snack bar in the atmospheric old covered market hall, with sandwiches from €4 and soft drinks around €3. Mid-June to Aug daily.

The Luberon

The great fold of rock of the Luberon runs for fifty-odd kilometres between the Coulon and the Durance valleys, and sits at the heart of the **Parc Naturel Régional du Luberon**. The massif is divided by the **Combe de Lourmarin**, a narrow gorge through which a lone metalled road gives access south to Cadenet and Aix. The **Grand Luberon** is the portion of the massif to the east of the Combe de Lourmarin, while the **Petit Luberon** is the section to the west. Though many forestry tracks cross the ridge, they are barred to cars (and too rough for bikes), and where the ridge isn't forested it opens into tableland pastures where sheep graze in summer. The northern slopes have Alpine rather than Mediterranean leanings: the trees are oak, beech and maple, and cowslips and buttercups announce the summer. But it is still very hot and there are plenty of vines on the lower slopes.

North of the massifs, the lively market town of **Apt** is the chief urban centre of the Luberon: close to it the remnants of ochre extraction have created the extraordinary **Colorado Provençal**, the vibrant orange-red landscapes of **Roussillon** and the dramatic subterranean spaces of the **Mines de Bruoux**. The most beguiling of the Luberon's **villages** stand on high ground overlooking the vale of the Calavon: **Saignon**, **Bonnieux**, **Lacoste**, **Ménerbes** and, to the north, **Gordes**. Equally beguiling – and mysterious – are the ruined villages of **Buoux** and **Oppède-le-Vieux**.

The Colorado Provençal

Parking des Mille Couleurs, 12km southwest of Simiane-la-Rotonde on the D22 near Rustrel • Free access to site; car park open daily: May & June 9am–6pm, July & Aug 8am–6pm • Free; parking €4 (motorbikes €2); guided tour €6 • ☎ 04 90 04 96 07, w colorado-provencal.com.

OUTDOOR ACTIVITIES IN THE LUBERON

The Luberon's natural beauty acts as a perfect backdrop for all manner of activities. Hiking, cycling and horseriding all allow you to get to know the landscape at a more gentle pace, but there's plenty to please more adventurous spirits too, from ballooning to rock climbing.

Cycling The 236-kilometre bike circuit of the Luberon is particularly well supported: the Vélo Loisir en Luberon scheme (ⓦveloloisirluberon) brings together cycle rental shops, accommodation providers, restaurateurs and others to support cycle-based tourism, providing advice, secure cycle parking, transfers from rail stations or airports and transfers of luggage as well as a breakdown service.

Horseriding There are many places where you can ride in the region, from Vaugines and Cucuron on the Luberon's southern flank to Céreste, east of Apt, Joucas near Gordes and Lauris near Cadenet. Those where English is spoken include: Cap Rando (3hr €55; ☎04 90 08 41 44, ⓦcaprando.com); Les Cavaliers du Luberon (€65/day; ☎06 11 23 26 08); Cheval Enjeu (1–2hr €35; ☎06 87 55 42 09, ⓦcheval-enjeu.fr); La Florentine (1hr 30min–3hr, from €20; ☎04 92 79 05 64, ⓦlaflorentine.fr); Ferme Équestre de Joucas (€85/day;

☎06 07 60 04 18, ⓦchevauxetponeysdejoucas .ffe.com); Centre de Randonnée Équestre Janssaud (3hr €30; ☎06 16 50 47 11).

Hot-air ballooning Get a bird's-eye perspective of the Luberon's ochre with a one-hour balloon ride over Roussillon (April–Oct daily; €230; ☎06 03 54 10 92, ⓦmontgolfiere-luberon.com).

Paragliding Take a beginner's flight over the Luberon from the ochre village of Rustrel (advance booking required; €80; ☎06 69 41 01 07, ⓔphilippelutz @yahoo.fr).

Rock climbing Buoux is the main centre for rock climbing, with qualified instruction (from around €50) available for beginners and more advanced climbers as well as mini-climbs for children. Outfits include Provence Escalade (☎04 90 71 82 51, ⓦprovence-escalade-buoux.com) and Aptitudes Escalade (☎04 90 04 68 41, ⓦaptitude84.free.fr).

4

Immediately to the east of the little village of Rustrel on the D22 lies a series of dramatic former ochre quarries known as the **Colorado Provençal,** the weathered remains of six generations of ochre extraction and iron-ore mining. You'll be given a map of the hiking trails at the car park; the site is quite extensive, with trails leading through both private and public properties, extending to 5.5km. The paths through the site lead you past pumps, quarries, streams, sluice gates and settling basins – the vestiges of nineteenth- and twentieth-century industrial activity. The quarry has weathered into striking and bizarre shapes, and the colours range from luminous yellow to deep red. You'll need to take a guided tour if you want to visit the refurbished Barriès sector of the quarry, where the industrial processes – from extraction to packaging – are explained.

Saignon

Fourteen kilometres south of Rustrel, **SAIGNON** is 4km from Apt but sits high enough to have an eagle-eye view not just of the town, but of the whole region. From below, the village rises like an immense fort with natural turrets of rock; on closer inspection it has an almost troglodyte charm, its houses – some exquisitely restored, others still in a crumbly state – set among the rocky outcrops on which the village's castle once stood. The very best of the views are from the pulpit-like **Rocher de Bellevue** at the far end of the village. The panorama here is almost 360 degrees; given the exposed, windy vantage point, the experience is properly breathtaking, but bear in mind that the steps to the top are a little uneven.

EATING AND DRINKING

SAIGNON

La Petite Cave Rue le Quai ☎04 90 76 64 92, ⓦlapetitecave-saignon.com. Smart, Michelin- and Gault Millau-listed dining in a vaulted stone space, with the likes of rillettes of smoked mackerel or confit duck leg with curried chickpeas and cauliflower purée; two courses will set you back €24, three courses €29. Wed–Sat 7.30– 9.30pm & Sun lunch.

Fort de Buoux

Signposted off the D113; from the gateway at the end of the road it's a 400m uphill walk to the entrance • Daily sunrise till sunset • €4 •
Ⓦ buoux-village.com

From the village of **BUOUX**, 8km south of Apt, a minor road leads the short distance to the fortified, abandoned hilltop village known as the **Fort de Buoux**; the 'x' in the name is pronounced. It stands on the northern flank of the Grand Luberon massif, overlooking a canyon forged by the once powerful River Aiguebrun at the start of its passage through the Luberon.

Numerous relics of prehistoric life have been found in the Buoux Valley, and in the earliest Christian days anchorite monks survived against all odds in tiny caves and niches in the vertical cliff face. In the 1660s, Fort de Buoux was demolished by command of Louis XIV for being a centre of Protestantism, but the ruins – including cisterns, storage cellars with thick stone lids, arrow-slitted ramparts, the lower half of a Romanesque chapel and a near-intact keep – give a good impression of life here over the centuries. Today, the spot is popular with **climbers**, many of whom can be seen clinging to the cliff face as you approach the fort.

ACCOMMODATION AND EATING   BUOUX

Auberge de la Loube Buoux ☎ 04 90 74 19 58. Very pretty restaurant in a loop of the D113 at the entrance to Buoux village, with a flower-filled terrace. There's shoulder of lamb stuffed with ceps on a €32.50 *menu* plus a three-course lunch for €24. Tues, Wed, Fri & Sat lunch & dinner, Sun lunch; closed Jan.

Auberge des Seguins Buoux ☎ 04 90 74 16 37, Ⓦ aubergedesseguins.com. Nestling at the foot of a gorge close to the Fort de Buoux, this busy hotel has a restaurant, pool and informal café, with accommodation in dorm beds or rooms; the cheapest rooms share WC, while for the more expensive rooms and dorms *demi-pension* or full *pension* is required. Closed mid-Nov to March. Doubles with shared WC €55; dorms (*demi-pension*) €40; doubles (*demi-pension*) €110

Apt

The main settlement in the Luberon, **APT**, lies northeast of the Combe de Lourmarin, nestling beneath the northern slopes of the Grand Luberon on the banks of the River Coulon. Best known for its crystallized fruit and preserves, Apt, like so many of the surrounding villages, is gentrifying rapidly as foreigners and wealthy Parisians move in. For now, though, the balance between timeless market town and fashionable urban oasis is about right, and Apt is a likeable and bustling little place with one of the oldest cathedrals in Provence, excellent shops and a lively Saturday **market** (see box, p.188). In July *Les Tréteaux de Nuit* **festival** provides a choice of shows with concerts, plays, café-theatre and exhibitions.

Cathédrale de Ste-Anne

Off rue des Marchands • Summer Mon–Sat 9am–noon & 3–6pm, Sun 3–6pm; winter Mon–Sat 10am–noon & 3–5pm, Sun 3–5pm •
☎ 04 90 74 36 60, Ⓦ apt-cathedrale.com

The **Cathédrale de Ste-Anne** is one of the oldest cathedrals in Provence – not the most coherent architecturally, but an agreeable enough mishmash of styles. The oldest parts of the cathedral include a beautiful fourth-century carved stone ceiling in the *crypte inferieure*; elsewhere slabs dating from the eighth and ninth centuries were reused in the twelfth. The cathedral's chief relic is a veil said to have belonged to St Anne herself. Outside, the **Tour de L'Horloge** (bell tower) spans the rue des Marchands.

Musée de l'Aventure Industrielle

14 place du Postel • June–Sept Mon & Wed–Sat 10am–noon & 3–6.30pm, Sun 3–7pm; Oct–May Mon & Wed–Sat 10am–noon & 2–5.30pm • €4 • ☎ 04 90 74 95 30

Apt's industrial heritage is the subject of the **Musée de l'Aventure Industrielle**, laid out over three floors and covering the major industries of the town and surrounding area:

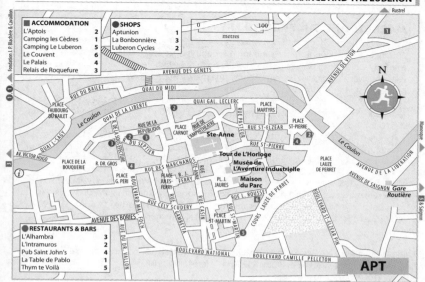

ochre, candied fruits and the production of fine *faïence*. Exhibits include the re-creation of a potter's studio, plus works by the sculptor Alexis Poitevin, who was inspired by industrial themes. The adjacent **Atelier d'Art Fernand Bourgeois** (Wed–Sat 10am–noon & 3–6.30pm; free) is the occasional venue for temporary art exhibitions.

Fondation J.P. Blachère

384 av des Argiles • Tues–Sun 2–6.30pm • Free • ☎ 04 32 52 06 15, ⓦ fondationblachere.org

The industrial district of les Bourguignons to the west of the town is the unlikely setting for the **Fondation J.P. Blachère**, which stages two or three exhibitions each year devoted to contemporary African sculpture and painting.

ARRIVAL AND DEPARTURE

APT

By bus Buses drop you off either at the focal place de la Bouquerie or at the *gare routière* on av de la Libération at the eastern end of the town (☎ 04 90 74 20 21).

Destinations Aix (2 daily; 2hr); Avignon (up to 8 daily; 1hr 10min); Avignon TGV (up to 8 daily; 1hr 30min); Bonnieux (3 daily; 20min); Cadenet (3 daily; 1hr); Lourmarin (3 daily; 40min); Pertuis (3 daily; 1hr 15min); Simiane la Rotonde (2–3 daily; 1hr 10min).

By car Arriving by car, park either along the river or to the east of the town centre.

INFORMATION

Tourist office 20 av Philippe-de-Girard, facing place de la Bouquerie (May to mid-June & second half Sept Mon–Sat 9am–12.30pm & 2–6.30pm; second half June & first half Sept Mon–Sat 9am–12.30pm & 2–6.30pm, Sun

---

PARC NATUREL RÉGIONAL DU LUBERON

The **Parc Naturel Régional du Luberon** is administered by the Maison du Parc in Apt at 60 place Jean-Jaurès (May–Sept Mon–Fri 8.30am–noon & 1.30–6pm, Sat 9am–noon; Oct–April Mon–Fri 8.30am–noon & 1.30–6pm; free; ☎ 04 90 04 42 00, ⓦ www.parcduluberon.fr). It's a centre of activity with laudable aims – nature conservation and the provision of environmentally friendly tourist facilities – and also the place to go for information about the fauna and flora of the Luberon, footpaths, cycle routes, pony trekking, *gîtes* and campsites. The maison has a geology display and also mounts temporary exhibitions.

MARKETS AND SHOPPING IN APT

Saturday is the best day to visit Apt, when cars are barred from the town centre to allow artisans and cultivators from the surrounding countryside to set up stalls at Apt's weekly **market** – on summer weekends there can be up to three hundred of them. As well as featuring every imaginable Provençal edible, the market is accompanied by barrel organs, jazz musicians, stand-up comics, aged hippies and notorious local characters. Everyone, from successful Parisian artists with summer studios here, to military types from the St-Christol base, serious ecologists, rich foreigners and local Aptois, can be found milling around the central rue des Marchands for this weekly social commerce.

The great local speciality of **fruits** – crystallized, pickled, preserved in alcohol or turned into jam – features at the market, but during the rest of the week you can go to La Bonbonnière, 57 rue de la Sous-Préfecture (Mon–Sat 9am–12.30pm & 3–7pm; ☎04 90 74 12 92, ⊕labonbonniere84 .com), for every sort of sweet and chocolate, as well as the Provençal speciality *tourron*, an almond paste flavoured with coffee, pistachio, pine kernels or cherries. If you're really keen on sticky sweets you can contact Aptunion, the **confectionery factory**, in *quartier* Salignan, 2km from Apt on the Avignon road, for a free tour, video and tasting (school holidays only; ☎04 90 76 46 66, ⊕aputunion.com) or just visit the shop (Mon–Sat 9am–noon & 2–6pm).

9.30am–12.30pm; July & Aug Mon–Sat 9am–1pm & 2.30–7pm, Sun 9.30–12.30; Oct–April Mon–Sat 9.30am–12.30pm & 2–6pm; ☎04 90 74 03 18, ⊕luberon-apt.fr).

Bike rental Luberon Cycles, 86 quai Général-Leclerc (☎04 86 69 19 00).

ACCOMMODATION

L'Aptois 289 cours Lauze de Perret ☎04 90 74 02 02, ⊕aptois.fr. Overlooking place Lauze de Perret and the Saturday market, this clean, simple two-star hotel is reasonably priced, cyclist-friendly and has some a/c rooms and some that sleep three. **€60**

★ **Le Couvent** 36 rue Louis-Rousset ☎04 90 04 55 36, ⊕loucouvent.com. Stylish *maison d'hôtes* in a seventeenth-century convent in the centre of the town, with simple, spacious rooms, wi-fi and a private garden with pool. Depending on the weather, breakfast is either served in the former convent refectory or on the terrace outside. **€95**

Hôtel le Palais 24bis place Gabriel-Péri ☎04 90 04 89 32, ⊕hotel-le-palais.com. Inexpensive two-star option bang in the centre of town, above a pizza and pasta place. There's free wi-fi and some rooms have beams or balconies. **€65**

Relais de Roquefure Quartier de Roquefure-Le Chêne, 6km from Apt on the D900 towards Avignon ☎04 90 04 88 88, ⊕relaisderoquefure.com. A large, renovated country house with a pool, restaurant and ochre-tinted rooms with en-suite bathrooms. Closed late Dec to late Jan. **€84**

CAMPING

Camping les Cèdres 63 impasse de la Fantaisie ☎04 90 74 14 61, ⊕camping-les-cedres.fr. A leafy two-star site with just 75 pitches, within easy walking distance of the town, across the bridge from place St-Pierre. Closed mid-Nov to Feb. **€9.50**

Camping le Luberon Av de Saignon ☎04 90 04 85 40, ⊕campingleluberon.com. Three-star campsite, less than 2km from the centre of town, with swimming and paddling pools, restaurant, bar, bakery, barbecue and laundry facilities. Closed Oct–March. **€25.50**

EATING AND DRINKING

L'Alhambra 128 rue de la République ☎04 90 04 08 82. Moroccan restaurant, deli and oriental *salon de thé* in Apt's Vieille Ville, with a three-course lunch for €16, a €24 *menu* and couscous and tagines from around €12. Mon, Tues & Thurs–Sat noon–1.30pm & 7–9.30pm or later.

★ **L'Intramuros** 120–124 rue de la République ☎04 90 06 18 87. Inventive bistro-style food served in eccentric, cluttered surroundings in Apt's Vieille Ville, with the likes of stuffed piquillo peppers with black olives; €26.50 for two courses, *plats* €17. Tues–Sat noon–2pm & 7–9pm.

St John's Pub Place St-Pierre ☎04 90 76 77 49. A good option for leisurely drinking in the Vieille Ville; it faces a tree-shaded square, has a/c and a decent selection of beers, including Kronenbourg and Grimbergen. *Pression* €2.30, cocktails €5.50. They also do salads. Mon–Sat 8am–9.30pm.

La Table de Pablo Petits Cléments ☎04 90 75 45 18, ⊕latabledepablo.com. Book 24 hours in advance to make the trek north of Apt to this restaurant close to the village of Villars for dishes such as scallops with truffled celeriac puree and wasabi foam, or confit Ventoux pork cheek with liquorice. *Menus* €17–55. Open for lunch &

dinner: mid-Feb to May & Sept–Dec closed all day Wed, & lunch Thurs & Sat; June–Aug closed Wed lunch; closed Jan to mid-Feb.
Thym te Voilà 59 place St-Martin ☎ 04 90 74 28 25. Relaxed and cosmopolitan with a chalked-up *selection* of

international dishes, from sea bass *en croute* with ratatouille to Indian-style sautéed aubergines with perfumed rice. Two-course *formule* €16.90. Tues–Sat noon–2pm & 7–9pm; closed Jan–March & evenings in Dec.

The Mines de Bruoux

Rte de Croagne, Gargas · Guided tours (45min) daily: mid-March to June & Sept to mid-Nov 10am–6pm; July & Aug 10am–7pm · €7.50 · ☎ 04 90 06 22 59, ⓦ minesdebruoux.fr

The extraordinary former ochre mine of **Bruoux** at Gargas, north of Apt on the route de Croagne, is entered via a bright orange cliff face into which a number of tall, arched entrances have been cut. These lead to a forty-kilometre network of subterranean passageways, 15m high in places. The guided tour takes you 650m underground, which is enough to give you a good impression of the strong colour, eerie atmosphere and strikingly beautiful, monumental form of the tunnels – altogether more reminiscent of the temple of some lost civilization than of a workaday place of mineral extraction.

Roussillon

Perched precariously atop soft-rock cliffs 10km northwest of Apt, the buildings of **ROUSSILLON** radiate all the different shades of the seventeen ochre tints once quarried here. A spiralling main street leads past potteries, antique shops and restaurants up to the top of the village, and it's worth the effort of walking up for the views over the Luberon and Ventoux.

Conservatoire des Ocres

Usine Mathieu · Feb, March & Oct daily 9am–1pm & 2–6pm; April–June & Sept daily 9am–6pm; July & Aug daily 9am–7pm; Nov–Jan Wed–Sun 9am–1pm & 2–6pm · Guided tours (50min) available; times vary according to season · €6 · ☎ 04 90 05 66 69, ⓦ okhra.com

Just outside Roussillon, on the Apt road, an old **ochre factory** has been renovated as the **Conservatoire des Ocres**. You can look round the various washing, draining, settling and drying areas, though you probably won't get much out of a visit without joining a guided tour. It also hosts excellent exhibitions on themes related to the use and production of ochre, with accompanying workshops for both adults and children, and there's a shop selling pigments and books.

The Sentier des Ocres

Daily: March 10am–5pm; April 9.30am–5.30pm; May & Sept 9.30am–6.30pm; June 9am–6.30pm; July & Aug 9am–7.30pm; Oct 10am–5.30pm; first half Nov 10am–4.30pm; mid-Nov to Dec & second half Feb 11am–3.30pm; closed Jan & first half Feb · €2.50 · ☎ 04 90 05 60 25

Roussillon's **ochre quarries** are close to the centre of the village and can be visited on the **Sentier des Ocres**, which is well worth the modest admission fee to see the strange landforms and vibrant colours of the former quarry, which range from soft pinks to

> ### OCHRE QUARRYING
>
> **Ochre quarrying** has been practised in the Vaucluse since prehistoric times, producing the natural dye that gives a range of colours (which don't fade in sunlight) from pale yellow to a blood red. By the nineteenth century the business had really taken off, with first donkeys and (by the 1880s) trains carrying truckloads of the dust to Marseille to be shipped round the world. At its peak in 1929, 40,000 tonnes of ochre were exported from the region. Twenty years later it was down to 11,500 tonnes, and in 1958 production at Roussillon was finally stopped, in part because the foundations of the village were being undermined. Production continues at Gargas, east of Roussillon, and at Rustrel.

deep orange. There are two circuits – a shorter one and a longer one – and it's hot work on a summer's day, but you'll get a reasonable impression of the quarries even on the shorter route. The ochre is ferrous and influences the type of vegetation found in the area, with species like heather, chestnut, laurel, furze and broom that are otherwise quite unusual in Provence.

INFORMATION ROUSSILLON

Tourist office Place de la Poste (Jan to mid-Feb & mid-Nov to Dec Mon–Sat 9.30am–noon & 1.30–5pm; mid-Feb to mid-May & late Sept to mid-Nov Mon–Sat 9.30am–noon & 1.30–6pm; mid-May to late Sept Mon–Sat 9am–noon & 1.30–6.30pm; in high season also open Sun and public holidays 1.30–5.30pm; ☎04 90 05 60 25, ⓦroussillon-provence.com).

ACCOMMODATION AND EATING

Camping L'Arc en Ciel Rte de Goult ☎04 90 05 73 96, ⓦcamping-arcenciel.monsite.orange.fr Three-star campsite in pine woods 2km along the D104 to Goult, with a pool, paddling pool, wi-fi, shop and (in high season) hot food. Closed Nov to mid-March. €15

Rêves d'Ocres Rte de Gordes ☎04 90 05 60 50, ⓦhotel-revesdocres.com. Two-star hotel on the quieter side of the village a little removed from the tourist hubbub,

with sixteen a/c rooms with views towards Gordes and the mountains, some with private terrace. There are also three- and four-bed rooms. Closed mid-Nov to Feb. €80

La Treille Rue du Four ☎04 90 05 64 47. "World cooking" under a white awning in the Vieux Village, with salads from €14, and Provençal platters featuring aubergine caviar, stuffed piquillo peppers, tapenade and *anchoïade* for €18. Tues–Sun noon–2.30pm & 7–10pm.

4 Gordes and around

GORDES, west of Roussillon and 6km north of the main Apt–Avignon road (but only as the crow flies), tumbles to spectacular effect down a steep hillside to create one of the most photographed views in all Provence. The approach at sunset is particularly memorable as the ancient stone turns gold. The village is popular with film directors, media personalities, musicians and painters, many of whom have added a Gordes address to their main Paris residence. As a result, the place is full of expensive restaurants, cafés and art and craft shops.

In the vicinity, you can see a superb array of dry-stone architecture in **Village des Bories**, as well as the **Abbaye de Sénanque**, and a couple of museums dedicated to glass and olive oil. Gordes' festival, **Les Soirées d'Été de Gordes**, takes place in the first two weeks of August and sees the village awash with theatrical performances, jazz and world music.

The castle

April–Sept daily 2–6pm • €4

In the past, near-vertical staircases hewn into the rock gave the only access to the summit of the village, where the church and houses surround a twelfth- to sixteenth-century **castle** with few aesthetic concessions to the business of fortification. By the early twentieth century most of Gordes' villagers had abandoned the old defensive site and it lay in ruins until the village was rediscovered by artists, including Chagall and the Hungarian scientist of art and design, Victor Vasarely. In summer the castle still occasionally hosts temporary art exhibitions; it's otherwise worth visiting primarily to see its monumental Renaissance staircase and chimney.

ARRIVAL AND INFORMATION GORDES

By bus Gordes does not lie on any major public transport routes and it's likely you'll arrive under your own steam. Infrequent buses connect it with Cavaillon, 16km to the west, and arrive at place du Château, before continuing to Roussillon.

Destinations Cavaillon (1–3 daily; 35–40min); Roussillon (1–2 daily; 15min).

Tourist office Le Château (Mon–Sat 9am–12.30pm & 2–6pm, Sun 10am–12.30pm & 2–6.30pm; ☎04 90 72 02 75, ⓦgordes-village.com).

ACCOMMODATION

La Bastide de Gordes Le Village ☎ 04 90 72 12 12, ⓦ bastide-de-gordes.com. The most luxurious hotel in the village, with spacious, elegant rooms, stunning views over the Luberon from its pool and terrace, and a Sisley spa. **€253**

Camping des Sources Rte de Murs ☎ 04 90 72 12 48, ⓦ campingdessources.com. Three-star campsite five minutes from the village on the D15 road to Murs, with a restaurant, bar, children's play area, minigolf, volleyball, multisports area and pool. Closed Oct–Feb. **€23.70**

Le Provençal Place du Château ☎ 04 90 72 10 01, ⓦ le-provencal.fr. The best-value option in the village, opposite the castle with just seven a/c rooms above a busy restaurant, with en-suite bath, TV and free wi-fi. **€66**

Les Romarins Rte de Sénaque ☎ 04 90 72 12 13, ⓦ masromarins.com. Overlooking the village, this three-star country-house hotel has comfortable, traditionally styled and mostly a/c rooms, plus a garden with terrace and swimming pool. **€128**

EATING

L'Artégal Place du Château ☎ 04 90 72 02 54. Right opposite the castle, serving veal tenderloin with girolle sauce or sea bass with olives and confit tomatoes, with big salads and *plats du jour* from €16, a two-course lunch for €22 and a three-course evening *menu* at €36. Daily except Tues 12.15–2pm & 7.15–9.15pm.

Le Jardin Rte de Murs ☎ 04 90 72 12 34. Gay-friendly café-gallery and souvenir shop, with a pretty garden terrace, Côtes de Ventoux wines, a €15 two-course *lunch*

formule and pasta or salad from €9. Daily noon–3pm; closed Mon Sept–June.

Le Mas Tourteron Chemin de St-Blaise, Les Imberts ☎ 04 90 72 00 16, ⓦ mastourteron.com. Southwest of Gordes on the D2, an old *mas* with an exceptionally pretty garden is the setting for this excellent restaurant; wild salmon tartare with wasabi cream and courgette flowers stuffed with chicken & mushrooms are on its €55 *menu*. Wed–Sat noon–2.30pm & 7.30–9.30pm, Sun noon–2.30pm; closed Nov–Feb.

Village des Bories

4km southwest of Gordes on the D15, signed off the D2 to Cavaillon • Daily 9am–sunset • €6 • ☎ 04 90 72 03 48

About 4km southwest of Gordes is an unusual rural agglomeration, the **Village des Bories**. This walled enclosure contains dry-stone houses, barns, bread ovens, wine stores and workshops constructed in a mix of unusual shapes: curving pyramids and cones, some rounded at the top, some truncated and the base almost rectangular or square. They are cleverly designed so that rain runs off their exteriors and the temperature inside remains constant whatever the season. To look at them, you might think they were prehistoric (and Neolithic rings and a hatchet have been found on the site), but most date from the eighteenth century and were inhabited until the early nineteenth century. Some may have been adapted from or rebuilt over earlier constructions, and there are extraordinary likenesses with huts and dwellings as far apart as the Orkneys and South Africa.

Abbaye de Sénanque

4.7km northwest of Gordes, off the D177 • Guided tours Jan & mid-Nov to Dec daily at 2.15pm & 3.30pm; Feb–April & Oct to mid-Nov 4 daily 10.30am–4.30pm; May 5 daily 10.10am–4.30pm; June & Sept 7 daily 10.10am–4.30pm; July & Aug 10 daily 10.10am–4.30pm; closed Sun mornings and certain religious festivals; non-guided visits are sometimes possible, for individuals only (not groups) • €7 • ☎ 04 90 72 05 72, ⓦ senanque.fr

The **Abbaye de Sénanque** is one of a trio of twelfth-century monasteries established by the Cistercian order in Provence, and predates both the *bories* and Gordes' castle. It stands alone, amid fields of lavender in a hollow of the hills, its weathered stone sighing with age and immutability. Though it has become one of the most familiar Provençal views, visitor numbers are tightly regulated and visitors are asked to dress modestly and to respect the silence to which the abbey is consecrated. The shop at the end of the visit sells the monks' produce, including liqueur, jams and toiletries as well as books, CDs, honey and lavender essence.

From the abbey, the loop back to Gordes via the D177 and D15 reveals the northern Luberon in all its glory.

Les Bouilladoires

The area around Gordes was famous for its olive oil before severe frosts killed off many of the trees. A still-functioning Gallo-Roman press, made from a single slice of oak 2m in diameter, as well as ancient oil lamps, jars and soap-making equipment, can be seen at the **Moulin des Bouillons** (April–Oct daily except Tues 10am–noon & 2–6pm; €5, or €7.50 with Musée du Vitrail) in **LES BOUILLADOIRES**, on the D148 just west of St-Pantaléon, 3.5km south of Gordes, and well signed from every junction. The ticket also gives admittance to the **Musée de l'Histoire du Verre et du Vitrail** (same hours; €5, or €7.50 with Moulin des Bouillons; ☎04 90 72 22 11, ⍟musee-verre-vitrail.fr), housed in a semi-submerged bunker next to the Moulin; the museum contains strongly coloured contemporary stained-glass creations by Frédérique Duran, the artist whose work forms the core of the collection, and plenty of historical exhibits.

Musée de la Lavande

276 rte de Gordes Coustellet · Daily: Feb–April & Oct–Dec 9am–12.15pm & 2–6pm; May–Sept 9am–7pm · €6.50 · ☎04 90 76 91 23, ⍟museedelalavande.com

If you've travelled through Provence in high summer you will have seen, smelled and probably tasted lavender. The **Musée de la Lavande**, on the route de Gordes near the hamlet of Coustellet, offers a chance to learn more about lavender and its uses. Exhibits include copper stills dating back to the sixteenth century, plus there's a film show and free English-language audioguide, as well as the inevitable shop. In July and August there are also daily demonstrations of outdoor distillation.

The Petit Luberon

The **Petit Luberon** has long been popular as a country escape for Parisians, Germans, the Dutch and the British – it was the setting for Peter Mayle's *A Year in Provence* – and *résidences secondaires* are everywhere. It remains a beguiling pastoral idyll, though these day's it's a rich man's retreat, its hilltop villages increasingly chic and its ruins, like **de Sade's château** in **Lacoste** and the **Abbaye de St-Hilaire** near Bonnieux, being restored by their private owners.

Oppède-le-Vieux

Ravishingly beautiful **OPPÈDE-LE-VIEUX**, above the vines on the steeper slopes of the Petit Luberon, maintains an aloof distance from the tourist invasion – literally so, for car-borne visitors are forced to park at quite a distance downhill and huff and puff their way up to the village along a meandering footpath. There's not much commerce either – a couple of cafés and a shop selling classy pottery. It's worth the climb, though. With its Renaissance gateway, the square in front of the ramparts suggests a monumental town within, and indeed at the settlement's zenith in the fourteenth century, nine hundred people lived here. But behind the line of restored sixteenth-century houses there are only the romantic, overgrown ruins that stretch up to the remains of the medieval **castle**; here and there isolated new homes have been crafted from restored fragments of the complex. "No entry" symbols warn you away from some of the more hazardous and crumbly portions of the ruin, while signs in English and French recount the history of the village. From the Vieux Château at the very top, the views are every bit as lovely as Oppède itself.

ACCOMMODATION AND EATING	OPPÈDE LE VIEUX
Petit Café Place de la Croix ☎04 90 76 74 01, ⍟petitcafe.fr. Pretty little *chambres d'hôte* on the main square, with three simply-furnished rooms in suitably rustic style, plus a bistro	serving Luberon wines and duck breast *brochette* with raspberry sauce & ratatouille. The bistro is open for lunch and dinner; closed Tues eve & all day Wed. **€75**

Ménerbes and around

If you head east from Oppède-le-Vieux, **MÉNERBES** is the next hilltop village you come to. Shaped like a ship, its best site, on the prow as it were, is given over to the dead:

from this cemetery – if it's not locked – you can look down onto an odd jigsaw of fortified buildings and mansions, old and new. In the other direction houses with exquisitely tended terraces and gardens, all shuttered up outside holiday time, ascend to the mammoth wall of the citadel, including the beautiful house that belonged to Dora Maar (1907–97) – artist, photographer, and mistress and muse of Pablo Picasso.

Maison de la Truffe et du Vin

Place de l'Horloge • April–Oct daily 10am–12.30pm & 2.30–6.30pm • Free • ☎ 04 90 72 38 37, ⓦ vin-truffe-luberon.com

The exquisite seventeenth-century Hôtel d'Astier de Montfaucon – a former boys' school and hospital – is now home to the **Maison de la Truffe et du Vin**, which has an *oenothèque* where you can taste and buy local wines at vineyard prices, a shop selling soaps, olive oil, flavoured vinegars and (in season) fresh truffles, and a restaurant and *bar à vins* (see below). There's a lovely garden at the back of the house.

Musée du Tire-Bouchon

Rte de Cavaillon, left off the D103 towards Beaumettes • April–Oct daily 10am–noon & 2–7pm; Nov–March Mon–Sat 9am–noon & 2–5pm • €4 • ☎ 04 90 72 41 58, ⓦ musee-tirebouchon.com

Outside Ménerbes is the wine-producing Domaine de la Citadelle's **Musée de Tire-Bouchon**, or Museum of Corkscrews, housed in a château dating back to the seventeenth century. The intriguing collection includes a Cézar compression, a corkscrew combined with pistol and dagger, others with erotic themes and many with beautifully sculpted and engraved handles. You can also visit the wine cellars for a free tasting.

Abbaye de St-Hilaire

Between Ménerbes and Lacoste off the D109 • Daily: week before Easter to June 9am–7pm; July–Oct 9am–8pm; Dec 26 to New Year's Day 10am–6pm • €2 • ⓦ prieuresainthilaire.com

The Carmelite **Abbaye de St-Hilaire**, with its fine seventeenth-century cloisters, exquisite Renaissance stairway and ancient dovecotes, is a handsome work of ecclesiastical architecture, though it's undergoing gradual restoration and at any one time parts of it may be off limits. The abbey is tucked down a rutted track; it isn't large and you won't see much sign of life – you pay your admission fee into an honesty box – but the peace and tranquility are impressive and the setting a delight.

ACCOMMODATION AND EATING   **MÉNERBES**

★ **Café du Progrès** Rue Raoul et Raymond Sylvestre ☎ 04 90 72 22 09. As featured in *A Year in Provence*, this friendly bar/*tabac* is good for cheap snacks and drinks, with sandwiches around €3–4, Paulaner beer and a terrace with superb views over the surrounding countryside. Just in case you're thinking it's all delightfully rustic, check out the titles on the newsstand, which include *Die Zeit* and *The Financial Times*. Daily 7am–9/10pm.

Maison de la Truffe et du Vin Place de l'Horloge ☎ 04 90 72 38 37, ⓦ vin-truffe-luberon.com. Classy restaurant in the seventeenth-century Hôtel d'Astier de Montfaucon, with a luxurious, truffle-dominated menu; *menus* €45 and €72. Tues–Sat 12.30–5pm & from 7.30pm, Mon & Sun from 7.30pm.

Le Roy Soleil Le Fort, Rte des Baumettes ☎ 04 90 72 25 61, ⓦ roy-soleil.com. Quiet and pretty hotel amid olive trees just outside the village, with a pool, bistro (closed Oct–April) and a *restaurant gastronomique* (closed mid-Oct to mid-April). €110

Lacoste

LACOSTE and its château can be seen from all the neighbouring villages, and are particularly enticing in moonlight, while a wind rocks the hanging lanterns on the narrow cobbled approaches to the château, and the castle itself is a floodlit beacon, visible from many kilometres around. These days you're as likely to hear American as French voices in Lacoste, since much of the village forms an outpost of the Savannah College of Art and Design.

4

The château

Daily June–Sept 11am–6pm • €10 • 📞 06 82 25 36 06, 🌐 chateau-lacoste-luberon.com

Lacoste **château**'s most famous owner was the Marquis de Sade, who retreated here when the reaction to his writings got too hot, but in 1778, after seven years here, he was locked up in the Bastille and the castle destroyed soon after. Semi-derelict, it was bought by *couturier* Pierre Cardin in 2001 and greatly restored, and it now hosts a **festival** of music and theatre each year in July. In summer you can visit the château to admire Pierre Cardin's eclectic furnishings and his selection of contemporary art.

ACCOMMODATION AND EATING   LACOSTE

Café de France Lacoste 📞 04 90 75 82 25. Simple rooms – cheaper ones with shared facilities – are available at this café, where the terrace offers views of Bonnieux. The menu ranges from omelettes (€6.50), salads or pasta (from €10) to a few meaty main courses. Café open daily noon–2.30pm and 7.30–9.30pm for food, later for drinks. **€38**

Bonnieux and around

From the *terrasse* by the old church on the heights of the village of **BONNIEUX** you can see Gordes, Roussillon and neighbouring Lacoste, 5km away. But the open aspect and lovely views aren't the only reason to pause here. Larger and livelier than its near-neighbour without being anything like as overrun as Roussillon or Gordes, Bonnieux makes an ideal touring base – if you're fit. Rising in a series of terrace-like switchbacks up a long, steep slope, it's the kind of place where you're forever huffing up the hill or tripping down it.

Bonnieux has its own **Bories**, an abandoned dry-stone walled village, located deep in the forest south of the village off the D36 (daily April–Nov 10am–7pm; €5; 🌐 enclos-des-bories.fr). The village is also home to one of the Luberon's oldest wine-producing *domaines*, the family-owned **Château La Canorgue** on route du Pont Julien (📞 04 90 75 81 01), where the production is organic and follows biodynamic principles in part; you can visit to buy and taste, but it's advisable to phone ahead. Further along the Pont Julien road you'll reach the triple-arched **Pont Julien**, which spans the river Coulon 5km north of Bonnieux, and dates back to the time when Apt was the Roman base of Apta Julia.

Musée de la Boulangerie

12 rue de la République • April–June & Sept Mon & Wed–Sun 10am–12.30pm & 2.30–6pm; July & Aug Mon & Wed–Sun 10am–1pm & 2–6pm; Oct Sat & Sun 10am–12.30pm & 2.30–6pm • €3.50 • 📞 04 90 75 88 34

Bonnieux has long had a reputation for the quality of its bread, which is why, in the upper part of the old village, there's a museum of traditional bread-making, the **Musée de la Boulangerie**. It's housed in a seventeenth-century former bakery with a handsomely proportioned oven of volcanic rock and a period baker's shop on the ground floor. The cellar contains baking implements, the first floor an archive and collection of cake moulds, and the second floor is devoted to the depiction and symbolism of baking, its customs and costumes across the centuries.

Église Louise Bourgois

Le Couvent d'Ô, rte de Lacoste • Guided tours daily in July & first 10 days of Sept • €6 • 📞 04 90 75 80 54

The seventeenth-century Couvent d'Ô, also known as the **Église Louise Bourgeois**, provides a graceful backdrop for several major works by French-American sculptor Louise Bourgeois. The pieces were especially commissioned for the church, and the installation was inaugurated by Jack Lang in 2004.

ACCOMMODATION AND EATING

Le César Place de la Liberté ☎04 90 75 96 35, ⓦhotel-cesar.com *Logis de France* place at the top of the village, with classy furnishings in the lobby, a restaurant serving a €17 two-course lunch, and breathtaking views from some rooms. The cheapest rooms share facilities; other rooms start at €80. €46

★ **Le Clos du Buis** Rue Victor Hugo ☎04 90 75 88 48, ⓦleclosdubuis.com. Very pleasant *chambre d'hôtes* in a former boulangerie close to the centre of the village, with eight a/c rooms, a pool, private parking and views of Mont Ventoux. €129

Le Fournil 5 place Carnot ☎04 90 75 83 62. Lovely Provençal dishes laced with olive oil and garlic, Luberon and Ventoux wines and a pretty terrace fringing a fountain-dominated *place*; two courses are €22.80, three €27.80. Tues–Fri & Sun open for lunch from noon & dinner from 7.30pm, Sat open for lunch from noon.

4

The Haut Var and Haute Provence

GRAND CANYON DU VERDON

5

The Haut Var and Haute Provence

Stretching from the Chaîne de la Ste-Baume up to the Alpes-de-Haute-Provence, the unspoiled geographical heartland of Provence is characterized by deep valleys and snowcapped mountains in the north, the source of several rivers that flow down to the gentle undulating fields of vines, lavender, sunflowers and poppies in the south. Small towns and villages such as Aups and Cotignac still thrive on their traditional industries of making honey, tending sheep, digging for truffles and pressing olive oil; and in isolated areas it's hard to believe this is the same country, never mind province, as the Côte d'Azur. Landscapes are exceptional, from the gentle countryside of the Haut Var or Pays de Forcalquier to the wild emptiness of the Plateau de Canjuers, the untrammelled forests east of Draguignan, and, most spectacularly of all, Europe's largest ravine, the Grand Canyon du Verdon.

Food is fundamentally Provençal: lamb from the high summer pastures, goat's cheese, honey, almonds, olives and wild herbs. The soil is poor and water scarce, but the Côtes de Provence **wine** *appellation* extends to the Upper Var.

The towns, like busy but workaday **Draguignan**, are not the prime appeal. First and foremost, this is an area for **walking** and **climbing**, or **canoeing** and **windsurfing** on the countless lakes that provide power and irrigation. The Grand Canyon du Verdon is a must, even if only seen from a car or bus. The best way to discover the area, however, is simply to stay in a village that takes your fancy, eating, dawdling and letting yourself drift into the rhythms of local life.

The mountainous northeastern corner of Provence, **Haute Provence**, is a different world from season to season. In **spring** the fruit trees in the narrow valleys blossom, and melting waters swell the Verdon, the Vésubie, the Var, the Tinée and the Roya, sometimes flooding villages and carrying whole streets away. In the foothills, the groves of chestnut and olive trees bear fruit in **summer** and **autumn**, while higher up the pine forests are edged with wild raspberries and bilberries, and the moors and grassy slopes with white and gold alpine flowers. Above the line where vegetation ceases lie rocks with eagles' nests and snowcaps that never melt. In **winter** the sheep and shepherds retreat to warmer pastures, leaving the snowy heights to antlered mouflons and chamois, and the perfectly camouflaged ermine. The villages, where the shepherds came to summer markets, are battened down for the long cold haul, while modern conglomerations of Swiss-style chalet houses, sports shops and late-night bars come to life around the ski lifts. From November to April many of the mountain passes are closed, cutting off the dreamy northern town of **Barçelonnette** from its lower neighbours.

This is not an easy place to live. Abandoned farms and overgrown terraced slopes bear witness to the declining viability of mountain agriculture. But the **ski resorts** bring in money, while summer sees an influx of trekkers, naturalists and climbers. One area, covering 75km from east to west, protected as the **Parc National du Mercantour**, has no permanent inhabitants at all.

ABBAYE DU THORONET

Highlights

❶ Abbaye du Thoronet An exquisite rose-coloured monastic complex, and the oldest of Provence's three great Cistercian monasteries. **See p.205**

❷ Aups With its fabulous crop of well-priced hotel-restaurants, this lovely rural town makes a perfect overnight stop. **See p.208**

❸ Grand Canyon du Verdon Walk, drive, cycle, raft or bungee, but whatever you do, don't miss Europe's largest and most spectacular gorge. **See p.216**

❹ Parc National du Mercantour An unspoiled alpine wilderness that is home to the Vallée des Merveilles and its mysterious four-thousand-year-old rock carvings. **See p.225**

❺ Entrevaux and Colmars-les-Alpes Both these picturesque towns retain beautifully preserved fortifications designed by Vauban. **See p.232 & p.229**

❻ Skiing in the Alpes-Maritimes Slide down the mountain in the resorts of Auron and Allos. **See p.234 & p.228**

❼ The Clues of Haute Provence A hidden landscape of rocky gorges, tiny villages and rural tranquillity, a mere 40km from the Riviera. **See pp.242–245**

HIGHLIGHTS ARE MARKED ON THE MAP ON P.200

5

For centuries the border between Provence and Savoy ran through this part of France, a political divide embodied by the impressive fortifications of **Entrevaux** and **Colmars**, the principal town of the Haut Verdon. To this day, most of the region is not considered to be part of Provence. The French refer to it by the geographical term, the **Alpes-Maritimes**, which is also the name of the *département* that stretches from between the Haut Var and Verdon valleys and just above the source of the Tinée Valley to the Italian border, and includes the Riviera. Where Provence ends and the Alps begin is debatable, but the **Tinée Valley** is usually cited as definitely belonging to the latter – the mountains here are pretty serious and the Italian influence becomes noticeable.

Running along the southern limit of the Alps, the **Nice–Digne rail line**, known as both the Chemins de Fer de Provence and the **Train des Pignes**, is the only remaining segment of the region's nineteenth- and twentieth-century narrow-gauge network. One of the great train rides of France, it takes in the isolated Var towns of **Puget-Théniers** and Entrevaux, and ends at low-key **Digne**, the centre of the lavender industry. Away from the Nice–Digne line, public transport is a problem except in the **Roya Valley**, over

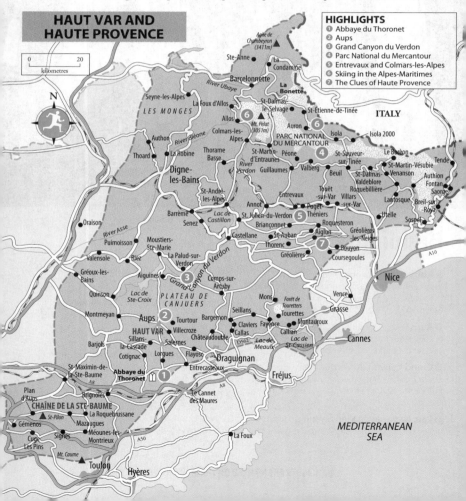

HAUT VAR AND HAUTE PROVENCE

0   20
kilometres

HIGHLIGHTS
1 Abbaye du Thoronet
2 Aups
3 Grand Canyon du Verdon
4 Parc National du Mercantour
5 Entrevaux and Colmars-les-Alpes
6 Skiing in the Alpes-Maritimes
7 The Clues of Haute Provence

in the east, where the **Nice–Turin rail line** links the Italianate towns of **Tende** and **Sospel**. Buses are infrequent and many of the best starting points for walks or the far-flung pilgrimage chapels are off the main roads. With your own transport, you'll face tough climbs and long stretches with no fuel supplies, but you'll be free to explore the most exhilaratingly beautiful corner of Provence.

The Chaîne de la Ste-Baume

East of **Aubagne**, described on p.72, the urban sprawl that surrounds Marseille finally slips away in the unspoiled **Chaîne de la Ste-Baume**, a sparsely populated region of rich forests. The plateau to the north is wonderful territory for walking and cycling, its northern face holding a profusion of woods, flowers and wildlife rare in these hot latitudes. The entire area north to **St-Maximin**, south to **Signes**, west to **Gémenos** and east to **La Roquebrussanne** is protected. You are not allowed to camp in the woods or light fires, and an ancient royal edict still forbids the picking of orchids.

Gémenos

Thanks to the beautiful seventeenth-century château that serves as its Hôtel de Ville, **GÉMENOS**, 3km east of Aubagne, makes a tempting place to stop. Cafés, bars and patisseries surround the château, while there are some welcoming hotels further out.

Plan-d'Aups and the Ste-Baume summit

Northeast of Gémenos, the D2 follows the narrow valley of St-Pons, past an open-air municipal theatre cut into the rock and the **Parc Naturel de St-Pons**, where beech, hornbeam, ash and maple trees surround the ruins of a thirteenth-century Cistercian abbey, before beginning the zigzagging ascent to the Espigoulier pass. A footpath beyond the park soon links to the GR98, which climbs directly up the Ste-Baume massif and then follows the ridge, with breathtaking views.

At **PLAN-D'AUPS**, which also has a tiny Romanesque church, the dramatic climb levels out to a forested plateau running parallel to the ridge of Ste-Baume, which cuts across the sky like a massively fortified wall. The Hôtellerie de la Ste-Baume, a roadside pilgrimage centre 3km east of Plan d'Aups that's run by Dominican friars, is the starting point for a **pilgrimage** based on Provençal mythology, or simply a walk up to the peaks. The myth takes over from the sea-voyage arrival in Stes-Maries-de-la-Mer of Mary Magdalene, Mary Salomé, Mary Jacobé and St-Maximin (see box p.108). **Mary Magdalene**, for some unexplained reason, gets transported by angels to a cave (*grotte*) just below the summit of Ste-Baume. There she spends 33 years, before being flown to St-Maximin-de-la-Ste-Baume (see p.202) to die.

The difficult **paths** up from the Hôtellerie are dotted with oratories, calvaries and crosses. It takes roughly an hour to reach the suitably sombre *grotte* at the top, where Mass is held daily at 10.30am. The path beyond, leading to the **St-Pilon summit**, makes you wish for some of Mary's winged pilots.

East to La Roquebrussanne

East of Plan-d'Aups, the D95 crosses many kilometres of unspoiled forest. These groves of spindly, stunted oaks and beeches have exerted a mystical pull since ancient times, and are said to have been sacred to the Druids. Around the village of **MAZAUGUES**, you pass huge, nineteenth-century covered stone wells, built to hold ice that could then be transported on early summer nights down to Marseille or Toulon. The **Musée de la**

5

Glace (June–Sept Tues–Sun 9am–noon & 2–6pm; Oct–May Sun 9am–noon & 2–5pm; €2.50; ☎04 94 86 39 24, ⓦmuseedelaglace.free.fr) traces the history of ice-making in Provence and worldwide.

From Mazaugues the GR99 footpath takes you, after an initial steep climb, on a gentle three- to four-hour walk down to Signes. Continuing east by road will bring you to the attractive village of **LA ROQUEBRUSSANNE**, home to a large Saturday food **market**.

Signes

Beside the lovely Gapeau stream 14km southwest of La Roquebrussanne, **SIGNES** is an appealing little village where palm trees and white roses grow around the war memorial, the clock tower is more than four hundred years old, and the people make their living from wine, olives, cereals and market gardening. Its Thursday **market** centres on place Marcel-Pagnol.

St-Maximin-de-la-Ste-Baume

The handsome old town of **ST-MAXIMIN-DE-LA-STE-BAUME** is where, in 1279, the count of Provence supposedly discovered a crypt containing the relics of Mary Magdalene and Saint Maximin, hidden during a Saracen raid. He set about building a basilica and **monastery**, which was consecrated in 1316, though building continued in stages up until 1532. The medieval streets that surround the basilica have considerable charm, with their uniform tiled roofs at anything but uniform heights, and there's a reasonable assortment of **cafés** and **brasseries**, congregating on place Malherbe, as well as shops selling the work of local artisans.

Basilica and monastery of St-Maximin

Basilica Daily 8am–6pm • **Cloisters and chapterhouse** Daily 8am–6pm • Free

St-Maximin's basilica and adjoining monastery took their present shape in the fifteenth century, and have since been extravagantly decorated in stone, wood, gold, silk and oil paint. There is, therefore, plenty to look at in the substantial Gothic **basilica**, including beautiful wood panelling in the choir and paintings on the nave walls, as well as Ronzen's lovely *Retable de la Passion* (1520). Also look out for the wonderfully sculpted fourth-century sarcophagi, and the grotesque skull once venerated as that of Mary Magdalene, encased in a glass helmet framed by a gold neck and hair, in the **crypt**.

The thirteenth-century **cloisters** and chapterhouse of the monastery, reached via the *Couvent Royal* (see opposite), are much more delicate. Look down the well to see the escape route used by the Dominican friars during several sixteenth-century sieges.

South of the church, a covered passageway leads into the arcaded rue Colbert, a former Jewish ghetto.

INFORMATION	THE CHAÎNE DE LA STE-BAUME
SIGNES	**ST-MAXIMIN-DE-LA-STE-BAUME**
Tourist office In the *médiathèque* on rue Frédéric-Mistral (Wed–Sat 10am–noon & 2–6.30pm; ☎04 94 98 87 80, ⓦsignes.com).	**Tourist office** Place Jean Salusse (Mon–Sat 9am–12.30pm & 2–6pm, Sun 10am–12.30pm & 2–5pm; ☎04 94 59 84 59, ⓦst-maximin.fr).

ACCOMMODATION AND EATING	
GÉMENOS	
Le Provence 200 av du 2ème Cuirassier ☎04 42 32 20 55, ⓦhotel-le-provence.fr. Friendly, good-value hotel, 600m northwest of the old centre, where the cheapest of the bright, simple rooms share toilets, while larger family suites have balconies and sleep up to five. **€39**	**Relais de la Magdeleine** Rond pont de la Fontaine ☎04 42 32 20 16, ⓦwww.relais-magdeleine.com. Magnificent luxury hotel, set in a lovely, vine-covered eighteenth-century manor house in a park designed by Le Nôtre, just off the N396 route d'Aix. Lunch *menu* €33, otherwise €46 and €60; closed mid-Nov to mid-March. **€130**

PLAN-D'AUPS

Lou Pèbre d'Aï Quartier Ste-Madeleine ☎ 04 42 04 50 42, ⓦ loupebredai.com. Comfortable small hotel, where five of the six rooms have mountain-view balconies, there's a heated pool, and the restaurant serves good seasonal *menus*, from €15 for lunch, €27 for dinner. **€58**

SIGNES

Château de Cancerilles Route de Belgentier ☎ 04 94 90 81 45, ⓦ chateaudecancerilles.com. The Garcia family's wonderful *chambres d'hôtes* in an old stone farm surrounded by vines, where rooms rent by the week in high season but by the night for the rest of the year. **€90**

ST-MAXIMIN-DE-LA-STE-BAUME

★ **Couvent Royal** Place Jean-Salusse ☎ 04 94 86 55 66, ⓦ www.hotelfp-saintmaximin.com. This enormous, imposing thirteenth-century monastery has been converted into a comfortable and highly atmospheric hotel. Some of its clean, excellent-value rooms used to be monks' cells; look for bargain rates online. *Menus* in the elegant restaurant adjoining the cloister (closed Sun eve) start at €39. **€140**

Plaisance 20 place Malherbe ☎ 04 94 78 16 74, ⓦ plaisance-hotel.com. A short walk west of the monastery, this well-run, friendly hotel offers simple but spacious rooms in a grand townhouse, but no restaurant. **€65**

Provençal Chemin de Mazaugues ☎ 04 94 78 16 97, ⓦ camping-le-provencal.com. Three-star campsite, 2km southeast of the centre towards Marseille, with pool, bar, restaurant and shop. Closed Oct–March. **€21**

Table en Provence 50 rue Général-de-Gaulle ☎ 04 94 59 84 61. Relaxed café-restaurant, with its outdoor tables facing the basilica entrance, that's ideal for a coffee or a simple meal, with a pasta *menu* at €14 and a full lunch *menu* for €19. Tues, Wed & Sun noon–2pm, Thurs–Sat noon–2pm & 7–9pm; closed Feb.

Brignoles

BRIGNOLES, 18km east of St-Maximin, is an ordinary, reasonably well-preserved provincial centre that can make for a convenient night's stay. At its heart, beyond the sprawling commercial zones and busy ring roads, lies a gentrified, warren-like medieval town full of quiet, shaded squares and old facades with faded adverts and flowering window boxes.

Rue des Lanciers, with its fine old houses where the rich Brignolais used to live, leads up from place des Comtes-de-Provence to the twelfth-century **St-Sauveur** church. Behind that, the stepped street of rue Saint-Esprit runs down to rue Cavaillon and place Carami, the café-lined central square of the modern town.

Musée du Pays Brignolais

Place des Comtes-de-Provence • April–Sept Wed–Sat 9am–noon & 2.30–6pm, Sun 9am–noon & 3–6pm; Oct–March Wed–Sat 10am–noon & 2.30–5pm, Sun 10am–noon & 3–5pm • €4 • ☎ 04 94 69 45 18, ⓦ museebrignolais.com

Displays in the fascinating, old-style **Musée du Pays Brignolais**, housed in a thirteenth-century summer residence of the counts of Provence, dip into every aspect of local life, and include an ancient paleo-Christian sarcophagus and a reinforced concrete boat made by the inventor of concrete in 1840. There's a statue of a saint whose navel has been visibly deepened by the hopeful hands of infertile women, a reconstruction of a bauxite mine, a crèche of *santons*, some Impressionist Provençal landscapes by Frédéric Montenard and a chapel cluttered with religious statuary.

ARRIVAL AND INFORMATION   BRIGNOLES

Tourist office Carrefour de l'Europe roundabout, north of the River Carami (Mon–Fri 9.30am–noon & 2–5.30pm; ☎ 04 94 72 04 21, ⓦ la-provence-verte.net).

ACCOMMODATION AND EATING

La Bastide de Messine Chemin de Cante Perdrix ☎ 04 94 72 09 06, ⓦ bastide-messine.com. Nice five-room *chambres d'hôtes*, 2km northwest of the centre, in a renovated old farmhouse with a pool. **€85**

Camping de Brignoles 786 route de Nice ☎ 04 94 69 20 10, ⓦ camping-brignoles.com. Two-star municipal campsite, in a pleasant leafy setting 1km east of the centre down the route de Nice. Closed late Oct to early March. **€13.90**

L'Oustau Place Carami ☎ 04 94 69 11 10. The pick of several similar café-restaurants on the main square, with shaded outdoor tables and a €9 daily *plat*, as well as good *aïoli*. Tues–Sun 11am–7pm; July & Aug also Fri 11am–10pm.

5

The Haut Var

Northeast of Brignoles, the rocky **Haut Var** holds some of Provence's most delightfully picturesque medieval villages, including **Cotignac** and **Villecroze**. Further north, the **Argens Valley** to the Verdon Gorge is the true heart of Provence, with its soft enveloping countryside of woods, vines, lakes and waterfalls, streaked with rocky ridges before the high plateaux and mountains. To the outsider, the villages rather merge together; to know them properly you'd have to live here for winter after winter, limiting your world to just a few square kilometres. The region is also home to the **Abbaye du Thoronet**, Provence's oldest surviving Cistercian monastery.

Barjols

Fountains are the chief attraction of **BARJOLS**, 21km north of Brignoles. No fewer than 28 mossy water features are dotted around the village, mostly in its older, eastern half, the **quartier du Réal**. The glum, rickety buildings of the long-defunct local tanning industry have been taken over by artists and craft workers; you can visit their studios (follow signs to Art-Artisanal) down the old road to Brignoles, east of the Vieille Ville. Looking back upwards from here at the industrial ruins is a spooky night-time experience.

Cotignac

COTIGNAC, the loveliest of all the Haut Var villages, stands 23km northeast of Brignoles. From its photogenic place de la Mairie, rue de l'Horloge heads under the clock tower and up to the church, from which a path leads to the foot of the spectacular eighty-metre cliff that forms the back wall of the village. A splendidly colourful and flower-bedecked, if at times nerve-racking, **cliffside trail** (April & early Oct Tues–Sun 2–5pm; May & June Tues–Sun 2–5.30pm; July & Aug Mon & Sun 2–6.30pm, Tues–Sat 10am–noon & 2–6.30pm; Sept Tues–Sat 10am–noon & 2–6.30pm, Sun 2–6.30pm; €2) leads past a troglodyte's dream of passageways, precarious stairways and strange little structures to the two ruined towers at the summit, relics of a long-abandoned castle. The rock between them is riddled with further caves and tunnels.

Long venerated as a saviour from the plague, the miraculous Virgin in the **Chapelle de Notre-Dame-des-Grâces**, on the summit across the valley to the south, hit the big time in 1638 when Louis XIII and Anne of Austria – married for 22 childless years – made their supplications to her. Nine months after the royal visit, the future Sun King let out his first demanding squall.

Entrecasteaux

ENTRECASTEAUX, 9km east of Cotignac along the minor D50, is scarcely more than a stone frame for its **château**, which rises from box-hedged formal gardens to dominate the village.

Château d'Entrecasteaux

Château Easter–Oct daily except Sat, guided visits 4pm, extra tour 11.30am in Aug · €8 · ☎ 04 94 04 43 95, ⓦ chateau-entrecasteaux.com **Gardens** Dawn–dusk · Free

Both Entrecasteaux's seventeenth-century **château**, and the publicly owned **Le Nôtre** gardens that separate it from the village, are open to visitors. The château owes its current condition to Scottish painter Ian McGarvie-Munn (1919–81), who retired in 1974 after a career that included a stint as head of the Guatemalan navy, and devoted the rest of his life to this massive restoration job. Its interior is spacious, light and charmingly rustic, typified by the terracotta tiles, a style that was all the rage when the Count and Countess of Grignan used the château as their summer residence.

Abbaye du Thoronet

Off the D79, 16km southeast of Cotignac • April–Sept Mon–Sat 10am–6.30pm, Sun 10am–noon & 2–6.30pm; Oct–March Mon–Sat 10am–1pm & 2–5pm, Sun 10am–noon & 2–5pm • €7.50 • T 04 94 60 43 90, W thoronet.monuments-nationaux.fr

The austere, rose-coloured **Abbaye du Thoronet**, one of Provence's three great Cistercian monasteries, stands deep in the forest of La Daboussière. Like Silvacane and Sénanque (see p.166 & p.191), it was founded in the first half of the twelfth century, but Thoronet is the oldest, and was completed in the shortest time, so its aesthetic coherence transcends its relatively modest size. Although abandoned in 1791, it was kept intact during the Revolutionary era. Restoration started in the 1850s, and a more recent campaign has brought it to graceful, melancholy perfection.

Salernes

Compared with Cotignac, **SALERNES**, 13km northeast, is quite a metropolis, with a thriving tile-making industry and enough near-level irrigated land for productive agriculture. Twenty or so studios and shops, large and small, sell a huge range of **pottery** and **tiles**, while on Sunday and Wednesday a **market** takes place beneath the ubiquitous plane trees on the *cours*.

Sillans-la-Cascade

Tiny **SILLANS-LA-CASCADE**, 6km west of Salernes, is a nice, sleepy little village that has clung on to a brief stretch of ancient ramparts. Down below, on the Bresque River, a stunning **waterfall**, reached by a twenty-minute walk along a delightful and clearly signed path from the main road, gushes into a turquoise pool that's perfect for swimming.

Villecroze

VILLECROZE, five kilometres northeast of Salernes, is a charming village, though it would be easy to drive straight through and fail to realize that its lovely, peaceful old quarter was even there. The inconspicuous walled medieval town lies immediately south of the main road, the D557, and is entered beneath an unadorned terracotta clock tower. With its vaulted stone arcades, it's a joy to stroll around.

Like Cotignac, Villecroze sits beneath a water-burrowed cliff, on its northern side. The gardens around the base are delightfully un-Gallic and informal, and intriguing **grottoes** in its flanks are open to visitors in summer (April & May Sat & Sun 2–6pm; June–Sept Wed & Fri–Sun 2–6pm; July & Aug daily 10.30am–12.30pm & 2.30–7pm; €2.50; T 04 94 67 50 00).

The centre of community life in Villecroze, the place du Général-de-Gaulle across the road from the old town, hosts a **market** on Thursday mornings.

Tourtour

TOURTOUR, 6km north of Villecroze via the tortuous D51, sits 300m higher, atop a ridge with views extending to the massifs of Maures, Ste-Baume and Ste-Victoire. The village has a seemingly organic unity, its soft-coloured stone growing into stairways and curving streets, branching to form arches, fountains and towers. An old mill looks like it has always been in ruins, and the elephant-leg towers of the sixteenth-century bastion stand around the *mairie* as if of their own volition, while the twelfth-century **Tour du Grimaldi** might have erupted spontaneously from the ground. The two elms on the main square, planted when Anne of Austria and Louis XIII visited Cotignac, are almost as enormous as the bastion towers, though they're showing signs of decrepitude.

That said, Tourtour is all a bit unreal, full of *résidences secondaires* and *salons de thé* selling expensive fruit-juice cocktails.

5

ARRIVAL AND INFORMATION

THE HAUT VAR

BARJOLS
Tourist office Bd Grisolle (Tues–Fri 9am–noon & 2–4pm, Sat 9am–noon; ☎ 04 94 77 20 01, ⓦ barjols.fr).

COTIGNAC
Tourist office 475 rte de Carcès (Tues–Fri 9am–12.30pm & 2–5.30pm, Sat 9am–12.30pm & 2–5pm; ☎ 04 94 04 61 87,

ⓦ ot-cotignac.provenceverte.fr).

SALERNES
Tourist office Place Gabriel-Péri (July & Aug Mon–Fri 9.30am–6.30pm, Sat 9.30am–7pm, Sun 9.30am–1pm; Sept–June Tues–Sat 9.30am–12.30pm & 2–6pm; ☎ 04 94 70 69 02, ⓦ www.ville-salernes.fr).

ACCOMMODATION AND EATING

BARJOLS
Le Pont d'Or 2 rue Eugène Payan ☎ 04 94 77 05 23, ⓦ www.hotel-du-pont-d-or-barjols.cote.azur.fr. This pleasant *Logis de France* hotel-restaurant has attractive old-fashioned rooms, while its dining room (closed Sun eve & Mon) serves the best food in town, with *menus* at €25–39. Closed Dec to mid-Jan. **€65**

COTIGNAC
Camping des Pouverels Chemin des Pouverels ☎ 04 94 04 71 91. This municipal campsite, equipped with peaceful shaded sites 3km northeast of the village towards Aups, also offers dormitory accommodation. Closed Nov–March. Dorms **€12**; camping **€19**

Restaurant du Cours 18 cours Gambetta ☎ 04 94 04 78 50. Sun-kissed pavement restaurant – not to be confused with the *Brasserie du Cours* – at the heart of the village's social life, decked out with bright yellow tablecloths and serving top-quality *menus* that start at €13 for lunch and range from €17 to €30 in the evening. Despite the sign, it's not a hotel. Daily except Wed noon–2pm & 7.30–9pm.

Maison Gonzagues 9 rue Léon Gérard ☎ 04 94 72 85 40, ⓦ maison-gonzagues-cotignac.com. Cotignac being notably short of hotels, this gorgeous and very welcoming *chambres d'hôtes*, offering five antique-furnished rooms complete with four-poster beds, in a former tannery, is the best accommodation option in the village. **€115**

★ **Le Temps de Pose** Place de la Mairie ☎ 04 94 77 04 69 17. This quaint, flower-bedecked café on a quiet square makes an ideal spot for breakfast, a light lunch or a reviving cup of tea. Tasty, fresh sandwiches and quiches cost around €8; a large salad or daily *plat* more like €10. Daily 10.30am–10pm.

ENTRECASTEAUX
Bastide Notre Dame L'Adrech de Sainte Anne ☎ 04 94 04 45 63, ⓦ bastidenotredame.free.fr. Terracotta *chambres d'hôtes* just west of the village, with four pretty, colour-coordinated rooms and a pool in the shaded garden. **€98**

Lou Cigaloun 93 chemin Caravane, St-Antonin-du-Var ☎ 04 94 04 42 67, ⓦ hotel-restaurant-loucigaloun.com. The friendly, family hotel-restaurant, in Entrecasteaux's

even smaller neighbour 4km east, has just six nicely modernized rooms, along with a pool and a park alongside. Its restaurant (closed Wed) offers simple but fine cooking, with lunch from €15. Closed Nov–Feb. **€90**

ABBAYE DU THORONET
La Sarrazine 375 Chemin de Pendedi, Lorgues ☎ 04 94 73 20 27, ⓦ lasarrazine.com. Very pleasant, comfortable three-room *chambres-d'hôtes*, in a spacious modern house just outside Lorgues, 12km northeast of the abbey. Set in extensive gardens, it has its own olive grove and swimming pool. **€110**

SALERNES
Les Arnauds Rte de Sillans ☎ 04 94 67 51 95, ⓦ village-vacances-lesarnauds.com. This riverfront campsite forms part of a larger municipally run holiday complex that includes a block of rental apartments; very much geared towards families, it incorporates an artificial beach. Closed Oct–April. **€26**

L'Odyssée 5 rue des 4 Coins ☎ 04 94 67 56 43, ⓦ restaurant-83-salernes-var.com. Friendly, high-class restaurant with seating on the main square, serving changing daily *menus* that focus on local, and especially organic, produce; *plats* like beef tartare or risotto typically cost €15–18. Concerts and theatre performances in winter. Daily except Thurs noon–1.30pm & 7.30–9.30pm.

SILLANS-LA-CASCADE
Les Pins 1 Grand Rue ☎ 04 94 04 63 26, ⓦ restaurant-lespins.com. The five simple en-suite rooms in this attractive hotel-restaurant, beside the main road, are well priced but very ordinary; the food, served on a colourful patio, is considerably better, with lunch at €18 and dinner *menus* from €24. **€50**

VILLECROZE
Au Bien Être Quartier Les Cadenières ☎ 04 94 70 67 57, ⓦ aubienetre.com. Secluded and very comfortable hotel, 3km south of the village along the D557, where you can step through French windows from your room to reach the pool. Dinner menus in the dining room (closed for lunch Mon–Wed) start at €28. **€82**

CLOCKWISE FROM TOP COTIGNAC (P.204); ENTREVAUX (P.232); AUPS (P.208) >

5

★ La Bohème Villecroze ☎ 04 94 70 80 04. Delightful, very floral café and tearooms, just inside the walls of the medieval enclave, with tables out on the alley. Breakfast (€6) is served, along with cooked brunches, afternoon tea, smoothies and cakes. Daily 9am–1pm & 4–7pm.

Le Colombier Rte de Draguignan ☎ 04 94 70 63 23, ⦿ lecolombier-var.com. Very charming hotel-restaurant, south of the village along the D557, with six sizeable and tastefully decorated rooms with terraces, and a lovely peaceful garden. *Menus* in the restaurant (closed Sun eve & Mon) start at €29. Closed mid-Nov to mid-Dec. **€90**

TOURTOUR
Bastide de Tourtour Rte de Flayosc ☎ 04 98 10 54 20, ⦿ bastidedetourtour.com. Upscale hotel-restaurant, housed in a modern version of a traditional fortified farmhouse, equipped with jacuzzis, tennis courts and a gym, and serving classic local cuisine on *menus* from €28 (closed lunch Mon–Fri Sept–June). **€190**

Aups

The neat and very pleasant village of **AUPS**, 10km north of Salernes, makes an ideal base for drivers touring the Haut Var or the Grand Canyon du Verdon. While it has all the facilities visitors might need, it remains a vibrant, lived-in community, still earning its living from agriculture, and at its best on Wednesdays and Saturdays, when market stalls fill its central squares and the surrounding streets. There's even a dedicated **truffle market** on Thursdays between November and the end of February.

Though only 500m or so above sea level, this was considered by the ancients to be the beginning of the Alps; its Roman name, Alpibus, became first Alps and then Aups. It now centres on three ill-defined and interconnected squares, where the D557 reaches the southern end of the village: place Frédéric-Mistral, the smaller place Duchâtel slightly uphill to the left and the tree-lined gardens of place Martin-Bidouré to the right. Beyond these, the tangle of old streets, and the sixteenth-century clock tower with its campanile, make it an enjoyable place to explore.

Musée Simon Segal

Av Albert 1ᵉʳ • Daily except Tues: June–Aug 10am–noon & 4–7pm; Sept 10am–noon & 4–6pm; Oct–May by appointment only • Free • ☎ 04 94 70 00 07, ⦿ aups.fr

Surprisingly, for such a small place, Aups holds a museum of modern art, the **Musée Simon Segal** in the former chapel of a convent. Its best works are those by the Russian-born painter Simon Segal, but there are interesting local scenes in the other paintings, such as the Roman bridge at Aiguines, now drowned beneath the artificial lake of Sainte-Croix.

ARRIVAL AND INFORMATION | AUPS

By bus Buses stop on place Frédéric-Mistral.
Destinations Aiguines (1 daily; 35min); Cotignac (3 daily; 25min).
Tourist office Place Frédéric-Mistral (May–June & Sept Mon–Sat 8.45am–12.15pm & 2–5.30pm; July & Aug

Mon–Sat 9am–12.30pm & 3.30–7pm, Sun 9am–12.30pm; Oct–April Mon, Tues, Thurs & Fri 8.45am–12.15pm & 1.30–5pm, Wed & Sat 8.45am–12.15pm; ☎ 04 94 84 00 69, ⦿ aups-tourisme .com).

REPUBLICAN RESISTANCE IN AUPS

An obelisk on Aup's **place Martin-Bidouré**, inscribed "To the memory of citizens who died in 1851 defending the Republic and its laws", commemorates a period of republican resistance all too rarely honoured in France. Peasant and artisan defiance of **Louis Napoleon's coup d'état** that year was at its strongest in Provence, and the defeat of the insurgents was followed by a massacre of men and women alike. At Aups, the badly wounded Martin Bidouré escaped, but was swiftly found being succoured by a peasant, and shot dead on the spot. That event may well explain the strident "République Française, Liberté, Egalité, Fraternité" sign on the **Église St-Pancrace** nearby, a building originally designed by an English architect five centuries ago.

ACCOMMODATION AND EATING

There can hardly be another village in France with such a perfect array of good and extraordinarily well-priced **hotels**, both in the centre and in the neighbouring countryside, along with several nearby **campsites** for good measure.

★ **Auberge de la Tour** Rue Aloisi ☎ 04 94 70 00 30, ⒲ aubergedelatour.net. Appealing and great-value hotel, where the beds have duvets, and the tasteful, airy, well-equipped rooms sleep up to four. They surround a sunny, peaceful, plant-filled courtyard restaurant that serves good *menus* from €19.50, so in a ground-floor room you can have diners right outside your window. Closed Oct–March, restaurant also closed Tues Sept– June. **€55**

Bastide du Calalou Moissac-Bellevue ☎ 04 94 70 17 91, ⒲ bastide-du-calalou.com. Imposing country-house hotel in a small village 5km northwest of Aups on the D9. The building itself is nothing special, but it's set in grand gardens and has 32 plush rooms, a pool and a fine restaurant. **€165**

Bastide de l'Estré Chemin de la Croix de Pins ☎ 04 94 84 00 45, ⒲ estre.com. B&B accommodation in an attractive rural location, off the road to Moustiers-Ste-Marie 3km north of town. There's also a *gîte* to rent, a camping barn for walkers and cyclists with dorm beds, and they serve evening meals by reservation for €25. Dorms **€18**; B&B **€56**

Camping Les Prés Rte de Tourtour ☎ 04 94 70 00 93, ⒲ campinglespres.com. This well-shaded two-star site, to the right off allée Charles-Boyer just 300m southeast of the town centre, stays open all year, and has a bar, snack bar and pool. **€19**

Grand Hôtel Place Duchâtel ☎ 04 94 70 10 82, ⒲ grand-hotel-aups.com. Traditional village hotel, just off the main square, with six plain but adequate en-suite rooms, including some that sleep up to four. The popular and hugely efficient garden restaurant in front serves excellent *menus* at €15.50–27, and there's also a nice bar. **€50**

★ **St-Marc** Rue Aloisi ☎ 04 94 70 06 08, ⒲ lesaintmarc .com. Rickety, earthy, but very characterful old rooms (sleeping up to five; not all en-suite) in a former olive-oil mill overlooking a tiny little square and above a good restaurant, where the €21 dinner *menu* features a delicious octopus stew; they also make pizzas over a wood fire. Closed Tues & Wed Sept–June, plus second half Nov. **€40**

Northwest of Aups: Quinson and Riez

For those who have time, two little towns northwest of Aups make potential stops before you embark on the Grand Canyon du Verdon: **Quinson**, which marks the start of the lower gorges, and workaday **Riez**, with its smattering of Roman ruins.

Quinson

QUINSON, on the attractive D13 22km northwest of Aups, sits at the head of the **Basses Gorges du Verdon**. If you haven't yet seen the Grand Canyon du Verdon, these 500-metre depths will strike you as quite dramatic, but, unfortunately, they're rather difficult to reach. The GR99 trail makes a short detour to the south side of the gorge a couple of kilometres downstream from Quinson, and paths off the road between Quinson and Esparron also lead to the edge of the gorge.

Musée de Préhistoire des Gorges du Verdon

Rte de Montmeyan • **Musée** May, June & Sept daily except Tues 10am–7pm; July & Aug daily 10am–8pm; Oct to mid-Dec & Feb–April daily except Tues 10am–6pm • €7 **Guided tours** July & Aug Wed & Sat 9.15am; otherwise see website • €4 • ⒲ museeprehistoire.com

A huge, bare and deeply incongruous modern edifice at the edge of Quinson, the **Musée de Préhistoire des Gorges du Verdon** was a millennium project, designed by British architect Norman Foster and opened in 2001. Europe's largest museum of human prehistory, it charts a million years of human habitation in Provence, with a multimedia presentation of the cave of Baume Bonne and a 15-metre-long reconstruction of the caves of the canyon of Baudinard, with their six-thousand-year-old red sun paintings. Sadly, though, many visitors find the museum unsatisfying, with its dry displays veering erratically between targeting kids and adults. Non-French speakers are dependent on poor English audioguides.

5

If you have time to join a four-hour guided tour, you can hike to the most important of the sixty or so archeological sites in and around Quinson, the cave of **Baume Bonne** itself, where human occupation has been traced back 400,000 years.

Riez

The main business of **RIEZ**, 21km north of Quinson, is derived from the lavender fields that cover this corner of Provence – hence the hideous **lavender distillery**, 1km south across the river, which produces essence for the perfume industry. Riez is more village than town today, but its antiquity is readily apparent. Four stately **Roman columns** stand in a field just off avenue Frédéric-Mistral at the bottom of the main allées Louis-Gardiol, while over the river stand the disappointingly scanty remains of a sixth-century **cathedral** (open access).

For a **walk** with good views over the town, head first for the clock tower above Grande Rue, then go up the steps past the cemetery, where a stony curving path brings you to a cedar-shaded platform on the hilltop where the pre-Roman Riezians lived. The only building there today is the eighteenth-century **Chapelle St-Maxime**, with its gaudily patterned interior.

ARRIVAL AND INFORMATION

QUINSON AND RIEZ

QUINSON

Tourist office Rue de St-Esprit (July & Aug daily 9.30am–1pm & 3–6.30pm; Sept–June Mon & Wed–Sat 9.30am–1pm & 2.15–5.45pm; ☎04 92 74 01 12, ⓦ quinson.fr).

By bus Quinson is connected by a daily bus to Riez (1 daily; 35min).

RIEZ

Tourist office Place de la Marie (July & Aug Mon–Sat 9.30am–12.30pm & 2.30–6.30pm, Sun 9.30am–12.30pm; Sept–June Mon, Tues, Thurs & Fri 8.30am–noon & 1.30–5pm, Wed & Sat 8.30am–noon; ☎04 92 77 99 09, ⓦ ville-riez.fr).

By bus Riez has connections with Barjols (1 daily; 45min); Digne (3 daily; 1hr 15min); Manosque (1 daily; 1hr); Marseille (1–2 daily; 2hr); Moustiers-Ste-Marie (2 daily; 20min); Quinson (1 daily; 35min).

ACCOMMODATION AND EATING

QUINSON

Relais Notre-Dame ☎04 92 74 40 01, ⓦ relaisnotredame-04.com. A short walk south of the prehistory museum, this pleasant, old-fashioned hotel, offers simple but attractive en-suite rooms, while its restaurant (closed Mon eve & Tues) serves a €20.50 vegetarian *menu* and others from €24.50, outdoor seating across the main road, above a sunflower field. Closed mid-Nov to March. **€74**

RIEZ

Rose de Provence Rue Edouard-Dauphin ☎04 92 77 75 45, ⓦ rose-de-provence.com. Two-star campsite, across the river 400m southeast of the centre, with a hot tub, table tennis and *boules*, but no pool. Closed Oct to early April. **€17.30**

Digne-les-Bains

The retirement spa town of **DIGNE-LES-BAINS**, 42km north of Riez and the capital of the Alpes-de-Haute-Provence *département*, is by far the largest town in northeastern Provence. While it enjoys a superb location between the Durance Valley and the start of the real mountains, and holds some interesting museums, it's really not a holiday destination in its own right. Consisting of a couple of busy boulevards that connect some yawningly empty squares, and a small network of faded lanes in the old town, it's best seen as a convenient overnight base for trips into the surrounding mountains.

Wednesday and Saturday **markets** bring animation to the windswept **place Général-de-Gaulle**, north of the cathedral, with lots of lavender products, including honey, on sale.

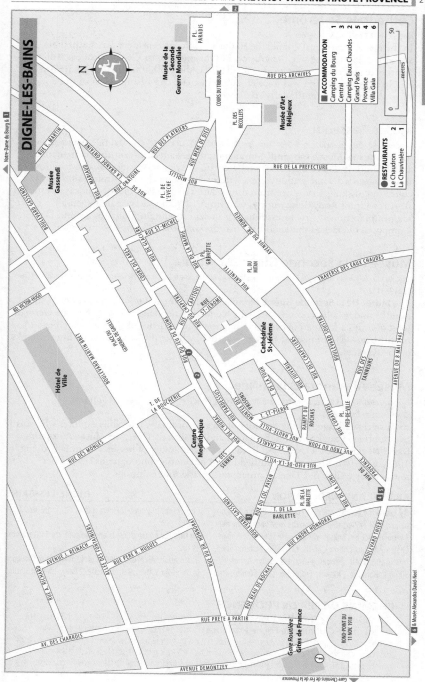

DIGNE-LES-BAINS

N

◄ Notre-Dame du Bourg & 1

RUE E. MARTIN

BOULEVARD GASSENDI

Musée Gassendi

LA GRANDE FONTAINE

RUE MARTIN BRET

RUE GRANDIE

RUE DE

PL. DE L'EVECHE

RUE ST-MICHEL

RUE DE LA MAIRIE

RUE DE LAGACHE

COURS DES ARÈS

Hôtel de Ville

BD VICTOR-HUGO

BOULEVARD MARTIN BRET

RUE DES PLATRIERS

RUE MÈRE DE DIEU

PL. DE PARADIS

PL. PARADIS

Musée de la Seconde Guerre Mondiale

COURS DU TRIBUNAL

RUE DES ARCHIVES

PL. DES RECOLLETS

Musée d'Art Réligieux

RUE DE LA PREFECTURE

RUE MIOLLIS

AVENUE DU 8 MAI 1945

RUE GRANETTE

PL. GRANETTE

PL. DU MITAN

TRAVERSE DES EAUX CHAUDES

AVENUE DU 8 MAI 1945

RUE ST-JÉRÔME

RUE DU CAPITOUL

RUE DU FEU DE PLAYME

Cathédrale St-Jérôme

BOULEVARD SOUSTRE

BOULEVARD GASSENDI

RUE DES TANNEURS

RUE DES CHAFFAUTS

RUE HUBERT

RUE DES CHAFFETTES

T. DE LA TOUR

RUE DE LA BOUCHERIE

RUE DES MONGES

GEORGES DE CAULLE

PLACE PARADIS

Centre Mediathèque

RUE DE THURIE

RUE PARDISSONS

T. DES SERRES

MONTÉE DES PRISONS

RUE HAUTE-VILLE

M. ST-CHARLES

M. ST-PIERRE

RUE TROU DU TOUR

RAMPE DU ROCHAS

RUE CUIRATERIE

PL. PIED-DE-VILLE

RUE DE PROVENCE

AVENUE J. REINACH

RUE A. RICHARD

ALLÉES FONTAINIERS

RUE PERE R. HUGUES

RUE DU DR. HONNORAT

RUE PIED-DE-LA-VILLE

RUE DU COL PAYAN

PL. DE LA BARLETTE

T. DE LA BARLETTE

RUE ANDRÉ HONNORAT

RUE DE LA LUNE

RUE DE PROVENCE

BOULEVARD THIERS

AV. DES CHARROIS

RUE PRETE A PARTIR

RUE BEAU DE ROCHAS

RUE BEAU DE ROCHAS

Gare Routière Gîtes de France

ROND-POINT DU 11 NOV. 1918

AVENUE DEMONTZEY

◄ Gare Chemins de fer de la Provence

▶ 6 & Musée Alexandra David-Neel

◼ **ACCOMMODATION**		
Camping du Bourg	1	
Central	3	
Camping Eaux Chaudes	2	
Grand Paris	5	
Provence	4	
Villa Gaia	6	

0 ——— 50
metres

● **RESTAURANTS**		
Le Chaudron	2	
La Chauvinière	1	

5

Cathédrale St-Jérôme

June–Oct Tues, Wed, Thurs & Sat 3–6pm

In the heart of medieval Digne, the **Haute Ville**, the fifteenth-century **Cathédrale St-Jérôme** has become weed-encrusted and dilapidated. Its Gothic facade is still impressive and the features inside, in particular the Gothic stained-glass windows, clearly indicate that this was once an awesome place of worship. Most of the surrounding streets are similarly run-down.

Musée Gassendi

64 bd Gassendi • Daily except Tues: April–Sept 11am–7pm; Oct–March 1.30–5.30pm • €4 • ☎ 04 92 31 45 29, ⓦ musee-gassendi.org

The municipal **Musée Gassendi** commemorates seventeenth-century mathematician and astronomer **Pierre Gassendi**, who grew up in Digne. As well as displays on his life, it holds assorted, largely anonymous sixteenth- to nineteenth-century paintings, and a collection of skulls that range from dromedaries to gorillas. The top floor is devoted to British sculptor **Andy Goldsworthy**, who from 1999 onwards created open-air sculptures in ruined structures along the ancient mountain footpaths around Dignes. Composed of cracked mud and hair, his *River of Earth* fills one enormous wall.

Musée de la Seconde Guerre Mondiale

Place Paradis • July & Aug Mon–Thurs 2–6pm, Fri 2–5.30pm; mid-April to June & Sept to mid-Nov Wed 2–5pm, by appointment • Free • ☎ 04 92 31 28 95

The **Musée de la Seconde Guerre Mondiale**, east of the old town, recalls Digne's nine months under Italian occupation, which ended in September 1943 when the Germans took over. It's a fascinating exposé of one town's experience of the war, which left people here – as throughout France – scarred by bitter divisions, even within the ranks of the Resistance.

Musée Alexandra David-Néel

27 av du Maréchal Juin, 1.2km southwest of the centre • Tours daily 10am, 2pm & 3.30pm • Free • ☎ 04 92 31 32 38, ⓦ alexandra-david-neel.org

Exclusively dedicated to the memory of an extraordinary, tenacious explorer who spent over fourteen years travelling the length and breadth of Tibet, the **Musée Alexandra David-Néel** is where David-Néel lived out the remainder of her life, eventually dying in 1969, aged 101. The house is stuffed full of fascinating photographs tracing her journeys, as well as old Tibetan ornaments, masks and paintings.

ARRIVAL AND INFORMATION

By train The *gare Chemins de Fer de la Provence* (see box below) is on av Pierre Sémard, on the west bank of the river. A regular *SNCF* bus links it with the *gare SNCF at* St-Auban–Château-Arnoux (30min), on the Marseille–Sisteron line. Destinations All services 4–5 times daily: Annot (1hr 30min); Barrême (40min); Entrevaux (1hr 50min); Nice (3hr 15min); Puget-Théniers (2hr); St-André-des-Alpes (1hr).

By bus The *gare routière* is on *rond point* du 11 Novembre 1918. Destinations Aix (4 daily; 2hr); Aups (2 daily; 40min); Avignon (3 daily; 3hr 30min); Barçelonnette (2 daily; 1hr–1hr 30min);

CHEMINS DE FER DE PROVENCE

Also known as the **Train des Pignes**, in honour of the pine cones originally used as fuel, the narrow-gauge **Chemins de Fer de Provence** connects Dignes-les-Bains with Nice, with stops including Annot and St-André-les-Alpes. It's a stupendous ride, taking 3hr 30min in total for a one-way fare of €20.30; the scenery en route includes glittering rivers, lush dark-green forests, dramatic cliff faces and plunging gorges. For full details, see ⓦ trainprovence.com.

Castellane (1 daily; 1hr 10min); Marseille (4 daily; 2hr–2hr 30min); Moustiers-Ste-Marie (1 daily; 1hr 20min); Nice (4 daily; 3hr 15min); Puget-Théniers (1 daily; 2hr); Riez (3 daily; 1hr 15min); St-André-les-Alpes (2–3 daily; 1hr); Seyne-les-Alpes (1 daily; 40min); Sisteron (3 daily; 1hr 15min).

Tourist office Rond point du 11 Novembre 1918 (July & Aug Mon–Sat 8am–7pm, Sun 9.30am–noon & 3.30–5.30pm; Sept–June Mon–Sat 9am–noon & 2–6pm, Sun 9.30am–noon & 3.30–5.30pm; ☎04 92 36 62 62, ⊚ot-dignelesbains.fr).

ACCOMMODATION

Central 26 bd Gassendi ☎04 92 31 31 91, ⊚lhotel -central.com. Spacious, comfortable budget hotel, on a bustling street in the heart of town near the tourist office. The cheapest of its simple antique-furnished rooms lack en-suite facilities. **€48**

Grand Paris 19 bd Thiers ☎04 92 31 11 15, ⊚hotel -grand-paris.com. Seventeenth-century former convent with large, tastefully decorated rooms, a surprising menagerie in the lobby, and a high-class gourmet restaurant (closed lunchtime Mon–Wed in low season), where excellent Provençal dinner menus start at €37. Closed Dec–Feb. **€120**

Provence 17 bd Thiers ☎04 92 31 32 19, ⊚hotel -alpes-provence.com. Set back behind a tiny garden courtyard, this renovated hotel, very close to the centre, is bright and friendly, with cheerful if small en-suite rooms. Almost all are equipped with queen-sized double beds, but there's also one tiny, cheaper single room. **€58.50**

Villa Gaia 24 rte de Nice ☎04 92 31 21 60, ⊚hotel -villagaia-digne.com. Stately, peaceful eighteenth-century country house, 3km southwest of the centre and offering ten very comfortable guest rooms of varying sizes, along with spa facilities. There's no public restaurant, but you can have dinner for €26. Closed Nov to mid-April. **€92**

CAMPING

Camping du Bourg Rte de Barçelonnette ☎04 92 31 04 87, ⊚campingdigne.com. Two-star municipal campsite, with a tennis court but no pool, 1.5km northeast of the centre along the D900 to Seynes-les-Alpes; follow av Ste-Douceline left from the top of bd Gassendi. Closed mid-Oct to March. **€17.50**

Eaux Chaudes Av des Thermes ☎04 92 32 31 04. Pleasantly situated three-star campsite, 1km east of town towards the Établissement Thermal. Closed Nov–March. **€19.50**

EATING

★ **Le Chaudron** 40 rue de l'Hubac ☎04 92 31 24 87. This excellent old-town restaurant, run by a very friendly husband-and-wife team, offers pavement seating in summer, a cosy upstairs dining room in winter. Menus from €21 to €32.50 focus on substantial baked dishes from their wood-fired oven. Mon, Tues & Fri–Sun noon–1.30pm & 7.30–9.15pm.

La Chauvinière 54 rue de l'Hubac ☎04 92 31 40 03. Intimate spot in the Haute Ville, serving traditional Provençal dishes on menus from €15 for lunch, €27 for dinner; some outdoor seating, in a courtyard below the cathedral that's crammed with multicoloured parasols. Mon–Sat noon–1.30pm & 7–9.15pm.

Draguignan

DRAGUIGNAN, the main settlement of the inland Var, less than 30km northwest of the coast at Fréjus, is a bustling place, if not particularly exciting. One of this region's few truly urban spots, it has a couple of worthwhile **museums**, a lively **market** on Wednesdays and Saturdays around place du Marché, and a striking **theatre**. Its boulevards and compact medieval centre hold enough moderately priced hotels and restaurants to make it a potential touring base.

Draguignan's compact old town is dominated by the distinctive seventeenth-century **Tour d'Horloge** (July & Aug guided tours only; free), which stands next to the twelfth-century Chapelle Saint-Sauveur atop a small hill just north of place du Marché.

Musée des Arts et Traditions Populaires de Moyenne Provence

15 rue Roumanille • Tues–Sat 9am–noon & 2–6pm, plus Sun 2–6pm April–Sept • €4 • ☎04 94 47 05 72

The **Musée des Arts et Traditions Populaires de Moyenne Provence** beautifully showcases the old industries of the Var. Nineteenth-century farming techniques and the manu-facturing processes for silk, honey, cork, wine, olive oil and tiles are presented within the context of daily working lives, though some scenes are spoilt by rather dire wax models.

5

Musée Municipal

Rue de la République • Tues–Sat 9am–noon & 2–6pm • Free • ☎ 04 98 10 26 85

Highlights at the **Musée Municipal**, housed in a former bishop's palace, include a delicate marble sculpture by Camille Claudel; Greuze's *Portrait of a Young Girl*; two paintings of Venice by Ziem; a Renoir; and upstairs in the library, a copy of the *Romance of the Rose* and early Bibles and maps. Rembrandt's *Child with a Soap Bubble*, stolen from the museum in 1999, remains conspicuous by its absence.

ARRIVAL AND INFORMATION   DRAGUIGNAN

By bus The *gare routière* and the redundant *gare SNCF*, connected by shuttle bus with the main line at Les Arcs, are at the bottom of boulevard Gabriel-Péri, south of the town centre.

Destinations Aix (3 daily; 2hr 30min); Aups (1 daily; 1hr 20min); Bargemon (5 daily; 45min); Barjols (1 daily; 1hr 10min); Brignoles (3 daily; 1hr); Entrecasteaux (2 weekly; 45min); Fayence (4 daily; 1hr 40min); Grasse (2 daily; 2hr 45min); St-Raphaël (12 daily; 1hr 30min); Salernes (3 daily; 1hr 30min); Tourtour (1 daily; 50min); Villecroze (2 weekly; 1hr).

Tourist office 2 av Carnot (July & Aug Mon–Sat 9.15am–12.15pm & 1.45–7pm, Sun 9.30am–12.30pm; Sept–June Mon–Fri 9.15am–12.15pm & 1.45–6pm, Sat 9.15am–12.15pm; ☎ 04 98 10 51 05, ⓦ tourisme-dracenie.com).

ACCOMMODATION AND EATING

Le Domino 28 av Carnot ☎ 04 94 67 15 13, ⓦ ledomino .fr. Fine old antique-furnished townhouse in which two pretty B&B rooms upstairs overlook the courtyard garden, while downstairs there's a good restaurant (closed Sun & Mon) that serves an eclectic mix of Provençal staples and world cuisines, on *menus* that start at €17 for lunch. **€75**
La Foux Quartier de la Foux ☎ 04 94 68 18 27. This

two-star campsite, 2km south towards Les Arcs, stays open year-round, and has a bar, restaurant and even mini-golf as well as a good pool complex. **€20.50**
Victoria 52 av Carnot ☎ 04 94 47 24 12, ⓦ hotelrestaurantvictoria.fr. Central, somewhat dated *belle époque* hotel, with a garden. It's on a main road, so for a quieter night, ask for a room at the back. **€75**

North and east of Draguignan

Of the two principal routes onwards and upwards from Draguignan, the **D955** heads north towards the mighty Grand Canyon du Verdon (see p.216), with the dramatic **Gorges du Châteaudouble** as a foretaste of the scenic splendours ahead, while the **D562** sets off northeast towards Grasse, with several medieval villages as potential detours along the way.

South of the D562 lies a wonderful, almost uninhabited expanse of forest where, between January and June, you may see untended cattle with bells round their necks and sheep chewing away at the undergrowth. That these animals are once more roaming the former pasturing grounds of the transhumance routes has great ecological benefits in maintaining the diversity of the forest fauna.

Châteaudouble

Beyond the exquisitely peaceful village of **Rebouillon**, beside the River Nartuby 5km northwest of Draguignan along the D955, the scenery changes dramatically with the start of the **Gorges du Châteaudouble**. A mere scratch it may be, compared to the great Verdon gorge, but it holds some impressive sites, not least the village of **CHÂTEAUDOUBLE** hanging high above the cliffs. Nostradamus predicted that the river would grind away at the base until the village fell, but has yet to be proved right. All but deserted out of season, Châteaudouble consists of little more than a couple of churches, a handful of houses, a potter's workshop, a beekeeper and his hives, and a ruined tower and ramparts.

Callas

The village of **CALLAS**, 15km northeast of Draguignan, can be reached by turning left onto the D525 12km along the road to Grasse. It's a pleasant place to stop for lunch or spend the night, with a lovely square by the church at its highest point.

Bargemon

The steep, narrow D25 climbs through luscious valleys for 6km north of Callas before reaching **BARGEMON**, tucked behind fortified gates and best known these days as the site of David and Victoria Beckham's Provençal retreat. With its fountained squares shaded by towering plane trees, the village is especially picturesque in spring, when its streets are filled with orange petals and mimosa blossom.

Musée-galerie Honoré Camos

Chapelle St-Étienne • July–Sept Mon 2–5pm, Wed–Sat 10am–12.30pm & 3.30–7pm; Oct–June Mon 2–5pm, Wed–Sat 10am–12.30pm & 2.30–6pm • Free • ☎ 04 94 76 72 88

The little Chapelle St-Étienne, originally constructed in the eleventh century and forming part of Bargemon's defences, is now home to the **Musée-galerie Honoré Camos**. As well as displays on local history, it hosts exhibitions of local painters, with a permanent collection of works by Honoré Camos himself (1906–91). The two angel heads on its high altar are attributed to the great Marseillais sculptor Pierre Puget.

Seillans

The village of **SEILLANS**, 13km east of Bargemon along the minor D19, consists of the tiny and very picturesque Vieux Village, shielded behind medieval walls from a sprawl of modern villas. The Romanesque **Chapelle de Notre-Dame-de-l'Ormeau**, 1km beyond the village on the road to Fayence, holds a wonderful Renaissance altarpiece, attributed to an inspired Italian monk; for details of guided tours, contact Seillans' tourist office (see p.216).

Collection Tanning-Ernst

Rue de l'Église • Mon–Sat 2.30–6.30pm, Sun 2.15–5.30pm • €2 • ☎ 04 94 76 85 91

Seillans was home to the painter **Max Ernst** (1891–1976) in his final years. He moved here in 1953, five years after marrying fellow artist **Dorothea Tanning**, whom he met after seeing her self-portrait, *Birthday*. The three-storey **Collection Tanning-Ernst** displays that painting, along with some lesser-known lithographs by Ernst himself, and even a mirrored bed, complete with mink bedspread, that he designed.

Fayence

Larger and livelier than most of its neighbours, **FAYENCE**, 6km east of Seillans, makes a good base for exploring the surrounding countryside. It was known to the Romans as Favienta Loca (favourable place), and its modern charm lies in the contrast between its small-town bustle and the peaceful traffic-free side streets spilling over with flowers. The Vieille Ville curls tightly around the steep slopes of a hill, with the imposing porchway of the *mairie* guarding its entrance; within the Vieille Ville stands a fourteenth-century gateway, the **Porte Sarrazine**. There's a **market** on place de l'Église on Tuesdays, Thursdays and Saturdays, as well as the inevitable ateliers and souvenir shops, and great views over the countryside.

5

ARRIVAL AND INFORMATION

SEILLANS
Tourist office Place du Thouron, beneath the Ernst exhibition (Mon–Sat 10am–12.30pm & 2.30–6.30pm, Sun 2.15–5.30pm; ☎ 04 94 76 85 91, ⓦ www.seillans.fr).

FAYENCE
By bus Buses stop on the central Place Léon-Roux.
Destinations Draguignan (Mon–Sat 3 daily; 1hr 30min); Grasse (Mon–Sat 3 daily; 1hr); St Raphaël (Mon–Sat

NORTH AND EAST OF DRAGUIGNAN

4 daily; 1hr 20min).
Tourist office Place Léon-Roux (mid-April to mid-June Mon–Sat 9am–noon & 2–6pm; mid-June to mid-Sept Mon–Sat 9am–12.30pm & 2–6.30pm, Sun 10am–noon; mid-Sept to mid-April Mon–Sat 9am–noon & 2–5.30pm; ☎ 04 94 76 20 08, ⓦ ville-fayence.fr).
Bookshop The Castle, 1 rue St-Pierre, sells local guides and maps in English (Mon 2.30–7pm, Tues–Sat 9am–12.30pm & 2.30–7pm; ☎ 04 94 84 72 00).

ACCOMMODATION AND EATING

CHÂTEAUDOUBLE
La Tour Place Purgatoire ☎ 04 94 70 93 08, ⓦ latour-chateaudouble.eresto.net. There's food to match the stunning location at this restaurant on the village's verdant central square, with a terrace overlooking the gorge, and satisfying Provençal *menus* from €25. Closed mid-Nov to mid-Dec. Mon, Tues & Thurs–Sat noon–1.30pm & 7–9pm, Sun noon–1.30pm.

CALLAS
Hôtel de France 1 rue de Portail de Blancon ☎ 04 94 76 61 02. Tiny, inexpensive hotel-restaurant, adjoining the shaded place Georges-Clemenceau; dinner *menus* in its restaurant start at €18. **€55**
Hostellerie des Gorges de Pennafort On the D25, below the D525 ☎ 04 94 76 66 51, ⓦ hostellerie-pennafort.com. Grand hotel-restaurant complex, overlooking the Pennafort waterfalls 7km south of the village, with its own heliport, pool, lake and olive grove. The restaurant (closed all day Mon, plus Wed lunch & Sun eve) spreads across a huge outdoor terrace, and serves a weekday lunch *menu* for €49, and dinner *menus* from €70. Closed mid-Jan to mid-March. **€220**

SEILLANS
★ **Les Deux Rocs** 1 place Font-d'Amont ☎ 04 94 76 87 32, ⓦ hoteldeuxrocs.com. Exquisitely restored hotel in a townhouse by the old wash house, opposite the two eponymous rocks on a little fountained square. It's a great place both to stay and to eat, with beautiful antiques, warm decor, and full dinner *menus* that start at €49. Closed Tues & Jan to mid-Feb. **€73**
Gloire de Mon Père Place du Thouron ☎ 04 94 76 98 68, ⓦ lagloiredemonpere.fr. Delightful restaurant, almost filling the tiny square that squeezes between the tourist

office and the village walls, and serving delicious Provençal food on dinner *menus* from €29. Daily except Wed noon–2pm & 7–9.30pm.

FAYENCE
Auberge de la Fontaine 1740 route de Fréjus ☎ 04 94 76 07 59. Seven-room hotel, 3km south of the village on the D563. The rooms are plain, and the building unremarkable, but it's a nice rural spot, with lots of outdoor space, and the hearty Provençal cooking adds to the appeal of its isolation. **€60**
Farigoulette 1 place du Château ☎ 04 94 84 10 49, ⓦ la-farigoulette.com. Peaceful restaurant, in a former stable at the top of the village, serving tasty traditional *menus* from €17.50 for lunch, €26.50 for dinner. Mon & Thurs–Sat 12.15–1.30pm & 7.15–9pm, plus Tues 7.15–9pm in July & Aug only.
Lou Cantaire D562 ☎ 04 94 76 23 77, ⓦ camping-lou-cantaire.fr. Three-star campsite in wooded surroundings 5km southwest towards Draguignan, with a couple of pools plus, in July & Aug, organized activities for kids, and night-time entertainment. Closed Dec & Jan. **€21.30**
Moulin de la Camandoule Chemin de Notre-Dame-des-Cyprès ☎ 04 94 76 00 84, ⓦ camandoule.com. English-owned converted mill, 1km northwest of town, which offers a dozen tasteful and comfortable rooms in really special surroundings. There's also a top-notch restaurant, *L'Escourtin*, serving *menus* from €20.50 lunch, €30 dinner (Sept–June closed all day Wed & Thurs lunch). **€128**
Les Oliviers 18 av St-Christophe ☎ 04 94 76 13 12, ⓦ lesoliviersfayence.fr. Straightforward, friendly little modern hotel, just below the village on the D19, with clean a/c rooms plus a nice garden and pool, and a bar but no restaurant. **€85**

The Grand Canyon du Verdon

Europe's widest and deepest gorge, the breathtaking **Grand Canyon du Verdon** – a V-shaped chasm also known as the Gorges du Verdon – cuts a 21km-long east–west swathe through the limestone foothills of the Alps. Peppered with spectacular viewpoints, plunging crevices up to 700m deep, and glorious azure-blue lakes, the area is absolutely irresistible; try not to leave Provence without spending at least a day here. The river falls from **Rougon** at the eastern end of the gorge, disappearing into tunnels, decelerating for shallow languid moments, and finally exiting in full steady flow at the **Pont de Galetas** to fill the huge artificial **Lac de Ste-Croix**.

The main overnight bases near the canyon are the villages of **Moustiers-Ste-Marie** and **Aiguines** at its western end; the even smaller community of **La Palud-sur-Verdon** halfway along the north rim; and the larger town of **Castellane** beyond its eastern end.

With so many hairpin bends and twisting, narrow roads, it takes a full, rather exhausting day to **drive** right around the canyon, particularly in the fearsome midsummer traffic. The entire circuit being 130km long, many visitors choose instead to explore just one rim, along either the **Route des Crêtes** on the north side or the **Corniche Sublime** to the south. This is **cycling** country only for the preternaturally fit, but **walking** is the ideal way to explore; the best trails start on the northern side, as described on p.219 onwards.

Before you hike in the gorge itself, always get details of the route and advice on **weather conditions** (ⓦmeteoconsult.fr). You'll also need water, a torch for the tunnels, and warm clothing for the cold shadows of the narrow corridors of rock. Always stick to the path and don't cross the river except at the *passerelles* (footbridges); water levels change very abruptly when the dams open upstream (ⓣ04 92 83 62 68 for recorded information), and drownings can and do occur.

Moustiers-Ste-Marie

The loveliest village on the fringes of the gorge, **MOUSTIERS-STE-MARIE** occupies a magnificent site near its western end. Seven kilometres north of Lac de Ste-Croix, but set

---

GRAND CANYON DU VERDON ACTIVITIES

Outfitters and guides based around the gorge offer activities of all kinds. Most operate in summer only, between April and September. For general information, contact the Parc Naturel Région du Verdon (ⓦparcduverdon.fr).

Only attempt to **canoe** or **raft** the full length of the gorge if you are very experienced and strong; you'll have to carry your craft for long stretches. However, you can pay (in the region of €35 for 2hr, €75 for a full day) to join a group and tackle certain stretches of the river. No trips take place during hydroelectric operations, so be prepared for disappointment.

MULTI-ACTIVITY OPERATORS

UCPA La Palud ⓣ04 92 77 31 66, ⓦucpa-vacances .com. Climbing, walking, cycling, canoeing and canyoning with a trained guide.

Verdon Passion Moustiers ⓣ06 08 63 97 16, ⓦverdon-passion.com. Canyoning, climbing and paragliding.

WALKING AND CLIMBING

Des Guides Pour l'Aventure La Palud ⓣ06 85 94 46 61, ⓦguidesaventure.com. Professional walking guides, rock climbers and canyoneers.

Maison des Guides du Verdon La Palud ⓣ04 92 77 30 50, ⓦescalade-verdon.fr. Association of professional guides for walks, canyoning and rock climbing.

Le Perroquet Vert La Palud ⓣ04 92 77 33 39, ⓦleperroquetvert.com. Climbing shop and *chambres d'hôtes* (see p.222).

ON THE WATER

Aboard Rafting Castellane ⓣ04 92 83 76 11, ⓦaboard-rafting.com. Water-based activities including rafting, canoeing, canyoning, hydrospeeding and water rambling.

Base Sport et Nature Castellane and Entrevaux ⓣ04 93 05 41 18, ⓦbasesportnature.com. Rafting, canoeing and canyoning.

CYCLING

Le Petit Ségriès Moustiers ⓣ04 92 74 68 83, ⓦverdon-vtt.com. Cycle rental and guided cycling tours.

BUNGEE JUMPING

Latitude Challenge Marseille ⓣ04 91 09 04 10, ⓦlatitude-challenge.fr. Bungee jumps from the 182m Pont de l'Artuby.

5

Comps-sur-Artuby & Draguignan
Comps-sur-Artuby & Draguignan

kilometres

Castellane

Pont de Soleils

D955

Trigance

River Jabron

D90

Clue de Carejuan

D71

D71

Rougon

Point
Sublime

CORNICHE SUBLIME

Balcons de la Mescla

Pont de l'Artuby

Couloir Samson

Belvédère
de l'Escalès

Sentier Martel

River Verdon

R. Artuby

GR4

ROUTE DES CRÊTES

Belvédère des
Glacières

D17

Belvédère
du Tilleul

La Palud-
sur-Verdon

Chalet de
la Maline

Falaise des
Cavaliers

D123

Passerelle
de l'Estellié
(Closed)

CORNICHE SUBLIME

D952

GR4

D71

Mayreste

CORNICHE SUBLIME

Col d'Ayen

Moustiers-Ste-Marie

River Verdon

Pont
du Galetas

N

GR4

D952

Aiguines

D619

D957

Lac de Ste-Croix

D957

Riez

Aups

Aups

GRAND CANYON DU VERDON

high enough to command fine views down to it, it straddles a plummeting stream that cascades between two golden cliffs. A mighty star slung between them on a chain, said to have been originally suspended by a returning Crusader, completes the perfect picture.

Not surprisingly, however, Moustiers gets very crowded in summer, when visitors throng its winding lanes and pretty bridges, and fill the many shops and galleries that sell the traditional local speciality, **glazed pottery**. To learn more about that, drop in at the small **Musée de la Faience** (Feb, March, Nov & Dec Sat & Sun 2–5pm; April–June, Sept & Oct daily except Tues 10am–12.30pm & 2–6pm; July & Aug daily 10am–12.30pm & 2–7pm; €3, free on Tues July & Aug; ☎04 92 74 61 64, ⓦmoustiers.eu) in the Hôtel de Ville on the east side of the stream.

Coming to Moustiers out of season is more of an unalloyed pleasure, but you can escape the commercialism year-round by puffing your way uphill to the aptly named chapel of **Notre Dame de Beauvoir**, high above the village proper.

Lac de Ste-Croix

At its western end, the canyon emerges abruptly into the enormous turquoise reservoir of the **Lac de Ste-Croix**. From the Pont de Galetas, where the D957 crosses the river, you can often see river rafts rounding the final bend of the gorge. At the beach just to the north, rowing boats and pedalos are available to rent; when no floodgates are open, the waters are placid enough to set off upstream between the cliffs. **Swimming** is also good here, though when the lake levels are low, things can get a bit muddy around the edges.

The north rim

The spectacular and tortuous D952 runs more or less parallel to the north bank of the Verdon river for 45km east from Moustiers to Castellane. For the best close-up views of the gorge, however, head south near the village of La Palud-sur-Verdon halfway along, and follow the **Route des Crêtes** to the lip of the abyss.

La Palud-sur-Verdon

Peace, tranquillity and breathtaking scenery reign supreme in the principal pit stop along the northern rim, **LA PALUD-SUR-VERDON**, 20km southeast of Moustiers. Even if you're just passing through, take the time to wander around the narrow, rambling streets and enjoy a meal or drink at a traditional restaurant or café. Note that out of season, however, the village all but closes down.

The Route des Crêtes

To admire the very best of the Gorges du Verdon, detour off the D952 onto the dramatic **Route des Crêtes**, which loops away both from the centre of La Palud, and from another intersection a short distance east. Along its 23-kilometre circuit, it offers a succession of stunning canyon viewpoints. There's nothing to stop you driving straight off into the abyss on its highest stretches, and at some points you look down a sheer 800m drop to the sliver of water below. As the mid-section of the Route des Crêtes is one-way (westbound only), to see it all you have to start from the more scenic eastern end. The road closes each winter from November 15 to March 15.

For walkers, the best trail down to the river itself starts at La Maline, halfway along. Hiking to the Verdon, then following it on the **Sentier Martel** footpath and climbing back up at **Point Sublime**, near Rougon on the D952, takes seven hours, and is best done as part of a guided group, with one of the operators listed on p.217.

Unaccompanied shorter excursions into the canyon include the relatively easy **Sentier du Lézard**, marked from Point Sublime. Alternative routes, ranging from thirty minutes to four hours, offer the chance to pass through the **Couloir Samson**, a 670-metre tunnel with occasional "windows", and a stairway down to the chaotic sculpture of the river banks.

5

Rougon

Immediately opposite Point Sublime, at a sharp, blind curve in the D952, a narrow side road doubles back up from the main road, away from the river. It takes three sinuous kilometres to snake its way up to the hilltop village of **ROUGON**, a lovely little place that feels very far removed from the summer crowds. Assorted café and restaurant terraces offer quite extraordinary views out over the canyon, surrounded by majestic cliffs and stark karst crags straight from some Chinese scroll painting.

The south rim

The aptly named **Corniche Sublime**, delineating the southern rim of the Grand Canyon du Verdon, is every bit as dramatic as its northern counterpart. The tortuous, precarious, but exhilarating D71 follows its entire course, starting at **Aiguines** at its western end, and eventually meeting the D955 up from Draguignan at **Comps-sur-Artuby**.

Aiguines

AIGUINES, perched at the western end of the Corniche Sublime 30km north of Aups, effectively consists of a single long promenade high above the Lac de Ste-Croix. Its one landmark, a château of pepperpot towers that dazzle with their coloured tiles, is not open to the public. Until tourism came along, it made its living from wood-turning, and in particular crafting *boules* for *pétanque* from ancient boxwood roots.

Along the Corniche Sublime

The **Corniche Sublime** itself was built expressly to provide the most jaw-dropping and hair-raising views. Drivers with any fear of heights – and of course their passengers – are best advised not to come this way.

The most spectacular viewpoint of all comes towards its eastern end, 24km along from Aiguines. Overlooking the **Balcons de la Mescla**, it's a memorable *coup de théâtre*. As the view is withheld until you are almost upon it, the 250-metre drop at your feet comes as a visceral body blow. Beyond the Balcons, the D71 drops southeast for its final 16km down to Comps, descending through end-of-the-earth heath and hills.

Comps-sur-Artuby

The isolated settlement of **COMPS-SUR-ARTUBY** stands 20km north along the D955 from Châteaudouble (see p.214), beyond the increasingly bleak military camp of Canjuers. Though the surrounding scenery is magnificent, the village itself holds few specific sights, other than the fortified chapel of **St André**.

Castellane

Huddled at the foot of a sheer 180-metre cliff, the grey and rather severe-looking town of **CASTELLANE** is these days primarily a gateway community for visitors to the **Gorges du Verdon**, 17km southwest. In summer, thanks to its wide range of restaurants, hotels and cafés, it enjoys an animation rare in these parts.

Houses in Castellane's old quarter, the Vieille Ville, are packed close together; some of the lanes are barely shoulder wide. At 34 rue Nationale, a house where Napoleon stopped to dine on March 3, 1815, is now the **Musée du Moyen Verdon** (May, June & Sept Wed, Sat & Sun 10am–1pm & 3–6.30pm; July & Aug daily 10am–1pm & 3–6.30pm; €4; ☎04 92 83 19 23), which holds temporary exhibitions of variable interest.

A footpath from behind the parish church at the head of place de l'Église winds its way up to the chapel of **Notre Dame du Roc** atop the cliff. Less demanding than it might at first appear, the path soon passes the machicolated **Tour Pentagonal**, which stands uselessly on the lower slopes. Twenty to thirty minutes should see you at the top; you won't actually see the gorge, but there's a pretty good view of the river disappearing into it and the mountains circling the town.

GETTING AROUND

THE GRAND CANYON DU VERDON

By bus Public transport connections are poor. You can find the latest timetables on ⊚ lapaludsurverdon.com, but broadly speaking there's one bus between Marseille, Aix, Riez, Moustiers, La Palud, Rougon and Castellane (July &

Aug Mon–Sat; Sept–June Mon & Sat only); and three daily services between La Palud, Rougon and Castellane (July & Aug daily; Easter–June & first half of Sept Sat & Sun only, plus hols).

INFORMATION

MOUSTIERS-STE-MARIE

Parc Naturel Région du Verdon Overall information on the gorge is available from the park office, Domaine de Valx (☎ 04 92 74 68 00, ⊚ parcduverdon.fr).

Tourist office Place de l'Église (March, Oct & Nov daily 10am–noon & 2–5.30pm; April–June daily 10am–12.30pm & 2–6pm; July & Aug Mon–Fri 9.30am–7pm, Sat & Sun 9.30am–12.30pm & 2–7pm; Sept daily 10am–12.30pm & 2–6.30pm; Dec–Feb daily 10am–noon & 2–5pm; ☎ 04 92 74 67 84, ⊚ moustiers.fr).

LA PALUD-SUR-VERDON

Bureau des Guides Grande Rue (hours erratic; ☎ 04 92 77 30 50, ⊚ escalade-verdon.fr); this is the best place to find out about guided walks, climbing, canyoning, rafting and other activities.

Tourist office The Maison des Gorges du Verdon, in the central château, incorporates the tourist office and also

holds displays on the gorge (daily except Tues: mid-March to mid-June and mid-Sept to mid-Nov 10am–noon & 4–6pm; mid-June to mid-Sept 10am–1pm & 4–7pm; ☎ 04 92 77 32 02, ⊚ lapaludsurverdon.com; exhibition €4).

AIGUINES

Tourist office Allées de Tilleul (July & Aug Mon–Sat 8.30am–6pm, Sun 10am–noon & 2–6pm; Sept–June Mon–Fri 9am–noon & 2–5pm; ☎ 04 94 70 21 64, ⊚ aiguines.com).

CASTELLANE

Tourist office Rue Nationale (May, June & Sept Mon–Sat 9am–noon & 2–6pm, Sun 10am–1pm; July & Aug daily 9am–7.30pm; Oct–April Mon–Sat 9am–noon & 2–6pm; ☎ 04 92 83 61 14, ⊚ castellane.org).

ACCOMMODATION AND EATING

MOUSTIERS-STE-MARIE

Bastide de Moustiers ☎ 04 92 70 47 47, ⊚ bastide -moustiers.com. Moustiers' most luxurious accommodation, beside the main D952 just below the village, and run by celebrity chef Alain Ducasse. Each of the dozen exquisite rooms has its own theme, there's a herb garden and a helicopter pad in the grounds, and the restaurant offers weekday set *menus* at a (relatively) modest €60. Closed Jan & Feb, plus Mon. **€250**

Clerissy Place du Chevalier du Blacas ☎ 04 92 74 62 67, ⊚ clerissy.fr. Among the nicest of the many *chambres d'hôtes*, where the four white-walled, en-suite rooms are simple, clean and full of character, and the colourful pizzeria downstairs offers good-value dining. Closed mid-Nov to mid-March. **€48**

Le Colombier Quartier St-Michel ☎ 04 92 74 66 02, ⊚ le-colombier.com. Very comfortable, good-value hotel on the main road, 600m below the village centre. The cheapest rooms are in the older original building, with larger and fancier options in a motel-style annexe, and there's a pleasant garden and pool, but no restaurant. Closed Nov–March. **€78**

Domaine du Petit-Lac ☎ 04 92 74 67 11, ⊚ lepetitlac .com. Two-star campsite, beside the eponymous "little lake" halfway along the D957 between Moustiers and the Lac de Saint Croix. Nice shaded sites, and lots of family-oriented activities, including canoeing and mini-golf. Closed early Oct to late April. **€25.80**

Hotel-Café du Relais ☎ 04 92 74 66 10, ⊚ lerelais -moustiers.com. Central hotel in a great location beside the main bridge; some rooms are a little faded, but the views are fantastic, and the brasserie serves good Provençal dishes, like lamb cutlets for €13, on a glassed-in terrace overlooking the stream. Closed Nov–March, plus Wed except in July & Aug. **€75**

LA PALUD-SUR-VERDON

Auberge de Jeunesse Rte de la Maline ☎ 04 92 77 38 72, ⊚ fuaj.org. Beautifully sited, nicely modernized hostel, poised on the hillside 500m south of the village, offering beds in rooms that sleep from two to six. Rates include breakfast. Closed Oct–March. **€18.50**

Camping Municipal Rte de Castellane ☎ 04 92 77 38 13, ⊚ lapaludsurverdon.com. Two-star municipal campsite, 800m east of the village along the D952. Minimal

5

facilities, but it's a nice setting. No reservations necessary. Closed Oct–March. **€11.30**

Les Gorges du Verdon Rte de la Maline ☎ 04 92 77 38 26, ⊛ hotel-des-gorges-du-verdon.fr. Smart, very comfortable and beautifully isolated, this luxurious upscale hotel is an incongruous but welcome presence, 500m down the Route des Crêtes from the village, just a few minutes' walk from the trails down into the gorge. Closed late Oct to early April. **€190**

Perroquet Vert Grande Rue ☎ 04 92 77 33 39, ⊛ leperroquetvert.com. Right in the village centre, this townhouse B&B offers three plain but comfortable bedrooms plus simple meals, and also serves as a shop-cum-rendezvous for climbers and walkers. Closed Nov–March. **€53**

Le Provence Rte de la Maline ☎ 04 92 77 38 88, ⊛ verdonprovencehotel.com. Good-value ivy-covered hotel, in a panoramic location 100m below the village, set back from the Route des Crêtes. The large courtyard garden is a great place to relax over a drink, while you can eat there or indoors, with *menus* from €17 for lunch, €22 for dinner. Rates include breakfast. Closed Dec–March. **€51–65**

ROUGON

Le Mur des Abeilles Eastern end of village ☎ 04 92 83 76 33. Walk right through Rougon to reach this delightful crêperie-café, where the tables on the garden terrace enjoy utterly sublime long-range views of the canyon. Substantial filled crêpes range from €5 to €9, and they offer a wide range of other snacks and drinks. Easter–Oct daily 10am–7pm.

AIGUINES

Altitude 823 Grande Rue ☎ 04 98 10 22 17, ⊛ hotel -altitude823-verdon.com. The best of the nine rooms in this small hotel-restaurant, at the hairpin bend where the main road reaches the centre, enjoy far-reaching views down to the lake. Rates include breakfast. Closed Nov to mid-March. **€103**

Le Galetas Quartier Vernis ☎ 04 94 70 20 48, ⊛ aiguines.com/galetas. Aiguines' large and rather plain municipal campsite is a long way down from the village, almost within diving distance of the lake. Closed mid-Oct to March. **€12.50**

Hôtel du Grand Canyon du Verdon Falaise des Cavaliers ☎ 04 94 76 91 31, ⊛ hotel-canyon-verdon .com. Perched atop a dramatic precipice on the Corniche Sublime, 20km east of Aiguines, this has to be the finest place to stay on the south side – so long as you don't suffer from vertigo. The restaurant (closed Tues eve & Wed

except July & Aug) serves good meals on *menus* from €24. Rates are for compulsory *demi-pension*. Closed Nov–March. **€125**

Le Vieux Château Place de la Fontaine ☎ 04 94 70 22 95, ⊛ hotelvieuxchateau.fr. Appealing *Logis de France* hotel, housed in an eighteenth-century coaching inn in the heart of the village, with bright, simple rooms and a nice terrace bar and restaurant that serves a €25 *menu terroir*. Closed Nov–March. **€75**

COMPS SUR ARTUBY

Grand Hotel Bain Av de Fayet ☎ 04 94 76 90 06, ⊛ grand-hotel-bain.fr. Pleasant old ochre-painted hotel-restaurant in the heart of town, with old-fashioned but cosy rooms, a reasonable traditional restaurant serving *menus* from €20 at tables set out along the pavement, and a sunny garden. **€84**

CASTELLANE

Bon Accueil Place Marcel Sauvaire ☎ 04 92 83 62 01, ⊛ auberge-du-bon-accueil.com. Inexpensive hotel on the main square, with faded but perfectly acceptable rooms and a restaurant downstairs that serves pretty good pizzas, along with conventional *menus* from €16. Closed Oct to mid-April. **€55**

Camping Frédéric Mistral 12 av Frédéric-Mistral ☎ 04 92 83 62 27, ⊛ camping-fredericmistral.com. Small, well shaded campsite, close to the river a mere hundred metres west of the central place Marcel Sauvaire. While not a rural idyll, it's very convenient for the town itself. Closed mid-Nov to Feb. **€16**

★ **Commerce** Place Marcel Sauvaire ☎ 04 92 83 61 00, ⊛ hotel-du-commerce-verdon.com. Comfortable and very central, Castellane's finest hotel holds recently modernized rooms that sleep up to four, plus a small pool. Its restaurant (closed Mon) serves wonderful food, both indoors and outside. Closed Nov–Feb. **€100**

Domain du Verdon ☎ 04 92 83 61 29, ⊛ camp-du -verdon.com. Leafy four-star campsite, 1.5km west of town, which has several pools, including one with big water slides; a restaurant and bar; and a crazy golf course. Closed mid-Sept to mid-May. **€35**

★ **Gite Chasteuil** Chasteuil ☎ 04 92 83 72 45, ⊛ gitedechasteuil.com. Beautiful five-room B&B, enjoying spectacular mountain views from its hillside perched in the hamlet of Chasteuil, north of the D952 7km west of Castellane, and reached by a very steep minor road with eleven switchback bends. Meals are served by arrangement, and they'll also prepare picnics. One room has a kitchenette. **€73**

Lac de Castillon and around

Following the D955 north of Castellane brings you after 5km to the southern shore of the hundred-metre-deep **Lac de Castillon**, created by another of the many hydroelectric projects that have progressively tamed the awesome power of the River Verdon. Slightly milky and an unearthly shade of aquamarine, the Lac de Castillon is a popular bathing spot in high summer, with closely supervised **beaches, boats** for rent, and plenty of opportunities for **waterskiing**. At its southern tip, the D955 crosses the awe-inspiring **Barrage de Castillon**, where there's a small parking area if you want to stop for a closer look, though bathing is forbidden. The gleam of gold up in the hills on the opposite bank is the Buddhist centre of Mandarom.

With good train and road access, plenty of accommodation in the Alpine village of **St-André-des-Alpes** (see below) as well as Castellane (see p.220), and well-organized facilities for outdoor activities, particularly water- and airborne sports, this is an easy corner of Haute Provence to explore. Traditional Provence is never far away, as the sight of sheep taking over the roads en route to or from their summer pastures may well remind you.

St-Julien-du-Verdon

The village of **ST-JULIEN-DU-VERDON**, 5km north of the dam, was a casualty of the creation of the lake. Today it's a tiny place, with nothing to suggest that this was once Sanctus Julienetus, on the Roman road from Nice to Digne. Still, it's a pleasant, quiet spot if you just want to laze about by calm water with a gorgeous backdrop of mountains.

St-André-les-Alpes

Unlike so many tightly huddled Provençal villages, **ST-ANDRÉ-LES-ALPES**, 8km north of St-Julien, sprawls amid open meadows. Low-key but ever-increasing tourist development, with the construction of wooden chalets and villas to all sides, has given it a straggly feel, though its central streets and squares lie open to magnificent views of the surrounding mountains. Beautiful **hiking** and **biking** trails radiate out from St-André; whether the lake itself is visible depends on current water levels, but as a rule it ends 1km or more south.

ARRIVAL AND INFORMATION — ST-ANDRÉ-LES-ALPES

By train The *gare Chemins de Fer de Provence*, across the N202 northeast of the centre, is served by trains between Dignes and Nice (see box, p.212).

By bus St-André is served by buses from Allos (1–3 daily in high season; 1hr); Barrême (1 daily; 10min); Digne (1 daily; 1hr); La Foux d'Allos (1–3 daily; 1hr 15min); and Nice (1 daily; 2hr).

Tourist office Place Marcel-Pastorelli (May Mon–Fri 9am–noon & 1.30–5.30pm, Sat 10am–12.30pm & 3.30–5.30pm; June & Sept Mon–Sat 9am–12.30pm & 2–6pm, Sun 10am–12.30pm; July & Aug daily 9am–1pm & 1.30–7pm; Oct–April Mon–Fri 9am–noon & 1.30–5.30pm; T 04 92 89 02 39, W ot-st-andre-les-alpes.fr).

ACTIVITIES

Paragliding and hang-gliding Aerogliss, based south of the village (T 04 92 89 11 30, W aerogliss.com), offer well-organized paragliding and hang-gliding around Mont Chalvet to the west. Short flights for the less experienced take place in the morning, and five-day beginners' courses start at €495.

Walking tours and watersports Natur Elements (T 06 28 33 23 15, W naturelements.com) organize walks, as well as rafting, canyoning and canoeing on the Lac de Castillon and Gorges du Verdon.

5

ACCOMMODATION AND EATING

Les Iscles ☎ 04 92 89 02 29, ⊛ camping-les-iscle s.com. This large two-star municipal campsite, set in the pine woods by the confluence of the Verdon and the Issole, offers good facilities at a very good price. Closed mid-Oct to March. **€11.70**

Lac et Forêt Route de Nice ☎ 04 92 89 07 38,

⊛ lacforet.com. This imposing 1930s hotel, beside the main road 1km south towards St-Julien, offers thirty somewhat old-fashioned en-suite rooms. The cheapest "economy" rooms are quite basic; a better lake-view one costs €25 extra. They have a restaurant, and bikes are available for rent. **€40**

Massif les Monges

North of Digne, the mountains that reach their highest peak at Les Monges (2115m) form an impassable barrier, as far as roads are concerned, between the valleys running down to Sisteron and the Durance and those of the Bléone's tributaries. There are footpaths for serious **walkers**, and just one road loops south of Les Monges linking Digne and Sisteron across the **Col de Font-Belle**. Fantastic forested paths lead off past vertical rocks from the pass.

The D900a, which follows first the course of the Bléone, and then the Bès torrent, before joining the main D900 and continuing north to **Seyne-les-Alpes**, passes many of the protected sites of the **Réserve Naturelle Géologique de Haute Provence**, where shrubs, flowers and butterflies are now the sole visible wildlife. After heavy rain the waters tear through the **Clues de Barles and Verdaches** like a boiling soup of mud in which it's hard to imagine fish finding sustenance.

Making a livelihood from the land here is difficult. A lot of "*marginaux*" (hippies or anyone into alternative lifestyles) manage to survive, making goat's cheese and doing seasonal work; the indigenous *paysans* are more likely to be opening *gîtes* and servicing the city dwellers who come for **trekking** or **skiing** trips. But it's still very wild and deserted, with little accommodation other than *gîtes* and *chambres d'hôtes*; petrol stations are also few and far between.

Seyne-les-Alpes

SEYNE-LES-ALPES lies in a distinctly alpine landscape 40km north of Digne, its highest point topped by a Vauban fort. Quiet for most of the year, Seyne experiences its main influx in winter, when its three skiing stations, **St-Jean**, **Chabanon** and **Le Grand Puy**, are in operation. It also has the only surviving **horse fair** in southeast France – held on the second Saturday of October – and a mule breeder's competition at the start of August.

INFORMATION

Tourist office Place d'Armes, off Grande Rue (July & Aug Mon–Sat 9am–12.30pm & 2.30–6.30pm, Sun

9am–12.30pm; Sept–June Mon–Fri 9am–noon & 2.30–5pm; ☎ 04 92 35 11 00, ⊛ valleedelablanche.com).

ACCOMMODATION AND EATING

Les Prairies ☎ 04 92 35 10 21, ⊛ campinglesprairies .com. Three-star, summer-only campsite, beside the river 800m below town, with a nice pool, bar and snack bar. Closed early Sept to late April. **€19.90**

Au Vieux Tilleul Les Auches, 1km from town centre ☎ 04 92 35 00 04, ⊛ vieux-tilleul.fr. Looking like a

mountain chalet, and remaining open in winter, this hotel offers twenty spacious, comfortable rooms, a happy combination of pool and skating rink, and a restaurant with dinner *menus* from €20. Lunch served Aug only; closed first three weeks in Dec. **€65**

Parc National du Mercantour

5

Strictly speaking, the **Parc National du Mercantour**, which stretches across the Alps for 75km from east to west, holds no permanent inhabitants. That's just the central core of a much wider area, however, in which the park sprawls across the peaks while a succession of delightful high-mountain valleys cradle towns that cater to a steady stream of visitors, from hikers and wildlife enthusiasts in summer to skiers in winter. The park itself, meanwhile, is crossed by numerous paths, equipped with refuge huts that provide basic food and bedding for trekkers.

As you head into the region from the little town of **Barçelonnette**, four potential routes cross the watershed of Mont Pelat, La Bonette, Chambeyron and their high gneiss and granite extensions. The Col d'Allos leads into the **Haut-Verdon** Valley; the Col de la Cayolle into the **Haut-Var** Valley; the road across the summit of La Bonette to the **Tinée** Valley; and the Col de Larche into Italy. All but the last are snowed up between November and April, and sometimes stay closed as late as June. Further east, the **Vésubie** rises just below the Italian border; like the Tinée and the Verdon it runs into the Var.

WILDLIFE OF THE MERCANTOUR

The mountains of the Mercantour are renowned as a habitat for all sorts of **wildlife**. Camping, lighting fires, picking flowers, playing loud music or doing anything else that might disturb the delicate environment is strictly outlawed.

MAMMALS

The least shy mammal hereabouts is the **marmot**, a cream-coloured, badger-sized creature often seen sitting on its haunches in the sun. Chamois, mouflon and ibex are similarly unwary of humans. The male **ibex** is a wonderful, big, solid beast with curving, ribbed horns that grow to 1m long; almost hunted to extinction, the population is now stable. Another species of goat, the **chamois**, is also on the increase; the male is recognizable by the shorter, grappling-hook horns and white beard. The **mouflon**, introduced to the Mercantour in the 1950s, is the ancestor of domestic sheep. Other animals you might see include **stoats**, rare species of **hare**, and **foxes**, the latter the most abundant predator since bears and lynxes became extinct here. The most problematic predator, however, is the **wolf**, formerly extinct, but now stalking the region again, having crossed the border from Italy. With eight hundred sheep killed by wolves in a single year, sheep farmers are not happy.

BIRDS

The Mercantour is a perfect habitat for **eagles**, which can build their nests on any number of crags, and have plenty to eat – including marmots. Pairs of **golden eagles** are breeding, while a rare vulture, the **lammergeier**, has been successfully reintroduced. Other birds of prey – **kestrels**, **falcons** and **buzzards** – wing their way down from the scree to the Alpine lawn and its torrents to swoop on lizards, mice and snakes. The **great spotted woodpecker** and the black-and-orange **hoopoe** are the park's most colourful inhabitants. **Ptarmigan**, which turn snowy-white in winter, can sometimes be seen in June parading to would-be mates on the higher slopes in the north. **Blackcocks**, known in French as *tétras-lyre* for their lyre-shaped white tails, burrow into the snow at night and fly out in a flurry of snowflakes when the sun rises.

FLORA

The **flowers** of the Mercantour are an unmissable glory. Around forty of the over two thousand species represented are unique to the region. The moment the snow melts, the lawn between the rocky crags and the tree line begins to dot with golds, pinks and blues. Rare species of **lily** and **orchid** grow here, as do the elusive **edelweiss** and the wild ancestors of various cultivated flowers – pansies, geraniums, tulips and gentian violets. Rarest of all is the **multi-flowering saxifrage** (*saxifraga florulenta*), a big spiky flower that looks as if it must be cultivated, though it would hardly be popular in suburban gardens since it flowers just once every ten years. Wild strawberries, raspberries and bilberries tempt visitors into the woods.

5

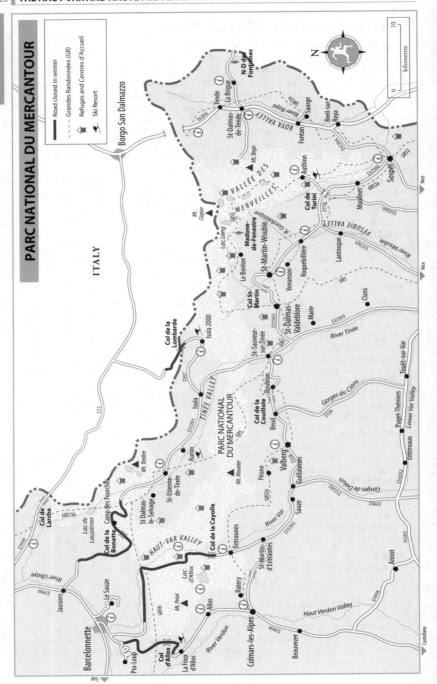

PARC NATIONAL DU MERCANTOUR

Road closed in winter
Grandes Randonnées (GR)
Refuges and Centres d'Accueil
Ski Resort

Borgo San Dalmazzo

ITALY

N-D des Fontaines
Tende
La Brigue
St-Dalmas-de-Tende
Mt. Bego
VALLÉE DES
MERVEILLES
Mt. Clapier
Lac Long
R. Gordolasque
Madone-de-Fenestre
Le Boréon
St-Martin-Vésubie
Col de la Lombarde
Isola 2000
Col St-Martin
St-Dalmas-Valdeblore
Marie
Clans
St-Sauveur-sur-Tinée
TINÉE VALLEY
Isola
D2205
River Tinée
PARC NATIONAL
DU MERCANTOUR
Roubion
Col de la Couillole
Beuil
Gorges du Cians
Mt. Mounier
Péone
Valberg
Guillaumes
Sauze
Touët-sur-Var
Puget-Théniers
Entrevaux
Lower Var Valley
Mt. Ténibre
Auron
St-Étienne-de-Tinée
Camp des Fourches
Col de Larche
Lac de Lauzanier
St-Dalmas-le-Selvage
Col de la Bonette
HAUT-VAR VALLEY
Col de la Cayolle
Entraunes
River Var
St-Martin-d'Entraunes
Gorges de Daluis
Annot
Jausiers
Le Sauze
Mt. Pelat
Lac d'Allos
Allos
Ratery
Pra-Loup
Col d'Allos
La Foux d'Allos
River Verdon
Colmars-les-Alpes
Haut Verdon Valley
Beauvezer
Barcelonnette
River Ubaye

Auron
Lantosque
Roquebillière
Venanson
Mt. Gordolasque
Col de Turini
Auther
Fontan
River Royá
Saorge
Breil-sur-Roya
Sospel
Modinet
VÉSUBIE VALLEY
River Vésubie

ROYA VALLEY

Nice

Nice

Castellane

kilometres

N

Barçelonnette

From the northern border of Provence at the Lac de Serre-Ponçon, the D900 follows the River Ubaye to little **BARÇELONNETTE**, passing through a dramatic landscape of tiny, irregular fields backed by the jagged silhouettes of mountains that look like something out of a vampire movie. The town owes its Spanish-sounding name, "Little Barcelona", to its foundation in the thirteenth century by Raimond Béranger IV, count of Provence, whose family came from the Catalan city. Although snow falls here around Christmas and stays until Easter, and there are several **ski resorts** nearby, summer is the main tourist season.

Barçelonnette is an immaculate little place, with sunny squares where old men wearing berets play *pétanque*, backed by views of snowcapped mountains. All the houses have tall gables and deep eaves, and a more ideal spot for doing nothing would be hard to find. In the central square, place Manuel, a white clock tower commemorates the centenary of the 1848 revolution.

Musée de la Vallée

10 av de la Libération • Jan–May & Oct to mid-Nov Wed–Sat 2.30–6pm; June to early July & Sept Tues–Sat 2.30–6pm; early July to Aug daily 10am–noon & 2.30–7pm • €4 • ☎ 04 92 81 27 15, ⓦ barcelonnette.com

Barçelonnette has a surprising connection with **Mexico**: many local sheep farmers and wool merchants emigrated to Latin America in the late nineteenth century to make their fortunes, before returning home to build their dream houses. In one of these grand villas, *La Sapinière*, the **Musée de la Vallée** details the life and times of the people of the Ubaye Valley, and the emigration to Mexico and the travels of a nineteenth-century explorer from the town.

ARRIVAL AND INFORMATION   BARCELONNETTE

By bus Buses from Marseille, Digne or Gap arrive on place Aimé-Gassier.
Destinations Digne (2 daily; 1hr 30min); Gap (4 daily; 1hr 30min); Marseille (2 daily; 3hr 50min).
Parc National du Mercantour information centre In the Musée de la Vallée at 10 av de la Libération (mid-June to mid-Sept daily 10am–noon & 3–7pm;

☎ 04 92 81 21 31, ⓦ mercantour.eu). Staff provide maps, advise on walks and mountain refuges, and explain the fauna and flora.
Tourist office Off place Frédéric Mistral (July & Aug daily 9am–12.30pm & 1.30–7.30pm; Sept–June Mon–Sat 9am–noon & 2–6pm; ☎ 04 92 81 04 71, ⓦ barcelonnette .com).

ACTIVITIES

Walking and biking Rando Passion/Maison de la Montagne, 31 rue Jules-Béraud (☎ 04 92 81 43 34, ⓦ rando-passion.com), provide guidance for walks and VTT mountain biking in summer, and offer snow-shoeing and igloo building in winter. They also offer bike rental.
Water-based activities More than a dozen companies offer every conceivable whitewater activity from canyoning and canoeing to rafting, including Alligator

(☎ 04 92 81 06 06; ⓦ alligator-rafting.com) and Aqua'Rider (☎ 06 32 42 50 15, ⓦ aquarider.net).
Skiing Local ski resorts include Pra-Loup (ⓦ praloup.com), where the pistes link up with La Foux d'Allos (see p.228); Ste-Anne/La Condamine (ⓦ sainte-anne.com); Jausiers (ⓦ jausiers.com); and Le Sauze/Super-Sauze (ⓦ sauze .com). During the skiing season, a free bus loops between the resorts and Barçelonnette.

ACCOMMODATION

★ **L'Azteca** 3 rue François-Arnaud ☎ 04 92 81 46 36, ⓦ azteca-hotel.fr. Extremely pleasant hotel, in a nineteenth-century villa built by an emigrant returned from Mexico, steps away from the centre and enjoying superb views of the mountains. **€88**
★ **Chalet les Blancs** Hameau les Blancs, Pra Loup ☎ 04 92 84 04 21, ⓦ hotel.lesblancs.free.fr. Lovely mountain-chalet hotel, ideal for families, 9km drive southwest of Barçelonnette. As well as wonderful valley

views and thirty large well-equipped rooms, they have a heated indoor pool and a restaurant in which full meals, with a dessert buffet, cost €22. **€94**
Cheval Blanc 12 rue Grenette ☎ 04 92 81 00 19, ⓦ www.chevalblancbarcelonnette.com. Inexpensive, central *Logis de France*, consisting of a rambling labyrinth of widely varying rooms above an attractive bar and restaurant (closed Sun) where *menus* start at €18. Closed Nov. **€66**

5

5

Grand Hôtel 6 place Manuel ☎ 04 92 81 03 14, ⓦ grandhotel-barcelonnette.fr. Old-fashioned but cosy and very central hotel, with 21 wood-panelled bedrooms, some capable of sleeping five guests. **€80**

Grande Épervière 18 rue des Trois Frères Arnaud ☎ 04 92 81 00 70, ⓦ hotelgrandeperviere.com. This imposing Mexican-era mansion, set in its own peaceful park an easy 500m walk west of the centre, now holds an upmarket hotel. All the comfortable, sizeable rooms have balconies, and there's a bar but no restaurant. **€88**

CAMPSITES

Camping du Plan 52 av Émile-Aubert ☎ 04 92 81 08 11, ⓦ campingduplan.fr. This three-star site is the closest to town, 500m southwest along the D902 towards the Col de la Cayolle. It centres on a chalet-style building that doubles as shop, bar and deli. Closed Oct to mid-May. **€14.35**

EATING AND DRINKING

Barçelonnette holds enough **restaurants** to feed the whole valley. At the Wednesday and Saturday **markets** on place Aimé-Gassier and place St-Pierre, you'll find all manner of sweets, jams and alcohol made from locally picked bilberries, pâtés made from local birds – thrush, partridge, pheasant – and the local juniper liquor, *Génépi*.

L'In Attendu 4 place St-Pierre ☎ 04 92 31 30 95, ⓦ linattendu-restaurant.com. Great-value Provençal restaurant on a peaceful and otherwise empty square, with a snug dining room and a handful of tables beneath the clock tower of the St-Pierre church. The one dinner *menu* changes daily, with two courses for €18 and three for €21. Daily noon–1.30pm & 7.30–9.30pm.

La Plancha Place Paul Reynaud ☎ 04 92 81 12 97, ⓦ laplancha-barcelonnette.fr. On the less attractive of Barçelonnette's linked central squares, this welcoming restaurant serves mountain specialities such as the cheese-and-potato dish *tartiflette* (the menu calls it *Le Farçon*), and grilled-meat platters, for around €15. For lunch, €10 buys *moules-frites* plus dessert. Daily noon–2pm & 7–9pm.

Villa Morelia Le Château, Jausiers ☎ 04 92 84 67 78, ⓦ villa-morelia.com. This gastronomic restaurant, 9km east of Barçelonnette in a neo-Mexican folly that also houses a plush spa hotel, serves a delicious nouvelle cuisine *menu* for €54. Jan, Feb & May–Oct daily noon–1.30pm & 7.30–9pm.

The Haut-Verdon Valley

The beautiful **Haut-Verdon Valley** forms the easiest and most direct route between Barçelonnette in the north and Castellane in the south. In its upper reaches, before it's forced to squeeze into the dramatic Gorges du Verdun, the Verdun river runs through a bucolic landscape that's at its most seductive around the pretty village of **Colmar-les-Alpes**. This is also prime ski country in winter, especially in the vicinity of **Allos**.

To reach the valley from Barçelonnette, however, you have first to cross the 2250m **summit of the Col d'Allos**, 20km southwest of town on the D908, which is usually closed from November to May. In late June pale wild pansies and deep-blue gentians flower between patches of ice. The panorama is magnificent, though once you start switchbaching your way down the side of the pass to reach the Verdon, the hideous vast hotels of **La Foux d'Allos** come into view.

A mountain refuge on the pass, *Col d'Allos* (☎ 04 92 83 85 14; June–Sept only), marks the junction with the GR56, which leads west to the Ubaye Valley and Seyne-les-Alpes, and east to the Col de Larche and the Tinée Valley.

La Foux d'Allos

Scruffy **LA FOUX D'ALLOS** is probably the cheapest Provençal resort in which to **ski** or snowboard, and its fifty lifts and 180km of pistes are open from late December to mid-April. The area joins up with Pra-Loup to the north, and the resort is quite high (1800–2600m) with over 250 snow cannons, so melting shouldn't be a problem.

La Foux d'Allos and its neighbours are also keen to promote themselves as summer resorts. A handful of lifts operate in July and August to transport mountain bikers to well-marked trails around the mountain.

Allos

The medieval village of **ALLOS**, 9km south of La Foux d'Allos, was all but destroyed by fire in the eighteenth century; one tower of the ramparts half-survived and was turned into the current clock tower. The old livelihoods of tending sheep and weaving woollen sheets were all but dying out when tourism began at the start of the twentieth century, with the discovery of the nearby **Lac d'Allos**. Once skiing became an established pastime the agricultural days of Allos were numbered. Even so, despite all its *résidences secondaires*, it's not a bad place to spend a day or two.

In summer, Allos's **Parc de Loisirs** offers all kinds of activities, from trampolining to horseriding, archery, courses in wildlife photography and watersports (July & Aug daily 10am–6.45pm; €6; ☎04 92 83 01 89, ⓦvaldallos.com).

Lac d'Allos

At 2228m, the round and impossibly blue surface of the **Lac d'Allos**, 13km east and 800m above Allos, reflects the amphitheatre of towering peaks that curves around its flanks. The lake nourishes trout and char in its pure cold waters and mouflon and chamois bound around its banks. Looking in the direction of the one-time glacier flow, you can just see the peak of **Mont Pelat**, the highest mountain in the Parc National du Mercantour.

To walk the whole way to the lake from Allos, follow the path that starts by the church. Alternatively, there's an uneven, single-track road that weaves up 46 bends in 6km through a dense forest of larch trees to a busy car park, from which a 45-minute walk brings you to what was once the head of a glacier.

Colmars-les-Alpes

COLMARS-LES-ALPES, 7km downstream from Allos or 29km northeast of St-André-les-Alpes, is an extraordinarily well-preserved stronghold, whose name comes from a temple to Mars built by the Romans high on the adjacent hill. Colmars' all-but-intact sixteenth-century ramparts, complete with arrow slits and small square towers, were constructed on the orders of François I of France to reinforce the defences that had existed since 1381, when Colmars became a border town between Provence and Savoy. When Savoy declared war on France, in 1690, Vauban was called in to make the town even more secure, and designed the **Fort de Savoie** and the **Fort de France** at either end. Their corresponding gateways, the Porte de France and Porte de Savoie, now form the town's two principal entrances, adorned with climbing roses.

Inside the walls, you find yourself in a quiet, atmospheric, somewhat rough-hewn old Provençal town, with cobbled streets and fountained squares. The Fort de Savoie is only open in summer (mid-June to mid-Sept Mon, Wed, Thurs, Sat & Sun 10am–2.30pm & 3–6.30pm, Tues & Fri 3–6.30pm; €3), when exhibitions of local customs and costumes are set up beneath the magnificent larch-timbered ceilings. All in all, there's not a lot to do in Colmars except wander around and soak up the atmosphere, or take a twenty-minute walk east to the Lance waterfall.

Colmars lies at the junction of the Verdon Valley road with the D78, which climbs northeast between the Frema and Encombrette mountains and descends to the Var Valley at St-Martin-d'Entraunes.

INFORMATION AND ACTIVITIES   **THE HAUT-VERDON VALLEY**

LA FOUX D'ALLOS

Tourist office Maison de la Foux (July, Aug & late Dec to April daily 9am–noon & 2–6.30pm; ☎04 92 83 02 81, ⓦvaldallos.com).

Ski and bike rental Lantelme Sports, Le Centre (☎04 92 83 80 09, ⓦla-foux-d-allos.skiset.com).

ALLOS

Tourist office Northern end of the old village (July, Aug & mid-Dec to mid-April Mon–Sat 8.30am–noon & 2–6.30pm, Sun 9am–noon & 3–6.30pm; Sept to mid-Dec and mid-April to June Mon–Sat 9am–noon & 2–5pm, Sun 9am–noon; ☎04 92 83 02 81, ⓦvaldallos.com).

5

Parc National du Mercantour information office In the same building as the tourist office (☎ 04 92 83 04 18, ⓦ mercantour.eu).

Ski and bike rental Au Petit Allossard, rue du Pré de Foire ☎ 04 92 83 14 62, ⓦ aupetitallossard.sport2000.fr).

COLMARS-LES-ALPES

Tourist office Outside the walls, by the Porte de la Lance (July & Aug daily 8am–7pm; Sept–June Tues–Sat 9am–12.15pm & 2–5.45pm; ☎ 04 92 83 41 92, ⓦ colmars -les-alpes.fr).

ACCOMMODATION AND EATING

ALLOS

Auberge Les Gentianes Grande Rue ☎ 04 92 83 03 50, ⓦ aubergelesgentianesallos.com. Simple, inexpensive hotel-restaurant in the old village, with plain but acceptable rooms and a restaurant that serves full meals and crêpes. **€70**

La Ferme Girerd-Potin 5km northwest on rte de la Foux ☎ 04 92 83 04 76, ⓦ chambredhotes-valdallos.com. Sixteenth-century farmhouse, open year-round, that offers five very comfortable en-suite B&B rooms plus a 3-bedroom *gîte*. Two-night minimum stay, half-board compulsory, so rates here include breakfast and dinner. **€114**

L'Ours Blanc Le Seignus ☎ 04 92 83 01 07, ⓦ hotel -loursblanc.com. Small hotel near the foot of the ski lifts, with simple but bright and comfortable rooms, a warm welcome, and a restaurant specializing in hearty mountain food. Closed April, May & mid-Sept to mid-Dec. **€75**

COLMARS-LES-ALPES

Bois Joly Le Bois Joly ☎ 04 92 83 40 40. Small and very scenic campsite, amid the riverside trees a 10min walk from the village. Closed Oct–April. **€11.70**

Le France Place de France ☎ 04 92 83 42 93, ⓦ hotel-lefrance-colmars.com. Colmars' one hotel, just across the D908 opposite the walled town, has a garden restaurant that serves pizza in summer. Closed Jan to late Feb. **€51**

Gassendi Rue St-Joseph ☎ 04 92 83 42 25, ⓔ eeric .dini@orange.fr. This year-round *gîte d'étape*, housed in a twelfth-century Templar hospice, holds six dorms with ten or twelve beds each, and a handful of private double rooms. Rates include breakfast; an evening meal costs €14 extra. Dorms **€22**; doubles **€60**

The Haut-Var Valley

Confusingly, the dramatic **Haut-Var Valley**, carved by the upper reaches of the Var river southeast of Barçelonnette, is entirely distinct from the region known as the Haut Var. To reach it from Barçelonnette, follow the D902 due south, climbing through a deep gorge cut by the **River Bachelard**. It then turns abruptly east, continuing beside the river as it squeezes between Mont Pelat to the south and the ridge of peaks to the north, named for their shapes – Pain de Sucre (Sugarloaf), Chapeau de Gendarme (Gendarme's Hat) and Chevalier (Horseman). At the *Bayasse* refuge, the D902 turns south once more, towards the **Col de la Cayolle**, while a track and the GR56 continue east towards La Bonette and the Tinée Valley.

Having switchbacked down south from the Col de la Cayolle, the road becomes the D2202. The **Var** now makes its appearance, pouring southwards towards Guillaumes, and beyond that down through the **Gorges de Daluis** to Entrevaux. Its banks are punctuated with chapels built before and after disasters of avalanches, floods, landslides and devastating storms. Many are superbly decorated, like the Renaissance Chapelle de St-Sébastien, just north of **Entraunes**, and the church at **St-Martin-d'Entraunes**, with its Bréa retable.

Guillaumes

Tucked beneath the ruined Château de la Reine Jeanne, **GUILLAUMES**, the valley's minor metropolis and a favourite with cyclists in summer, served for centuries as a resting place for sheep on their way between the Haut-Var summer pastures and Nice. Most flocks now travel by lorry, but the old **sheep fairs** still take place on September 16 and the second Saturday of October. Winter sees a migration in the opposite direction, as the residents of the Côte d'Azur flock to the ski resorts of Valberg and Beuil, east of Guillaumes, on the fabulous road that climbs over to the Tinée Valley.

Tourist office Opposite the town hall (daily 10am–noon & 2–6pm; ☎ 04 93 05 57 76, ⓦ pays-de-guillaumes.com).
Renaissance 7 place Napoléon III ☎ 04 93 05 59 89. Old-fashioned hotel, 100m up on the right from the tourist office, just past the bridge, with simple, brightly coloured rooms and a restaurant serving *menus* at €15 and €22, with seating outdoors in summer. **€80**

The Gorges de Daluis

The Var enters the dramatic red-rocked **Gorges de Daluis** around 5km south of Guillaumes. Drivers heading upstream here (northwards) enjoy better views; the downstream carriageway is in tunnels much of the way. Walkers can take a closer look at the gorge by following the two-kilometre **Sentier du Point Sublime** from Pont de Berthèou on the D2202 to the Point Sublime itself. The Pont de la Mariée is a popular spot for **bungee jumping** (mid-July to Aug daily 1–5pm; €60; ⓦ saut-elastique.com /bon-spot-pont-mariee.htm).

The Lower Var Valley

East of St-Julien-du-Verdon (see p.223), the main N202 climbs to meet the Var river after 24km. From there, as first the D4202 and then the D6202, it follows the **Lower Var Valley** for another 40km to its semi-subterranean confluence with the Tinée, and thus provides direct access to Nice along the spectacular gorge known as the **Défilé de Chaudan**. This riverside route is also followed by the Chemins de Fer de Provence (see box, p.212), and by steam trains in summer. The major highlight along the way is the medieval fortified town of **Entrevaux**, but several lesser communities also make good stops.

Annot

Surrounded by hills a couple of kilometres north of the N202, 17km east of St-Julien-de-Verdon, the town of **ANNOT** centres on a large open *cours*, lined by plane trees. This is bounded to one side by the river Vaire and to the other by a compact **Vieille Ville**, a flavourful tangle of pretty arcades, mysterious passageways, thick arches and gateways that nonetheless lacks any businesses or particular tourist attractions. While Annot is not in itself as lovely or picturesque as Entrevaux, it's a popular holiday centre, and makes an excellent base for walks, up past strange sandstone formations to rocky outcrops with names like Chambre du Roi (the King's Chamber) and Dent du Diable (the Devil's Tooth).

Entrevaux

The absurdly photogenic village of **ENTREVAUX** stands on the north bank of the River Var 15km east of Annot, 6km beyond the southern end of the Gorges de Daluis. Entrevaux was once a key border town between France and Savoy, and the only access to its old walled centre is via a single-arched drawbridge across the rushing river. The bridge was fortified by Vauban, whose linking of the town with a ruined **château** (access at any time; €3), perched atop a steep spur 135m above the river, gives the site a menacing character. Originally the château could only be reached by scrambling up the rock, but by the seventeenth century that had become unacceptable, and Vauban built the double-walled ramp, plus attendant bastions, which zigzags up the rock with ferocious determination.

The former **cathedral** (summer 9am–7pm; winter 9am–5pm), in the lower part of the old town, is well integrated into the military defences, with one wall forming part of the ramparts and its belfry a fortified tower. The interior, however, is all twirling Louis Quinze, with misericords, side altars and organ as over-decorated as they could possibly be. Just beyond the church, through the **Porte d'Italie**, you can escape from Baroque opulence and military might alike.

Musée Moto

Rue Serpente • May–Sept daily 10am–12.30pm & 2–6pm • Free, donations accepted

A bizarre labour of love, the **Musée Moto**, in the heart of the village, consists of a rather amazing collection of old motorcycles squeezed into a tiny house. Prize specimens include a gleaming Harley-Davidson from 1917, and a Narcisse tandem from 1951.

Puget-Théniers

East of Entrevaux, the broad Var Valley abounds in pear, apple and cherry orchards. **PUGET-THÉNIERS**, 13km along, is a presentable but not especially attractive country town, though its **Vieille Ville**, on the right bank of the River Roudoule, is full of thirteenth-century houses, some still bearing symbols of their original owners' trades on the lintels. The left bank is dominated by the great semicircular apse of the Romanesque **church**, outreaching even the ancient cedar alongside, and more suggestive of a fort or prison than a place of worship.

On the *cours* below the old town, in front of the station, a statue of a naked woman with bound hands commemorates **Auguste Blanqui**, born here in 1805. A leader of the Paris Commune of 1871, Blanqui spent forty years in prison for – as the inscription states – "fidelity to the sacred cause of workers' emancipation". There are few French revolutionaries for whom the description "heroic defender of the proletariat" is so true, and none who came from a more isolated, unindustrialized region.

Touët-sur-Var

The River Cians joins the Var 8km east of Puget-Théniers. As described on p.236, the road along this tributary, the D28, climbs beside the spectacular **Gorges du Cians** to reach the ski resort of Beuil. Crammed against a cliff not far beyond the confluence, **TOUËT-SUR-VAR** holds a remarkable church, built over a small torrent that's visible through a grille in the floor of the nave. The village's highest houses look as if they're falling apart, but in fact the gaps between the beams are open galleries where the midday sun can reach the rows of drying figs.

ARRIVAL AND INFORMATION   **THE LOWER VAR VALLEY**

ANNOT

By train The *gare Chemins de Fer de Provence* (see box, p.212), on the Nice–Dignes line, is not far southeast of place du Germe.

Tourist office Place du Germe, just outside the old quarter (mid-May to June & Sept to mid-Oct Mon–Sat 9am–noon & 2–6pm; July & Aug Mon–Sat 9am–6.30pm; mid-Oct to mid-May Tues–Sat 9am–noon & 2–5pm; ☏ 04 92 83 23 03, ⓦ annot.fr).

ENTREVAUX

By train The *gare Chemins de Fer de Provence* (see box, p.212) is just downstream from the centre, on the south bank.

Tourist office Set into the left-hand tower of the drawbridge (July & Aug daily 10am–6pm; March–June &

Sept daily 10am–12.30pm & 2–5pm; Oct Mon, Tues, Thurs & Fri 10am–12.30pm & 2–5pm; ☏ 04 93 05 46 73, ⓦ entrevaux.info).

PUGET-THÉNIERS

By train The *gare Chemins de Fer de Provence* (see box, p.212) is on the N202.

By bus Buses stop in front of the *gare Chemins de Fer de Provence*.

Destinations Annot (1 daily; 20min); Barrême (1 daily; 1hr 10min); Digne (1 daily; 2hr); Entrevaux (1 daily; 10min); St-André-les-Alpes (1 daily; 1hr).

Tourist office Alongside the *gare Chemins de Fer de Provence* (June–Aug Mon–Fri 9am–12.30pm & 2–6pm, Sat & Sun 9am–7pm; Sept–May Mon–Sat 9am–noon and 2–5.30pm; ☏ 04 93 05 05 05, ⓦ www.provence-val-dazur.com).

ACCOMMODATION AND EATING

ANNOT

Beau Séjour Place du Révelly ☏ 04 92 83 21 08, ⓦ hotel-beausejour-annot.com. This well-priced *Logis de France*, beside the entrance to the Vieille Ville, has fifteen clean and comfortable rooms, plus a restaurant that serves

good food both indoors and out, with *menus* at €15 and €21. €58

L'Avenue Av de la Gare ☏ 04 92 83 22 07, ⓦ hotel -avenue.com. Smart little hotel, a few metres south of the old town, with small, tasteful rooms and a good restaurant (open for dinner only), with *menus* at €20 and €30. Closed Nov–March. **€80**

La Ribière On the D908 ☎ 04 92 83 21 44, ⓦ la-ribiere .com. Very pleasant two-star campsite, just north of town towards Fugeret; you can swim in the river alongside. Pizzas and simple meals available in summer. Closed late Oct to Feb. **€15**

ENTREVAUX

L'Ambassade Place du Marché ☎ 04 93 05 49 98, ⓦ lambassadeentrevaux.com. Appealing bar/restaurant in the walled village, with outdoor tables on an attractive lane. All of its five different *menus*, at €16–22, include a plate of the delicious house speciality, *secca* (dried beef). Mon–Sat 11am–11pm.

Vauban 4 place Moreau ☎ 04 93 05 42 40, ⓦ hotel-le -vauban.com. With no hotels in the old town proper, the *Vauban*, immediately across the river, is the most convenient option, with reasonable rooms – the two cheapest are not en-suite – and a restaurant (closed Sun pm & Mon, Sept to mid-July) specializing in trout, pasta and the local dry beef sausage (*secca de boeuf*), with *menus* from €14 at lunchtime, €19 at dinner. **€49.50**

PUGET-THÉNIERS

Les Acacias 1km east on the D6202 ☎ 04 93 05 05 25. Much the best food in the vicinity of Puget-Théniers. *Cuisine de terroir* using the local produce can be enjoyed on a €13.20 lunch *menu*, or for €30 in the evenings. Mon, Tues & Thurs–Sun noon–1.30pm & 7.30–9pm.

The Tinée Valley

The longest tributary of the Var, the **Tinée**, rises just below the 2800-metre summit of **La Bonette**, roughly 30km southeast of Barçelonnette (see p.227) by road. The mountains on its left bank – under whose shadow **St-Étienne** and **Auron** nestle – rise up to the Italian border, while the river heads south to cut a steep, narrow valley before joining the Var 30km from the sea.

Across La Bonette

Claiming to be the highest stretch of tarmac in Europe, the D64 across **La Bonette** gives a feast of high-altitude views. The actual summit of the mountain, a ten-minute scrabble up scree from a lesser loop road that branches off the main road, is not particularly exciting, and all the more ugly for its military training camp. The green and silent spaces of the long approach, however, circled by barren peaks, are magical.

Before the hairpins begin for the southern descent, at **Camp des Fourches**, you can abandon your wheels and take the **GR5/56** north and parallel with the Italian border to the Col de Larche. While it's not exactly a stroll, once you've climbed to the Col de la Cavale (after 5km or so) it's more or less downhill all the way, with the Ubayette torrent as your guide; the **Lac de Lauzanier**, 5km on from the Col de la Cavale, is a spot you may never want to leave..

St-Étienne-de-Tinée

On the south side of La Bonette, the D2205 descends, with the Tinée alongside, to the small, isolated town of **ST-ÉTIENNE-DE-TINÉE**, which comes to life only during its sheep fairs, held twice every summer, and the Fête de la Transhumance at the end of June. On its western side, off boulevard d'Auron, a cable car then chairlift climb to the summit of **La Pinatelle**, thereby linking the village to the ski resort of Auron.

Auron

Seven kilometres south of St-Étienne and accessible on a dead-end road, the resort of **AURON** has 21 lifts and 135km of pistes used by skiers in winter (Dec–April; €30 per day). A few remain open for hikers and mountain bikers in summer (July & Aug; €9 per day; ⓦ auron.com).

Isola 2000

Downstream from St-Étienne, the D2205 runs between nothing but white quartz and heather. Only the silvery sound of crickets competes with the water's roar until you reach **Isola**, an uneventful village at the bottom of the climb to the purpose-built ski resort of **ISOLA 2000** (ⓦisola2000.com), a jumble of concrete apartment blocks high in the mountain, just below the tree line, built to accommodate the skiers who use its 22 lifts and 120km of piste (Dec–April; €31 per day).

From Isola, both the D2205 and the Tinée river head south through the Gorges de Valabre towards St-Sauveur-sur-Tinée. The drop in altitude is marked by sweet chestnut trees taking over from the pines.

St-Sauveur-sur-Tinée

The pleasantly sleepy village of **ST-SAUVEUR-SUR-TINÉE**, 13km south of Isola, is dominated by its medieval needle belfry, which perches above the river in Mediterranean rather than Alpine fashion. The adornments of the Romanesque gargoyled church include a fine fifteenth-century retable, behind the bloodied crucifix. There's not a lot to do here, other than sit in the sun above the river or head off along the GR52A, but it's an attractive place to pause, perhaps in one of its small cafés.

From St-Sauveur, you can either head west along the D30 towards Valberg and the Haut-Var Valley, a dramatically precipitous climb, or follow the Tinée south, passing far below the charming perched villages of Marie, Clans and La Tour, all of which have medieval decorations in their churches.

Roubion

To enjoy spectacular bird's-eye views over the Tinée Valley, it's well worth turning west at St-Sauveur-sur-Tinée onto the D30. After 12km of slowly snaking its way up the sheer valley walls, it passes just below the dramatic hilltop village of **Roubion**. Park at the edge and walk up into its tangled alleyways, and the centuries simply seem to drop away. On the first Sunday of October, in a celebration of the traditional annual **Transhumance**, the squares and streets of Roubion fill once more with sheep.

ARRIVAL AND INFORMATION   **THE TINÉE VALLEY**

ST-ÉTIENNE-DE-TINÉE

By bus Auron (1–5 daily; 15min); Isola (1–4 daily; 15min); Nice (1–4 daily; 2hr 30min); St-Sauveur-de-Tinée (1–4 daily; 45min).

Tourist office 1 rue des Communes-de-France (daily 9am–noon & 2–5pm; ☎04 93 02 41 96, ⓦauron.com).

Maison du Parc At the northern end of the village (daily; July & Aug 9.30am–noon & 2–6pm; Oct–May 9.30am–noon & 2–5.30pm; ☎04 93 02 42 27; ⓦmercantour.eu).

Ski and bike rental Georges Sports, place Central, Auron (☎04 93 23 00 28, ⓦauron.skimium.fr), rents bikes in summer and ski equipment in winter.

ROUBION

Tourist office Village centre (Jan–Sept Mon, Tues & Fri–Sun 9.30am–12.30pm & 2–6pm; ☎04 93 02 10 30, ⓦroubion.com).

ACCOMMODATION AND EATING

ST-ÉTIENNE-DE-TINÉE

Camping du Plan d'Eau ☎04 93 02 41 57, ⓦcampingduplandeau.com. Small, summer-only municipal site, in a nice verdant location at the edge of the village, beside a little lake and near the Maison du Parc. Closed Oct to mid-May. **€9.90**

Regalivou 8 bd d'Auron ☎04 93 02 49 00, ⓦleregalivou.free.fr. Lively hotel-restaurant, perched above the village centre that a large terrace, and has open year is round. Fourteen en-suite rooms and a hearty dining room. **€75**

ST-SAUVEUR-SUR-TINÉE

Auberge de la Gare 1 av des Blavets ☎04 93 02 00 67.

Very cosy restaurant, at the southern end of the village, serving good filling mountain food, with a strong emphasis on local produce, and a good-value €16 *menu*. July & Aug daily noon–1.30pm & 7.30–9pm, Sept–June Mon, Tues & Thurs–Sun noon–1.30pm.

ROUBION

Crêperie de Païsot Place Adolphe-Ramin ☎06 81 68 40 22. Right at the entrance to the village, this friendly place offers pizzas, salads and drinks as well as a full *menu* of inexpensive crèpes, served on an enormous sunny south-facing terrace. March, April & Sept–Dec Fri–Sun 11am–9pm; May–Aug daily 10am–9.30pm.

5

The Cians Valley

For anyone driving westward across Haute Provence, towards the Grand Canyon du Verdon and beyond, a compelling potential shortcut leaves the Tinée Valley by taking the D30 west from St-Sauveur-sur-Tinée, via Roubion on the D30. Once out of the valley, the road drops once more to reach the small ski resort of **Beuil**, where you can join the D28 to follow the wild River Cians on its compelling course south through the **Gorges du Cians**.

Beuil

Perched beneath a stern grey pyramidal peak, at the northern end of the Gorges du Cians, **Beuil** is a sturdy old mountain town that's established a new identity as a relatively low-key winter ski resort. The nearby slopes hold 28 lifts and 56 distinct runs.

The Gorges du Cians

The sinuous **Gorges du Cians**, one of the lesser-known natural wonders of Provence, stretches south for 22km from just below Beuil to the point where the River Cians joins forces with the Var. An ominous chaos of water, tumbling between looming red schist cliffs, it's paralleled by the D28 on its west bank, though the canyon's so narrow that the road repeatedly burrows through tunnels in the rock. It finally emerges into the lower Var valley a total of 46km southwest of St-Sauveur, 2km west of Touët-sur-Var (see p.233).

INFORMATION	THE CIANS VALLEY
BEUIL	
Tourist office Bd du Col Marcel Pourchier (March–June & Sept–Nov Mon–Sat 10am–noon & 2–5pm; July, Aug &	Dec–Feb daily 9am–noon & 2–6pm; ☎ 04 93 02 32 58, ⓦ beuil.com).

ACCOMMODATION AND EATING

BEUIL

★ **L'Escapade** Bd du Col Marcel Pourrchier ☎ 04 93 02 31 27, ⓦ premiumorange.com/hotelescapade. Cosy, old-fashioned mountain hotel on the main approach to town, festooned inside with ancient farming implements. The cheapest of the simple but comfortable wood-panelled rooms share toilets; having your own costs €13 extra. The food, savoured on an outdoor terrace in summer, is utterly magnificent; all diners can start by helping themselves from a huge jar of preserved mushrooms as well as platters of pâté and *fromage de tête*, then move onto substantial meat and fish dishes, such as trout smothered in parsley, or pasta specials. *Menus* from €24 for both lunch and dinner. Closed Oct–Christmas. **€63**

The Vésubie Valley

For anyone who's followed the Tinée Valley south from the summit of La Bonette, it makes a rewarding scenic detour to head east on the D2565, 4km south of St-Sauveur-sur-Tinée, to reach the dramatic **Vésubie Valley**. The road first has to climb through the scattered **Commune of Valdeblore**, home to the ancient village of **St-Dalmas**, before descending to **St-Martin-Vésubie** in the Vésubie Valley itself.

South from St-Martin, road and river head for the Var, passing **Roquebillière**, the perched village of **Lantosque**, and the approach to the pilgrimage chapel of **Madonne d'Utelle**. An alternative southern route from the valley crosses east to the **Col de Turini** and down the **River Bévéra** towards Sospel.

The Commune de Valdeblore

Straddling the Col St-Martin between the Tinée and Vésubie valleys, the **COMMUNE DE VALDEBLORE** consists of a series of villages strung along the D2565. The most interesting, **ST-DALMAS**, was built on the remains of a Roman outpost, and lies at the strategic crossroads between the most accessible southern route across the lower Alps, linking Piedmont with Provence, and a north–south route that connects Savoy with the sea. The former importance of this region is clear from the dimensions of the **Église Prieurale Bénédictine** (mid-June to mid-Sept daily 3–5pm), parts of which date from the tenth century. A gruesome glazed tomb reveals a 900-year-old skeleton; more appealing are the fragments of fourteenth-century frescoes in the north chapel. The present structure is Romanesque, plain and fierce with its typically Alpine bell tower and rounded apsidal chapels.

Across the Col St-Martin, 3km east of St-Dalmas, chairlifts at the ski resort of **La Colmiane** provide stunning views from the **Pic de Colmiane** (daily: Christmas–March 10am–4.50pm; July & Aug 10am–6pm; ☎04 93 23 25 90, ⍟colmiane.com; ski pass €19 daily, chairlift alone €5).

St-Martin-Vésubie

The lovely little town of **ST-MARTIN-VÉSUBIE**, at the head of the Vésubie Valley 11km east of St-Dalmas, is at its busiest in July and August. Even at the height of the season, however, it's not jam-packed. In late spring and early autumn it makes a perfect base for exploring the surrounding mountains, while in winter you can go for wonderful walks in snowshoes, or tackle assorted cross-country skiing routes.

The main artery of the old quarter, the **rue du Docteur-Cagnoli**, is a single-file cobbled street of Gothic houses with overhanging roofs and balconies, with a channelled stream flowing through its centre. Halfway along on the left, is the **Chapelle des Pénitents Blancs** which is decorated with eighteenth-century paintings, while St-Martin's **church** at the end holds works attributed to Louis Bréa. Southeast of the church you can look down at the Madone de Fenestre torrent from place de la Frairie. In the opposite direction a narrow lane leads to the junction of rue Kellerman and the main road, beyond which is the old wash house and the **Musée du Patrimoine** (July & Aug Tues–Sun 2.30–6.30pm; €3; ⍟saintmartinvesubie.fr), housed in a former watermill, which illustrates the traditional Vésubien way of life.

Alpha wolf reserve

8km north of St-Martin on the D89 • Mid-April to June, Sept, Oct & school hols daily 10am–5pm, last admission 3.30pm; July & Aug daily 10am–6pm, last admission 4.30pm • €12 • ☎04 93 02 33 69, ⍟alpha-loup.com

At **LE BORÉON**, a small, scenic mountain retreat, just inside the Parc du Mercantour, the **Alpha wolf reserve** is home to three distinct wolf packs. Wolves were reintroduced to this region in 1992, and their presence remains controversial. The reserve represents an attempt to explain the often-misunderstood creatures to locals, and explore their current and historic interaction with humans. Despite its shortage of English-language information and signage, it's a fascinating place to visit – and if you come in spring, you can watch the new-born cubs from three observation points.

Roquebillière

The old village of **ROQUEBILLIÈRE**, on the left bank of the Vésubie 13km southeast of St-Martin, has been rebuilt six times since the Dark Ages following catastrophic landslides and floods. After the last major disaster, in 1926, when half the buildings disappeared under mud, a new village was created high above the right bank of the river. The wide, tree-lined avenues of the *nouveaux village* lie in stark contrast to the crumpling, leaning, medieval houses bearing down over narrow passageways in the dark and sad *vieux village*.

The Gordolasque Valley

The D171 along the **Gordolasque Valley** above old Roquebillière heads northeast for 16km, with paths leading off eastwards towards the Vallée des Merveilles. From the end, hikers can continue upstream past waterfalls and high crags to Lac de la Fous, to meet the GR52 running west to Madone de Fenestre and east to the northern end of the Vallée des Merveilles (see p.240). This triangle between Mont Clapier on the Italian

5

border (3045m), Mont Bego (2873m) to the east and Mont Neiglier (2785m) to the west is a fabulous area for walking, but not to be taken lightly. All the **mountain refuges** here belong to the Club Alpin Français (⬥ffcam.fr), and may well be unsympathetic if you turn up unannounced.

The Col de Turini

South of Roquebillière, the D70 leaves the Vésubie Valley to head east through the chic resort of La-Bollène-Vésubie to the **Col de Turini**, where four roads and two tracks meet. All give access to the **Forêt de Turini**, which covers the area between the Vésubie and Bévéra valleys. Larches grow in the highest reaches of the forest, giving way further down to firs, spruce, beech, maples and sweet chestnuts.

The road north from the col through the small ski resort of **Camp d'Argent** to L'Authion gives a strong impression of limitless space, following the curved ridge between the two valleys and overlooking a hollow of pastures. There are plenty of walks hereabouts, but the sun, the flowers and the wild strawberries and raspberries are so pleasant you might just want to stop in a field and listen to the cowbells.

Lantosque

South of Roquebillière, the D2565 follows the Vésubie Valley south to **LANTOSQUE**, which, like Roquebillière, has had its share of earth tremors and floods; nonetheless, its pyramid of winding, stepped streets survives in picturesque form.

Utelle

Just north of the point where the Vésubie river starts to pick up speed through the gorge that leads to its confluence with the Var, 11km south of Lantosque, the switchbacking D32 climbs east to reach yet another far-flung **chapel**, dedicated to **La Madone d'Utelle**. Set on a plateau above the village of **UTELLE**, it's high enough to be visible from the sea at Nice. According to legend, two Portuguese sailors lost in a storm in the year 850 navigated safely into port by a light they saw gleaming from Utelle. They erected a chapel here to give thanks, though the current one dates from 1806. Pilgrimages still take place on Easter Monday, the Monday of Pentecost, August 15 and September 8, and conclude with a communal feast on the grassy summit.

ARRIVAL, INFORMATION AND ACTIVITIES	THE VÉSUBIE VALLEY

ST-MARTIN-DE-VÉSUBIE
By bus Lantosque (3 daily; 30min); Nice (3 daily; 1hr 45min); Roquebillière (3 daily; 15min).
Tourist office Place Félix-Faure (July & Aug daily 9am–12.30pm & 2–7.30pm; Sept–June Mon–Sat 10am–12.30pm & 2–6pm, Sun 10am–12.30pm;

⬥ 04 93 03 21 28, ⬥ saintmartinvesubie.fr).
Outdoor activities Guides du Mercantour, place de Marché (⬥ 04 93 03 31 32, ⬥ guidescapade.com), can guide and organize canoeing, canyoning, climbing, walking and skiing expeditions.

ACCOMMODATION AND EATING

ST-MARTIN-DE-VÉSUBIE
Châtaigneraie Allée de Verdun ⬥ 04 93 03 21 22, ⬥ raiberti.com. Imposing, summer-only hotel, set in lovely gardens near the village centre. Comfortable en-suite rooms, many with balconies, which sleep up to five, plus a pool and a good restaurant. Closed Oct–May. **€70**
Ferme St-Joseph Quartier St-Joseph, rte de Nice ⬥ 06 70 51 90 14, ⬥ camping-alafermestjoseph.com. This small and very leafy campsite is the closest to town, beside the lower bridge over La Madone, and offers basic but attractive rental cabins – cheaper if you use your own bedding – as well as tent pitches. Closed Oct to late April.

Cabins **€52**; camping **€17.70**
★ **La Pierre Bleu** 163 bd Raoul Audibert ⬥ 04 93 03 37 86, ⬥ lapierrebleue.fr.st. Delightful, secluded B&B, set in lush gardens and offering five lovely en-suite rooms; the friendly hosts also cook superb dinners for €28, using fresh local ingredients. **€102**
Treille 68 rue Cagnoli ⬥ 04 93 03 30 85. The nicest local restaurant, an unpretentious and inexpensive place where the shaded terrace enjoys fabulous mountain views. *Menus* from €15 for lunch, €22 for dinner. Mid-April to June, Sept & Oct Mon, Tues & Fri–Sun noon–2pm & 7.30–9pm, Wed noon–2pm; July & Aug daily noon–2pm & 7.30–9pm.

LANTOSQUE

Hostellerie de L'Ancienne Gendarmerie Quartier Rivet ☎04 93 03 00 65, ⓦvesubian.com/sites/hotel_ancienne_gendarmerie.htm. Swish, white-painted, *Logis de France* hotel, down below the village on the other side of the river, and equipped with eight nice rooms, a pool and an excellent restaurant. Closed mid-Nov to Feb. €85

The Roya Valley

The most easterly valley of Provence, the Roya is also the most accessible, being served by train lines from Nice, via the lovely riverfront town of **Sospel**, and from Ventimiglia in Italy, which converge just south of **Breil-sur-Roya**. When Nice became part of France in 1860, the upper Roya Valley was kept by the new King Victor Emmanuel II of Italy to indulge his passion for hunting, despite a plebiscite in which only one person in Tende and La Brigue voted for the Italian option. Only in 1947 was the valley finally incorporated into France, but everyone speaks French, albeit with a distinctly Italian intonation.

Sospel

The ruggedness of the surrounding terrain only serves to emphasize the placid idyll of **SOSPEL**, which straddles the main road and rail links from the French coast to the Roya Valley. This dreamy Italianate town, spanning the gentle River Bévéra, is worth at least half a day of anyone's time. Its main street, avenue Jean-Médecin, follows the river on its southern bank before crossing the most easterly of the three bridges to become boulevard de Verdun, heading for the Roya Valley.

The central bridge, the impossibly picturesque, eleventh-century **Vieux Pont**, has a tower poised between the two spans for collecting tolls, and forms the architectural lynchpin of the townscape. The scene is made yet more alluring by the balconied houses along the north bank, which back on to the grimy rue de la République: the banks are lush with flowering shrubs and trees, and one house even has a trompe-l'oeil street facade. Viewed from the eastern end of avenue Jean-Médecin, with the hills to the west and the bridge tower reflected in the water, this scene would be hard to improve.

Place St-Michel, a block back from the river at the west end of town, is adorned by a ravishing series of peaches-and-cream Baroque facades. Stand facing the **Église St-Michel** with its detached, austere Romanesque clock tower, and the **Chapelle des Pénitents Gris** and **Chapelle des Pénitents Rouges** are to your left, while to the right are the medieval arcades and trompe-l'oeil decoration of the **Palais Ricci**.

The road behind the church, rue de l'Abbaye, reached via steps between the two chapels, climbs to an ivy-covered **castle ruin** that offers good views of town.

Breil-sur-Roya

Eight kilometres short of the Italian border, the town of **BREIL-SUR-ROYA** sits in a deep, narrow valley 23km north of Sospel, over the Col de Brouis. Here, the River Roya has picked up enough volume to justify a barrage, behind which a placid and aquamarine lake is ideal for canoeing. A place of modest industries – leather, olives and dairy products – Breil spreads back from both banks, with the old town on the eastern edge. A Renaissance chapel, with a golden angel blowing a trumpet from its rooftop cross, faces place Biancheri, while the vast eighteenth-century **Église Santa-Maria-in-Albis** (daily 9am–noon & 2–6pm) by the pont Charabot, is topped by a belfry with shiny multicoloured tiles. Concealed behind the faded, crumbling plasterwork of its facade, its interior is quite splendid.

Several good **walks** are signed from the village. For a short stroll, follow the river downstream past the barrage and the wash houses, then fork upwards through an olive grove to a tiny chapel and an old Italian gatehouse. The path eventually leads up to the summit of the Arpette, which stands between Breil and the Italian border.

5

Saorge

The fascinating and very pretty village of **SAORGE**, reached by a side road that climbs steeply east from the main road at **Fontan**, 7km north of Breil, consists of a clutter of houses in grey and mismatched shades of red tumbling across a hillside. The scene is brightened by the church and chapel towers, shimmering with gold Niçois tiles.

Almost nothing in the village is level. Vertical stairways turn into paths lined with bramble; there's just one near-horizontal main street, and even that goes up and down flights of steps and through arches formed by the houses. At the end of this street a path leads across the cultivated terraces to **La Madone del Poggio**, an eleventh-century chapel guarded by an impossibly high bell tower topped by an octagonal spire; the chapel is private property, however, and can't be visited.

Back in the village, there's a seventeenth-century **Franciscan convent** (daily except Tues: Feb, March, Oct & Nov 10am–noon & 2–5pm; May–Sept 10am–noon & 2–6pm; €5; ☏04 93 04 55 55), with rustic murals around its cloisters; and the **Église** which **St-Sauveur** (daily 9am–5pm); holds rich examples of ecclesiastical art.

La Brigue

The very appealing village of **LA BRIGUE**, 8km northeast of Fontan, lies on an eastern tributary of the Roya, just south of Tende, surrounded by pastures and with the perennial snowcap of Mont Bego visible to the west. Its Romanesque church, the **Église St-Martin**, is full of medieval paintings, including several by Louis Bréa, mostly depicting hideous scenes of torture and death. The octagonal seventeenth-century **Chapelle St-Michel** stands alongside.

Notre-Dame-des-Fontaines

4km east of La Brigue • May–Oct daily 10am–12.30pm & 2–5.30pm • €3 • ⓦ labrigue.fr

From the exterior, the sanctuary of **Notre-Dame-des-Fontaines** seems to be a plain, graceful place of retreat. Inside, however, it's more akin to a slasher movie. Painted in the fifteenth century by Jean Baleison (the ones above the altar) and Jean Canavesio (all the rest), the sequence of restored **frescoes** contains 38 episodes. Each one, from Christ's flagellation, through the torment on the Cross to devils claiming their victims and, ultimate gore, Judas's disembowelment, is full of violent movement and colour.

The Vallée des Merveilles

2hr 30min guided walks start from the Lac des Mesches, 8km west of St-Dalmas-de-Tende on the D91 • June & Sept Fri–Sun 8am & 1pm; July & Aug daily 8am, 11am, 1pm & 3pm • €10 • ☏ 04 93 04 73 71, ⓦ tendemerveilles.com

The **Vallée des Merveilles** lies between two lakes over 2000m up on the western flank of Mont Bego. The first person to record his experience of this high valley of lakes and bare rock, a fifteenth-century traveller who had lost his way, described it as "an infernal place with figures of the devil and thousands of demons scratched on the rocks". These were no delusions: the rocks of the valley are carved with thousands of images, of animals, tools, people working and mysterious symbols, the oldest of which are believed to date from 3200 BC. More are to be found in the **Vallée de Fontanable** on the northern flank of Mont Bego, and west from the Vallée des Merveilles across the southern slopes of Mont des Merveilles.

Over the centuries other travellers, shepherds and eventually tourists have added their own engravings to the collection. As a result explorations of the Vallée de Fontanable, and the Mont des Merveilles area, are restricted to one path unless accompanied by an official Mercantour guide. Joining one of these **guided walks** is recommended: venturing into the area alone, it's perfectly possible to miss the engravings altogether, while blue skies and sun can quickly turn into violent hailstorms and lightning.

If you're determined to explore more thoroughly, however, note that the easiest route to the Vallée des Merveilles is the ten-kilometre trek (6–8hr) that starts at *Les Mesches* refuge, 8km west of St-Dalmas-de-Tende. The first part of the climb is through woods full of wild raspberries, mushrooms and bilberries, not all of it steeply uphill. Eventually you rise above the tree line and **Lac Long** comes into view. A few pines still manage to grow around the lake, and in spring the grass is full of flowers, but encircling you is a mountain wilderness. From the *Refuge des Merveilles* by the lake, you continue up through a fearsome valley where the rocks turn from black to green according to the light. From here to just beyond the **Lac des Merveilles** you can start searching for the engravings.

The path to the Vallée de Fontanable starts 4.5km further up the D91 from *Les Mesches* refuge, just before the Casterino information point.

Tende

TENDE, the highest town on the Roya, guards the access to the Col de Tende, which connects Provence with Piedmont but is now bypassed by a road tunnel. Part of Italy until 1947, Tende is not especially attractive, but it's a bustling place, with plenty of cheap accommodation, places to eat, bars to lounge around in and shops to browse in which.

The town's old and gloomy houses are built with green and purple schist, but blackened by fumes from the heavy trucks that cross to and from Italy. Above them rise the cherry-coloured belfry of the **collegiate church**, the peachy-orange towers and belfries of various **chapels**, and a twenty-metre needle of wall that's all that remains of a château destroyed in the seventeenth century.

The **Vieille Ville** is fun to wander through, looking at the symbols of old trades on the door lintels, the overhanging roofs and the balconies on every floor. On place de l'Église, the **Collégiale Notre-Dame de l'Assumption** is more a repository of the town's wealth than a place of contemplation, with Baroque excess throughout.

Musée des Merveilles

Av 16 Septembre 1947 • July–Sept daily 10am–6.30pm; Oct–June daily except Tues 10am–5pm; closed 2 weeks in March & 2 weeks in Nov • Free • ☎ 04 93 04 32 50, Ⓦ museedesmerveilles.com

Tende's beautifully designed **Musée des Merveilles** details the geology, archeology and traditions of the Vallée des Merveilles. Alongside dioramas depicting the daily lives of Copper- and Bronze-Age peoples, reproductions of the rock designs are displayed, with attempts to decipher the beliefs and myths that inspired them. They're placed in the context of the contemporaneous and much better known civilizations of the ancient Near East, with considerable emphasis on the motif of the primordial couple, the bull-god and the earth goddess. There's also a model of Otzï, the so-called "Iceman" whose frozen body was discovered on the Italy/Austria border in 1991. Whether or not you go to the valley itself, the museum provides an invaluable insight into an intriguing subject, though you'll need reasonable French to understand the displays.

ARRIVAL, INFORMATION AND ACTIVITIES   THE ROYA VALLEY

SOSPEL

By train The *gare SNCF* is southeast of town on av A-Borriglione.

Destinations La Brigue (1–3 daily; 50min); Nice (4 daily; 50min); St-Dalmas-de-Tende (3 daily; 45min); Tende (3 daily; 55min).

Tourist office 19 av Jean-Médecin (Mon–Fri 9am–6pm, Sat & Sun 9am–5pm; ☎04 93 04 15 80, Ⓦ sospel-tourisme.com).

BREIL-SUR-ROYA

By train The large *gare SNCF* is 600m north of the centre.

Destinations Nice (5 daily; 55min).

Tourist office 17 place Biancheri (June–Sept Mon 1.30–5.30pm, Tues–Fri 9am–noon & 1.30–5.30pm, Sat 9am–noon; ☎04 93 04 94 76, Ⓦ breil-sur-roya.fr).

Outdoor activities Roya Evasion, 11 bd Rouvier ☎04 93 04 91 46, Ⓦ royaevasion.com), rents equipment and organizes guided canoeing and whitewater rafting trips.

5

SAORGE
By train Saorge shares a *gare SNCF* with Fontan; it's a short way up the eastern valley slope from Fontan.
Destinations Nice (3 daily; 1hr 15min–1hr 40min).

LA BRIGUE
Tourist office Place St-Martin (daily 9am–12.30pm & 2–5.30pm; ☎ 04 93 79 09 34, ⊛ labrigue.fr).

TENDE
By train The *gare SNCF* is set back from the top of the main street, av 16 Septembre 1947. In addition to regular services on the same line, the **Train des Merveilles**, designed for sightseers and offering English commentary in summer, leaves Nice daily at 9.24am, and reaches Tende at 11.05am (€25 return).
Destinations Nice (3 daily; 1hr 40min–2hr 30min).
Tourist office 103 av 16 Septembre 1947 (daily 9am–noon & 2–6pm; ☎ 04 93 04 73 71, ⊛ tendemerveilles.com).

ACCOMMODATION AND EATING

SOSPEL
Bar Moderne 17 av Jean-Médecin ☎ 04 97 00 00 42. This spacious café-bar, with tables on the main square as well as on the south bank of the river, and free wi-fi, is a prime local rendezvous that's particularly good for an early-evening drink. Daily 6am–11pm.

Étrangers 7 bd de Verdun ☎ 04 93 04 00 09, ⊛ sospel .net. Smart hotel, just across the town's eastern bridge, with a pool; its riverfront restaurant (closed Tues & Wed lunch) serves *menus* from €25. Closed Dec–Feb. **€70**

Le Mas Fleuri Quartier La Vasta ☎ 04 93 04 14 94, ⊛ camping-mas-fleuri.com. The closest of the four local campsites, 2km upstream along the D2566, this two-star site has a pool. Closed Oct–March. **€16.40**

Relais du Sel 3 bd de Verdun ☎ 04 93 04 00 43. Attractive restaurant at the east end of town, where you dine on a terrace that's well below street level and just above the river. Excellent *menus* at €23 and €33. Also open as a tearoom in the afternoons. Tues–Sat noon–2pm & 7–10pm, Sun noon–2pm.

Souta Loggia 5 place St-Nicolas ☎ 04 93 04 24 23. Very cool bar and café, stretching beneath and beyond the arcades of a fine old square just north of the river, with a hip soundtrack and a *menu* of €12 salads and changing daily *plats* including steaks and pasta specials. Daily 11am–11pm.

BREIL-SUR-ROYA
Camping Azur et Merveilles 650 promenade Georges Clemenceau ☎ 04 93 62 47 04, ⊛ camping-azur -merveilles.com. The municipal two-star campsite, part of a complex that also includes a large indoor swimming pool, is in a pleasant spot by the river, just upstream from the village. Bikes available for rent. Closed Oct–March. **€21.50**

Castel du Roy 146 rte de l'Aigara ☎ 04 93 04 43 66, ⊛ castelduroy.com. Very comfortable eighteen-room villa

hotel, with a pool and large garden, off the route de Tende. Its excellent dining room serves *menus* from €28. Closed early Oct to March. Summer rates include breakfast. **€95**

Roya 3 place Biancheri ☎ 04 93 04 48 10. This very central hotel has very plain, somewhat ageing rooms above a Spar supermarket. All overlook the river, some have balconies; the cheapest lack en-suite facilities. **€48**

SAORGE
Lou Pountin 56 rue Revelli ☎ 04 93 04 54 90, ⊛ loupountin.fr. Perched just above the main alleyway through the village, with a few tables crammed onto the pavement, this good-value pizzeria and Italian restaurant (closed Tues eve & Wed) also owns the only accommodation here, a modernized rental apartment that sleeps four and is available for weekends or entire weeks, at bargain rates. **€60**

LA BRIGUE
Le Mirval 3 rue Vincent-Ferrier ☎ 04 93 04 63 71, ⊛ lemirval.com. Large, renovated century-old *Logis de France* by the bridge, offering eighteen rooms overlooking the Levenza stream, and decent food in its light conservatory dining room. Closed Nov–March. **€48**

TENDE
La Marguerita 19 av du 16 Septembre ☎ 04 93 04 60 53. Popular pizzeria, with beams strung with dried herbs and garlic, stuffed foxes on the walls, and a good range of other Italian specialities. Daily noon–2pm & 7.30–9.30pm; closed Tues Oct–June.

Miramonti 5 rue Antoine Vassalo ☎ 04 93 04 61 82, ⊛ lemiramonti-restaurant.fr. Inexpensive and very central hotel-restaurant that's handy for the station. The cheapest of its six clean, plain rooms lack en-suite facilities. Closed mid-Nov to mid-Dec. **€39**

Clues de Haute Provence

The area known as the **Clues de Haute Provence** lies west of the River Var, north of Vence and the Route Napoléon, in the Pre-Alpes de Grasse. *Clues* is the word for the gorges cut by torrential rivers through the limestone mountain ranges. The seclusion of this arid, sparsely populated region is disturbed only by the winter influx of skiers heading to the 1777-metre summit of the **Montagne du Cheiron**.

Each claustrophobic and seemingly collapsible *clue* opens onto a wide and empty landscape of white and grey rocks with a tattered carpet of thick oak and pine forest. All the horizons are closed off by mountains, some erupting in a space of their own, others looking like coastal cliffs trailing the **Cheiron**, the **Charamel** or the 1664-metre-high **Montagne de Thorenc**. It's the sort of scenery familiar from fantasy films, where wizards might throw laser bolts from the mountains.

Not all the passes stay open in winter – roadside notices forewarn of closures. Routes that go through the *clues* rather than over passes are manageable for cyclists: this is gorgeous, clean-air, long-freewheeling and panoramic terrain. There are plenty of footpaths, with the **GR4** as the main through-route for walkers from Gréolières to Aiglun across the Cheiron. **Accommodation** is scarce. What hotels there are tend to be very small, with a faithful clientele booking them up each year, while campsites, too, are thin on the ground. Even winter accommodation at **Gréolières** and **Gréolières-les-Neiges** is minimal, as visitors tend to come up for a day's skiing or have their own weekend places.

From Vence, you approach the *clues* via the Col de Vence, which brings you down to **Coursegoules**. Approaching from Grasse and the Loup Valley, the road north leads to Gréolières.

Coursegoules

The bare white rocks that surround **COURSEGOULES** are not the most hospitable of sites for a working village, so it's no surprise that many of its houses are now second homes. The local population has steadily declined to just three hundred or so people who don't need to eke a living from the soil-scoured terrain.

Gréolières

GRÉOLIÈRES, 11km west of Coursegoules, seems a similarly unpromising site for habitation. Originally a stopping point on the Roman road from Vence to Castellane, it's now surrounded by ruins, of Haut-Gréolières to the north and a fortress to the south. While the village is liveliest during the winter, it passes as a summer resort as well, and is a popular site for paragliding.

Gréolières-les-Neiges

An 18km drive around the mountains from Gréolières – first west, then doubling back east – brings you through the Clue de Gréolières, carved by a tributary of the Loup, to **GRÉOLIÈRES-LES-NEIGES**, barely 5km north as the crow flies. The closest ski resort to the Mediterranean, this is a centre for **cross-country skiing** (ⓦstations-greolieres-audibergue.com). Fourteen lifts ascend Mont Cheiron in winter, while a single chairlift operates in July and August for summer panoramas. While there are no hotels, just some furnished apartments, a handful of cafés and restaurants stay open year-round.

Thorenc

The paragliding and cross-country-skiing resort of **THORENC**, 13km west of Gréolières off the D2, was originally founded by English and Russians a century ago. The dense woods and style of the older buildings give it an almost Central European atmosphere. Nicknamed the "Suisse Provençale", it remains lively in both winter and summer.

5

North of Thorenc, the narrow and rough D5 crosses the Montagne de Thorenc by the Col de Bleine. Beyond the summit, the D10 branches over for the ascent of Charamel, without a moment's pause in the twisting climb as it heads towards Aiglun; known as the Route des Crêtes, its course is described below. Stay on the D5, on the other hand, and the easier westward route leads to St-Auban and its *clue*.

St-Auban

With its back to the mountainside, tiny **ST-AUBAN** rises above the grassy valley, its wide southern views making up for the plainness of the village itself. The gash made by the River Esteron has left a jumble of rocks through which the water tumbles beneath overhanging cliffs riddled with caves and fissures. In summer, rock climbing and canyoning are possible in the narrow *clue*.

Briançonnet

Downstream from St-Auban, 7km northeast along the D2211, **BRIANÇONNET** enjoys one of the most stunning positions in all inland Provence. Views from its cemetery stretch southwards past the edge of the Montagne de Charamel across kilometres of uninhabited space. The Romans had a settlement here and the present houses are built with stones from the ancient ruins; odd bits of Latin are still decipherable in the walls. There's just one street with a boulangerie, a *tabac*, a small museum of local history, and a church.

From here you can head north across the **Col de Buis** (usually closed Nov to mid-April) to Entrevaux or Annot, or east towards the Clue d'Aiglun and the Clue de Riolan.

The Route des Crêtes

Clinging to the steep southern slope of the Montagne de Charamel, the switchbacking **Route des Crêtes** (D10) requires concentration and nerve. For long stretches there are no distracting views, only thick forest matted with mistletoe. After the hamlet of Le Mas, which hangs on the edge of a precipitous spur below the road, trees can no longer get a root-hold in the near-vertical golden and silver cliffs; the narrowing road crosses high-arched bridges over cascading streams that fall to smoothly moulded pools of aquamarine.

Roughly 14km east of its junction with the D5, just before **Aiglun**, the D10 crosses the Esteron as it shoots out from the high-pressure passage (too narrow for a road) that splits the Charamel and the Montagne St-Martin. The most formidable of all the *clues*, it's impossible to explore. You can, however, walk for roughly 3km south along the GR4 from the D10, 1.5km west of the *clue*, to the **Vegay waterfall**, halfway between Aiglun and Gréolières-les-Neiges, where water destined for the Esteron plummets down a vertical cliff face.

From **ROQUESTERON**, 10km east of Aiglun – which was divided for a century by the France–Savoy border – you can either follow the D17 above the Esteron to the river's confluence with the Var, or take the tangled D1. That leads, via passages of rock seamed in thin vertical bands, to **BOUYON**, from where the D8 loops back to Coursegoules. Both routes lead through a succession of eagle's-nest villages.

ARRIVAL AND INFORMATION   CLUES DE HAUTE PROVENCE

GRÉOLIÈRES

By bus Gréolières has daily connections with Grasse (1–2 daily; 35–50min).

Tourist office 21 Grande Rue (Mon–Fri 9am–noon & 2–6pm; ☎ 04 93 59 97 94, ⓦ greolieres.fr).

5

ACCOMMODATION AND EATING

COURSEGOULES

L'Auberge de l'Escaou 8 place de la Castre ☎ 04 93 59 11 28, ⓦ auberge-escaou.com. Welcoming hotel on a lovely square in the old town, with a really nice restaurant on its terrace, serving a €25 dinner *menu*. €85

GRÉOLIÈRES

La Vieille Auberge 7 place Pierre-Merle ☎ 04 93 59 03 02. This café-restaurant enables visitors to eat well and cheaply on Gréolières' central square; there are tables out on the street and a hearty menu of meaty Provençal classics. Mon–Sat 11am–11pm.

THORENC

Les Merisiers 24 av du Belvédère ☎ 04 93 60 00 23, ⓦ aubergelesmerisiers.com. Very pleasant small hotel-restaurant, with twelve simple en-suite rooms, and *menus* at €28 and €36. Hotel and restaurant open daily July & Aug; Sept–June hotel open Thurs–Sun only, restaurant open Sat & Sun only. €60

ST-AUBAN

Le Tracastel 13 rue Tracastel ☎ 04 93 60 43 06, ⓦ letracastel.fr. St-Auban's only hotel-restaurant offers seven old-fashioned but comfortable rooms, and a wide-ranging *menu* of local specialities, including wood-fired pizzas. Closed Nov–Easter. €50

Toulon and the southern Var

PORQUEROLLES, ÎLES D'HYÈRES

6

Toulon and the southern Var

The shoreline of the Var *département* represents a sizeable chunk of the Côte d'Azur and, thus, of the fabled allure of the south of France. Though much of the coast has been developed, the resorts are mostly small, and between the oversized marinas and dull apartment complexes, the characteristic landscape of pines, glimmering rocks and translucent sea still sometimes takes precedence – cheered in February by mimosa blossom and in autumn by the brilliance of the turning vines. Development notwithstanding, this is still a coastline that conjures up the visual magic that attracted Impressionists, Post-Impressionists and their 1950s cinematic successors. The nexus of the Côte's artistic fame and cinematic glamour – but also of vulgar display and hype – is the erstwhile fishing village of St-Tropez, possessed of charisma which none of its neighbours can match, though its prices and peak-season crowds trump all rhyme or reason just as emphatically.

Elsewhere, the pleasures are those of the seaside, which for the most part is neither conspicuously fashionable nor unduly dowdy. In the west, highlights include the wines of the **Bandol** *appellation contrôlée* and the literary and historic associations of **Sanary-sur-Mer**. **Hyères** has attracted foreign visitors since the eighteenth century, while the crystal-clear waters and pristine ecosystems of the **Îles d'Hyères** lie just offshore. To the east is the **Corniche des Maures**, a long procession of small coastal villages turned resorts, and though it's hard to gauge quite where **Cavalière**, **Pramousquier** or **Le Rayol** start or stop, each is a little paradise of dense pinewoods and clean, sandy beaches, with the sublime garden at **Le Rayol** providing a standout diversion.

Behind this coast, the mournful **Massif des Maures** is more pristine still, its endless forests sheltering ancient monasteries and the timeless agricultural industries of cork oak and chestnut. The principal villages of **Collobrières** and **La Garde Freinet** still preserve (for now at least) some of their rural character in the face of the encroaching wealth of **St-Tropez**, its chic neighbours and beautiful peninsula. Facing St-Tropez across its bay is the middle-class resort of **Ste-Maxime**, beyond which the coast road follows the shoreline's twists and turns – without ever quite shaking off suburbia – all the way to **Fréjus**. This, the most ancient of the Var's coastal towns, is replete with monuments from its Roman and medieval heyday. The sun, sea and sand theme reasserts itself in Fréjus's twin town of **St-Raphaël**, before the coast turns wilder along the dramatically red, rocky corniche of the **Esterel**.

The Var's one great urban agglomeration – an important transport hub that you're quite likely to pass through – is the naval port (and departmental capital) of **Toulon**, blessed with a magnificent natural harbour, cursed by its past reputation for racism and sleaze, and now slowly making good the political and aesthetic mistakes of its recent past.

ESTEREL CORNICHE

Highlights

❶ Bandol Appellation Contrôlée Sample the fine wines and explore the peaceful wine-growing country a little way inland from the bustle of the coast. **See p.253**

❷ The island of Port-Cros Take a glass-bottomed boat to explore the fascinating marine life off France's smallest national park. **See p.270**

❸ St-Tropez Suspend your cynicism for a day and enjoy the art, the absurdity, the glamour and sheer excess of the Côte d'Azur's best-known resort. **See p.276**

❹ Massif des Maures Escape the glitz and development of the coast to explore the sombre wooded hills, and the unspoilt country towns of Collobrières and La Garde-Freinet. **See p.284 & p.287**

❺ Fréjus Founded by Julius Caesar as a naval base, Fréjus has some of the best-preserved Roman remains along this coast, including a theatre, an amphitheatre and a ruined aqueduct. **See p.291**

❻ The Esterel Drive or walk in the most distinctive, rugged and ancient of the coast's landscapes, the craggy, red Esterel. **See p.298**

HIGHLIGHTS ARE MARKED ON THE MAP ON PP.250–251

Les Lecques and St-Cyr-sur-Mer

Wedged between the D559 coast road and the sea at the Var's western extremity, sedate **LES LECQUES** is a beach resort, pure and simple – the coastal extension of the inland town of **ST-CYR-SUR-MER,** with which it shares a municipality. Les Lecques is strung along a sand-and-shingle beach that curves east from the town's marina to the pleasant little fishing port of La Madrague, from where a wonderful

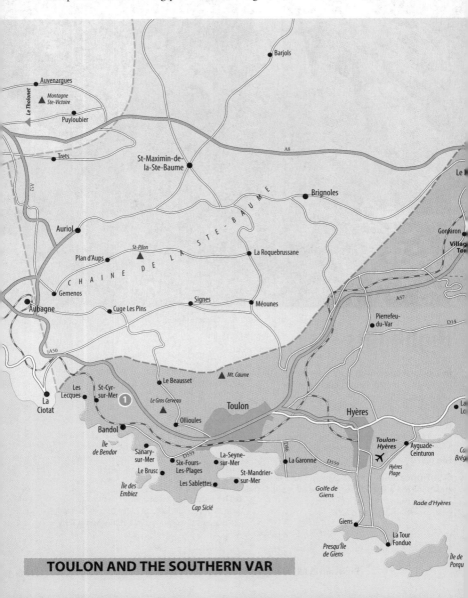

TOULON AND THE SOUTHERN VAR

twelve-kilometre coastal path meanders around Pointe Grenier to the *calanque* of Port d'Alon – where there's a simple snack bar, *Chez Tonton Jou* (☎4 94 26 20 08; daily 9am–8pm, closed Nov–Easter) – before continuing to Bandol. Meanwhile, across the D559 in St-Cyr-sur-Mer proper, there is a miniature, golden **Statue of Liberty**, sculpted by Bartholdi, the artist who created its better-known New York sister. The twin towns' other great draw is wine from the local **vineyards**, which belong to the Bandol *appellation* (see box, p.253).

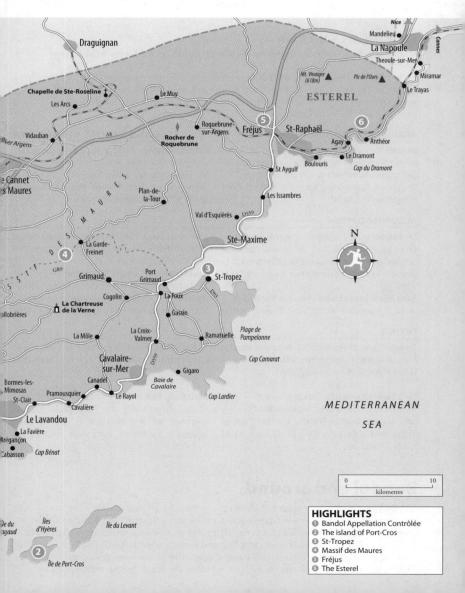

HIGHLIGHTS
1. Bandol Appellation Contrôlée
2. The island of Port-Cros
3. St-Tropez
4. Massif des Maures
5. Fréjus
6. The Esterel

6

Musée de Tauroentum

131 rte de la Madrague • June–Sept daily except Tues 3–7pm; Oct–May Sat & Sun 2–5pm • €3 • ☎ 4 94 26 30 46

Les Lecques claims to have been the Greek trading post of Tauroentum, site of a decisive naval battle between Caesar (the eventual victor) and Pompey for the control of Marseille. The remains of a **Roman villa**, now the **Musée de Tauroentum**, on the coast between Les Lecques and La Madrague, date from the first century AD and boast three extant mosaics, patches of frescoes, a couple of interesting sarcophagi, numerous beautiful Greek and Roman vases and other household items.

Centre d'Art Sébastian

10 bd Jean-Jaurès, St-Cyr-Sur-Mer • July–Sept Wed–Sun 9am–noon & 3–7pm; Oct–June Wed–Sun 9am–noon & 2–6pm • €1 • ☎ 04 94 26 19 20

In St-Cyr, the small **Centre d'Art Sébastien** displays the paintings and tender terracotta statues of Sébastien, the Parisian-born artist (and friend of Picasso) in a beautifully restored former caper storehouse. It also hosts regular temporary exhibitions of painting, sculpture and photography.

ARRIVAL AND INFORMATION · LES LECQUES AND ST-CYR-SUR-MER

By train The *gare SNCF* serving Les Lecques and St-Cyr-dur-Mer lies between the two at the north end of avenue des Lecques, a twenty-minute walk from Les Lecques. Destinations Bandol (every 30min–1hr; 6min); La Ciotat (every 20min–1hr; 4min).

Tourist office Place de l'Appel du 18 Juin, off av du Port, Les Lecques (May–June, Sept & Oct Mon–Fri 9am–6pm, Sat 10am–6pm; July & Aug Mon–Sat 9am–7pm, Sun 10am–1pm & 4–7pm; Nov–April Mon–Sat 9am–5pm; ☎ 4 94 26 73 73, ⓦ saintcyrsurmer.com).

ACCOMMODATION

Les Baumelles 1 rte de la Madrague ☎ 04 94 26 21 27, ⓦ campinglesbaumelles.net. A spacious three-star campsite, close to the beach between Les Lecques and La Madrague and with plenty of shade. Closed late Oct to March. **€27**

Beau Séjour Les Palmiers 34 av de la Mer ☎ 04 94 26 54 06, ⓦ beausejour-lespalmiers.fr. Pleasant two-star hotel in Les Lecques with fourteen individually themed rooms – from lavender to Moroccan – close to the sea, plus an Italian restaurant on site. **€139**

Grand Hôtel des Lecques 24 av du Port ☎ 04 94 26 23 01, ⓦ grand-hotel-les-lecques.com. A handsome three-star hotel set in a large garden with a pool, *pétanque* pitch and tennis courts, 100m from the sea in Les Lecques. **€199**

EATING

The widest choice of restaurants in Les Lecques is along the traffic-free seafront promenade near the marina, while there's a smaller cluster of unpretentious eating places around the fishing harbour at La Madrague. St-Cyr has a **market** on Sunday at place G. Péri in the Vieille Ville.

Les 2 Soeurs Nouveau Port des Lecques ☎ 04 94 26 24 15. Right on the marina in Les Lecques, with a fish-heavy carte, prix fixe menus at €18.80 or €24.70 and *aioli* on Fridays. Daily noon–2.15pm & 7.15–10.30pm; closed mid-Nov to mid-Dec.

Restaurant Samantha 74 av du Port ☎ 04 94 26 13 68. Tiny, cluttered 1970s-style bistro offering basic but inexpensive fare on a two-course €17 *prix fixe menu*, including a few Spanish dishes. Daily noon–2pm & 7–9.30pm.

Bandol and around

BANDOL is a lively resort screened from the open sea by its vast marina. The town bustles with yachties and with day-trippers browsing in its many clothes shops, which range from cheap to chic. Bandol is rightly proud of its wines, which have their own, distinct *appellation contrôlée*, and sampling and buying wine is much the best reason to stop over; the attractive countryside around town also holds some gentle attractions. Other than this, the sea is the main draw, whether for beach lazing, watersports or

THE WINES OF BANDOL

Winemaking in these relatively infertile coastal hills dates back to the Phoenician colony that later became Roman Tauroentum. The quality of the wines – which is boosted by the unusually low yields – was acknowledged as early as the eighteenth century, when despite decrees promoting cereal production over wine, Bandol's vines were spared by official *dérogation*. The Bandol **appellation d'origine contrôlée** (or AOC) was established in 1941, making it one of France's oldest. *Domaines* were replanted with the region's traditional cinsault, grenache and **mourvèdre** grapes, the last-named of Spanish origin and the dominant grape in the superb reds and sublime pale, dry rosés; the whites, though rare, are also worth trying. Bandol **reds** must contain a minimum of 50 percent mourvèdre, though some winemakers push this percentage far higher. The result is a rich, dark red wine that develops notes of leather, truffle and black fruits as it matures.

The Bandol AOC spreads in an arc along the A50 autoroute from **St-Cyr** in the west to **Ollioules** in the east, with the densest concentration of vineyards still focused on La Cadière. Most can be visited for tasting and buying; those with international reputations include the **Domaine Tempier** at Le Plan du Castellet (Mon–Fri 9am–noon & 2–6pm; ☎04 94 98 70 21, ⓦdomainetempier.com), **Château de Pibarnon** at La Cadière (Mon–Sat 9am–noon & 2–6pm; ☎04 94 90 12 73, ⓦpibarnon.com) and the organic **Domaine de Terrebrune** at 724 chemin de la Tourelle, Ollioules (July & Aug 9am–12.30pm & 3–6.30pm; Sept–June Mon–Sat 9am–12.30pm & 2.30–6pm; ☎04 94 74 01 30, ⓦterrebrune.fr), which has an excellent *restaurant gastronomique*, *La Table du Vigneron* (☎04 94 88 36 19).

excursions to the **Île de Bendor**, which houses France's largest exposition of wines, spirits and alcohols.

Oenothèque des Vins de Bandol

Place Lucien Artaud • Mon–Sat 10am–1pm & 3–7pm, Sun 10am–1pm • ☎ 04 94 29 45 03, ⓦ maisondesvins-bandol.com

Given that **wine** is Bandol's main claim to fame, the obvious first port of call is the modern **Oenothèque des Vins de Bandol** at the eastern end of the quai Charles-de-Gaulle opposite the casino. You can obtain information and maps of the various *domaines* here, but if you don't have the time for a self-guided tour of the local vineyards, this is also a good place to taste and buy, with its helpful, friendly staff.

The beaches

Bandol's most scenic sandy **beach** curves around **Anse de Rènecros**, an almost circular cove west of the port along boulevard Louis-Lumière. More secluded are the little coves and beaches along the coastal path to Les Lecques, which you reach from avenue du Maréchal-Foch on the western side of the Anse de Rènecros.

The Île de Bendor

ⓦ bendor.com • Boat trips from Bandol's port: April–June & Sept 7am–11.30pm; July & Aug 7am–2am; Oct–March 7.45am–4.30pm • €11 mid-April to mid-Oct, €9 mid-Oct to mid-April

If you're at all susceptible to the allure of islands, you may want to take the short boat trip from Bandol's quay to the rocky **ÎLE DE BENDOR**. Uninhabited when it was bought by *pastis* tycoon **Paul Ricard** in the 1950s, it's nowadays more tourist honeypot than desert island: picnics aren't allowed and it is cluttered from end to end with attractions of various kinds, including a **museum** dedicated to Ricard advertising (summer only: daily 10.30am–12.30pm & 3–6pm; free), and the **Musée des Vins et des Spiritueux EUVS** (July & Aug only: daily except Wed 1–6pm; free), which in addition to its vast display of wines, spirits and bottles also organizes cocktail nights and workshops. The man who created all this, Paul Ricard, died in 1997 and is buried at the highest point of the island.

6

A LITERARY HAVEN

In the interwar years, Sanary was not the most fashionable place in the south of France, but its lack of cachet made it affordable to writers and intellectuals. **Aldous Huxley** wrote *Eyeless in Gaza* and *Brave New World* at his Villa Huley on allée Thérèse in between dips at the Gorguette beach; later, after the Nazis came to power, many of Germany's cultural elite found temporary refuge here. **Thomas Mann** held court at his villa on chemin de la Colline, later torn down by the Nazis to make way for coastal defences; his near-neighbour was Alma Mahler, widow of the composer, while **Brecht** sang anti-Hitler songs in the cafés on the *quai*. A plaque on the tourist office wall commemorates Sanary's German connection; the office will supply you with information on landmarks associated with the exiles, many of which are now marked with plaques. Huxley's villa, now known as Les Flots, and Sybille Bedford's house in chemin du Diable are among the survivors.

For most of the year, outdoor activities on the island revolve around the **Centre International de Plongée** (☎4 94 29 55 12, ⓦcipbendor.com), which offers diving training from beginner to instructor level, including classes for children from the age of eight upwards.

ARRIVAL AND INFORMATION

By train From Bandol's *gare SNCF*, head down avenue de la Gare and avenue du 11 Novembre 1918 to reach the town centre and port. Infrequent free shuttle buses link it with Embarcadère, close to the tourist office.
Destinations Bandol (every 30min–1hr; 6min); Toulon (for Hyères; every 30min–1hr; 15min).

BANDOL AND AROUND

Tourist office On Bandol's quayside at allée Vivien (July & Aug daily 9am–7pm; Sept–June Mon 9am–noon & 3–6pm, Tues–Sat 9am–noon & 2–6pm; ☎04 94 29 41 35, ⓦbandol.fr).

ACCOMODATION

Camping Vallelongue 936 ave Deï Reganeu ☎04 94 29 49 55, ⓦcampingvar.com. A two-star campsite on the D559, 2.5km from the town centre and port, with a pool, pitches for tents and bungalows to rent. Closed Oct–March. **€22**
Golf Hotel Plage de Rènecros ☎04 94 29 45 83, ⓦgolfhotel.fr. You couldn't be closer to the beach than at this pleasant two-star hotel on the pretty sandy cove of Rènecros, a short walk from the centre of Bandol; it has wi-fi and secure private parking. **€84**

Île Rousse 25 bd Louis Lumière ☎04 94 29 33 00, ⓦile-rousse.com. Bandol's top hotel is a five-star affair, with a pool, direct access to a private stretch of Rènecros beach, vast, light rooms and a choice of restaurants (see below). **€285**
Le Key Largo 19 corniche Bonaparte ☎04 94 29 46 93, ⓦhotel-key-largo.com. A pleasant two-star hotel right by the sea near the port. Rooms are simple but bright; some have balconies and the more expensive have views of the Île de Bendor. **€78.60**

EATING AND DRINKING

In the centre of Bandol, you'll find plenty of restaurants, brasseries and bars – some of them quite sophisticated – along rue de la République and allée Jean-Moulin, parallel to the port. For picnic fare try the Tuesday-morning **market** on the quayside.

Auberge du Port 9 allée Jean-Moulin ☎04 94 29 42 63, ⓦauberge-du-port.com. Classy restaurant and informal brasserie with a terrace facing the port: oysters and seafood from €7, a €24 lunch *menu* and a *parrillada de la mer* – seafood mixed grill – for €26. Daily 9am–late; last lunch orders 2.30pm, last dinner orders 11pm (10pm outside high season).
Le Clocher 1 rue de la Paroisse ☎04 94 32 47 65, ⓦleclocher.fr. *Gault Millau*-rated restaurant just back from the port serving *pastilla* of slow-cooked lamb with bulghar wheat and Toblerone™ *nems* with Snickers™ ice cream on its creative carte. Mon & Thurs–Sun open for lunch and dinner

Les Oliviers 25 bd Louis Lumière ☎04 94 29 33 00, ⓦile-rousse.com. Elegant *restaurant gastronomique* at the hotel *Île Rousse*, with delights like courgette flowers with summer truffle & *piquilo* jam, and roast sea bass with seasonal vegetables, plus Bandol and Cassis wines; *menus* €70–85. Daily 12.15–2pm & 7.15–10pm; open evenings only in July & Aug

The Cap Sicié peninsula

The coastal approach to Toulon from the west takes you via the congested neck of the **Cap Sicié peninsula**. On the western side, **Six-Fours-les-Plages** sprawls between pretty **Sanary-sur-Mer** and **Le Brusc**, from where you can get boats to another of Ricard's islands, **Île des Embiez**. The eastern side of the peninsula merges with Toulon's former shipbuilding suburb of La Seyne-sur-Mer (see p.260), while at the southern end a semi-wilderness of high cliffs and forest reigns.

6

Sanary-sur-Mer

"Next morning the sun came through the French window, the window gave onto a balcony, the balcony to a sea front; small boats bobbing at harbour. Pretty, my mother said."

Sybille Bedford, *Quicksands, a Memoir*

So the little harbour of **SANARY-SUR-MER**, 5km east of Bandol, seemed to the novelist and travel writer Sybille Bedford in the mid-1920s, when she saw it for the first time. And so it remains, with its pastel pink and yellow facades and comically dignified little *mairie*. The harbour preserves its fishing-port character, the headland to the west its discreetly desirable villas. It may not be the most fashionable spot in the south of France, but Sanary's intact charm draws day-trippers from a wide area, and on warm summer evenings the portside hums with life.

Literary fame aside, the pleasures of Sanary are those of the coast: café-lounging on the port and swimming or diving in the clear waters west of the town, at La Gorguette or the coves of Portissol and Beaucours. It livens up on Wednesday, which is market day.

La Tour Romane

Place de la Tour • July & Aug Mon & Thurs–Sun 10am–12.30pm & 4–7pm; Sept–June Wed, Sat & Sun 2.30–6pm • Free

The thirteenth-century **Tour Romane** by the port holds a small **museum** devoted to undersea archaeology, with finds including fragments of Carthaginian amphorae dating from the fifth to the third century BC and discovered off the Île des Embiez.

ARRIVAL AND INFORMATION

SANARY

By train The *gare SNCF*, which Sanary shares with neighbouring Ollioules, is 2.5km north of the centre; buses into town (4 daily; 11min) don't necessarily link up with train arrivals.
Destinations Bandol (every 30min; 5min); Toulon (every 30min–1hr; 9min).

By bus Buses from Toulon, Bandol or Six-Fours stop at the post office, two blocks back from the port.

Destinations Bandol (hourly; 10min); Six-Fours (hourly; 10min); Toulon (hourly; 40 min).

Tourist office By the port at 1 quai du Levant (April–June, Sept & Oct Mon–Fri 9am–6pm, Sat 9am–1pm & 2–5pm; July & Aug Mon–Sat 9am–7pm, Sun 9.30am–12.30pm; Nov–March Mon–Fri 9am–12.30pm & 2–5.30pm, Sat 9am–12.30pm & 2–5pm; ☎04 94 74 01 04, ⓦ sanarysurmer.com).

ACCOMMODATION

Campasun Parc Mogador 167 chemin de Beaucours ☎04 94 74 53 16, ⓦ campasun-mogador.eu. Three-star campsite west of the town centre, with a heated pool, sports facilities and with mobile homes as well as pitches for tents or caravans. Closed Nov to late March. **€42**

Centre Azur des UCJG 149 av du Nid ☎04 94 74 18 87, ⓦ ymca-sanary.org. Sanary's YMCA, in the quiet district of Portissol, offers accommodation in tents, dorms or double rooms with en-suite facilities. High season half-board or

full board only. Camping (per person, half/full board) **€31/42**; dorms (half/full board) **€38/50**; doubles (half/full board) **€90/114**

La Tour 24 quai Général de Gaulle ☎04 94 74 10 10, ⓦ sanary-hoteldelatour.com. Attractive and historic hotel from which Sybille Bedford first glimpsed Sanary, with a/c en-suite rooms, free wi-fi and a good quayside restaurant. There's also private parking. **€95**

6

EATING

L'enK 13 rue Louis Blanc ☏04 94 74 66 57. Creative cuisine with a few Asian touches (they also own the neighbouring sushi bar), in dishes such as whole grilled sea bass with tomato & coriander. *Menu* €29. Daily noon–2pm & 7–11pm.

Le Nautique 6 quai Général de Gaulle ☏04 94 74 00 64. Once the haunt of Sanary's interwar literary exiles, the *Nautique* is rather classy as bar *tabacs* go, with an impressive selection of cigars, cocktails from €9 and sandwiches and croissants from around €1.40. They also serve breakfast. Drinks prices are higher after 10pm. Open daily 6am–2am.

★ **Quai 16** 16 quai Esmenard ☏06 31 34 62 10. Tiny place on Sanary's port – the interior is all kitchen and you sit on the narrow terrace outside – serving traditional Provençal fare with an emphasis on fish and seafood. Service is friendly and prices low; the lunchtime *formule* is around €15. Tues–Sun noon–2pm & 7–9.30pm.

Six-Fours-les-Plages

Sanary merges seamlessly along the D559 into **SIX-FOURS-LES-PLAGES**, which at first seems nothing but sprawling suburbs littered with hoardings, though it has its charms – not least its well-kept sand and shingle beaches (of which the **Plage du Cros**, just before Le Brusc, is the nicest). A small lane off the D11 Sanary-Ollioules road on the northern fringes of Six-Fours takes you up to the **Chapelle de Pépiole** (daily 3–6pm), a stunning sixth-century pre-Romanesque chapel with three naves, restored during the 1950s and set in the midst of pines, cypresses and olive trees.

Le Brusc and Cap Sicié

From the pleasant harbour of **LE BRUSC**, a **coastal footpath** winds its way along the wild headlands of **Cap Sicié** itself. The path offers heady views in every direction, but as it can get pretty windy up here, exploring the cliffs should be done with a certain amount of caution even on a calm day. The sturdy sentinel of **Notre-Dame-de-Mai** (Oct–April every first Sat of the month, plus May daily 9am–noon & 2.30–5.30pm for pilgrimages; free), once a primitive lighthouse, provides a suitable objective.

EATING LE BRUSC

Au Royaume de la Bouillabaisse 909 corniche des Îles, Le Brusc ☏04 94 34 00 40, ⊚auroyaume delabouillabaisse.fr. In an idyllic setting on the presqu'île de Gaou at the southern tip of Le Brusc, with sweeping views along Cap Sicié and a fish-focused *carte* that includes *bourride* (€38) and bouillabaisse (€38). Wed–Sat for lunch & dinner, Sun lunch only. Closed Mon & Tues & mid-Dec to mid-Jan.

Île des Embiez

ⓦ les-embiez.com • Ferry crossings from Le Brusc daily: April–June & Sept 7am–11.30pm; July & Aug 7am–12.30am; Oct–March 7am–7.20pm; 10min; €13.50 mid-April to mid-Oct, €11.50 mid-Oct to mid-April

Larger than its sister island to the west, Paul Ricard's second island, the **Île des Embiez** offers more in the way of natural beauty, with a couple of pocket-handkerchief beaches and low cliffs that are a riot of flowers in spring; there's even a themed nature trail to follow. With its vast marina and miniature road train, tennis courts and football pitch, it's not exactly Robinson Crusoe country, however. The major attraction is the **Institut Océanographique Paul Ricard** (July & Aug daily 10am–12.30pm & 1.30–5.30pm; April–June, Sept & Oct closed Sat am; first half Nov, Feb & March closed all day Sat & Sun am; mid-Nov to Jan closed all day Sat & Sun; €4.50; ⓦinstitut-paul-ricard.org), which has an aquarium and exhibitions on underwater matters.

Toulon and around

Viewed from the heights of Mont Faron or Notre-Dame-du-Mai, it's clear why **TOULON** had to be a major port, for the city stands on a magnificent natural harbour. The heart-shaped bay of the Petite Rade (the inner harbour) gives over 15km of shoreline around Toulon and its neighbour **La Seyne-sur-Mer** to the west. Facing the city, about 3km out to sea, is **St-Mandrier**, a virtual island connected to the Cap Sicié peninsula by the isthmus of Les Sablettes and protecting the Grande Rade (the outer harbour) both northwards and eastwards.

Though the high apartment buildings and wide highways slicing through the centre don't make the approach to Toulon very alluring, a gentrification programme is slowly beautifying the Vieille Ville. A smart **gallery** of modern art attracts touring shows from Paris, and the port is increasingly a stopover for cruise liners. There are also no fewer than 25 **fountains** dotted around the city centre. Other attractions of a stay here include good markets and the superb views from **Mont Faron**; in addition, there are fine sand-and-shingle **beaches** to the east of town in Le Mourillon and across the Petit Rade at La-Seyne-sur-Mer.

Some history

Toulon is home to the French Navy's Mediterranean Fleet, continuing a naval tradition that dates back to the fifteenth century. The city's strategic importance made wartime destruction almost inevitable; the entire fleet was scuttled here in November 1942 to avoid it falling into the hands of the Germans, while the waterfront was severely battered during the Allied landings of 1944. Postwar reconstruction did Toulon few aesthetic favours, and its stock fell further in 1995 when local elections returned a racist *Front National* administration to the town hall with a policy of "preference for the French". Long since returned to the political mainstream, Toulon has slowly set about regenerating its historic core and rebuilding its tattered image.

The Vieille Ville

Vieux Toulon, crammed in between boulevard de Strasbourg and avenue de la République on the old port, has a fine scattering of fountains, a decent selection of shops (particularly clothing stores), and an excellent **market** (Tues–Sun) around rue Landrin and cours Lafayette. The nicest (and liveliest) parts of the old town are around the **Cathédrale Notre Dame de la Seds** and the imposing nineteenth-century **Opéra**, with plenty of café terraces that offer people-watching opportunities. Big chunks of the eastern side of Vieux Toulon disappeared with the construction of the ugly but useful **Mayol** shopping centre; traffic-free quai Cronstadt fronting the **port** is more alluring, with plenty more sunny café terraces.

Musée National de la Marine

Place Monsenargue, quai de Norfolk • July & Aug daily 10am–6pm; Sept–June Mon & Wed–Sun 10am–6pm • €5.50; English audioguide • ☎ 04 22 42 02 01, ⓦ musee-marine.fr

The vast expanse of the **Arsenal**, on place Monsenergue, marks the western end of the Vieille Ville, with its grandiose eighteenth-century gateway leading to the **Musée National de la Marine**, where visitors are greeted by Pierre-Louis Ganne's depiction of the battle of Trafalgar. The museum displays figureheads, an extensive collection of model ships and an enormous fresco showing the old arsenal before it was burnt by the British (see p.260), as well as stark black-and-white photos that illustrate the after-effects of the scuttling of the French fleet in 1942.

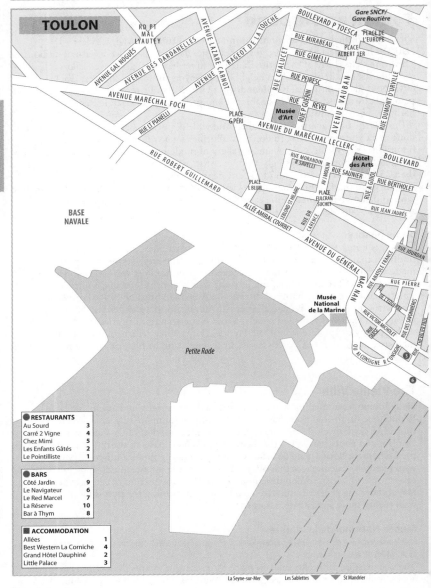

Hôtel des Arts

236 bd Maréchal-Leclerc • Tues–Sun 10am–6pm • Free • ⓦ hdatoulon.fr

Housed in the Beaux Arts former Conseil General building on boulevard Maréchal-Leclerc – Toulon's Haussmann-inspired main east–west artery – the handsome **Hôtel des Arts** attracts big touring exhibitions from the major Parisian galleries; a vigorous acquisitions policy is also helping the museum to assemble a permanent collection.

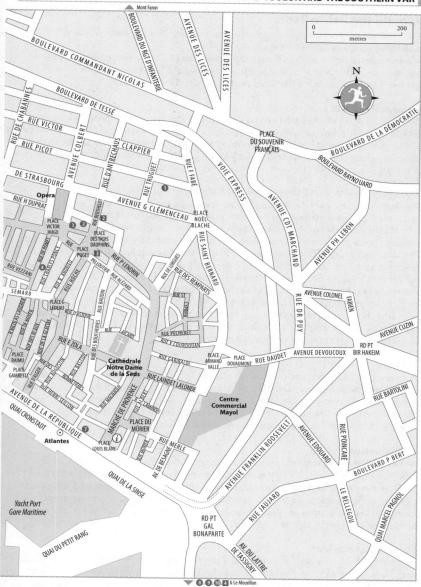

Musée d'Art

113 bd Maréchal-Leclerc • Tues–Sun noon–6pm • Free • ☎ 04 94 36 81 01

The grandiose **Musée d'Art** has a small but eclectic collection spanning eighteenth- and nineteenth-century works by Toulon artists, paintings by Fragonard and Felix Ziem and more modern pieces by the likes of Niki de St Phalle and Yves Klein. The museum stages themed exhibitions that draw on its own collection, as well as hosting temporary exhibitions.

Around the Petite Rade

Regular municipal ferries connect Toulon's *gare maritime* with La Seyne-sur-Mer (#8M; 20min); Les Sablettes via Tamaris (#18M; 30min); and St-Mandrier (#28M; 20min) • ⓦ reseaumistral.com

It's worth taking the time to discover the attractions of Toulon's magnificent natural harbour, from the forts and shoreline of La Seyne-sur-Mer to the sandy beaches of Les Sablettes and the charm of the small port of St Mandrier-sur-Mer.

La Seyne-sur-Mer

The loss of **LA SEYNE-SUR-MER**'s naval shipyards at the end of the 1980s took a heavy toll on this old industrial community, though a smart new waterfront complete with a public park has now taken their place. Away from the centre, La Seyne has an attractive shoreline along the Petite Rade and the Baie du Lazaret's dotted with pines and eccentric villas and popular with joggers.

The Musée Naval du Fort Balaquier and Fort Napoléon

Musée Naval 924 Corniche Bonaparte • Tues–Sun: July & Aug 10am–noon & 3–7pm; Sept–June 10am–noon & 2–6pm • €3 • ☎ 04 94 94 84 72 Fort Napoléon Chemin Marc Sangnier • Open during exhibitions Tues–Sat 2–6pm • Free • ☎ 04 94 87 83 43

The **Musée Naval du Fort Balaguier** explores La Seyne's long association with naval history. It occupies a fort built in 1634 and later reinforced by Vauban. In 1793, after Royalists had handed Toulon over to the British and Spanish fleet, it was the scene of fierce fighting between the British and Napoleon's forces, during which the British set up a line of immensely secure fortifications between this bastion and the one now known as **Fort Napoléon**, 1km or so to the west. Despite its ability to rain down artillery on any attacker, Balaguier was taken by Napoleon with a bunch of volunteers, who sent the enemies of revolutionary France packing, though not before they burnt the arsenal, the remaining French ships and part of the town. Fort Napoléon now houses a cultural centre and contemporary art gallery.

Tamaris

Between Fort Balaguier and the sand spit of Les Sablettes is the peaceful former resort of **TAMARIS**, with its lovely shoreline of rickety wooden jetties and fishing huts on stilts overlooking the mussel beds of the Baie du Lazaret. The beautiful oriental building on the front, now the Michel Pacha Marine Physiology Institute, was built in the nineteenth century by a local man who made his fortune in Turkey.

Les Sablettes

At **Les Sablettes** you can lounge on an impressive, south-facing sandy beach with a view towards Cap Sicié. It's very much bucket-and-spade, family territory, with no St-Tropez-style airs and graces, and there's a smattering of bar–glaciers and restaurants catering to day-trippers. To the southwest is a series of charming and progressively more low-key bays, from the perfect sandy cove of Anse de Fabrégas to a trio of naturist beaches on the eastern side of Cap Sicié.

St Mandrier-sur-Mer

Beyond Les Sablette's neck of sand is the pretty little port of **ST-MANDRIER-SUR-MER**, with the security gates of a *terrain militaire* beyond it. The juxtaposition of portside cafés and hulking frigates anchored offshore is delightfully odd; that aside, there are several beaches, including some of fine sand.

Mont Faron

Cable car Bd Amiral Vence • Daily: May, June & Sept 10am–7pm; July & Aug 10am–8pm; March, April & Oct 10am–6/6.30pm; first half Nov and second half Feb 10am–5.30pm; closed mid-Nov to mid-Feb • €6.80 Bus #40 direction Super Toulon • ⓦ telepherique-faron.com

The best way to appreciate the magnificence of Toulon's harbour is to ascend the

542-metre **Mont Faron**. By road, avenue Emile-Fabre becomes route du Faron, snaking up to the top and descending again from the northeast, a journey of 18km in all. The **road** is a one-way slip of tarmac with few barriers on the hairpin bends, looping up and down through a pristine landscape of pine and rock – and with a wonderful if somewhat vertigo-inducing belvedere just before the summit. For speed of access, the **cable car** is the way to go.

Mont Faron's **summit** is threaded with paths and dotted with picnic spots, and the views over Toulon are quite breathtaking. The peak area also holds a **memorial museum** (July & Aug daily 10am–noon & 2–5.30pm; Sept–June Tues–Sun 10am–noon & 2–4.30pm; €4), dedicated to the Allied landings in Provence that took place in August 1944, with gripping screenings of original newsreel footage. There's a restaurant, *Le Drap d'Or*, close to the museum and another by the cable-car station. Further along the summit is a **zoo** (daily: May–June & Sept Tues–Sun 10am–6.30pm; July & Aug 10am–7.15pm; Oct–April Tues–Sun 10am–5.30pm; €9), which specializes in big cats.

6

Le Mourillon

Bus #3 (direction "Mourillon") or #23 (direction "Quatre Saisons") from the centre

Neat artificial beaches stretch along the shoreline of Toulon's smart eastern suburb of **Le Mourillon**, east of the city centre. In the mid-nineteenth century it became the favoured residence of naval officers, before developing as a bathing resort around the turn of the twentieth century. The artificial beaches were constructed in the 1960s; nowadays Le Mourillon's pleasant coastal strip is also home to many of the city's most fashionable bars and restaurants.

ARRIVAL AND DEPARTURE
TOULON

By train The *gare SNCF* is on place de l'Europe on the northern side of the city centre, next to the *gare routière*. Destinations Hyères (8 daily; 20min); La Seyne-Six-Fours (every 20min–1hr; 5min); Les Arcs (1–2 per hr; 35–50min); Marseille (every 10–20min at peak times; 50min–1hr 5min); Ollioules–Sanary (every 20min–1hr; 9min).

By bus The *gare routière* is on place de l'Europe on the northern side of the city centre, next to the *gare SNCF*. Destinations Aix (up to 14 daily; 1hr 15min); Bandol (hourly; 50min); Brignoles (1–2 daily; 1hr 20min);

Draguignan (7 daily; 1hr 50min); Hyères (every 30min–1hr; 55min–1hr); Le Lavandou (up to 7 daily; 1hr 15min); St-Tropez (6 daily; 1hr 40min); Sanary (hourly; 40min); Six-Fours (hourly; 30min); Toulon-Hyères airport (5 daily; 40min).

By ferry Corsica Ferries (ⓦcorsica-ferries.fr) and SNCM (ⓦsncm.fr) operate ferry services between Toulon and Corsica; frequency depends on the season, but even in winter there's usually at least one daily sailing by Corsica ferries to Bastia (10hr) and several per week to Ajaccio (10–13hr).

INFORMATION

Tourist office 12 place Louis Blanc (Mon & Wed–Sat 9am–6pm, Tues 10am–6pm, Sun 9am–1pm; ☎04 94 18 53 00, ⓦtoulontourisme.com).

GETTING AROUND

Buses and ferries Buses and the ferries across the Rade are run by Réseau Mistral (☎04 94 03 87 03, ⓦreseaumistral.com). The tourist office can supply you with a city bus map.

Tickets Single fares on buses cost €1.40 and on the ferries

€2; these are sold only on the bus or ferry. Abonnement 1 Jour tickets (€3.90) allow unrestricted travel for one day on buses and ferries; the Abonnement 1 Jour Téléphérique (€6) offers the same plus one return trip on the Mont Faron cable car (see p.260). One-day tickets are sold in bars and *tabacs*.

ACCOMMODATION

Des Allées 18 allée Amiral Courbet ☎04 94 91 10 02, ⓦhoteljaures.fr. One of the cheapest in town, opposite the Base Navale, with soundproofed, a/c rooms including one that sleeps four. Reception is at its sister hotel, *Le*

Jaurès, one block back at 50 rue Jean Jaurès. **€45**
Best Western La Corniche 17 littoral Frédéric Mistral ☎04 94 41 35 12, ⓦhotel-corniche.com. Very pleasant hotel overlooking a small fishing port in the seaside suburb

of La Mourillon, with a/c, soundproofed rooms, parking and free wi-fi. Some rooms have sea views. **€109**

Grand Hôtel Dauphiné 10 rue Berthelot ☎04 94 92 20 28, ⓦgrandhoteldauphine.com. Impressively smart two-star hotel in the pedestrian zone close to the Opéra, with 55 soundproofed, a/c rooms, free wi-fi and a lift. There's no parking on site, but the hotel offers concessionary rates at a nearby car park. **€71**

Little Palace 6 rue Berthelot ☎04 94 92 26 62, ⓦhotel-littlepalace.com. Smart and comfortable two-star hotel in the Vieille Ville, close to the Opéra with 23 rooms decorated in attractive, Provençal style. There's also secure parking nearby. **€60**

6 EATING, DRINKING AND NIGHTLIFE

There's a strip of **brasseries**, **cafés** and **restaurants** facing Toulon's port, though greater culinary ambition is to be found in the cluster of streets around the Opéra; there's plenty of choice, too, along the littoral Frédéric-Mistral in Le Mourillon, which is also a good spot to immerse yourself in Toulon's lively, student-orientated **nightlife** scene; pick up the free *Le Petit Bavard* **guide** from the tourist office for hints on where to go.

RESTAURANTS

Au Sourd 10 rue Molière ☎04 94 92 28 52, ⓦausourd .com. Toulon's oldest restaurant serves wonderful fish dishes like monkfish *feuilleté* with basil cream or poached turbot with morels and green asparagus. *Menus* €27 and €33. Tues–Sat noon–2pm and 7.15–10pm.

Carré 2 Vigne 14 rue de Pomet ☎04 94 92 98 21, ⓦcarre2vigne.com. Provençal and Italian influences blend on the menu of this chic small restaurant close to the Opéra, with dishes like seared tuna with Provençal condiments, mini ratatouille & meat jus for around €18. Menus €26–33. Tues–Sat noon–1.30pm & 7–9pm.

Chez Mimi 83 av de la République ☎04 94 24 97 42. Good meat and veggie couscous and tagines from around €12.50, plus grills and Merguez sausage with ratatouille, all served in suitably Moorish blue-and-white tiled surroundings. Tues–Sun noon–2pm and 7–10pm.

Les Enfants Gâtés 9 rue Corneille ☎04 94 09 14 67. Charmingly informal place close to the Opéra, with a chalked-up menu of international dishes, from risotto with speck and Bayonne ham to stir fries with ginger, chicken and sesame; main courses around €13.50, starter-sized salads from €7. Mon–Fri noon–2.30pm and 7–10.30pm.

Le Pointilliste 43 rue Picot ☎04 94 71 06 01, ⓦlepointilliste.com. *Restaurant gastronomique* serving treats such as rabbit with foie gras, roast figs and sautéed girolles or turbot with courgette *mousseline*; main courses cost €20–40. Tues–Fri noon–1.30pm & 7.45–9.30pm, Sat 7.45–9.30pm.

BARS

Bar à Thym 32 bd Dr Cuneo ☎04 94 41 90 10, ⓦbarathym.com. Big, Irish-pub-style bar and live venue midway between the city centre and Le Mourillon's beaches, with regular live rock bands and DJ sets. Mon–Sat 6pm–3am.

Côté Jardin 437 av Frédéric Mistral, Le Mourillon ☎04 94 41 38 33. Big, slick Le Mourillon bar/brasserie with a bougainvillea-shaded terrace facing the sea and DJs on Fridays and Saturdays. A perfect spot after a day at the beach, with cocktails from €6 and beers from €2.70. Daily 7am–3am.

Le Navigateur 128 av de la République ☎04 94 92 34 65. Big portside bar/brasserie with 150 draught or bottled beers from around the world, including a big selection of premium bottled Belgian brands. Beers from around €4.50. Daily 6am–1am.

Le Red Marcel 377 av de la République ☎04 94 89 14 10, ⓦredmarcel.fr. Small but effervescent gay bar just back from the port, with a variety of themed nights and a party-minded crowd that spills into the street outside. Tues–Sun 9pm–2.30am.

La Réserve 401 av Frédéric Mistral, Le Mourillon. Very popular Le Mourillon bar/*tabac* with funky modern decor in zingy shades of lime green and purple, attracting a mainly young, trendy crowd. Tapas from €2.50. Daily 7am–1am.

Cap Garonne

Bus #23 from Toulon Gare (direction "4 Saisons", stop "Flamencq"; every 30min; 30min), then bus #91 (direction "Oursinières") from Le Pradet to La Garonne and Les Oursinières (approx hourly; 20min)

Beyond Le Mourillon, Toulon merges with **Le Pradet**, from where the D86 winds south along the eastern side of Cap Garonne to the little resorts of **La Garonne** and **Les Oursinières**. La Garonne has a pleasant west-facing shingle-and-sand beach and a scattering of restaurants; further on, at Les Oursinières, there's a small curve of shingly beach, clear water and a diving school.

Musée de la Mine de Cap Garonne

Chemin du Baou Rouge, Le Pradet • Wed, Sat, Sun & public holidays 2–5pm; guided tours only • €6.50 • ⓦ mine-capgaronne.fr

Between La Garonne and Les Oursinières a side road leads to the protected, pine-clad 300-hectare headland of Cap Garonne and the **Musée de la Mine de Cap Garonne**, a treasure trove of semi-precious minerals, including malachite, azurite and cyanotrichite. There's also some information on the history of the miners themselves. Napoléon III granted the licence for mining of copper and lead on this site in the mid-nineteenth century; the first miners were Italians and the raw copper was exported to Swansea in the UK for processing. The history of mineral extraction here was of frequent changes of ownership interspersed with lengthy periods of idleness; the mine closed for good in 1917 and its tunnels were thereafter used to grow mushrooms. It reopened as a museum in 1994.

ACCOMMODATION AND EATING   **CAP GARONNE**

L'Escapade Port des Oursinières ☎04 94 08 39 39, ⓦ hotel-escapade.com. Delightful small family-run hotel just back from the port at Oursinières, tucked into a quiet lane, with plenty of exposed wood and stone, beautiful lush gardens and a pool. The hotel also has an excellent restaurant, *La Chanterelle*. **€125**

Hyères

HYÈRES is the oldest resort of the Côte d'Azur, listing among its pre-twentieth-century admirers Empress Joséphine, Queen Victoria, Tolstoy and Robert Louis Stevenson. It was particularly popular with the British, being closer, and more southerly, than its rival Nice. To winter at Hyères in style one needed one's own villa, hence the expansive gardened residences that spread seawards from the Vieille Ville, giving the town something of the atmosphere of a spa. By the early twentieth century, however, Nice and Cannes began to upstage Hyères, and when the foreign rich switched from winter convalescents to summer sunbathers, Hyères, with no central seafront, lost out.

Today it has the rare distinction on the Côte of not being totally dependent on the summer influx, with the export of flowers, exotic plants and trees important to the local economy. It's also a garrison town, home to the French army's 54th artillery regiment and to a naval air station. Hyères is consequently rather appealing: the Vieille Ville is neither a sanitized tourist trap nor a slum, and the locals aren't out to squeeze maximum profit from the minimum number of months.

The Vieille Ville

Hyères' **Vieille Ville** lies on the slopes of Casteou hill, 5km from the sea, with avenue des Îles d'Or and its continuation, avenue Général-de-Gaulle, marking its border with the modern town to the south. The best approach to the Vieille Ville is through the **Porte Massillon**, a medieval gatehouse which opens onto rue Massillon which is lined with tempting shops selling fruit and vegetables, chocolate, soaps, olive oil and wine.

Tour des Templiers

Place Massillon • Open during exhibitions: April–Oct daily except Tues 10am–noon & 4–7pm; Nov–March Wed–Sun 10am–noon & 2–5pm • Free

The twelfth-century **Tour des Templiers**, the remnant of a Knights Templar lodge, overshadows place Massillon, a perfect Provençal square filled with café terraces. The tower now hosts art exhibitions, though these are sometimes less impressive than their dramatic setting: don't miss the narrow staircase that leads to the roof for a bird's-eye view of the medieval centre.

6

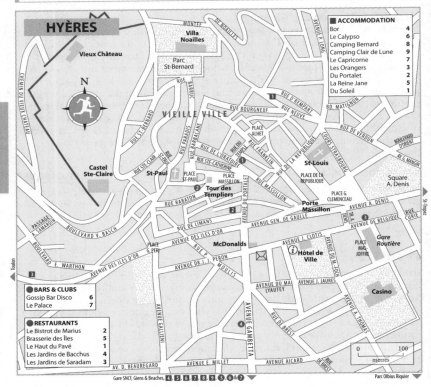

Collégiale St-Paul

Place St-Paul • April–Oct Wed–Sat 9am–noon & 2–6pm, Sun 10am–noon; Nov–March Wed–Sat 9am–noon & 2–6.30pm, Sun 10am–noon • Free

Dominating place St-Paul is the former collegiate church of **St-Paul**, whose wide steps fan out from a Renaissance door. Its distinctive belfry is pure Romanesque, as is the choir, though the simplicity of the design is masked by the collection of votive offerings hung inside. The decoration also includes some splendid wrought-iron candelabras and a Christmas crib with over-life-size *santons*.

The **place St-Paul** gives panoramic views over a section of medieval town wall to the Golfe de Giens. It's around here, where the crumbly lanes are festooned with bougainvillea, wisteria and yuccas, that the real charm of the Vieille Ville begins to be apparent.

Parc Ste-Claire

Entrance on rue St-Claire • Daily 8am–7pm • Free

The exotic gardens of **parc Ste-Claire** surround **Castel Ste-Claire**, which now houses the offices of the Parc National de Port Cros; the castle was originally owned by the French archeologist Olivier Voutier (who discovered the Venus de Milo), before becoming home to the American writer Edith Wharton.

Villa Noailles and around

Villa Noailles Along montée des Noailles – which can be reached by car from cours de Strasbourg and avenue Long • July–Sept Mon, Wed, Thurs, Sat & Sun 2–7pm, Fri 4–10pm; Oct–June Mon, Wed, Thurs, Sat & Sun 1–6pm, Fri 3–8pm • Free • ☎ 04 98 08 01 98, ⓦ villanoailles-hyeres.com Parc St-Bernard Daily 8am–7pm • Free

> ### SEMAINE OLYMPIQUE DE VOILES
>
> Thanks to its idyllic waters and consistently strong winds, the Hyères bay is one of the world's best-known sailing centres, bustling year-round with windsurfers, kite surfers and sailors alike. Each April, for the last forty-odd years, the town has hosted the **Semaine Olympique de Voiles** (ⓦ sof.ffvoile.com), a major six-day regatta when some fifty national teams and more than a thousand ships descend on the bay in what amounts to a rehearsal for the Olympic Games, with many countries using the competition to select their future teams. With sponsors, support teams and around a thousand crew thronging the streets and bars, a festive atmosphere prevails in town, with flags of all nations hanging from balconies and windows; while down by the port, crowds brace the weather for glimpses of boats offshore. During the event hotels around the port are at a premium, and although those in the Vieille Ville are less in demand, it's still advisable to book at least three months in advance.

The **Villa Noailles**, an angular Cubist mansion, was designed by Mallet-Stevens in the 1920s, with gardens enclosed by part of the old citadel walls. All the luminaries of Dada and Surrealism stayed here and left their mark, including Man Ray who used it as the setting for one of his most inarticulate films, *Le Mystère du Château de Dé*. It now hosts contemporary art and design exhibitions.

The Villa sits at the top of the **parc St-Bernard**, an enjoyable warren full of almost every Mediterranean flower known. To the west of the park and further up the hill you come to the remains of Hyères' **Vieux Château** (free access), whose keep and ivy-clad towers outreach the oak and lotus trees and give stunning views out to the Îles d'Hyères and east to the Massif des Maures.

The modern town

The switch from medieval to eighteenth- and nineteenth-century Hyères is particularly abrupt, with wide boulevards and open spaces, opulent villas, waving palm fronds and fanciful Moorish architectural details marking the modern town. Most of the former aristocratic residences and grand hotels now have more prosaic functions, though the **casino** is still in use (see p.267). Unfortunately its elegant Beaux Arts exterior and interior have lost much of their original character due to crude modernization, and the interior will disappoint all but the most hardened gamblers.

Parc Olbius Riquier
Av Ambroise Thomas • Summer 7.30am–8pm; winter 7.30am–6pm • Free

South of the casino, at the bottom of avenue Ambroise Thomas, is Hyères' botanic garden, the **Parc Olbius Riquier**, which opened in 1868. Pride of place is given to the palms, of which there are 28 varieties, plus yuccas, agaves and bamboos. There's a hothouse full of exotics including banana, strelitzia, hibiscus and orchids, and a small zoo and miniature train to keep children amused.

The coast
Buses from Hyères' *gare routière* to Tour Fondue (#67; 8 daily; 30min), L'Almanarre (#39; every 30min; 14min), Hyères-Plage (#63; hourly; 12min; or #67; 8 daily; 14min) and Le Ceinturon (#102; 5 daily; 37min).

Hyères' coastal suburbs offer plenty of opportunities for bathing, though mosquitoes can be a problem, so bring insect repellent. Hyères' main port is at **Hyères-Plages**, with the village-resorts of **Le Ceinturon**, **Ayguade** and **Les Salins d'Hyères** strung out along the coast to the northeast. Traffic fumes and proximity to the airport detract from the charms of the seaside between Hyères-Plage and Le Ceinturon, despite the pines and ubiquitous palms, but it's more pleasant further up by the little fishing port of Les Salins. East of here, where the coastal road finally turns inland, you can follow a path

6

between abandoned salt flats and the sea to a secluded beach, part of which is naturist. The less sheltered **L'Almanarre** beach runs the length of the west side of Les Salins; it's a popular kite-surfers' hangout.

Presqu'Île de Giens

The peculiar **Presqu'Île de Giens** is leashed to the mainland by an isthmus, known as **La Capte**, and a parallel sandbar enclosing the salt marshes. The eastern side of the isthmus is a series of narrow sand-and-pebble beaches, with warm, shallow water, packed out in summer; **plage de la Bergerie** in the south is about the nicest. The **route du Sel** (closed 9pm–5am and Oct–April) leads down the sandbar on the western side of the Presqu'Île, giving you glimpses of the salt pans and flamingos that lie between the sandbar and the beach resorts on the eastern side. At the south end of the sandbar sits the placid seaside community of **Giens**, with its **Tour Fondue**, built by Richelieu, on the eastern side overlooking the port that serves Porquerolles on the Îles d'Hyères (see p.268).

Site Archéologique d'Olbia

April–June, Sept & Oct Mon & Wed–Sat 9.30am–noon & 2–5.30pm; July & Aug daily 9.30am–noon & 3.30pm–7pm; Nov–March call to arrange a visit • €2.50 • ☎ 04 94 65 51 49

L'Almanarre is the site of the ancient Greek town of **Olbia**, a maritime trading post founded in the fourth century BC on a small knoll by the sea. Excavations here have revealed Greek and Roman remains, including baths, temples and homes, plus parts of the medieval abbey of St-Pierre de L'Almanarre.

ARRIVAL AND DEPARTURE   HYÈRES

By plane Hyères-Toulon airport (☎ 0825 018 387, ⓦ toulon-hyeres.aeroport.fr) lies between Hyères and Hyères-Plage, 3km from the centre, to which it's connected by an infrequent bus service (#102).
Destinations London City (2 weekly in summer; 2hr); London Stansted (5 weekly in summer; 2hr 5 min); Paris Orly (daily; 1hr 25min).
By train The *gare SNCF* is on place de l'Europe, with frequent buses (#29, #39 or #67) connecting to the town

centre, 1.5km north.
Destinations Toulon (8 daily; 22min).
By bus The *gare routière* (☎ 04 94 03 87 03, ⓦ reseaumistral.com) is on place Mal-Joffret, two blocks south of the entrance to the old town.
Destinations Le Lavandou (8 daily; 35min); St-Tropez (8 daily; 2hr); Toulon (frequent; 1hr); Tour Fondue (for Porquerolles); every 1–2hr; 30min).

INFORMATION AND ACTIVITIES

Tourist office Near the *gare routière* at Rotonde du Park Hôtel, av de Belgique (July & Aug daily 9am–7pm; Sept–June Mon–Fri 9am–6pm, Sat 9am–4pm; ☎ 04 94 01 84 50, ⓦ hyeres-tourisme.com).
Bike rental Holiday Bikes, 10 rue Jean d'Agrève, near Port St Pierre (☎ 04 94 38 79 45, ⓦ holidaybikes.fr).

Kitesurfing There's a kitesurf school based at the port (☎ 06 16 18 49 91, ⓦ kitesurf-var.com); courses at all levels from €110; half-day kitesurfing session €30 up.
Sailing The International Yacht Club de Hyères (IYCH), 61 av du Docteur-Robin (☎ 04 94 57 00 07, ⓦ iych.fr), has a sailing school.

ACCOMMODATION

BOR 3 allée Emile-Gérard, Les Pesquiers ☎ 04 94 58 02 73, ⓦ hotel-bor.com. Smart, timber-clad designer hotel right on the beach, with an elegant but pricey restaurant. Rooms have flatscreen TV, a/c and wi-fi. Closed Nov to early March. **€150**
Le Calypso 36 av de la Méditeranée ☎ 04 94 58 02 09, ⓦ lecalypso.fr. Basic and friendly hotel close to the port, handy for the beach and for trips to the islands. The eleven rooms have double glazing, wi-fi and flatscreen TVs; some also have a terrace or small garden. **€49**
Les Orangers 64 av des Îles d'Or ☎ 04 94 00 55 11, ⓦ orangers-hotel.com. This pleasant small hotel is

situated in a historic villa district, west of the modern centre, and has an attractive garden and terrace. Closed Jan. **€65**
Du Portalet 4 rue de Limans ☎ 04 94 65 39 40, ⓦ hyeres-hotel-portalet.com. In the lower (and busier) part of the old town, with nineteen tastefully designed rooms with en-suite bath or shower, double glazing and satellite TV, and a brace of suites with terraces. Pets are accepted on payment of a small fee. **€90**
La Reine Jane le port de l'Ayguade ☎ 04 94 66 32 64, ⓦ reinejane.com. Small, a/c hotel overlooking the port at Ayguade and just 30m from the beach, with a restaurant,

bar and terrace to make up for its out-of-town location. Closed Jan and early Feb. **€75**

Du Soleil Rue du Rempart ☎ 04 94 65 16 26, ⊛ hotel -du-soleil.fr. Twenty assorted en-suite rooms with wi-fi and TV in a renovated house at the top of the Vieille Ville, close to parc St Bernard and the Villa Noailles. Decor is simple, and the location peaceful. **€94**

CAMPING

Camping Bernard Rue des Saraniers 5 ☎ 04 94 66 30 54, ⊛ campingbernard.fr. Two-star campsite just 50m from the sea in Le Ceinturon, with 100 pitches and plenty of shade; facilities include a barbecue area, washing machine, snack bar and children's games. Closed Oct– Easter. **€20.20**

Camping Clair de Lune 27 av du Clair de Lune ☎ 04 94 58 20 19, ⊛ campingclairedelune.fr. Three-star campsite and caravan park on the Presqu'île de Giens, with mobile homes, bungalows and free wi-fi. Closed mid-Nov to early Feb. Two-berth caravans (per week) **€325**; mini-bungalows (per week) **€359**; camping **€28**

Le Capricorne Rte des Vieux Salins ☎ 04 94 66 40 94, ⊛ campingcapricorne.com. Three-star site 1.5km from the beach at Les Salins, with a pool, volleyball and basketball courts and boules pitch and a snack bar. Closed Oct–March. **€20**

EATING AND DRINKING

The best places to eat and drink in Hyères are the **restaurant** terraces on place Massillon. There's a **food market** on place Clémenceau on Tuesday and Thursday mornings and along avenue Gambetta on Saturday morning. Hyères' **nightlife** is a rather scattered affair, with the portside café terraces having the edge over the more sedate old town. The **casino** (1 av Ambroise Thomas; daily 10am–4am; ⊛ casinohyeres.com) is south of the *gare routière*.

RESTAURANTS

Le Bistrot de Marius 1 place Massillon ☎ 04 94 35 88 38. One of the nicest options in the Vieille Ville, with dishes like octopus daube with polenta and *rouille* and lamb tagine with olives and lemon on its *carte*. Menus €19–26. Wed–Sun noon–2pm & 7–10.30pm.

Brasserie des Îles Port St Pierre ☎ 04 94 57 49 75, ⊛ brasserie-des-iles.com. A swish brasserie at the port serving a big *plateau de fruits de mer*, and a €29.90 *menu*. Mon–Sat noon–2.30pm & 7–11pm; closed Tues out of season.

★ **Le Haut du Pavé** 2 rue du Temple ☎ 04 94 35 20 98, ⊛ lehautdupave.fr. Excellent Provençal and Mediterranean-style cooking in the Vieille Ville facing place Massillon. *Menus* €26 and €33. Daily noon–2pm & 7–10pm; closed Mon & Tues out of season.

Les Jardins de Bacchus 32 av Gambetta ☎ 04 94 65 77 63, ⊛ bacchushyeres.com. Creative fusion cooking in the modern town, with dishes like fillet of beef glazed with honey and mustard or roast sea bass with artichokes and fondant courgettes. Evening *menus* €22 and €29; lunch *menus* €14 and €19. Tues–Sat noon–1.30pm & 7.30–9.30pm.

★ **Les Jardins de Saradam** 35 av de Belgique ☎ 04 94 65 97 53. Reliable North African restaurant close to the *gare routière* with a pretty garden and filling couscous and tagines from around €13. Book ahead. July & Aug daily 7–9.30pm; Sept–June Tues–Sat noon–2pm & 7–9.30pm, Sun noon–2pm.

NIGHTLIFE

Gossip Bar Disco Carré 15 av du Docteur Robin Port St Pierre ☎ 04 94 48 84 53. A popular bar and disco down on the port with a huge, lively terrace; cocktails from €12, and ice creams from €5. Daily 7am–1am.

Le Palace Rte de Giens ☎ 06 52 11 30 39. Newly revamped discotheque on the coast between Hyères-Plage and La Tour Fondue, with a variety of themed nights from Old Skool to Roman, and free entry before 1am – there's generally a charge after that; expect to pay around €10 with *conso*. Thurs–Sat 11.45pm–6am.

The Îles d'Hyères

The wild, scented greenery and fine sand beaches of the **Îles d'Hyères** are a reminder of what much of the mainland was like half a century ago. You can stay on all three main islands – **Porquerolles**, **Port-Cros** and **Île du Levant** – though accommodation is scarce, coveted and expensive. Today the Parc National de Port-Cros and the Conservatoire Botanique de Porquerolles protect and document the islands' rare species of wild flowers. Port-Cros and its small neighbour Bagaud are just about uninhabited, so the main problem there is controlling the flower-picking and litter-dropping habits of visitors. On Levant, the military rule all but a tiny morsel of the island.

Visitors should observe signs forbidding smoking (away from the ports); the **fire risk** in summer is extreme: at times large sections of the islands are closed off and visitors must stick to marked paths.

Some history

A haven from tempests in ancient times, then the peaceful habitat of monks and farmers, in the Middle Ages the Îles d'Hyères (also known as the Îles d'Or) became a base for **piracy** and coastal attacks by a relentless succession of aggressors, against whom the few islanders were powerless. In 1550, Henri II tried to solve the problem by turning the islands into penal colonies, but the convicts themselves turned to piracy, even attempting to capture a ship of the royal fleet from Toulon. **Forts** were built all over the islands from the sixteenth century onwards, when François I started a trend of fort building that lasted into the twentieth century, when the German gun positions on Port-Cros and Levant were knocked out by the Americans. The military presence endures, and has at least spared the islands from the otherwise inevitable pressure for development.

GETTING TO THE ISLANDS

There are ferries to the Îles d'Hyères from numerous ports along the Côte d'Azur, though some services only operate in summer. Compagnies Maritimes TLV-TVM – which operates the ferry services from La Tour Fondue and Port d'Hyères – also runs glass-bottomed boat trips from Tour Fondue to see the national park's marine treasures (June–Sept daily except Sat 9am–noon & 2–4pm; hourly; 35min; €13.50).

From Bandol Quai d'Honneur ☎04 94 32 51 41, ⓦatlantide1.com. Thrice-weekly excursions to Porquerolles in summer; the trip includes 6hr on the island.

From Cavalaire ☎04 94 00 45 77, ⓦvedettesilesdor.fr. To Porquerolles (July & Aug daily; April–June, Sept & Oct Mon, Wed & Fri) and Port-Cros (July & Aug Mon, Thurs & Fri; April–June, Sept & Oct Mon & Fri).

From La Croix Valmer ⓦvedettesilesdor.fr. To Porquerolles (July & Aug daily) and Port-Cros (July & Aug Mon, Thurs & Fri).

From La Tour Fondue Presqu'Île de Giens ☎04 94 58 21 81, ⓦtlv-tvm.com. The closest port to Porquerolles; year-round services (daily).

From Le Lavandou Gare maritime ☎04 94 71 01 02, ⓦvedettesilesdor.fr. The closest port to Port-Cros and Levant, with year-round services to both (mid-April to early Oct daily; early Oct to mid-April daily except Wed); plus services to Porquerolles (daily July & Aug; 3 weekly April–early Oct).

From La Londe Port Miramar ☎04 94 05 21 14, ⓦbateliersdelacotedazur.com. Services to Porquerolles (April–Aug daily; Sept daily except Sat; Oct to mid-Nov Tues, Thurs & Sun) and Port-Cros (July & Aug daily except Sat; April–June & Sept Tues, Wed, Fri & Sun; Oct & Nov Tues, Thurs & Sun).

From Port d'Hyères Hyères-Plage ☎04 94 57 44 07, ⓦtlv-tvm.com. Year-round services to Port-Cros and Levant (April–Sept daily; Oct & March Mon, Wed & Fri– Sun; Nov–Feb Mon, Wed, Fri & Sat).

From Sanary Port de Sanary ☎06 75 71 81 76, ⓦcroixdusud5.com. Service to Porquerolles (July & Aug Mon, Wed & Sun; Sept–Nov Wed).

From St-Raphaël Quai Nomy, Vieux Port ☎04 94 95 17 46, ⓦbateauxsaintraphael.com. Excursions to Porquerolles (July & Aug weekly).

From Toulon Quai Cronstadt ☎04 94 93 07 56, ⓦlesbateliersdelacotedazur.com. Excursions to Porquerolles (June Wed & Sun; July & Aug Wed, Fri & Sun).

Porquerolles

PORQUEROLLES is by far the most easily accessible of the islands, with a permanent village around the port, a few hotels and plenty of places to eat. In summer, the island's population expands dramatically, but there is some activity year-round. This is the only cultivated island and it has its own wine, with three Côte de Provence *domaines* which can be visited.

The village

The **village** began life as a nineteenth-century military settlement, with its central square, the place d'Armes, being the old parade ground. It achieved notoriety of the non-military kind in the 1960s, when Jean-Luc Godard filmed the bewildering finale of his film *Pierrot le Fou* here, as well as at the Calanque de la Treille, at the far end of the plage de Notre-Dame.

Fort Ste-Agathe
Mid-June to mid-Sept daily 10am–1pm & 2–5pm · €4

Overlooking the village is the ancient **Fort Ste-Agathe**, whose origins are unknown, though evidence suggests it was already in existence by 1200, and was refortified in the sixteenth century by François I, who built a tower with five-metre-thick walls to resist cannon fire. The fort has a small **museum**, which traces the history of the island and the work of the national park. The ticket also gives access to the **Bonheur windmill** behind the fort.

Maison du Parc and the south shore
Daily: Feb–June, Sept & Oct 9.30am–12.30pm & 2–6pm; July & Aug 9.30am–12.30pm & 2.30–6.30pm · Free

Five minutes south of the village is the **Maison du Parc**, which opens its gardens and orchards to the public to wander around. The orchards are particularly interesting, as the Conservatoire is concerned with preserving biodiversity through protecting traditional and local varieties of fruit trees. It also offers tours of the nearby Mediterranean botanic garden of **Le Hameau** (groups only; on application). If you prefer a wilder environment, however, you're better off continuing south to the **lighthouse** and the **calanques** to its east, both of which make good destinations for an hour's walk. Be aware, though, that it's not safe to swim on this side of the island, as the southern shoreline is all cliffs.

Beaches
The most fabled (and distant) of the beaches is the **plage de Notre-Dame**, 3km northeast of the village just before the *terrain militaire* on the northeastern tip. The nearest to the village is the sandy **plage de la Courtade**, which you pass on the way to Notre Dame. Facilities are minimal – there are earth toilets and places to park bikes at Courtade. The much smaller **plage d'Argent** on the west of the island has a pleasant **restaurant**. You can hire **kayaks** from Aventures Porquerolles (ⓦaventuresporquerolles. com) on the plage d'Argent or from Ileo Porquerolles (ⓦileo-porquerolles.fr) on the plage de la Courtade, and at the port from Locamarine 75 (ⓦlocamarine75.com).

INFORMATION AND GETTING AROUND PORQUEROLLES

Tourist information There's a booth by the harbour in Porquerolles (daily: April–Sept 9am–5.30pm; Oct–March 9am–12.30pm; ☎04 94 58 33 76, ⓦporquerolles .com), where you can get basic maps – though for €2 you'll get an info pack and much better map from the Maison du Parc (see above).

Bike hire Gravel tracks criss-cross the island, so it's worthwhile renting bikes. There are several outlets in Porquerolles village, including La Bécane, rue de la Poste (☎04 94 58 36 00), and L'Indien, place d'Armes (☎04 94 58 30 39).

ACCOMMODATION

L'Arche de Porquerolles 12 rue de la Ferme ☎04 94 58 33 71, ⓦlarchedeporquerolles.com. Eleven a/c rooms above a restaurant in the village with modern decor, en-suite showers, wooden floors and flatscreen TVs. Some rooms also have terraces and sea views. Closed mid-Nov to March. **€170**
Les Mas du Langoustier ☎04 94 58 30 09, ⓦlangoustier.com. The most luxurious hotel on Porquerolles, at the western tip of the island close to the

beach, with a restaurant, pool and a minibus link to the port. It insists on half board. Closed Oct–late April. Half board for two **€450**
Les Medes 2 rue de la Douane ☎04 94 12 41 24, ⓦhotel-les-medes.fr. Quite smart, modern three-star hotel close to place d'Armes with a/c, wi-fi and a garden with an artificial waterfall. Closed early Nov to late Dec. **€165**

EATING

Place d'Armes in the village is ringed by restaurant terraces, though they tend to be pricey for what they are. There are places in the village selling ice creams or sandwiches to take away, plus a small supermarket and a fruit stall.

6

L'Olivier Le Mas du Langoustier ☏ 04 94 58 30 09, ⓦ langoustier.com. If you want gourmet cuisine you'll need to make the trek to the idyllic and Michelin-starred restaurant of the *Mas du Langoustier* hotel in the west of the island *menus* start from €62 and dishes like lobster and foie gras cannelloni on the *carte*. May–Sept daily 12.30–2pm & 7–9.30pm.

Le Pélagros Place d'Armes ☏ 04 94 58 38 63. One of the more affordable options in the village, with grilled meats and fish for around €9.50–12.50, including *kefta* with fresh coriander or herb-crusted lamb. April–Sept.

La Plage d'Argent Plage d'Argent ☏ 04 94 58 32 48, ⓦ plage-dargent.com. Right on the beach, serving salads from around €17 and seafood from around €21, plus snacks. April–Sept daily noon–3.30pm.

Port-Cros

With just 35 permanent residents, the island of **PORT-CROS** is France's smallest national park and a protected zone – smoking is forbidden outside the port area, as is picking any flowers. It's the only one of the islands with natural springs, and boasts the richest **fauna and flora**: kestrels, eagles and sparrowhawks nest here; there are shrubs that flower and bear fruit at the same time, while more common species such as broom, lavender, rosemary and heather flourish in abundance. If you come armed with a botanical dictionary, and the information pack and map sold by the **Maison du Parc** (☏ 04 94 01 40 70, ⓦ portcrosparcnational.fr; hours vary in accordance with boat arrivals) at the port, you'll have no problem spotting all the different species.

Exploring the island

The dense vegetation and hills make exploring considerably harder going than on Porquerolles, even though it is less than half the size. Aside from ruined forts and a handful of buildings around the port, the only interventions on the island's wildlife are the classification labels on some of the plants and the paths that crisscross the island from the port via the **Vallon de la Solitude** and **Vallon de la Fausse-Monnaie** to the cliff-bound south coast; alternatively, there's a signed ten-kilometre **circuit of the island**. You are not supposed to stray from these paths, though given the thickness of the undergrowth, doing so would be difficult.

Plage de la Palud and the Fort de l'Estissac

One kilometre northeast of the port is the nearest beach, the **plage de la Palud**, backed by dense vegetation and with an underwater trail for snorkellers – the **Sentier Sous-Martin** (mid June to mid-Sept; free); Sun Plongée (ⓦ sun-plongee.com) hire out equipment and organize dives. On the way to the beach, you'll find the **Fort de L'Estissac** (July–Sept daily 10.30am–5.30pm; free), which houses an exhibition on the national park and the island's protected marine life – most easily seen by taking a glass-bottomed boat trip (see p.268) from La Tour Fondue. Divers will want to head for the island's southern shore to explore the waters round the **Ilot de la Gabinière**.

ACCOMMODATION AND EATING	**PORT-CROS**
Le Manoir ☏ 04 94 05 90 52, ⓦ hotel-lemanoirportcros .com. The island's principal hotel, in a leafy garden beneath tall eucalyptus and with a pool. Doubles with shower; half board only. Main courses in its *restaurant gastronomique* cost from €28. Closed Nov–March. Half board for two **€370**	**Provençale** ☏ 04 94 05 90 43, ⓦ hostellerie -provencale.com. En-suite, a/c rooms above a restaurant, with terrace or balcony. More luxurious rooms have sea views and access to a swimming pool. Half board only. Closed mid-Nov to March. Half board for two **€290**

Île du Levant

Ninety percent military missile testing range, the **ÎLE DU LEVANT** is almost always humid and sunny. Cultivated plant life grows wild with the result that giant geraniums and nasturtiums climb three-metre hedges, overhung by immense eucalyptus trees and yucca plants.

The tiny bit of the island spared by the military is dominated by the nudist colony of **Héliopolis**, founded in the early 1930s; nudity is also compulsory on the beaches of Bain de Diane and Les Grottes. About sixty people live at Héliopolis year-round, joined by thousands of summer visitors and many more day-trippers. The residents' preferred street dress is "*les plus petits costumes en Europe*", on sale as you get off the boat. Visitors who come just for a few hours tend to be treated as voyeurs. If you stay, even for one night, you'll generally receive a much friendlier reception, but in summer without advance booking you'd be lucky to find a room or camping pitch.

6

ACCOMMODATION AND EATING   **ÎLE DU LEVANT**

La Brise Marine ☎ 04 94 05 91 15, ⊛ labrisemarine .net. One of the better-value options, this small hotel has fourteen simple en-suite rooms with sea views and free wi-fi. There's a pool and a restaurant (open for lunch only). Closed Nov–Easter. €85

Héliotel ☎ 04 94 00 44 88, ⊛ heliotel.net. Larger and a bit more fancy than the *Brise Marine*, this three-star hotel has a pool, a terrace with sea views and a restaurant

(two-course *formule* €16, three courses €19). Rooms have a/c and wi-fi. €120

La Pinède ☎ 04 94 05 92 81, ⊛ campingdulevant.free .fr. The island's campsite has a pool, jacuzzi and sauna and also rents out bungalows and an apartment with kitchen and private terrace. Closed Oct–March. Bungalows €65; apartment €130; camping €26

The Corniche des Maures

The Côte d'Azur really gets going to the east of Hyères in the resorts of the **Corniche des Maures**, a twenty-kilometre stretch of coast from Le Lavandou to the Baie de Cavalaire. Multi-million-dollar residences lurk in the hills, pricey yachts in the bays, and seafront prices start edging up, yet the attractions are primarily natural: beaches that shine silver from the mica crystals in the sand, shaded by tall dark pines, oaks and eucalyptus; glittering rocks of purple, green and reddish hue; and chestnut-forested hills keeping winds away. There are even unspoilt stretches where it's possible to imagine what all this coast looked like in bygone years, notably around **Cap de Brégançon**, at the **Domaine de Rayol gardens**, and between **Le Rayol** and the resort of **Cavalaire-sur-Mer**.

GETTING AROUND   **THE CORNICHE DES MAURES**

Transport around the Corniche is the biggest problem. The coast road is narrow and littered with hairpin bends, so progress – whether by car or bus – is slow, particularly in high season. Regular buses on the Toulon–St Tropez route #7801 link the settlements along this stretch of coast, and a cycle track runs parallel to the coast.

Bormes-les-Mimosas

You can almost smell the money as you spiral uphill from the D559 into immaculate **BORMES-LES-MIMOSAS**, 20km east of Hyères. It's indisputably medieval, with a restored castle at the top, protected by spiralling lines of pantiled houses backing onto short-cut flights of steps. The castle is private, but there is a public terrace alongside it with attractive views. The winding alleys of the village are oddly named, with addresses such as "alleyway of lovers", "street of brigands", "gossipers' way", and "arse-breaker street". They're stuffed full of arts and crafts ateliers.

Bormes-les-Mimosas' name is apt, particularly in February when you'll see a spectacular display of the tiny yellow pom-poms. Despite its popularity along the whole of the Côte d'Azur, mimosa is no more indigenous to the region than Porsches, having been introduced from Mexico in the 1860s.

The Musée d'Art de d'Histoire

103 rue Carnot • June–Sept Mon, Tues & Thurs–Sat 10am–noon & 3–6.30pm, Wed 3–6.30pm, Sun 10am–noon; Oct–May Mon, Tues & Thurs–Sat 10am–noon & 2–5.30pm, Wed 2–5.30pm, Sun 10am–noon • Free • ☎ 04 94 71 56 60

Bormes' small **Musée d'Art et d'Histoire** occupies a renovated seventeenth-century house and displays nineteenth- and early twentieth-century painting by artists associated with the region. It also stages temporary exhibitions.

The coast

Bormes' bland pleasure port at **La Favière** is flanked by spot-the-spare-metre-of-sand beaches. To the south the tip of **Cap Bénat** can be reached on foot along a coastal path from La Favière's beach. From Cap Bénat westwards to the bland modern seaside extension of **La Londe**, vineyards and private woods will block your way, as will the security arrangements around the château at **Cap de Brégançon**, which is the holiday home of the president of the Republic. In summer you will have to pay for parking if you want to use the public tracks down to the shore from the La Londe–Cabasson road (cars €8–9). However, once you've reached the water you can wander along the gorgeous beaches as far as you like, with no apartment buildings amongst the pine trees, not even villas, just the odd mansion in the distance surrounded by its vineyards.

ARRIVAL AND INFORMATION   BORMES-LES-MIMOSAS

By bus Buses from Hyères stop at Pin below the medieval village, from where there's a free shuttle bus daily in summer; otherwise, you'll have to walk up.

Tourist office Place Gambetta (April–June & Sept daily 9.30am–12.30pm & 2.30–6.30pm; July & Aug daily 9.30am–12.30pm & 2.30–7pm; Oct–March Mon–Sat 9am–12.30pm & 2–5.30pm; ☎ 04 94 01 38 38, ⊕ bormeslesmimosas.com).

ACCOMMODATION

Bellevue Place Gambetta ☎ 04 94 71 15 15, ⊕ bellevuebormes.com. Simple but attractive hotel/restaurant at the entrance to the medieval village with a/c en-suite rooms with wi-fi, flatscreen TV and safe. Full or half board available. Closed mid-Nov to late Jan. €50

Camp du Domaine Rte de Bénat, La Favière ☎ 04 94 71 03 12, ⊕ campdudomaine.com. Four-star site right by the sea, with plenty of sports facilities including tennis courts and *pétanque*, plus film nights and live entertainment. Closed Nov–Feb. €45

Clau Mar Jo 895 chemin de Bénat ☎ 04 94 71 53 39, ⊕ www.camping-clau-mar-jo.fr. Four-star mobile-home park just below the main road between the village and Le Lavandou, with good facilities including a swimming pool, children's play area and *boules* pitch. Closed mid-Sept to mid-June. Mobile homes sleeping four (per week). €721

Hostellerie du Cigalou Place Gambetta ☎ 04 94 41 51 27, ⊕ hostellerieducigalou.com. Classy three-star hotel opposite the *Bellevue*; a member of *Châteaux & Relais de France*, with a mimosa-shaded swimming pool and twenty tastefully decorated, a/c rooms with bath, safe, wi-fi and flatscreen TV. €189

Les Palmiers 240 chemin du Petit Fort, Cabasson ☎ 4 94 64 81 94, ⊕ hotellespalmiers.com. Very attractive and peaceful hotel by the coast, with seventeen rooms, private parking and its own path to the beach. Closed mid-Oct to late Feb. €142

EATING

La Cassole 1 ruelle du Moulin ☎ 04 94 71 14 86. Provençal specialities in unpretentious surroundings on a pretty terrace in the medieval village. Three-course *menu* €28, otherwise €15 and up for the likes of sautéed chicken with chorizo and green olives. Mon–Sat 7.30–9pm or later.

Pâtes...et Pâtes Place du Bazar ☎ 04 94 64 85 75, ⊕ bormeslesmimosas.com/patesetpates. At the foot of the medieval village, this restaurant serves good pasta from around €9.50, with a big choice of varieties and sauces; fancier dishes include the four-cheese ravioli with cream sauce for €14.90. July & Aug Mon & Wed–Sun 7–9.15pm; Sept–June Mon, Tues & Fri–Sun noon–1.45pm & 7–9.15pm, Wed noon–1.45pm.

La Tonnelle de Gil Renard Place Gambetta ☎ 04 94 71 34 84, ⊕ la-tonnelle-bormes.com. Rather chic, *Gault Millau*-listed restaurant at the entrance to the old village, with dishes like veal kidneys sautéed with port sauce and polenta or *aioli* with seasonal vegetables. *Menus* from €19, otherwise around €20. May, June & Sept Mon, Tues & Thurs–Sun noon–1.30pm & 7.15–9.30pm; July & Aug daily 7.15–9.30pm; Oct–April Mon, Tues & Fri–Sun noon–1.30pm & 7.15–9.30pm.

FROM TOP SAINT CLAIR BEACH, LE LAVANDOU (P.274); BANDOL GRAPE HARVEST (P.253) >

6

Le Lavandou

LE LAVANDOU, five kilometres from Bormes, is an out-and-out seaside resort, with sandy beaches, a scattering of pastel-painted high-rise hotels and an unpretentious atmosphere. Its origins as a Mediterranean fishing village are betrayed by the dozen or so remaining fishing vessels, which are kept in business by the region's upmarket seafood restaurants. Merging with Bormes to the west and St-Clair to the east, Le Lavandou concentrates its charm in the tiny area between avenue du Général-de-Gaulle and quai Gabriel-Péri, where café tables overlook the *boules* pitch and the traffic of the seafront road. Three narrow stairways lead back from here to rue Patron-Ravello, place Argaud and rue Abbé Helin, each lined with specialist shops and cafés.

However, it's the coast that is the real attraction, and there's no shortage of watersports and boat trips on offer: the Lavandou Plongée diving school offers initiation **dives** (☏04 94 71 83 65, ⦿lavandou-plongee.com; from €30) while the École de Voile Municipale (☏06 26 58 39 55, ⦿le-lavandou.fr) offers **sailing lessons** to groups and individuals from March to mid-November. For **bathing**, the sands of St-Clair and the very pleasant cove of Aiguebelle mark the start of a string of excellent beaches, with crescents of silver sand interspersed with rocky headlands between here and Cavalaire-sur-Mer.

INFORMATION

Tourist office Opposite the port at quai Gabriel-Péri (Mon, Wed & Thurs–Sat 9am–12.30pm & 2.30–7pm, Tues 9.30am–12.30pm & 2.30–7pm, Sun 9.30am–12.30pm & 3.30–6.30pm; ☏04 94 00 40 50, ⦿ot-lelavandou.fr).

ACCOMMODATION

Auberge de la Calanque 62 av du Général-de-Gaulle ☏04 94 71 05 96, ⦿aubergelacalanque.fr. Upmarket and comfortable, if slightly faded hotel close to the centre of town, with a shady garden, pool and a/c rooms including some with balconies. Room styles vary quite widely. Closed Nov–March. **€135**

L'Oustaou 20 av du Général-de-Gaulle ☏04 94 71 12 18, ⦿lavandou-hotel-oustaou.com. Le Lavandou's best budget option – a clean, family-run two-star in the town centre, just minutes from the beach and port. It's well known and gets busy, so it might be worth booking ahead. **€56**

La Plage 14 rue des Trois-Dauphins, Aiguebelle ☏04 94 05 80 74, ⦿lhoteldelaplage.com. Classy, modernized two-star hotel right on the pretty sandy cove of Aiguebelle, with uncluttered modern decor, a restaurant (three-course *menu* €22.90) and a broad terrace with bar. Rooms have en-suite bath and a/c. **€90**

EATING AND DRINKING

Bistr'eau Ryon Bd des Dryades, plage Saint-Clair ☏04 94 15 26 97, ⦿bistreauryon.com. A cut above the average tourist fare, right on the beach at Saint-Clair, with a short, weekly-changing market-based regional *carte* and a €24 three-course *menu*. Tues–Sat noon–2pm & 7.15–9.30pm, Sun noon–2pm; closed early Nov to early Dec.

Brasserie du Centre 3 place Ernest Reyer ☏04 94 71 10 50, ⦿labrasserieducentre.fr. Much the smartest and most animated of Le Lavandou's bar/brasseries, with a big shady terrace and a woody, yacht-like interior. Cocktails €12.50 up; €26 *menu*. Daily 7am–3am; closes earlier outside summer season.

Le Nautique Av des Trois Dauphins, Aiguebelle ☏04 94 05 81 20, ⦿nautiquelavandou.com. Fish and meat grilled over charcoal at this deceptively simple place right on the beach at Aiguebelle; grilled fish with spiced butter €24; salmon, crab & avocado *millefeuille* €16.50. Open for lunch and dinner; closed Mon eve.

The silver beaches

The D559 east from Le Lavandou curves its way through steep wooded hills that reach down to the sea. This, along with the St-Tropez peninsula it leads to, is the most beautiful part of the Côte d'Azur, boasting silvery beaches and sections of unspoiled tree-backed coastline.

East of Aiguebelle, there's silver sand at the **Plage de Jean Blanc** in Rossignol before you come to the tiny, secluded *calanques* either side of **Pointe du Layet**, at Plage de l'Éléphant, Plage du Rossignol and the naturist Plage du Layet. The village of

CAVALIÈRE has a particularly fine beach: long, wide and pale, with undeveloped hilltops that at last outreach the houses. A couple of kilometres further on at **PRAMOUSQUIER**, you can look up from the turquoise water to woods undisturbed by roads and buildings. A further 4km east, the villages of **LE CANADEL** and **LE RAYOL** have gradually merged and colonized the hills behind them. At Le Canadel, the sinuous D27 to La Môle leaves the coast road and spirals up past cork-oak woodland to the **Col du Canadel**, giving unbeatable views en route.

East from Le Rayol, the corniche climbs away from the coast through 3km of open countryside, sadly scarred most years by fire, before ending with the sprawl of **CAVALAIRE-SUR-MER**. Here the tiny *calanques* give way to a long stretch of sand and flat land that has been exploited for the maximum rentable space. In its favour, Cavalaire is very much a family resort and not too stuck on glamour.

6

Domaine du Rayol gardens

Av des Belges, Rayol-Canadel-sur-Mer • Daily: Jan–March & Nov–Dec 9.30am–5.30pm; April–June & Sept–Oct 9.30am–6.30pm; July & Aug 9.30am–7.30pm • Snorkelling tours of the "Jardin Marin" bookable in advance June ro early Oct • €9; English audioguide €2.50; snorkelling tours €18 • ☎ 04 98 04 44 00, ⓦ domainedurayol.org

Le Rayol is best known for the beautiful **Domaine du Rayol gardens**, which extend down to the Figuier bay and headland. The land originally belonged to a banker who, before going bust at Monte Carlo in the 1930s, built the Art Nouveau mansion through which you enter the gardens; it's nowadays rather dilapidated, as is the beautifully situated Art Deco villa at the far side of the *domaine*. Areas of the garden are dedicated to plants from different parts of the world that share the climate of the Mediterranean: Chile, South Africa, China, California, Central America, Australia and New Zealand. Apart from the extraordinary diversity of the vegetation, the garden is memorable for the loveliness of its setting, with cooling breezes and views of its small sandy beach (off limits to visitors) and crystal-clear turquoise waters, which you can explore on **snorkelling tours**. There are also various engaging themed tours of the garden given by professional gardeners.

INFORMATION	THE SILVER BEACHES

LE RAYOL

Tourist office Place Michel-Goy (Mon–Sat 9.30am–1pm & 2–6.30pm, Sun 9.30am–12.30pm; ☎ 04 94 05 65 69, ⓦ lerayolcanadel.fr).

CAVALAIRE-SUR-MER

Tourist office In the Maison de la Mer on the seafront (mid-June to mid-Sept daily 9am–7pm; mid-Sept to mid-June Mon–Fri 9am–12.30pm & 2–6pm, Sat 9am–12.30pm; ☎ 04 94 01 92 10, ⓦ cavalairesurmer.fr).

ACCOMMODATION

Le Bailli de Suffren Av des Américains, Le Rayol-Canadel ☎ 04 75 75 21 91, ⓦ lebaillidesuffren.com. Four-star luxury in an idyllic beachside setting in Le Rayol, with a/c suites, a heated pool and a *restaurant gastronomique*. Closed mid-Oct to mid-April. €425

La Calanque Rue de la Calanque, Cavalaire-sur-Mer ☎ 04 94 01 95 00, ⓦ residences-du-soleil.com /lacalanque. Small, upmarket hotel beautifully perched on a low cliff overlooking the sea a little way out of town. Closed mid-Oct to early April. €208

Camping de Pramousquier Chemin de la Faverolle, Pramousquier ☎ 04 94 05 83 95, ⓦ camping pramousquier.com. Two-star site 400m from Pramousquier's fine sandy beach, with a bar, restaurant and food store on site. Closed early Oct to early April. €25.70

EATING, DRINKING AND NIGHTLIFE

Le Maurin des Maures Avenue du Touring Club, Le Rayol ☎ 04 94 05 60 11, ⓦ maurin-des-maures.com. Lively place with sea views on the main road through Le Rayol, serving fresh grilled fish, *bourride* and aioli. There's a €15.50 lunch *menu*. March–June, Sept & Oct 12.15–2.30pm & 7.15–9pm; July & Aug 12.15–10.30pm.

Le Rescator Résidence du Port, Cavalaire-sur-Mer ☎ 04 94 15 42 10. Smart *restaurant gastronomique* facing the port in Cavalaire-sur-Mer, with bouillabaisse for €48, *plateaux de fruits de mer* from €28 and a three-course *menu* for €25. Open all year round.

La Croix-Valmer and Cap Lardier

At the eastern end of Cavalaire-sur-Mer's bay lies another exceptional stretch of wooded coastline, the **Domaine de Cap Lardier**. This pristine coastal conservation area snakes around the southern tip of the St-Tropez peninsula, and is best accessed from **LA CROIX-VALMER**, even though the somewhat bland village centre is some 2.5km from the sea; some of the land between is taken up by vineyards that produce a decent wine. To reach the best beach in the vicinity, **plage du Gigaro**, catch the *navette* or **shuttle bus** (June–Sept; every 45min) from outside the tourist office (see below).

ARRIVAL AND INFORMATION — LA CROIX-VALMER AND CAP LARDIER

By bus Buses stop at the plage du Débarquement and at the Croix de Constantin in the village.
Destinations Le Lavandou (7 daily; 35min); Hyères (7 daily; 1 hr 15min) St-Tropez (up to 8 daily; 20min).
Tourist office 287 rue Louis Martin, just up from the junction of the D559 and D93 (April–June & Sept Mon–Sat 9am–noon & 2–6pm, Sun 9am–noon; July & Aug daily 10am–7pm; Oct–March Mon–Fri 9am–noon & 2–6pm, Sat 9am–noon; ☎ 04 94 55 12 12, ⓦ lacroixvalmer.fr).

ACCOMMODATION

Le Château de Valmer Rte de Gigaro ☎ 04 94 55 15 15, ⓦ chateauvalmer.com. Luxurious old mansion in an idyllic setting between pines, palms and vines just back from the plage de Gigaro, with 42 rooms plus cottages on the estate and a few treehouses. Spa and leisure facilities include an indoor pool, sauna, hammam and gym. Closed Oct–April. **€355**
La Ricarde Bd de St Raphaël, plage du Débarquement ☎ 04 94 79 64 07, ⓦ hotel-la-ricarde.com. A good-value family-run *chambres d'hôte* just 150m from the plage du Débarquement, west of Gigaro, with eight tasteful and individually styled, a/c rooms with en-suite shower and WC. Closed Nov–Feb. **€73**
Sélection 12 bd de la Mer ☎ 04 94 55 10 30, ⓦ selectioncamping.com. Four-star campsite, 400m from the plage du Débarquement and with excellent facilities including a heated pool, bar, restaurant, takeaway, shop and plenty of activities. Closed mid-Oct to mid-March. **€42**

EATING AND DRINKING

L'Italien/Pepe le Pirate Plage de Gigaro ☎ 04 94 79 67 16, ⓦ lesmoulinsdepaillas.com. Two-in-one restaurant near the conservation area. It's quite smart and formal at lunch (two-course *menu* €29) and more casual in the evening, with a menu dominated by pasta and pizza (from €10). The adjacent *restaurant gastronomique*, *Brigantine*, is run by the same people. Mid-May to Sept daily 12.15–2pm & 7.30–9pm.
Souleias Plage de Gigaro ☎ 04 94 55 10 55; ⓦ souleias .com. *Restaurant gastronomique* with a terrace facing the sea and *menus* from €48 to €78; there's simpler fare at lunchtime around the hotel pool. Restaurant: May–Sept Mon & Wed–Sun evenings only.

St-Tropez and around

As the summer playground of Europe's youthful rich, the one-time fishing village turned VIP hangout of **ST-TROPEZ** remains undeniably glamorous, its oversized yachts and infamous champagne "spray" parties creating an air of hedonistic excess; on warm nights there's a delicious buzz of excitement around the port. Be warned, however, that its beaches aren't the cleanest, and that if you don't have the holiday budget of a supermodel or Formula One racing driver, St-Tropez's sheer expense and occasional haughtiness towards visitors, particularly in high season, can make it feel like a party you're not invited to. Time your visit for a fine late spring or early autumn day, though and the crowds will be more manageable, and you may just discern some of the old St-Tropez magic.

The Vieux Port

The **Vieux Port**, rebuilt after its destruction in World War II, is where you get the classic St-Tropez experience: the quayside café clientele eyeing the Martini-sippers on their

BIRTH OF A LEGEND

The origins of St-Tropez are not unusual for this stretch of coast: a fishing village that grew up around a port founded by the Greeks of Marseille. It was destroyed by the Saracens in 739 and finally fortified in the late Middle Ages. Its sole distinction was its inaccessibility, stuck out on a peninsula that never warranted real roads. St-Tropez could be reached easily only by boat as late as the 1880s, when the novelist **Guy de Maupassant** sailed his yacht into the port during his final high-living binge before the onset of syphilitic insanity. Soon after Maupassant's' visit, the Neo-Impressionist painter **Paul Signac** sailed down the coast in his boat, named after Manet's notorious painting *L'Olympia*. Bad weather forced him to moor in St-Tropez and – being rich and impulsive – he decided to have a house built there: *La Hune*, on what is now rue Paul-Signac, was designed by fellow painter Henri van de Velde. Signac opened his doors to impoverished friends who could benefit from the light, the beauty and the distance from the respectable convalescent world of Cannes and Nice. **Matisse** was one of the first to take up his offer; the locals were shocked again, this time by Madame Matisse modelling in a kimono. **Bonnard**, **Marquet**, **Dufy**, **Derain**, **Vlaminck**, **Seurat**, **Van Dongen** and others followed, and by the end of World War I St-Tropez was fairly well established as a hangout for bohemians.

The 1930s saw a further artistic influx, this time of writers as much as painters: **Jean Cocteau** came here, **Colette** lived for fourteen years in a villa outside the village, describing her main concerns as "whether to go walking or swimming, whether to have rosé or white, whether to have a long day or a long night", while **Anaïs Nin**'s journal records "girls riding bare-breasted on the back of open cars; an intensity of pleasure" and undressing between bamboo bushes that rustled with concealed lovers.

But it wasn't until after World War II that St-Tropez achieved international celebrity. In 1955 Roger Vadim arrived to film **Brigitte Bardot** in *Et Dieu Créa La Femme*, and the cult of Tropezian sun, sex and celebrities took off, creating a tourist boom. The village has been groaning under the sheer weight of visitor numbers ever since.

6

gin-palace motor yachts, with the latest fashions parading in between, defining the French word *frimer* (derived from sham) which means exactly this – to stroll ostentatiously in places like St-Tropez. You may be surprised at how entertaining the spectacle can be, though it's undeniably a little vulgar – a sort of human zoo in which the conspicuously rich are willing exhibits. The portside is at its most magical in late September and early October during **Les Voiles**, the regatta which sees the harbour swap ugly motor yachts for beautiful sailing vessels, and cruise liners dot the Golfe de St-Tropez beyond.

Musée de l'Annonciade

2 rue de l'Annonciade • Jan–Oct & Dec Mon & Wed–Sun 10am–noon & 2–6pm • €5 • ☎ 04 94 17 84 10, ⓦ saint-tropez.fr

The marvellous **Musée de l'Annonciade** occupies a deconsecrated sixteenth-century chapel on place Georges-Grammont, right on the Vieux Port and reason in itself for a visit to St-Tropez. It was originally Signac's idea to have a permanent exhibition space for the Neo-Impressionists and Fauves who painted here, though it was not until 1955 that collections owned by various individuals were put together in this building. The museum features representative works by Signac, Matisse and most of the other artists who painted in St-Tropez: grey, grim, northern scenes of Paris, Boulogne and Westminster, and then local, brilliantly sunlit landscapes by the same brush. Two winter scenes of the village by Dufy contrast with Camille Camoin's springtime *Place des Lices* and Bonnard's boilingly hot summer view. The museum is a real delight, both for its contents – unrivalled outside Paris for the 1890 to 1940 period – and for the fact that it is often the least crowded place on the port.

6

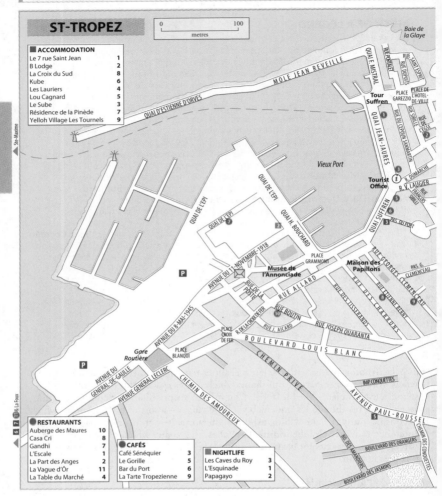

ST-TROPEZ

0   100
metres

ACCOMMODATION

Le 7 rue Saint Jean	1
B Lodge	2
La Croix du Sud	8
Kube	6
Les Lauriers	4
Lou Cagnard	5
Le Sube	3
Résidence de la Pinède	7
Yelloh Village Les Tournels	9

RESTAURANTS

Auberge des Maures	10
Casa Cri	8
Gandhi	7
L'Escale	1
La Part des Anges	2
La Vague d'Or	11
La Table du Marché	4

CAFÉS

Café Sénéquier	3
Le Gorille	5
Bar du Port	6
La Tarte Tropezienne	9

NIGHTLIFE

Les Caves du Roy	3
L'Esquinade	1
Papagayo	2

Place des Lices and around

The other pole of St-Trop's life is **place des Lices**, southeast of the Vieux Port, with its battered old plane trees, *pétanque* players and benches on which to sit and watch – a rather nicer option than the café-brasseries fringing the *place*, which are a bit too smugly Champs-Élysées in style. In the streets between here and the port – rue François Sibilli and rue Georges Clemenceau – and the smaller lanes in the heart of the old village you can window-shop or buy haute couture, antiques, *objets d'art* and classy trinkets to your heart's content.

Maison des Papillons

9 rue Etienne Berny • Tues & Thurs 2–6pm, Wed, Fri & Sat 10am–12.30pm & 2–6pm • €3 • ☎ 04 94 97 63 45

One of the narrowest lanes in St-Tropez is rue Etienne Berny, where you'll find the **Maison des Papillons**, a butterfly museum housing more than 20,000 pinned specimens, including many rare and endangered species.

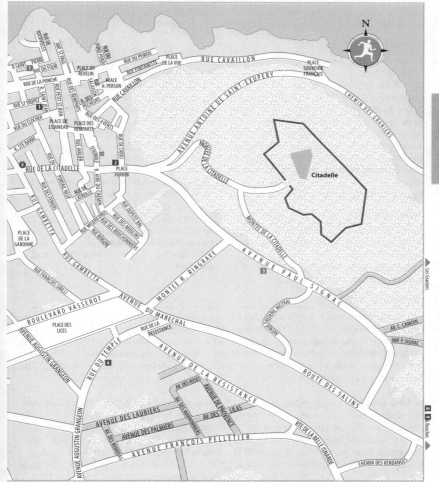

The quartier de la Ponche and the Citadelle

Heading east from the port, from the top end of quai Jean-Jaurès, you pass the **Tour Suffren**, originally built in 980 by Count Guillaume I of Provence, and enter the **quartier de la Ponche,** the oldest and most atmospheric part of the village. Here, place de l'Hôtel-de-Ville is dominated by the *mairie*, which, with its attractive earthy pink facade and dark green shutters is one of the few reminders that this is a real town. A street to the left takes you down to the tiny, rocky **Baie de la Glaye**; straight ahead, rue de la Ponche passes through an ancient gateway to place du Revelin, which overlooks the lovely **fishing port** and its tiny beach. Overlooking this picturesque *quartier* is the Citadelle.

The Citadelle

1 Montée de la Citadelle • Daily: April–Sept 10am–6.30pm; Oct–March 10am–12.30pm & 1.30–5.30pm • €2.50 • ☎ 04 94 97 59 43, Ⓦ saint-tropez.fr

The sixteenth-century **Citadelle** is worth a visit for the walk round the ramparts, whose

6

excellent views of the gulf and the back of the town have not changed since their translation into oil on canvas in the early twentieth century.

ARRIVAL AND DEPARTURE — ST-TROPEZ

By bus Buses drop you at the *gare routière* on av Général-de-Gaulle.

Destinations Hyères (up to 8 daily; 1hr 40min); Le Lavandou (up to 8 daily; 1hr 5min); Sainte Maxime (up to 13 daily; 45min), Saint Raphaël (up to 11 daily; 1hr 35min).

By car Beware of driving to St-Tropez in summer – traffic jams start in earnest at Sainte Maxime, where the D25 from the autoroute joins the coast road; it can take 2hr to crawl the remaining 16km into St Tropez. There is (paid) parking in the vast Parking du Nouveau Port at the entrance to the village.

By ferry The quickest way to reach St-Tropez in summer

– except by helicopter – is the ferry (15min) operated by Les Bateaux Verts (☎ 04 94 49 29 39, ⓦ bateauxverts.com) from Sainte-Maxime on the opposite side of the Golfe de St-Tropez. Les Bateaux Verts also runs seasonal ferries from Port Grimaud and Les Issambres. A more frequent service between Port Grimaud and St-Tropez is offered by Les Navettes Grimaldines (ⓦ navette-bateau.com).

Destinations Les Issambres (June–Sept; hourly); Port Grimaud (Les Bateaux Verts: April–Oct; hourly); Port Grimaud (Les Navettes Grimaldines: July & Aug; every 30min); and Sainte-Maxime (year-round except Jan & early Feb; every 15min in high season; 15min).

INFORMATION

Tourist office Quai Jean-Jaurès (daily: April–June, Sept & Oct during Les Voiles 9.30am–12.30pm & 2–7pm; July & Aug 9.30am–1.30pm & 3–7.30pm; Oct after les Voiles–March 9.30am–12.30pm & 2–6pm; ☎ 04 94 97 45 21, ⓦ ot-saint-tropez.com). In high season there's also an

office at the Parking du Nouveau Port.

Bike rental Bikes and motorbikes can be rented at Rolling Bikes, 12 av G.-Leclerc (☎ 04 94 97 09 39, ⓦ rolling-bikes.com).

ACCOMMODATION

You'll be lucky to find a room in high season. The tourist office can help (for a €10 fee), but – transport permitting – you might be better off staying elsewhere. A lot of the classiest accommodation is out of town on the peninsula – there's no price advantage but you may gain in tranquillity what you lose in convenience; some outlying hotels run shuttle services into town. Campsites are out on the peninsula (see p.283) and are geared more towards glamping in fancy chalets than pitches for tents. In summer it's worth checking out the signs for **camping à la ferme** that you'll see along the D93, but make sure you know the charges first.

Le 7 Rue Saint-Jean 7 rue Saint-Jean ☎ 06 16 05 21 76, ⓦ aucoeurdesainttropez.com. Stylish *chambres d'hôte* with two individually decorated rooms in the oldest part of the village. The larger of the two is a duplex with views of the Citadelle and sea; it sleeps up to three. **€135**

B. Lodge 23 rue de l'Aïoli ☎ 04 94 97 06 57, ⓦ hotel-b-lodge.com. Overlooking the Citadelle, this attractive boutique-style hotel is in a quieter setting than places in the centre and has stylish decor and its own bar. Lack of a/c in cheaper rooms is a downside, and there's no parking. **€140**

★ **Kube** Rte de St-Tropez ☎ 04 94 97 20 00, ⓦ kubehotel.com. Gorgeous white designer hotel on the road from La Foux, with an infinity pool facing the sea and an ice bar in the basement; there's a free chauffeur-driven shuttle to the Vieux Port. **€400**

Les Lauriers Rue du Temple ☎ 04 94 97 04 88, ⓦ hotel-les-lauriers.com. Just behind Place des Lices, this friendly, relaxed two-star hotel has eighteen a/c rooms and

a pleasant garden. Relatively good value for Saint Tropez. Closed Nov–April. **€90**

Lou Cagnard 18 av Paul-Roussel ☎ 04 94 97 04 24, ⓦ hotel-lou-cagnard.com. The best budget option. Nineteen Provençal-style rooms – fifteen of them with a/c – in a tranquil location with a garden and secure private parking. Seven-night minimum stay in July & Aug. **€75**

Le Sube 15 quai Suffren ☎ 04 94 97 30 04, ⓦ hotelsube.net. One of St Tropez's oldest-established hotels, right in the thick of the action with 25 rooms, a/c and a bar. Some – more expensive – rooms offer fantastic views over the port. Closed mid-Nov to Easter. **€140**

Résidence de la Pinède Plage de la Bouillabaisse ☎ 04 94 55 91 00, ⓦ residencepinede.com. With a wonderful location on its own private beach, this luxurious hotel has just 39 spacious rooms tastefully decorated in pale colours, with marble-lined bathrooms. Prices are eye-watering, though. Closed Oct–April. **€1020**

EATING AND DRINKING

Eating in St-Tropez is notoriously expensive. The correlation between price and quality is weaker here than anywhere else on the Côte d'Azur, even at the top end of the market. As a rule of thumb, avoid the obvious hotspots of the Vieux Port or place des Lices, and instead browse the restaurant menus in the lanes that climb towards the church and Citadelle to find the best value. Prime **drinking** spots are along the port and on place des Lices. Place aux Herbes has a daily fish **market**, and the main food market is on place des Lices on Tuesday and Saturday mornings from 7am to 1pm.

CAFÉS AND SNACKS

Café Sénéquier Quai Jean-Jaurès ☎ 04 94 97 00 90, ⓦ senequier.com. The top quayside café: it's horribly expensive, particularly for drinks, but aside from its sunglass-posing potential it sells sensational nougat (also available from the shop at the back). Breakfast €17, ice-cream *coups* from around €11. Daily 8am–7pm.

Le Gorille 1 quai Suffren ☎ 04 94 97 03 93. Straightforward quayside café, where you can get omelettes, salads and the like from around €10.50, *moules-frites* for €16 and beer from €4.50. Mon, Tues & Thurs–Sun 7am–7pm.

Bar du Port 7 quai Suffren ☎ 04 94 97 00 54. With its stylish, modern but vaguely retro-1960s decor, this café-bar is the epitome of St-Tropez idling – and not as expensive as some. Breakfast €11, wine by the glass €5. Daily 7am–3am.

La Tarte Tropezienne 36 rue G.-Clemenceau ☎ 04 94 97 71 42, ⓦ tropezienne.com. This patisserie claims to have invented the rather sickly but moreish eponymous sponge and custard cake (€2.90 for an enormous slice), though you no longer have to come to St-Tropez to sample it – the company is now a chain. Good, too, for cheap takeaway lunch *formules* (€5.90). Daily 6.30am–7.30pm.

RESTAURANTS

Auberge des Maures 4 rue du Dr-Boutin ☎ 04 94 97 01 50, ⓦ aubergedesmaures.fr. Twee, pretty Michelin and *Gault Millau*-rated place specializing in classic Provençal cooking, chargrilled fish and meat, with a *menu* at €52. March–Nov daily from 7pm; closing time varies.

Casa Cri 12 rue Berny ☎ 04 94 97 42 52. Classy if rather pricey Italian, set in a lovely courtyard garden down a quiet side street just back from the Vieux Port. Pasta dishes from €16; meat dishes such as *scaloppine* in white wine sauce from around €22. Mid-April to June & Sept to mid-Oct

Tues–Sun from 7.30pm; July & Aug daily from 7.30pm; closing time varies.

Gandhi 3 quai de l'Épi ☎ 04 94 97 71 71, ⓦ gandhisai .com. Small, busy Indian restaurant close to the Parking du Nouveau Port and with a few fusion dishes like fillet of rascasse in masala sauce alongside the familiar vindaloos and biryanis. Lunch *formule* €16.50; most dishes around €12. Tues & Thurs–Sun noon–2pm & 7–10.30pm, Mon & Wed 7–10.30pm.

l'Escale 9 quai Jean-Jaurès ☎ 04 94 97 00 63, ⓦ alpazurhotels.com. Upmarket seafood restaurant and lounge on the Vieux Port with a stylish beige-and-white interior. Pasta dishes from around €23, *plats* from €26 and – if you're pushing the boat out – *plateaux de fruits de mer* kicking off at €68. Daily noon–2.30pm & 8.30–10.30pm.

La Part des Anges 6 rue de l'Église ☎ 04 94 96 19 50. Very pleasant little restaurant serving decent food at modest prices in a pretty, atmospheric lane just down from St-Tropez's church, with pasta from €11 and fish dishes from around €13. There's also a three-course dinner *menu*. Mon, Tues & Thurs–Sun noon–3pm & 7–11pm.

La Vague D'Ôr, Résidence La Pinède Plage de la Bouillabaisse ☎ 04 94 55 91 00. Michelin two-star chef Arnaud Donckele presides over the kitchens at St-Tropez's most renowned restaurant, where you might feast on turbot *yuzu gremolata* with slipper lobster ravioli and marjoram-scented crab; *menus* €160–235. Late April–Sept daily 7.30–10pm.

La Table du Marché 11 rue des Commerçants ☎ 04 94 97 01 25. Smart but casual place that recently moved to bigger premises, with chicken Caesar salad for €12, club sandwiches for €16 and *plats du jour* from the chalked-up menu for around €14. May–Oct daily noon–3pm & 7–11pm.

NIGHTLIFE

In season, St-Tropez stays up late, as you'd expect. The **pétanque games** on place des Lices continue till well after dusk, the portside spectacle doesn't falter till the early hours, and even the shops stay open well after dinner. **Clubs** open every night in summer, and usually weekends only in winter; your chances of getting in will depend on who's on the door, and whether they think you look the part.

Les Caves du Roy Byblos, entrance av du Maréchal Foch ☎ 04 94 56 68 00, ⓦ lescavesduroy.com. Still the place to see and be seen, the *Caves du Roy* is where you can rub shoulders with rap stars and supermodels. Music is a mix of current dance hits and oldies from the 1970s and 80s. €28 with *conso*. July & Aug daily midnight–dawn; Sept to mid-Oct & mid-April to June Fri & Sat only.

L'Esquinade 2 rue du Four ☎ 04 94 97 87 44, ⓦ facebook.com/discotheque.esquinadesainttropez.

Gay-friendly club spinning house, disco, R&B and world music. Unlike most of St-Tropez's clubs it's open year round.

Papagayo Port de Saint Tropez ☎ 04 94 97 95 95, ⓦ papagayo-st-tropez.com. Fifty-year-old veteran of the St-Tropez nightlife scene with a restaurant terrace (*plats* from €19) overlooking the yachts. Club entry from €25 with *conso*. May–Aug midnight to 5/6am; restaurant daily noon–1am.

6

The beaches and the St-Tropez pensinula

Transport from St-Tropez is provided by a minibus service in summer from place des Lices to Salins (5 daily; 15min), or the infrequent bus #7705 to Ramatuelle (6 daily in summer; 9min) which passes Pampelonne; by car, you'll have to pay high parking charges at all the beaches – the approach roads are designed to make it impossible to park for free on the verge.

St-Tropez's fabled beaches stretch along the eastern flank of the **St-Tropez peninsula**. They may lack the Blue Flags of their neighbours but more than make up for it in glamour; it was here back in the 1960s that topless bathing and G-string bikinis were seen for the first time. The nearest beach to St-Tropez, within easy walking distance, is **Les Graniers**, below the Citadelle beyond the Port des Pêcheurs along rue Cavaillon. From here a path follows the coast around the **Baie des Canebiers**, which has a small beach, to Cap St-Pierre, Cap St-Tropez, the very crowded **Salins** beach and right round to **Plage Tahiti** at the top end of the famous **plage de Pampelonne**, 12.5km from St-Tropez. This eastern area of the peninsula is where the rich and famous have their vast villas, with helipads and artificial lakes in acres of heavily guarded grounds.

In contrast to its crowded coastline, the **interior** of the St-Tropez peninsula is almost uninhabited, thanks to government intervention, complex ownerships and the value of some local wines. The best view of this richly green, wooded and flowering countryside is from the hilltop village of **Gassin**, its lower neighbour **Ramatuelle**, or the tiny road between them, the beautiful route des Moulins de Paillas where the ruined windmills once caught every wind.

The Plage de Pampelonne and beyond

The almost straight five-kilometre north–south **Plage de Pampelonne** is the famous bronzing belt of St-Tropez and initiator of the topless bathing cult. The water is shallow for 50m or so and exposed to the wind, and it's sometimes scourged by dried sea vegetation, not to mention slicks of pollutants from the offshore traffic. But spotless glitter comes from the rash of **beach bars and restaurants** built out over the coarse sand, all with patios and sofas, all serving cocktails and ice creams (as well as full-blown meals), and all renting out beach mattresses and matching parasols.

The beach ends with the headland of **Cap Camarat**, beyond which the private residential settlement of Villa Bergès grudgingly allows public access to the Plage de l'Escalet. Another coastal path leads to the next bay, the **Baie de la Briande**, where you'll find the least populated beach of the whole peninsula. You can continue to **Cap Lardier** with a choice of paths upwards and downwards and along the gorgeous shore all the way round to La Croix-Valmer (see p.276).

Gassin

The highly chic village of **GASSIN** gives the impression of a small ship perched on a summit. Once a Moorish stronghold, it's a perfect place to have a dinner (see opposite), as you sit outside by the village wall enjoying a spectacular panorama east over the peninsula.

Ramatuelle

RAMATUELLE is bigger than its neighbour Gassin, though just as old, and is surrounded by some of the best Côte de Provence **vineyards** – the top selection of wines can be tasted at Les Maîtres Vignerons de la Presqu'île de St-Tropez by the La Foux junction on the N98. The twisting and arcaded streets of Ramatuelle itself are inevitably full of arts and crafts shops selling works by artists of dubious talent, but the village is very pleasant nonetheless. The central Romanesque **Église Notre-Dame** that formed part of the old defences has heavy gilded furnishings from the Chartreuse de la Verne (see p.285) and an impressive early seventeenth-century door carved out of serpentine. Gérard Philippe, perhaps the most beautiful French actor ever to have appeared on screen, is buried in Ramatuelle's cemetery.

ACCOMMODATION

ST-TROPEZ PENSINSULA

Chez Tony 31 av Georges Clémenceau, Ramatuelle ☎04 94 79 20 46. Fairly simple but good-value accommodation for these parts – double rooms with shower and TV (but shared WC facilities) above a revamped bar in the old village. **€60**

La Croix du Sud Rte des Plages, 3km from Ramatuelle ☎04 94 55 51 23, ⓦwww.camping-saint-tropez.com. A three-star site 3km from Ramatuelle towards the Plage de Pampelonne (see opposite), with plenty of shade and a pool. Closed Oct–March. **€21.10**

L'Ecurie du Castellas Rte des Moulins de Peillas,

Ramatuelle ☎04 94 79 20 67, ⓦlecurieducastellas .com. Just outside Ramatuelle village on the road to Gassin with panoramic views over the village to the sea, and eleven stylish en-suite rooms with wi-fi; some also have terraces. **€90**

Yelloh Village Les Tournels Rte de Camarat, 3km from Ramatuelle ☎04 94 55 90 90, ⓦtournels.com. Four-star site with good facilities including an extensive, heated outdoor pool with water slides, plus an indoor pool and spa. It's more geared to chalet lets than tents, but they do welcome campers too. Closed Jan to mid-March. **€46**

EATING

★ **Bello Visto** 9 place des Barrys, Gassin ☎04 94 56 17 30, ⓦbellovisto.eu. Good Provençal specialities on a €28 *menu*, with dishes like endive *tarte tatin* with honey and pine nuts or john dory with saffron. They also have rooms. April–Oct daily noon–2pm & 7–10pm.

Club 55 43 bd Patch, plage de Pampelonne ☎04 94 55 55 55, ⓦleclub55.fr. The classic among Pampelonne's chic beach concessions, named after the year when Vadim's film crew scrounged food from what was then a family beach hut. *Plats du jour* around €25. April–Oct & Christmas.

L'Ecurie du Castellas Rte des Moulins de Peillas, Ramatuelle ☎04 94 79 11 59, ⓦlecurieducastellas .com. Michelin-listed restaurant with a pretty outdoor

terrace and a €33 *menu* featuring goats cheese Bavarois with basil and a €49 *menu* featuring cold lobster with ratatouille and herb-crusted lamb with aubergine caponata. Daily noon–2pm and 7–9.30pm.

Au Fil à la Pâte 7 rue Victor Léon, Ramatuelle ☎04 94 79 16 40. Diminutive, rustic place on the main street in the old village, serving fresh pasta from €13, salads from around €10 and meat or fish mains from €17. Daily except Wed noon–2.30pm & 7pm–midnight.

Nikki Beach Rte de l'Epi ☎04 94 79 82 04, ⓦnikkibeach.com. The hot celebrity haunt on the plage de Pampelonne, with simple fare at VIP prices: salads from €22, pasta dishes from €24 and sharing platters €65 up. June–Sept daily 11am–8pm.

The Massif des Maures

The secret of the Côte d'Azur is that despite the crowds and traffic of the coast, Provence is still just behind – old, sparsely populated, village-oriented and dependent on the land for its produce, not its real-estate value. Between Marseille and Menton, the most bewitching hinterland is the sombre **Massif des Maures** that stretches from Hyères to Fréjus. Darkly forested, its name derives from the Provençal and Latin words for dark, *mauram* and *mauro*.

The highest point of these hills stops short of 800m, but the quick succession of ridges, the sudden drops and views, and the curling, looping roads are pervasively mountainous. Where the lie of the land gives a wide bowl of sunlit slopes, vines are grown. Elsewhere the hills are thickly forested, with Aleppo pines, holly, sweet chestnuts and gnarled cork oaks, their trunks scarred in great bands where their bark has been stripped.

Exploring the Massif

Much of the massif is inaccessible even to **walkers**. However, the GR9 follows the most northern and highest ridge from Pignans on the N97 past Notre-Dame-des-Anges, La Sauvette, La Garde-Freinet and down to the head of the Golfe de St-Tropez. There are other paths and tracks, such as the one following the Vallon de Tamary from north of La Londe-des-Maures to join one of the roads snaking down from the Col de Babaou to Collobrières. Some of the smaller back roads don't go very far and many are closed to the public in summer for fear of forest fires, but when they are open, this makes exceptional countryside for exploring by mountain bike or on foot. Bear in mind, however, that at certain times of the year the entire Massif is thick with rifle-toting hunters. Local tourist offices have information on routes.

For **cyclists**, the D14 that runs through the middle of the Massif, parallel to the coast, from Pierrefeu-du-Var north of Hyères to Cogolin near St-Tropez, is manageable and stunning.

6 Collobrières and around

At the heart of the massif is the ancient village of **COLLOBRIÈRES**, reputed to have been the first place in France to adopt **cork-growing** from the Spanish. From the Middle Ages until recent times, cork production has been the major business of the village; however, the main industry now is *marrons glacés* and every other confection derived from sweet chestnuts. The annual *Fête de la Châtaigne*, the **chestnut fair**, takes place at the height of the harvest on the last three Sundays of October, when special dishes are served in restaurants and roast chestnuts sold in the streets.

Confiserie Azurienne

Bd Koenig • Daily 9.30am–12.30pm & 1.30–6.30pm • ☏ 04 94 48 07 20, ⓦ confiserieazureenne.con

The **Confiserie Azurienne** factory has a small exhibition of old machinery used for processing chestnuts, and a shop that sells the signature *marrons glacés* plus ice cream, jam, nougat and bonbons, all made with chestnuts, as well as a sunny terrace on which to enjoy the delicious chestnut-flavoured ice cream.

ARRIVAL AND INFORMATION   COLLOBRIÈRES

By bus Collobrières is served by infrequent buses from Hyères (1 daily; 90min) and Toulon (1–2 daily; 1hr 45min).
By car Parking can be a headache at Collobrières, with the main tourist car park a five-minute walk from the village centre.

Tourist office Bd Charles-Caminat (Tues, Wed, Fri & Sat 9am–noon & 3–5pm; ☏ 04 94 48 08 00, ⓦ collobrieres -tourisme.com). They can supply details of walks in the surrounding hills.

ACCOMMODATION

Camping Municipal St Roch On the eastern of the village near place Charles-de-Gaulle ☏ 04 94 48 08 00, ⓦ collobrieres-tourisme.com. Fairly basic campsite (bookings only through the tourist office), open summer only. *Camping sauvage* is forbidden. €9.40
Des Maures 19 bd Lazare Carnot ☏ 04 94 48 07 10, ⓦ hoteldesmaures.fr. Simple but spacious and very good-value rooms above a restaurant and bar in the centre of the

village, facing the river at the back. Competitive half board available. €33
★ **Notre Dame** 15 av de la Libération ☏ 04 94 48 07 13, ⓦ hotel-notre-dame.eu. Surprisingly chic for the deeply rural location, this trendy boutique-style hotel has ten individually decorated rooms with huge bathrooms, a/c and wi-fi, plus a lovely patio restaurant by the river with excellent wines. €98

EATING AND DRINKING

La Ferme du Peïgros South of the village, signed off the D41 to Bormes at the Col de Babaou ☏ 04 94 48 03 83. An isolated farmhouse in wonderful surroundings serving its own produce, including goats cheese and – in season – ceps. Dishes from around €15. Open for lunch all year round, plus dinner in July & Aug.

La Petite Fontaine 6 place de la République ☏ 04 94 48 00 12. Congenial and affordable *Gault Millau*-listed restaurant with an excellent reputation, serving classic Provençal dishes on €26 and €31 *menus*. It books up fast. Tues–Sat noon–2pm & 7.30–9pm, Sun noon–2pm.

SHOPPING

Les Vignerons de Collobrières Near Hôtel Notre-Dame at the western entrance to the village ☏ 04 94 48

07 26. A good place to buy the local Côtes de Provence wines. Mon 2–6pm, Tues–Sat 8.30am–noon & 2–6pm.

La Chartreuse de la Verne

Off the D14 • Feb–May & Oct–Dec Mon & Wed–Sun 11am–5pm; June–Sept daily except during high fire risk 11am–6pm • €6 •
☎ 04 94 43 48 28 or ☎ 04 94 48 08 00 for fire risk information, ⓦ diocese-frejus-toulon.com/Monastere-Notre-Dame-de-Clemence •
Visitor car park is several hundred metres back from the monastery

Writing at the end of the nineteenth century, Maupassant declared that there was
nowhere else in the world where his heart had felt such a pressing weight of melancholy
as at the ruins of **La Chartreuse de la Verne**. Since then a great deal of restoration work
has been carried out on this Carthusian monastery, abandoned during the Revolution
and hidden away in total isolation, 12km east of Collobrières on a winding but largely
paved track off the D14 towards Grimaud. It remains a desolate spot, though; the
buildings of this once vast twelfth-century complex, in the dark reddish-brown schist
of the Maures, combined for decorative effect with local greenish serpentine, appear
gaunt and inhospitable, but the atmosphere is indisputable.

Le Village des Tortues

Quartier les Plaines, Gonfaron • Daily noon–7pm • €12 • ☎ 04 94 78 26 41, ⓦ www.villagetortues.com

About 20km north of Collobrières and 2km east of Gonfaron on the D75 to Les
Mayons, **Le Village des Tortues** is not just a tourist attraction but a serious conservation
project to repopulate the native Hermann tortoise. A million years ago the tortoises
populated a third of France, but now, due to the ever-increasing threat of urbanization,
forest fires, theft of eggs and sale as pets, this rare creature only just survives in the
Massif des Maures. The tortoises are cared for and protected here, and you can look
round their large enclosures where you'll see the tiny babies, "juveniles" and those soon
to be released back into the wild.

Cogolin

Just 8.5km from St-Tropez, **COGOLIN** is renowned for its craft industries, including
reed-making for wind instruments, pipes for smoking, wrought-iron furniture, silk
yarn and knotted wool carpets, all offering one-off, made-to-order, high-quality and
high-cost goods for the Côte d'Azur market. It's possible to visit some of the **craft
factories**; the helpful tourist office (see below) can provide a *guide pratique*, and help
with making appointments. Alternatively, you can just pop into the retail outlets. The
production of **pipes** from briarwood is on show at Courrieu, 58 avenue Clemenceau
(Mon–Sat 9am–noon & 2–6pm; ⓦ courrieupipes.fr). Typically pretty Provençal **faïence**
is on sale at La Poterie de Cogolin, 24 rue Carnot (Mon–Sat 10am–12.30pm &
3.30–7pm). On the way out of town, before joining the N98 heading west, the **Cave
des Vignerons**, on rue Marceau (closed Sun, plus Mon Oct–March; ☎ 04 94 54 40 54),
is worth a visit to sample some of the local wines, said to have impressed Julius Caesar.

ARRIVAL AND INFORMATION COGOLIN

By bus Buses from Grimaud, La Garde Freinet and
St-Tropez stop in avenue Clémenceau, which leads to the
central place de la République
Destinations Grimaud (5 daily; 5min); La Garde Freinet (3
daily; 20min); St-Tropez (5 daily; 20min).
Tourist office Place de la République (April–June &

Sept–Oct Mon–Fri 9am–12.30pm & 2–6.30pm, Sat
9.30am–12.30pm & 2–6pm; July & Aug Mon–Sat
9am–1pm & 2–6.30pm, Sun 9am–1pm; Nov–March
Mon–Fri 9am–12.30pm & 2–6pm, Sat 9.30am–12.30pm;
☎ 04 94 55 01 10, ⓦ cogolin-provence.com).

ACCOMMODATION

Bliss Place de la République ☎ 04 94 54 15 17, ⓦ bliss-
hotel.com. Three-star upmarket hotel, with a hint of
St-Tropez trendiness in its minimalist decor. Rooms have
a/c and flatscreen TV. **€119**

Coq Hôtel Place de la République ☎ 04 94 54 13 71,
ⓦ coqhotel.com. Congenial and affordable hotel above a
restaurant on Cogolin's main square, with private parking;
rooms have satellite TV. Pets are welcome. Closed Jan. **€75**

6

EATING

La Petite Maison 34 bd de Lattre de Tassigny ☎ 04 94 54 58 49. Semi-gastronomic restaurant in an eponymous little house, with a pretty garden, pasta from €16 and meat or fish mains from around €20. There are *menus* at €25 and €32. Mon–Sat noon–1.30pm & from 7.15pm.

Côté Jardin 1 rue Gambetta ☎ 04 94 54 10 36. Grilled meat and fish (around €15) and salads from €13.90 in a very pretty garden setting in the centre of Cogolin; there's also an indoor café serving patisserie and light meals. Mon–Sat 8am–6pm; garden open April–Sept only.

6 Grimaud and around

GRIMAUD is a film set of a *village perché*, where the cone of houses enclosing the twelfth-century church, culminating in the spectacular ruins of a medieval castle, appears as a single, perfectly unified entity, decorated by its trees and flowers. The most vaunted street in this ensemble is the narrow **rue des Templiers**, which leads up past the arcaded Gothic house of the Knights Templar to the pure Romanesque **Église St-Michel**. The views from the **château ruins** (free access) are superb, and the monumental, sharply cut serpentine window frames of the shattered edifice stand in mute testimony to its former glory.

ARRIVAL AND INFORMATION   GRIMAUD

By bus Bus #7701 links St-Tropez to Grimaud village; bus #7601 links St-Tropez with Grimaud, Port Grimaud and Sainte Maxime.
Destinations: St-Tropez (up to 9 daily; 25min); La Garde Freinet (3 daily; 15min); Port Grimaud (7 daily; 5min); Ste-Maxime (4 daily; 20min).

Tourist office On the RD558 next to the lift up to the old village (Mon–Sat: April–June & Sept 9am–12.30pm & 2.30–6pm; July & Aug 9am–12.30pm & 3–7pm; Oct–March 9am–12.30pm & 2–5.30pm; ☎ 04 94 55 43 83, ⓦ grimaud-provence.com).

ACCOMMODATION

Camping Charlemagne Le Pont de Bois, rte de Collobrières ☎ 04 94 43 22 90, ⓦ camping-charlemagne.com. Four-star campsite on the road to Collobrières. Facilities include a restaurant, pizzeria, barbecue, bakery and games room, and there's wi-fi too. __€28__

Le Coteau Fleuri Place des Pénitents ☎ 04 94 43 20 17, ⓦ coteaufleuri.fr. Fourteen rooms above an excellent restaurant (see below) in a peaceful corner of the medieval village. Cheaper rooms lack a/c and have showers rather than baths; more expensive ones have views across open countryside. __€99__

EATING AND DRINKING

Le Café de France 5 place Neuve ☎ 04 94 43 20 05. Pleasant place in the old village, with a shady terrace, a two-course lunchtime *formule* for €18 and the likes of chicken *brochettes* or entrecote with truffle butter from around €18–20. March–Oct daily 9am–3pm & 6–10pm; closed Mon & Tues in March.
Le Coteau Fleuri Place des Pénitents ☎ 04 94 43 20 17, ⓦ coteaufleuri.fr. In a tranquil garden setting at the western end of the village, this good hotel restaurant offers

a two-course lunch *menu* at €24, with three courses at €27 and dishes like white asparagus *velouté* with chicken mousse and *fines herbes*. Jan–Oct & last 2 weeks of Dec 12.15–10pm; closed Tues except July & Aug.
Le Pâtissier du Château Bd des Aliziers ☎ 04 94 43 21 16, ⓦ patisserie-du-chateau.com. Bakery and tearoom selling wonderful cakes and fresh, nutty breads, plus breakfasts (€8.50), omelettes from €4.30 and an €11.50 set lunch. Mon, Tues & Thurs–Sun 7am–7pm.

Port Grimaud

The main visitors' entrance is well-signed 800m off the N98, surrounded by parking areas • Boat rental €25 for 30min; boat tours €5.50

Avoiding the St-Tropez traffic chaos is tricky if you're visiting **PORT GRIMAUD**, the ultimate Côte d'Azur property development, half standing, half floating at the head of the Golfe de St-Tropez just north of La Foux and quite separate from Grimaud village itself, though it's part of the same *commune*. It was created in the 1960s by developer François Spoerry – whose tomb is in the village church – as a private pleasure lagoon with waterways for roads and yachts parked at every door. The houses are in exquisitely tasteful old Provençal style, and their owners, amongst them Joan Collins, are extremely well-heeled. Anyone can wander in for a gawp: you don't pay to get in, but you can't explore all the islands without renting a **boat** or taking a crowded boat tour. There are plenty of places to eat and drink, though they are clearly aimed at visitors rather than the residents.

La Garde-Freinet

The attractive village of **LA GARDE-FREINET**, 10km north of Grimaud, was founded in the late twelfth century by people from the nearby villages of St-Clément and Miremer. The original fortified settlement sat further up the hillside, and the foundations of its **fort** are visible above the present-day village. To explore it, you'll have to make the steep one-kilometre clamber along a path from the car park at place de la Planète; the tourist office can supply a simple map, and it's also signposted from place de l'Hubac above the tourist office.

Although attempts have been made to give La Garde-Freinet the chic airs of the nearby coast, it still retains an authentic, rural feel for now, with tempting food shops selling organic produce and good local wines. The **Conservatoire du Patrimoine de la Garde** (Tues–Sat 10am–12.30pm & 2.30–5.30pm, free), next door to the tourist office, has displays on local natural and cultural interest. For hikers, the spectacular 21-kilometre GR9 **route des Crêtes** to the west of the village passes along a tremendously scenic forested ridge, though if the fire risk is high the paths are likely to be closed; the tourist office has information (in English) on the route.

ARRIVAL AND INFORMATION

LA GARDE-FREINET

By bus Buses from Grimaud (up to 4 daily; 15min) and St-Tropez (up to 4 daily; 40min–1hr 5min) arrive at Parking du Stade on the main road at the entrance to the village.

Tourist office Chapelle St Jean, place de l'Hôtel de Ville (April–June, Sept & Oct Mon–Sat 9am–12.30pm &

2–6pm; July & Aug Mon–Sat 9am–1pm & 3–6.30pm, Sun 9am–1pm; Nov–March Mon–Fri 9am–12.30pm & 2–5.30pm; ☎04 94 43 67 41, ⓦwww.la-garde-freinet -tourisme.fr). The office can provide details for the entire Maures region, including suggested walks and hikes.

ACCOMMODATION

Camping de Bérard 5km along the RD558 to Grimaud ☎04 94 43 21 23, ⓦcampingberard.com. Three-star campsite with a swimming pool, free wi-fi, a shop, restaurant and bar, plus musical evenings and plenty of games facilities. Closed Nov–Feb. **€13.70**

Le Mouron Rouge Quartier Le Défend Nord, 1km

north of La Garde Freinet ☎04 94 43 66 33, ⓦlemouronrouge.com. Lovely *chambres d'hôte* in a rustic setting, with well-equipped apartments (for 2–5 people), studios (2–4 people) and a double room with private terrace. There's a *boules* pitch and a large pool. Double **€110**; apartments **€155**; studios **€130**

EATING AND DRINKING

Le Carnotzet 7 place du Marché ☎04 94 43 62 73. Lively bar, art gallery and restaurant with a terrace on the village's most exquisite square. *Plats du jour* from €14 and a *menu* at €24; occasional live jazz July–Sept. Daily noon–2.30/3.30pm & 5.30–11.30pm; closed Tues eve.

La Faucado Av de l'Esplanade ☎04 94 43 60 41. *Restaurant gastronomique* serving beautiful dishes like fillet of beef with pork or lamb *brochette* from local produce in a pretty garden setting; mains around €35. Daily noon–2pm & 7–10pm; closed Tues outside high season.

Ste-Maxime and around

STE-MAXIME, which faces St-Tropez across the gulf, is an archetypal Côte resort: palmed corniche and enormous pleasure-boat harbour, beaches crowded with confident, bronzed windsurfers and waterskiers, a local history museum in a defensive tower that no one goes to, and a proliferation of estate agents. It sprawls a little too far

6

MARKETS OF STE-MAXIME

Ste-Maxime's rather pretty Vieille Ville has several good **markets**: a covered flower and food market on rue Fernand-Bessy (July & Aug Mon–Sat 8am–1pm & 4.30–8pm, Sun 8am–1pm; Sept–June Tues–Sun 8am–1pm); a daily fish market on the port (8am–noon); a Thursday morning food market on place du Marché; a weekly flea market on promenade Simon Lorière (Wed 8am–6pm); and arts and crafts in the pedestrian streets (mid-June to mid-Sept daily 4–11pm).

– most of the coast road to Fréjus is built up – but the magnetic appeal of the water's edge is hard to deny. Compared to its more famous neighbour, though, it's all rather lacking in atmosphere.

Its sandy **beaches**, however, have the Blue Flags for cleanliness that St-Tropez's lack, and there's a string of fancy concessions along the east-facing **Plage de la Nartelle**, 2km from the centre round the Pointe des Sardinaux towards Les Issambres. The Plage de la Nartelle merges seamlessly into the **Plage des Eléphants**, named after the cartoons of Jean de Brunhoff, creator of Babar the elephant, who had a holiday home in Ste-Maxime.

Musée du Phonographe et de la Musique Mécanique

Parc St-Donat, rte de Muy • Wed–Sun: May, June & Sept 10am–noon & 4–6pm; July & Aug 10am–noon • €3 • ☎ 04 94 96 50 52

Ten kilometres north of town on the road to Le Muy, the marvellous **Musée du Phonographe et de la Musique Mécanique** at parc St-Donat is the result of one woman's forty-year obsession with collecting audio equipment. The facade resembles Hansel and Gretel's fantastical biscuit house, but is actually modelled on an eighteenth-century Limonaire mechanical music machine. Inside, displays include one of Thomas Edison's "talking machines" of 1878, the first recording machines of the 1890s and an amplified lyre (1903). Almost half the exhibits still work, and you may find yourself listening to the magical, crackling sounds of an original wax cylinder recording from the 1880s played on the equipment it was made for.

ARRIVAL AND INFORMATION STE-MAXIME

By bus Buses from St-Tropez (up to 12 daily; 35min–1hr) and Saint Raphaël (up to 12 daily; 50min) stop outside the tourist office.

By ferry Ferries to and from St-Tropez run all year except Jan and early Feb (every 15min in high season; 15min; ☎ 04 94 49 29 39, ⦿ bateauxverts.com).

Tourist office 1 promenade Simon-Lorière (June–Aug daily 9am–1pm & 3–7pm; Sept–May Mon–Sat 9am–noon & 2–6pm; ☎ 04 94 55 75 55, ⦿ sainte-maxime.com).

Bike rental ADA/Holiday Bikes, 16 bd Frédéric-Mistral (☎ 04 94 96 16 25, ⦿ holiday-bikes.com).

ACCOMMODATION

Auberge Provençale 19 rue Aristide-Briand ☎ 04 94 55 76 90, ⦿ sainte-maxime.com. Central and very welcoming, this simple, greenery-swathed budget hotel has doubles with showers, a/c, and wi-fi, and some triples and rooms for four. There's also a restaurant with tables in the pretty garden. **€50**

La Baumette 142 rte du Plan de la Tour ☎ 04 94 96 10 92, ⦿ www.labeaumette.com. Three-star campsite some 2km inland from the port, up in the hills off the D25, with a pool, ping pong and *pétanque*. Closed Oct–March. **€28**

Castellamar 8 av G.-Pompidou ☎ 04 94 96 19 97, ⦿ hotelcastellamar.wordpress.com. The best of the cheaper hotels, on the west side of the river, but still close

to the town centre and the sea, with a bar, lounge and tree-shaded terrace. Closed mid-Oct to mid-March. **€67**

Les Cigalons 34 av di Croiseur Léger le Malin ☎ 04 94 96 05 51, ⦿ campingcigalon.com. Two-star seaside option east of town, just 50m from the beach, with wi-fi, children's games and *boules*. It also rents out holiday bungalows. Closed mid-Oct to early April. Bungalows (per week) **€640**; camping **€27**

De la Poste 11 bd Frédéric-Mistral ☎ 04 94 96 18 33, ⦿ hotellieriedusoleil.com. Smart, very central three-star hotel with Cuban-themed decor and a pool. There are various categories and styles of room but all have a/c and either bath or shower. Closed most of Dec. **€145**

EATING

De la Belle Aurore 5 bd Jean-Moulin ☎04 94 96 02 45, ⓦbelleaurore.com. Elegant *restaurant gastronomique* with a stunning setting on the water's edge with views across to St-Tropez. There's a three-course *menu*; otherwise it's around €38 for a main course. April to mid-Oct Mon 12.30–2.30pm, Tues–Sun 12.30–2.30pm & 7.30–9.15pm; closed Wed outside high season.

La Dérive 14 rue Courbet ☎06 12 43 30 75. Lively brasserie with a smart terrace in an atmospheric part of the old town. Pasta from €14, meat dishes from €15 and fish from around €18. There's a sister restaurant, *La Petite Dérive*, next door. Daily lunch & dinner.

Les Issambres to St-Aygulf

Beyond Ste-Maxime, its suburb **Val d'Esquières** merges with **Les Issambres**, the seaside extension of Roquebrune, and **St-Aygulf**, belonging to the *commune* of Fréjus, along the fast and rather dangerous coast road. For all its relentless suburban sprawl, this stretch has its attractions, notably a shoreline of rocky coves and *calanques*, shaded by shapely pines and alternating with golden crescents of sand.

Inland: the Argens Valley

The **River Argens** meets the Mediterranean in unspectacular style between St-Aygulf and St-Raphaël. It's an important source of irrigation for orchards and vines, but as a waterway it has little appeal, being sluggish, full of breeding mosquitoes and on the whole inaccessible. The geographical feature that dominates the lower Argens Valley, and acts as an almost mystical pole of attraction, is the **Rocher de Roquebrune** between the village of **Roquebrune-sur-Argens** and the town of Le Muy.

Roquebrune-sur-Argens and around

The village of **ROQUEBRUNE-SUR-ARGENS** lies on the edge of the Massif des Maures, 12km from the sea, facing the flat valley of the Argens which opens to the northeast. Some of its sixteenth-century defensive towers and ramparts remain, and almost every house within them is four hundred years old or more, joined together by vaulted passageways and tiny cobbled streets. Two fountains face each other across picturesque rue des Portiques, where the houses are arcaded over the pavement; beyond it, ancient houses huddle around the imposing village church.

Maison du Chocolat

Chapelle Saint-Jacques, rue de l'Hospice • Feb–June & Sept Tues–Sat 10am–noon & 2.30–5.30pm; July & Aug Mon–Sat 10am–12.30pm & 3–6.30pm, Sun 10am–1pm; Oct–Dec Thurs–Sat 10am–noon & 2.30–5.30pm • Free • ☎04 94 45 42 65

A seventeenth-century chapel in Roquebrune village is the setting for a delightful collection of chocolate-related ephemera, from antique packaging and advertising to toys and even a chocolate sculpture. It's the private collection of *maître chocolatier* Gérard Courreau, whose boutique is nearby at 2, montée St-Michel.

Rocher de Roquebrune

Three kilometres west of Roquebrune, the rust-red mass of the **Roquebrune rock** erupts unexpectedly out of nothing, as if to some purpose. Even the A8 autoroute thundering past its foot fails to bring it into line with the rest of the coastal scenery glimpsed from the fast lane. To reach it, coming from Roquebrune, take the left fork just after the village, signed to La Roquette; at the next fork you can go left or right depending on which side of the mountain you want to skirt. The right-hand route runs alongside the highway towards **Notre-Dame-de-la-Roquette**, an erstwhile place of pilgrimage (now closed to the public), while the left-hand fork takes you round the quieter, steeper southern side.

The tourist office in Roquebrune can sell you a map outlining four **hiking routes** which ascend the rock from the north, east and west. All but one are challenging in their latter stages, so wear appropriate walking boots.

Chapelle de Ste-Roseline

Château Sainte-Roseline, Les-Arcs-sur Argens, on the D91 • **Chapelle de Ste-Roseline** Tues–Sun: Feb, March & Oct–Dec 2.30–5pm; April & May 2.30–5.30pm; June–Sept 2.30–6pm • Free • **Château Sainte-Roseline** Wine-tasting & buying daily 9am–7pm • Cellar tours Mon–Fri at 2.30pm • Cellar tours €4 • ☎ 04 94 99 50 30, ⓦ sainte-roseline.com

Beneath a crudely buttressed ceiling, the crumbly interior of the **Chapelle de Ste-Roseline** is really rather ghoulish. Saint Roseline was born in 1263 and spent her adolescence disobeying her father by giving food to the poor. On one occasion he caught her and demanded to see the contents of her basket; the food miraculously turned into rose petals. She became the prioress of the abbey and when she died her body refused to decay and it now, supposedly, lies in a glass case in the chapel, shrivelled and brown but not quite a skeleton. What's worse are her eyes – one lifeless, the other staring at you – displayed in a gaudy frame on a wall. Horror objects apart, the chapel has a fabulous mosaic by **Chagall** showing angels laying a table for the saint; some beautifully carved seventeenth-century choir stalls; and an impressive Renaissance rood-loft in which peculiar things happen to the legs of the decorative figures.

The old abbey buildings of which the chapel is part are a private residence belonging to a **wine** grower, and you can also taste and buy the *cru classé* named after the chapel and visit the châteaux's cellars.

Les Arcs-sur-Argens

Eighteen kilometres west of Roquebrune, the picturesque medieval village of **LES ARCS-SUR-ARGENS** has been immaculately restored, with its skyline dominated by a Saracen lookout tower, the sole remnant of a thirteenth-century castle. Les Arcs is one of the centres for the Var wine industry, and at the **Maison des Vins** (open daily: April– Sept Mon– Sat 10am– 7pm, Sun 10am– 6pm; Oct–March Mon–Sat 10am– 6pm, Sun 10am–5pm; ⓦ maison-des-vins.fr) you can taste and buy wine and cheeses and pick up details of local *vignerons* to visit and *routes du vin* to follow: it's on the DN7 just west of the village towards Vidauban.

ARRIVAL AND INFORMATION
THE ARGENS VALLEY

ROQUEBRUNE-SUR-ARGENS

Tourist office 12 av Gabriel-Péri (July & Aug daily 9.30am–12.30pm & 2.30–6.30pm; Sept–June Mon–Sat 9.30am–12.30pm & 2.30–6pm, Thurs opens 10.30am except in June & Sept; ☎ 04 94 19 89 89, ⓦ paysmeresterel .com).

LES ARCS-SUR-ARGENS

By train Les Arcs' *gare SNCF* is on the south side of the village; turn left out of the station and then right into avenue Jean Jaurès to reach the centre.

Destinations Fréjus (11 daily; 13min); St-Raphaël (up to 4 per hr at peak times; 14–17min); Toulon (1–3 per hr; 30min–1hr).

ACCOMMODATION AND EATING

ROQUEBRUNE-SUR-ARGENS

La Tour 401 bd Jean Jaurès ☎ 04 94 81 22 16. Creative cooking in an inconspicuous setting on the edge of the old village, close to the Maison du Terroir, and with a €19 *menu*. Mon noon–2pm, Tues–Sat noon–2pm & 7–10pm.

LES ARCS-SUR-ARGENS

Le Logis du Guetteur Place du Château ☎ 04 94 99 51 10, ⓦ logisduguetteur.com. Charming three-star hotel in a lovely setting at the top of Les Arcs' beautiful Vieux Village,

clustering at the base of the Saracen tower and with just twelve rooms. The good restaurant has *menus* from €29.50 to €99. Daily noon–2pm & 7–9.30pm. €154

La Vigne à Table At the Maison des Vins DN7 ☎ 04 94 47 48 47, ⓦ francois-pillard.com. The Maison des Vins' very beautiful restaurant offers classic flavour combinations like roast sea bass with fennel and *sauce vierge*, or fillet of beef Rossini with morel sauce, plus a three-course lunch *menu* for €25. Tues, Thurs, Fri & Sat noon–2pm & 7–10pm, Wed & Sun noon–2pm.

Fréjus

FRÉJUS – along with its neighbour St-Raphaël (see p.295) 3km east – dates back to
the Romans. It was established as a naval base under Julius Caesar and Augustus, and
its ancient port, known as Forum Julii, consisted of 2km of quays connected by a
walled canal to the sea (which was considerably closer then). After the battle of
Actium in 31 BC, the ships of Antony and Cleopatra's defeated fleet were brought
here. Little remains of the Roman walls that circled the city, and the once-important
port silted up and was filled in after the Revolution. Today you can see a scattering of
Roman remains, along with the medieval **Cité Episcopale**, or cathedral complex, which
takes up two sides of **place Formigé**, the marketplace and heart of both contemporary
and medieval Fréjus.

The area between Fréjus and the sea is now the suburb of **Fréjus-Plage**, with its vast
1980s marina, **Port-Fréjus**, a little over 2km from the centre of the old city. Both Fréjus
and Fréjus-Plage merge seamlessly with St-Raphaël, which in turn merges with
Boulouris to the east.

The Roman remains

A tour of the Roman remains gives you a good idea of the extent of Forum Julii,
but they are scattered throughout and beyond the town centre and take a full day
to get around. As you turn right out of the *gare SNCF* it's a 400m walk down
boulevard Severin-Decuers to the **Butte St-Antoine**, against whose east wall the
waters of the port would have lapped, and which once was capped by a fort. It
was one of the port's defences, and one of the ruined **towers** may have been a
lighthouse. A lane around the southern wall follows the quayside (some stretches
are visible) the short distance from boulevard Severin-Decuers to the medieval
Lanterne d'Auguste, which was built on the Roman foundations of a structure
marking the entrance of the canal into the ancient harbour. Retracing your steps

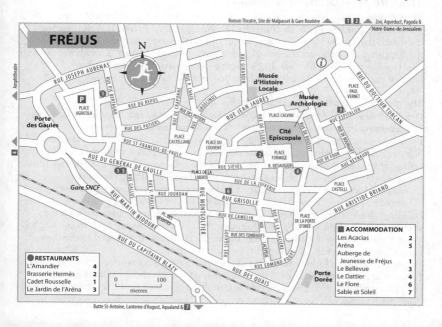

FRÉJUS

RESTAURANTS
L'Amandier 4
Brasserie Hermès 2
Cadet Rousselle 1
Le Jardin de l'Aréna 3

ACCOMMODATION
Les Acacias 2
Aréna 5
Auberge de
Jeunesse de Fréjus 1
Le Bellevue 3
Le Dattier 4
Le Flore 6
Sable et Soleil 7

FREJUS PASSES

If you're planning to visit most of Fréjus's sights, it may be worth getting the seven-day **Fréjus'Pass** (€4.60), which gives access to the amphitheatre, Roman theatre and Musée Archéologique, or the **Pass Intégral** (€6.60), which adds access to the cathedral cloisters and baptistry. The passes are available from the individual sights.

6

to the centre, on rue des Moulins, are the arcades of the **Porte d'Orée**, positioned on the former harbour's edge alongside what was probably a **bath complex**.

The amphitheatre

Rue Henri-Vadon • Tues–Sun: May–Oct 9.30am–12.30pm & 2–6pm; Nov–April 9.30am–12.30pm & 2–5pm • €2 • ☎ 04 94 51 34 31, Ⓦ www.frejus.fr

On the southwestern fringe of the old town, the Roman **Porte des Gaules** marks the approach on rue Henri-Vadon to the **amphitheatre**, which had a capacity of around ten thousand. Fit to host concerts again after a refurbishment in 2012, its upper tiers have been reconstructed, but the vaulted galleries on the ground floor are largely original.

The Roman theatre and around

Rue du Théâtre Romain • Tues–Sun: May–Oct 9.30am–12.30pm & 2–6pm; Nov–April 9.30am–12.30pm & 2–5pm • €2 • ☎ 04 94 53 58 75, Ⓦ www.frejus.fr

The **Roman theatre** is immediately north of the old town, around 300m from the tourist information office. Its original seats have long gone, though it's still used for shows in summer. To the northeast, in the parc Aurelienne at the far end of avenue du XVème-Corps-d'Armée, six arches are visible of the 40km **aqueduct**, which was once as high as the ramparts.

The Cité Episcopale and around

The **Cité Episcopale**, or cathedral close, takes up two sides of **place Formigé**, the marketplace and heart of both contemporary and medieval Fréjus. It comprises the cathedral, flanked by the fourteenth-century bishop's palace, now the Hôtel de Ville, the baptistry, cloisters and archeological museum. You can wander through the modern courtyard of the Hôtel de Ville, but you get a better view of the orange Esterel stone walls of the Episcopal Palace from rue de Beausset.

The cloisters, baptistry and cathedral

48 rue du Cardinal Fleury • June–Sept daily 9am–6.30pm; Oct–May Tues–Sun 9am–noon & 2–5pm • Cloisters & bapistry same ticket €5.50; guided tours in English available; cathedral free • ☎ 04 94 51 26 30, Ⓦ cathedrale-frejus.monuments-nationaux.fr

By far the most beautiful and engaging component of the ensemble is the **cloisters**. Slender marble columns, carved in the twelfth century, support a fourteenth-century ceiling of wooden panels painted with apocalyptic creatures. Out of the original 1200 pictures, 400 remain, each about the size of this page. The subjects include multiheaded monsters, mermaids, satyrs and scenes of bacchanalian debauchery.

The oldest part of the complex is the **baptistry**, one of France's most ancient buildings, built in the fourth or fifth century and, as such, contemporary with the decline and fall of the city's Roman founders. Its two doorways are of different heights, signifying the enlarged spiritual stature of the baptized, and it was used in the days of early Christianity when adult baptism was still the norm.

Parts of the early Gothic **cathedral** may belong to a tenth-century church, but its best features, apart from the coloured diamond-shaped tiles on the spire, are Renaissance: the choir stalls, a wooden crucifix on the left of the entrance, and the intricately carved doors with scenes of a Saracen massacre.

Musée Archéologie

Place Calvini • Tues–Sun: May–Oct 9.30am–12.30pm & 2–6pm; Nov–April 9.30am–12.30pm & 2–5pm • €2 • ☎ 04 94 52 15 78, Ⓦ www.frejus.fr

The **Musée Archéologie** on the upper storey of the cloisters has as its star pieces a complete Roman mosaic of a leopard and a copy of a renowned double-headed bust of Hermes, alongside various archeological finds from the Roman town, from workaday ceramics to domestic artefacts and tombs.

Musée d'Histoire Locale

153 rue Jean-Jaurès • April–Sept Tues–Sun 9.30am–12.30pm & 2–6pm; Oct–March Tues–Sun 9.30am–12.30pm & 2–5pm • €2 • ☎ 04 94 51 64 01

Close to the Cité Episcopale in an old bourgeois townhouse on Jean-Jaurès, the small **Musée d'Histoire Locale** has reconstructions of past life, including an old school classroom, plus displays on traditional local trades and a film about the Malpasset dam tragedy of 1959 (see box, p.294).

Around Fréjus

The environs of Fréjus hold several reminders of France's colonial past, a beautiful chapel decorated by Cocteau and evidence of a terrible disaster which befell Fréjus half a century ago. More light-hearted diversions are to be found in the town's zoo and water park.

Pagode Hong Hien and the Mémorial des Guerres en Indochine

Pagoda Hong Hien 13 rue Henri-Giraud • Daily: April–Oct 10am–7pm; Nov–April 10am–noon & 2–5pm • €2 • ☎ 04 94 53 25 29 Mémorial des Guerres en Indochine Av du général Calliès • ☎ 04 94 44 42 90 • Mon & Wed–Sun 10am–5.30pm • Free

About 2km north of the town centre at the junction of rue Henri-Giraud and the DN7 to Cannes, there's a Vietnamese pagoda, the **Pagode Hong Hien**, built by colonial troops and still maintained as a Buddhist temple. Alongside it stands the massive **memorial** to the dead of the Indo-Chinese wars of the 1940s and 1950s. It is inscribed with the name of every fallen Frenchman; the sheer length of the lists suggests that the years 1950–54 were the most bloody.

The Mosquée Missiri de Djennè

Rte des Combattants d'Afrique du Nord • July–Sept Tues–Sun 9.30am–12.30pm & 2–6pm • €2

An unlikely remnant of France's imperial past comes in the shape of an abandoned mosque, built by French colonial troops. The **Mosquée Missiri de Djenné** is on the left

---

OUTDOOR AND KIDS' ACTIVITIES AROUND FRÉJUS

Around Fréjus, rugged terrain for **cyclists** is found in the forested hills of the **Massif de l'Esterel** to the northeast of town; there are more than 100km of signposted trails in and around Fréjus. The tourist office in St Raphaël (see p.296) sells a **map/guide** to the Esterel for €8.50. There are cycle trails at the **Base Nature François Leotard** (daily: mid-June to mid-Sept 8am–midnight; mid-Sept to mid-June 8am–11pm; free; ☎ 04 94 51 91 10), a large public park just west of Port-Fréjus on the coast, as well as a beach, a public swimming pool and sports pitches.

Opposite the Base Nature is Fréjus's water park, **Aqualand**, with all manner of water slides and pools (daily: last 2 weeks of June & late Aug to early Sept 10am–6pm; July to late Aug 10am–7pm; ☎ 04 94 51 82 52, Ⓦ aqualand.fr). Equally appealing to children is the **zoo** in Le Capitou, close to exit 38 from the autoroute on the D4 heading north, which has everything from big cats to marsupials and apes (daily: March–May & Sept–Oct 10am–5pm; June–Aug 10am–6pm; Nov–Feb 10.30am–4.30pm; €14.50, children aged 3–9 €10; children under 3 free; ☎ 04 98 11 37 37, Ⓦ zoo-frejus.com; bus #1 or #2).

6

THE MALPASSET DAM DISASTER

The bleakest day in Fréjus's recent history is recalled by the **site de Malpasset**, deep in the Forêt Communale de Fréjus and signposted off the *rond point* du Gargalon on the D37. At 9.13pm on the rainy night of December 2 1959, the new Malpasset dam across the Reyran valley collapsed, releasing 50 million cubic metres of water to create a forty-metre wave which swept along the narrow valley, obliterating everything – including the construction workers' camp on the site of the A8 autoroute, just below the dam. As the wave neared the coast it fanned out, widening the trail of destruction; it was still 3m high when it raced through Fréjus twenty minutes later. Fifty farms were swamped and some 423 people killed; the death toll was never accurately established as many victims were swept out to sea. Afterwards, it was found that the geological survey had failed to pinpoint a fault line at the site, which allowed pressure to build up under the dam. Far from failing structurally, the entire left side of the dam was simply pivoted off its foundations by the water. Long before you reach Malpasset, great chunks of steel-reinforced concrete litter the riverbed like outsized boulders. The road fords the river then passes under the autoroute to a car park, from which a path (free access during daylight hours) climbs to a viewing point. The dam is left more or less as it was, its graceful arc poignantly terminated a few metres from the valley side. Forest has re-colonized the valley floor behind it. At the time of writing the access road – undermined, ironically, by the stream in the valley bottom – was being reconstructed.

---

off the D4 to Bagnols, in the middle of an army camp 2km from the RN7 junction. A strange, guava-coloured, fort-like building, it's a replica of a Sudanese mosque in Mali, sadly fenced off most of the time, though much of the interior is visible from outside.

Notre-Dame-de-Jerusalem

Rte de Cannes • Tues–Sun: May–Oct 9.30am–12.30pm & 2–6pm; Nov–April 9.30am–12.30pm & 2–5pm • Free • ☏ 04 94 53 27 06

Just off the DN7 at La Tour de Mare, 5.6km from the centre of Fréjus, is the last of Jean Cocteau's artistic landmarks, the chapel of **Notre-Dame-de-Jerusalem**. Conceived as the church for a failed artistic community, the octagonal building was not completed until after Cocteau's death in 1963, and the interior was completed to Cocteau's plans by Edouard Dermit. The Last Supper scene inside includes a self-portrait of Cocteau; the building's exterior is covered in elegantly simple mosaics and its floors with vibrant blue tiles.

ARRIVAL AND INFORMATION   FRÉJUS

By train Trains to St-Raphaël are much more frequent than those to Fréjus, so it's often easiest to alight there and take the #3, #4, #5, #6, #7 or #14 Agglobus, which run frequently between the two towns (15min). There are also trains between St-Raphaël and Fréjus *gare SNCF*, which is on the south side of the Vieille Ville (9 daily; 3–4min).

By bus The *gare routière* is on the east side of the town centre at Clos de la Tour, close to the tourist office (☏ 04 94 53 78 46). Note that the inter-town coastal bus route #7601 doesn't serve Fréjus town centre but continues to St-Raphaël's *gare routière*.

Tourist office Le Florus II, 249 rue Jean-Jaurès (June–Sept daily Mon–Fri 9am–1pm & 2–7pm; Oct–May Mon–Sat 9.20am–noon & 2–6pm; ☏ 04 94 51 83 83, ⓦ www.frejus.fr).

Bike rental Holiday Bikes, 238 av de Verdun (☏ 04 94 44 22 37, ⓦ holidaybikes.fr).

ACCOMMODATION

Aréna 145 rue de Général-de-Gaulle ☏ 04 94 17 09 40, ⓦ hotel-frejus-arena.com. Comfortable three-star hotel in three buildings grouped around a pool and luxuriant garden, close to the *gare SNCF*. Rooms have flatscreen TV, a/c and free wi-fi. There's also a good restaurant. **€130**

Auberge de Jeunesse de Fréjus Chemin du Counillier ☏ 04 94 53 18 75, ⓦ www.fuaj.org. Located in a small pine grove, 2km from Fréjus centre on bus #7 or #10 (stop "Auberge de Jeunesse"). Reception closed 11am–5.30pm.

Dorms **€13.20**

Le Bellevue Place Paul-Vernet ☏ 04 94 17 12 20, ⓦ hotelbellevue-frejus.com. Basic two-star hotel with fairly simple, a/c rooms above a bar next to the bus station and a large car park. Rooms have flatscreen TV and free wi-fi; most have shower and WC. **€69**

Le Flore 35 rue Grisolle ☏ 04 94 51 38 35, ⓦ hotelleflore.com. The nicest budget option in the old town is this pretty, wisteria-clad two-star. It won't win any awards for decor but rooms have shower and WC, a/c, free wi-fi and flatscreen TV. **€60**

Sable et Soleil 158 rue Paul-Arène, Fréjus-Plage ☎06 73 09 84 44, ⓦhotel-sableetsoleil.com. A pleasant, small, modern hotel, 300m from the sea near the port. All rooms have free internet and private terrace, and there's secure parking. **€89**

CAMPING

Les Acacias 370 rue Henri-Giraud, 2.5km from the old town, close to the pagoda Hong Hien ☎04 94 53 21 22, ⓦcampingacacias.fr. Leafy, moderate-sized three-star campsite with 83 pitches, children's play facilities, a swimming pool and spa. Closed Nov–March. **€36.50**

Le Dattier 1156 rue des Combattants d'Afrique du Nord ☎04 94 40 88 93, ⓦcamping-le-dattier.com. A four-star site 3.5km north of Fréjus, with a restaurant and bar, pool and sports faciltiies. They also rent out mobile homes. Oct–March. **€28.50 per tent**

6

EATING AND DRINKING

Fréjus is not a bad place for menu-browsing and café-lounging, with a scattering of reasonably priced places to **eat** in the Vieille Ville. There's a string of options to choose from at Fréjus-Plage, and more upmarket seafood outlets at Port-Fréjus. For **nightlife**, the port and beach are the places to aim for.

CAFÉS AND RESTAURANTS

L'Amandier 19 rue Desaugiers ☎04 94 53 48 77, ⓦrestaurant-lamandier.com. Critically lauded restaurant in the Vieille Ville, with a €25 *menu* with baked fillet of sea bream with herb mash and a €38 *menu gourmand*. Mon & Wed 7.30–9.30pm, Tues & Thurs–Sat noon–1.30pm & 7.30–9.30pm.

Brasserie Hermès 15 place Formigé ☎04 94 17 26 02. Unpretentious and affordable brasserie with a terrace facing the cathedral. There's a €13.50 two-course lunchtime *formule* and a big choice of salads and pizza from around €9, plus a few pasta dishes at slightly higher prices. Daily 11am–11pm.

Cadet Rousselle 25 place Agricola ☎04 94 53 36 92. Perennially popular crêperie with a wide choice of sweet crêpes and savoury *galettes* and a three-course weekday *menu* for €13. They also serve main-course-sized salads from €6. Tues, Wed & Fri–Sun noon–1.30pm & 6.30–8.30pm, Thurs 6.30–8.30pm.

Le Jardin de l'Aréna 145 rue de Général-de-Gaulle ☎04 94 17 09 40, ⓦhotel-frejus-arena.com. You can dine on the leafy terrace at the *Aréna* hotel's *restaurant gastronomique*, with dishes like prawns with mesclun and balsamic caramel or lobster with olive oil and *bisque*. *Menus* €23–38. Tues–Fri & Sun noon–2pm & 7–9.30pm, Mon & Sat 7–9.30pm.

St-Raphaël

A large resort and now one of the richest towns on the Côte, **ST-RAPHAËL** became fashionable at the turn of the twentieth century. It lost many of its *belle époque* mansions and hotels in the bombardments of World War II; some, like the *Continental*, have been rebuilt from scratch in a modern style, others have undergone more subtle restoration. The sea is the main draw, with family-friendly sandy beaches and plenty of watersports options.

The Vieille Ville

The **Vieille Ville**, beyond place Carnot on the inland side of the railway line, is no longer the town's commercial focus but a good place to stroll and browse. On rue des Templiers the fortified Romanesque church of **San Raféu** has fragments of the Roman aqueduct that brought water from Fréjus in its courtyard, along with a local **history and underwater archeology museum** (Tues–Sat 9am–noon & 2–6pm; free; ⓦwww.musee-saintraphael .com). You can climb to the top of the fortified tower for views over the town and sea.

The modern town

Dominating the modern town is St-Raphaël's principal landmark, the towering, florid late nineteenth-century church of **Notre Dame de la Victoire de Lépante**, on boulevard Félix-Martin. Its interior houses a representation of St Raphaël, the symbol of the city.

6

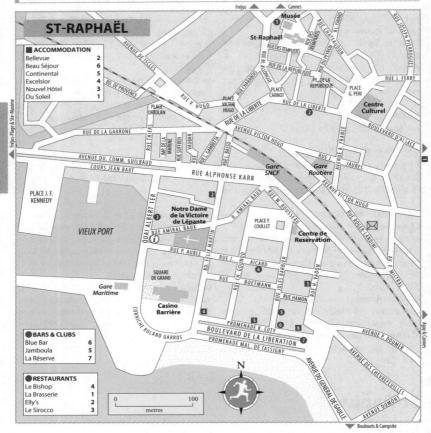

From here, it's a brief stroll to the broad promenade René-Coty which is lined with grand hotels – look out for the opulent stucco flowers adorning La Rocquerousse apartment buildings, next to the *Hôtel Beau Séjour*. The promenade culminates with the grandiose Résidence La Méditerranée, built in 1914, at 1 avenue Paul-Doumer: continue along here, and you'll find a fine *fin-de-siècle* villa, Les Palmiers.

The beaches and coast

St-Raphaël's **beaches** stretch west of the port into Fréjus-Plage and east of the Jardin Bonaparte at the entrance to the old port to the modern **Marina Santa Lucia**, where there are opportunities for every kind of **watersport** (see box opposite).

ARRIVAL AND INFORMATION

ST RAPHAËL

By train St-Raphaël's *gare SNCF* is in rue Waldeck-Rousseau in the centre of town on the Marseille–Ventimiglia line.
Destinations Cannes (2–5 per hour; 25–40min); Fréjus (9 daily; 3–4min); Nice (2–5 per hour; 55min–1hr 15min).
By bus The *gare routière* is at 100 rue Victor Hugo, across the rail line behind the *gare SNCF*.
Destinations Fréjus (frequent; 15–20min); Ste-Maxime

(up to 16 daily; 50min); St-Tropez (up to 12 daily; 1hr 25–1hr 55min).
Tourist office Quai Albert-1er (July & Aug daily 9am–7pm; Sept–June Mon–Sat 9am–12.30pm & 2–6.30pm).
☎ 04 94 19 52 52, ⍟ www.saint-raphael.com).
Bike and moped rental JLP Bike, 345 av du Général Leclerc ☎ 04 94 83 95 57.

ST-RAPHAËL WATERSPORTS AND BOAT TRIPS

With the pristine coast of the Corniche de l'Esterel on its doorstep, the sea is a strong draw here. You can explore the Esterel coast on a **boat trip**, dive to discover the coast's rich marine archeology or simply hire a boat. There are more than thirty **diving sites** between the bay of St-Raphaël and Agay, and the area is well-known for its numerous wrecks, ranging from Gallo-Roman ships to the minesweepers, barges and landing ships lost during the 1944 Allied landings. In addition to the activities listed below, the tourist office has information on a wide range of sea- and land-based activities in and around St-Raphaël.

6

BOAT TRIPS

Les Bateaux de Saint Raphaël Quai Nomy on the south side of the Vieux Port (☎ 04 94 95 17 46, 🌐 bateauxsaintraphael.com). Boat trips to St-Tropez (daily; 1hr; €24 return), the *calanques* of the Esterel coast (Mon, Wed, Thurs, Fri & Sun; half-day/day €16/€25) and Porquerolles (July & Aug; weekly; €45). Ticket office: April & May Mon–Sat 9am–noon & 2–5pm, Sun 2–5pm; June & Sept daily 9am–noon & 2–5pm; July & Aug Mon–Sat 9am–7pm, Fri also 9–10.30pm, Sun 9–11.45am & 1.30–7pm; Oct Mon 2–5pm, Tues–Sat 9am–noon & 2–5pm.

DIVING

Club Sous l'Eau Port Santa Lucia, east of the town centre (☎ 04 94 95 90 33, 🌐 clubsousleau.com). Takes divers out to the numerous wartime wrecks and underwater archeological sites off the coast.

SAILING

Club Nautique Saint Raphaël Bd Général de Gaulle ☎ 04 94 95 11 66. Sailing courses for adults and children during the school holidays: one-week Catamaran course €102 child/€143 adult. One-hour sailing tuition from €51.

ACCOMMODATION

Bellevue 22 bd Félix-Martin ☎ 04 94 19 90 10, 🌐 hotel-bellevue-saintraphael.com. Budget two-star hotel in the town centre. It's nothing fancy but rooms do have a/c, flatscreen TV plus wi-fi. It smells nice, being above a bakery, and it's open all year round. **€55**

Beau Séjour Promenade René-Coty ☎ 04 94 95 03 75, 🌐 beausejour-hotel.com. Seafront hotel, with a pleasant bar and terrace and 41 soundproofed, a/c rooms – some of them very spacious, with balconies and sea views, and all with flatscreen TV. **€172**

Continental Promenade René-Coty ☎ 04 94 83 87 87, 🌐 hotels-continental.com. A modern seafront hotel rebuilt on the site of its illustrious predecessor in 1993, with a/c, private parking and light, spacious, soundproofed non-smoking rooms, each with minibar, satellite TV and safety deposit box. **€135**

Excelsior 192 Bd Félix-Martin ☎ 04 94 95 02 42, 🌐 excelsior-hotel.com. The handsome old *Excelsior* is one of the rare seafront survivors from St-Raphaël's prewar heyday, with forty tastefully decorated a/c rooms plus a restaurant and English-style pub. More expensive rooms have sea views. **€160**

Nouvel Hôtel 66 rue Henri-Vadon ☎ 04 94 95 23 30, 🌐 nouvelhotel.net. A cheerful and pleasant two-star budget option, with two stars, simple but attractive decor and double rooms with TV, en-suite shower and WC. **€60**

Du Soleil 47 bd du Domaine du Soleil ☎ 04 94 83 10 00, 🌐 hotel-dusoleil.com; bus #8 to Les Plaines. Charming non-smoking hotel occupying a very pretty old villa east of the town centre. Rooms have flatscreen TV, free wi-fi, bath or shower and most have a balcony or terrace. **€88**

EATING

You'll find plenty of pizzerias, crêperies and restaurants around the Vieux Port, Port Santa Lucia and along the promenades, but the more interesting options are all inland. There are daily **food markets** on place Victor Hugo and place de la République (7am–1pm; closed Mon in winter).

Le Bishop 84 rue Jean Aicard ☎ 04 94 95 04 63 Popular restaurant dishing up the Provençal staples at reasonable prices, a couple of blocks back from the beach. Niçoise-style tripe €13, *andouillette* €13; *menus* from €19.90. Mon–Sat noon–2pm & 7–10pm.

La Brasserie 6 av de Valescure ☎ 04 94 95 25 00,

🌐 labrasserietg.fr. Traditional Provençal dishes are cooked to a high standard at this smart modern restaurant on the edge of the Vieille Ville. *Bourride* €18.90, aioli €17.90, and *pieds et paquets* Marseille-style €14.90. Mon–Sat noon–2.30pm & 7–11pm.

Elly's 54 rue de la Liberté ☎ 04 94 83 63 39,

6

ⓦ www.elly-s.com. Elegant restaurant serving the likes of seared *tournedos* of tuna with truffled gnocchi or fillet beef with bordelaise sauce, with fancy Bordeaux and Burgundies alongside Provençal wines. *Menus* €30–65. Mon–Sat 7–9.30pm, Sun noon–1.30pm & 7–9.30pm.

Le Sirocco 35 quai Albert 1ᵉʳ ☏ 04 94 95 39 99, ⓦ lesirocco .fr. Smart but rather staid portside restaurant specializing in fish, with bouillabaisse or *bourride* at €38 and a €52.50 *menu* with lobster. The cheapest *menu* is €19.50, and there's plenty of Provençal wine. Wed–Sun noon–1.30pm & 7–9.30pm.

DRINKING, NIGHTLIFE AND ENTERTAINMENT

If you're in St-Raphaël in early July, try to catch some of the bands playing in the international Festival des Jazz: ask at the tourist office for details of venues. St-Raphaël's **casino** is on Square de Gand overlooking the Vieux Port (daily 10am–3/4am; ☏ 04 98 11 17 77, ⓦ lucienbarriere.com).

Blue Bar 133 rue Jules Barbier ☏ 04 94 95 15 87. There's a big range of Belgian beers from €5.20 at this unpretentious, pub-like place on the seafront. Cocktails start at around €7.20 and they serve fancy ice creams (€6.50), inexpensive snacks and salads. Daily 7am–3am.
Jamboula 133 rue Jules-Barbier ☏ 04 94 40 61 97. Disco with a bias towards black music and a hip-hop to R&B playlist,

plus karaoke. Entry with *conso* €13. Wed–Sun 10pm–7am.
La Réserve Promenade René Coty ☏ 06 09 87 25 58, ⓦ la-reserve.fr. Swish seafront disco, improbably situated beneath a road junction, that attracts some big-name international DJs. Entry with *conso* €15, spirits priced by the bottle, beers €9. Summer nightly 11.30pm–7am; winter Fri & Sat only.

The Esterel

The 32-kilometre **Corniche de l'Esterel**, the sole stretch of wild coast between St-Raphaël and the Italian border, remains untouched by property development – at least between **Anthéor** and **Le Trayas** – its backdrop a 250-million-year-old arc of brilliant red volcanic rock tumbling down to the sea from the harsh crags of the **Massif de l'Esterel**. From the two major routes between Fréjus and La Napoule (the coastal D559 and rail line, and the inland DN7), minor roads lead into this steeply contoured and once deeply wooded wild terrain. The **shoreline**, meanwhile, is a mass of little beaches – some sand, some shingle – cut by rocky promontories.

The inland route

The high, hairpin **inland route** along the old DN7 route de Cannes is a dramatic drive, and once you pass Notre Dame de Jerusalem on the northernmost tip of the Fréjus-St-Raphaël agglomeration it's largely free of development. It's an ancient route, in parts following the Roman Via Aurelia.

Because of the fire risk many of the minor roads and paths are subject to closure during the summer months: call the **fire information line** on ☏ 04 98 10 55 41 to check the current situation. All fires, and even cigarettes, are banned all year round, and vehicles are restricted to authorized routes. This makes **walking** even more enjoyable, though camping is strictly forbidden. The tourist office in St-Raphaël (see p.296) can provide details of paths and of the peaks that make the most obvious destinations. The highest point is **Mont Vinaigre**, which you can almost reach by road on the N7; a short, signposted footpath leads up to the summit. At 618m it's hardly a mountain, but the view from the top is spectacular.

The corniche

The long, winding coastal route east of St-Raphaël is one of the most exhilarating drives on the Côte d'Azur, its rugged scenery and deep-blue waters made more memorable still by the extraordinary, rust-red colour of the rock. Along the twisting coast road between Anthéor and Le Trayas, each easily reached **beach** has its summer snack-van, and by clambering over rocks you can usually find a near-deserted cove.

Prior to the twentieth-century creation of the corniche, the coastal communities here were linked only by sea; these days, the coast is altogether more accessible even for non-drivers, with half a dozen train stations and at least four buses a day between St-Raphaël and Le Trayas on weekdays. Boats also run along the coast from St-Raphaël's *gare maritime* (see p.296). Hikers can follow the *sentier littoral* as far as Agay, though the route is occasionally blocked by the campsites along the shoreline.

6

Le Dramont

The merest snatch of clear hillside separates Boulouris from the hamlet of **LE DRAMONT**, 7km east of St-Raphaël, where the landing of the 36th American division in August 1944 is commemorated by a memorial and by the name of the largest beach – plage du Débarquement. The path around the wooded, lighthouse-capped **Cap du Dramont** gives fine views out to sea, with the Île d'Ôr – a rocky islet capped by a mock-medieval tower – providing a popular target for camera-snapping 200m offshore. East of the Cap du Dramont there's another modest crescent of beach at Camp Long.

Agay and Anthéor

Le Dramont's close neighbour **AGAY** is one of the least pretentious resorts of the Côte d'Azur, beautifully situated around a deep horseshoe bay edged by sand beaches, red porphyry cliffs and pines. Both Agay and its eastern neighbour **ANTHÉOR** suffer a little from the creeping contagion of housing estates edging ever higher up their hills, but once you get above the concrete line, at the **Sommet du Rastel**, for example (signposted from Agay's avenue du Bourg or boulevard du Rastel), you can begin to appreciate this wonderful terrain. Note, however, that many of the roads leading off the corniche are open to residents only.

Le Trayas

LE TRAYAS is on the highest point of the corniche and its shoreline is the most rugged, with wonderful inlets to explore. You can also trek to the Pic de l'Ours from here (about 3hr; the route starts from the *gare SNCF*).

ACCOMMODATION AND EATING   THE ESTEREL

Agay Soleil 1152 bd de la Plage, Agay ☎ 04 94 82 00 79, ⓦ agay-soleil.com. Three-star campsite on the horseshoe-shaped bay of Agay on the breathtaking corniche de l'Esterel, with mobile homes and chalets to rent as well as pitches. Closed Nov to late March. **€29.80**

Les Flots Bleus Bd Eugène Brieux, Anthéor ☎ 04 94 44 80 21, ⓦ www.hotel-restaurant-les-flots-bleus.com. Good-value two-star *Logis de France* hotel in Anthéor, with sea views, individually decorated rooms, private parking and a restaurant. Closed Nov–March. **€70**

Relais des Calanques Rte des Escalles, Le Trayas ☎ 04 94 44 14 06, ⓦ relaisdescalanques.fr. Small hotel/restaurant on the corniche in Le Trayas, nestling above a small cove and with just twelve rooms and a private terrace right on the water's edge. The restaurant menu is fish-focused; the speciality is *marmite du pêcheur* (€37). Closed Oct–March. **€120**

Les Rives de l'Agay Av du Gratadis, Agay ☎ 04 94 82 02 74, ⓦ camping-agay.fr. Well-equipped campsite 400m inland on the D100 road to Valescure in Agay, with a heated pool, grocery store and restaurant and just 103 pitches. **€38**

Cannes and the western Riviera

STE-MARGUERITE, ÎLES DE LÉRINS

Cannes and the western Riviera

The stretch of coast between the Massif de l'Esterel and the River Var makes up the western French Riviera. As much legend as reality, the region has been a playground for the rich and famous for the better part of two centuries. Such names as Cannes, Juan-les-Pins and Antibes conjure up powerful images, of a fantasy land where the sparkling blue sea is speckled with boards, bikes and skis, and where extravagant yachts moor tantalizingly out of reach, disgorging their privileged cargo to fill the glamorous bars and restaurants or populate the latest event in the celebrity-studded calendar. To some extent, that's still true, even though it's long since lost any sense of exclusivity: this now ranks among the most developed and densely populated coastal strips in Europe.

7

Summer crowds and traffic can make travelling slow and unpleasant – speedy **train** connections offer a convenient alternative to driving – but once you're here, each individual resort has its own appeal. It's also possible simply to visit the coast on day-trips, and stay inland in historic towns like **Vence** and **Grasse**, or lovely villages such as **St-Paul-de-Vence** and **Tourrettes-sur-Loup**.

Though it shares much in common with the coast east of the Var, the western Riviera has a rather different **history**. Unlike the formerly Savoyard (and strongly Italianate) Nice and Menton, Cannes and Antibes were always Provençal, the latter almost a border town, just west of the frontier on the Var. The fishing village of **Cannes** itself was discovered in the 1830s by a retired British chancellor, Lord Brougham, who couldn't get to Nice because of a cholera epidemic. From the start, tourism here was more exclusive than in bustling, raffish Nice, with aristocrats and royals from across Europe and North America building opulent mansions in the years before World War I. During the 1920s, as Coco Chanel popularized the suntan and the glamorous *Eden Roc* on Cap d'Antibes stayed open year-round for the first time, the season switched from winter to summer. A new kind of elite took centre stage, notably film stars like Charlie Chaplin and Maurice Chevalier; the era was immortalized in F. Scott Fitzgerald's *Tender is the Night*. Then, in 1936, the socialist government of Léon Blum granted French workers their first paid holidays, and the democratization of the Riviera began.

War in 1939 interrupted everything – including Cannes' first film festival – but by the 1950s **mass tourism** took off in earnest and the real transformation began. Locals quickly realized that servicing visitors was far more profitable than working on the land or at sea, and over-zealous property development and sheer pressure of numbers have been problems ever since. The coast is now built up for its entire length, while inland the hills between the villages are carpeted with disorientating, featureless suburbia.

The appeal of the coast, however, remains clear enough, most notably in the legacies of the **artists** who stayed here: **Picasso** in Antibes and Vallauris; **Léger** in Biot; **Matisse** in Vence; **Renoir** in Cagnes-sur-Mer; and all of them in St-Paul-de-Vence and Haut-de-Cagnes.

BOULEVARD DE LA CROISETTE, CANNES

Highlights

❶ Boulevard de la Croisette, Cannes Pop on your shades, turn on your iPod and rollerblade along the Riviera's most glamorous seafront. **See p.305**

❷ Îles de Lérins Clean, pine-scented air, peaceful walks and shimmering rocks and water, just minutes from the centre of Cannes. **See p.312**

❸ Musée d'Art Classique, Mougins As well as Classical and contemporary art, this new museum owns a staggering array of beautiful ancient arms and armour. **See p.314**

❹ Jazz à Juan The Riviera's most renowned jazz festival brings big names to Juan-les-Pins every summer. **See p.318**

❺ Plage de la Salis, Cap d'Antibes This beautiful, sandy public beach is the laziest way to enjoy the millionaires' cape. **See p.321**

❻ Chapelle du Rosaire Matisse's final masterpiece – the modern master oversaw every stunning detail of this profoundly moving convent chapel in Vence. **See p.335**

❼ St-Paul-de-Vence A favourite haunt of Riviera artists, this quintessential Provençal hill village makes an exhilarating escape from the coast. **See p.338**

❽ Fondation Maeght Art and architecture fuse with landscape and the dazzling Provençal light to create this astonishing museum of contemporary art and sculpture. **See p.338**

HIGHLIGHTS ARE MARKED ON THE MAP ON P.304

Cannes

With its immaculate seafront hotels and exclusive beaches, glamorous yachts and glitzy designer boutiques, **CANNES** is in many ways the definitive Riviera resort. It's a place where appearances truly count, especially during the **film festival** in May, when the orgy of self-promotion reaches its annual peak.

Although its urban sprawl stretches several kilometres east, west and inland, Cannes lacks the must-see sights and general dynamism of a genuine city. At heart, it's just a

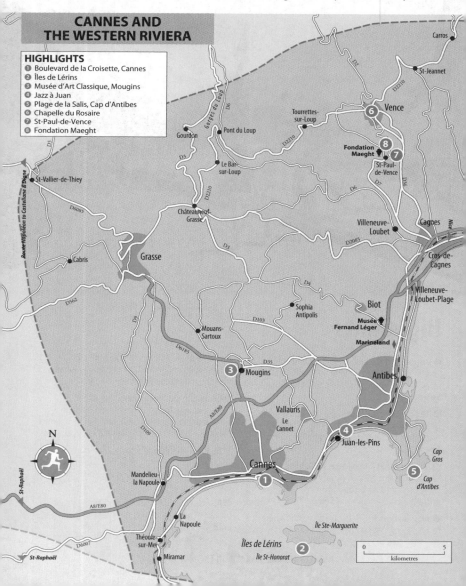

CANNES AND THE WESTERN RIVIERA

HIGHLIGHTS
❶ Boulevard de la Croisette, Cannes
❷ Îles de Lérins
❸ Musée d'Art Classique, Mougins
❹ Jazz à Juan
❺ Plage de la Salis, Cap d'Antibes
❻ Chapelle du Rosaire
❼ St-Paul-de-Vence
❽ Fondation Maeght

beach resort, and while the central **Plage de la Croisette** remains the preserve of an opulent elite, it's actually possible to come here for a straightforward, unpretentious seaside holiday, as there are plenty of free sandy **beaches** west of the port, and hotels and restaurants to suit all pockets. In terms of sightseeing, the two most enjoyable attractions are the self-contained old town quarter of **Le Suquet**, and the sublimely peaceful **Îles de Lérins**, just a short boat-ride out to sea.

Modern Cannes is not as large as you might expect, consisting basically of the five or so blocks between the seafront boulevard of **La Croisette** and the parallel rue d'Antibes. Old Cannes, or **Le Suquet**, is even smaller, just a few tight streets spiralling up the hill immediately west. If you're just popping into Cannes for a quick look, take a stroll beside the main beach then climb up to the fortifications atop Le Suquet, and you'll have seen the best of both.

La Croisette

Although Cannes' *raison d'être*, the celebrated, swanky **Plage de la Croisette**, stretches for well over 1km, only a few meagre scraps of sand are freely accessible to the public. The rest is swallowed up by chic private beach concessions, many belonging to specific hotels and clubs. During the film festival especially, you can spot the most exclusive and expensive by the paparazzi who buzz around them. Those that allow mere mortals entry tend to cost upwards of €20 per day, with supplementary charges for parasols or prime locations on their jetties (*pontoons*), as well, of course, for food and drink. If you can't get onto the beach, you can at least take advantage of the little blue chairs provided free along the elegant **boulevard de la Croisette**, the broad promenade which curves all the way from the Pointe de la Croisette to the Vieux Port. Here you can watch the endless display of rollerbladers, rubbernecking visitors and genteel retired folk with tiny dogs.

Although much of central Cannes has fallen victim to redevelopment, the buildings that line La Croisette still include a few palatial hotels from the town's nineteenth-century golden age, notably the **Carlton Intercontinental**, whose cupolas were inspired by the breasts of a famous courtesan, and the Art Deco **Martinez**. Rather overshadowed by the seafront glitz, the beautiful **La Malmaison**, at no. 47, started life as the tearoom of the now-vanished *Grand Hotel*, which was built in 1863 and demolished a century later. It now stages temporary exhibitions of modern and contemporary art (hours and admission fees vary; ☎04 97 06 44 90). Further east is, the **Espace Miramar** which also hosts short-term exhibitions (hours vary, admission usually free; ☎04 93 43 10 92).

THE CANNES FILM FESTIVAL

In the second half of May each year, Cannes hosts the world's most famous movie festival, the **Festival International du Film** (ⓦwww.festival-cannes.com). It was first conceived in 1939, as a rival to the Venice film festival, which had fallen under the influence of Mussolini; as only pro-fascist films had any chance of winning prizes there, an alternative competition was planned for Cannes. However, World War II intervened, and the first Cannes festival took place in 1946.

Winning Cannes' top prize, the **Palme d'Or**, may not compete with Oscars for box-office effect, but for prestige within the movie world it remains unrivalled. Some years it seems as if the big names are all too busy talking finance in LA to come to Cannes; the next they're all begging for the accolades. In contrast to all the attendant glitz and froth, the Festival has become renowned for rewarding politically committed (and/or controversial) film-makers.

The festival is strictly an event for film professionals and the associated media, and without proper accreditation you won't get into the Palais des Festivals. However, it is possible to gain entry to the open-air *Cinéma de la Plage*, which screens certain official selections to the public (tickets available at the tourist office).

7

● BARS		
Cavok	3	
Coco Loco	5	
Morrison's	2	
● RESTAURANTS		
Auberge Provençale	9	
Aux Bon Enfants	7	
Barbarella	11	
Chaperon Rouge	10	
Chez Vincent & Nicolas	8	
Côté Jardin	1	
La Mère Besson	4	
La Palme d'Or	6	
Le Salon des Indépendants	12	

■ ACCOMMODATION	
Alizé	9
Alnea	8
Camping Bellevue	1
Canberra	4
Carlton Intercontinental	11
Chanteclair	13
Cybelle	7
Idéal Séjour	3
Mistral	10
Provence	5
Le Ranch Camping	2
Splendid	12
La Villa Tosca	6

■ CLUBS	
Backstage	1
Le 7	2
Le Baôli	3

0 ————— 300
metres

Palais des Festivals

Dominating the western end of La Croisette, the vast, ugly **Palais des Festivals** resembles a misplaced concrete missile silo. The main focus of the film festival, it also hosts a steady stream of conferences, tournaments and trade shows throughout the year. Outside, you can compare hand sizes with film stars from Sharon Stone to Mickey Mouse, whose imprints have been set, Hollywood-style, in tiles on the pavement. As the tradition pretty much stopped at the end of the 1980s, the stardust is wearing off names and tiles alike.

The Vieux Port

Cannes' **Vieux Port**, west of the Palais des Festivals, fills up with extraordinarily sumptuous yachts in summer; tourists gather to watch white-frocked crews serve

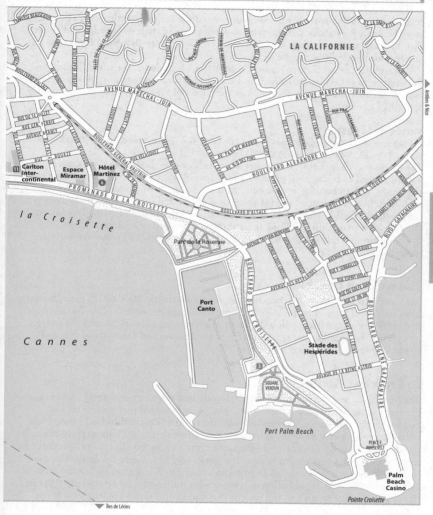

dinner to millionaires on their decks. Inland from here, the streets in between the western end of La Croisette and the rue d'Antibes form the South of France's most extensive luxury **shopping** district, stuffed with designer names such as Bulgari, Cartier, Chanel, Lacroix and Vuitton, and also hold the city's most stylish **nightclubs**. This part of town looks its best in the weeks leading up to Christmas, when the streets glitter with tasteful white lights and the crowds of summer are long forgotten.

Le Suquet

Back in the eleventh century, the hill known as **Le Suquet** became the property of the Îles de Lérins monks. It still holds a castle built by the *abbé* in 1088, with the white stone twelfth-century Romanesque **Chapelle de Ste-Anne** alongside. After several centuries in which a small town took root around the religious settlement, a dispute arose between the monks and the townsfolk who wanted their own parish and priest. Two hundred years after their initial demand in 1648, **Notre-Dame de l'Espérance** was finally built beside the Chapelle de Ste-Anne.

Although Le Suquet used to house the city's poorer residents, the streets leading to the summit have become gentrified, and the various places to **eat** and **drink** increasingly tourist-oriented and chic, if, for the most part, less overtly trendy than in the streets behind La Croisette.

Musée de la Castre

Place de la Castre • April & May Tues–Sun 10.30am–1.15pm & 2.15–5.45pm; June–Sept daily 10am–5.45pm; Oct–March Tues–Sun 10.30am–1.15pm & 2.15–4.45pm • €6 • ☏ 04 93 38 55 26, ⓦ cannes.travel

The castle and chapel atop Le Suquet are now home to the **Musée de la Castre**, which, as well as fascinating pictures and prints of old Cannes, displays strong ethnology and archeology collections, with an emphasis on the south Pacific. Its highlight, however, is the brilliant collection of musical instruments from all over the world, including Congolese bell bracelets, an Ethiopian ten-string lyre, an Asian "lute" with a snakeskin box, and an extraordinary selection of drums. Climb the medieval tower in the museum courtyard for the best view of Le Suquet and the town below.

The western beaches

Extensive and very sandy **free beaches** line the **boulevard du Midi**, which extends west from boulevard Jean-Hibert, below Le Suquet, towards the suburb of La Bocca. Although the road is backed by a distinctly unglamorous railway line and the water isn't always the cleanest, the atmosphere is unpretentious and family-oriented, and kiosks sell simple snacks and ice creams.

La Croix des Gardes

The best place to get a sense of Cannes' largely lost nineteenth-century elegance is the leafy suburb of **La Croix des Gardes**, just a few hundred metres west of Le Suquet. From the outset, Cannes' aristocratic visitors preferred to build their own villas, many of which survive. Thus Lord Brougham's elegant **Château Eléonore** still stands on avenue du Dr Raymond-Picaud on the plot he bought after his enforced sojourn in the then-unknown village of Cannes in 1834. Close by, across the road, is the **Villa Victoria**, constructed in unmistakeably English Victorian Gothic style in 1852 by Sir Thomas Woolfield, a developer who built and sold around 30 villas in the town. Neither is open to the public, but you can visit the opulent **Villa Maria Thérèse**, a Beaux-Arts mansion just around the corner at 1 avenue Jean-de-Noailles, built in 1881 for the Dowager Baroness Rothschild. Set in a lovely garden with winding paths and waterfalls, it now houses Cannes' **Mediathèque**, or multimedia library, along with the city archive (Tues–Sat 9.30am–6pm; ☏ 04 97 06 44 83, ⓦ mediatheque.ville-cannes.fr).

Le Cannet

Although nominally a town in its own right, **Le Cannet**, 4km northeast of the city centre along the busy boulevard Sadi-Carnot (bus routes #1A or #4 from the Hôtel de Ville), forms an indistinguishable part of Cannes' urban sprawl. It was originally built on land belonging to the Îles de Lérins monks to house 140 Ligurian families brought here to tend the orange trees, and its old part, along rue St-Sauveur, still preserves a certain villagey charm.

Musée Bonnard

16 bd Sadi-Carnot, Le Cannet • Mid-April to mid-Oct Tues, Wed & Fri–Sun 10am–8pm, Thurs 10am–9pm; mid-Oct to mid-April Tues, Wed & Fri–Sun 10am–6pm, Thurs 10am–9pm; occasional closures between temporary exhibitions • €5, or €7 during exhibitions • ☎ 04 93 94 06 06, ⓦ museebonnard.fr

Perhaps the most private of the Riviera's great artists, **Pierre Bonnard** bought the Villa le Bosquet in Le Cannet in 1926. He lived here from 1939 until his death in 1947, and is buried in the town's Notre Dame des Anges cemetery. Born in the suburbs of Paris in 1867, Bonnard found fame early as a member of Les Nabis, followers of Gauguin, and subsequently created his own style, distinguished by intense colour and a highly domestic choice of subject matter.

Opened in 2011, the **Musée Bonnard** is housed not in Bonnard's former home but in a *belle époque* villa transformed by recent concrete-and-glass extensions. As well as displaying an extensive collection of Bonnard's own work, it hosts temporary exhibitions focusing on his contemporaries.

ARRIVAL AND DEPARTURE

By bus Cannes has two *gares routières*: one on place Bernard Cornut Gentille between the *mairie* and Le Suquet, serving coastal destinations; and the other, next to the *gare SNCF*, for buses inland.

Destinations Aéroport Nice-Côte-d'Azur (every 20min; 1hr 10min); Antibes (every 20min; 35min); Grasse (every 20min; 40–50min); Mougins (every 20min; 20min); Nice (every 20min; 1hr 55min); Vallauris (every 45min; 15min).

By train The *gare SNCF* is on rue Jean-Jaurès, five blocks north of the Palais des Festivals.

Destinations Antibes (every 10–30min; 9–13min);

Grasse (hourly; 25–30min); Marseille (every 30min–1hr; 2hr); Nice (every 10–20min; 35min), via Juan-les-Pins (10min), Antibes (15min), Biot (18min), Villeneuve-Loubet-Plage (22min), Cagnes-sur-Mer (25min) and Cros-de-Cagnes (30min); St Raphaël (up to 32 daily; 21–38min).

By car Cannes' narrow, traffic-clogged streets are cramped and unpleasant for drivers. Multistorey car parks in the centre charge around €4 per hour, or €22 overnight; there's free street parking east of the Parc de la Roseraie, beyond the eastern end of the Croisette.

INFORMATION

Tourist offices Cannes has three tourist offices (all ☎ 04 92 99 84 22, ⓦ cannes.travel): at Palais des Festivals, 1 bd de la Croisette (daily: March–June, Sept & Oct 9am–7pm; July & Aug 9am–8pm; Nov–Feb 10am–7pm);

at the train station (Mon–Sat 9am–1pm & 2–6pm); and at 1 rue Pierre-Sémard in La Bocca (Tues–Sat: July & Aug 9am–12.30pm & 3.30–7pm; Sept–June 9am–noon & 2.30–6.30pm).

GETTING AROUND

By bus Bus Azur runs 24 lines and five night buses from outside the Hôtel de Ville, facing the Vieux Port, which serve all of Cannes and the surrounding area (☎ 08 25 82 55 99, ⓦ busazur.com); a single ticket costs €1, a carnet of ten €9.50 and a weekly pass, the *Carte Palm'Hebdo*, €11. The enjoyable, open-top #8 bus runs along the seafront from the quai Max-Laubeuf to Palm Beach Casino on Pointe

Croisette, at the other end of the bay.

By taxi Cannes Allo Taxi ☎ 08 90 71 22 27, ⓦ allo-taxis -cannes.com.

Bike rental Elite Rent a Bike, 32 av Maréchal Juin, who also rent scooters (☎ 04 93 94 30 34, ⓦ elite-rentabike .com); Holiday Bikes, 44 bd Lorraine (☎ 04 97 06 07 07, ⓦ www.holidaybikes.fr).

ACCOMMODATION

Cannes has **hotels** to suit all budgets, though it has to be said that €80 or €90 here doesn't get you nearly as nice a room as it might inland. Book well in advance for the cheaper options. Room rates in winter (Nov–March) tend to be less than half what's indicated below. The tourist office runs a **reservation website**, on ⓦ cannes-hotel-reservation.fr.

Alizé 29 rue Bivouac Napoleon ☎ 04 97 06 64 64, ⓦ hotel-alize-cannes.fr. A central hotel with large, renovated and soundproofed rooms with a/c, cable TV and wi-fi: great value, considering the location. **€92**

Alnea 20 rue Jean de Riouffe ☎ 04 93 68 77 77, ⓦ hotel-alnea.com. Centrally located two-star with

pleasant service and simple but colourful and well-equipped rooms with a/c, double glazing, flatscreen TV and wi-fi, plus pleasant service. **€85**

★ **Canberra** 120 rue d'Antibes ☎ 04 97 06 95 00, ⓦ hotel-cannes-canberra.com. Classy, understated and intimate four-star hotel with elegant, 1950s-inspired decor and large rooms with wi-fi, a/c and flatscreen TV. There's a heated pool in the garden plus a sauna, gym, restaurant and cocktail bar. **€196**

Carlton Intercontinental 58 La Croisette ☎ 04 93 06 40 06, ⓦ ichotelsgroup.com. Legendary landmark *belle époque* seafront palace hotel that featured in Hitchcock's *To Catch a Thief*, along with Cary Grant and Grace Kelly. Rooms are decorated in a tasteful but conservative style, with pay-per-view movies, voicemail and TV internet browser, plus individually controlled a/c. **€390**

Chanteclair 12 rue Forville ☎ 04 93 39 68 88, ⓦ hotelchanteclair.fr. About as cheap as you'll get in the centre of Cannes, right next to the old town, and with a private courtyard where you can eat breakfast. Rooms are small but all have shower; most also have WC. Free wi-fi. **€75**

Cybelle 14 rue du 24 Août ☎ 04 93 38 31 33, ⓦ hotelcybelle.fr. You get what you pay for at this small, very central budget hotel; there's no a/c, the walls are paper-thin, the cheapest rooms share bathrooms, and some are frankly a bit grotty, but the rates are great, so people keep coming back. The unnervingly friendly management insist on full payment when you make a reservation. Closed mid-Nov to mid-Dec. **€46**

Idéal Séjour 6 allée du Parc-des-Vallergues ☎ 04 93 39 16 66, ⓦ ideal-sejour.com. Nicely restored, gay-friendly villa hotel, set in spacious hillside gardens a 15min walk up from the centre. Small but very tasteful rooms, with attractive common areas that include an extensive library. Free parking and wi-fi; cheaper single rooms available. **€91**

Mistral 13 rue des Belges ☎ 04 93 39 91 46, ⓦ www.mistral-hotel.com. Smart little modernized hotel, in a

great position just back from the Croisette, with ten crisp, clean, en-suite rooms. **€99**

Provence 9 rue Molière ☎ 04 93 38 44 35, ⓦ hotel-de-provence.com. Charmingly decorated and well-appointed three-star hotel just off rue d'Antibes, with pale colours, a/c, wi-fi, a bar and a luxuriant garden. Some rooms have balconies and the deluxe suite has a large terrace. **€140**

Splendid 4–6 rue Félix-Fauré ☎ 04 97 06 22 22, ⓦ splendid-hotel-cannes.fr. Charmingly old-fashioned *belle époque* hotel where the white-painted rooms have wrought-iron trimmings; expect to pay extra for those that overlook the yachts of the old port. **€165**

La Villa Tosca 11 rue Hoche ☎ 04 93 38 34 40, ⓦ villa-tosca.com. Smartly renovated three-star hotel a few blocks from the sea, with well-equipped, a/c rooms with TV and wi-fi; some rooms also have balconies. The same management run a cheaper two-star sister hotel – the *PLM* – a few doors down. **€125**

CAMPING

Camping Bellevue 67 av Maurice-Chevalier ☎ 04 93 47 28 97, ⓦ parcbellevue.com. Three-star campsite, complete with pool, bar, shop and restaurant, 3km northwest of the centre in the suburb of Ranguin; bus #2 from Hôtel de Ville (stop "Sainte-Jeanne"). Closed Oct–March. **€25**

Le Ranch Camping Chemin St-Joseph, l'Aubarède ☎ 04 93 46 00 11, ⓦ leranchcamping.fr. Three-star site, with pool, set on a well wooded hillside 4km northwest of the centre in Le Cannet, very close to the A8 autoroute; bus #10 from the Hôtel de Ville (direction "Les Pins Parasols", stop "Le Ranch"). Closed Nov–March. **€25**

EATING

Cannes has hundreds of **restaurants**, though quality across the board can be patchy. Many stay open very late, so getting a meal after midnight is no great problem. The best areas for inexpensive dining are **rue Meynadier**, **Le Suquet** and **quai St-Pierre** on the Vieux Port, which is lined with **brasseries** and **cafés**. Reserving a table is advisable at almost all the places listed below. Thanks to the vigour of the **Forville market**, two blocks north of the Vieux Port (daily except Mon 7am–1pm), local chefs have access to the finest and freshest ingredients. Note that many Cannes visitors also make the pilgrimage to eat in nearby **Mougins** (see p.313), renowned for its gourmet restaurants.

Auberge Provencale 10 rue Saint-Antoine, Le Suquet ☎ 04 92 99 27 17, ⓦ www.auberge-provencale.com. Established in 1860, this stylish restaurant is the oldest in Cannes, serving Niçois specialities and creative dishes like crème brûlée with foie gras or sea bream with black olives, tomato, basil and saffron potatoes. *Menu* €29; two-course *lunch formule* €20. Daily noon–2.15pm & 7–11.15pm.

Aux Bons Enfants 80 rue Meynadier. Small, friendly and rustic, this family-run stalwart – established in 1920 – serves very reliable Provençal cuisine with *menus* at €26 and dishes like octopus with saffron potatoes or hazelnut

and foie gras terrine. Cash only. Jan–Nov Tues–Sat noon–2pm & 7–9.30pm.

★ **Barbarella** 16 rue Saint Dizier, Le Suquet ☎ 04 92 99 17 33, ⓦ barbarellarestaurant.fr. Stylish, fun and gay-friendly, with Philippe Starck ghost chairs on the terrace and a cosmopolitan fusion menu with Asian and other influences in dishes like cod fillet in ginger crust with baby vegetables. *Menus* from €29. Tues–Sat 7pm–midnight.

Chaperon Rouge 17 rue St-Antoine ☎ 04 93 99 06 22, ⓦ www.lechaperonrouge-cannes.fr. Friendly dinner-only restaurant, with tables squeezed onto a terrace beside a steep alley leading up to Le Suquet; this is a very touristy district, but the evening hurly-burly is fun and the food is actually pretty good, with a €27 *menu* that features gazpacho plus either a whole bream or salmon with ginger. March–June & Sept–Nov Tues–Sun 7–9.30pm; July & Aug daily 7–9.30pm.

Chez Vincent & Nicolas 90 rue Meynadier ☏ 04 93 68 35 39. Slightly quirky and original choice, with flamboyant staff and inventive food, in a lovely setting in a square just off the main street. Be sure to try the scallops wrapped in bacon. Meat or fish mains start at around €16. Daily 6.30–11.30pm.

Côté Jardin 12 av St-Louis ☏ 04 93 38 60 28, ⓦ restaurant-cotejardin.com. Intimate family-run restaurant with a small garden and terrace. Changing daily *menus* on the blackboard cost €31 and €40 and feature Provençal classics and plenty of fish. Tues–Sat 12.15–1.45pm & 7.15–10pm.

La Mère Besson 13 rue des Frères Pradignac ☏ 04 93 39 59 24. This smart, long-established restaurant in the thick of the nightlife quarter is an old Cannes favourite, with dishes like chicken with parsley cream or mesclun salad with lardons. *Menus* €28. Also open for weekday lunch during festivals or exhibitions. Mon–Fri 7–10.30pm.

La Palme d'Or Hôtel Martinez, 73 bd de la Croisette ☏ 04 92 98 74 1, ⓦ hotel-martinez.com. The place to go and celebrate if you've just won a film festival prize; it has held two Michelin stars for more than twenty years. Lunch *menu* €68; evening *menus* start at €95. Tues–Sat 12.30–2pm & 8–10pm.

Le Salon des Indépendants 11 rue Louis Perrissol ☏ 04 93 39 97 06. Inventive and very popular dinner-only restaurant on one of Le Suquet's quieter alleys, featuring dishes – and live music – from all around the Mediterranean. The one *menu*, at €39, includes coffee and a half-bottle of wine. Tues–Sun 7.15–10.30pm.

NIGHTLIFE AND ENTERTAINMENT

Cannes abounds with exclusive **bars** and **clubs**, nowhere more so than in the tight little grid of streets bounded by rue Macé, rue V. Cousin, rue Dr G Monod and rue des Frères-Pradignacs. As is so often the case in the South of France, the boundaries between restaurant, bar and club are somewhat blurred, so that you can frequently dine, drink and dance – at a price – in the same venue. Cannes' **lesbian and gay** bar scene is smaller than that in Nice, but smart and a good deal more relaxed, and some venues attract hetero as well as gay visitors. If you are determined to lose money, choose from **casinos** at the Palais des Festivals and at the Palm Beach at the eastern end of La Croisette.

BARS AND CLUBS

Backstage 17 rue Dr G Monod ⓦ backstage-cannes .com. The biggest and flashiest of the trendy restaurant/bar/clubs in the tight little knot of streets between rue d'Antibes and La Croisette, with dramatic black decor, and live music and cabaret Mon–Thurs. Main courses from €17 up, cocktails €10. Mon–Sat 6pm–5am.

Le Baôli Port Pierre Canto ☏ 04 93 43 03 43, ⓦ lebaoli. com. If you want to rub shoulders with celebrities and big-name international DJs, head to this exclusive exotic (and expensive) outdoor disco–restaurant (*menus* at €70 and €80) with palms lit up at night. Dress the part. April–Oct daily; Nov–March Sat & Sun: restaurant from 8pm, club midnight–5am.

Cavok 19 rue des Frères Pradignacs ☏ 09 62 53 60 04. Smaller than the average Cannes nightspot and with chilled music, this is a good place to relax from the

hustle and bustle of these streets. Cocktails €10. July & Aug daily 5pm–2.30am; Sept–June Tues–Sat 5pm–2.30am.

Coco Loco 4 rue des Frères Pradignacs ☏ 04 97 06 31 90. Cocktails with umbrellas, a punchy punch and a Creole vibe. Rum's the speciality, and during the film festival everything kicks off. Tues–Sun 6.30pm–2am.

Morrison's 10 rue Teisseire ☏ 04 92 98 16 17, ⓦ morrisonspub.com. The inevitable Irish pub, a few blocks back from the seafront, and also featuring an upscale lounge. Mon–Fri 5pm–2.30am, Sat & Sun noon–2.30am.

Le 7 7 rue Rouguière ☏ 06 09 55 22 79, ⓦ facebook .com/cabaretdiscotheque.leseptcannes?ref=ts. Gay disco and cabaret club just off rue Félix Faure, with drag shows on Fri and Sat. Free entry. Daily midnight–dawn; opens 5.30pm during the film festival.

DIRECTORY

Airport Cannes-Mandelieu, 6km southwest of the centre ☏ 08 20 42 66 66, ⓦ www.cannes.aeroport.fr.

Bookshop Cannes English Bookshop, 11 rue Bivouac-Napoleon (Mon–Sat 10am–6.45pm; ☏ 04 93 99 40 08, ⓦ cannesenglishbookshop.com).

Emergencies SOS médecins ☏ 08 25 00 50 04; Hôpital de Cannes, av des Broussailles ☏ 04 93 69 70 00,

ⓦ www.ch-cannes.fr.

Pharmacy Call ☏ 04 93 06 22 22 for address of emergency pharmacy after 7.30pm.

Police Commissariat Central de Police, 1 av de Grasse ☏ 04 93 06 22 22

Post office 22 rue Bivouac-Napoleon.

7

Îles de Lérins

The **Îles de Lérins** would be lovely anywhere, but at just a fifteen-minute ferry ride from Cannes, they make an idyllic escape from the modern city. Known as Lerina, or Lero, in ancient times, the two tiny islands, Ste-Marguerite and St-Honorat, have a long historical pedigree and today offer the gentle pace and tranquillity the Riviera so often lacks.

Ste-Marguerite

The more animated of the Îles de Lérins, **STE-MARGUERITE**, has plenty of day-trippers and a working boatyard, but also offers clear water and beautiful scenery. It's large enough to find seclusion if you're prepared to leave the crowded port and follow paths through the thick woods of Aleppo pines and evergreen oaks.

Fort Ste-Marguerite

April–May Tues–Sun 10.30am–1.15pm & 2.15–5.45pm; June–Sept daily 10am–5.45pm; Oct–March Tues–Sun 10.30am–1.15pm & 2.15–4.45pm • €6, includes museum • ☎ 04 93 38 55 26, ⓦ cannes.travel

The imposing **Fort Ste-Marguerite**, reached by a very obvious path that leads up from the ferry dock, past the boatyard, was a Richelieu commission that failed to prevent the Spanish occupying both Lérins islands between 1635 and 1637; the fortifications were later completed by Vauban.

A cell within is renowned for having held the **Man in the Iron Mask** for eleven years of his long captivity, between 1687 and 1698; a quasi-mythical character who died in the Bastille in 1703, and whose true identity has never been proved, his legend was popularized by novelist Alexandre Dumas. Other prisoners here included Huguenots imprisoned for refusing to submit to Louis XIV's vicious suppression of Protestantism. A series of murals created in the 1990s covers the cell walls, and depicts painter Jean le Gac as a prisoner. As well as three Roman **cisterns** – Ste-Marguerite has no natural springs, so water supply has always been a problem – the fort also holds a barracks-style hostel used by school and youth groups, and the **Musée de la Mer**, which displays artefacts discovered by underwater archeologists, such as amphorae from a Roman shipwreck and ceramics from a tenth-century Arab vessel.

Exploring the island

The quickest route to Ste-Marguerite's peaceful southern shore, the **allée des Eucalyptus**, heads south from roughly halfway around the fort. Follow the outer perimeter of the walls, and keep going straight on when you come to a sign pointing left towards *La Guérite* (see opposite). A pleasant fifteen-minute stroll from here ends abruptly at the seashore, where you can look across the lovely turquoise channel that separates Ste-Marguerite from St-Honorat. Picnic tables are scattered at the water's edge, and many visitors swim here, though the shore is lined by compacted masses of dried vegetation.

The most enjoyable way to get back to the ferry is to follow the coastal **Chemin de la Ceinture**, which offers great views back to Cannes once you round the headland at either end.

St-Honorat

ST-HONORAT, the smaller southern island, is an idyllic and utterly tranquil spot, devoid of both cars and hotels. It has belonged to monks almost continuously since Honoratus, a former Roman noble seeking peace and isolation, founded a monastery here in 410 AD. Visitors soon began to arrive, and a monastic order was established. By the end of Honoratus' life, the Lérins monks had monasteries all over France, held bishoprics in Arles and Lyon, and were renowned throughout the Catholic world for their contributions to theology. **St Patrick** trained here for seven years before setting out for Ireland.

Most of the present **abbey** buildings date from the nineteenth century, though vestiges of medieval and earlier construction survive in the church and cloisters. You can visit the austere church, but not the residential areas, where 25 Cistercian monks live and work, tending an apiary and a vineyard that produces a sought-after white wine, sold in the abbey's shop. Behind this complex, on the sea's edge, stands an eleventh-century **fortress**, a monastic bolthole connected to the original abbey by a tunnel, and used to guard against invaders, especially the Saracens. Of all the protective forts along this coast, only this one looks as if it could still serve its original function.

The other buildings on St-Honorat are the churches and chapels that served as retreats. **St-Pierre**, beside the modern monastery, **La Trinité**, to the east, and **St-Sauveur**, west of the harbour, remain more or less unchanged. By **St-Cabrais**, on the eastern shore, a furnace with a chute for making cannonballs shows that the monks did not lack worldly defensive skills.

The rest of the island is given over to cultivated vines, lavender, herbs and olive trees, mingled with wild poppies and daisies. Pine and eucalyptus trees shade the paths beside the white rock shore, mixing their scent with rosemary, thyme and wild honeysuckle.

ARRIVAL AND DEPARTURE — ÎLES DE LÉRINS

Ste-Marguerite from Cannes Three companies – Horizon (☎ 04 92 98 71 36, ⍾ horizon-lerins.com), Riviera Lines (☎ 04 92 98 71 31, ⍾ riviera-lines.com) and Trans Côte d'Azur (☎ 04 92 98 71 30, ⍾ trans-cote-azur.com) – run to Ste-Marguerite from Cannes' Quai des Îles, at the seaward end of the quai Max-Laubeuf (up to 18 daily 7.30am–5.30pm; last boat back to Cannes 5pm in winter, 6pm in summer; €12).

Ste-Marguerite from Juan-les-Pins Riviera Lines offers day-trips to Ste-Marguerite from Juan-les-Pins (April to mid-June and mid-Sept to mid-Oct 4–6 daily except Mon; mid-June to mid-Sept 4–6 daily; €16.50; ☎ 04 93 63 86 76, ⍾ riviera-lines.com).

Ste-Marguerite from Nice Trans Côte d'Azur offers day-trips to Ste-Marguerite from Nice in summer (June & Sept Tues, Thurs, Sat & Sun 9am; July & Aug daily 9am; €36; ☎ 04 92 98 71 30, ⍾ trans-cote-azur.com).

St-Honorat from Cannes Compagnie Planaria sail to St-Honorat from Cannes' Quai des Îles, at the seaward end of the quai Max-Laubeuf (May–Sept 9 daily; Oct–April 7 daily; last boat back to Cannes 5pm in winter, 6pm in summer; €14; ☎ 04 92 99 54 18, ⍾ lerins-sainthonorat.com).

EATING

Ste-Marguerite is an expensive place to eat and drink, and options are limited, so at the very least it's worth bringing plenty of water. A couple of summer-only snack stalls sell *pan bagnats* close to the ferry dock.

La Guérite Ste-Marguerite ☎ 04 93 43 49 30, ⍾ laguerite.fr. Walk all the way around the inland side of the fort, drop back down to sea level via the steep stairway on the far side, and you'll come to this absurd but very welcome beachfront Club-Med-style place, divided between a very expensive à la carte restaurant where lunch costs at least €40, and a shaded terrace snack bar serving sandwiches for €10–12 or a delicious salad Niçoise for €18.

Mid-April to June & Sept noon–2.30pm; July & Aug noon–9pm.

La Tonelle St-Honorat ☎ 04 92 99 54 08, ⍾ tonelle -abbayedelerins.com. St-Honorat's one small restaurant, by the landing stage, is open for lunch only. On weekdays, a three-course set *menu* costs €30; à la carte prices range from €17 for a burger up to €175 for lobster. Jan–Oct & second half of Dec daily noon–2pm.

Around Cannes

A couple of small towns in the hills immediately inland from Cannes are worth visiting before you head further afield. The hilltop village of **Mougins** is renowned as home to some of the finest restaurants in Provence, while the pottery town of **Vallauris**, a short way west, was where Pablo Picasso made his fascinating postwar experiments with ceramics.

Mougins

If **MOUGINS**, 8km north of Cannes, is the first Provençal village you visit, you may well be charmed by its hilltop site, exquisitely preserved lanes and associations with Man Ray and with Picasso, who had his last studio here and died here in 1973. If, however, you arrive with villages such as Cotignac, Simiane la Rotonde or even St-Paul-de-Vence fresh in mind, Mougins itself may strike you as rather over-praised, a pretty bauble adrift amid bland suburbs and lacking character of its own. Its winding streets are, however, thick with ateliers and small galleries, including the superb new **Musée d'Art Classique**.

More than anything else, modern Mougins is effectively a **culinary** theme park. It was at the **Moulin de Mougins** restaurant, across the Cannes–Grasse highway from the old village on avenue Notre Dame de Vie, that legendary, now-retired chef Roger Vergé perfected his *Cuisine of the Sun*, a modern reworking of Provençal cooking that won him (and Mougins) international acclaim in the 1970s. The *Moulin* and the village alike remain pilgrimage destinations for fans of contemporary cuisine – especially the moguls and mega-stars who attend the Cannes Film Festival – and have an astonishing number of high-class restaurants crammed into the gorgeous medieval centre. In September each year, the community hosts the **Festival International de Gastronomie Mougins** (W lesetoilesdemougins.com).

Musée d'Art Classique

32 rue du Commandeur • April–Oct daily 9.30am–8.30pm; Nov–March Tues–Sun 9.30am–7pm • €12, ages 10–17 €5 • ☎ 04 93 75 18 65, W mouginsmusee.com

Opened in 2011, Mougins' small but exquisite **Musée d'Art Classique** displays a remarkable collection of art, artefacts and sculpture acquired by British hedge-fund manager Christian Levett. Placing its emphasis on the continuing exploration by contemporary artists of themes from Egyptian, Greek and Roman art, it repeatedly juxtaposes original Classical works, for example some gorgeous Roman bronzes, with pieces by the likes of Damean Hirst, Alberto Giacometti and Andy Warhol. Picasso is especially well represented.

The most extraordinary section of the museum is the **armoury** on its topmost floor, which holds an amazing array of superbly preserved ancient arms and armour. Highlights include bronze Urartian helmets from Mesopotamia, dating from the eighth century BC; Thracian helmets, as worn by the troops of Alexander the Great; and Roman cavalry helmets, adorned with eagles.

Musée de la Photographie

Porte Sarrazine • Daily: July & Aug 10am–8pm; Sept–June 10am–12.30pm & 2–6pm • Free • ☎ 04 93 75 85 67, W mougins.fr

Mougins' excellent **Musée de la Photographie**, just beyond the Porte Sarrazine, hosts changing exhibitions by contemporary photographers. Its own small permanent collection includes some stunning portraits of Pablo Picasso, taken by Jacques Lartigue (1894–1986) during the 1950s. Lartigue, who was also a painter himself, had first met Picasso in Paris in 1915.

Le Lavoir de Mougins

Av J.C.-Mallet • March–Oct daily 11am–12.30pm & 2–7pm • Free • ☎ 04 92 92 37 20, W mougins.fr

At the top end of the village, the old wash house, **Le Lavoir de Mougins**, serves as an exhibition space for the visual arts. Its wide basin of water plays reflecting games with the images and the light, making it well worth checking out each year's changing temporary exhibitions.

ARRIVAL AND INFORMATION   MOUGINS

By bus Mougins is served by frequent #600 buses between Cannes and Grasse.

By car Driving up to Mougins involves negotiating a fiendishly complicated road network; just trust the signs, even when they seem to make no sense. Parking once you're there is straightforward, though; the village itself is pedestrianized, so you'll be directed to one of the peripheral car parks just below the hilltop.

Tourist office 18 bd G-Courteline, just below the village centre (July–Sept daily 9am–7pm; Oct–June Mon–Sat 9.30am–5pm; ☎ 04 93 75 87 67, W mougins.fr).

ACCOMMODATION AND EATING

L'Amandier 48 av J.C.-Mallet ☎04 93 90 00 91, ⓦamandier.fr. The attractive former cooking school of the *Moulin de Mougins*, close to the main car park, has a lunch *menu* at €19, and dinner from €35. It also has its own ice cream shop alongside. Mon, Tues & Thurs–Sun noon–1.30pm & 7–9.30pm.

Les Liserons de Mougins 608 av St-Martin ☎04 93 75 50 31, ⓦhotel-liserons-mougins.com. A good-value alternative to staying in Mougins itself, well beyond walking distance 2km north towards Mouans-Sartoux. It's a pretty old country house, with sun-splashed rooms of varying sizes, climbing flowers, a pleasant breakfast terrace and a pool. **€58**

Le Mas Candille Bd Clément-Rebuffel ☎04 92 28 43 43, ⓦlemascandille.com. Twenty romantic, tastefully decorated rooms in a gorgeous traditional farmhouse, complete with deluxe Zen-inspired spa, amid the olive groves and cypresses, 1km southwest of the village centre. Its renowned restaurant, under chef Serge Gouloumès, serves exquisite lunches and dinners daily year-round, on the €90 *Discovery* menu and the €130, 8-course *Roller Coaster*. **€450**

Moulin de Mougins ☎04 93 75 78 24, ⓦmoulindemougins.com. Six relatively simple but very handsome rooms and three suites, down near the main road 500m southeast of the village. This is also Mougins' most famous restaurant, where Alain Ducasse, as an assistant, absorbed the secrets of founding chef Roger Vergé's "cuisine de soleil". Guests are invariably here to enjoy the succulent Provençal cooking of the latest chef, Sébastien Chambru, with lunch at €45, and dinner *menus* from €50 to €110. Restaurant closed Mon & Tues Sept–May. **€200**

Restaurant de la Méditerranée 32 place du Commandant Lamy ☎04 93 90 03 47, ⓦrestaurantlamediterranee.com. Bright, cheerful brasserie on the main square, with a two-course lunch for €17. Dinner *menus* start with the €38 *Menu Gourmande*, which includes an "assortment of crudeness". Daily noon–1.30pm & 7–9.30pm.

Rendez-Vous de Mougins 84 place du Commandant Lamy ☎04 93 75 87 47, ⓦau-rendez-vous-mougins.fr. Excellent Provençal food, with indoor and outdoor seating on the village's central square. Dinner *menus* at €23.50 and €28.50. Daily noon–1.30pm & 7–9.30pm; closed Tues Oct–May.

Vallauris

The small town of **VALLAURIS**, 6km east of Cannes above Golfe-Juan, is remarkable only for its long-standing tradition of making **pottery**, and its more recent association with **Picasso**. Despite being set on sloping hills, it's not a hill village in the usual sense; it's just an ordinary and not particularly attractive little town. That said, the very fact that it feels genuinely lived-in, with backstreets close to the centre bustling with day-to-day activity, makes it a refreshing change from so many prettified Riviera communities.

Ceramics became established here in the sixteenth century, when the bishop of Grasse rebuilt Vallauris following a plague, and settled Genoese potters here to exploit the clay soil and abundant timber. By the end of World War II, however, aluminium had become a much more popular material for pots and plates. It took the intervention of Picasso to reverse Vallauris' decline. In 1946, while installed in the castle at Antibes, the artist met some of the town's few remaining potters, and was invited to Vallauris by the owner of a ceramics studio, Georges Ramié. Hooked on clay, Picasso spent the next two years working at Ramié's Madoura workshop.

A gift from Picasso to the town, the bronze **Man with a Sheep**, stands in the main square, beside the church and neat little castle. The municipality had some misgivings as to whether the sculpture might prove to be too "modern", but decided that the possible affront to their conservative tastes was outweighed by the benefits to tourism of Picasso's international reputation. They needn't have worried; the statue looks quite simply like a shepherd boy and sheep.

Today the main street, avenue Georges-Clemenceau, is almost entirely given over to **pottery shops**, while the **Madoura workshop** (Mon–Fri 10am–12.30pm & 3–6pm; closed Nov), off to the left halfway up, is now a gallery with exclusive rights to reproduce – and sell – Picasso's designs. Other classy commercial galleries include **Sassi-Milici**, 65bis avenue Georges-Clemenceau (daily 10.30am–noon & 3–6.30pm; ☎04 93 64 65 71, ⓦsassi-milici.com).

The Musée National Picasso

Place de la Libération du 24 Août 1944 • Daily except Tues: July & Aug 10am–7pm; Sept–June 10am–12.15pm & 2–6pm • €3.25, includes Musée de la Céramique/Musée Magnelli • ☎ 04 93 64 71 83, ⓦ musee-picasso-vallauris.fr

In 1952, Pablo Picasso took up the offer from local authorities and redecorated the early medieval deconsecrated **chapel** in the courtyard of Vallauris' castle. The tiny vault – now the **Musée National Picasso** – is covered with painted panels and has the architectural simplicity of an air-raid shelter, which indeed it was during the war. Picasso's subject is *War and Peace*. At first glance it's easy to be unimpressed (as many critics still are) – it looks mucky and slapdash, with paint runs on the unyielding plywood surfaces. Stay a while, however, and the passion of this violently drawn pacifism slowly emerges. On the *War* panel a music score is trampled by hooves and about to be engulfed in flames; the figure of "valiant resistance" tenuously holds the scales of justice; a shield bears the outline of a dove; and skeletons unleash creepy-crawlies and pestilence from a deathly chariot. *Peace* is represented by symbols of creativity and fecundity, including Pegasus, people dancing and suckling babies, trees bearing fruit, owls, books and general innocent mischief.

The ticket for the chapel also gives admission to the castle's **Musée de la Céramique/ Musée Magnelli**, which exhibits many of the ceramics Picasso made at the Madoura, ranging from plates and more complicated vessels to carved woodblocks, as well as works by the Florentine painter Alberto Magnelli.

ARRIVAL AND INFORMATION VALLAURIS

By bus Regular buses from Cannes (#18 from the gare *routière* by the *gare SNCF*) and from Golfe-Juan SNCF arrive at the rear of the castle.
Destinations Antibes (every 45–50min; 30min); Cannes (every 30min–1hr; 24min).

By car The main tourist car park is near the tourist office on square du 8-Mai-1945.
Tourist office Square du 8-Mai-1945, at the bottom of av Georges-Clemenceau (July & Aug daily 9am–7pm; Sept–June Mon–Sat 9am–12.15pm & 1.45–6pm; ☎ 04 93 63 82 58, ⓦ vallauris-golfe-juan.fr).

EATING

l'Escalier Gourmand 47 av Georges-Clemenceau ☎ 04 93 00 08 74. The pick of the restaurants, cafés and bars along the main tourist drag; lunch specials served on

the upstairs terrace cost around €12. Daily noon– 1.30pm & 7–9pm.

West of Cannes

Immediately **west of Cannes**, the western end of the Riviera holds a handful of little resorts, such as **La Napoule** and **Théoule-sur-Mer**. While they're not worth going out of your way to see, the coastal D6908 makes an enjoyable route west towards St-Raphaël (see p.295), running beyond Théoule-sur-Mer along the dramatic **Corniche de l'Esterel**.

La Napoule

The small former fishing port of **LA NAPOULE** stands 8km west of Cannes, beyond the city's small airport. Technically, it's just the seaside portion of the larger community of **Mandelieu-La Napoule**. Mandelieu, up the hill away from the sea, is a characterless golfing resort with minimal appeal to casual visitors.

Château de la Napoule

Gardens Early Feb to early Nov daily 10am–6pm; early Nov to early Feb Mon–Fri 2–5pm, Sat & Sun 10am–5pm; €3.50
Castle tours Early Feb to early Nov daily at 11.30am, 2.30pm, 3.30pm & 4.30pm; early Nov to early Feb Mon–Fri 2.30pm & 3.30pm, Sat & Sun 11.30am, 2.30pm & 3.30pm; €6; ☎ 04 93 49 95 05, ⓦ www.chateau-lanapoule.com

The fantasy castle that dominates the waterfront of La Napoule, the **Château de la Napoule**, was erected atop the three towers and gateway of a fourteenth-century fort by

American sculptor Henry Clews and his wife, Marie Clews. A classic pre-World War I folly, it features beautiful gardens, which host a quirky and hugely enjoyable treasure hunt for children, and also holds a collection of Clews' odd and gloomy works, represented on the outside by the grotesques on the gateway.

Théoule-sur-Mer and Miramar

The ruggedly picturesque **Corniche de l'Esterel** extends for 20km westwards from **THÉOULE-SUR-MER**, 2.5km down the coast from La Napoule, all the way to St-Raphaël. Théoule itself is a quiet, rather low-key place with a sandy beach, large marina, and a small castle that can't be visited. Beyond it the coast runs south, becoming wilder and more dramatic around the Pointe de l'Esquillon as it approaches the little village of **MIRAMAR**.

INFORMATION

LA NAPOULE

Tourist office 806 av de Cannes, Mandelieu-La Napoule (Feb–June, Sept & Oct Mon–Sat 9.30am–12.30pm & 2–6pm, Sun 9.30am–1pm; July & Aug Mon–Sat 9.30am–1pm & 2.30–6pm, Sun 9.30am–1pm & 2.30–5pm; Nov–Jan Mon–Sat

WEST OF CANNES

9.30am–12.30pm & 2–5pm, Sun 10am–1pm; ☎ 04 93 93 64 64, ⓦ ot-mandelieu.fr).

THÉOULE-SUR-MER

Tourist office 1 corniche d'Or (Mon–Sat 9am–7pm, Sun 9am–2pm; ☎ 04 93 49 28 28, ⓦ theoule-sur-mer.org).

ACCOMMODATION

LA NAPOULE

La Calanque 404 av Henri-Clews ☎ 04 93 49 95 11, ⓦ hotel-restaurant-lacalanque.fr. Just across from the beach, the best of the simple rooms in this pleasant hotel offer views of the castle and the sea; the cheapest lack en-suite facilities. A pretty restaurant serves fine Provençal fish dishes. Closed mid-Oct to mid-Feb. **€35**

MIRAMAR

Tour de l'Esquillon Place Vert Bisson ☎ 04 93 75 41 51, ⓦ esquillon.com. This splendid pink hotel, high up on the corniche in Miramar, is the best place to stay on this stretch of coast. All the attractive rooms enjoy breathtaking views, and it has its own beach and a fine restaurant. **€160**

Juan-les-Pins

Though perhaps not as glamorous as it used to be, **JUAN-LES-PINS**, just 9km east of Cannes, is still an appealing resort, with sandy beaches, haunting reminders of its former Art Deco glory, plenty of nightlife and a renowned **jazz festival**, Jazz à Juan. The one real drawback is that so much of its 2km stretch of fine sheltered sand is obscured by private beach and restaurant concessions.

Unlike St-Tropez, Juan-les-Pins was never a fishing village, just a pine grove by the sea. Its casino was built in 1908, but only in the late 1920s did it take off as the original summer resort of the Côte d'Azur. It was here, in the 1930s when Charlie Chaplin and Maurice Chevalier were regular visitors that revealing swimsuits were reputedly first worn, and waterskiing was invented. Juan-les-Pins' trail-blazing style continued to attract aristocrats, royals, writers, dancers and screen stars throughout the 1950s and 1960s.

For more than thirty years after it closed in 1976, the town's central landmark, the eerily beautiful Art Deco **Hotel Provençal**, slipped gradually into utter dereliction, and seemed to symbolize the decline in local fortunes. Built by the American railroad magnate Frank Jay Gould, who was also responsible for the Palais de la Méditerranée in Nice, it was finally converted into apartments in 2008. Gould's own home, the 1912 **Villa Vigie**, stands behind high walls across the road. Another wonderful, peeling remnant from Juan's heyday stands at the western end of the seafront; complete with minaret, cupolas and domes, the **Villa El Djezair**, at 1 boulevard

> ### JAZZ À JUAN
>
> Juan's international jazz festival – known simply as Jazz à Juan and by far the best in the region (Ⓦ jazzajuan.com) – is held in the middle two weeks of July in the central pine grove, the Jardin de la Pinède, and square Gould above the beach by the casino. Juan-les-Pins is twinned with New Orleans, so there's always a strong contingent of performers from the Crescent City. The music is always chosen with serious concern for every kind of jazz, both contemporary and traditional, rather than commercial popularity.

Charles-Guillaumont, was built in exuberant neo-Moorish style by Antibes architect Ernest Truch in 1922.

An ancient, beautiful pine grove near the eastern end of the promenade, **Jardin de la Pinède** (known simply as La Pinède), plays host to the **jazz festival**, and boasts a Hollywood-style **celebrity walk** with the handprints of Sydney Bechet, B.B. King, Stéphane Grappelli, Dave Sanborn and others.

7

ARRIVAL, INFORMATION AND TOURS   JUAN-LES-PINS

By train Trains from Cannes *gare SNCF* is 200m from the sea, on av de l'Esterel.

Destinations Cannes (every 10–20min; 10min).

By bus The most central local bus stops are "Pin Doré" and "Rond Point Joffre".

Destinations Antibes (#3; every 40min; 6min); Cannes (every 20min; 15min).

Tourist office 51 bd Guillaumont, at the western end of the seafront (July & Aug daily 9am–7pm; Sept–June Mon–Sat 9am–noon & 2–6pm, Sun in school hols only 10am–12.30pm & 2.30–5pm; Ⓣ 04 97 23 11 10,

Ⓦ antibesjuanlespins.com).

Bike rental Holiday Bikes, 93 bd Wilson (Ⓣ 04 93 20 90 20, Ⓦ holiday-bikes.com).

Boat trips Boats from Ponton Courbet in Juan-les-Pins run regular cruises around Antibes' fabled "bay of millionaires", east of Point de l'Ilette (April–June & Sept 4 departures daily, 11am–4.30pm; July & Aug 7 departures daily, 9.25am–6pm; Ⓣ 04 93 67 02 11, Ⓦ visiobulle.com; €13). Day-trips to the Îles Lerins are detailed on p.313.

ACCOMMODATION

Belles Rives 33 bd Edouard-Baudoin Ⓣ 04 93 61 02 79, Ⓦ bellesrives.com. This gorgeous Art Deco hotel preserves Juan-les-Pins' most authentic aura of 1930s glamour, but luxury comes at quite a price, and it's not the most peaceful of places in summer. €228

La Marjolaine 15 av du Docteur Fabre Ⓣ 04 93 61 06 60. Seventeen traditionally styled rooms in a beautiful a/c villa with a leafy terrace, in a handy location between Juan-les-Pins train station and the beach. Closed Nov to late Dec. €90

Mimosas rue Pauline Ⓣ 04 93 61 04 16, Ⓦ hotelmimosas.com. Grand but very welcoming white villa, in lush gardens ten minutes' walk up from the sea,

with rooms of varying sizes – the cheapest are rather small – and a lovely pool, but no restaurant. Free parking. Closed Oct–April. €99

De la Pinède 7 av Georges Gallice Ⓣ 04 93 61 03 95, Ⓣ hotel-pinede.com. Renovated, friendly two-star hotel in the centre of Juan-les-Pins, just a short walk from the beach, with a small sun terrace. Closed Nov to mid-Feb. €119

Pré Catelan 27 av des Palmiers Ⓣ 04 93 61 05 11, Ⓦ precatelan.fr. Peaceful and very comfortable hotel, in attractive gardens on the corner of av Lauriers, near the sea and the station, with large spacious rooms, some sleeping four, and a heated swimming pool. €144

EATING AND DRINKING

Café de la Plage 1 bd Edouard-Baudouin Ⓣ 04 93 61 37 61, Ⓦ cafe-de-la-plage.fr. This pleasant seafront spot offers everything from seafood to cocktails and ice cream, with lunchtime *plats* for €15. Daily: June–Sept 7.45am–midnight; Oct–May 7.45am–7pm.

Le Pam–Pam 137 bd Wilson Ⓣ 04 93 61 11 05, Ⓦ pampam.fr. Perennially popular cocktail bar with a Polynesian-meets-Brazilian ambience and frequent live music and dance spectacles. Fruit-and gewgaw-bedecked

cocktails from €9.60. Daily 3pm–4.30am.

★ **La Passagère** Hotel Belles Rives, 33 bd Edouard Baudoin Ⓣ 04 93 61 02 79, Ⓦ bellesrives.com. Modern Mediterranean delights using regional produce served in lovely, restored Art Deco surroundings with wonderful views over the bay; *retour du marché menu* €70, otherwise mains €45–58. June–Sept daily noon–2.30pm & 8–10.30pm; March–May & Oct–Dec Wed–Sun noon–2.30pm & 8–10pm.

THE ROUTE NAPOLÉON

The pines and silver sand between Juan-les-Pins and Cannes, now **Golfe-Juan**, witnessed Napoleon's return from exile in 1815. Having been in command of the Mediterranean defences as a general in 1794, with Antibes' Fort Carré as his base, the emperor knew the bay well. This time, however, his emissaries to Cannes and Antibes were taken prisoner upon landing, though the local men in charge decided not to capture him. The lack of enthusiasm for his return was enough to persuade the ever-brilliant tactician to head north, bypassing Grasse, and take the most isolated snowbound mule paths up to Sisteron and onwards – the path commemorated by the modern **Route Napoléon**. By March 6 he was in Dauphiné; on March 19 he was back in Paris's Tuileries Palace. One hundred days later he lost the battle of Waterloo and was finally and absolutely incarcerated on St Helena.

It's said that on the day he landed at Golfe-Juan, Napoleon's men accidentally held up the prince of Monaco's coach travelling east along the coast. The Revolution incorporated Monaco into France but the restored Louis XVIII had just granted back the principality. When the prince told the former emperor that he was off to reclaim his throne, Napoleon replied that they were in the same business and waved him on his way.

For **other sections of the Route Napoléon**, see "Grasse" on p.333, "Sisteron" on p.175, and "Castellane" on p.220.

7

Antibes

Centring on its walled old town, abutting against the waves 1.5km east of Juan-les-Pins and a total of 11km east of Cannes, the delightful resort of **ANTIBES** has largely escaped the overdevelopment that blights so many of its neighbours. Graham Greene lived here for over twenty years and described it as the only place on the Riviera to have preserved its soul. It remains a bustling little town, its animated streets full of bars and restaurants, swarming with Anglophones and yachting types, and hosting one of the finest **markets** along the coast. In addition to its stupendous seafront setting, its castle holds an extensive **Picasso collection**, and the views up from the ramparts towards the Alps are wonderful.

Very little remains of the medieval centre of Antibes, thanks to border squabbles from the fifteenth century until the Revolution, when Antibes belonged to France and Nice to Savoy. The finest surviving stretch of **walls** line the seafront near the little crescent of the old port, with a tiny little beach in front. Immediately north, luxury yachts and humble fishing boats jostle amicably for space in the harbour. The headland at its northern end is topped by the splendidly situated **Fort Carré** (Tues–Sun: mid-June to mid-Sept 10am–5.30pm; mid-Sept to mid-June 10am–4pm; €3), which was transformed by Vauban in the seventeenth century into an impregnable fortress.

Musée Picasso

Chateau Grimaldi, place Mariejol • Mid-June to mid-July & first 2wks of Sept Tues–Sun 10am–6pm; mid-July to end Aug Tues, Thurs, Sat & Sun 10am–6pm, Wed & Fri 10am–8pm; mid-Sept to mid-June Tues–Sun 10am–noon & 2–6pm • €6 or €10 with other municipal museums • ☎ 04 92 90 54 20, ⊛ antibes-juanlespins.com

Lording it over the ramparts, Antibes' **Château Grimaldi**, rebuilt in the sixteenth century but still with its twelfth-century Romanesque tower, is a beautifully cool, light space with hexagonal terracotta floor tiles. In 1946, Picasso was offered this dusty old building – by then already a museum – as a studio. Several prolific months followed before he moved to Vallauris, leaving all his Antibes output to what is now the **Musée Picasso**. Although he donated other works later on, the bulk of the collection belongs to this one period, when he was involved in one of his better relationships, with Françoise Gilot; Matisse was just up the road in Vence; the war was over; and the 1950s had not yet changed the Côte d'Azur forever.

7

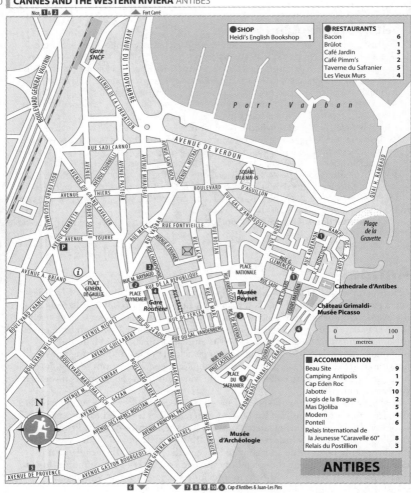

● SHOP
Heidi's English Bookshop   1

● RESTAURANTS
Bacon	6
Brûlot	1
Café Jardin	3
Café Pimm's	2
Taverne du Safranier	5
Les Vieux Murs	4

Port Vauban

Gare
SNCF

Plage
de la
Gravette

Cathedrale d'Antibes

Château Grimaldi-
Musée Picasso

Musée
Peynet

Gare
Routière

0   100
metres

■ ACCOMMODATION
Beau Site	9
Camping Antipolis	1
Cap Eden Roc	7
Jabotte	10
Logis de la Brague	2
Mas Djoliba	5
Modern	4
Ponteil	6
Relais International de la Jeunesse "Caravelle 60"	8
Relais du Postillion	3

Musée
d'Archéologie

N

ANTIBES

6 ▼   ▼ 7, 8, 9, 10, 6, Cap d'Antibes & Juan-Les Pins

For all but devotees, the Picassos on display will not be familiar; instead, the museum offers a chance to see lesser-known works in beautiful surroundings. There's an uncomplicated exuberance in the numerous still lifes of sea urchins, the goats and fauns and the wonderful *Ulysses and the Sirens*, a great round head against a mast, around which the ship, sea and sirens swirl. The materials reveal postwar shortages – odd bits of wood and board instead of canvas, and boat paint rather than oils. Picasso himself also makes a subject for other painters and photographers, including André Villers, Brassai, Man Ray and Bill Brandt.

The museum also holds several anguished works by **Nicolas de Staël**, who lived in Antibes for the last few months of his life, painting the sea, gulls and boats with great washes of grey, before he committed suicide in 1955. A wonderful terrace overlooking the sea is adorned by Germaine Richier sculptures, along with works by Miró, César and others.

Cathédrale d'Antibes

Rue du Saint-Esprit • Mon–Fri 8am–noon & 3–6.30pm, Sat & Sun 8am–noon & 3–7.30pm • ☎ 04 93 34 06 29

The **Cathédrale d'Antibes**, alongside the castle, was built on the site of an ancient temple. The choir and apse survive from the Romanesque building that served the city in the Middle Ages, while the nave and stunning ochre facade are Baroque. Inside, in the south transept, a sumptuous altarpiece by Louis Bréa is surrounded by immaculate panels of tiny detailed scenes.

Covered market

Cours Masséna • **Food market** June–Aug daily 6am–1pm; Sept–May Tues–Sun 6am–1pm • **Craft market** Mid-June to Sept Tues–Sun 3pm–midnight; Oct to mid-June Fri–Sun 3pm–midnight

Cours Masséna, one block inland from the castle, once marked the limit of Antibes' Greek settlement. Now it's the site of a morning **covered market** that overflows with Provençal goodies including delicious olives, and a profusion of cut **flowers**, a long-standing local speciality. Later in the day, a **craft market** takes over; as the stalls pack up, café tables take their place.

Musée d'Archéologie

Promenade Amiral-de-Grasse • Late June and early Sept Tues–Sun 10am–noon & 2–6pm; July & Aug Tues, Thurs, Sat & Sun 10am–noon & 2–6pm, Wed & Fri 10am–noon & 2–8pm; mid-Sept to mid-June Tues–Sun 10am–1pm & 2–3pm • €3 • ☎ 04 42 90 54 37

Set into the ramparts not far south of the castle, the Bastion St-André was built by Vauban in 1698, but from the outside at least still looks spanking new. It now houses the small but interesting **Musée d'Archéologie**, which gathers together Greek and Roman finds not only from the ancient settlement of Antipolis, the precursor of Antibes, but from all around the Mediterranean. The prettiest exhibits are the oldest: some lovely Duanian ceramics from southern Italy, dating from the sixth century BC.

Cap d'Antibes

South of the walled town, the peninsula known as the **Cap d'Antibes** is dominated by the world's super-rich, many of whom live – or at least maintain homes – here, though the southern Cap still retains pinewoods that hide the exclusive mansions. As well as offering intermittent access to the wonderful rocky shore and a couple of sandy beaches, the Cap holds a couple of beautiful gardens, the **Jardin Thuret** and the **Villa Eilenroc**. Walking or cycling up the western side of the Cap is a joy; you pass the tiny **Port de l'Olivette**, full of small, unflashy boats, as well as rocks, jetties, tiny sandy beaches, and grand villas hiding behind high walls.

The beaches

Antibes' longest beach, the sandy and utterly irresistible **Plage de la Salis**, runs along the eastern neck of the **Cap d'Antibes**. It's a rarity along the Riviera: access to it is free, with no big hotels blocking the way – the success of Juan-les-Pins spared this side of the Cap from unchecked development in the days before planning laws were tightened.

Above the southern end of the beach, at the top of chemin du Calvaire, stands the **Chapelle de la Garoupe** (daily 10am–noon & 2.30–5pm; ⓦgaroupe.free.fr), full of ex-votos for deliverances from accidents ranging from battles with the Saracens to collisions with speeding Citroëns. Much the best reason to make the trail up here, however, is for the stunning panoramic **views** across Cap d'Antibes towards both Juan-les-Pins and Antibes; you can see as far as the Esterel and to Nice and beyond. Next to the church is a powerful lighthouse whose beam is visible 70km out to sea.

A second public beach, **Plage de la Garoupe**, smaller than the Plage de la Salis but similarly sandy, stretches along boulevard de la Garoupe before the promontory of Cap Gros.

Villa Eilenroc

Avenue Mrs L.D. Beaumont • April–June Wed & Sat 10am–5pm; July–Sept Wed, Sat & Sun 3–7pm; Oct–March Wed & Sat 1–4pm • €2, Oct–March free

At the southern end of the Cap d'Antibes stands the grandiose **Villa Eilenroc**, completed in 1867 and designed by Charles Garnier, architect of the casino at Monte Carlo. Its unusual name is (almost) the Christian name of the wife of its original owner, spelled backwards – Cornelia. Both the house and its 27 acres of lush gardens are now owned by the municipality, and open to visitors; the real highlight is the superb rose garden.

From the gardens you may catch a glimpse the villa's equally magnificent neighbour, the **Château de la Croé**. Home, after the 1936 abdication, to the Duke and Duchess of Windsor, it now belongs to Russian billionaire Roman Abramovich.

Musée Napoléonien

Av J.-F.-Kennedy • Tues–Sat: mid-June to mid–Sept 10am–6pm; mid-Sept to mid-June 10am–4.30pm • €3 • ☎ 04 93 61 45 32

The **Musée Napoléonien**, at the Batterie du Graillon, close to the southwestern extremity of the Cap d'Antibes, documents the general's return from Elba with the usual paraphernalia of hats, cockades, model ships and signed commands. Both the fort itself, and the slightly grubby public beach alongside, enjoy lovely views.

Jardin Thuret

90 chemin Raymond • Mon–Fri: mid-June to mid–Sept 8am–6pm; mid-Sept to mid-June 8.30am–5.30pm • Free • ☎ 04 97 21 25 00, ⓦ jardin-thuret.antibes.inra.fr

Dominating the middle of the Cap, the **Jardin Thuret** was established in the nineteenth century by botanist Gustav Thuret. It now tests and acclimatizes subtropical trees and shrubs in order to diversify the Mediterranean plants of France.

ARRIVAL AND INFORMATION | ANTIBES

By train The *gare SNCF* is a 3min walk north of the old town along av Robert-Soleau.
Destinations Cannes (very frequent; 7–10min); Nice (very frequent; 20–25 min).
By bus The *gare routière* is on place Guynemer (☎ 04 93 34 37 60, ⓦ envibus.fr).
Destinations Aéroport Nice-Côte-d'Azur (every 20min; 20–45min); Biot (#10; every 20–35 min; 25min); Cannes (every 20min; 30–35min); Cap d'Antibes (#2; every 40min; 9min); Juan-les-Pins (#3; every 40min; 6min); Nice (every 20min; 45min–1hr 10min); Vallauris (hourly; 25min).

By car Driving in and around Antibes can be a nightmare; best to follow signs to one of the city's multi-storey car parks as soon as you arrive. The most convenient for the walled town is Parking J-M Poirier, accessed on av Tourre.
Tourist office 11 place du Général-de-Gaulle (July & Aug daily 9am–7pm; Sept–June Mon–Fri 9am–12.30pm & 1.30–6pm, Sat 9am–noon & 2–6pm, Sun 10am–12.30pm & 2–6pm; ☎ 04 97 23 11 11, ⓦ antibesjuanlespins.com).
Bookshop Heidi's English Bookshop, 24 rue Aubernon (Tues–Sat 10am–7pm, Sun & Mon 11am–6pm; ☎ 04 93 34 74 11) is the best-stocked English bookshop on the coast.

ACCOMMODATION

Beau Site 141 bd Kennedy, Cap d'Antibes ☎ 04 93 61 53 43, ⓦ hotelbeausite.net. This white-painted inn, set in a lovely garden amid some of the most exclusive villas on the Cap d'Antibes, offers spacious, plain, tiled rooms that represent great value, plus a very welcome pool. Closed Nov–Feb. **€95**
Cap Eden Roc bd Kennedy, Cap d'Antibes ☎ 04 93 61 39 01, ⓦ edenroc-hotel.fr. A celebrity haunt since F. Scott Fitzgerald used it as the setting for *Tender is the Night*, this luxury hotel has a prime seafront position in 25 acres on Cap d'Antibes. Along with all the comforts you'd expect at this price, it even has its own landing stage. Closed mid-Oct to mid-April. **€750**
La Jabotte 13 av Max Maurey, Cap d'Antibes ☎ 04 93

61 45 89, ⓦ jabotte.com. Just a short walk from the Plage de la Salis in Cap d'Antibes, and twenty minutes' walk from town, this tranquil, relaxing and gay-friendly place has ten cosy, beautifully decorated rooms in vibrant, cheerful colours – book in advance. The cheapest double has a shower, but WC on the landing. **€101**
Le Mas Djoliba 29 av de Provence, Cap d'Antibes ☎ 04 93 34 02 48, ⓦ hotel-djoliba.com. Fine old Provençal farmhouse that's now a three-star *Logis de France* with a pool, *boules* and a fabulous garden; it's a great hideaway from the bustle of town and not too far from the beach. Closed mid-Nov to early March. **€154**
Modern 1 rue Formillère ☎ 04 92 90 59 05, ⓦ modernhotel06.com. Welcoming and inexpensive

little hotel, tucked away in a pedestrian lane in the heart of the old town, though the very plain modern rooms are duller than the cute exterior might suggest. €82

Ponteil 11 impasse Jean-Mensier ☎04 93 34 67 92, ⓦleponteil.com. Friendly, pretty hotel with the feel of a B&B, in a quiet location at the end of a cul-de-sac near the sea, and surrounded by luxuriant vegetation. Small plain rooms, and free parking. Closed mid-Nov to Jan. €82

Relais International de la Jeunesse "Caravelle 60" 272 bd de la Garoupe, Cap d'Antibes ☎04 93 61 34 40, ⓦclajsud.fr. As this popular hostel is right by the beach, you'll need to book well in advance to secure a bed; meals are taken outdoors under the pine trees. Bus #2 from the *gare routière* stops right outside. Closed Oct–March. €28

Le Relais du Postillion 8 rue Championnet ☎04 93 34 20 77, ⓦrelaisdupostillon.com. Situated in the old town of Antibes above a low-key bar that's open until midnight, this charming, gay-friendly and very central little hotel has

the feel of an old inn, with a wide range of comfortable, individually decorated rooms, and lots of exposed stonework. €114

CAMPING

Camping Antipolis Av du Pylone, La Brague ☎04 93 33 93 99, ⓦcamping-antipolis.com. Four-star campsite, 3km north of Antibes (on bus #10)and 800m from the sea, with a pool, restaurant, bar, supermarket and nightly entertainment in summer. Closed late Sept to early April. €45

Logis de la Brague 1221 rte de Nice, La Brague ☎4 93 33 54 72, ⓦcamping-logisbrague.com. Like all Antibes' campsites, this three-star option is north of the city in the quartier of La Brague (bus #10 or one train stop). At 4km from central Antibes, this is the closest to the "Gare de Biot" station. It's just two minutes from the beach and has a restaurant but no pool. Closed Oct–April. €17

EATING AND DRINKING

Old Antibes has places to eat at every turn: place Nationale and cours Masséna are lined with **cafés**; rue James-Close has nothing but **restaurants**, and rue Thuret and its side streets also offer numerous menus to browse through. Places to **drink** are especially thick on the ground by the port.

Restaurant de Bacon 664 bd de Bacon, Cap d'Antibes ☎04 93 61 50 02, ⓦrestaurantdebacon.com. With excellent fish and a sea view, this locally renowned restaurant offers a €55 set lunch; the usual dinner *menu* costs €85, but in July & Aug you can only order à la carte, when a magnificent bouillabaisse, for example costs €125 per person. April–Oct Tues 7.30–10pm, Wed–Sun noon–2pm & 7.30–10pm.

Brûlot 3 rue Frédéric Isnard ☎04 93 34 17 76, ⓦbrulot .fr. A stalwart of the restaurant scene in Antibes' old town, dishing up classic regional dishes like *socca* chickpea pancakes from its wood-fired oven, salad Niçoise and tripe. *Lunch formule* €12.90, *menus* €19–42. Mon–Wed 4–9.30pm, Thurs–Sat 9am–3pm & 6–9.30pm.

Le Café Jardin 23 rue des Bains ☎04 93 34 42 66, ⓦlecafejardin.fr. Friendly little brasserie/café in a very peaceful spot in the back lanes of the old town, with a couple of tables out on the street, a nice bar, and a courtyard filled with twee ceramic frogs. Breakfast is €6, or you can just pick up a smoothie or hot drink; lunch *menus* start at €14.50, with a €16 vegetarian option. Daily 8am–7.30pm.

Café Pimm's 3 rue de la République ☎04 93 34 04 88, ⓦpimmscafe.fr. Daytime brasserie, with carousel decor and a friendly atmosphere, where the pavement tables on the corner of place Guynemer guard the approach to the old town. Whether you order salad, pasta, or a daily *plat*, it will cost in the range of €9–16. Daily 7am–8.30pm.

★ **Taverne du Safranier** 1 place Safranier ☎04 93 34 80 50, ⓦtaverne-du-safranier.fr. With outdoor tables spreading beneath a trellis of vines, close to both the centre and the sea, this is arguably Antibes' prettiest restaurant, even though it's set in a drab little square. Fresh-caught fish is the speciality, with whole, beautifully prepared bass or bream typically priced around €23, or available on the €28 set *menu*. Very friendly, with English-speaking service. Tues, Wed & Fri–Sun noon–2pm & 7.30–9.30pm, Thurs 7.30–9.30pm.

Les Vieux Murs 25 promenade Amiral-de-Grasse ☎04 93 34 06 73, ⓦlesvieuxmurs.com. *Restaurant gastronomique* serving classy food, like salt cod with shavings of Iberian ham or poached veal with artichokes, in a perfect setting on the castle ramparts. Lunch *menu* from €29, dinner *menus* €34–90. Tues–Sun 12.30–2pm & 7.30–10pm.

Biot

The pretty *village perché* of **BIOT**, 4km from the coast and 5km northwest of Antibes, is famous for its rich arts and crafts tradition. Long a centre of **pottery** production and now home to several glassworks, Biot is usually packed out in high season, as visitors drawn by the excellent **Fernand Léger museum** nearby stay on to browse around the village itself.

Most of Biot's wide array of shops, studios and galleries line up along the long, straight **rue St-Sébastien**, which runs along the crest of the hill to reach the old **walled village**, a much less developed labyrinth of narrow lanes and tiny squares.

Musée d'Histoire et de Céramique Biotoises

9 rue St-Sébastien • July–Sept Wed–Sun 11am–7pm; Oct–June Wed, Sat & Sun 2–6pm, Thurs & Fri 10am–6pm • €4 • ☎ 04 93 65 54 54, ⓦ musee-de-biot.fr

The artist **Fernand Léger**, who lived in Biot for a few years at the end of his life, was first attracted to the village by its potteries; one of his old pupils had set up shop here to produce ceramics of his master's designs. Today, the former Chapelle des Pénitents Blancs houses a small **Musée d'Histoire et de Céramique Biotoises**, which underlines the importance of the potteries to the historical development of the village.

Verrerie de Biot

Chemin des Combes • **Verrerie de Biot** Mid-June to mid-Sept Mon–Sat 9.30am–8pm, Sun 10.30am–1.30pm & 2.30–7.30pm; mid-Sept to mid-June Mon–Sat 9.30am–6pm, Sun 10.30am–1.30pm & 2.30–6.30pm • Free **Eco-musée du Verre** Guided tours only: mid-June to mid-Sept Mon–Sat 11.30am, 3.30pm & 5.30pm, Sun 3.30pm & 5.30pm; mid-Sept to mid-June daily 4.30pm • €6 • ☎ 04 93 65 03 00, ⓦ verreriebiot.com

Biot's **glass-makers** do all they can to encourage visitors to admire, and ideally buy, the famous and beautiful hand-blown bubble glass (*verre bullé*). You can watch glass-blowers at work at the **Verrerie de Biot** – established in 1956, a year after Léger's death – just north of the centre, and learn more by taking a tour of the on-site **Eco-musée du Verre**.

Musée Fernand Léger

316 chemin du Val de Pôme • Daily except Tues: May–Oct 10am–6pm; Nov–April 10am–5pm • €5.50, €7.50 during temporary exhibitions • ☎ 04 92 91 50 30, ⓦ musee-fernandleger.fr • Bus #10 from Antibes (every 20–35 min; 20min) to stop "F. Leger"

A stunning, life-affirming collection of paintings by Fernand Léger is displayed at the **Musée Fernand Léger**, 1km southeast of Biot. Even the museum building is a pleasure: with its giant mosaic murals, it transcends its mundane suburban setting.

Léger was turned off from the abstraction of Parisian painters by his experiences of fighting alongside ordinary working people in World War I. Not that he favoured realism, but he wanted his paintings to have popular appeal. Understanding that in the modern world, art competes with images generated by advertising, cinema and public spectacle, he set about producing work with a similar visual power. Without any realism in the form or facial expressions, the people in such paintings as *Four*

THEME PARKS ALONG THE COAST

Several large-scale attractions for children line up along the main coast road, well away from Biot village – everything from performing dolphins at Marineland to water slides at Aquasplash.

Marineland On the N7 ⓦ marineland.fr. Dolphin, killer whale and sea lion shows, aquariums, a shark tunnel and plenty of other marine animals, from penguins to polar bears, spread over an expansive site. Daily: mid-Feb to March & Oct–Dec 10am–6pm; April–June & Sept 10am–7pm; July & Aug 10am–11pm; closed Jan to mid-Feb. Adult €38, under-13 €34.

Aquasplash On the same site as Marineland, on the N7 ⓦ marineland.fr. Water toboggans, chutes and slides. Mid-June to Aug daily 10am–7pm. Adult €26, child €23.

Antibesland Almost opposite Marineland ⓦ azurpark.com. Large funfair with plenty of rollercoasters and rides. April to mid-June Sat, Sun & public hols 2–7pm; second fortnight of June Mon–Fri 8.30pm–1am, Sat 5pm–1am, Sun 3pm–1am; July & Aug Mon–Sat 5pm–2am, Sun 3pm–2am. Free entry, rides €2–5.

Bicycle Riders or the various *Construction Workers* are forcefully present as they engage in their work or leisure, and are visually on an equal footing with the objects. Almost all the collection is displayed in two very spacious white galleries upstairs; while it's not scrupulously chronological, Léger's earlier, Cubist works come first.

ARRIVAL AND INFORMATION

BIOT

By train and bus Although Biot does officially have a *gare SNCF*, it's not near the village itself, but down by the sea at La Brague, 4km south, along a road that's much too dangerous and unpleasant to walk. Regular buses between Biot and Antibes (#10; every 20–35 min; 25min) call at the *gare SNCF*.

Tourist office 46 rue St-Sébastien (June–Aug Mon–Fri 9.30am–6.30pm, Sat & Sun 11am–5pm; April, May & Sept Mon–Fri 9.30am–12.30pm & 1.30pm–6pm, Sat & Sun 2–6pm; ☎ 04 93 65 78 00, ⓦ biot.fr).

ACCOMMODATION AND EATING

★ **Hôtel des Arcades** 16 place des Arcades ☎ 04 93 65 01 04, ⓦ hotel-restaurant-les-arcades.com. Definitely the nicest place to stay in Biot; this very reasonably priced hotel, full of old-fashioned charm, offers huge rooms on a lovely little square in the heart of the medieval village. Book well in advance. Its café-restaurant, which doubles as an art gallery, serves delicious Provençal food at tables under the arcades (closed Sun evening & Mon; *plats du jour* around €17, dinner *menus* from €32). **€55**

Café de la Poste 24 rue St-Sébastien ☎ 04 93 65 19 32. The best of several restaurants that have outdoor tables in the main village square, as well as indoor dining rooms just off it. A very decent two-course lunch costs €16, or you can get a sandwich or even a horse steak for €9. Tues–Sun: May–Oct noon–2pm & 7–9pm; Nov–April 7–9.30pm.

L'Eden 243 chemin du Val-de-Pôme ☎ 04 93 65 63 70, ⓦ camping-eden.fr. Three-star campsite, a couple of hundred metres from the Léger museum, with a pool, bar and restaurant. Closed Nov–March. **€27**

Mistral 1780 route de la Mer ☎ 04 93 65 61 48, ⓦ campinglemistral.com. Good-value one-star campsite, near the Marineland theme park, 800m up from the sea. There's a bar but no pool. Closed Oct–April. **€21.30**

Villeneuve-Loubet

The Riviera shore reaches its trashy nadir at **Villeneuve-Loubet-Plage**, 6km straight up the coast from Antibes, where the giant **Baie des Anges** marina dominates the waterfront. The marina was built in the 1970s, and the petrified sails of its colossal residential blocks – a clever, well-maintained but hugely intrusive slice of modernism – are visible all the way from Cap d'Antibes to Cap Ferrat. The commercial squalor that surrounds it is even harder to stomach – an unsightly mess of drive-in restaurants, petrol stations and out-of-town retail sheds wedged between the autoroute and the sea.

Across the autoroute, the quieter, more attractive village of **VILLENEUVE-LOUBET**, on the River Loup, clusters around an undamaged twelfth-century castle (closed to the public), which was once home to François I.

Musée de l'Art Culinaire

3 rue Escoffier, Villeneuve-Loubet • July & Aug Mon, Tues, Thurs, Fri & Sun 2–7pm, Wed & Sat 10am–noon & 2–7pm; Sept, Oct & Dec–June daily 2–6pm; closed Nov • €5 • ☎ 04 93 20 80 51, ⓦ fondation-escoffier.org

The small village house in Villeneuve-Loubet where legendary chef **Auguste Escoffier** (1846–1935) was born is now the **Musée de l'Art Culinaire**. The son of a blacksmith, Escoffier began his restaurant career at thirteen, skivvying for his uncle in Nice, and was by the end of the century known as "the king of chefs and the chef of kings". In London he was the *Savoy*'s first head chef, then the *Carlton*'s; he fed almost every European head of state, and personally trained almost 2000 chefs. *Pêche melba* was his most famous creation, but his significance for the history of haute cuisine was in breaking the tradition of health-hazard richness and quantity. He was also a technical innovator, who invented dried potato and a breadcrumb maker.

As well as items related to Escoffier's own life, the museum tells the history of French cuisine, and includes a re-creation of an eighteenth-century Provençal kitchen. It was the invention of the stove or *potager* that revolutionized French cooking: by making it possible to cook dishes simultaneously at a wide range of temperatures, it paved the way for the development of elaborate menus. The top floor displays a collection of historic menus, while another entire floor, reeking of chocolate and sugar, is devoted to the art of the pastry chef.

In a gesture other museums would do well to emulate, all visitors are presented with a free *pêche melba*, to enjoy in the small courtyard.

ACCOMMODATION AND EATING

L'Auberge Fleurie 11 rue des Mesures ☎ 04 93 73 90 92, ⓦ laubergefleurievilleneuveloubetvillage.com. It's not just the web address that's flowery at this pretty, flower-bedecked village restaurant, which serves the likes of salmon escalope with saffron or carpaccio of beef with truffle oil, in a formal setting. *Menus* from €15 at lunch, €29 at dinner. Tues–Fri & Sun noon–1.30pm & 7.30–9.30pm, Sat 7.30–9.30pm.

Le Chat Plume 5 rue des Mesures ☎ 04 93 73 40 91, ⓦ chatplume.com. Good local restaurant in the pedestrianized centre, just down the hill from the museum,

VILLENEUVE-LOUBET

which serves hearty *cuisine de terroir* in cheerfully quirky surroundings, with dishes such as *cuisse de lapin* on marinated artichokes on *menus* that start at €18 for lunch, €29 for dinner. Tues 7.30–9.30pm, Wed–Sat noon–1.30pm & 7.30–9.30pm, Sun noon–1.30pm.

Parc 1 av de la Libération ☎ 04 93 20 88 13, ⓦ hotelduparcvilleneuve.com. Simple, inexpensive hotel, beside the bridge at the busy road junction at the entrance to the old town, with restaurant tables down on a terrace overlooking the river. *Menus* at €20 and €30. **€66**

Cagnes

Slashed through by three major roads and with an awe-inspiring traffic problem, **CAGNES** is a confusing agglomeration. The narrow coastal strip, known as **Cros-de-Cagnes**, consists of a small, pleasant old quarter, with fishing boats pulled up on its broad, pebbly beach. Scruffy, modern **Cagnes-sur-Mer**, which constitutes the town centre, is inland above the autoroute, a bustling but rather characterless place notable only for **Renoir's house**. The original medieval village, **Haut-de-Cagnes**, overlooks both town and coast from the northwest heights, and has a stunning **castle** that contains the fabulous **Donation Solidor**.

In early July Cagnes celebrates all manner of sea-related activities as part of the **Fête de la Saint-Pierre et de la Mer**; in early August there's free **street theatre** on place du Château and on the seafront; and late August sees a bizarre **square boules** competition down montée de la Bourgade.

Les Collettes – the Musée Renoir

Chemain des Collettes, 1km east of Cagnes-sur-Mer up av Renoir • Daily except Tues: May–Sept 10am–noon & 2–6pm; Oct–April 10am–noon & 2–5pm; check that it has reopened following extensive renovations • €4, or €6 with Château Grimaldi • ☎ 04 93 20 61 07, ⓦ www.cagnes-tourisme.com • Bus #49 from Cagnes-sur-Mer bus station

Surrounded by olive and rare orange groves, **Les Collettes**, the house that **Renoir** had built in 1907 and where he spent the last twelve years of his life, is now the **Musée Renoir**. Renoir was captivated by the olive trees and by the difficulties of rendering "a tree full of colours". One of the two studios in the house, north-facing to catch the late afternoon light, is arranged as though Renoir had just popped out. Despite the rheumatoid arthritis that had forced him to seek a warmer climate than Paris, he painted every day at Les Collettes, strapping the brush to his hand when moving his fingers became too painful.

Portraits of Renoir here by his closest friends, displayed in the house, include Albert André's *À Renoir Peignant*, showing the ageing artist hunching over his canvas; a bust by Aristide Maillol; a crayon sketch by Richard Guido; and Dufy's *Homage to Renoir*. Renoir's work is represented by several sculptures including two bronzes – *La Maternité* and a medallion of his son Coco – some beautiful, tiny watercolours in the studio, and ten paintings from his Cagnes period (the greatest, the final version of *Les Grandes Baigneuses*, hangs in the Louvre).

Haut-de-Cagnes

As perfect a hilltop village as you'll find on the Riviera, **HAUT-DE-CAGNES**, an easy walk up from Cagnes-sur-Mer and also accessible on bus #44, was for many years the haunt of successful artists. No architectural excrescences spoil its tiers of tiny streets, and even the flowers spilling over terracotta pots or climbing soft stone walls appear perfect.

Château Grimaldi

Place Grimaldi, Haut de Cagnes • Daily May–Sept 10am–noon & 2–6pm; Oct–April 10am–noon & 2–5pm • €4, or €6 with Les Collettes • ☎ 04 92 02 47 30 • Free shuttle bus #44 from bus station; on foot, it's a steep ascent from av Renoir along rue Général-Bérenger and montée de la Bourgade

Ancient Haut-de-Cagnes backs up to the crenellated **château**, which once belonged to the Grimaldis of Monaco and now houses the **Château Grimaldi**, comprising the **Musée de l'Olivier**, the **Donation Solidor** and exhibition space for **contemporary art**. The castle's Renaissance interior is itself a masterpiece, with tiers of arcaded galleries, vast frescoed ceilings, stuccoed historical reliefs and gorgeously ornamented chambers and chapels.

The **Donation Solidor** consists of wonderfully diverse portraits of cabaret star Suzy Solidor, by the likes of Dufy, Cocteau, Laurençin, Lempicka, Van Dongen and Kisling. Solidor's career spanned the 1920s to the 1970s, and she spent her last 25 years in Cagnes. She was quite a character: extremely talented and independent, she declared herself a lesbian years before the word, let alone the preference, was remotely acceptable, and was the inspiration for the British music-hall song "*If you knew Suzy, like I know Suzy*". Each canvas clearly reveals the qualities that most endeared her to each artist, or the fantasies she provoked, giving a fascinating insight into the art of portraiture as well as a multifaceted image of the woman.

The **Musee de l'Olivier** explains the history and practice of olive cultivation and oil production, with sundry old wooden presses and other artefacts.

ARRIVAL AND INFORMATION   CAGNES

By train The Cagnes-sur-Mer *gare SNCF* (as opposed to Cros-de-Cagnes, one stop along) is southwest of the centre alongside the autoroute. Buses #42, #49, #56 and #200 all make the short run from the *gare SNCF* to the gare routière on place M. Bourdet in Cagnes-sur-Mer.
Destinations Antibes (every 20–30min; 11min); Cannes (every 20–30min; 23min); Nice (every 15–30min; 15min).
By bus The *gare routière* is on place M. Bourdet in Cagnes-sur-Mer. From there, bus #41 runs to Cros-de-Cagnes and the seafront; bus #49 to the Renoir museum; and #44 up to Haut-de-Cagnes.
Destinations Cannes (every 15–20min; 57min); Nice (every 15–20min; 38min).

By car The narrow lanes of Haut-de-Cagnes present a phenomenal challenge to drivers. The extraordinary hilltop car park is well worth experiencing, however; you leave your vehicle in what looks like a car wash, from which it's whisked away and filed in some subterranean cavern until you return.
Tourist office Each component of Cagnes has its own office. In Cagnes-sur-Mer, it's at 6 bd Maréchal-Juin (July & Aug Mon–Sat 9am–12.30pm & 2–6pm; Sept–June Mon–Fri 9am–noon & 2–6pm, Sat 9am–noon; ☎ 04 93 20 61 64, ⓦ cagnes-tourisme.com); up in Haut-de-Cagnes, it's on place du Dr-Morel (July & Aug daily 9.30am–noon & 1.30–6pm; June & Sept Wed–Sun 9.30am–noon & 1.30–6pm; Oct–May Wed–Sun 1.30–5.30pm; ☎ 04 92 02 85 05).

ACCOMMODATION

Although the largest choice of **hotels** is down in Cros-de-Cagnes, assuming you don't mind not being by the sea it's much nicer to stay up in the peace of Haut-de-Cagnes. There are also plenty of **campsites** around, most of them in wooded locations inland.

Aéva 22–23 promenade de la Plage, Cros-de-Cagnes ☎ 04 93 73 39 52, ⓦ _hotel-aeva.fr. Stylishly revamped seafront hotel. Elegant, modern, a/c en-suites have soundproofing, satellite TV, safes and wi-fi. There's a glassy restaurant facing the sea, and a separate aparthotel, too. **€100**

Le Grimaldi 6 place du Château, Haut-de-Cagnes ☎ 04 93 20 60 24, ⓦ hotelgrimaldi.com. Charming old village house, with five cosy modernized rooms, set behind a large terrace restaurant on the square. It's really hard to get a car anywhere near here, but once you find it, it's a delightful place to spend a few days, absorbing the life of the village. **€135**

Les Terrasses du Soleil Place Notre Dame de la Protection, Haut-de-Cagnes ☎ 04 93 73 26 56, ⓦ www.terrassesdusoleil.com. Attractive *chambre d'hôte* in the former village home of songwriter Georges Ulmer, with two B&B rooms and two suites. **€115**

Le Val Fleuri 139 chemin Vallon des Vaux ☎ 04 93 31 21 74, ⓦ campingvalfleuri.fr. Two-star campsite approximately 4km from the sea (bus #41) with a heated pool, snack bar and children's play area. They also rent out studio flats and mobile homes. Closed mid-Oct to Jan. **€23**

EATING AND DRINKING

Fleur de Sel 85 montée de la Bourgade, Haut-de-Cagnes ☎ 04 92 20 33 33, ⓦ restaurant-fleurdesel.com. This lovely old hilltop house serves delicious Provençal cuisine such as langoustines in creamy risotto and tournedos of beef with duck foie gras and black truffle sauce; *menus* from €33. April–Sept daily except Wed 7.30–9.30pm; Oct–March Mon, Tues & Fri–Sun 7.30–9pm.

Josy-Jo 2 rue du Planastel, Haut-de-Cagnes ☎ 04 93 20 68 76, ⓦ restaurant-josyjo.com. Charming restaurant in the space that served as the workshop for artist Chaim Soutine during the interwar years, with an oleander-shaded terrace and refined Provençal dishes. *Menus* €29–42, otherwise around €25 for main courses à la carte. July & Aug Mon–Sat 7.30–9.30pm; Sept–June Tues–Sat noon–1.30pm & 7.30–9pm.

Grasse

Enjoying stunning uninterrupted views over the Côte d'Azur from its hillside location 16km inland from Cannes, **GRASSE** has been capital of the **perfume industry** for almost three hundred years. It's a far cry now, though, from the medieval town depicted in Patrick Süskind's novel *Perfume*. If you're at all interested in the scent business, various perfume museums and factories make Grasse worthy of a day-trip, and it also has a gritty sense of being a genuine lived-in community that many of its neighbours lack, but it's not really a place to plan a long stay, especially as it's very short of decent hotels.

By the time Grasse experienced the aristocratic tourist boom of the late nineteenth century, its most desirable addresses – including one where Queen Victoria stayed for a month in 1891 – lay outside the old town, to the east. These days, however, the residential suburbs hold minimal appeal for the visitors who flock to the restored **Vieille Ville**, a hubbub of life and noise where the former homes of sixteenth-century tanning merchants, seventeenth-century perfumed-glove manufacturers and eighteenth-century *parfumiers* have become museums, boutiques and municipal offices. Walking the narrow lanes of the old town is a pleasure in itself, as is emerging into the public gardens at the southern end, where the terrace above Boulevard Fragonard commands fabulous views down to the distant Mediterranean.

At the north end of town, **Place aux Aires** hosts a daily **flower and vegetable market** (mornings only). Ringed by arcades of different heights, it was at one time the exclusive preserve of the tanning industry.

Musée International de la Parfumerie

2 bd du Jeu du Ballon • April daily 11am–6pm; May–Sept Mon–Fri & Sun 10am–7pm, Sat 10am–9pm; Oct–March Mon & Wed–Sun 11am–6pm; closed 3wks in Nov • €4, under-18s free • ☎ 04 97 05 58 00, ⓦ museesdegrasse.com

Housed in a much-altered eighteenth-century mansion alongside the public gardens, the **Musée International de la Parfumerie** tells the story of the creation and uses of scent ever since ancient Egyptian priests became the first *parfumiers*. A fascinating parallel account describes how perfumes have been marketed and sold – often using Egyptian or other "exotic" iconography – and there's also a general history of the beauty and make-up industries. Prize exhibits include a travelling case that belonged to Marie

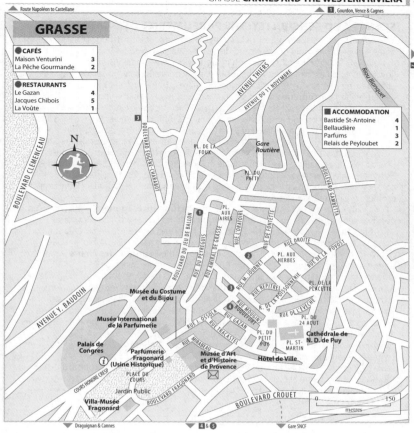

Antoinette, and there's a greenhouse filled with gently scented herbs and flowers. Visits culminate by exploring Grasse's role in industrializing the whole process.

Musée Provençal du Costume et du Bijou

2 rue Jean-Ossola • April–Oct daily 10am–1pm & 2–6pm; Nov–March Mon–Sat 10am–1pm & 2–6pm • Free • ☎ 04 93 36 44 65, ⓦ fragonard.com

The small, **Musée Provençal du Costume et du Bijou**, owned by the Parfumerie Fragonard, does exactly what it claims. Besides a room filled with jewels, several more hold mannequins dressed in various traditional regional costumes, dimly lit to preserve their vivid colours.

Musée d'Art et d'Histoire de Provence

2 rue Mirabeau • April daily 11am–6pm; May–Sept daily 10am–7pm; Oct–March Mon & Wed–Sun 11am–6pm; closed 3wks in Nov • Free • ☎ 04 97 05 58 00, ⓦ museesdegrasse.com

A luxurious townhouse commissioned by the sister of the Comte de Mirabeau, a leading figure in the French Revolution, now serves as the **Musée d'Art et d'Histoire de Provence**. As well as retaining many of its gorgeous fittings and original eighteenth-century kitchen, it displays a historical collection that includes wonderful

SCENTS AND SENSIBILITY: THE PARFUMERIES OF GRASSE

Making perfume is usually presented as a mysterious process, an alchemy, turning the soul of the flower into a liquid of luxury and desire. The reality, including traditional methods of *macération* – mixing the blossoms with heated animal fat – and *enfleuration* – placing the flowers on cold fat, then washing the result with alcohol and finally distilling it into the ultimately refined essence – is distinctly less romantic, but every bit as intriguing.

There are ten **parfumeries** in and around Grasse, most of them making not perfume but essences-plus-formulas, that are then sold to Dior, Lancôme, Estée Lauder and the like, who make up their own brand-name perfumes. Although synthetic ingredients have long formed an essential part of their repertoire, they still use copious amounts of locally grown lavender, jasmine and roses. To extract 1kg of essence of lavender takes 200kg of lavender; 1kg of cabbage rose essence needs over 3000kg of roses. Perfume contains twenty percent essence (eau de toilette contains ten percent; eau de Cologne five or six percent), and the bottles are extremely small. The major cost to this multi-billion-pound business is marketing. On strictly cost-accounting grounds, the clothes created by the grand Parisian couturiers serve simply to promote their latest fragrances.

For a fairly close-up look at production, visit the **Parfumerie Fragonard**, which is spread over two venues. The first, the **Usine Historique** at 20 bd Fragonard (Feb–Oct daily 9am–6pm; Nov–Jan Mon–Sat 9am–12.30pm & 2–6pm; free; ☎04 93 36 44 65, ⓦfragonard .com), shows traditional methods of extracting essence and has a collection of antique cosmetics bottles and bejewelled flagons. The second, the **Fabrique des Fleurs** – 3km southeast towards Cannes, at Les Quatre Chemins (same hours; free; ☎04 93 77 94 30, ⓦfragonard.com), is more informative, and at least admits to modernization of the processes. A world map shows the origins of various strange ingredients: resins, roots, moss, beans, civet (extract of a wild cat's genitals), ambergris (whale intestines), bits of beaver, and musk from Tibetan goats all help to produce the array of scents that the "nose" – as the creator of the perfume's formula is known – has to play with. A professional "nose" (of whom there are fewer than fifty) can recognize five or six thousand different scents.

Two other *parfumeries* offer tours in French and English: **Galimard**, 4km southeast of the centre at 73 route de Cannes (guided visits daily: June–Sept 9am–7.30pm; Oct–May 9am–12.30pm & 2.30–7pm; free; ☎04 93 09 20 00, ⓦgalimard.com), and **Molinard**, 1.5km southwest of the centre at 60 bd Victor-Hugo (April–June & Sept daily 9.30am–1pm & 2–6.30pm; July & Aug daily 9am–7pm; Oct–March Mon–Sat 9.30am–1pm & 2–6.30pm; free; ⓦmolinard.com).

eighteenth- to nineteenth-century faïence from Apt and Le Castellet, Mirabeau's death mask, a tin bidet, six prehistoric bronze leg bracelets, *santons* and oil presses.

Villa-Musée Fragonard

23 bd Fragonard • April daily 11am–6pm; May–Sept daily 10am–7pm; Oct–March Mon & Wed–Sun 11am–6pm; closed 3wks in Nov • Free • ☎04 97 05 58 00, ⓦmuseesdegrasse.com

The delightful **Villa-Musée Fragonard** celebrates Rococo painter Jean-Honoré Fragonard. The son of an early and not very successful Grassois perfumed-glove maker, he returned to live in this villa when his work fell out of favour after the Revolution. The staircase features impressive wall paintings by his son Alexandre-Evariste, while the salon is graced by copies of the panels depicting *Love's Progress in the Heart of a Young Girl*, which Jean-Honoré painted for Louis XV's mistress, Madame du Barry.

The Cathédrale Notre-Dame du Puy

Place du Petit Puy • July–Sept daily Sat 9.30–11.30am & 3–6.30pm; Oct–June Mon–Sat 9.30–11.30am & 3–5.30pm • Free

Cradled in the alleyways at the south end of the old town is the former Bishop's Palace

– now the Hôtel de Ville – and the **Cathédrale Notre-Dame du Puy** which were built in the twelfth century, replacing a two-hundred-year-old fortress. Despite endless alterations, the cathedral still has its high gaunt nave, in which the starkly unadorned ribbed vaulting is supported from the side walls. Its astonishing, weighty columns and the walls surrounding the altar were fractured in a fierce fire after the Revolution, giving the masonry an incredible, organic cave-like feel.

ARRIVAL AND INFORMATION   GRASSE

By bus Grasse's *gare routière* is on place de la Buanderie, just north of the old town.
Destinations Le-Bar-sur-Loup (11 daily; 15min); Cagnes (every 45min; 50min); Cannes (every 30min; 1hr); Digne (1 daily; 2hr 25min); Mougins (every 15–45min; 20–30min); Nice (every 30–50min; 1hr 30min); Tourrettes-sur-Loup (3 daily; 35min); Vence (3 daily; 50min).

By train Trains from Cannes (hourly; 31min) arrive at Grasse's *gare SNCF*, 1.6km south of the Vieille Ville by road, but just 300m on foot; it's a stiff walk uphill, so take bus #2, #4 or #5 into town.
Tourist office Cours Honoré-Cresp (July to mid-Sept daily 9am–8pm; mid-Sept to June Mon–Sat 9am–12.30pm & 2–6pm; ☎ 04 93 36 66 66, ⓦ grasse.fr).

ACCOMMODATION

The fact that Grasse sprawls over an extended and very hilly urban area means that it would be preferable to stay right in the heart of town. However, not only does the centre have surprisingly few **hotels**, but some of the few there are are best avoided. Many visitors choose to stay instead in more rural locations nearby.

Bastide St-Antoine 48 av Henri-Dunant ☎ 04 93 70 94 94, ⓦ jacques-chibois.com. Gorgeous and extremely luxurious country-house hotel, 1km south of the centre, that's best known for its restaurant (see below). Its nine rooms and seven even fancier suites cost up to €1000; even breakfast will cost you €29. **€330**
Bellaudière 78 av Pierre Ziller ☎ 04 93 36 02 57. *Logis de France* enjoying long-distance sea views from the slopes 3km east of town. Set in an eighteenth-century farmhouse, it has simple, good-value rooms and a nice terrace restaurant, serving dinner *menus* from €21. **€75**

Hôtel des Parfums 2 bd Eugène-Charabot ☎ 04 92 42 35 35, ⓦ hoteldesparfums.com. Large, unremarkable but adequate business-oriented modern hotel at the top of town, with panoramic views plus a terrace restaurant, pool and gym. Closed mid-Nov to mid-Dec & Jan. **€93**
Relais de Peyloubet 65 chemin de la Plâtrière ☎ 04 93 70 69 90, ⓦ relais-peyloubet.com.fr. Five very comfortable B&B rooms and suites, in an eighteenth-century *bastide*, perched on a hillside 2km east of town, with magnificent views and a large pool, and barbecue facilities in summer. **€115**

EATING AND DRINKING

Old Grasse is disappointingly short of good **restaurants**, though one or two hidden gems are tucked away on the lanes. As for **bars**, there a couple of lively spots on the place aux Aires; sitting outside here makes a very pleasant way to spend a summer evening, and offers the best chance to meet the locals.

La Bastide Saint Antoine Jacques Chibois 48 rue Henri-Dunant ☎ 04 93 70 94 94, ⓦ jacques-chibois .com. This elegant, expensive Michelin-starred hotel restaurant, 1km south of the centre, is the best place to eat in Grasse. *Cuisine gourmande* with a Provençal twist produces dishes like lobster bouillabaisse-style with olives. Lunch *menus* €59; otherwise *menus* from €169. Daily noon–2pm & 8–10pm.
Le Gazan 3 rue Gazan ☎ 04 93 36 22 88. Pretty, friendly and very traditional little place, in the heart of the old town, with a small terrace and intimate dining room. *Menus* from €15 lunch, €25 dinner. Mon–Sat noon–3pm & 6.30–9pm, Sun noon–6pm.
Maison Venturini 1 rue Marcel-Journet ☎ 04 93 36 20 47. *Confiserie* where you can buy *fougassettes* – a sweet flatbread flavoured with orange blossom (€1.60).

They also sell candied fruits, candied rose petals and Marseille-style *navettes* (€3 a pack). Tues–Sat 9am–12.30pm & 3–6.30pm.
La Pêche Gourmande 6 rue de l'Oratoire ☎ 06 15 11 30 15. This lovely little tearoom in the old town offers delicious teas, coffees, pastries and ice creams, plus, until 6pm, a well-priced array of salads and hot dishes, with *plats* €9–15 and *formule* €13–25. Tues–Sat 10am–7pm, Sun 10am–6pm.
La Voûte 3 rue du Thouron ☎ 04 93 36 11 43. Popular local restaurant in the old town, serving up €11–14 pizzas as well as Provençal specialities from its wood-fired oven, with open-air seating in summer. Lunch *menu* €17; dinner *menus* at €24 and €27. Daily noon–3pm & 7–11pm.

Around Grasse

The main highlight of the countryside immediately surrounding Grasse is the attractive village of **Cabris**, but two routes out of the area offer wonderful scenic views. The **Route Napoléon** heads northwest through the mountains towards Castellane, while to the northeast the gorges of the **Loup River** pass the cliff-hanging stronghold of **Gourdon**, and **Le-Bar-sur-Loup**, home to an intriguing medieval chapel. East of the river, the hillside road towards Vence holds one final treat, the delightful village of **Tourrettes-sur-Loup**.

Cabris

CABRIS, just 6km southwest of Grasse, has all the trappings of a picture-postcard village: a ruined château providing panoramas from the Lac de St-Cassien to the Îles de Lérins, sometimes as far as Corsica; arty residents who decamped here from Grasse; and no shortage of *immobiliers* trading on fat local property prices. It's a lovely place to stroll around for an hour or two, but most visitors press onto the region's larger towns.

7

The Route Napoléon: St-Vallier-de-Thiey

Built in the 1930s to commemorate the path taken by the emperor in March 1815 after his escape from Elba, the D6085 north from Grasse is known as the **Route Napoléon**. The road doesn't follow the imperial boot-tracks precisely, going far off course in places, but it serves a useful purpose. After several kilometres of zigzagging bends you get fantastic views back to Grasse, its basin and the coast.

The first village you come to – **ST-VALLIER-DE-THIEY**, 12km from Grasse – holds some prehistoric dolmens and tumuli. From there, the Route Napoléon heads, almost uninterrupted by settlements, towards Castellane (see p.220). Wayside stalls sell honey and perfume; each little hamlet has a hotel-restaurant; and every so often you see a commemorative plaque carved with Napoleon's winged eagle.

Along the Gorges de Loup

Of the two alternative routes that follow the stunning Gorges de Loup, the lower, along the east bank of the Loup, is the more compelling. Both leave the main D2085 at **Châteauneuf-Grasse**, 6km east from Grasse.

Le Bar-sur-Loup

The lower Gorges de Loup road, the D2210, passes through the pretty hillside village of **LE BAR-SUR-LOUP** after just 3.5km. The little **Église de St-Jacques** here contains an altarpiece attributed to the Niçois painter, Louis Bréa, while a tiny but detailed fifteenth-century *Danse Macabre*, painted on a wooden panel, shows courtly dancers being picked off by Death's arrows, and their souls being thrown by devils into the toothed and tongued mouth of hell.

From here, you can follow the **gorges road** itself, the D6, through dark, narrow twists of rock beneath cliffs that look as if they might tumble at any minute, through the sounds of furiously churning water, to corners that appear to have no way out.

Gourdon

The higher of the two roads from Châteauneuf-Grasse, the D3, climbs 8km along the northern balcony of the gorges to tiny **GOURDON**, a *village perché* teetering on the very brink of the abyss. The village itself is swamped in souvenir shops, but the view from place Victoria at the top is extraordinary.

Tourrettes-sur-Loup

TOURRETTES-SUR-LOUP is an artisans' paradise, preserving just the right balance between crumbly attractiveness and modern comforts. The three towers from which the village derives its name – and the rose-stone houses that cling to the high escarpment – almost all date from the fifteenth century; the best views can be had from the curious rock shelf known as Les Loves, just above the town.

The oldest and most charming part of the village is accessed via two gateways that lead south from the main place de la Libération, which adjoins the D2210. Beyond the fine portals, the Grande Rue loops between the two, lined with expensive ateliers selling clothes, sculpture, jewellery, leather, fine art and the like. A viewing platform at the southern end commands a majestic prospect all the way to the Mediterranean.

During Tourrettes' famous **violet festival**, on the first or second Sunday in March, floats are decorated with thousands of blooms. Violets, which thrive in the mild microclimate, are grown here in vast quantities for the perfume trade as well as for subsidiary cottage industries such as old-fashioned candied violets; be sure to try the local violet-flavoured ice cream while you're here.

INFORMATION   AROUND GRASSE

ST-VALLIER-DE-THIEY
Tourist office 10 place du Tour (Mon–Sat: March–Oct 9am–noon & 3–6pm; Nov–Feb 9am–noon & 3–5pm; ☎ 04 93 42 78 00, ⊛ saintvallierdethiey.com).

TOURRETTES-SUR-LOUP
Tourist office 2 place de la Libération (July & Aug daily 10am–1pm & 2–6.30pm; Sept–June Mon–Sat 9.30am–1pm & 2–5.30pm; ☎ 04 93 24 18 93, ⊛ tourrettessurloup.com).

ACCOMMODATION

CABRIS
★ **Auberge du Vieux Château** Place du Panorama ☎ 04 93 60 50 12, ⊛ aubergeduvieuxchateau.com. With just four tasteful rooms, this lovely hotel is a great place to stay, with wonderful views, though dinner *menus* in its high-class dining room (closed Mon & Tues Sept–June) start at €45. **€85**

ST-VALLIER-DE-THIEY
Le Préjoly Place Rougière ☎ 04 93 60 03 20, ⊛ leprejoly.com. Presentable, reasonably priced little hotel at the entrance to the village. Some of the en-suite rooms have large mountain-view terraces. The adjoining restaurant is run by separate management, but recommended. Closed Jan. **€75**

TOURRETTES-SUR-LOUP
★ **L'Auberge de Tourrettes** 11 route de Grasse ☎ 04 93 59 30 05, ⊛ aubergedetourrettes.fr. At Tourrettes' classiest accommodation option, on the edge of the village, most of the tasteful and very comfortable bedrooms enjoy great views. There's also a very nice restaurant, open for dinner only, serving classy Provençal food on its outdoor terrace, with a €39 *menu*. **€120**

Rives du Loup 2666b route de la Colle ☎ 04 93 24 15 65, ⊛ rivesduloup.com. Fancy three-star campsite – only a couple of kilometres south of the village on the other side of the gorges but 9km by road – with a restaurant, snack bar and pool, and offering hotel-style rooms as well as tent pitches and mobile homes. Closed Oct–March. Rooms **€89**; camping **€26.50**

EATING

CABRIS
Petit Prince 15 rue Frédéric-Mistral ☎ 04 93 60 63 14, ⊛ lepetitprince-cabris.com. Delicacies at this warm and welcoming restaurant, overlooking a park lined with chestnut trees, include a *parmentier* of *boudin noir* with apples and a cider sauce. Lunch from €17; dinner *menus* €23–40. Daily noon–2.30pm & 7–10pm; closed Thurs Nov–May.

TOURRETTES-SUR-LOUP
Lou Coucoun 1 rue du Château ☎ 04 93 24 16 12. Quirky restaurant, in a cellar, which serves *socca* pancakes for €10 or a *plat du jour* for €11.50. Tues–Sat noon–2pm & 7–9.30pm, Sun noon–2pm.

Médiéval 6 Grand Rue ☎ 04 93 59 31 63. Good restaurant in the historic core, serving traditional Provençal *menus* at €25 and €37. Mon, Tues & Fri–Sun noon–2pm & 7–9.30pm, Wed noon–2pm.

Vence

Sheltered by the Pre-Alpes that rise to its rear, the delightful hill town of **VENCE**, 10km up from the sea, is unusual in having an appealing modern quarter that for once complements rather than simply engulfs its ravishing historic core, **Vieux Vence**. It helps, of course, that **Henri Matisse** chose the new town as the site of his magnificent **Chapelle du Rosaire**, but more generally the bustle of the boulevards outside the walls, and particularly the lively main place du Grand-Jardin, with its cafés, carousel and summer concerts, make a pleasing contrast to the tranquil ancient lanes of the old town.

Vence was originally founded by a Ligurian tribe, the Nerusii. They put up stiff opposition to Augustus Caesar, but to no avail; Roman funeral inscriptions and votive offerings remain embedded in the fabric of its cathedral. During the Dark Ages, the local bishop, **Saint Véran**, organized the city's defence. The Saracens, however, subsequently razed both the town and St-Véran's cathedral to the ground. Thereafter, Vence was plagued until the Revolution by rivalry between its barons and its bishops.

In the 1920s Vence became a haven for **painters and writers**: André Gide, Raoul Dufy, D.H. Lawrence (who died here in 1930 while being treated for tuberculosis contracted in England) and Marc Chagall were all long-term visitors. Matisse moved here towards the end of World War II, to escape the Allied bombing of the coast.

Vieux Vence

With its ancient houses, gateways, fountains and chapels, the diminutive old town of **Vieux Vence** is absolutely exquisite. It remains encircled by medieval ramparts, though they're not so much walls as the backs of people's homes. While holding its fair share of chic boutiques and arty restaurants, it also has an everyday feel, with ordinary townsfolk going about their business, seeking out the best market deals, and stopping for a chat and a *petit verre* at little cafés.

More or less untouched since the twelfth century, the **Porte du Peyra**, and the tower that surmounts it, provide the best entry into Vieux Vence. **Place du Peyra**, within the walls, focuses on the town's oldest fountain. The narrow, cobbled **rue du Marché** off to the right is a busy street of tiny and delectable food shops, all with stalls (and all closed Mon). Behind it, **place Clemenceau**, centring on the cathedral, hosts a Tuesday and Friday clothes **market**.

East of the cathedral is **place Godeau** which is almost totally medieval save for the column in the fountain, presented to the city, along with its twin on place du Grand-Jardin, by the Republic of Marseille during the third century. Follow rue St-Lambert and rue de l'Hôtel-de-Ville down from here to reach the original eastern gate, the **Porte du Signadour**, outside which another fifteenth-century fountain on place Antony-Mars celebrates the town's expansion.

St-Véran Cathedral

St-Véran Cathedral is a tenth- and eleventh-century replacement for the church over which St-Véran presided in the fifth century, which had in turn been built on the ruins of a Roman temple to Mars and Cybele. Like so many of the oldest Provençal churches, it's basically square in shape, with an austere exterior. Although centuries of subsequent alterations have left none of the clear lines of Romanesque architecture, fragments of its Merovingian and Carolingian predecessors, and of Roman Vence, still remain.

In the chapel beneath the belfry, two reliefs from the old church show birds, grapes and an eagle, while more stone birds, flowers, swirls of leaves and interlocking lines are embedded in the walls and pillars throughout the church. The purported **tomb of St-Véran**, in the southern chapel nearest the altar, is a pre-Christian sarcophagus. Later adornments include some superb, irreverent Gothic carved **choir stalls**, housed alongside powerfully human, if crude, polychrome wooden statues of the Calvary, up above the western end of the nave. In the baptistry, a Chagall **mosaic** depicts the infant Moses being saved from the Nile by the Pharaoh's daughter.

Château de Villeneuve Fondation Emile Hugues

2 place du Frêne • Tues–Sun 10am–12.30pm & 2–6pm • €7 • ☎ 04 93 58 15 78, ⊛ museedevence.com

Vence's castle, the **Château de Villeneuve Fondation Emile Hugues**, was built just outside the city walls during a calm period of fifteenth-century expansion. Rebuilt in the seventeenth century, it was renovated in 1992 to become a beautiful space for displaying modern and contemporary art. Each year sees a different themed exhibition. Out in front, **place du Frêne** is named for its 450-year-old ash tree.

Matisse's Chapelle du Rosaire

466 av Henri-Matisse, beside the D2210 to St-Jeannet, 1km east of Vieux Vence • Mon, Wed & Sat 2–5.30pm, Tues & Thurs 10–11.30am & 2–5.30pm, Sunday Mass 10am; closed mid-Nov to mid-Dec • €4 • ☎ 04 93 58 03 26

It's worth travelling a very long way indeed to see the beautiful and profoundly moving **Chapelle du Rosaire**, which **Henri Matisse** spent four of the final years of his life designing in every meticulous detail; be sure to time your visit to Vence to coincide with its limited opening hours. A simple modern structure, the chapel is inconspicuous but for its blue-and-white tiled roof, topped by a wrought-iron cross. Matisse was too ill to attend its dedication in 1951, but in a statement read out at the ceremony he said "in spite of all its imperfections, I consider it as my masterpiece".

The **murals** on the chapel walls – faceless black outlines on white tiles – so thoroughly achieve this goal that some visitors are disappointed, not finding the "Matisse" they expect. The east wall is the most shocking; it shows the *Stations of the Cross*, each one numbered and scrawled as if it were an angry doodle on a pad. The full-length windows in the west and south walls are the aspect of the chapel most likely to live up to expectations. They provide the only source of colour, which changes with the day's light through opaque yellow, transparent green and watery blue, playing across the black-and-white murals, floor and ceiling.

Despite the prominent signs requesting silence, the chapel repeatedly fills with excited, chattering tour groups. A nun is usually on hand to calm things down, and point out the symbolism of every aspect of Matisse's vision: the overall configuration of the chapel; the stone of the east-facing altar, chosen for its resemblance to bread; the raw anguish of the figures; the door of the confessional, alluding to the artist's trips to Morocco; and the chasubles, crucifix and candelabra.

MATISSE AND THE CHAPELLE DU ROSAIRE

In 1941, while convalescing from an operation for cancer, Matisse advertised for a "young and pretty nurse". Having developed a strong rapport with successful applicant Monique Bourgeois, who also posed for him, he bought a home in Vence after she joined the Dominican convent here, in 1943, as Sister Jacques-Marie. Although he did not consider himself a Christian, Matisse agreed to help the young nun with the new convent chapel, the **Chapelle du Rosaire**. As he later put it "my only religion is the love of the work to be created, the love of creation, and great sincerity".

The artist moved back to his huge rooms in Nice in 1949, to work on the designs using the same scale as the chapel. A photograph shows him in bed, drawing studies for the figure of St-Dominic on the wall with a paintbrush tied to a long bamboo stick. It's not clear how much this bamboo technique was a practical solution to his frailty, and how much a solution to an artistic problem. Some critics suggest Matisse wanted to pare down his art to the basic essentials of human communication, and thus needed to remove his own stylistic signature from the lines.

Matisse was even responsible for the various resplendently colourful silk **vestments**, which match different moments in the liturgical calendar; ideally you'd see them worn by the priest at Sunday Mass, but during the week they're displayed in the gallery beyond, which also holds a gift shop.

ARRIVAL AND INFORMATION
VENCE

By bus Vence's *gare routière* is at place Maréchal Juin, a short walk from the tourist office.
Destinations Nice (every 35min–1hr; 55min–1hr 10min), via St-Paul-de-Vence (5–10min) and Cagnes (25min).
By car The best place to park is the large underground car park beneath place du Grand-Jardin.

Tourist office Place du Grand-Jardin (July & Aug Mon–Sat 9am–7pm, Sun 10am–6pm; March–June, Sept & Oct Mon–Sat 9am–6pm; Nov–Feb Mon–Sat 9am–5pm; ☎ 04 93 58 06 38, ⓦ vence.fr).
Bike rental Tendanas Cycles, av Henri Giraud (☎ 04 93 32 59 92).

ACCOMMODATION

Home to an excellent range of well-priced **hotels**, Vence makes a very popular and peaceful base for visitors who plan to explore not just the town itself, and the surrounding hills, but all the way down to the coast as well.

★ **Auberge des Seigneurs** 1 rue du Dr Binet ☎ 04 93 58 04 24, ⓦ auberge-seigneurs.com. Lovely, very friendly old inn, set into the walls of Vieux Vence. Each of its six huge, quirky rooms is named after a different painter associated with the town; but for the very decent bathrooms, they're minimally updated. The restaurant, which spreads onto a panoramic terrace just outside the walls, is excellent, serving a fine array of Provençal specialities on *menus* costing from €23 at lunch, €32 at dinner. Closed Nov to mid-March. **€90**
Closerie des Genêts 4 impasse Maurel ☎ 04 93 58 35 18. Peaceful, slightly old-fashioned and very welcoming ten-room hotel on the southern edge of Vieux Vence, with an attractive garden and sea views from some rooms. The good-value restaurant is closed Sun & Mon. **€80**
Le 2 des Portiques 2 rue des Portiques ☎ 04 93 24 42 58, ⓦ le2avence.fr. Four stylish a/c rooms – including a junior suite and a loft with private roof terrace – in a *chambres d'hote* in the heart of Vieux Vence, above a bistro with live music in the evenings. **€90**
Diana 79 av des Poilus ☎ 04 93 58 28 56, ⓦ hotel-diana.fr. Modern building in a quiet and convenient location just 200m west of the centre, and enjoying lovely views. Comfortable rooms, some with

balconies and half with kitchenettes, and an open-air jacuzzi. **€109**
Victoire 4 place du Grand-Jardin ☎ 04 93 24 15 54, ⓦ hotel-victoire.com. Soundproofed, very central hotel beside the tourist office on the main square in the modern town, and offering spruced-up rooms at reasonable prices. **€109**
Villa Roseraie 128 av Henri-Giraud ☎ 04 93 58 02 20, ⓦ www.villaroseraie.com. Three-star comforts in a 1929 villa on the road to the Col de Vence 1km northwest of town, with ancient cedars and magnolias overhanging the terrace. There's a palm-fringed pool, a garden, private parking and a bar. The rooms are decorated in Provençal style and some have their own patios. **€107**

CAMPSITE
Domaine de la Bergerie 1330 chemin de la Sine ☎ 04 93 58 09 36, ⓦ camping-domainedelabergerie .com. Three-star campsite in the woods 3km west of town off the road to Tourettes-sur-Loup, with a summer-only pool, restaurant and *pétanque* pitch. They also rent small chalet-like pods (3-night min). Closed Oct–April. Chalets **€40**; camping **€24.50**

EATING, DRINKING AND NIGHTLIFE

The squares and lanes of Vieux Vence abound in restaurants, bars and cafés in all price ranges, and there are also several appealing alternatives in the newer streets beyond. Between early July and early August, in **Les Nuits du Sud** (ⓦ nuitsdusud.com), big-name Latin and World musicians perform open-air concerts on the place du Grand-Jardin, mostly on Friday and Saturday evenings.

Les Agapes 4 place Clemenceau ☎ 04 93 58 50 64, ⓦ les-agapes.net. Lively, sophisticated old-town restaurant, in a quiet spot close to the cathedral, serving Provençal dishes like roast salmon with sun-dried tomato risotto on dinner *menus* at €27 and €35. June–Sept Mon–Sat noon–2pm & 7–10pm; Oct–May Tues–Sat noon–2pm & 7–9.30pm.

La Farigoule 15 av Henri-Isnard ☎ 04 93 58 01 27, ⓦ lafarigoule-vence.fr. Just outside the old town behind the tourist office, this very pretty restaurant – with white limed beams inside and a courtyard garden – is a good bet for a special meal. Dinner *menus* at €29 and €45 offer small, precise portions of exquisitely flavoured dishes such as roast cod, and excellent desserts. July & Aug Tues–Sun

7

noon–1.30pm & 7.30–9.30pm; Sept–June Wed–Sun noon–1.30pm & 7.30–9.30pm.

★ **La Litote** 5 rue l'Évêché ☎ 04 93 24 27 82, ⓦ lalitote.com. The outdoor tables of this lovely, secluded old-town restaurant fill the delightful little place de l'Évêché, beneath its single spreading tree. Changing daily *menus* of Provençal specialities, including bouillabaisse, start at €15 for lunch, €28 for

dinner. Tues–Sat noon–2.30pm & 7–10pm, Sun noon–2.30pm.

Le Pêcheur du Soleil 1 place Godeau ☎ 04 93 58 32 56, ⓦ pecheurdusoleil.com. Tiny place in Vieux Vence, in a pretty location close to the cathedral with seats out on the square. An astounding choice of pizzas – they claim 600 – at €9.50–14, plus salads from €6.50 and omelettes from €8.50. Feb–Nov Tues–Sat noon–2pm & 7–9pm, Sun noon–2pm.

St-Paul-de-Vence

The beautiful fortified village of **ST-PAUL-DE-VENCE** squeezes onto a hilltop just 3km south of Vence towards Cagnes, although the combination of twisting roads and undulating hills can make it unexpectedly hard to find. While the village itself is a delight, and is usually crammed with visitors throughout the summer, its popularity owes as much to the **Fondation Maeght**, a wonderful museum of modern art and sculpture tucked into the woods nearby, as it does to its medieval core. As most visitors just come for the day, St-Paul is a very quiet place to spend a night.

St-Paul stands on its own separate eminence alongside the D7. You can't miss its most famous landmark, right outside the walls on the only approach road – the **Colombe d'Or**, a hotel-restaurant (see opposite) that's celebrated not so much for its food as for the art on its walls, donated in lieu of payment for meals by the then-impoverished Braque, Picasso, Matisse and Bonnard in the lean years following World War I.

Beyond that, you pass through the ramparts to find a miniature jewel of a village, where the old stone cottages that line the winding lanes hold around seventy contemporary **art galleries and ateliers**. Most of those are concentrated along the central rue Grande, so it's normally possible to escape the crowds simply by exploring any alleyway that catches your eye, or heading for the walls.

Up on the top of the hill, facing the stark whitewashed belfry of the Église Collégiale across place de l'Église, a peculiar little **museum** holds dioramas of local history (daily: April–Oct 10am–noon & 3–6pm; Dec–March 2–5pm; €3). At the far end of the village, a little **cemetery** (daily: summer 7.30am–8pm; winter 8am–5pm) outside the ramparts, perched above the fields, holds the simple grave of **Marc Chagall**.

Fondation Maeght

623 Chemin des Gardettes • Daily: April–June 10am–6pm; July–Sept 10am–7pm; Oct–March 10am–1pm & 2–6pm • €14 • ☎ 04 93 32 81 63, ⓦ www.fondation-maeght.com

The remarkable **Fondation Maeght**, ten minutes' walk west of the village, encapsulates the link between the Côte d'Azur and modern European art. It was established in 1964 by art collectors Aimé and Marguerite Maeght, who knew all the great artists who worked in Provence. Spanish architect José Luis Sert designed the building, and it was decorated by assorted painters, sculptors, potters and designers. Both structure and ornamentation were conceived as a single project, to create a museum in which the concepts of entrance, exit and *sense de la visite* would not apply.

Once through the gates, any idea of dutifully checking off a catalogue of priceless museum pieces crumbles. Giacometti's *Cat* is sometimes stalking along the edge of the grass, Miró's *Egg* smiles above a pond, and his totemed *Fork* is outlined against the sky. It's hard not to be bewitched by the Calder mobile swinging over watery tiles, by Léger's flowers, birds and a bench on a sunlit rough stone wall, by Zadkine's and Arp's metallic forms hovering between the pine trunks, or by the clanking tubular fountain by Pol Bury. And all this is just a portion of the garden.

The **building** itself is superb: multilevelled and flooded with daylight, with galleries opening on to terraces and courtyards, blurring the boundaries between inside and outside. It houses an impressive collection, including sculpture, ceramics, paintings and graphic art by Braque, Miró, Chagall, Léger, Kandinsky, Dubuffet, Bonnard, Dérain and Matisse, along with work by more recent artists. Not all the works are exhibited at any one time, however, and in summer, when the main annual exhibition is mounted, only those that make up the decoration of the building are on show.

ARRIVAL AND INFORMATION   ST-PAUL-DE-VENCE

By bus St-Paul is on bus route #400 between Nice and Vence, via Cagnes. There are two stops: to reach the Fondation from the first, beside the roundabout on the way up from Nice, head left up the hill; from the village centre, head uphill along the steep street opposite the village entrance.

Destinations Nice (every 35min–1hr; 1hr 3min); Vence (every 35min–1hr; 10min).

By car or bike Parking is limited and expensive; if you're visiting both the Fondation and the village, it's usually easier and cheaper to park at the Fondation, which is clearly signposted off both the D7 and the D2.

Tourist office 2 rue Grande, just inside the walled village (daily: June–Sept 10am–7pm; Oct–May 10am–6pm; ☎04 93 32 86 95, ⓦ saint-pauldevence.com).

ACCOMMODATION AND EATING

As St-Paul-de-Vence is primarily a day-trip destination, it has many more places to eat than to sleep. You'll need to book well in advance if you want to stay overnight in summer; if you manage to find a **room**, though, you'll find it delightfully tranquil once the crowds have gone. As for **restaurants**, most are firmly poised at the more expensive end of the spectrum, but a few reasonably priced options are scattered through the village.

La Colombe d'Or Place du Général-de-Gaulle ☎04 93 32 80 02, ⓦ la-colombe-dor.com. Famed for its stellar collection of modern art, the sixteenth-century *Colombe d'Or* also has a *restaurant gastronomique*, valet parking, a heated outdoor pool, sauna and gardens, plus 13 comfortable wood-beamed rooms and 12 apartments. Closed Nov–Christmas. €295

Hostellerie Les Remparts de St-Paul 72 rue Grande ☎04 93 32 09 88, ⓦ hostellerielesremparts.com. The least expensive central option, in the heart of the village.

All except one of its 9 pretty but far from luxurious rooms, which vary widely in price, have en-suite facilities, while a good-value restaurant (closed Sun pm & Mon) occupies a nicely shaded terrace with huge views out over the hills. Closed Jan and second half of Nov. €45

La Sierra Rempart Ouest, just below rue Grande ☎04 93 32 82 89. Anything from an *assortiment Provençal* for €20, to €11–14 pizzas and crêpes, served on a lovely garden terrace beside the western ramparts. Daily: June–Sept noon–2.30pm & 7–10.30pm; Oct–May noon–6pm.

7

Nice and the eastern Riviera

THE PERCHED VILLAGE OF PEILLON

Nice and the eastern Riviera

East of the River Var, the Riviera is subtly different. For much of its history the coastline between Nice and the Italian border was part of the Kingdom of Savoy, only becoming securely French in 1860. Even today a certain Italian influence lingers, in the cooking of Nice and in the architecture of Vieux Nice, Villefranche and Menton. The landscape changes, too: east of Nice the Alpes-Maritimes come crashing down to the sea and the coastline is often thrillingly scenic. The contrast between the littoral and the interior is stark: opulent villas dot the coast's green hillsides and jostle for the best position on its headlands, while behind the coast the landscape is rugged and unspoilt and the villages timeless in their appeal.

The Riviera's largest city, **Nice** became fashionable as a winter resort in the eighteenth century, as aristocratic visitors – many of them invalids – made the journey south to escape the brutal northern winters. Right up to World War I they built their villas here or sojourned in the opulent palace hotels, most of which have long since been converted to apartments, though their architecture remains and often lends the city an appealing, eccentric face. Gradually, other resorts grew to rival Nice, each with its own speciality: **Menton** for tuberculosis sufferers; **Monte Carlo** in the comic-opera principality of Monaco with its casino.

After World War I many of the old aristocratic visitors never returned: they were dead, impoverished or scattered by revolution and war. In their place came artists and intellectuals: **Matisse** and **Dufy** made Nice their home, **Isadora Duncan** met her end there; **Cocteau** favoured Villefranche, and **Somerset Maugham** Cap Ferrat. The introduction of *congés payés* (paid holiday) in 1936 brought thousands of ordinary French men and women to a coast that had hitherto been an elite retreat for wealthy foreigners. The democratization continued after the war, and though the marriage in 1956 of film star Grace Kelly to Prince Rainier of Monaco set the seal on the Riviera's glamour image, the reality was increasingly different. The bucolic Mediterranean coast that the author Tobias Smollett saw in eighteenth century is nowadays a thing of distant memory.

Nevertheless, there's much to enjoy: the food, vivacious street life and superb culture of **Nice**, and the unspoilt **villages** in the city's hinterland; the thrills of the **corniches** along the mountainous coast between Nice and Menton; and – last but not least – the vicarious pleasures of the independent principality of **Monaco**.

Nice

The capital of the Riviera and fifth-largest town in France, **NICE** lives off a glittering reputation, its former glamour now gently faded. First popularized by English

MONTE CARLO CASINO

Highlights

❶ Vieux Nice From the flower market at dawn to bar-hopping in the early hours, Nice's mellow, Mediterranean heart buzzes with street life the whole day long. **See p.345**

❷ The Musée Chagall Custom-built to house Marc Chagall's Biblical Message paintings, the Musée Chagall is unmissable for fans of the artist's work. **See p.354**

❸ Niçois villages Explore craggy Peillon and unspoilt Lucéram, the *villages perchés* of Nice's wild and underpopulated hinterland, where villagers still live off the land, producing olives, goat's cheese, herbs and vegetables. **See p.361 & p.362**

❹ Villa Ephrussi de Rothschild Visit this handsome mansion and its exquisite gardens to find out how the Riviera's aristocratic other half used to live. **See p.367**

❺ Plage Mala Relax on this secluded, idyllic Riviera beach in classy Cap d'Ail, just a leisurely stroll along the coast from the hustle and bustle of Monaco. **See p.370**

❻ The Casino at Monte Carlo Break the bank – or merely admire the *belle époque* architectural and decorative opulence – at the world's most famous casino. **See p.375**

HIGHLIGHTS ARE MARKED ON THE MAP ON P.344

> ## NICE ORIENTATION
>
> Shadowed by mountains that curve down to the Mediterranean east of its port, Nice divides fairly clearly between old and new. **Vieux Nice**, the old town, groups about the hill of **Le Château**, its limits signalled by **boulevard Jean-Jaurès**, which was built along the course of the River Paillon. Along the seafront, the celebrated **promenade des Anglais** runs a cool 5km until forced to curve inland by the sea-projecting runways of the airport. The central square, **place Masséna**, is at the bottom of the modern city's main street, **avenue Jean-Médecin**; to the north is the exclusive hillside suburb of **Cimiez**, while the port lies on the eastern side of **Le Château**.

aristocrats in the eighteenth century, Nice reached its zenith in the *belle époque* of the late nineteenth century.

The city has retained its historical styles almost intact: the medieval labyrinth of **Vieux Nice**, the Italianate facades of **modern Nice** and the rich exuberance of *fin-de-siècle* residences dating from when the city was Europe's most fashionable winter retreat. It also preserves mementoes from the **Roman** period, when the region was ruled from here, and from the era of its Greek founders. Of late, Nice has smartened up its act with extensive **refurbishment** of its public spaces and the construction of a **tramway**; it may be a politically conservative – at various times even reactionary – city, but Nice

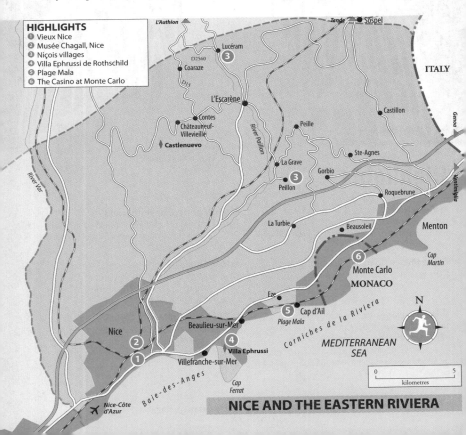

HIGHLIGHTS
1. Vieux Nice
2. Musée Chagall, Nice
3. Niçois villages
4. Villa Ephrussi de Rothschild
5. Plage Mala
6. The Casino at Monte Carlo

NICE AND THE EASTERN RIVIERA

FRENCH RIVIERA PASS

The **French Riviera Pass** allows unlimited access to many of the most important museums, monuments and gardens on the Riviera and in Monaco, including guided tours in some cases; it also allows reduced-price or free entry to water parks and reductions or gifts at certain businesses, from diving schools to casinos or boat trips. A one-day pass costs €26, a two-day pass €38 and a three-day pass €56, or you can get passes that allow unlimited use of Ligne d'Azur's public transport network for €30, €46 or €68 respectively. The cards are available online at ⓦ frenchrivierapass.com and at Nice's tourist offices. Before you buy, it's worth noting that admission to Nice's municipally controlled museums is free anyway, so if you're visiting Nice alone, the pass is probably not worth bothering with.

---

does not rest on its laurels. Its many **museums**, meanwhile, are a treat for art lovers: within France, Nice is second only to Paris for the sheer range on offer.

Far too large to be considered simply a resort, Nice has all the advantages and disadvantages of a major Mediterranean city: superb cultural facilities, wonderful street life and excellent shopping, eating and drinking, but also a high crime rate, graffiti blight and horrendous traffic. Yet for all that, the sun shines, the sea sparkles and a thousand sprinklers keep the lawns and flowerbeds lush. On summer nights the old town buzzes with contented crowds, and it's hard not to be utterly seduced by the place.

Parc de la Colline du Château

8

Daily 8am–6/7/8pm according to season • Climb the steps from rue de la Providence or montée du Château in the old town, or take the lift by the Tour Bellanda at the eastern end of quai des États-Unis (daily: April, May & Sept 9am–7pm; June–Aug 9am–8pm; Oct–March 10am–6pm)

For initial orientation, with brilliant sea and city views, fresh air and a cooling waterfall, head for the **Parc de la Colline du Château**. There's no fortress here today; it was destroyed by the French in the early eighteenth century when Nice belonged to Savoy. This is, however, where Nice began as the ancient Greek city of Nikea – hence the mosaics and stone vases in mock Grecian style. Excavations have revealed Greek and Roman levels beneath the foundations of the city's first, eleventh-century cathedral on the eastern side of the summit. Rather than ruin-spotting, however, the real pleasure here lies in looking down on the scrambled rooftops and gleaming mosaic tiles of Vieux Nice, the yachts and fishing boats in the port on the eastern side, and along the sweep of the promenade des Anglais. In the **cemetery** to the north of the park are buried the two great Niçois revolutionaries, Giuseppe Garibaldi and Léon Gambetta, though casual visitors aren't particularly welcome. A moving Jewish war memorial includes an urn of ashes from the crematoria of Auschwitz.

Vieux Nice

Most of Nice's wonderful street life – and a fair amount of its street crime – is concentrated in the dense warren of medieval streets that make up **Vieux Nice**. Once considered little more than a slum, it has changed markedly over the years, yet despite decades of gradual gentrification, the teeming *quartier* is still very far from sanitized. It's an intriguing and often charming place, full of contradictions: churches of the most opulent Italianate Baroque rub shoulders with mean, scruffy alleyways where washing hangs high overhead, while the flipside of the elegant restaurant terraces and colourful markets is a dodgy undercurrent, particularly at night. Vieux Nice is, without doubt, the repository of Nice's Mediterranean soul, but though it has an almost Neapolitan vibrancy and chaos in high summer, it can seem eerie and deserted in winter once the tourists have departed.

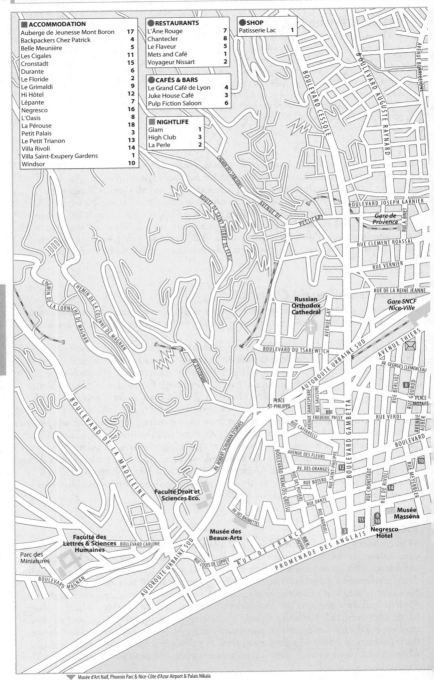

■ ACCOMMODATION

Auberge de Jeunesse Mont Boron	17
Backpackers Chez Patrick	4
Belle Meunière	5
Les Cigales	11
Cronstadt	15
Durante	6
Le Floride	2
Le Grimaldi	9
Hi Hôtel	12
Lépante	7
Negresco	16
L'Oasis	8
La Pérouse	18
Petit Palais	3
Le Petit Trianon	13
Villa Rivoli	14
Villa Saint-Exupery Gardens	1
Windsor	10

● RESTAURANTS

L'Âne Rouge	7
Chantecler	8
Le Flaveur	5
Mets and Café	1
Voyageur Nissart	2

● CAFÉS & BARS

Le Grand Café de Lyon	4
Juke House Café	3
Pulp Fiction Saloon	6

■ NIGHTLIFE

Glam	1
High Club	3
La Perle	2

● SHOP

Patisserie Lac	1

Musée d'Art Naïf, Phoenix Parc & Nice-Côte d'Azur Airport & Palais Nikaïa

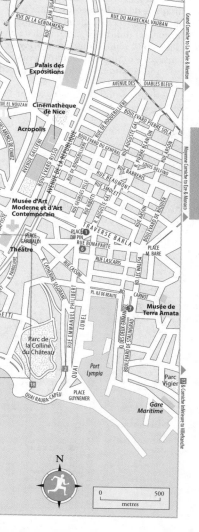

The streets are too narrow for buses and much of it is effectively car- (though not necessarily scooter-) free. It's an area made for walking.

Place Rossetti

The central square is **place Rossetti**, where the soft-coloured Baroque **Cathédrale de Ste-Réparate** (Mon–Fri 9am–noon & 2–6pm, Sat 9am–noon & 2–7.30pm, Sun 9am–1pm & 3–6pm; ⓦcathedrale-nice.com) just manages to be visible from the eight narrow streets which meet here. There are cafés to relax in, with the choice of sun or shade, and a magical ice-cream parlour, *Fenocchio*.

Cours Saleya

The real magnet of Vieux Nice is the **cours Saleya**, with its splendidly Baroque **Chapelle de la Miséricorde** (Tues 2.30–5pm), and its adjacent places Pierre-Gautier and Charles-Félix. These wide-open, sunlit spaces, lined with grandiloquent municipal buildings and Italianate chapels, are the site of the city's main **market** (see p.360), where there are gorgeous displays of fruit, vegetables, cheeses and sausages – along with cut and potted flowers and scented plants. Summer nights see café and restaurant tables filling the **cours Saleya** to create the Riviera's most animated free show.

Leading west off the *cours* is rue St-François-de-Paule, home to the suitably grand *belle époque* **Opéra**, which opened in 1885, with its plush red and gold interior.

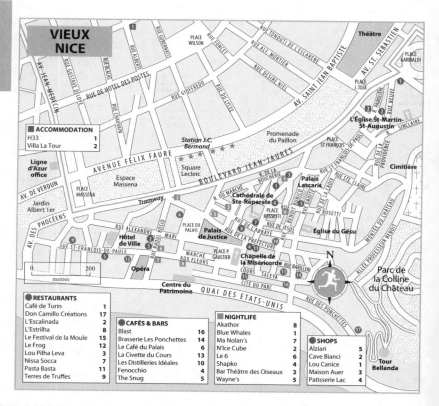

THE GALLERIES OF VIEUX NICE

Vieux Nice has some small art galleries worth seeking out. The municipal **Galerie des Ponchettes**, 77 quai des États-Unis (Tues–Sun 10am–6pm; free), and the neighbouring **Galerie de la Marine**, 59 quai des États-Unis (same hours; free), both host temporary exhibitions displaying the work of promising young artists. Also work tracking down is **Galerie a**, 4 rue St-Réparate (Tues–Sun 10am–1pm & 2–6pm; free).

Palais Lascaris

15 rue Droite • Daily except Tues 10am–6pm • Free • ☎ 04 93 62 72 40, ⓦ palais-lascaris-nice.org

Grandest survivor of Vieux Nice's baroque town mansions is the **Palais Lascaris**, a seventeenth-century palace built by the Duke of Savoy's Field-Marshal, Jean-Paul Lascaris, whose family arms, engraved on the ceiling of the entrance hall, bear the motto "Not even lightning strikes us". It's all very sumptuous, with frescoes, tapestries and chandeliers, along with a five-hundred-strong collection of historic musical instruments.

Centre du Patrimoine

75 quai des États-Unis • Mon–Thurs 8.30am–1pm & 2–5pm, Fri 8.30am–1pm & 2–5.45pm • Free; walking tours €5 • ☎ 04 92 00 41 90

A worthwhile detour onto the quai des États-Unis brings you to the **Centre du Patrimoine**, a mine of information (in French) on Nice's rich artistic, architectural and historic heritage. The Centre also organizes numerous bookable themed **walking tours** of the city.

Place Masséna

The stately, red-ochre **place Masséna** is the hub of the city and the meeting point of Vieux Nice and the modern city. It was built in 1835 across the path of the River Paillon and is now crossed by the city's gleaming modern tramway. Renovated in 2007, the square is graced by seven human figures by Spanish artist Jaume Plensa; they're suspended high above the ground and are most beautiful by night, when they're illuminated.

Steps lead up from Vieux Nice to the south side of the square; the new town lies to the north. To the west, the **Jardins Albert-1er** lead down to the promenade des Anglais; to the east, the **Espace Masséna** provides cooling fountains and a focus for the city's Christmas festivities. By 2013 a major urban regeneration project will turn the course of the Paillon from the sea to MAMAC into a 12-hectare wooded garden in the heart of the city.

Musée d'Art Moderne et d'Art Contemporain (MAMAC)

Promenade des Arts • Tues–Sun 10am–6pm • Free • ☎ 04 97 13 42 01, ⓦ mamac-nice.org

Nice's most impressive museum is the futuristic **Musée d'Art Moderne et d'Art Contemporain,** composed of four marble-clad towers linked by steel and glass bridges, with the giant **Tête Carrée** sculpture terminating the view to the northeast. It's undeniably a bold and confident work of architecture, though the building hasn't aged well; crumbling cladding panels have necessitated recladding work after just two decades, while the piazza outside is a favourite gathering place for Nice's drunks. Nevertheless, MAMAC is one of the cultural highlights of Nice and not to be missed. It has a rotating exhibition of its collection of the avant-garde French and American movements of the 1960s to the present. **Pop Art** highlights include Lichtenstein cartoons and Warhol's Campbell's soup tin, while more contemporary exhibits include works by Anish Kapoor and Antony Gormley. Pride of place goes to Nice's own **Yves Klein,** who has a room devoted to him, his celebrated 1960s happenings and his uniquely vibrant shade of blue. There's also a room given over to the colourful work of the Franco-American sculptor, painter and Vogue fashion model Niki de Saint Phalle, who died in 2002 having donated 170 works to the museum. Don't miss the roof terrace, which offers wonderful views over Vieux Nice.

The modern city centre

Running north from place Masséna, **avenue Jean-Médecin** is the city's rather dull main **shopping** street. The late nineteenth-century architecture and trees make it indistinguishable from any other big French city, as do the usual chain stores – including FNAC, Galeries Lafayette and Virgin – though the extensive refurbishment work on the Centre Nice Etoile mall and the opening of the tramway have cheered things up a little. More inviting shopping, including Nice's densest knot of **designer boutiques**, is concentrated west of place Masséna on rue du Paradis and rue Alphonse-Karr. Both intersect with the pedestrianized **rue Masséna**, an out-and-out tourist haunt full of bars, *glaciers* and fast-food outlets.

Théatre de la Photographie et de l'Image
27 bd Dubouchage • Tues–Sun 10am–6pm • Free • ☏ 04 97 13 42 20 • ⓦ tpi-nice.org

A side turning off avenue Jean-Médecin brings you to the **Théatre de la Photographie et de l'Image**: a photographic museum which displays the fascinating works of Charles Nègre, who shot local views of Nice between 1863 and 1866, just after the city and surrounding area had been ceded to France. There are also regular temporary exhibitions on photographic themes.

Russian Orthodox Cathedral
Av Nicolas II • Daily 9am–noon & 2–6pm • Free • Bus #17 (stop "Tzaréwitch")

The chief interest of the modern town is its architecture: eighteenth- and nineteenth-century Italian Baroque and Neoclassical, florid *belle époque*, the occasional slice of Art Deco, and unclassifiable exotic aristo-fantasy. The most gilded, elaborate edifice is the early twentieth-century **Russian Orthodox Cathedral**, beyond the train station, at the end of avenue Nicholas II, off boulevard Tsaréwitch. The subject of a bitter battle over its ownership in recent years, it is now under the aegis of the Moscow patriarchate.

The promenade des Anglais

The point where the Paillon flows into the sea marks the start of the famous palm-fringed **promenade des Anglais**, which began as a coastal path created by nineteenth-century English residents for their afternoon stroll. It was here that the dancer **Isadora Duncan** met a dramatic death one September evening in 1927, throttled by her own scarf as it caught in the wheel of the open car in which she was travelling. Today, the broad beachfront promenade itself is separated from the town by multiple lanes of traffic, which crawls past some of the most fanciful architecture on the Côte d'Azur.

Past the first building, the glittery Casino Ruhl, is the 1930s Art Deco facade of the **Palais de la Méditerranée**, all that remains of the original municipal casino, closed due to intrigue and corruption, and finally demolished; a new casino and hotel have subsequently been inserted behind the original facade.

Galerie Ferrero
2 rue du Congrès • Mon–Sat 10am–12.30pm & 2.30–7pm • ⓦ galerieferrero.com

Something of an institution in the art world, the commercial **Galerie Ferrero** is associated strongly with the artists of the Nice School and with Nouveau-Réalisme, and nowadays also sells works by a new generation of artists from the Côte d'Azur.

FROM TOP VILLA EPHRUSSI DE ROTHSCHILD, CAP FERRAT (P.367); COURS SALEYA, VIEUX NICE (P.348) >

Musée Masséna

65 rue de France/35 Promenade des Anglais • Daily except Tues 10am–6pm • Free • ☎ 04 93 91 19 10

The **Musée Masséna**, the city's local history museum, charts Nice's development from Napoleonic times up to the 1930s. It was built at the turn of the twentieth century as a private residence for Prince Victor d'Essling, Duc de Rivoli, and it's worth a look to see the sumptuous interior of an aristocratic villa from Nice's heyday.

Negresco Hotel

37 promenade des Anglais • ☎ 04 93 16 64 00, Ⓦ hotel-negresco-nice.com

Most celebrated of all the Riviera's hotels is the **Negresco**, built in 1906 and occupying the block between rues de Rivoli and Cronstadt. It's one of the great surviving European palace hotels, still independently run and with an interior that is both opulent and occasionally downright odd. You'll have to be staying there or dining at one of the restaurants if you want to see it though, as they don't encourage casual visitors.

Musée des Beaux-Arts

33 av des Baumettes • Tues–Sun 10am–6pm • Free • ☎ 04 92 15 28 28, Ⓦ musee-beaux-arts-nice.org • Bus #23, stop "Grosso"

A kilometre or so west of the *Negresco Hotel* and a couple of blocks inland is the **Musée des Beaux-Arts**, housed in a mansion built by a Ukrainian princess in 1878. Highlights include 28 works by Raoul Dufy, the result of a bequest to the city from Mme Dufy. There are also works by Monet, Sisley, Degas and Ziem, as well as whimsical canvases by Jules Chéret, who died in Nice in 1932, a room dedicated to Vanloo, and some very amusing Van Dongens.

Musée International d'Art Naïf Anatole Jakovsky

Château Sainte-Hélène, av de Fabron • Daily except Tues 10am–6pm • Free • ☎ 04 93 71 78 33 • Bus #23, stop "Fabron/Art Naïf"

A kilometre or so west of the Musée des Beaux-Arts and on the inland side of the Voie Rapide expressway is the **Musée International d'Art Naïf Anatole Jakovsky**, home to a surprisingly good collection of amateur art from around the world. Housed in the former home of the parfumier Coty, the museum displays six hundred examples of art naïf from the eighteenth century to the present day, including works by Vivin, Rimbert, Bauchant and the Yugoslavian masters Ivan and Josep Generalić.

Phoenix Parc Floral de Nice

405 promenade des Anglais • Daily: April–Oct 9.30am–7.30pm; Nov–March 9.30am–6pm • €2 • ☎ 04 92 29 77 01, Ⓦ parc-phoenix.org • Exit St-Augustin from the highway from Nice or Promenade des Anglais from Cannes, or bus #9, #10 or #23 from Nice

The Phoenix Parc Floral de Nice, right out by the airport, the is a cross between botanical gardens, bird-and-insect zoo, and theme park: a curious jumble of automated dinosaurs and mock Mayan temples, alpine streams, ginkgo trees and cockatoos. The greenhouse full of fluttering butterflies is the star attraction.

Musée Départemental des Arts Asiatiques

Within Phoenix Parc Floral, 405 promenade des Anglais • Daily except Tues: May to mid-Oct 10am–6pm; mid-Oct to April 10am–5pm • Free • ☎ 04 92 29 37 00

The Phoenix Parc Floral is home to the **Musée Départemental des Arts Asiatiques**, beside the lake. Housed in a beautiful building designed by Japanese architect Kenzo Tange, the museum displays artworks from India, China, Japan and Cambodia, as well as hosting touring exhibitions: there are also regular afternoon tea ceremonies.

The beaches

Nice's main beach stretches west of the Château along the shores of the Baie des Anges and is backed by the promenade des Anglais. Although the water is reasonably clean the beach itself is painfully pebbly, and though much of it is public it's broken up by fifteen private beach concessions that, from April to October, charge fees for loungers, parasols, mattresses and towels, and are more interested in serving you a meal or cocktail than in the state of your tan. East of the port a string of rocky coves includes the **Plage de la Réserve** opposite Parc Vigier (bus #20 or #30), and **Coco Beach**, popular with the local gay community.

The port and around

The **port**, flanked by gorgeous red-ochre eighteenth-century buildings and headed by the Neoclassical Notre-Dame du Port, is full of bulbous yachts but has little quayside life despite the restaurants along quai Lunel, though a new programme of improvement has somewhat tamed the ferocious traffic. There is a **flea market** at place Robilante (Tues–Sat 10am–6pm).

Musée de Terra Amata

25 bd Carnot · Wed–Sun 10am–6pm · Free · ☎ 04 93 55 59 93, ⓦ musee-terra-amata.org · Bus #81 or #100, stop "Gustavin"

Just to the east of the port is the **Musée de Terra Amata**, a museum of human paleontology on the site of an early human settlement dating back 400,000 years – a time when the sea level was much higher than it is today and much of the site of present-day Nice was submerged. The site was the camp of a tribe of hunters, located on a pebbly beach.

Cimiez

Nice's northern suburb, **Cimiez**, has always been posh. The approach up boulevard de Cimiez is punctuated by vast *belle époque* piles, many of them former hotels; at the foot of the hill stands the gargantuan *Majestic*, while the summit is dominated by the equally vast *Hôtel Régina*, built for a visit by Queen Victoria.

Musée d'Archéologie

160 av des Arènes de Cimiez · Daily except Tues 10am–6pm · Free · Take bus #15, #17 or #22, stop "Les Arènes"

The heights of Cimiez were the social centre of the town's elite some 1700 years ago, when the city was Cemenelum, capital of the Roman province of Alpes-Maritimes. Part of a small amphitheatre still stands, and excavations of the Roman baths have revealed enough detail to distinguish the sumptuous facilities for the top tax official and his cronies from the plainer public and women's baths. The **archeological site** is overlooked by the impressive, modern **Musée d'Archéologie** which displays all the finds and illustrates the city's history up to the Middle Ages.

Musée Matisse

164 av des Arènes de Cimiez · Daily except Tues 10am–6pm · Free · ☎ 04 93 81 08 08, ⓦ musee-matisse-nice.org

Adjacent to the Musée d'Archéologie is the **Musée Matisse**, housed in a seventeenth-century villa painted with trompe l'oeil. The museum's collection has work from every period of Matisse's long career, including an almost complete set of his bronze sculptures. There are sketches for one of the *Dance* murals; models for the Vence chapel plus the priests' robes that matisse designed; book illustrations including those for a 1935 edition of Joyce's *Ulysses*; and excellent examples of his cut-out technique, of which the most delightful are *The Bees* and *The Creole Dancer*.

Monastère Notre-Dame de Cimiez

Place du Monastère · **Monastère** Mon–Sat 9am–6pm · Free **Gardens** Daily: June–Aug 8am–8pm; April, May & Sept 8am–7pm; Oct–March 8am–6pm · Free **the Musée Franciscain** Mon–Sat 9am–noon & 3–5.30pm · Free

The Musée Matisse and the Roman remains back onto an old olive grove, the **Parc des Arènes de Cimiez**, one of the best open spaces in Nice. At its eastern end on place du

---

MATISSE IN NICE

Matisse wintered in Nice from 1916 onwards, staying in hotels on the promenade – from where he painted *Storm over Nice* – and then, from 1921 to 1938, renting an apartment overlooking place Charles-Félix. It was in Nice that he painted his most sensual, colour-flooded canvases featuring models as oriental odalisques posted against exotic draperies. In 1942, when he was installed in the *Régina*, he said that if he had gone on painting in the north "there would have been cloudiness, greys, colours shading off into the distance". As well as the Mediterranean light, Matisse loved the cosmopolitan life of Nice and the presence of fellow artists Renoir, Bonnard and Picasso in neighbouring towns. He returned to the *Régina* from Vence in 1949, having developed his solution to the problem of "drawing in colour" by cutting out shapes and putting them together as collages or stencils. He died in Cimiez in November 1954, aged 85.

Monastère is the **Monastère Notre-Dame de Cimiez**, which has a flamboyant pink Gothic facade of nineteenth-century origin topping a much older and plainer porch. Inside there's more gaudiness, reflecting the rich benefactors the Franciscan order had access to, but also three masterpieces of medieval art: a *Pietà* and *Crucifixion* by Louis Bréa and a *Deposition* by Antoine Bréa.

Adjoining the monastery is the **Musée Franciscain**, which paints a picture of the mendicant friars and relates the gruesome fate that befell some early martyrs. You can also look into the first cloister of the sixteenth-century **monastic buildings**, and visit the peaceful **gardens**.

On the north side of the monastery is the **Cemetery** of Cimiez (daily: March, April, Sept & Oct 8am–5.45pm; May–Aug 8am–6.45pm; Nov–Feb 8am–4.45pm); the simple tomb of **Matisse** is signposted on the left-hand side.

Musée Chagall

Av du Docteur-Ménard • Daily except Tues: May–Oct 10am–6pm; Nov–April 10am–5pm • €5.50, €7.50 during temporary exhibitions • ☎ 04 93 53 87 20, ⓦ musees-nationaux-alpesmaritimes.fr • Bus #22, stop "Musée Chagall"

At the foot of Cimiez hill, just off boulevard Cimiez on avenue du Docteur-Ménard, the **Musée Chagall**, custom-built to house the artist's Biblical Message paintings, and opened by him in 1972. The rooms are light, white and cool, with windows allowing you to see the greenery of the garden beyond the pinky red shades of the *Song of Songs* canvases. The seventeen paintings are all based on the Old Testament and are complemented by etchings and engravings. To the building itself, Chagall contributed a mosaic, the painted harpsichord and the *Creation of the World* stained-glass windows in the auditorium.

ARRIVAL AND DEPARTURE

NICE

BY PLANE

Aeroport Nice Côte d'Azur (☎ 0820 423 333, ⓦ nice .aeroport.fr) is at the western end of the Promenade des Anglais.

Getting into town Two fast buses connect with the city: #99 goes to the *gare SNCF* on av Thiers (every 30min 8am–9pm); #98 goes to the *gare routière* (every 20min 5.52am–11.37am). A €4 day-pass is needed for either. The slower regular bus #23 (€1; last bus 8.50pm) also serves the *gare SNCF* from the airport. Taxis are plentiful and cost about €22–32 into town.

Airlines Aer Lingus ☎ 0821 23 02 67; Air France ☎ 36 54; Air Transat ☎ 0825 12 02 48; British Airways ☎ 0825 82 54 00; Delta ☎ 0892 70 26 09; EasyJet ☎ 0820 42 03 15; Ryanair ☎ 0892 78 02 10.

Destinations Belfast (3 weekly; 2hr 40min); Birmingham (daily in summer; 2hr 20min); Bristol (daily; 2hr 5min); Cork (2 weekly; 2hr 35min); Dublin (daily; 2hr 30 min); East Midlands (up to 6 weekly; 2hr 20min); Edinburgh (up to 6 weekly; 2hr 35min); Glasgow (2 weekly in summer; 2hr 40min); Liverpool (daily; 2hr 20min); London City (up to 8 weekly; 1hr 55min); London Gatwick (up to 9 daily; 1hr 55 min); London Heathrow (9 daily; 2hr 5min); London Luton (2 daily; 2hr 5min); London Stansted (daily; 2hr 5min); Lyon (up to 6 daily; 1hr); Monaco (every 15min; 6min); Montreal (2 weekly; 8hr 25min); Newcastle (4 weekly in summer; 2hr 25min); New York JFK (daily; 9hr 10min); Paris Orly (every 30min–1hr; 1hr 25min); Southampton (4 weekly; 2hr 5min).

CHEMIN DE FER DE PROVENCE

The **Chemin de Fer de Provence** (☎04 97 03 80 80, ⊛trainprovence.com) runs one of France's most scenic and fun railway routes, from the Gare de Provence on rue Alfred-Binet (4 daily; 3hr 15min). The line runs up the Var valley into the hinterland of Nice to Digne-les-Bains (see p.210), and climbs through some spectacular scenery as it goes. There are also special steam train excursions on Sundays in summer.

BY TRAIN

Nice's *gare SNCF* (☎03635) is on av Thiers on the northern edge of the city centre next to the *voie rapide*.

Destinations Antibes (every 10–30min; 18–29 min); Beaulieu (every 15min–1hr; 8–10min); Breil-sur-Roya (9 daily; 1hr); Cannes (every 10–30min; 27–42min); Cap d'Ail (every 30min–1hr; 18min); Digne (4 daily; 3hr 15min); Entrevaux (5 daily; 1hr 30min); L'Escarène (9 daily; 40min); Èze-sur-Mer (every 30min–1hr; 14min); Marseille (17 daily; 2hr 32min–2hr 45min); Menton (every 15min–1hr; 28–35min); Monaco (every 30min–1hr; 15–22min); Peille (9 daily; 30min); Peillon (9 daily; 18–23min); Roquebrune-Cap Martin (every 30min–1hr; 28min); St Raphaël (every 30min–1hr; 53min–1hr 15min); Sospel (9 daily; 48 min); Tende (2 daily; 1hr 40min); Villefranche (every 15min–1hr; 6min).

BY BUS

Most buses arrive or depart from Station J.C Bermond on bd Jean-Jaurès between Place Masséna and MAMAC.

Destinations Antibes (every 10–20min; 50min); Èze-sur-Mer (up to 5 per hr; 32min); Cannes (every 10–30min; 1hr 30min); Coaraze (2 daily; 55 min); Contes (13 daily; 45min); Grasse (every 25–45min; 1hr 35min); Èze village (6 daily; 30min); La Turbie (5 daily; 40min); L'Escarène (9 daily; 40–50min); Lucéram (6 daily; 1hr–1hr 10min); Menton (up to 5 per hr; 1hr 25min); Monaco (up to 5 per hr; 43min); Peille (3 daily; 55min); Peillon (Le Moulin: 3 daily; 35min); St-Paul-de-Vence (every 30min–1hr; 1hr); Vence (every 30min–1hr; 1hr 10min); Villefranche (up to 5 per hr; 18min).

BY FERRY

SNCM and Corsica Ferries operate ferries to Corsica from the port: SNCM's services run during July & August only but Corsica Ferries serves Ajaccio and Bastia all year round.

Corsica Ferries, *gare maritime*, quai du Commerce (☎0825 095 095, ⊛corsica-ferries.fr).

SNCM *gare maritime*, quai du Commerce (☎04 93 13 66 59, ⊛sncm.fr).

INFORMATION AND TOURS

Tourist office At the *gare SNCF* on av Thiers (mid-June to mid-Sept Mon–Sat 8am–8pm, Sun 9am–7pm; mid-Sept to mid-June Mon–Sat 8am–7pm, Sun 10am–5pm; ☎0892 707 407, ⊛en.nicetourisme.com). There are annexes at 5 promenade des Anglais (mid-June to mid-Sept Mon–Sat 8am–8pm, Sun 9am–7pm; mid-Sept to mid-June Mon–Sat 9am–6pm), and at terminal 1 of the

airport (April–Sept daily 9am–8pm; Oct–March Mon–Sat 9am–6pm).

Boat trips Trans Côte d'Azur, quai Lunel (☎04 92 00 42 30, ⊛trans-cote-azur.com), run summer trips to Îles de Lérins (July & Aug daily except Mon), Monaco (June to mid-Sept Tues, Thurs & Sat) and St-Tropez (July & Aug daily except Mon).

GETTING AROUND

BY BUS AND TRAM

Buses and trams in Nice and surrounding towns are provided by **Lignes d'Azur**, 3 place Masséna (Mon–Fri 7.30am–6.45pm, Sat 8.30am–6pm; ☎08 1006 1006, ⊛lignesdazur.com). A single **tram** line loops in a "V" shape from the northern suburbs through the city centre to the northeastern suburbs. **Buses** are frequent until early evening (roughly 7.30–9.15pm), after which five Noctrambus night buses serve most areas from Station Bermond, close to place Masséna until 1.10am; the tram continues until 12.50am to Las Planas and until 1.35 am to Pont Michel.

Tickets You can buy a single ticket (€1) or a day pass (€4) on the bus; ten-journey multipasses (€10) and seven-day passes (€15) are available from *tabacs*, kiosks, newsagents

and from the Lignes d'Azur office, where you can also pick up a free route map.

BY TAXI

Central Taxi Riviera (☎04 93 13 78 78, ⊛taxis-nice.fr); Taxis Niçois Indépendents (☎04 93 88 25 82). Taxis cost €1.80/km by day and €2.40/km by night (7pm–7am) and on Sundays and public holidays. Note that there are supplementary charges for the airport run, for each item of baggage and for being stuck in traffic; the minimum fare is €6.40.

BY CAR

Autobleue rental scheme You can rent an electric car using the Autobleue scheme (⊛auto-bleue.org); there are

8

42 rental stations around the city, and the registration fee is €25, after which the hourly rate is €8, or €50/day.

Car hire Major commercial agencies are based at the airport and *gare SNCF*.

Car parks At Acropolis; promenade du Paillon; promenade des Arts; *gare SNCF*; place Masséna; cours Saleya.

BY BIKE

Vélo Bleu Nice's on-street bicycle rental scheme, Vélo Bleu

(☎ velobleu.org), has 120 rental stations scattered throughout the city. You have to sign up online or at the bike station (€1/day, €5/week; ☎ 04 30 00 30 01), after which the first 30min is free; it costs €1 for the next 30min and €2 per hr thereafter. Payment is by credit card.

Bike, scooter and motorbike hire If you want to hire a mountain bike, electric bike, scooter or motorbike, try Holiday Bikes, 23 rue de Belgique (☎ 04 93 16 01 62, ☎ holidaybikes.fr).

ACCOMMODATION

Before hunting for **accommodation**, it's worth taking advantage of the **online reservation service** on the tourist office website. The area around the station teems with cheap hotels, some of them seedy, though there are a few gems. Sleeping on the beach is illegal and for campsites you'll need to head west to Cagnes-sur-Mer (see p.327).

Les Cigales 16 rue Dalpozzo ☎ 04 97 03 10 70, ☎ hotel-lescigales.com; map pp.346–347. Clean, a/c and renovated three-star hotel 150m from the promenade des Anglais, with soundproofed en-suite rooms with satellite TV and safe, plus a sun terrace for guests. Good value for the price and location. **€99**

Cronstadt 3 rue Cronstadt ☎ 04 93 82 00 30, ☎ hotelcronstadt.com; map pp.346–347. Hidden inside the garden courtyard of a large residential block, slightly gloomy but extremely tranquil for its location, close to the *Negresco* and the sea, with old-fashioned, clean and comfortable rooms. **€90**

Hôtel Durante 16 av Durante ☎ 04 93 88 84 40, ☎ hotel-durante.com; map pp.346–347. Great-value mid-range hotel in a quiet side turning near the *gare SNCF*, with smart, pretty a/c rooms with flatscreen TV, free parking and an attractive garden. **€115**

★ **Le Floride** 52 bd de Cimiez ☎ 04 93 53 11 02, ☎ hotel-floride.fr; map pp.346–347. Clean, friendly and good-value two-star hotel in Cimiez, with some spacious en-suite doubles and a few cheap singles with WC and shower. There's no a/c – which might be an issue in high season – but rooms have electric fans. Free wi-fi and private parking. **€67**

★ **Le Grimaldi** 15 rue Grimaldi ☎ 04 93 16 00 24, ☎ le-grimaldi.com; map pp.346–347. Highly successful boutique-style reworking of a *belle époque* hotel on the fringe of Nice's prime designer shopping district: smart, central, and with chic, individually designed rooms. **€115**

H33 33 rue Pastorelli ☎ 04.93.62.18.82, ☎ h33-hotel-nice.com; map pp.348. Frill-free but renovated budget hotel with simple modern decor, a/c, soundproofing, wi-fi and a convenient, central location. It's gay-friendly, and prices take a tumble outside the summer season. **€99**

Hi Hotel 3 av des Fleurs ☎ 04 97 07 26 26, ☎ hi-hotel. net; map pp.346–347. Swish designer hotel with bold colour schemes, individually themed rooms and a lobby that resembles a fashionable beauty parlour. It also has a rooftop pool, spa and its own stretch of beach. **€178**

Lépante 6 rue Lépante ☎ 04 93 62 20 55, ☎ hotellepante.com; map pp.346–347. Gay-friendly two-star hotel in a refurbished, central, *belle époque* building, with wi-fi, a/c and a first-floor sunny balcony with lots of seating. Decor is traditional, but there's a wide variety of room types and tarifs. **€99**

Negresco 37 promenade des Anglais ☎ 04 93 16 64 00, ☎ hotel-negresco-nice.com; map pp.346–347. This legendary, free-spirited seafront palace hotel is a genuine one-off, with its own private beach, masses of art and a few wacky touches, including some occasionally garish colour schemes. **€330**

★ **L'Oasis** 23 rue Gounod ☎ 04 93 88 12 29, ☎ hotelniceoasis.com; map pp.346–347. Tucked off the street in a peaceful garden setting, this freshly renovated three-star hotel has nice, upgraded and a/c rooms, secure private parking and an outdoor terrace where you can take breakfast in fine weather. **€109**

La Pérouse 11 quai Rauba-Capeu ☎ 04 93 62 34 63, ☎ hotel-la-perouse.com; map pp.346–347. The best-situated hotel in central Nice, at the foot of Le Château, with a rooftop pool and fabulous views over the promenade des Anglais and Baie des Anges. Rooms have marble bathrooms and individually controlled a/c. **€290**

Petit Palais 17 av Émile-Bieckert ☎ 04 93 62 19 11, ☎ petitpalaisnice.com; map pp.346–347. Set in hilly Cimiez, this attractive, quiet and comfortable *belle époque* mansion was the former home of writer and actor Sacha Guitry. There are 25 rooms, some with views over the Baie des Anges. **€130**

Le Petit Trianon 11 rue Paradis ☎ 04 93 87 50 46, ☎ lepetittrianon.fr; map pp.346–347. Prettily renovated, in a modern yet slightly frou-frou style that matches the name, these a/c and soundproofed rooms have a great location in an old apartment block in the pedestrian zone close to the beach. **€95**

Villa Rivoli 10 rue Rivoli ☎ 04 93 88 80 25, ☎ villa-rivoli.com; map pp.346–347. Sweet hotel in a *belle époque* building a short walk from the promenade des Anglais and beach, with refurbished, a/c en-suite rooms with pretty, traditional decor, plus free wi-fi. Some rooms have small balconies; parking is available. **€80**

Villa la Tour 4 rue de la Tour ☎ 04 93 80 08 15, ⓦ villa-la-tour.com; map pp.348. The only hotel in the heart of Vieux Nice, with fourteen a/c en-suite rooms with satellite TV and safe, including a few with balconies or views over the city. Room styles (and rates) vary quite widely. There's also a roof terrace. **€59**

Windsor 11 rue Dalpozzo ☎ 04 93 88 59 35, ⓦ hotelwindsornice.com; p.346–347. Smart boutique-style and gay-friendly "art hotel" with individually styled rooms, some with frescoes, and many of them quite striking. There's also a spa with sauna and steam bath, and small pool in a partially shaded garden, overgrown with bamboo. **€128**

HOSTELS

Auberge de Jeunesse Mont Boron Rte Forestière du Mont-Alban ☎ 04 93 89 23 64, ⓦ fuaj.org; bus #14 from J.C. Bermond (direction "place du Mont-Boron", stop "L'Auberge"), last bus 7.30pm; map pp.346–347. HI hostel 4km from the centre of town, just off the Moyenne Corniche on the forested slopes of Mont Boron. Reception

7am–noon & 5pm–midnight. Rates include breakfast. Closed Nov–May. **€19.60**

Backpackers Chez Patrick First floor, 32 rue Pertinax ☎ 04 93 80 30 72, ⓦ backpackerschezpatrick.com; map pp.346–347. Clean, a/c first-floor hostel (there's another hostel downstairs), close to the station. There are no cooking facilities but there's a fridge and washing machine, a safe, and no curfew. Accommodation is in four- to six-bed dorms or doubles. Dorms **€30**; doubles **€70**

La Belle Meunière 21 av Durante ☎ 04 93 88 66 15, ⓦ bellemeuniere.com; map pp.346–347. Efficient, clean and friendly backpacker hotel in a lovely old bourgeois house, with accommodation in double, twin, triple or four-bed rooms, or dorms that sleep up to five. There's free wi-fi, laundry service, private parking and a terrace at the front; public areas have recently been spruced up. Dorms **€22**; doubles **€76**

★ **Villa Saint-Exupery Gardens** 22 av Gravier ☎ 04 93 84 42 83, ⓦ vsaint.com; tram from Place Masséna (direction "Las Planas", stop "Comte de Falicon"), from where staff will pick you up; map pp.346–347. Impressively well-equipped, family-run hostel in an old nunnery, some way out of central Nice, with bar, internet, kitchen and laundry facilities. There's also a sister hostel in the city centre. Dorms **€30**; twins **€90**

EATING AND DRINKING

Nice is a great place for **food**, whether you're picnicking on market fare, snacking on **Niçois specialities** like *pan bagnat* (a bun stuffed with tuna, salad and olive oil), *salade Niçoise*, *pissaladière* (onion tart with anchovies) or *socca* (a chickpea flour pancake), or dining in the palace hotels. The **Italian** influence is strong, with pasta on every menu; *seafood* and **fish** are also staples, with good *bourride* (fish soup), *estocaficada* (stockfish and tomato stew), and all manner of sea fish grilled with fennel or Provençal herbs. The local Bellet wines from the hills behind the city provide the perfect light accompaniment. For **snacks**, many of the cafés sell sandwiches with typically Provençal fillings such as fresh basil, olive oil, goat's cheese and mesclun, the green-salad mix of the region.

Despite the usual fast-food chains and tourist traps dotted around, most areas of Nice have plenty of reasonable **restaurants**. Vieux Nice has a dozen on every street catering for a wide variety of budgets, while the port quaysides have excellent, though pricey, fish restaurants. From June till September it's wise to **reserve** tables, or turn up before 8pm, especially in Vieux Nice – and though browsing menus is half the fun it's best not to leave your selection too long, as not all Niçois kitchens stay open particularly late.

VIEUX NICE RESTAURANTS

The restaurants below are all marked on the Vieux Nice map on p.348.

Café de Turin & Le Petit Turin 5 place Garibaldi ☎ 04 93 62 29 52, ⓦ cafedeturin.fr. A local institution, the *Café de Turin* has spread into the premises next door so that it dominates one corner of place Garibaldi. The emphasis is on raw seafood, with panachés of *fruits de mer* from €34, plus a few shellfish-based cooked options. They don't take reservations, so be prepared to queue. Daily 8am–10pm.

Don Camillo Créations 5 rue des Ponchettes ☎ 04 93 85 67 95, ⓦ doncamillo-creations.fr. Elegant, modern *restaurant gastronomique* between Vieux Nice and the château, with contemporary Niçois/Italian cooking and

dishes like roast langoustines with *cèpes* or foie gras marinated in Sauternes on a €45 *menu*. Tues–Sat noon–2.30pm & 7–10.30pm.

L'Escalinada 22 rue Pairolière ☎ 04 93 62 11 71, ⓦ escalinada.fr. Good Niçois specialities at this old restaurant at the foot of a stepped side street in Vieux Nice: stuffed sardines with mesclun €15.50, courgette fritters €13, *plats du jour* from €15, *menu* €26. Service is efficient, but occasionally a bit gruff. Daily lunch & dinner.

L'Estrilha 13 rue de l'Abbaye ☎ 04 93 62 62 00. Reservations essential in summer for this popular restaurant that serves *bourride*, *civet de lapin* with ravioli and tuna *à la Niçoise*. *Menus* €18 and €22. Tues–Sun 6–11pm.

8

Le Festival de la Moule 20 cours Saleya ☎ 04 93 62 02 12. If you like mussels, come to this unpretentious all-you-can-eat *moules-frites* place on cours Saleya. There are ten sauces to choose from, and a pot is €14.90 with free refills; they also serve pasta and grilled fish. Daily 11am–11pm.

Le Frog 2 rue Milton Robbins ☎ 04 93 85 85 65, ⓦ frog-restaurant.fr. Quirky, trendy little restaurant close to the Opera serving up inventive variations on classic French cooking, with dishes like duck foie gras with fig ice cream or warm goat's cheese salad with truffles & apple. *Menu* €19 including a glass of wine. Mon 7–11pm, Tues–Sun noon–2pm & 7–11pm.

Lou Pilha Leva 10 rue Collet ☎ 04 93 13 99 08. One of a number of places in Vieux Nice where you can try street food *à la Niçois* at rock-bottom prices: *socca* costs €2.80, *pissaladière* €3, *petits farçis* €5.70. You can take away or eat at the benches outside. Daily 11am–9.30pm, later in summer.

★ **Nissa Socca** 7 rue Sainte Réparate ☎ 04 93 80 18 35. Right in the thick of Vieux Nice and better than its touristy location might suggest, particularly for the Niçois specialities, which include huge portions of *soupe de poissons* and a good and generous *daube de boeuf* with gnocchi (€12). *Menu* €18. Daily except Wed noon–2.30pm & 7–10.30pm.

Pasta Basta 18 rue de la Préfecture ☎ 04 93 80 03 57. No-frills pasta place with eleven types of fresh and three dried pasta varieties and a choice of twenty sauces. Pasta from €4.80, sauce from €3.50, and rough wine by the *pichet* from €4. Try the *merda de can* – buckwheat gnocchi. Daily noon–10.30pm.

Terres de Truffes 11 rue St-François-de-Paule ☎ 04 93 62 07 68, ⓦ terresdetruffes.com. Intimate, upmarket and tasteful restaurant with a wide variety of dishes – from pasta to meat and fish – all cooked or served with truffles. Lunch *menu* €24; otherwise €39–85. Mon–Sat noon–2pm & 7–10pm.

GREATER NICE RESTAURANTS

The restaurants below are all marked on the Nice map on pp.346–347.

L'Âne Rouge 7 quai des Deux-Emmanuel ☎ 04 93 89 49 63, ⓦ anerougenice.com. Lobster is the speciality of this portside gastronomic haunt, where the *menu* has a bias towards fish and seafood but also includes the likes of roast lamb with swiss chard & artichoke-stuffed cannelloni. Lunch *menu* €23, dinner *menus* from €35. Mon, Tues & Fri–Sun noon–2pm & 7.30–10pm, Thurs 7.30–10pm.

Chanteclerc 37 promenade des Anglais ☎ 04 93 16 64 00, ⓦ hotel-negresco-nice.com. The *Negresco's* restaurant *gastronomique* is the grandest in Nice, with two Michelin stars. It's seriously expensive in the evening, but chef Jean-Denis Rieubland's €58 Sunday lunch *menu* provides a good idea of how sublime Niçois food is at its best. Wed–Sat 7–10pm, Sun 12.20–2pm & 7–10pm.

Le Flaveur 25 rue Gubernatis ☎ 04 93 62 53 95, ⓦ flaveur.net. Friendly gastro restaurant with creative dishes, such as lobster with green curry and coconut milk or maki-style jamon Serrano, that make this a new local favourite. *Menus* €45–70. Tues–Fri lunch & dinner, Sat dinner only.

Mets and Café 28 rue Assalit ☎ 04 93 80 30 85. Busy lunchtime-only budget brasserie close to many of the backpacker hostels, serving up traditional French food and with a €9.80 lunchtime *formule*. Mon–Sat 11.30am–3pm.

★ **Voyageur Nissart** 19 rue Alsace Lorraine ☎ 04 93 82 19 60, ⓦ voyageurnissart.com. Excellent food like *maman* used to make, in a setting that couldn't be more typically French – chequered tablecloths and all. *Menus* start at €16.50; one focuses on Niçois specialities like *daube* and *petits farcis*. Tues–Fri & Sun noon–2.30pm & 7–10.30pm, Sat 7–10.30pm.

VIEUX NICE CAFÉS AND BARS

The places below are all marked on the Vieux Nice map on p.348.

Blast 8 place Charles Felix ☎ 04 93 80 00 50. The vast terrace of this lively bar is an ideal vantage point for observing the comings and goings on cours Saleya. There's finger food to soak up the €8.50 cocktails, draught beers start at €4 and bottled Belgian beer at €6.50. Daily from 8pm.

Brasserie Les Ponchettes 3 place Charles Félix ☎ 04 93 92 16 13. Bar/brasserie with a blingy but diminutive interior and a vast terrace for al fresco people-watching. Sandwiches from €6, bruschetta and pasta from around €10 and good, strong classic cocktails for €10. Daily 8am–midnight.

Le Café du Palais 1 place du Palais. Classic pavement café ambiance and a prime alfresco lounging spot on the handsome square by the Palais de Justice, dishing up cocktails (around €10), simple meals and draught beer (from around €3.50). Daily 7am–11pm.

La Civette du Cours 1 cours Saleya ☎ 04 93 80 80 59. Classier and more intimate than its neighbours, this is the best-loved of the cours' café terraces, with a mixed gay/straight crowd, a vaguely Art Deco look and a wide terrace for people-watching. Snacks from around €3; expect to pay upwards of €10 for *plats du jour*. Daily 7.30am–1am.

Les Distilleries Idéales 24 rue de la Préfecture ☎ 04 93 62 10 66, ⓦ lesdistilleriesideales.fr. Undoubtedly the prettiest bar in Vieux Nice, with high vaulted ceilings and a florid, *fin de siècle* look including wall paintings by a local artist. Eight beers on draught, classic cocktails and light snacks from €4.10. Happy hour 6–8pm. Daily 3pm–1am.

★ **Fenocchio** 2 place Rossetti ☎ 04 93 80 72 52, ⓦ fenocchio.fr. A firm Vieux Nice favourite, this excellent *glacier* serves a vast range of ice creams, with flavours like salty caramel, violet or beer sorbet alongside more familiar offerings. On warm nights, skip the restaurant desserts and head here instead. One scoop €2, two €3.50. Daily 9am–midnight.

The Snug 22 rue Droite ☎04 93 80 43 22, ⓦsnugandcellar.com. Smaller and more low-key than most of Nice's Irish bars, with a friendly, pubby atmosphere, live music on Mondays and Guinness and Kilkenny to drink. *Pression* beer from €2.80; they also serve food, including a Sunday roast. Daily noon–12.30am.

GREATER NICE CAFÉS AND BARS

The places below are all marked on the Nice map on pp.346–347.

Le Grand Café de Lyon 33 av Jean-Médecin ☎04 93 88 13 17, ⓦcafedelyon.fr. Big *bar/brasserie and* café on

Nice's main shopping street, with Art Deco touches to the interior and a big terrace for people-watching. Big selection of Belgian and German beers from €4.20; *plats du jour* €12.90. Daily 7.30am–10pm.

Juke House Café 8 rue Defly ☎04 93 80 02 22. Tiny, American-style cocktail and tapas bar that draws a young crowd. Happy hour is 6–8pm; otherwise, cocktails cost upwards of €8 and beers start at €3.30. The food menu is a mix of tapas, burgers and salads, and as the name suggests, there's a jukebox. Tues–Sat noon–midnight.

★ **Pulp Fiction Saloon** 7 rue Emmanuel Philibert, at place du Pin ☎04 93 55 25 35. Stylish new lesbian and gay bar on a corner site in the newly emerging "Petit Marais" gay district, with black decor, skull-and-crossbones wallpaper and Philippe Starck "Ghost" chairs on the terrace. Bottled beers €4.50. Mon & Sun 5–12.30pm, Tues–Sat noon–12.30pm.

NIGHTLIFE

Vieux Nice's British- and Irish-style **pubs** have long been very popular with young expat travellers – in fact, you're more likely to hear English than French spoken in some of them. Along with their encyclopedic range of beers or whiskies they often feature live **bands**, though the music tends not to be very original. For the older, more affluent generation, the luxury **hotel bars** with their jazzy singers and piano accompaniment have held sway for decades. As for the **clubs**, bouncers judging your wallet or exclusive membership lists are the rule. Nice's **lesbian and gay scene** is quite sizeable; of late rue Bonaparte is the focus of a new gay district between place Garibaldi and the port – the so-called "Petit Marais". The annual Pink Parade takes place in early summer.

8

VIEUX NICE NIGHTLIFE

The places below are all marked on the Vieux Nice map on p.348.

Akathor 32 cours Saleya ☎04 93 80 89 22. Much the busiest of cours Saleya's rock and sports bars, with live bands upstairs from 10.15pm (no cover), salsa nights, €3 happy hour shots until 9pm and inexpensive, nachos-to-houmous food (€3.80). It's a bit less Anglophone than some Vieux Nice places, too. Daily 5.30pm–2.30am.

Blue Whales 1 rue Mascoïnat ☎04 93 62 90 44. Intimate Vieux Nice late bar with a friendly, boozy atmosphere, pool tables and regular live bands. Happy hour 6.30pm–midnight, live rock, funk or jazz from 11pm. Daily 6.30pm–4.30am.

Ma Nolan's 2 rue St-François-de-Paule ☎04 93 80 23 87, ⓦma-nolans.com. Vast, slick Irish pub with live bands most nights at 10pm, televised Irish and British sport plus a big range of draught and bottled beer from €3.70 and pies to eat (€13.50). You might as well not be in France, but it's popular with a younger crowd. There's a second branch on the port. Daily 11am–2am.

N'îce Cube 1 rue de la Préfecture ☎04 97 09 82 39. Lively, clubby little DJ bar that gets packed and sweaty later on and offers free tapas and €2 drinks during its 6–10pm happy hour. Free admission. Daily 6pm–2.30am.

★ **Shapko** 5 rue Rossetti ☎09 54 94 69 31, ⓦshapko .com. Intimate and friendly Vieux Nice music bar on two

levels, with a relaxed crowd and eclectic live music, from slap bass jazz to live electronica, plus Mexican bar food. Wed–Sun 7pm–12.30am.

Le 6 6 rue Raoul Bosio ☎04 93 62 66 64, ⓦle6.fr. Smart Vieux Nice lesbian and gay music bar with regular live entertainment including chanson, go-go dancers taking showers and karaoke nights, plus DJs. Daily 10pm–5am.

Bar Théâtre des Oiseaux 65 rue de l'Abbaye ☎04 93 80 21 93, ⓦbardesoiseaux.com. Named for the birds that once nested in the loft, this bar serves Niçois tapas (4 for €10) and cocktails (€7 up). There's also an old-fashioned, small cabaret stage, which is a good place to hear traditional French chanson. Bar Mon–Sat lunch & dinner; Theatre Wed & Thurs from 8.30pm, Fri & Sat from 9pm.

Wayne's 15 rue de la Préfecture ☎04 93 13 46 99, ⓦwaynes.fr. This big, boisterous bar is one of the lynchpins of the Vieux Nice nightlife scene, very popular with Anglophone expats and with sport on big screen TVs plus regular live rock bands. Daily noon–2am.

GREATER NICE NIGHTLIFE

The places below are all marked on the Nice map on pp.346–347.

Glam 6 rue Eugène Emanuel ☎06 60 55 26 61, ⓦleglam.org. Nice's liveliest lesbian and gay club, with guest DJs, a dance and pop-oriented music policy and theme nights ranging from bears to underwear. Entry with *conso* €10 Fri, €13 Sat; free on Sun. Fri–Sun 11pm–4.30am.

High Club 45 promenade des Anglais ☎ 06 16 95 75 87, ⊕highclub.fr. Large seafront disco that attracts big-name international DJs and live PAs. There's also an 1980s-themed club, *Studio 47*, that targets the over-25s, plus a lesbian and gay-friendly club, *Sk'high*. Expect to pay €10, except for the occasional free nights. Fri–Sun 11.45pm–6am.

La Perle 26 quai Lunel ☎ 04 93 26 54 79, ⊕perle-club .com. Smart restaurant and disco on the port, with regular Thursday mojito nights (€12) and a catch-all 1980s-to-R&B music policy. "Tenue correcte" is expected, so dress up. Restaurant 8–11pm; club Thurs–Sun from 11pm until at least 5am.

ENTERTAINMENT

The best place for up-to-date **listings** for concerts, plays, films and sporting events is FNAC at 44–46 av Jean-Médecin (Mon–Sat 10am–7.30pm, Sun 11am–7pm), where you can also buy **tickets** for most events.

Cinémathèque de Nice 3 esplanade Kennedy ☎ 04 92 04 06 66, ⊕cinematheque-nice.com. Arthouse cinema which shows subtitled films in the original language (v.o), including black-and-white classics and documentaries.

Opéra de Nice 4 & 6 rue St-François-de-Paule ☎ 04 92 17 40 79, ⊕opera-nice.org. Nice's opulent late nineteenth-century opera house provides a magnificent venue for classical opera, ballet and concerts. Opera tickets range from €12 to €78. Performances generally start at 8pm.

Palais Nikaïa 163 route de Grenoble ☎ 04 92 29 31 29, ⊕nikaia.fr. Indoor auditorium in the west of the city that is Nice's major venue for big-name touring rock concerts, major musicals and ice spectaculars.

Théâtre de la Cité 3 rue Paganini ☎ 04 93 16 82 69, ⊕theatredelacite.fr. Small, independent theatre with an eclectic programme that embraces everything from live chanson and flamenco to cabaret, drama and film.

Théâtre National de Nice Promenade des Arts ☎ 04 93 13 90 90, ⊕tnn.fr. Nice's most prestigious stage for serious drama is part of the same iconic arts complex as MAMAC, staging everything from Molière to new works by up-and-coming dramatists.

SHOPPING

MARKETS

Cours Saleya, place Pierre-Gautier and Charles-Félix The city's main food market (Tues–Sun 6am–1.30pm), sells fruit, vegetables, cheeses and sausages. On Monday the stalls sell bric-a-brac and secondhand clothes (7.30am–6pm).

Place du Palais de Justice Fortnightly Saturday market (first & third Sat of month: summer 7am–7pm; winter 7am–5pm) of old paintings, books and postcards.

Place St-François Fish market (Tues–Sun 6am–1pm).

SHOPS

Alziari 14 rue St François de Paule ☎ 04 93 85 76 92, ⊕alziari.com.fr; map pp.348. Legendary (and very pretty) olive oil emporium established in 1868. You can taste and buy the oils, and they sell beautifully wrapped packs of oil, tapenade, olives, honey and other luxury nibbles to take home. Mon–Sat 8.30am–12.30pm & 2.15–7pm.

Cave Bianchi 7 rue Raoul Bosio ☎ 04 93 85 65 79, ⊕cave-bianchi.fr; map pp.348. This old-established wine merchant is a good place to sample wines from Nice's own *appellation contrôlée*, Bellet; it has a lovely vaulted stone wine cellar. Daily 9.30am–7.30pm and until 10.30pm Fri & Sat.

Lou Canice 7 rue Mascoïnat ☎ 04 93 85 41 62, ⊕loucanice.fr; map p.348. Artisan biscuit maker selling macaroons and *navettes* flavoured with lemon or orange blossom, plus jams, olives, olive oil and local Bellet wines. Daily 10am–8pm.

Maison Auer 7 rue St François de Paule ☎ 04 93 85 77 98, ⊕maison-auer.com; map p.348. Old established *confiserie* and *chocolatier* that has been selling its famous candied fruits, chocolates and *marrons glacés* from beautiful premises close to the Opera since the nineteenth century. Tues–Sat 9am–1.30pm & 2.30–6pm.

NICE FESTIVALS AND SPORTING EVENTS

Of Nice's many festivals – which begin with the celebrated Mardi Gras **Carnival** and associated flower processions in February – probably the most interesting is the **Nice Jazz Festival**, staged in July (for details, check ⊕nicejazzfestival.fr). The city's biggest sporting event is the **Triathlon de Nice** in June when competitors from all round the world swim 3.8km in the Baie des Anges, cycle 180km in the hills behind the city and run 42km, ending up along the promenade des Anglais.

Patisserie Lac 18 rue Barla, map pp.346–347; 12 rue de la Préfecture, Vieux Nice, map p.348; ☎ 04 93 55 37 74, ⊕ patisseries-lac.com. Classy chocolatier selling beautifully-presented chocolate, macaroons, nougat, marrons glacés and chocolate-coated ginger. Rue Barla Mon, Tues, Thurs & Fri 9am–12.30pm & 3–7.30pm, Sat 9am–1pm & 3–7.30pm, Sun 9am–1pm & 4–7pm; rue de la Préfecture Mon–Sat 9.30am–1pm & 2.30–7.30pm, Sun 9.30am–1pm & 3–7pm.

DIRECTORY

Consulates Canada, 2 place Franklin ☎ 04 93 92 93 22; USA, 7 av Gustave-V ☎ 04 93 88 89 55.
Disabled access Mobil Azur transport for people with reduced mobility ☎ 0805 20 06 06, ⊕ mobilazur.org
Health SOS Médecins ☎ 0810 85 01 01; Riviera Medical Services (English-speaking doctors; ☎ 04 93 26 12 70); Hôpital St-Roch, 5 rue Pierre-Dévoluy ☎ 04 92 03 33 33; SOS Dentaire ☎ 04 93 01 14 14.
Internet Taxi Phone Internet, 43 av Thiers.

Laundry Laverie 7/7, 10 rue Assalit; Assalit Pressing, corner rue Assalit & rue Lamartine.
Lost property 1 rue Raoul Bosio ☎ 04 97 13 44 10.
Money exchange American Express, Nice-Côte d'Azur airport; Change Méditerranée, 17 av Médecin.
Pharmacy 66 av Jean-Médecin (Mon–Sat 24hr, Sun 7pm–8am; ☎ 04 93 62 54 44).
Police 1 av Maréchal Foch ☎ 04 92 17 22 22.
Post office 21 av Thiers (Mon, Tues, Wed & Fri 8am–7pm, Thurs 8am–5.45pm, Sat 8.30am–noon).

The Arrière-Pays Niçois

The **foothills of the Alps** come down to the northern outskirts of Nice, and right down to the sea on the eastern side of the city: a majestic barrier, with the highest peaks snowcapped for much of the year. From the sea, the wide course of the Var to the west appears to be the only passage northwards. But the hidden river of Nice, the **Paillon**, also cuts its way to the sea through the mountains past small, fortified medieval settlements. The **Nice–Turin railway line** follows the Paillon for part of its way – one of the many spectacular train journeys of this region. If you have your own transport you'll find this is serious, hairpin-bend country where the views are a major distraction. **Buses** from Nice to its villages are infrequent.

With their proximity to the metropolis, the *villages perchés* of **Peillon**, **Peille**, **Lucéram**, **L'Escarène**, **Coaraze** and **Contes** are no longer entirely peasant communities, though the social make-up remains a mix. You may well hear Provençal spoken here and the **traditional festivals** are still communal affairs, even when the participants include the well-off Niçois escaping from the coastal heat. The links between the city and its hinterland are strong: the villagers still live off the land and sell their olives and olive oil, goat's cheese or vegetables and herbs in the city's markets; many city dwellers' parents or grandparents still have homes within the mountains, and for every Niçois this wild and underpopulated countryside is the natural remedy for city stress.

Peillon

For the first 10km or so along the River Paillon, after you leave the last of Nice, the valley is marred by quarries that supply the city's constant demand for building materials. However, shortly after Ste-Thècle – site of Peillon's nearest *gare SNCF* – a side road begins to climb, looping through olive groves, pine forest and brilliant pink and yellow broom to reach the gates of **PEILLON**'s medieval enclave. The ascent is little more than 1km from the valley floor as the crow flies, but in reality the journey is considerably further because of the twisting, circuitous road.

Peillon is beautifully maintained, right up to the lovely place de l'Église at the top. There is very little commerce and very little life during the week – most of the residents commute to their jobs in Nice. Just outside the village stands the **Chapelle des Pénitents Blancs**, which is decorated with violent fifteenth-century

8

frescoes similar to those by Jean Canavesio at La Brigue (see p.240). You can peer through the grille across the chapel door; depositing a twenty cent coin illuminates the interior. From the chapel a path heads off across the hills northwards to Peille. It's a two-hour walk along what was once a Roman road, and a more direct route than going via the valley.

Peille

PEILLE lies at the end of a long climb from the valley below, the journey up from the *gare SNCF* replete with hairpin bends. The atmosphere here is very different to that in Peillon. The village was excommunicated several times for refusing to pay its bishop's tithes, and its republicanism was later manifested by the domed thirteenth-century Chapelle de St-Sébastien being turned into the **Hôtel de Ville**, and the Chapelle des Pénitents Noirs into a communal **oil press**. Peille claims to be the birthplace of the Roman emperor Pertinax, who was assassinated within thirteen weeks of his election on account of his egalitarian and democratic tendencies.

The village

The main square, **place de la Colle**, is graced with a Gothic fountain and two half-arches supporting a Romanesque pillar. It's also home to the medieval **court house** which bears a plaque recalling Peille's transfer of its rights over Monaco to Genoa. On nearby rue St-Sébastien the former salt tax office, the **Hôtel de la Gabelle**, still stands. Peille's small **Musée du Terroir** on place de l'Armée (open 2–6pm on request; enquire at tourist office – see p.364; free) is fascinating, not so much for the exhibits but because the captions are written in the village's own dialect, Peilhasc. The only thing detracting from the beauty of the village is the view to the southwest which is marred by the cement-quarrying around La Grave, its suburb down in the valley by the rail line. You can, however, take labyrinthine winding routes to La Turbie, Ste-Agnes or L'Escarène from the village, on which precipitous panoramas – and slow progress – are assured. More adventurous visitors to Peille make the circuit of its **Via Ferrata**, which includes a rope bridge and rock face; there's a €3 charge to make the circuit and you need to book in advance; you can hire the necessary equipment locally. For more information enquire at the *Bar l'Absinthe* (see p.364).

L'Escarène

At **L'ESCARÈNE** the rail line leaves the Paillon and heads northeast to Sospel (see p.239). In the days before rail travel, this was an important staging post on the road from Nice to Turin, when drivers would harness up new horses to take on the thousand-metre Braus pass, which the rail line now tunnels under. There's not a great deal to see, other than the great Baroque church of **St Pierre-es-Liens**, with its wonderful eighteenth-century church organ inside.

Lucéram

Following the Paillon upstream for 6km from L'Escarène, you reach unpretentious but beautiful **LUCÉRAM**, with its outwardly unobtrusive fifteenth-century **Chapelle de St-Grat**, with gorgeous frescoes by Jean Beleison, a colleague of Louis Bréa, at the entrance to the village. You'll need to visit the tourist office (see p.364) to gain entry to the village's museums or church, which are otherwise locked; it's a good idea to phone in advance.

The Circuit des Crèches and Musée de la Crèche

Lucéram is well-known locally for its annual **Circuit des Crèches**, which brings thousands of visitors to the village in the weeks before Christmas. During this period more than four hundred nativity scenes are displayed in the streets of Lucéram and the neighbouring community of Peïra-Cava; there's a smaller selection at the **Musée de la Crèche** (open daily during the Circuit des Crèches; free; at other times enquire at tourist office – see p.364), which is midway between the tourist office and the church of Sainte Marguerite.

The church of Sainte-Marguerite
The belfry of **Ste-Marguerite** rises proudly above the village houses, its Baroque cupola glittering with polychrome Niçois tiles. Inside are some of the best late medieval artworks in the Comté de Nice, though several have been removed and taken to Nice's Musée des Beaux Arts (see p.352). All these works belong to the School of Nice, and both the Retable de Ste-Marguerite, framed by a tasteless Baroque baldaquin, and the painting of Saints Peter and Paul, with its cliff-hanging castle in the distance, are attributed to Louis Bréa.

Chapelle de Notre-Dame de bon Coeur
There are more examples of work by Jean Beleison on the walls and ceilings of the **Chapelle de Notre-Dame de Bon Coeur**, 2km northwest of the village off the road to the St-Roch pass and Coaraze. Although you can't go inside, you can view the paintings from outside.

Coaraze
COARAZE overlooks the valley of the Paillon de Contes, a tributary running west of the main Paillon. From Lucéram the D2566 ascends to the pass of St-Roch, from which the D15 hangs over near-vertical descents, turning corners onto thrilling vistas of these beautiful but inhospitable mountains.

Coaraze is one of the more chic Niçois villages, with many an artist and designer in residence, and it doesn't pander to the tourist trade in the slightest. The facades of the post office and *mairie*, and place Félix-Giordan near the top of the village, are decorated with **sundials** signed by various artists including Cocteau and Ponce de Léon. The latter decorated the **Chapelle Notre-Dame du Gressier**, northwest of the village, in 1962, known now as the Chapelle Bleue for the single colour he used in the frescoes. Place Félix-Giordan also has a **lizard mosaic** and a Provençal poem engraved in stone. The **church**, destroyed and rebuilt three times, is famous for the number of angels in its interior decoration, 118 in all. The tourist office (see p.364) holds the key to the church and chapel; on Sundays, enquire about the keys at the *Bar Les Arts* nearby.

Châteauneuf-Villevieille and Castelnuovo
Across the river from Contes, 9km downstream from Coaraze, the D815 road winds up the mountainside to **CHÂTEAUNEUF-VILLEVIEILLE**, a hilltop gathering of houses around an eleventh-century Romanesque church.

About 2km further on, a rutted track to the left leads to a more recent **ruined village**, the Bourg Mediéval (also called **Castelnuovo**) which was established by Châteauneuf-Villevieille's inhabitants in the sixth century for reasons of defence, but gradually abandoned from the first half of the eighteenth century as the political situation stabilized and defence was no longer the highest priority, at which point the community "deperched" itself to return to the village's original site. Ivy-clad towers and crumbling walls rise up among once-cultivated fig trees and rose bushes, while insects buzz in the silence and butterflies flit about the wild flowers that have replaced the gardens. The views over Contes, Coaraze and the surrounding rugged landscape are superb. A boom across the track leading to the site supposedly closes at night, but there's otherwise nothing to stop you wandering around at will.

ARRIVAL AND INFORMATION

PEILLON

By bus Bus #360 from Nice (3 daily; 35min) will get you as far as the "Le Moulin" stop after Ste-Thècle, from where it is a stiff walk uphill.

PEILLE

By bus Bus #116 makes the connection between Nice and Peille via La Turbie (3 daily; 55min).

By train The *gare SNCF* is at La Grave, 7km from the village via a twisting road.

Tourist information Pointe Info, 15 rue Centrale (Wed–Sun 10am–noon & 3–6pm; ☎04 93 82 14 40, ⊚www.peille.fr).

THE ARRIÈRE-PAYS NIÇOIS

LUCÉRAM

By bus Buses #340 and #360 run from Nice (6 daily; 1hr–1hr 10min).

Tourist office Place Adrien-Barralis (Mon, Tues & Thurs–Sat 9am–noon & 2–6pm; ☎04 93 79 46 50, ⊚luceram.com).

COARAZE

By bus Bus #300 runs from Nice (2 daily; 55min).

Tourist office Place Ste-Catherine below the village (Mon–Sat 10.30am–12.30pm & 3–5pm; ☎04 93 79 37 47). As it's volunteer-run and not always staffed, it's best to phone ahead.

ACCOMMODATION AND EATING

PEILLON

Auberge de la Madone 3 place August Arnulf ☎04 93 79 91 17, ⊚auberge-madone-peillon.com. Lovely, rambling hotel/restaurant at the entrance to the *vieux village*, with plenty of old-fashioned charm and a good restaurant serving a €32 two-course *lunch formule*. Restaurant and reception closed Wed; closed mid Nov–Christmas and second half of Jan. **€98**

PEILLE

L'Absinthe Place du Sarre ☎04 93 79 95 75. Friendly bar/*tabac* in the *vieux village*, serving *pan bagnat* and snacks from around €3–6, plus hot food in winter and with draught beer from €1.40. Daily except Thurs 7am–8pm.

★ **Restaurant Cauvin/Chez Nana** Place Carnot ☎04 93 79 90 41. For a real slap-up feed like your (Provençal) mother would make, it's worth making the pilgrimage to this wonderful restaurant for the €26 lunch buffet, complete with a generous selection of hors d'oeuvres. Mon & Thurs–Sun noon–3pm.

LUCÉRAM

Bocca Fina Place Adrien Barralis ☎04 93 79 51 54, ⊚boccafina.net. Unpretentious restaurant on the main road through the village close to the tourist office, with pizza from €8.50 and meat dishes from around €4. Tues, Wed & Sun 8am–6pm, Thurs–Sat 8am–10pm.

The Corniche Inférieure

The characteristic **Côte d'Azur mansions** that represent the unrestrained fantasies of the original owners parade along the **Corniche Inférieure**, a series of pale dots among the lush pines. Others pepper the promontory of **Cap Ferrat**, where some of the planet's priciest real estate hides behind high walls and equally high security.

Villefranche-sur-Mer

VILLEFRANCHE-SUR-MER, the resort closest to Nice, marks the beginning of one of the most picturesque and unspoilt sections of the Riviera, though the cruise liners attracted by the deep anchorage in Villefranche's beautiful bay ensure a steady stream of tour buses climbing the hill from the port. However, as long as your visit doesn't coincide with the shore excursions, the old town on the waterfront, with its active fishing fleet and its covered, medieval **rue Obscure** running beneath the houses, is a charming place to while away an afternoon.

Chapelle de St-Pierre

Tues–Sun: spring & summer 10am–noon & 3–7pm; autumn & winter 10am–noon & 2–6pm • €2.50

The fishing harbour is overlooked by the tiny medieval **Chapelle de St-Pierre**, decorated by **Jean Cocteau** in 1957 in shades he described as "ghosts of colours". In the guide to the chapel written by Cocteau, the artist invites travellers to enter without any aesthetic

THE CORNICHES

Three **corniche roads** run east from Nice to the independent principality of Monaco and on to Menton, the last town of the French Riviera. Napoleon built the **Grande Corniche** on the route of the Romans' Via Julia Augusta. The **Moyenne Corniche** dates from the first quarter of the twentieth century, when aristocratic tourism on the Riviera was already causing congestion on the coastal road, the **Corniche Inférieure**. The upper two are popular for shooting car commercials and action films, but they're dangerous roads: Grace Kelly, princess of Monaco, who was filmed driving the corniches in *To Catch a Thief*, died more than 25 years later when she took a bend too fast as she descended from La Turbie to the Moyenne Corniche.

VISITING THE CORNICHES

Buses serve all three routes; the train follows the lower corniche; and all three are superb means of seeing the most mountainous stretch of the Côte d'Azur. For long-distance panoramas you follow the **Grande Corniche**; for precipitous views the **Moyenne Corniche**; and for close-up encounters with the architectural riot of the continuous coastal resort, take the **Corniche Inférieure**. If you want to stay, you'll find that the biggest choice is along the Corniche Inférieure, or in the chic (and expensive) *village perché* of Èze.

preconceptions. The ghostly colours fill drawings in strong and simple lines, portraying scenes from the life of St Peter and homages to the women of Villefranche and to the gypsies. Above the altar Peter walks on water supported by an angel, to the amusement of Christ. The fishermen's eyes are drawn as fishes; the ceramic eyes on either side of the door are the flames of the Apocalypse and the altar candelabras of night-time fishing forks rise above single eyes. On June 29, the local fishermen celebrate the feast day of St Peter and St Paul with a Mass, the only time the chapel is used.

8

Citadelle de St-Elme

Museums June–Sept Mon–Sat 12am–noon & 3–6.30pm, Sun 3–6.30pm; Oct–May Mon–Sat 10am–noon & 2–5.30pm, Sun 2–5.30pm • Free

To the west of the fishing port, the massive **Citadelle de St-Elme** shelters the Hôtel de Ville, an open-air cinema, a conference centre and a series of **art museums**. One is dedicated to the voluptuous works of Villefranche sculptor **Volti**, whose bronze woman lies in the fountain outside the citadel gates; another, to the couple **Henri Goetz** and **Christine Boumeester**, contains two works by Picasso and one by Miró. A third collection, the **Roux**, is given over to ceramic figurines.

INFORMATION   VILLEFRANCHE-SUR-MER

Tourist office In the Jardin François-Binon just below the corniche as it changes from av Foch to av Albert-1ᵉʳ (Mon–Sat 9am–noon & 2–6pm, plus Sun in July & Aug; ☎04 93 01 73 68, ⓦ villefranche-sur-mer.com).

ACCOMMODATION

La Darse 32 av du Général-de-Gaulle ☎04 93 01 72 54, ⓦ hoteldeladarse.com. Reasonably priced two-star hotel west of the train station and close to the citadelle and the sea, with renovated a/c rooms, some with seaward-facing balconies and some sleeping up to four. Closed mid-Nov to March. €76

Villa Patricia 310 av de l'Ange Gardien, Pont St-Jean ☎04 93 01 06 70, ⓦ hotel-patricia.riviera.fr. Good-value, gay-friendly budget option just off the Corniche Inférieure between Villefranche and Cap Ferrat, with twelve rooms, some with sea views. There's parking and free internet access. €69

Welcome 3 quai Amiral-Courbet ☎04 93 76 27 62, ⓦ welcomehotel.com. Highly recommended four-star hotel in the former convent where Cocteau used to stay, in a prime position overlooking the port. The 35 rooms have a/c, balconies and sea views. Closed mid-Nov to mid-Dec. €180

EATING

La Grignotière 3 rue du Poilu ☎04 93 76 79 83. An affordable option in Villefranche's old town, with fillet of sea bream Provençal style or *salade niçoise* on a three-course *menu* (€16), plus pizza from €9; otherwise, main courses cost from around €10. April–Oct daily lunch & dinner.

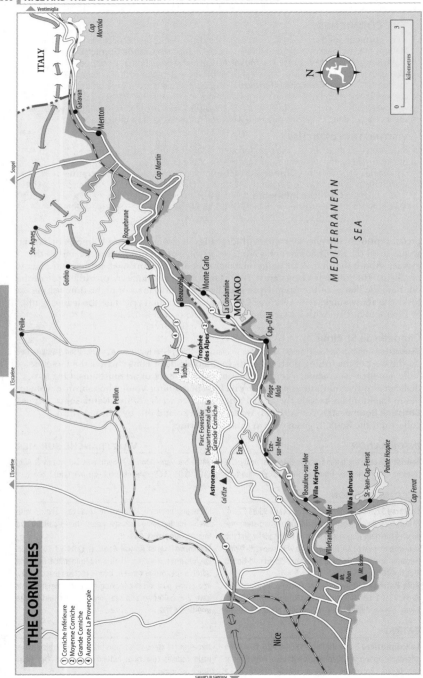

THE CORNICHES

① Corniche Inférieure
② Moyenne Corniche
③ Grande Corniche
④ Autoroute La Provençale

La Mère Germaine 7–9 quai Amiral-Courbet ☎ 04 93 01 71 39, ✆ meregermaine.com. The most famous of the quayside fish restaurants, founded in 1938 and known for its bouillabaisse; *menu* €43. Daily noon–2.30pm & 7–10pm.

Cap Ferrat

Closing off Villefranche's bay to the east is **Cap Ferrat**, justifiably among the Côte d'Azur's most desirable addresses due to the lack of through traffic and its pretty, indented coast; past residents include assorted Rothschilds and the King of Belgium, but also the actor David Niven and writer Somerset Maugham. The one town, **ST-JEAN-CAP-FERRAT**, is a typical Riviera hideout for the wealthy: old houses overlooking modern yachts in a fishing port turned millionaires' resort.

East of St-Jean's pleasure port you can follow avenue Jean-Mermoz then a **coastal path** out along the little peninsula, past the Plage Paloma to **Pointe Hospice**, where a nineteenth-century chapel cowers behind a twelve-metre-high turn-of-the-twentieth-century metal *Virgin and Child*. Back in St-Jean, another coastal path runs from avenue Claude-Vignon right round to chemin du Roy on the opposite side of the peninsula.

Villa Ephrussi

St-Jean-Cap-Ferrat • Mid-Feb to June, Sept & Oct daily 10am–6pm; July & Aug daily 10am–7pm; Nov to mid-Feb Mon–Fri 2–6pm, Sat & Sun 10am–6pm • €12, or €18 with Villa Kérylos (see p.368), or €13 with Jardin Exotique (see p.371) • ☎ 04 93 01 33 09, ✆ villa-ephrussi.com

The one exception to the Cap's formidable privacy is the **Villa Ephrussi**, which was built in 1912 for Baroness Ephrussi, née Rothschild, a woman of unlimited wealth and eclectic tastes. The result is a wonderful profusion of decorative art, paintings and sculpture from the fourteenth to the nineteenth century of European to Far Eastern origin. Highlights include a fifteenth-century d'Enghien tapestry of hunting scenes; paintings by Carpaccio and other works of the Venetian Renaissance; Sèvres and Vincennes porcelain; Ming vases; Mandarin robes; and canvases by Fragonard, Monet, Sisley and Renoir. The baroness had a particular love of the eighteenth century, and would receive guests dressed as Marie Antoinette; in order to make the beautiful **gardens**, she had a hill removed to level out the space for her formal French design, but one part of the park – the eastern slope – remained wild, because funds eventually ran out. Today, the highlights include the **musical fountains**, which perform every twenty minutes, and – when in bloom – the stunning **rose garden**, which offers wonderful views over the bay of Villefranche.

ARRIVAL AND INFORMATION

CAP-FERRAT

By bus The #81 bus service from Nice and Villefranche (every 20–30min) serves St-Jean's port, but beyond that there's no public transport.

Tourist office 5 av Dénis-Séméria, on St-Jean's port (June–Sept Mon–Fri 9am–6pm, Sat 9am–5pm, Sun 10am–2pm; Oct–May Mon–Fri 9am–5pm, Sat 9am–4pm; ☎ 04 93 76 08 90, ✆ saintjeancapferrat.fr).

ACCOMMODATION

Brise Marine 58 av J-Mermoz ☎ 04 93 76 04 36, ✆ hotel-brisemarine.com. Attractive old Italianate villa in an idyllic garden setting close to the sea; rooms have en-suite facilities and a/c, and more expensive ones have balcony or terrace. Closed Nov–Jan. **€164**

La Frégate 11 av Dénis-Séméria ☎ 04 93 76 04 51, ✆ hotellafregate.jimdo.com. The best bet for those on a limited budget; nothing fancy but it's in a central location by the port, with ten rooms with garden or sea views. **€55**

Grand Hôtel du Cap Ferrat 71 bd du Général-de-Gaulle ☎ 04 93 76 50 50, ✆ grand-hotel-cap-ferrat .com. Classic Riviera palace hotel in a stunning site near the southern tip of the Cap, with elegant, all-white rooms and suites – the very fanciest have their own swimming pools – and an excellent restaurant. **€684**

EATING

St-Jean-Cap-Ferrat's best (and most expensive) restaurants are in its luxury hotels, but for less eye-watering prices there's plenty of choice on the restaurant strip around the pleasure port, where you can tuck into excellent fresh fish and seafood.

La Goélette Quai du Nouveau Port ☎ 04 93 76 14 38. Dramatic black decor and a fish-focused menu right on the port, with bouillabaisse (€36) and *zarzuela* (€32.50) alongside paella and aioli. *Menu* €25. Daily noon–3pm & 6–10.30pm; closed Sun eve in winter.

Le Sloop Quai du Nouveau Port ☎ 04 93 01 48 63, ⓦ restaurantsloop.com. The pick of the restaurants fronting St-Jean's port, serving fresh fish cooked in delicate and original ways. *Menu* €32. Daily 9.30am–2pm & 7–10pm; closed Tues & Wed lunch in summer, Tues eve & all day Wed in winter.

Beaulieu-sur-Mer

To the eastern side of the Cap Ferrat peninsula, overlooking the pretty Baie des Fourmis and accessible by foot from St-Jean along the promenade Maurice-Rouvier, is **BEAULIEU-SUR-MER**, sheltered by a ring of craggy hills that ensures its temperatures are amongst the highest on the Côte, and that the town itself is one of its less developed spots. It's an appealing place, more tranquil than the bigger resorts and with a working harbour where you can buy freshly caught fish from the quayside, and it retains a couple of fine examples of *belle époque* architecture – most notably La Rotonde on avenue Fernand-Dunan, an opulent former hotel.

Villa Kérylos

Impasse Gustave-Eiffel • Mid-Feb to June, Sept & Oct daily 10am–6pm; July & Aug daily 10am–7pm; Nov–Feb Mon–Fri 2–6pm, Sat & Sun 10am–6pm • €10, €18 with Villa Éphrussi (see p.367) • ☎ 04 93 01 01 44, ⓦ villa-kerylos.com • The villa is a 5min walk from Beaulieu train station

Beaulieu's star attraction is the **Villa Kérylos**, a near-perfect reproduction of an ancient Greek villa, just east of the casino on impasse Gustave-Eiffel. The only concessions made by Théodore Reinach, the archeologist who had it built, were glass in the windows, a concealed piano, and a minimum of early twentieth-century conveniences. He lived here for twenty years, eating, dressing and behaving as an Athenian citizen, taking baths with his male friends and assigning separate suites to women. However bizarre the concept, it's visually stunning, with faithfully reproduced frescoes, ivory and bronze copies of mosaics and vases, authentic antiquities and lavish use of marble and alabaster. Not the least of its attractions is the fabulous waterside location with views across to St-Jean-Cap-Ferrat.

INFORMATION
BEAULIEU-SUR-MER

Tourist office Next to the *gare SNCF* on place Georges-Clemenceau (July & Aug Mon–Sat 9am–12.30pm & 1.30–6.30pm; Sept–June Mon–Fri 9am–12.30pm & 2–5.30pm, Sat 9am–12.30pm & 2–5pm; ☎ 04 93 01 02 21, ⓦ beaulieusurmer.fr).

ACCOMMODATION

Riviera 6 rue Paul Doumer ☎ 04 93 01 04 92, ⓦ hotel-riviera.fr. A tempting economical option, this family-run three-star hotel is right in the centre, close to the Villa Kérylos and the sea. Tastefully decorated rooms have a/c and double glazing. **€70**

Select 1 rue André Cane ☎ 04 93 01 05 42, ⓦ hotelselect-beaulieu.com. Good value two-star hotel in the centre of Beaulieu, facing the market and close to the *gare SNCF* and restaurants, with a/c and wi-fi. **€75**

EATING AND DRINKING

Le Beaulieu 45 bd Marinoni ☎ 04 93 01 03 36. Smart and central café/bar that's a good bet for drinks and coffee, with a chalked-up menu of salads, platters and simple main courses from around €14. Mon–Sat 7am–8.30pm.

Le Petit Darkoum 18 bd Maréchal-Leclerc ☎ 04 93 01 48 59. Atmospheric Moroccan restaurant serving up tagines and couscous with *menus* from €23.50; it doesn't look much from the outside but has a good reputation locally. Open Wed–Sun; evenings only during July & August.

La Restaurant des Rois At *La Réserve*, 5 bd du Maréchal-Leclerc ☎ 04 93 01 00 01, ⓦ reservebeaulieu .com. Beaulieu's best restaurant is in its best hotel, with two Michelin stars and a suitably palatial setting for dishes like milk-fed Limousin veal with roast sweetbreads, summer truffle & wild mushrooms. *Menus* cost €170–220, and in summer there's a poolside restaurant, *Vent Debout*, at lunchtime. Closed Nov to 21 Dec. Daily noon–2.30pm & 7.30–9.20pm.

PLAGE MALA, CAP D'AIL (P.370) >

Èze-sur-Mer

The next stop on the train is **ÈZE-SUR-MER**, the little seaside extension of **Èze** village (see below) on the Moyenne Corniche, with its long but narrow shingle beach and fewer pretensions than its western neighbours – though that doesn't stop Bono from U2 from owning a beachfront villa here. When you tire of the beach, you can struggle up the steep Sentier Nietzsche (see opposite) to reach Èze's *vieux village* – the uphill hike takes an hour and a half, or take the easy way with the shuttle bus from the *gare SNCF* (9.55am–6.15pm; 25min; €1).

Cap d'Ail

CAP D'AIL has an informal (but extremely affluent) feel, though it suffers from the noise and congestion of the lower and middle corniches running closely parallel. As you descend to the sea from the main road, however, the noise is quickly left behind, for Cap d'Ail's delightful secret is that its coast is fringed not by some multi-laned boulevard but by a peaceful and beautiful coastal path. From the tiny promontary of **Point des Douaniers**, the **sentier du Littoral** leads east into **Monaco** and also – rather more temptingly – winds west around the headland to the pretty little **Plage Mala**, one of the most secluded and attractive beaches on the eastern Riviera. The way there is dotted with imposing old villas; in places the path is a bit of a scramble, and it can get slippery if the sea is rough.

8

| ACCOMMODATION AND EATING | CAP D'AIL |

Hôtel de Monaco 1 av Pierre-Weck ☎ 04 92 41 31 00, ⓦ hoteldemonaco.com. Chic small boutique-style hotel in a quiet & classy residential area close to Plage Mala, recently renovated with tasteful contemporary decor and a private bar/terrace. **€139**

La Pinède 10 av R. Gramaglia ☎ 04 93 78 37 10, ⓦ wrestaurantlapinede.com. In a pine grove right on the water's edge on the sentier du Littoral, with a *carte* ranging from steak tartare to *moules-frites*, and *menus* from €32. Open daily except Wed for lunch & dinner; closed Nov–Feb.

Thalassa Relais International de la Jeunesse 2 av R-Gramaglia ☎ 04 93 81 27 63, ⓦ clajsud.fr. Youth hostel right on the sentier du Littoral close to the *gare SNCF*, with accommodation in four- to ten-bed dorms overlooking the sea. Closed Oct–April. **€20**

The Moyenne Corniche

The first views from the **Moyenne Corniche** are back over Nice as you grind up Mont Alban, which, with its seaward extension, Mont Boron, separates Nice from Villefranche. The wooded summit is crowned by a perfect little sixteenth-century fortress, the **Fort du Mont Alban,** a surprisingly endearing structure with its four tiny turrets glimmering in glazed Niçois tiles. You can wander freely around the fort and see why Villefranche's citadel, so unassailable from the sea, was so vulnerable from above. To reach it you turn sharp right off the corniche along route Forestière before you reach the Villefranche pass. The #14 bus from Nice stops at Chemin du Fort from which the fort is signed. At the opposite (southern) end of the summit, an old military battery has been laid out as a **belvedere** and public park, with views over the coast and a nature trail through lush woodland.

Once through the pass, the cliff-hanging car-chase stretch of the Moyenne Corniche begins, with great views, sudden tunnels and little habitation.

Èze

ÈZE is unmistakeable long before you arrive, its streets wound around a cone of rock below the corniche, whose summit is 470m above the sea. From a distance the village has the monumental medieval unity of Mont St-Michel and is a dramatic sight to behold, but seen up close, its secular nature exerts itself. Of the *villages perchés* in Provence, only St-Paul-de-Vence can compete with Èze for catering so single-mindedly to tourists, and it takes a mental feat to recall that the labyrinth of tiny vaulted passages and stairways was designed not for charm but from fear of attack.

Jardin Exotique

Daily: Feb & March 9am–5pm; April–May 9am–6pm; June & Sept 9am–7pm; July & Aug 9am–7.30pm; Oct 9am–5.30pm; Nov–Jan 9am–4.30pm • €6, or €13 with Villa Ephrussi

Èze's ultimate defence, the castle, no longer exists, but the **Jardin Exotique** which replaces it is worth a visit for the fantastic views it offers from the ruins – and for a respite from the commerce below. Cacti, agave and aloe thrive on the dry, stony site.

The Sentier Frédéric Nietzsche

From place du Centenaire, just outside the old village, you can reach the shore through open countryside via the **sentier Frédéric-Nietzsche**. The philosopher Nietzsche is said to have conceived part of *Thus Spoke Zarathustra* on this path. You arrive at the Corniche Inférieure at the eastern limit of Èze-sur-Mer (see opposite).

(see opposite)

INFORMATION ÈZE

Tourist office On place du Général-de-Gaulle just above the main car park (April–June & Sept Mon–Sat 9am–6pm; July & Aug daily 9am–7pm; Oct–March Mon–Sat 9am–5pm; ☎ 04 93 41 26 00, ✆ eze-tourisme.com). Pick up a free map here of the footpaths through the hills linking the three corniches.

ACCOMMODATION

Château de la Chèvre d'Or Rue de Barri ☎ 04 92 10 66 66, ✆ chevredor.com. Luxury hotel in the *vieux village* with a wide variety of room and suite styles, some of them very spacious with terraces and sea views; the presidential suite even has its own infinity pool. It oozes character, and the restaurant (see below) has two Michelin stars. **€383**
Château Eza Rue de la Pise ☎ 04 93 41 12 24, ✆ chateaueza.com. Award-winning luxury boutique hotel in the *vieux village*, with just twelve a/c rooms and suites that range from prettily Provençal to wood-panelled and grand, plus a Michelin-starred restaurant and fabulous views. **€360**
Le Golf Hôtel Place de la Colette ☎ 04 93 41 18 50, ✆ wgascogne-hotel-restaurant.fr. A reasonably priced option on the main road at the entrance to the *vieux village*, with eight a/c rooms, wi-fi and parking nearby; closed Jan. **€80**

EATING AND DRINKING

Auberge du Cheval Blanc Place de la Colette ☎ 04 93 41 03 17. Unpretentious place at the entrance to the *vieux village*, serving hearty pasta, pizza, salads and regional fare washed down with Provençal wines. Lunch *formule* €14.50, *menu* €24. Noon–3pm & 7–10pm.
Restaurant la Chèvre d'Or Rue de Barri ☎ 04 92 10 66 66, ✆ chevredor.com. Nosebleed prices match the dizzying location at the *Chèvre d'Or*'s two-Michelin-starred *restaurant gastronomique*: expect to pay €200 à la carte without drinks. Daily 12.30–3pm & 7.30–10pm; closed Mon in Nov.

The Grande Corniche

At every other turn on the **Grande Corniche** you're tempted to park your car and enjoy the distant views, which uniquely extend both seaward and inland, but there are frustratingly few truly safe places to do so. At certain points, such as **Col d'Èze**, you can turn off upwards for even higher views.

Col d'Èze

The upper part of Èze is backed by the **Parc Naturel Départemental de la Grande Corniche**, a wonderful oak forest covering the high slopes and plateaux of this coastal range. Paths are well signed, and there are picnic and games areas and orientation tables – in fact it's rather over-managed, but at least it isn't built on. If you take a left (coming from Nice) to cross the col and keep following route de la Revère, you come, after 1.5km or so, to an observatory, **Astrorama** (Jan & Feb Fri & Sat during school holidays 7–11pm; March–June & Sept–Oct Fri & Sat 7–11pm; July & Aug Tues–Sat 7–11pm; €10; ⓦastrorama .net), where you can admire the evening and night sky through telescopes.

ACCOMMODATION AND EATING   COL D'ÈZE

Hôtel L'Hermitage 1951 av des Diables Bleus ☎ 04 93 41 00 68, ⓦ ezehermitage.com. Three-star *Logis de France* hotel/restaurant on the Grande Corniche, with magnificent views of sea and forested hills, and a restaurant serving reasonable meals, with an €18 lunch *menu*. Restaurant open daily 12.30–3pm & 7.30–10pm. **€115**

La Turbie

Eighteen stunning kilometres from Nice, **LA TURBIE** boasts an eighteenth-century church, the **Église de St-Michel-Archange,** that is a Baroque concoction of marble, onyx, agate and oil paint, with pink the overriding colour, and, among the paintings, a superb *St Mark writing the Gospel* attributed to Veronese. In the old part of the village rough-hewn stone houses line rue Comte-de-Cessole, once part of the Roman Via Julia, leading to the Trophée des Alpes.

Trophée des Alpes

Av Albert 1er, La Turbie • Tues–Sun: mid-May to mid-Sept 9.30am–1pm & 2.30–6.30pm; mid-Sept to mid-May 10am–1.30pm & 2.30–5pm • €5.50 • ☎ 04 93 41 20 84, ⓦ monuments-nationaux.fr • Infrequent buses from Nice (#116; Mon–Sat)

La Turbie's chief glory is the **Trophée des Alpes**, a sixth-century monument to the power of Rome and the total subjugation of the local peoples. Originally, a statue of Augustus Caesar stood on the 45-metre plinth, which was inscribed with the names of 45 vanquished tribes and an equally long list of the emperor's virtues. In the fifth century the descendants of the suppressed were worshipping the monument – to the horror of St Honorat, who did his best to have the graven image destroyed. However, it took several centuries of barbarian invasions, quarrying and incorporation into military structures before the trophy was finally reduced to rubble in the early eighteenth century by Louis XIV's engineers, who blew the fortress up to prevent it being used by the king's enemies. Its painstaking reconstruction was undertaken in the 1930s, and it now stands, statueless, at 35m.

Viewed from a distance along the Grande Corniche, however, the Trophée can still hold its own as an imperial monument. If you want to take a closer look and see a model of the original, you'll have to buy a ticket for the fenced-off plinth and its little **museum**. You can climb up to the viewing platform and enjoy the spectacular view, extending to the Esterel in the west and Italy in the east.

ACCOMMODATION AND EATING   LA TURBIE

Café de la Fontaine 4 av Général-de-Gaulle, La Turbie ☎ 04 93 28 52 79. Excellent bistro on the main road through La Turbie, run by the same team as the *Hostellerie Jérôme* and with a chalked-up selection of classic dishes like roast *gigot* of lamb or *daube de boeuf* with carrots; main courses from €15. Daily 7am–midnight.

Hostellerie Jérôme 20 Comte-de-Cessole ☎ 04 92 41 51 51, ⓦ hostelleriejerome.com. There's plenty of style and atmosphere at this thirteenth-century hostelry on the Via Julia in the heart of the old village; its beautiful *restaurant gastronomique*; has two Michelin stars (*menus* €75 & €130). Restaurant open 7–11pm; closed Mon & Tues except in July & Aug. **€95**

Roquebrune-Cap Martin

As the corniche descends towards Cap Martin, it passes the eleventh-century castle of **ROQUEBRUNE** and its fifteenth-century village nestling round the base of the rock.

The castle

Daily: Jan & Oct–Dec 10am–12.30pm & 2–5pm; Feb–May 10am–12.30pm & 2–6pm; June–Sept 10am–12.30pm & 2–7pm • €4.50 • ☎ 04 93 35 07 22

Roquebrune's **castle** might well have become yet another Côte-side architectural aberration, thanks to its English owner in the 1920s. He was prevented from continuing his "restorations" after a press campaign brought public attention to the mock-medieval tower by the gateway, now known as the *tour Anglaise*. The local authority has since made great efforts to kit the castle out in medieval fashion, and one of the best, if perhaps not most authentic, ideas has been to create an **open-air theatre** for the concerts and dance performances held here in July and August, with a spectacular natural backdrop down the precipitous slopes to Monaco and the coast.

The village

Roquebrune itself is a real maze of passages and stairways that eventually lead either to one of the six castle gates or to dead ends. If you find yourself on rue de la Fontaine you can leave the village by the Porte de Menton and see, on the hillside about 200m beyond the gate, an incredible spreading **olive tree** that was perhaps one hundred years old when the count of Ventimiglia first built a fortress on Roquebrune's spur in 870 AD.

Cap Martin

Southeast of the old village, just below the joined middle and lower corniches and the station, is the peninsula of **Cap Martin**, that has **coastal path** giving access to a wonderful shoreline of white rocks and wind-bent pines. The path is named after **Le Corbusier**, who spent several summers in Roquebrune and drowned off Cap Martin in 1965. His grave – a work of art designed by himself – is in the cemetery (square J near the flagpole), high above the old village on promenade 1er DFL, and his beach house, the **Cabanon Le Corbusier** (guided visits Tues & Fri mornings booked in advance through the tourist office – see below; €8) is on the shore just east of the pretty **Plage du Buse**, the beach just below the station. It's a restful, low-key spot, with a simple café right on the beach. Further west, the **Plage du Golfe Bleu** is similar. East of Plage du Buse, a coastal path threads its way right round the tip of Cap Martin, linking up with avenue Winston Churchill on the eastern side to bring you to Roquebrune-Cap Martin's main beach, the **Plage de Carnolès**. It's a spacious enough stretch of shingle, though much less restful than the beaches west of the Cap.

At the junction of the Via Aurelian and Via Julia on avenue Paul Doumer is a remnant from the Roman station. Known as the **Tombeau de Lumone**, it comprises three arches of a first-century BC mausoleum, with traces of frescoes still visible under the vaulting.

ARRIVAL AND INFORMATION | ROQUEBRUNE-CAP MARTIN

By train It's a steep walk uphill from the *gare SNCF*: turn right out of the station, ascending to av de la Côte d'Azur by the path at the end of sentier de la Gare and its continuation, the escalier Saint Louis; from av de la Côte d'Azur a second stepped route (the escalier Saft) ascends to the Grande Corniche, crossing it to join the final stretch – the escalier Chanoine Grana – to reach the village.

By car There's limited parking at the entrance to Roquebrune's *vieux village*.

Tourist office In the modern town centre and just up from the beach, at 218 av Aristide-Briand (June & Sept Mon–Sat 9am–12.30pm & 2–6.30pm; July & Aug Mon–Sat 9am–7pm, Sun 10am–5pm; Oct–May Mon–Sat 9am–12.30pm & 2–6pm; ☎04 93 35 62 87, ☮ roquebrune-cap-martin.com).

ACCOMMODATION

Les Deux Frères Place des Deux Frères, Roquebrune ☎04 93 28 99 00, ☮ lesdeuxfreres.com. The best-located hotel in Roquebrune village, worth booking in advance to try to get a sea-view room; there are just nine a/c rooms, varying widely in style and price. The hotel also has a good restaurant with €28 and €48 *menus*. Restaurant open Tues–Sat noon–1.30pm & 7.30–9.30pm, Sun noon–1.30pm. **€75**

Hôtel Victoria 7 promenade du Cap ☎ 04 93 35 65 90, ⓦ hotel-victoria.fr. Stylish, refurbished upmarket seafront hotel overlooking the Plage de Carnolès on the coast, with crisp blue-and-white contemporary decor, bar/terrace, a/c and wi-fi. **€172**

EATING

Au Grand Inquisiteur 18 rue du Château ☎ 04 93 35 05 37, ⓦ auxgrandinquisiteur.com. Atmospheric, almost cave-like restaurant in one of the darker crannies of Roquebrune's *vieux village*, with *menus* at €25, €29 & €33. Open Tues–Sat for dinner, Sun for lunch.

Le Vistaero at the *Vista Palace Hotel*, 1551 Grande Corniche ☎ 04 92 10 40 20, ⓦ vistapalace.com. A gourmet and visual treat with spectacular views over Monaco to accompany the refined cooking. *Menus* at €49 and €75. Smart dress is required. Noon–2.30pm & 7.30–10pm.

Monaco

Viewed from a distance, there's no mistaking the dense cluster of towers that is **MONACO**. Though rampant property development rescued the principality from postwar decline, much of its former Italianate prettiness was elbowed aside in the process, leaving it looking like nowhere else on the Riviera. Not for nothing was **Prince Rainier**, who died in 2005, known as the Prince Bâtisseur ("Prince Builder"). For all its wealth it's nowadays a city-state of apartment dwellers, built up from end to end and almost entirely lacking the leisured elegance of the Riviera's other plutocrat hangouts.

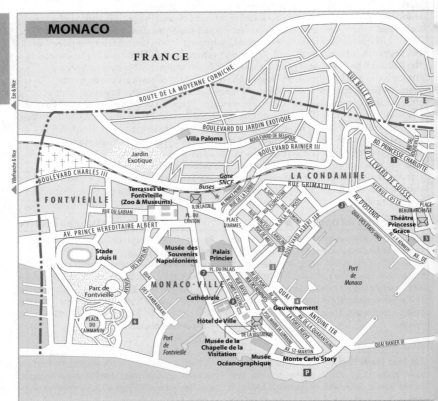

Despite this, Monaco actually has quite a lot to offer the visitor, from the famous casino to the Grimaldis' palace and a string of museums.

One time to avoid Monaco – unless you're a motor-racing fan – is the end of May, when racing cars burn around the port and casino for the **Formula 1 Monaco Grand Prix**. Every space in sight of the circuit is inaccessible without a ticket, making casual sightseeing – or sneaky free views of the race – out of the question.

Monte Carlo

The heart of **MONTE CARLO** is its **casino**, the one place not to be missed on a trip to Monaco. It forms the focus of place du Casino, which with its lush gardens and palace hotels is in turn the focus of Monte Carlo itself – the one part of the principality which, more than any other, really does live up to the jet-set image.

Casino de Monte-Carlo and the Opera House

Place du Casino Salons Européens • Open from 2pm • €10 Salons Privés May & June Fri & Sat from 8pm; July & Aug Mon–Fri daily from 8pm • €20 • ☎ +377 98 06 21 75, ⓦ montecarlocasinos.com • Bus #1, #2 or #6

Entrance to **Casino de Monte-Carlo** is restricted to over-18s and you may have to show your passport; dress code is rigid, with shorts and T-shirts frowned upon, though most visitors are scarcely the last word in designer chic. Skirts, jackets and ties are obligatory for the more interesting sections. Bags and large coats are checked

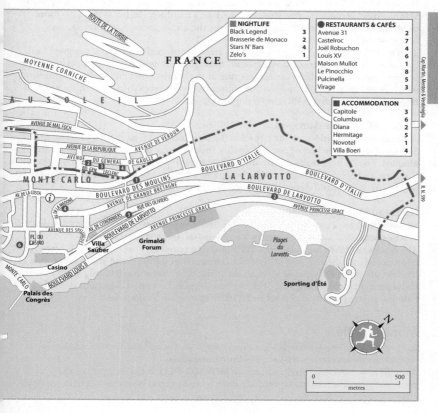

■ NIGHTLIFE	
Black Legend	3
Brasserie de Monaco	2
Stars N' Bars	4
Zelo's	1

● RESTAURANTS & CAFÉS	
Avenue 31	2
Castelroc	7
Joël Robuchon	4
Louis XV	6
Maison Mullot	1
Le Pinocchio	8
Pulcinella	5
Virage	3

■ ACCOMMODATION	
Capitole	3
Columbus	6
Diana	2
Hermitage	5
Novotel	1
Villa Boeri	4

MONACO PRACTICALITIES

For visitors arriving from France there are no **border** formalities and the currency used is the euro. Note, however, that wearing just bathing costumes, or displaying bare feet or chests, is **illegal** once you step off the beach.

Monaco's international code is 00377 and **telephone numbers** have eight digits (omit 0 when dialing from outside the principality).

ORIENTATION

The three-kilometre-long state consists of several distinct quarters. The pretty old town of **Monaco-Ville** around the palace stands on the high promontory, with the densely built suburb and marina of **Fontvieille** in its western shadow. **La Condamine** is the old port quarter on the other side of the rock; **Larvotto**, the rather ugly bathing resort with artificial beaches of imported sand, reaches to the eastern border; and **Monte Carlo** is in the middle. French **Beausoleil**, uphill to the north, is merely an extension of the conurbation – the border is often unmarked and always easily crossed on foot.

---

at the door. The first gambling hall is the **Salons Européens** where slot machines surround the American roulette, craps and blackjack tables, the managers are Vegas-trained and the lights are low. Above this slice of Nevada, however, the decor is *fin-de-siècle* Rococo extravagance, while the ceilings in the adjoining Pink Salon Bar are adorned with female nudes smoking cigarettes. The heart of the place is the **Salons Privés**. To get in, you have to look like a gambler. Rather larger and more richly decorated than the European Rooms, the atmosphere is of intense concentration.

Charles Garnier, the nineteenth-century architect of the Paris Opera, designed both the casino and the adjacent **Opera House**, though you'll need to take in a performance or join a guided tour of the casino (enquire at the tourist office) to see the auditorium, which is an excess of gold and marble with statues of pretty Grecian boys, frescoed classical scenes and figures waving palm leaves.

Place du Casino and around

Around **place du Casino** are the city's *hôtels-palais* and *grands cafés*, all owned by the SBM monopoly (see box opposite). Luxury shops cluster here and along **boulevard des Moulins**. People here really do live up to their stereotypes: you may not catch sight of Caroline and Stéphanie, but you can be sure of a brilliant fashion parade of clothes and jewels, luxury cars and designer luggage.

Nouveau Musée National

Villa Sauber 17 av Princesse Grace • Daily: June–Sept 11am–7pm; Oct–May 10am–6pm • €6 • ☎ +377 98 98 91 26 **Villa Paloma** 56 bd du **Jardin-Exotique** • Daily: June–Sept 11am–7pm; Oct–May 10am–6pm • €6 • ☎ +377 98 98 48 60 • ⓦ nmnm.mc

The **Nouveau Musée National** presents interesting temporary art exhibitions, often on Monaco-related themes, and is divided between two buildings: the **Villa Sauber**, one of the few surviving *belle époque* villas in the principality, set incongruously amid towering concrete apartment blocks east of the casino towards Larvotto beach; and the **Villa Paloma**, a dazzling white villa set in an Italian garden in Fontvieille.

Monaco-Ville

Bus #1 or #2 from place d'Armes by the *gare SNCF* • Vehicle access to Monaco-Ville is restricted; head for the Parking du Chemin des Pêcheurs, from where there's a lift up to av St-Martin by the Musée Océanographique

Though rather over-restored and lifeless, **MONACO-VILLE** is the one part of the principality where the developers have been reined in, and it retains a certain toy-town charm despite the surfeit of shops selling Grimaldi mugs and assorted junk.

Palais Princier

April–Oct daily 10am–6pm • €8 • ☎ +377 93 25 18 31, ⓦ palais.mc

Monaco-Ville is home to the **Palais Princier**, whose state apartments and throne room can be visited on a self-guided tour, with Prince Albert's voice on the audioguide. Despite the palace's modest size and military origins as a thirteenth-century Genoese fortress, the part you see certainly feels suitably palatial, thanks in part to major embellishment by the Grimaldis during the latter half of the sixteenth century. The palace courtyard conceals a massive sixteenth-century cistern designed to ensure a water supply in time of siege. These days, the main group besieging it is camera-clicking tourists; if you're outside the palace at 11.55am, you'll catch the daily changing of the immaculate, white-uniformed guard.

Musée de la Chapelle de la Visitation

Place de la Visitation • Tues–Sun 10am–4pm • €3 • ☎ +377 93 500 700

If you've had your fill of Grimaldis, check out the **Musée de la Chapelle de la Visitation**, which displays part of the religious art collection of Barbara Piasecka Johnson (an heir to the Johnson & Johnson fortune). This small but exquisite collection includes works by Zurbarán, Rivera, Rubens, and a rare, early religious work by Vermeer, *St Praxedis*.

Musée Océanographique

Av Saint-Martin • Daily: April–June & Sept 9.30am–7pm; July & Aug 9.30am–7.30pm; Oct–March 10am–6pm • €14 • ☎ +377 93 15 36 00, ⓦ oceano.org

One of Monaco's best sights is the aquarium in the basement of the imposing **Musée Océanographique**, where the fishy beings outdo the weirdest Kandinsky or

8

A HISTORY OF INDEPENDENCE

It may have lost its looks, but the tiny state of **Monaco** – no bigger than London's Hyde Park – retains its comic-opera independence. It has been in the hands of the **Grimaldi family** since the fourteenth century (save for the two decades following the French Revolution) and, in theory, Monaco would again become part of France were the royal line to die out. For the last hundred years the principality has lived off gambling, tourism and its status as a tax haven. Among its inhabitants, French citizens outnumber native-born Monegasques.

Along with the Pope and the house of Liechtenstein, **Prince Albert II** is one of Europe's few remaining constitutionally autocratic rulers, with right of refusal over any changes to the constitution – though since the late Prince Rainier's constitutional 1962 reforms, the monarch's power is no longer absolute. Monaco has a 24-member **parliament** of limited power, elected by universal suffrage and (since 2003) with competing parties, but the prince has the power to dissolve it. The only other authority is the **Société des Bains de Mer (SBM)**, which owns the casino, the opera house and some of the grandest hotels.

Along with its reputation for great wealth, Monaco latterly acquired an unwelcome reputation for wheeler-dealer **sleaze**. On his accession in July 2005, the US-educated Albert declared that he no longer wished it to be known – in the words of Somerset Maugham – as "a sunny place for shady people". He signaled that the principality would be more discriminating in granting residence, and in 2005 Sir Mark Thatcher, the son of former British Prime Minister Margaret Thatcher, was declared persona non grata. Albert then set about complying with EU banking regulations and trying to get Monaco off an OECD list of uncooperative tax havens – a policy which finally came to fruition in 2009. The principality now levies a withholding tax on the interest income of EU citizens resident here, which it rebates to the resident's country of origin.

Even so, Monaco remains home to large numbers of non-French **expats**, many of them British – including Roger Moore and Shirley Bassey. Hopes that Monaco under Albert might take a more sensitive line on **development** were dashed in 2009, when plans for the 49-storey Tour Odéon skyscraper hard against the French border were approved despite protests from residents in Beausoleil, who feared the tower would blot out their views and cast them into perpetual shade.

GRIMALDI ATTRACTIONS IN MONACO-VILLE

Monaco-Ville has several Grimaldi-related attractions beyond the Palais Princier. You can examine Napoleonic relics at the **Musée des Souvenirs Napoléoniens et Collection des Archives Historiques du Palais** on the same square as the Palais Princier (Jan–April & Dec 10.30am–5pm; May–Oct 10am–6.15pm; €4); see the tombs of Prince Rainier and Princess Grace in the slightly dull nineteenth-century **cathedral** (daily 8.30am–6/7pm; free) and even watch "Monaco the movie", at the **Monte-Carlo Story** on the Parking des Pêcheurs (on the hour Jan–June & Sept–Nov 2–5pm; July & Aug 2–6pm; €8; ⓦ monaco-memory.com).

Hieronymus Bosch creations. A serious scientific institution as well as a visitor attraction, the museum celebrated its centenary in 2010. The attractions also include a giant shark lagoon with coral reefs.

Fontvieille

Tucked behind Monaco-Ville at Monaco's southwestern extremity, **Fontvieille** is the newest of the principality's main districts, built on land reclaimed from the sea. For the most part it's a standard-issue development of apartments and yacht moorings, but it's worth a visit for the museums in the Terrasses de Fontvieille.

Les Terrasses de Fontvielle

Collection de Voitures Anciennes de SAS le Prince de Monaco Daily 10am–6pm • €6 • ☏ +377 92 05 28 56 **Musée Naval** Daily 10am–6pm • €4 **Musée des Timbres et des Monnaies** Daily: July & Aug 9.30am–6pm; Sept–June 9.30am–5pm • €3 • ⓦ oetp-monaco .com **Zoo** March–May 10am–noon & 2–6pm; June–Sept 9am–noon & 2–7pm; Oct–Feb 10am–noon & 2–5pm • €5

Overlooking Fontvieille's harbour and the Palais Princier, and with a public garden on its roof, the **Terrasses de Fontvieille** complex houses a number of interesting museums: the **Collection de Voitures Anciennes**, an enjoyable miscellany of old and not-so-old cars, with everything from a 1928 Hispano-Suiza worthy of Cruella de Ville to Princess Grace's elegant 1959 Renault Florida Coupé; the **Musée Naval**, containing 250 model ships; and a museum of stamps and coins, the **Musée des Timbres et des Monnaies**, which has rare stamps, money and commemorative medals dating back to 1640. It also contains a small **zoo**, with exotic birds, hippopotamuses and lemurs.

The Jardin Exotique

62 bd du Jardin-Exotique • Daily: mid-May to mid-Sept 9am–7pm; mid-Sept to mid-May 9am–6pm or dusk • €7 • ☏ +377 93 15 29 80, ⓦ jardin-exotique.mc • Bus #2

High above Fontvieille there are breathtaking panoramas of the coast as far as Italy from the **Jardin Exotique**, where cacti and succulents alternate with mineral-rich caverns.

La Condamine

The yachts in the **Port de Monaco** in **La Condamine** are, as you might expect, gigantic. Also on the port at quai Albert-1er is a fabulous public Olympic-size, saltwater **swimming pool** with high-dive boards (May to mid-Oct Tues–Sun 9am–6pm, until 8pm in high season; €5.10). From December to early February it's transformed into an ice rink.

ARRIVAL AND DEPARTURE
MONACO

By train The *gare SNCF* is wedged between bd Rainier III and bd Princess Charlotte and has several exits, signposted clearly. Destinations Menton (up to 4 per hr; 10min); Nice (up to 4 per hr; 20min).

By bus Buses following the lower corniche or autoroute stop at place d'Armes by the *gare SNCF* and in Monte Carlo; there's also a service from Nice via Èze to Beausoleil.

Destinations Èze (6 daily; 15min); Menton (up to 4/hr; 42min); Nice (via Corniche, up to 4/hr; 58min); Nice airport (every 30min; 50min).

INFORMATION

Tourist office 2a bd des Moulins (Mon–Sat 9am–7pm, Sun 11am–1pm; ☎+377 92 16 61 16, ⊛visitmonaco .com), with an annexe at the *gare SNCF* (Tues–Sat 9am–5pm). Monaco's main tourist office is helpful and friendly, with English-speaking staff and plenty of information in English; you can also pick up a free map here.

GETTING AROUND

By bus Municipal buses ply the length of the principality from 7am to 9pm (€2 single; ten-trip card €10); after 9pm a single night bus route runs (Mon–Fri until 12.20am, Sat & Sun until 4am).

By ferry A ferry (8am–8pm; €2) shuttles across the harbour every 20min.

Lifts Clean and convenient lifts – marked on the tourist office's map – link the lower and higher streets and can save you a lot of breathless hill climbing.

Bike hire Monte-Carlo-Rent, quai des États-Unis, on the port (☎+377 99 99 97 79).

ACCOMMODATION

Monaco has relatively few **hotels**, and most are pitched firmly at the top end of the market. If you're on a tight budget, it's not really worth trying to stay in Monaco itself: you'll get more for your money by staying just across the invisible border in **Beausoleil**. The most prestigious hotels cluster around the casino in **Monte Carlo**. Monaco has no **campsite**, and **caravans** are illegal in the state; camping vehicles must be parked at the Parking des Écoles in Fontvieille, but can't stay overnight.

Capitole 19 bd du Général-Leclerc, Beausoleil ☎04 93 28 65 65, ⊛hotel-capitole.fr. This three-star hotel is one of Beausoleil's nicest, just 300m from the Casino, with tastefully decorated renovated rooms with a/c, soundproofing, safe and flatscreen TV. There's free wi-fi, and a breakfast room on the ground floor. **€130**

Colombus 23 av des Papalins, Fontvieille ☎+377 92 05 90 00, ⊛columbusmonaco.com. Overlooking the sea in Fontvieille, offering boutique hotel comforts in cool shades and natural materials for a fraction of the price of the palace hotels. Rooms are soundproofed, with a/c, and there's a brasserie and a cocktail bar. **€170**

Diana 17 bd du Général-Leclerc, Beausoleil ☎04 93 78 47 58, ⊛monte-carlo.mc/hotel-diana-beausoleil. This two-star hotel in Beausoleil is the cheapest option around. It's a little tired, but it's soundproofed and has a/c and it's very close to Monte Carlo's sights. The cheapest rooms have washbasin and bidet but no WC. **€50**

Hôtel Hermitage Square Beaumarchais ☎+377 98 06 40 00, ⊛hotelhermitagemontecarlo.com. One of two opulent *belle époque* palace hotels owned by the Societé des Bains de Mer, the *Hermitage* boasts a glass dome by Gustav Eiffel, a Michelin-starred restaurant and fabulous views over the harbour. **€506**

Novotel 16 bd Princesse Charlotte ☎+377 99 99 83 00, ⊛novotel.com. One of the best mid-priced options, with 218 modern, comfortable rooms and suites – some with views over the principality – plus a pool, gym and sauna. **€160**

Villa Boeri 29 bd du Général-Leclerc, Beausoleil ☎04 93 78 38 10, ⊛hotelboeri.com. Cheerful Beausoleil cheapie almost hidden behind a screen of oleander, with a nice shady terrace. The a/c rooms are soundproofed, with satellite TV and bath or shower and WC. **€78**

EATING

La Condamine and Monaco-Ville are replete with **restaurants**, **brasseries** and **cafés**, and there's a scattering of mid-priced options along Larvotto beach and the port, but good food and reasonable prices don't always coincide in Monaco: the best-value cuisine is usually Italian. The best daily food **market** is in rue du Marché in Beausoleil.

Avenue 31 31 av Princesse Grace ☎+377 97 70 31 31, ⊛avenue31.mc. Stylish, modern brasserie just across from the beach in Larvotto, with an eclectic *carte* that ranges from sushi and fish to burgers and Italian dishes. Lunchtime *formules* from around €17. Daily noon–2.30pm & 8–10.45pm (11.45pm on Fri & Sat).

Castelroc Place du Palais ☎+377 93 30 36 68, ⊛restaurant-castelroc.com. Opposite the Palais Princier with a terrace overlooking Fontvieille, this smart restaurant isn't cheap, but it's a good place to sample traditional Monegasque dishes like *barbajuans* – samosa-like triangles stuffed with Swiss chard and cheese. Mains €25. Feb, March & Oct to mid-Dec daily noon–3pm; April–Sept Mon–Fri & Sun noon–3pm.

Joël Robuchon Monte Carlo *Hôtel Metropole*, 4 av de la Madone ☎+377 93 15 15 10, ⊛metropole.com. The inventive, refined Mediterranean-accented cooking of this two-Michelin-starred restaurant is under the aegis of one

8

of France's most respected chefs. It may not be the very grandest dining room in the principality, but it's pretty close. Lunch €49–79, *Discovery menu* €119. Daily 12.15–2pm & 7.30–11pm.

Louis XV *Hôtel de Paris*, place du Casino T98 06 88 64. Alain Ducasse's Monaco flagship, in the *belle époque* splendour of one of the grandest palace hotels and making plentiful use of excellent local produce. Around €200 à la carte. Mon & Thurs–Sun 12.15–1.45pm & 8–9.45pm; closed late Nov to late Dec & mid-Feb to early March.

Maison Mullot 19 bd des Moulins ☎ +377 92 05 99 10. Clean, bright patisserie and *chocolatier* on Monte Carlo's main strip, with a good selection of ice creams (€3 up) and a €13 *lunch formule*. Mon–Fri 7.45am–7pm, Sat 8am–6pm.

Le Pinocchio 30 rue Comte-Félix-Gastaldi ☎ +377 93 30 96 20. A good-value Italian place in a narrow street in Monaco-Ville dishing up hearty portions from a long menu of antipasti and pasta, including *vitello tonnato* with salad for €15 and *penne alla sorrentina* for €13. Feb–Dec daily until 11.30pm.

Pulcinella 17 rue du Portier ☎ +377 93 30 73 61, ⊕ pulcinella.mc. Traditional Italian between the Casino and Larvotto beach. The view – of a motorway flyover – isn't the best, but the food is relatively good value for the location. *Salade niçoise* €15, risotto with *cèpes* €18; more elaborate dishes include breaded veal Milanese and roast sea bass. Daily noon–2pm & 7.30–11pm.

Virage 1 quai Albert 1er ☎ +377 93 50 77 21, ⊕ virage .mc. Light-flooded, glassy modern restaurant on the port, serving simple bistro-type food including salads, risotto and fish: *fritti misto* with tartare sauce or roast chicken with five spices, for example. Around €20 or more. Mon–Sat noon–11.30pm, Sun 11.30am–5pm.

BARS AND NIGHTLIFE

There are better places for **nightlife** than Monaco. Prices can be astronomical, service haughty and the top discotheques like *Jimmy'z* (in the Sporting Monte-Carlo in Larvotto in summer; on place du Casino in winter), are not going to let you in unless you're decked out in designer finery.

Black Legend Rte de la Piscine ☎ +377 93 30 09 09, ⊕ black-legend.com. A portside restaurant and lounge bar that morphs into a disco and live music venue as the evening progresses, with an emphasis on black American music. DJ sets nightly 7.30–11.30pm in summer, after which the club proper gets going – until 5am.

Brasserie de Monaco 36 rte de la Piscine ☎ +377 97 98 51 20, ⊕ brasseriedemonaco.com. Situated on the port and with Monaco's only beer brewed on the premises – including wheat beers and amber ale – this smart place is often guested by internationally known DJs and there are occasional live bands. Pints €7. Daily 11am–5am.

Stars 'N' Bars 6 quai Antoine 1er ☎ +377 97 97 95 95, ⊕ starsnbars.com. Big, American-themed bar/diner and cocktail bar on the port, with crash helmet & pit-stop motifs, games machines and sport on TV. Bottled beers from €6.50, cocktails from €9.50, plus a huge food menu with everything from buffalo wings to salad, steak and pizza; mains €15 up. Mon–Fri 7.30am–1am, Sat & Sun 11am–1am.

Zelo's 10 av Princesse Grace, atop the Grimaldi Forum ☎ +377 99 99 25 50, ⊕ zelosworld.com. Stylish combination of a restaurant, lounge, DJ bar and disco, with a sea-facing terrace and plush interior complete with chandeliers. Occasional sets from internationally known DJs. Light food menu until 9pm. Daily 6pm–2.30am.

ENTERTAINMENT

The programme of **theatre, ballet** and **concerts** throughout the year is impressive, with the **Printemps des Arts** festival (March & April) seeing performances by famous classical and contemporary dance troupes from all over the

---

MONACO FESTIVALS AND SPORTING EVENTS

Monaco's **festivals** are spectacular, particularly the **International Fireworks** in July and August, which can be seen from as far away as Cap d'Ail or Cap Martin. Mid- to late January sees vast trailers entering Monaco for the **International Circus Festival** at the Espace Fontvieille, a rare chance to witness the world's best in this underrated performance art (details on ☎ +377 92 05 23 45).

As for sporting spectaculars, the principality's name is synonymous with motorsport: the **Monte-Carlo Automobile Rally** takes place in mid-January and the **Formula 1 Grand Prix** at the end of May. Every space in sight of the circuit, which runs round the port and the casino, is inaccessible without a ticket (☎ +377 93 15 26 00). Monaco also has a first-division **football team**, AS Monaco, whose home ground is the enormous Stade Louis II in Fontvieille, 3 av des Castelans (☎ +377 97 77 74 74, ⊕ asm-fc.com).

world. The main **booking office** for ballet, opera and concerts is the casino foyer, place du Casino, Monte Carlo (Tues–Sat 10am–5.30pm; ☎+377 98 06 28 28).

Opera Place du Casino ☎+377 98 06 28 00, ⊛ opera.mc. Monaco's opera house is in the Casino in Monte Carlo. The season runs from November to April and is pretty exceptional, the SBM being able to book up star companies and performers before Milan, Paris or New York get hold of them.
Théâtre Princesse Grace 12 av d'Ostende, Monte Carlo ☎+377 93 25 32 27. The principality's main venue for drama.

DIRECTORY

Banks Most banks have a branch in Monaco around bd des Moulins, av de Monte-Carlo and av de la Costa; hours are Mon–Fri 9am–noon & 2–4.30pm.
Emergencies ☎18 or ☎+377 93 30 19 45; Centre Hospitalier Princesse Grace, av Pasteur ☎+377 97 98 99 00.
Lost property 3 rue Louis-Notari ☎+377 93 15 30 18.
Money exchange Cie Monégasque de Change, parking du Chemin des Pêcheurs; Monafinances, 17 av des Spélugues.
Pharmacy Call ☎141.

Police ☎17 (emergency).
Post office PTT Palais de la Scala, av Henri Dunant (Mon–Fri 8am–7pm & Sat 8am–noon).
Public holidays Similar to those in France, with the addition of January 27 (Fête de Ste-Dévote) and November 19 (Fête Nationale Monégasque), and without Bastille (July 14), VE (May 8) or Armistice (Nov 11) days.
Radio Riviera Radio 106.3 FM English-language radio station (106.5 FM in France); ⊛ rivieraradio.mc

Menton and around

Of all the big Riviera resorts, **MENTON**, the warmest and the most Italianate, is the one that most retains an atmosphere of genteel, aristocratic tourism. It's also a classic border town, and in summer the streets and beaches are thronged with relaxed Italian day-trippers munching ice cream. Menton does not go in for the ostentatious wealth of Monaco and it has little of Nice's big-city buzz: its lush gardens and associations with Cocteau aside, what it chiefly glories in is its climate and its famous lemon crop. Ringed by protective mountains, hardly a whisper of wind disturbs the suntrap of the city. Winter is when you notice the difference most, with Menton several vital degrees warmer than St-Tropez or St-Raphaël. The beaches, though stony, are popular, and in summer the gritty plage des Sablettes on the harbour has a fashionable edge.

Perched in the hills around Menton, the stunning little unspoilt village of **Ste-Agnes** is known for its arts and crafts studios and stunning views, while its near neighbour **Gorbio** is just as scenic, but more sleepy and traditional.

Brief history

Menton's history, like that of Monaco, almost took an independent path. In the revolutionary days of 1848, Menton and Roquebrune, both at the time under Monaco's jurisdiction, declared themselves an **independent republic** under the protection of Sardinia. When the Prince of Monaco came to Menton in the hope that his regal figure would sway the people, he had to be rescued by the police from a furious crowd and locked up overnight for his own protection. Eventually, following an 1860 vote by Roquebrune and Menton to remain in France, Grimaldi agreed to the sale of the towns to the French state for four million francs.

Menton got its first boost as a resort the following year when a British doctor, James Henry Bennet, published a treatise on the benefits of Menton's mild winter climate to tuberculosis sufferers, and soon thousands of well-heeled invalids were flocking to the town in the vain hope of a cure. Menton's sedate feel and well-preserved historic architecture makes it easy to imagine the presence of archduchesses, grand dukes, tsars and other autocrats, as well as convalescing artists such as Guy de Maupassant and Katherine Mansfield.

8

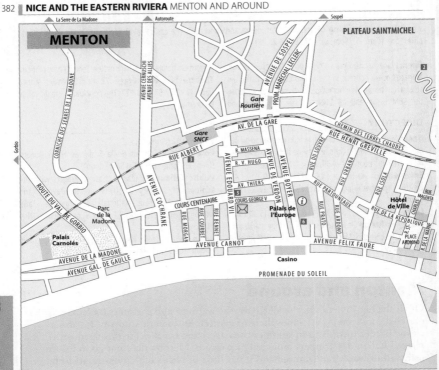

8

The modern town

Roquebrune and Cap Martin merge into Menton along the three-kilometre shore of the Baie **Baie du Soleil**. The modern town is arranged around three main streets parallel to the promenade du Soleil, with an impressive boulevard – **av Boyer/av de Verdun** – running inland from the sea. Menton's old palace hotels, now almost all converted into apartments, add touches of architectural grandeur, whimsy and exotica to the townscape, but the main cultural draw is the town's association with Cocteau. The pedestrianized **rue St-Michel**, lined with cafés and restaurants, links the old and modern towns.

Salle des Mariages

Mairie de Menton, place Ardoïno o Mon–Fri 8.30am–noon & 2–4.30pm • €2 • ☎ 04 92 10 50 00

The **Salle des Mariages**, or registry office, in the Hôtel de Ville on place Ardoïno, was decorated in inimitable style by **Jean Cocteau** (1889–1963) and can be visited by asking the receptionist by the main door. On the wall above the official's desk a couple face each other, with strange topological connections between the sun, her headdress and his fisherman's cap. The *Saracen Wedding Party* on the right-hand wall reveals a disapproving mother of the bride, spurned girlfriend of the groom and her armed vengeful brother amongst the cheerful guests. On the left wall is the story of *Orpheus and Eurydice* at the doomed moment when Orpheus has just looked back. Meanwhile, on the ceiling are *Poetry rides Pegasus*, tattered *Science juggles with the Planets*, and *Love*, open-eyed, waiting with bow and arrow at the ready.

Musée de Préhistoire Régionale

Rue Lorédan-Larchey • Daily except Tues 10am–noon & 2–6pm • Free • ☎ 04 93 35 84 64

The **Musée de Préhistoire Régionale**, at the top of rue Lorédan-Larchey close to the

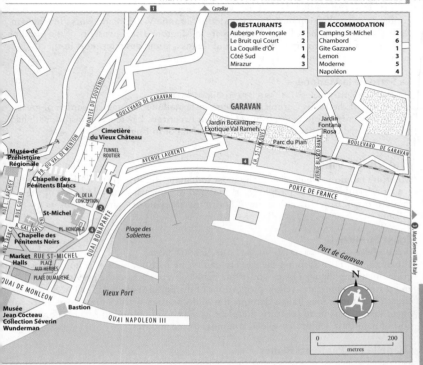

Hôtel de Ville, is one of the best on the subject. There are good videos to watch, life-size re-created scenes of early human life, and the famous 27,000-year-old skull of "Menton Man" found in a cave near the town, encrusted with shells and teeth from his headgear.

Musée Jean Cocteau Collection Séverin Wunderman

2 quai de Monléon • **Museum and bastion** Daily except Tues 10am–6pm • €6, temporary exhibitions €5, combined ticket €8 • ☎ 04 89 81 52 50, ⓦ museecocteaumenton.fr

The seafront's most diverting building is the striking new structure opened in 2011 to house the **Musée Jean Cocteau Collection Séverin Wunderman.** Designed by North African-born Provençal architect Rudy Ricciotti, the new museum exhibits all facets of the polymath artist's work from before World War I to the 1950s; it also mounts temporary exhibitions.

On the same ticket you can visit the seventeenth-century **bastion**, by the quai Napoléon-III nearby, which was restored according to Cocteau's plans between 1958 and 1963. It contains ceramics and pictures of his Mentonaise lovers in the *Inamorati* series.

Palais Carnolès

3 av de la Madone • Daily except Tues 10am–noon & 2–6pm • Free • Bus #7 • ☎ 04 93 35 49 71

At the far western end of the modern town, on avenue de la Madone, an impressive collection of paintings from the Middle Ages to the twentieth century can be seen in the sumptuous **Palais Carnolès**, the old summer residence of the princes of Monaco. Of the early works, the *Madonna and Child with St Francis* by Louis Bréa is exceptional; there are excellent Dutch and Venetian portraits; and an anonymous sixteenth-century École Français canvas of a woman holding a scale. The small modern and contemporary collection includes a wonderful Suzanne Valadon and works by Graham Sutherland, who spent some of his last years in Menton. The downstairs of the building is given over to temporary exhibitions, and there's a **jardin des sculptures** in the adjoining lime, lemon and orange grove.

La Serre de la Madone

74 route du Val de Gorbio • Guided tours Tues–Sun at 3pm • €8 • ⓦ jardins-menton.fr

Due north of the Palais Carnolès is **La Serre de la Madone**, a botanical garden of great tranquillity created in the interwar years by an American, Lawrence Johnston, who had already created a celebrated garden at Hidcote Manor in England.

The Vieille Ville

Menton's fabulous **Vieille Ville** is the most Italianate and beautiful on the Riviera – a wonderful huddle of pastel campaniles and disappearing stairways east of the modern town, towering above the old port and the Baie de Garavan from its hillside site.

Église St-Michel

Parvis de la Basilique St-Michel • Mon–Fri 10am–noon & 3–5.15pm, Sat & Sun 3–5.15pm

Where the *quai* bends round the western end of the Baie de Garavan from the Cocteau museum, a long flight of black-and-white pebbled steps leads to the **parvis St-Michel** and the perfect pink and yellow proportions of the **Église St-Michel**. The interior of the church is a stupendous Italian Baroque riot of decoration, with an impressive, vast organ casing, a sixteenth-century altarpiece in the choir by Antonio Manchello, and a host of paintings, sculptures, gilded columns, stucco and frescoes.

Chapelle des Pénitents Blancs

Visits by guided tour in summer; contact the tourist information office (see opposite) for details

A few steps higher than St-Michel is the apricot-and-white marbled **Chapelle des Pénitents Blancs**, home to a collection of processional lanterns and with a fine trompe l'oeil over the altar.

Cimetière du Vieux Château

Daily May–Sept 7am–8pm; Oct–April 7am–6pm • Free

At the summit of the Vieille Ville you'll reach the bewitchingly beautiful and hauntingly sad **Cimetière du Vieux Château**. Its cream-coloured mid-nineteenth-century sculpted gravestones bear diverse foreign names from Russian princes to William Webb-Ellis, credited, in public schools throughout England, with the invention of rugby; his grave is signposted. Many of Menton's young, consumptive visitors were buried here, and the grief etched in the gravestones is palpable, from the grave of 24-year-old Englishman James MacEwan – "gentle in spirit, patient in suffering" – to the Liverpool-born Arthur Edward Foster, who died aged 23 in 1887 – "God's finger touched him, and he slept" – and the achingly romantic tribute (in German) from a widowed husband to the "unforgettable" Henriette van der Aue of Prague, who died at 33. If all this untimely death is a tad gloomy, there can at least be few lovelier final resting places, with sweeping views along the coast into Italy. The cemetery is in rather crumbly condition, and parts are undergoing restoration.

Garavan

Extending to the Italian border, **Garavan** is Menton's most exclusive residential area, overlooking the modern marina. If it's cool enough for walking, you'll find that the public **parks** up in the hills and the **gardens** of Garavan's once-elegant villas make a

---

MENTON FESTIVALS

In August the pebbled mosaic of the Grimaldi arms on the parvis St-Michel is covered by chairs, music stands, pianos and harps for the **Festival de Musique de Menton** (W musique-menton.fr). The nightly concerts are superb and can be listened to from the quaysides without buying a ticket. If you want a proper seat, make a reservation at the tourist office.

More bizarrely, Menton's biggest event of the year is the **Fête du Citron** in February, when the lemon-flavoured bacchanalia includes processions of floats decorated entirely with the fruit.

---

change from shingle beaches. From the Vieux Cimetière you can walk or take bus #8 along boulevard de Garavan past houses hidden in their large, exuberant gardens.

Jardin Exotique Val Rameh

Av St Jacques • Daily except Tues: April–Sept 10am–12.30pm & 3.30–6.30pm; Oct–March 10am–12.30pm & 2–5pm • €6 • W jardins-menton.fr

The closest public garden to the Vieille Ville along the boulevard de Garavan is the **Jardin Exotique Val Rameh** which surrounds a nineteenth-century villa that acquired its current name from a past owner, a former British governor of Malta. Open to the public since 1967, it's nowadays dedicated to the acclimatization and conservation of rare species, including *sophora toromiro*, a species of flowering tree native to Easter Island, where it has almost disappeared.

Jardin Fontana Rosa

Av Blasco-Ibañez • Guided tours Mon & Fri at 10am • €6 • W jardins-menton.fr

The garden of **Fontana Rosa** surrounds the late nineteenth-century villa that was, from 1921, the home of the Spanish author Vincente Blasco-Ibañez. Figs, palms and bananas give the garden an almost tropical feel, emphasized by its brightly coloured ceramic decoration, and monuments to great writers include a rotunda dedicated to Cervantes, the "father of Spanish literature". The garden is a scheduled historic monument, and is slowly undergoing restoration.

Jardin Maria Serena

21 promenade Reine Astrid • Guided tours Tues at 10am • €6 • W jardins-menton.fr

The very last house on the seafront before the Italian border is the **Maria Serena Villa**, designed by Charles Garnier – architect of the Paris opera and the casino in Monte Carlo – for the family of Ferdinand de Lesseps. Reputed to be the most temperate garden in France, it has an important collection of palms and tropical plants.

ARRIVAL AND INFORMATION   MENTON

By train Menton's *gare SNCF* is at the end of av de la Gare, off av de Verdun/ Boyer.
Destinations Monaco (every 15–30min; 11min); Nice (every 15–30min; 35min).
By bus The *gare routière* is north of the *gare SNFC* on av de Sospel, which is the northern continuation of av de Verdun. Local buses (€1; W carfenbus.fr) all pass through the *gare routière*.

Destinations Monaco (up to 5 per hr; 32min); Nice (up to 5 per hr; 1hr 30min); Nice airport (hourly; 1hr).
Tourist office 8 av Boyer (July to mid-Sept daily 9am–7pm; mid-Sept to June Mon–Sat 8.30am–12.30pm & 2–6pm, Sun 9am–12.30pm; ☎ 04 92 41 76 76, W tourisme-menton.fr).

ACCOMMODATION

Chambord 6 av Boyer ☎ 04 93 35 94 19, W hotel-chambord.com. Sister hotel to the *Moderne* (see p.386), and slightly swisher, with large, modern en-suite rooms, many with balconies. Close to the tourist office, the sea and the town centre. **€115**
Gîte Gazzano 151 route de Castellar ☎ 04 93 57 39 73.

Very pleasant double rooms 2km inland from Menton and with a pool looking down over the wooded slopes to the sea. Minimum 3-night stay. **€70**
★ **Lemon** 10 rue Albert-1er ☎ 04 93 28 63 63, W hotel-lemon.com. Newly renovated budget hotel a couple of minutes' walk from the train station, run by a

8

friendly young couple. Simple but modern en-suite rooms, and a pretty garden. A good choice at the price. **€59**

Moderne 1 cours George V ☎ 04 93 57 20 02, ⓦ hotel-moderne-menton.com. Good-value two-star between the *gare SNCF* and the tourist office. The a/c and soundproofed rooms have wi-fi and cable TV; some have balconies. The decor isn't as up to the minute as the name might suggest, but it's comfortable enough. **€90**

Napoléon 29 porte de France, Baie de Garavan ☎ 04 93 35 89 50, ⓦ napoleon-menton.com. Menton's smartest hotel is modern, friendly and right on the seafront between the old town and Italian border, with

understated contemporary decor, a private beach and an ice-cream parlour 100m from the hotel, and a bar and pool on site. **€175**

CAMPSITE

Camping St-Michel 1 rte des Ciappes ☎ 04 93 35 81 23, ⓦ hotelmenton.fr/hotel-menton/menton-camping-saint-michel; bus #6 via les Ciappes or #903 from the *gare routière*. Menton's municipal campsite sits in an olive grove overlooking the town. It's a gruelling walk uphill, so take the bus. No bookings. Closed mid-Oct to March, except for the Fête du Citron. **€19.80**

EATING AND DRINKING

The pedestrianized **rue St-Michel** is promising ground for cheap eats, with plenty of snack stops and an excellent Italian *gelato* stand, while the pretty **covered market** off quai Monléon is a good place to assemble a picnic. In summer, the **Plage des Sablettes** between the Vieux Port and the Port de Garavan is lined with beach bars, some of them quite stylish.

Auberge Provencale 11 rue Trenca ☎ 04 93 18 14 51. Unpretentious restaurant in a side street in the modern town, dishing up Provençal and French bistro staples – from *salade niçoise* to *blanquette de veau* – on a €17 three-course menu. Closed Sun eve & Mon.

Le Bruit qui Court 31 quai Bonaparte ☎ 04 93 35 94 64, ⓦ lebruitquicourt.fr. Foie gras is a speciality at this smart restaurant facing the port and plage des Sablettes, but there's a lot of fish on the menu too – John Dory with béarnaise sauce, grilled salmon with fennel – plus lamb with *herbes de Provence*. *Menu* €23. Wed–Sat noon-1.30pm & 7pm–late, Tues 7pm–late.

La Coquille d'Ôr 1 quai Bonaparte ☎ 04 93 35 80 67. Excellent fish and seafood restaurant overlooking the bay of Garavan, with bouillabaisse for two for €72, paella to

share and *menus* at €25 and €29. Daily except Tues noon–2pm & 7–10pm.

Côté Sud 15–17 quai Bonaparte ☎ 04 93 84 03 69. One of the more promising budget options facing the port, with stylish modern decor, a vast selection of pizzas from €7.50, pasta from €9.50 and main-course salads around €11; meat or fish mains from around €14.50. Daily 7am–midnight.

Mirazur 30 av Aristide Briand ☎ 04 92 41 86 86, ⓦ mirazur.fr. Rising culinary star Mauro Colagreco has bagged two Michelin stars for this swish 1930s-style dining room hard by the Italian border, making it one of the Riviera's hottest culinary tickets. Three courses €85; €29 two-course weekday lunch. Mid-July to Aug Tues–Sun 7.15–10pm, Sat & Sun noon–3pm; Sept to mid-July Wed–Sun noon–3pm & 7.15–10pm.

Ste-Agnes

Ten kilometres northwest of Menton and 800m above sea level, **STE-AGNES** claims to be the highest coastal village in Europe – something you'll readily believe after completing the tortuous journey up and getting a glimpse of the breathtaking views over Menton. Though packed with crystal engravers, painters, herbalists, jewellers and leather workers, it's still a peaceful spot. When it's not up in the clouds the village commands breathtaking views, especially from the twentieth-century **fort** at the seaward end of the village (June–Sept daily 3–6pm; Oct–May Sat & Sun 2.30–5.30pm; €5), built into the mountain top as part of the Maginot Line defences of the 1930s. Clamber higher still and you'll reach the ancient Saracen fortress at the top of **St Agnès crag**, from which you'll get properly 360-degree panoramas of sea and mountain – though if the views over Menton and the coast are all you're after save your breath, as the seaward view is no better than from the Maginot fort below.

Ste-Agnes is also an excellent starting point for **walks**; download route descriptions and maps in the Randoxygène Pays Côtier guide from the *département*'s website (ⓦ cg06.fr), or pick up a copy from one of the local tourist offices. One popular route is the four-hour ascent and circuit of **Pointe Siricocca** (1051m).

ARRIVAL AND DEPARTURE   STE-AGNES

By bus Bus #10 (3 daily; 30min) makes the trek up to the village from the *gare routière* in Menton.

EATING AND DRINKING

Le Righi 1 place du Fort ☎ 04 92 10 90 88. The views from this restaurant bar/*glacier* and *salon de thé* just beyond the fort are breathtaking; they serve home-made pasta or gnocchi with daube or *blettes* sauces, plus meat-based main courses. *Menus* €18–28. Daily except Wed 9am–10pm; meals noon–2pm & 7–9pm.

Gorbio

GORBIO, to the southwest of Ste-Agnes, is an exquisite hilltop village with very few arts and crafts boutiques or other tourist fodder, lending it a tranquil atmosphere that's rare for so scenic a place. Though the two villages are only 2km apart as the crow flies, the roads between them meet approximately 8km away, below the autoroute. The walkers' route – which partly follows the GR51 footpath – cuts out some of the road's twists and turns, but it's steep and in places narrow.

On the Thursday after Corpus Christi in June, the annual rite of the **Procession des Limaces** takes place, when the streets are illuminated by tiny lamps of snail shells filled with olive oil – a custom dating back to medieval times and occurring in villages throughout this area (check with the tourist office in Menton for exact dates).

ARRIVAL AND DEPARTURE   GORBIO

By bus Bus #7 (Mon–Sat 6, Sun 4; 30min) make the trek up to the village from the *gare routière* in Menton.

8

EATING AND DRINKING

Beau Séjour Place de la République ☎ 04 93 41 46 15. Very pretty restaurant on Gorbio's main square, with a pergola-shaded terrace and sautéed rabbit and *daube de* *boeuf* on its €27 *menu*. They don't accept cards. Daily except Wed noon–1.30pm; closed Oct–Easter.

LEOPARD MOSAIC, MUSÉE ARCHÉOLOGIE, FRÉJUS

Contexts

History

While it's hard today to think of Provence and the Côte d'Azur as anything other than definitively French, the region has a long and varied history. Colonized by the Greeks, occupied by the Romans, fought over by Normans and Saracens, and prized as the personal fiefdom of medieval counts and popes, it has only belonged to France for little more than five centuries.

From the Stone Age to the Celto-Ligurians

Although it can safely be assumed that Provence and southeastern France held substantial populations during the Stone Age – including in large areas that now lie beneath the sea – all the great discoveries dating from that era in France are in the southwest of the country. A few Paleolithic traces have been found at Nice and in Menton, but there's nothing to compare with the cave drawings of Lascaux.

The development of farming, which characterizes the **Neolithic Era**, began in Provence around 6500 BC, with the domestication of wild sheep. Around 3000 BC **Ligurian** settlers reached southern France from the east, and cultivated the land for the first time. These were the people responsible for the carvings in the Vallée des Merveilles, the few megalithic standing stones, and the earliest *bories*. Certain Provençal word endings, such as *-osc, -asc, -auni* and *-inc*, which endure in place names, derive from Ligurian dialects passed down through Greek and Latin.

At some later point **Celts** from the north moved into western Provence, bringing bronze technology with them. A new ethnic mix emerged, the **Celto-Ligurians**; they built the earliest fortified hilltop retreats, the *oppidi*, of which traces remain in the Maures, the Luberon, the upper Durance and the hills in the Rhône Valley.

The Greeks discover Provence

As the Celto-Ligurian civilization developed, so did its trading links with other Mediterranean peoples. The River Rhône may have been named by traders from the Greek island of Rhodes (in French the name can be made into an adjective, *Rhodien*). Etruscans, Phoenicians, Corinthians and Ionians all had connections with Provence. Starting with **Massalia** (Marseille) around 600 BC, the **Greek colonies** that appeared along the coast were the result not of military conquest but of gradual economic integration. While Massalia was a republic with great influence over its hinterland, it was not a base for wiping out the indigenous peoples. Deriving prestige and wealth from its port, the city prided itself on its independence, which was to last well into the Middle Ages.

The Greeks introduced olives, figs, cherries, walnuts, cultivated vines and money. In the succeeding two centuries, further **colonies** were set up in La Ciotat, Almanarre (near Hyères), Bréganson, Cavalaire, St-Tropez (known as Athenopolis), Antibes, Nice and Monaco, while Mastrabala at St-Blaize and Glanum by St-Rémy-de-Provence

400,000 BC	6500 BC	3200 BC	600 BC
Human beings inhabit the cave of Baume Bonne, near Quinson, and use fire at Terra Mata, Nice.	Neolithic shepherds introduce farming to the lower Alpine slopes.	Ligurian settlers create enigmatic rock carvings in the Vallée des Merveilles.	Greek colonists establish a coastal settlement at Massalia (Marseille).

developed within Massalia's sphere of influence. The **Rhône** was the corridor for commercial expeditions, including journeys as far north as Cornwall to acquire tin. Away from the coast and the river, however, the Celto-Ligurian lifestyle was barely affected.

Roman conquest

Unlike the Greeks, the **Romans** were true imperialists, imposing their organization, language and laws by military subjugation on every corner of their empire. During the third century BC Roman expansion focused on Spain, from where the Carthaginian general Hannibal set off with his elephants to cross first southern Gaul and then the Alps, before attacking the Romans in upper Italy. Massalia's good diplomatic relations with Rome served the city well when Spain was conquered, and the Romans set about securing the land routes to Iberia.

This they achieved remarkably quickly. Between 125 and 118 BC, **Provincia** (the origin of the name Provence) became part of the Roman Empire. Encompassing all southern France from the Alps to the Pyrenees, it stretched as far north as Vienne and Geneva.

While Massalia and other areas remained neutral or collaborated with the invaders, many Ligurian tribes fought to the death. Thus the Oppidum d'Entremont of the Salyens was demolished, and a victorious new city, Aquae Sextiae (Aix), built at its foot in 122 BC. Pax Romana was still a long way off, however. **Germanic Celts** moving south from the Baltic managed to decimate several Roman legions at Orange in 105 BC, only to be defeated by a major campaign designed to keep the barbarians out of Italy. Massalia exploited every situation to gain more territories and privileges, while the rest of Provence grudgingly submitted. Finally, from 58 to 51 BC all of Gaul was conquered by **Julius Caesar**.

At that crucial moment, Massalia blew its hitherto successful diplomatic strategy by supporting Pompey in the Civil War. Caesar laid siege, defeated the city and confiscated all its territories, from the Rhône to Monaco. Unlike earlier emperors, Julius Caesar implanted his own people in Provence – St-Raphaël was founded for his veterans – and so too did his successor Octavian. While the coastal areas duly Latinized themselves, the **Ligurians** in the mountains, from Sisteron to the Roya Valley, refused to give up their identity. They kept Roman troops busy until their eventual defeat in 14 BC, which the Trophie des Alpes at La Turbie gloats over to this day.

This monument to Augustus Caesar was erected on the newly built **Via Aurelia**, which linked Rome with Arles, by way of Cimiez, Antibes, Fréjus and Aix (pretty much the route of today's N7). The **Via Agrippa** continued north from Arles, through Avignon and Orange. Only the rebellious mountainous area was heavily garrisoned. Western Provence, with Arles as its main town, dutifully served the imperial interests, providing oil, grain and, most importantly, ships for the superpower that ruled western Europe and the Mediterranean for five centuries.

Christianity appeared in Provence during the third century and spread rapidly, becoming the official religion of the Roman Empire in the fourth. The **Lérins Monastery** was founded around 410 AD and the **Abbey of St-Victor** in Marseille six years later.

450BC	218 BC	175 BC	Second century BC
Arrival of the Gauls.	Hannibal, plus army and elephants, crosses the Rhône above Orange, en route for Italy.	Celto-Ligurian establish the oppidum of Entremont, outside Aix-en-Provence.	Gallo-Greeks found Glanum, just outside modern St-Rémy; Provincia joins the Roman Empire, with Narbonne as its capital.

Rome falls: more invasions

During the early fifth century, as the Roman Empire began to split apart, Germanic invaders initially bypassed Provence. By the time the Western Roman Empire finally collapsed in 476 AD, Provence was dominated by both the **Visigoths**, who had captured Arles and were terrorizing the lower Rhône valley, and the **Burgundians**, who had moved in from the east. The new rulers confiscated land, took slaves and generally made life miserable.

Over the next two centuries, **Goths** and **Franks** fought over Provence: famine, disease and bloodshed diminished the population, lands that had been drained returned to swamp, and intellectual life declined. Under the eighth-century **Merovingian dynasty**, Provence, in theory, formed part of the **Frankish empire**. But a newly emergent world power – **Islam** – had spread from the Middle East into North Africa and most of Spain. In 732 a Muslim army reached as far as Tours before being defeated by the Franks at Poitiers. At this point the local ruler of Provence rebelled against the central authority, and called on the **Saracens** (Muslims) to assist. Armies of Franks, Saracens, Lombards and locals rampaged through Provence, putting the Franks back in control.

Though the ports had trouble carrying on their lucrative trade while the Mediterranean was controlled by Saracens, agriculture developed under the Frankish **Carolingian dynasty**, particularly during the relatively peaceful reign of **Charlemagne**. When Charlemagne's sons and then grandsons squabbled over the inheritance, during the ninth century, Provence once again became easy prey.

Normans took over the lower Rhône, and the **Saracens** returned, pillaging Marseille and destroying its abbey in 838, sacking Arles in 842, and attacking Marseille again in 848. From a base at Fraxinetum (La Garde-Freinet), they controlled the whole Massif des Maures for a century.

In response to the Saracen threat, the people of Provence constructed the **hilltop villages** that still, albeit in much altered form, characterize the Provençal coast. Far inland, they similarly retreated to whatever defensive positions were available, which in cities would be the strongest building, for example the Roman theatre at Orange. The Rhône Valley villagers took refuge in the Luberon and the Massif de la Ste-Baume.

Despite the terrors and bloodshed, the period also saw progress. The Saracens introduced basic medicine, the use of cork bark, resin extraction from pines, flat roof-tiles, and the most traditional Provençal musical instrument, the tambourine.

The counts of Provence

Towards the end of the tenth century, **Guillaume Le Libérateur**, count of Arles, expelled the Saracens and claimed Provence as his own feudal estate. A period of relative stability ensued. Forestry, fishing, irrigation, land reclamation, vine cultivation, beekeeping, salt-panning, river transport and renewed learning began to pull Provence out of the Dark Ages.

While Guillaume and his successors retained considerable independence from their overlords – first the kingdom of Burgundy, then the Holy Roman Empire – their influence was largely confined to the area around Arles and Avignon. Local lords held sway in rural areas, and the cities developed their own autonomy. Although the Rhône officially formed the border between France and the Holy Roman Empire, the old

49 BC	First century AD	c.100 AD
Having constructed a fleet in Arles and defeated Pompey's forces off Les Lecques, Julius Caesar successfully besieges Massalia.	According to legend, Mary Jacobé, Mary Salomé and their Egyptian servant Sarah, later the Gypsies' patron saint, reach Les Stes-Maries-de-la-Mer.	Completion of amphitheatre in Arles, the largest Roman building in Gaul.

economic, cultural and linguistic links between its two sides endured.

During the **twelfth century**, Provence passed to the counts of Toulouse. It was then divided with the counts of Barcelona, although various fiefdoms – including Forcalquier, Les Baux and Beuil – refused integration. Power shifted repeatedly but, sporadic armed conflicts apart, the titleholder to Provence hardly affected ordinary people, who were bound in serfdom to their immediate *seigneur*.

Thanks to the Crusades, **maritime commerce** flourished once again, as did trade along the Rhône, giving prominence to Avignon, Orange, Arles and, most of all, Marseille. In Nice, then under the control of the Genoese Republic, a new commercial town developed below the castle rock. The cities took on the organizational form of the Italian consulates, increasingly separating themselves from feudal power.

Troubadour poetry made its appearance in the *langue d'oc* language that was spoken from the Alps to the Pyrenees (and from which the **Provençal dialect** developed). Church construction looked back to the Romans for inspiration, producing the great Romanesque edifices of Montmajour, Sénanque, Silvacane, Thoronet and St-Trophime in Arles.

Raymond Béranger V, Catalan count of Provence in the early thirteenth century, took the unprecedented step of spending time in his domains. While fighting off the count of Toulouse and the Holy Roman Emperor, he made Aix his capital, founded Barçelonnette and travelled throughout the Alps and the coastal regions. For the first time since the Romans, Provence became an organized mini-state with a more or less **unified feudal system** of law and administration.

The Angevins

After Béranger's death, Provence turned towards France. It fell under the control of the **house of Anjou** until the end of the fifteenth century. The borders changed: Nice, Barçelonnette and Puget-Théniers passed to Savoy in 1388 and remained separate from Provence until 1860. Extraneous powers claimed or bought territories: the **popes at Avignon** (see p.115) and in the **Comtat Venaissin**; the Prince of Nassau in Orange. Though armed conflicts, revolts and even civil war chequered its medieval history, Provence was at least spared the Hundred Years' War, which never touched the region.

By the end of this period the trading routes from the Orient to Genoa and Marseille, and from Marseille to Flanders and London, were forming the basis of **early capitalism**, and spreading new techniques and learning. Marseille was not a great financial centre, but its population became ever more cosmopolitan. For a shepherd or forester in the mountains, meanwhile, life in Marseille or in the extravagant papal city of Avignon would have appeared to belong to another planet.

Provençal Jews exercised equal rights with Christians, owning land and practising assorted professions in addition to finance and commerce. Though concentrated in the western towns, they were not always ghettoized. But the moment disaster struck, such as the **Black Death** in the mid-fourteenth century, latent hostility became violently manifest. The Plague itself made no distinctions: half the population died in the recurring epidemics.

In **cultural and intellectual life** the dominant centres were the **papal court at Avignon**,

410	Fifth century	Ninth century	973
Honoratus founds a monastery on the Île St-Honorat.	With the Roman Empire collapsing, Visigoths and Burgundians contend for control.	Saracen armies sack Arles in 842 and Marseille in 848.	Count Guillaume of Arles expels the Saracens from Provence, following the battle of Tourtour.

and later the court of **King René of Anjou** at **Aix**. However, Angevin rulers and foreign trade, art and architecture remained surprisingly unmarked by the major contemporary movements. Only in the mid-fifteenth century did native art develop around the **Avignon School**, while the **School of Nice**, more directly under Italian influence, also emerged. Avignon acquired great **Gothic architecture** – the Palais des Papes and many of the churches – but elsewhere the only major examples of the new style were Tarascon's castle and the basilica of St-Maximin-de-la-Ste-Baume.

Founded in 1303, the **university in Avignon** became famous for jurisprudence. Aix university was established a century later and in the mid-fourteenth century the first paper mills were in use. By King René's time, French was the official language of the court.

Union with France

After the short-lived Charles III of Provence, René's heir, bequeathed all his lands to **Louis XI of France**, the *parlement* of Aix glossed over, and approved, the transfer of power in 1482. Within twelve months every top Provençal official had been replaced by a Frenchman; the castles at Toulon and Les Baux were razed to the ground; and garrisons were placed in five major towns.

Louis XI's successors took a more careful approach to this crucial border province. The **Act of Union**, ratified by *parlement* in 1486, declared Provence to be a separate entity within France, enshrining the rights to its own law courts, customs and privileges. In reality, the ever-centralizing power of the French state systematically eroded these rights.

The **Jewish population** provided a convenient diversion for Provençal frustrations. Encouraged, if not instigated, by the Crown, there were massacres, expulsions and assaults in Marseille, Arles and Manosque at the end of the fifteenth century. The royal directive was convert or leave – some, like the parents of **Nostradamus**, converted, while others fled to the Comtat, where Jews lost their papal protection in turn in 1570.

Meanwhile Charles VIII, Louis XII and François I involved Provence in their **Italian Wars**. **Marseille** became a **military port** in 1488, and in 1496 **Toulon** was fortified and its first **shipyards** opened. While the rest of the province suffered troop movements and requisitions, Marseille and Toulon benefited from extra funds and unchecked piracy against the enemies of France. Genoese, Venetian and Spanish vessels were regularly towed into Marseille.

The war took a more serious turn in the 1520s. After the French conquered Milan, **Charles V**, the new Holy Roman Emperor, sent a large army across the Var and into Aix. The French sought to protect Marseille at all costs. When the imperial forces failed to take Marseille, the city was rewarded with a royal wedding between François' second son, the future Henri II, and **Catherine de Médicis**. The Château d'If was built to protect the roadstead.

Charles V then re-took Milan, so the French invaded Savoy and occupied Nice. In 1536 an even bigger **imperial army invaded**, and again the French abandoned inland Provence to protect Marseille and the Rhône Valley. At **Le Muy**, fifty local heroes, subsequently hanged for their pains, stopped the emperor for one day. **Marseille** and **Arles** held out; French troops moved south down the Durance; and the weakened Savoyards returned whence they came.

Twelfth century	1309	1334
The Cistercian order establishes the Abbaye de Sénanque.	Clement V becomes the first pope to move to Avignon.	Benedict XII builds the Vieux Palais.

As a result of the Italian Wars, Provence finally identified itself with France, making it easier for the Crown to diminish the power of the *États*, impose greater numbers of French administrators, and, in 1539, decree that all administrative laws were to be translated from Latin into French, not Provençal.

Life in the early sixteenth century

Sixteenth-century Provence was ruled by two royal appointees – a governor and grand *sénéchal* (the chief administrator) – but the **feudal hierarchy** had little control over the structure of society. Those few nobles who lived on their estates were often poorer than the merchants and financiers of the major cities. In remoter areas people cultivated their absent *seigneur*'s land as if it were their own; elsewhere towns bought land off the feudal owners, and nearly half the population owned land. Advances in irrigation, such as **Craponne's canal through the Crau**, were carried out independently from the aristocracy.

While not self-sufficient in grain, Provence exported wine, fish and vermilion from the Camargue; textiles, tanneries, soap and paper thrived; and new foods, such as oranges, pepper, palm dates and sugar cane, were imported. Olives provided the basic oil for food, commercial orchards appeared, and most families kept pigs and sheep: only vegetables were rare luxuries. People lived on their land, with the **old fortified villages** populated only in times of insecurity. Epidemics continued, however, and sanitation left much to be desired.

Certain larger towns set up **free schools**, while Aix, Marseille, Arles and Avignon established secondary colleges. **Nostradamus** (1503–66) achieved renown throughout France, although his books had to be printed in Lyon – there was as yet no market for printers in Provence.

The Wars of Religion

While the Italian Wars disrupted social and productive advances, they were nothing compared with the **Wars of Religion** that threw all France into **civil war** later in the sixteenth century. The clash between the reforming ideas of Luther and Calvin and the old Roman Catholic order was particularly violent in Provence. Avignon was a rigid centre of Catholicism, whereas Orange allowed Huguenots to practise freely. Haute Provence and the Luberon became centres for the new religion due to the influx of Dauphinois and Piedmontais settlers.

Incidents began to build up in the 1540s, culminating in the massacre of Luberon Protestants and the destruction of Mérindol (see box, p.169). In Avignon heretics were displayed in iron cages; in Haute Provence churches were smashed by the reformers; and in Orange Protestants pillaged the cathedral and seized control of the city. The regent Catherine de Médicis' **Edict of Tolerance** in 1562 only made matters worse. The *parlement* chose to resign rather than ratify a new Edict of Tolerance in 1563, even though by now Orange had been won back to the established Church, the garrison of Sisteron had been massacred for protecting the Protestants and the last armed group of reformers had fled north.

When Catherine de Médicis and her son Charles XIV toured Provence in 1564, all seemed well. But within a few years fighting again broke out, with Sisteron once more

1388	1409	1434–80	1482
Civil war in Provence; Nice and Barçelonnette pass to Savoy.	The antipope Benedict XIII, following a siege that prompts him to build the city's still-extant walls, flees from Avignon.	Under King René of Anjou, Aix-en-Provence reaches its apogee as capital of Provence.	Provence passes into French control, following the death of Charles III of Provence.

under siege. This state of civil war was only terminated by another major outbreak of **plague** in **1580**.

The *Guerres de Religion* hotted up once more after the Protestant **Henri de Navarre** (the future Henri IV) became heir to the throne in 1584. The pope excommunicated Henri; and the leaders of the French Catholics (the de Guises) formed the **European Catholic League**, seized Paris and drove out the king, Henri III. Provence found itself with two governors – the king's and the League's appointees; two capitals – Aix and Pertuis; and a split *parlement*. After Henri III's assassination, Catholic Aix called in the duke of Savoy, whose troops trounced Henri de Navarre's supporters at Riez. By now the main issue for the Provençaux was loyalty to the French Crown against invaders, rather than religion. Even the Aix *parlement* stopped short of giving Savoy the title to Provence, and after Marseille again withstood a siege, the duke gave up and went back home to Nice in 1592. For another year battles continued between the Leaguers and the Royalists. Finally Henri IV said his Mass; troops entered Marseille; and Provence reverted, war-damaged and impoverished, to **royal control**.

Louis XIII and Louis XIV

The **consolidation of the French state** initiated by Louis XIII's minister, **Richelieu**, saw Provençal institutions and ideas of independence whittled away, along with ever-increasing tax demands and enforced "free gifts" to the king.

As the power and prestige of the *États* and *parlement* dwindled, political power switched to *intendants*, servants of the state with powers over every aspect of provincial life, including the military. Having refused to provide the royal purse with funds in 1629, the *États* were not convoked again. The *noblesse d'épée* (the real aristos) were left disgruntled but impotent, while the clergy (the First Estate) also lost a measure of power.

It was a time of **plague, famine**, and yet more **religious strife and conflict. War with Spain** increased taxation, decimated trade and cost lives. When Marseille attempted to preserve its ancient independence by setting up a rebel council in 1658, the royal response was swift. Troops were sent in, rebels condemned to the rack or the galleys, and a permanent garrison established.

Despite taxes and upheavals, progress in manufacture (including the faïence industry), education and social provision carried on apace. The townhouses of Aix, Marseille and Avignon, the Hospice de la Charité in Marseille, the Baroque additions to churches and chapels, all show wealth accumulating – gained, as ever, by maritime commerce.

As the reign of **Louis XIV**, the **Sun King**, became more grandiose and more aggressive, Provence, like all France beyond Versailles and Paris, was eclipsed. The **war with Holland** saw Orange and the valley of Barçelonnette annexed; Avignon and the papal Comtat swung steadily into the French orbit; attempts were made again to capture Nice. With the *ancien régime* slowly digging its own grave, the rest of France stagnated. The pattern for Provence of wars, invasions and trade blockades became entrenched. Aix had its grandiose town planning, Avignon its mansions, and Grasse its perfume industry, but elsewhere there was complete stagnation.

1503	1584	1632
Nostradamus is born in St-Rémy.	With the Wars of Religion at their peak, Provence finds itself with two governors, and two capitals – Aix and Pertuis.	Louis XIII of France destroys the feudal citadel at Les Baux.

The Revolution

Conditions were ripe for revolution in Provence. The region had suffered a disastrous silk harvest and a sharp fall in the price of wine in 1787, and the severe winter of 1788–89 killed off olive trees. Unemployment and starvation were rife and the soaring cost of bread provoked riots in the spring of 1789.

In **July 1789**, while the Bastille was stormed in Paris, Provençal peasants pillaged local châteaux and urban workers rioted against the mayors, egged on by the middle classes. There was only one casualty, at Aups. The following year **Marseillaise revolutionaries** seized the forts of St-Jean and St-Nicolas, with again just one dose of violence when the crowd lynched St-Jean's commander. **Toulon** was equally fervent in its support for the new order, and at **Aix** a counter-revolutionary lawyer and two aristocrats were strung up on lampposts. In the **papal lands**, where the crucial issue was reunion with France, Rome's representative was sent packing, and a revolutionary municipality installed.

Counter-revolutionaries regrouped in Carpentras, but 1792 saw Marseille's staunchly Jacobin National Guard, the **Féderés**, demolish counter-revolutionary forces in the Comtat and aristocratic Arles. Marseille's authorities declared kingship to be contrary to the principles of equality and national sovereignty. When the Legislative Assembly summoned the Féderés to Paris, five hundred Marseillais marched north singing Rouget de Lisle's **Hymn to the Army of the Rhine**. Written for troops in that April's war with Germany and Austria, it was a major hit with the Parisian *sans-culottes*, and as the **Marseillaise** it became France's national anthem – especially after the attack on the Tuileries Palace was swiftly followed by the dethronement of the king.

Provence had by now incorporated the papal states and was divided into **four départements**. Peasants were once again on the pillage, and still starving, while royalists and republicans fought it out in the towns. In 1793 the Var military commander was ordered to take Nice, a hotbed of émigré intrigue. Twenty thousand people fled the city but no resistance was encountered. The Alpes-Maritimes *département* came into existence.

That summer, political divisions between the factions of the Convention and the growing fear of a dictatorship by the Parisian *sans-culottes* provoked the **provincial Federalist revolt**. Fed up with conscription to wars on every frontier, the populace hankered after their former Provençal autonomy. Revolutionary cities found themselves fighting against government forces – a situation exploited by the real **counter-revolutionaries**. In Toulon the entire fleet and the city's fortifications were handed over to the English. Besides the almost daily executions of the Terror, reprisals cost thousands of lives.

Much of Provence, however, had remained Jacobin, and fell victim to the **White Terror of 1795** that followed the execution of Robespierre. The prisons of Marseille, Aix, Arles and Tarascon overflowed with people picked up on the street with no charge. Cannons were fired into the cells at point-blank range and sulphur or lighted rags thrown through the bars. The Revolution abandoned all hope of being revolutionary, and **anarchy reigned**. Provence was crawling with returned émigrés who readily attracted violent followers motivated by frustration, exhaustion and famine.

1661	1720	1789
Louis XIV, the "Sun King", introduces absolute monarchy to France.	Plague kills half the population of Marseille.	French Revolution ends the monarchy.

Napoleon and restoration

Provence's experience of **Napoleon** was much like that of the rest of France, despite the emperor's close connection with the region (childhood at Nice; military career at Antibes and Toulon; then the escape from Elba). Order was restored and power became even more centralized, with *préfets* enlarging on the role of Louis XIV's *intendants*. Although the **concordat with the pope** re-establishing Catholicism as the state religion was widely welcomed, secular power often reverted to the old *seigneurs* – the new mayor of Marseille, for example, was a marquise.

It was the **Napoleonic wars** that cost the emperor his Provençal support. Marseille's port was again blockaded; conscription and taxes for military campaigns were as detested as ever; the Alpes-Maritimes *département* became a theatre of war and in 1814 was handed over (with Savoy) to Sardinia. Monaco followed suit the following year, though with the Grimaldi dynasty reinstalled in their palace.

The **restoration of the Bourbons** after Waterloo unleashed another White Terror. Provence was again bitterly divided between royalists and republicans, but there was no major resistance to the **1830 revolution** that put Louis-Philippe, the "Citizen King", on the throne. The new regime represented liberalism – tinged with anti-clericalism and a dislike of democracy – and was welcomed by the Provençal bourgeoisie.

1848 and 1851

The first half of the nineteenth century saw the first major **industrialization** of France, and, overseas, the conquest of Algeria. Marseille was linked by rail with Paris and expanded its port to take steam ships; iron bridges over the Rhône and new roads were built; many towns demolished their ramparts to extend their main streets into the suburbs. By the 1840s the arsenal at Toulon employed over three thousand workers.

This emerging proletariat was highly receptive when socialist and feminist **Flora Tristan** toured France in 1844. A year later all the arsenal's different trades went on strike. Throughout industrialized Provence workers overturned their traditional *compagnons* (guilds) to form radical trade unions. Things hardly changed inland, however, as protectionist policies hampered the exchange of foodstuffs, and the new industries' demand for fuel eroded forestry rights. By 1847 the country (and most of Europe) was in severe economic crisis.

When news of the **1848 revolution** arrived from Paris, town halls, common lands and forests were instantly and peacefully reclaimed by the populace. The ensuing elections returned very moderate republicans, albeit including three manual workers in Marseille, Toulon and Avignon. Two months later, however, the economic situation was deteriorating again, and employers were clawing back by newly won improvements in working hours and wages. A demonstration in Marseille turned nasty and the **barricades** went up.

Elsewhere, the most militant action was in Menton and Roquebrune, both under the rule of **Monaco**, where locals refused to pay the prince's high taxes on oil and fruit. Sardinian military assistance failed to quell the revolt and the two towns declared themselves independent. His main source of income gone, the Grimaldi prince turned

1792	1793
Written for troops in the war with Germany and Austria, the Hymn to the Army of the Rhine becomes, as the Marseillaise, the French national anthem.	Revolutionary forces recapture Toulon, in an engagement that brings the young Napoleon to public attention.

his focus shrewdly towards **tourism** – already well-established in Nice and Hyères – and opened the casino at Monte Carlo.

The 1848 revolution turned sour with the election of **Louis-Napoleon** as president in 1850. Universal male suffrage was effectively annulled by a new residency requirement. Laws against "secret societies" and "conspiracies" followed. Ordinary *paysans* discussing prices over a bottle of wine could be arrested; militants from Digne and Avignon were deported to Polynesia for belonging to a democratic party; and cooperatives were seen as hotbeds of sedition.

When Louis-Napoleon made himself emperor in the **coup d'état of 1851**, Provence, like many other regions, turned again to revolt. Initially there were insufficient forces in the small towns and villages to prevent the rebels taking control. In order to take the *préfectures*, villagers and townspeople, both male and female, organized themselves into "*colonnes*" that marched beneath the red flag. Digne was the only *préfecture* they held, though, and then for only two days. Reprisals were bloody, with thousands of rebels caught as they tried to flee. Of all the insurgents shot, imprisoned or deported, one in five was from Provence.

The Second Empire

The **Second Empire** saw huge changes in everyday life. **Marseille** became France's premier port, its trade enormously expanded by the colonization of North and West Africa, Vietnam and parts of China. The depopulation of inland Provence suddenly became a deluge of migration to the coast and Rhône Valley. While the railway was extended along the coast, communications inland were ignored.

At the end of the **war for Italian unification** in 1860, **Napoléon III** regained the Alpes-Maritimes as reward for supporting Italy against Austria. A plebiscite in Nice gave majority support for **reunion with France**. To the north, Tende and La Brigue voted almost unanimously for France but the result was ignored: Italy's new king wished to keep his favourite hunting grounds. Menton and Roquebrune also voted for France. While making noises about rigged elections, Charles of Monaco agreed to sell the two towns – despite their independence – to France. The sum was considerably greater than the proceeds from the fledgling gambling and tourism industry, and saved the principality from bankruptcy. **Monaco's independence**, free from any foreign protector, was finally established.

One casualty of this dispersal of traditional Provence was the Provençal language. This prompted the formation of the **Félibrige** in 1854, by a group of poets including **Frédéric Mistral** – a nostalgic, backward-looking and intellectual movement in defence of literary Provençal. Other, more popularist, Provençal writers of the time were similarly conservative, railing against gas lighting and any other innovation. The attempt to associate the language with some past golden age of ultra-Catholic primitivism only encouraged the association of progress with the French tongue – particularly for the Left.

By the end of the 1860s the **socialism** of the First International was gaining ground in the industrial cities, and in Marseille most of all. In the plebiscite of 1870, in which the country as a whole gave Napoleon III their support, the Bouches-du-Rhône *département* was second only to Paris in the number of "nons". It was not surprising therefore that Marseille had its own commune (see box, p.55) when the Parisians took up arms.

1815	1830	1834
Napoleon defeated at Waterloo; monarchy re-established.	Frédéric Mistral, the writer largely responsible for re-establishing a Provençal identity, is born near St-Rémy.	Cholera sweeps Provence; Jean Giono later records its impact on his native Manosque in *A Horseman On The Roof*.

Honoré **Daumier**, the Marseillais caricaturist and fervent republican, was the great illustrator of both the 1851 and the 1871 events. In the middle of the century the **Marseille school of painting** developed under the influence of foreign travel and Orientalism, attracting such artists as Puvis de Chavannes and Félix Ziem. Provence's greatest native artist, **Cézanne**, though living in Paris from the 1860s to the 1880s, spent a few months of every year in his home town of Aix, or in Marseille and L'Estaque. He was sometimes accompanied by his childhood friend **Zola**, and by **Renoir**, whom he introduced to this coast. Meanwhile **Van Gogh** travelled south to Arles, and briefly persuaded **Gauguin** to join him.

Third Republic: 1890–1914

Under the **Third Republic**, the division between inland Provence and the coast and Rhône Valley accentuated. Port activity at Marseille quadrupled with the opening of new trade routes along the Suez Canal and further colonial acquisitions in the Far East. Manufacturing began to play an equal role with commerce. The Rhône Valley orchards were planted on a massive scale, and light industries developed in Aix and elsewhere to export clothes, foodstuffs and paper to the North African colonies. Chemical works in Avignon produced the synthetics that ensured the decline of the traditional industries of the interior – tanning, dyeing, silk and glass. Wine production, meanwhile, was devastated by phylloxera.

An especial area of brilliance was **art**, and painting in particular. A younger generation of artists discovered the Côte d'Azur, while the **Post-Impressionists** and Fauves flocked to St-Tropez in the wake of the ever-hospitable Paul Signac. Matisse, Dufy, Seurat, Dérain, Van Dongen, Bonnard, Braque, Friesz, Marquet, Manguin, Camion, Vlaminck and Vuillard were all intoxicated by the Mediterranean light, the climate and the ease of living. The escape from the rigours of Paris released a massive creative energy and resulted in works that, in addition to their radical innovations, have more *joie de vivre* than those of any other period in French art. Renoir retired to Cagnes for health reasons in 1907; for Matisse, Dufy and Bonnard the Côte d'Azur became their permanent home.

Meanwhile, the **winter tourist season** on the coast was taking off. **Hyères** and **Cannes** had been "discovered" in the first half of the nineteenth century (and Nice even earlier). But increased ease of travel and the temporary restraint of simmering international tensions encouraged aristocratic mobility. The population of **Nice** trebled between 1861 and 1911; luxury trains ran from St Petersburg, Vienna and London; *belle époque* mansions and grand hotels rose along the Riviera seafronts; and gambling, particularly at Monte Carlo, won the patronage of the Prince of Wales, the Emperor Franz Josef and scores of Russian grand-dukes.

The native working class, meanwhile, were forming the first **French Socialist Party**, which had its opening congress in Marseille in 1879. In 1881 Marseille elected the first socialist *député*. By 1892 the municipal councils of Marseille, Toulon, La Ciotat and other industrial towns were in socialist hands. In Aix, however, the old legitimist royalists (those favouring the return of the Bourbons) still held sway.

1846	1856	1871
Chef Auguste Escoffier is born in Villeneuve-Loubet.	Monte Carlo opens its first casino.	Marseille establishes its own commune, in response to events in Paris.

World War I and the interwar years

The battlefields of **World War I** may have seemed far away in northern France and Belgium, but conscription brought the people of Provence into the war. The socialists divided between pacifists and patriots, but when, in 1919, France took part in the attack on the Soviet Union, soldiers, sailors and workers joined forces in Toulon and Marseille to support mutinies on French warships in the Black Sea. The struggle to have the mutineers freed continued well into 1920, the year in which the **French Communist Party** (PCF) was born.

War casualties led to severe depopulation in the already dwindling villages of inland Provence. **Land use** also changed dramatically, from mixed agriculture to a monocrop of vines, to provide the army ration of one litre of wine per soldier per day. Quantity rather than quality was the aim, leaving acre upon acre of unviable vineyards after demobilization. With the growth in tourism, it was easiest to sell the land for construction.

The **tourist industry** recovered fairly quickly from the war. The *Front Populaire* of 1936 introduced paid holidays, encouraging native visitors to the still unspoiled coast. International literati – Somerset Maugham, Katherine Mansfield, Scott and Zelda Fitzgerald, Colette, Anaïs Nin, Gertrude Stein – and a new wave of artists, including Picasso and Cocteau, replaced the defunct grand-dukes.

Marseille during the interwar years saw the emergence of characteristics that have yet to be obliterated. The activities of the fascist *Action Française* led to deaths during a left-wing counter-demonstration in 1925. Modern-style **corruption** snaked its way through the town hall and gangsters on the Chicago model moved in on the vice industries. Elections were rigged; revolvers were used at the ballot box. The increasing popularity of the Communist Party in the city was due to its anti-corruption platform. After the failure of the *Front Populaire* (for which the great majority of Provençaux had voted, electing several Communist *députés*), Marseille saw constant pitched battles between Left and Right.

World War II

France and Britain declared **war on Germany** together on September 3, 1939. The French Maginot line, however, swiftly collapsed, and by June 1940 the Germans controlled Paris and all of northern France. On June 22, Marshall Pétain signed the **armistice with Hitler**, which divided France between the Occupied Zone – the Atlantic coast and north of the Loire – and "unoccupied" Vichy France in the south. Menton and Sospel were occupied by the Italians, to whom the adjoining Roya Valley still belonged.

With the start of the British counteroffensive in 1942, **Vichy France** joined itself with the Allies and was immediately occupied by the Germans. When the port of Toulon was overrun in November, the French navy scuppered its fleet rather than letting it fall into German hands.

Resistance fighters and passive citizens suffered executions, deportations and the wholesale destruction of Le Panier quarter in Marseille (see box, p.53). The **Allied bombings** of 1944 caused high civilian casualties and considerable material damage, particularly to Avignon, Marseille and Toulon. The **liberation** of the two great port cities was aided by armed popular revolt, but the fighting by the local populace was at its most heroic in the Italian sector, in Sospel and its neighbouring villages.

1888	1907	1920s	1936
Following a confrontation with Paul Gauguin in Arles, Vincent Van Gogh cuts off his ear.	The game of *pétanque* is invented in La Ciotat on the Côte d'Azur.	Celebrities including Charlie Chaplin, Maurice Chevalier, F. Scott Fitzgerald and the Prince of Wales flock to the Côte d'Azur.	The *Front Populaire* introduces paid holidays, encouraging French visitors to the coast.

Modern Provence

Before surrendering **Marseille**, the Germans made sure its harbours were blown to bits. In the immediate **postwar years** the task of repairing the damage was compounded by a slump in international trade and passenger traffic. The nationalization of the Suez Canal also hit the city, ending its prime position on world trading routes.

Marseille's solution was to orient its **port** and industry towards the Atlantic and the inland route of the Rhône. The **oil industries** that had developed in the 1920s around the Étang de Berre and Fos were extended. The mouth of the Rhône and the Golfe de Fos became a massive tanker terminal. **Iron and steel works** filled the spaces behind the new Port de Marseille that stretched for 50km beyond the Vieux Port. In the process, the city's population boomed. To meet the urgent demand for housing, badly designed, low-cost, high-rise estates proliferated out from the congested city centre.

While never halted, the depopulation of **inland Provence** was slowed by massive **irrigation and hydroelectric schemes**. The isolated *mas* or farmhouses, positioned wherever there happened to be a spring, were left to ruin or linked to the mains. Orchards, lavender fields and olive groves became larger, competition for early fruit and vegetables fiercer, and the market for luxury foods greater. The rich **Rhône Valley** continued to export fruit, wine and vegetables, while the river was exploited for irrigation and power, both nuclear and hydroelectric, and made navigable for sizeable ships.

After Algeria won back its independence in 1962, hundreds of thousands of French settlers, the **pieds noirs**, returned, bringing a virulent hatred of Arabic-speaking people. At the same time, the government encouraged immigration from its former colonies, North Africa in particular, with the (unkept) promise of well-paid jobs, civil rights and social security. The resulting tensions, not just in Marseille but all along the coast, made perfect fodder for the **parties of the Right**. From being a bastion of socialism at the end of World War II, Provence turned towards intolerance and reaction.

Ethnic tensions and the rise of the Front National

Corruption, waste and incompetence in the region's town halls was a significant element in the 1995 electoral breakthrough of **Jean-Marie Le Pen's neo-fascist Front National** (FN) party. Under the slogan "Priority for the French", by which it meant the "ethnically pure" French, it took control in Orange, Marignane and Toulon. The most important factor was fear, born of a toxic brew of racism, unemployment and high crime rates. In 1998 **internal feuding** split the party into two camps. Ousted members formed the *Mouvement National Républicain* (MNR), headed by Le Pen's former deputy, **Bruno Mégret**.

Le Pen however returned in full force for the 2002 **presidential elections**, with first-round victories in five out of six *départements* in the PACA (Provence, Alpes, Côtes d'Azur) region, soundly defeating both Chirac and Jospin. At about the same time, **ethnic tensions** of other kinds began to manifest themselves, notably among France's Arab and Jewish communities – both the largest of their kind in Europe. However, the **civic unrest** across France during 2005, which saw youths – many, though not all, from deprived ethnic minority backgrounds – clash with police and hundreds of cars torched, was focused on Paris, rather than the south and, perhaps surprisingly, Marseille was relatively unaffected.

1939–1945	**1946**	**1947**
World War II; Paris and northern France occupied by Nazis; the south, ruled at first by the puppet Vichy regime, falls under German occupation in 1942.	Cannes stages its first Festival International du Film; Pablo Picasso at work in Antibes' Château Grimaldi.	Tende and the upper Roya Valley revert from Italy to France.

CRIME, CORRUPTION AND POLITICS

The hidden ties between the Provençal mafia – known as the **milieu** – and the region's town halls date back to the 1920s, but only after the shocking assassination of Hyères' *député*, **Yann Piat**, in 1994 did the demand for a "clean hands" campaign begin in earnest.

Drug trafficking became a major problem in Marseille in the early 1970s as the notorious **French Connection** routed heroin from Turkey to the United States through the port, then controlled by Corsican mobsters. At the same time, regional politics were ripe for exploitation. **Municipal fiefdoms** evolved, offering opportunities for patronage, nepotism and corruption, along with the financial muscle that, until all too recently, ensured incumbents a more-or-less permanent position.

In 1982, Graham Greene accused Nice's police and judiciary of protecting organized crime; he claimed he slept with a gun under his pillow after he detailed the corruption in *J'Accuse* (which was banned in France). The late **Jacques Médecin**, who succeeded his father as mayor of Nice in 1966, controlled public life in the city until his downfall in 1990 for political fraud and tax evasion; only when he fled to Uruguay were his mafioso connections finally discussed. Despite this, most Niçois gladly supported his sister Géneviève Assemat-Médecin as his successor; and those who didn't backed his daughter, Martine Cantinchi-Médecin, a Le Pen supporter. Finally extradited in 1994, Médecin served a short prison term and used his popularity to back the successful candidate in the 1995 municipal elections – **Jacques Peyrat**, a close friend of Le Pen and former member of the *Front National*. Peyrat remained in power until 2008, when he lost the municipal elections to **Christian Estrosi** of the centre-right UMP party. Following his acquittal on corruption charges in 2012, however, he was as, this book went to press, promising to run for re-election in 2014.

Toulon was another classic fiefdom, run for four decades by **Maurice Arreckx** and his clique of friends with their underworld connections, until he was put away when financial scandals finally came to light. His successor, and former director of finances, tried in vain to win back the voters but merely ran up more debts and lost to the *Front National* in 1995. Arreckx was sentenced to prison on two separate occasions (in 1997 and 2000), before dying of cancer in 2001. Prior to his death, investigators had found several Swiss bank accounts, where some of the money paid to Arreckx's campaign fund in return for a major construction contract was secreted.

François Léotard, the right-wing mayor of Fréjus, who held cabinet office (under Chirac in the late 1980s) and a seat in the *Assemblée Nationale*, was investigated for financial irregularities, but the case eventually ran out of time and the charges were dropped. Cannes' mayor, **Michel Mouillot**, was debarred from public office for five years and given a fifteen-month suspended sentence in 1989, then won his appeal and returned to the town hall only to be given an eighteen-month suspended sentence in 1996. **Pierre Rinaldi**, mayor of **Digne**, was investigated for fraud; **Jean-Pierre Lafond**, mayor of **La Ciotat**, for unwarranted interference; two successive mayors of **La Seyne** for corruption and abuse of patronage … and so the list goes on.

Meanwhile, though the French Connection was ultimately smashed, **organized crime** continued to flourish, controlled both by the Italian mafia and – increasingly – by eastern European gangs. The faces and nationalities may change, but the criminals of the Côte d'Azur preserve their reputation for resourcefulness. The activities of the newer arrivals have included boat-jacking: yachts stolen to order, and often used for drug trafficking and smuggling illegal immigrants before being resold in the ports of the Black Sea.

1951	1953	1962
Matisse's final masterpiece, the Chapelle du Rosaire, is dedicated in Vence.	Roger Vadim films *Et Dieu Crea La Femme*, introducing St-Tropez, and Brigitte Bardot, to the world.	Following Algerian independence, former French settlers and North Africans add to the volatile mix of Marseille and other cities.

After the region's most prominent FN mayor, Jacques Bompard of Orange, defected to the rival *Mouvement pour la France* (MPF) in 2005, the FN tide seemed to be ebbing. The **elections of 2012** however showed that the far right remained a force to be reckoned with in Provence; neighbouring districts in the Vaucluse elected both Le Pen's 22-year-old granddaughter Marion Maréchal-Le Pen, and Jacques Bompard, nominally independent but with FN support, to the National Assembly.

Mass tourism and the environment

A crucial factor in the postwar history of Provence has been the rise of **mass tourism**. Since the 1960s, the number of visitors to the Côte d'Azur has grown beyond what – in any sane sense – could be considered manageable proportions. By the mid-1970s the coast had become a nearly uninterrupted wall of concrete, hosting eight million visitors a year. Agricultural land, save for a few profitable vineyards, was transformed into campsites, hotels and holiday housing. **Property speculation** and construction became the dominant economic activities, while the flaunting of planning laws and the ever-increasing threat to the **environment** were ignored.

When **Brigitte Bardot** complained in the 1980s that her beloved **St-Tropez** was becoming a mire of human detritus, the media saw it as a sexy summer story. Then **ecologists** began to warn that the Mediterranean's principal oxygenating sea grasses were disappearing. A non-native toxic algae, *Caulerpa taxifolia*, has spread from the Côte d'Azur around the Mediterranean, obliterating sea grasses and replacing them with largely sterile algal beds.

Urban expansion on the coast

Since the first three postwar decades, when sun-worshipping set the region's tone, different forces have been at work. While summer tourism exacted a heavy toll, a new type of visitor and resident has also become prevalent: the expense-account delegate to **business conferences** and the well-paid employee of **multinational firms**. Towns like Nice and Cannes led the way in attracting the former, while the business park of **Sophia-Antipolis** north of Antibes showed how easily information-technology firms could be persuaded to relocate to the beautiful Côte d'Azur hinterland. The result is a further erosion of Provençal identity and greater pressure on the environment. Rather than countering the seasonal imbalance of tourism, business visitors have made consumption and congestion a year-round factor.

The money from business services and industry on the Riviera now outstrips income from tourism. In the big cities, the distinctive Marseillais and Niçois identities have endured, but elsewhere along the coast, continuities with the past have become ever harder to detect.

Inland Provence

Inland Provence has undergone a parallel transformation – more social than physical, with less property development but a great deal of property price inflation, as high-salaried professionals from all over northern Europe buy their place in the sun. The Luberon in particular is especially prized as **second-home territory**.

While the influx rescued some villages from extinction, many are now lifeless out of season. In the Alpine valleys, the growth of ski resorts reversed centuries-old population

1967	**1986**	**1989**
British cyclist Tom Simpson dies on Mont Ventoux, during the Tour de France.	Film director Claude Berri releases *Jean de Florette* and *Manon des Sources*, based on the books by Marcel Pagnol, themselves novelizations of his own 1952 movie, *Manon des Sources*.	Peter Mayle publishes *A Year in Provence*, inspiring a new wave of British visitors to explore the region.

decline, and the resultant damage to trees, soil and habitats has in part been offset by the creation of the **Parc National du Mercantour**, which has saved several Alpine animal and plant species.

Meanwhile, those *paysans* who still keep goats and bees, a few vines and a vegetable plot, have reached pensionable age. The cheeses and honey, the vegetables, olive oil and wine (unless it's AOP) must compete with Spanish, Italian and Greek produce, from land that doesn't have the ludicrously high values of Provence. The emergence of successful international companies such as l'Occitane en Provence and Oliviers & Co, however, offers one pointer to a viable economic future, trading on the magic of a Provençal image to target upmarket consumers, with prices to match.

Transport mania

Fast access to the Côte d'Azur has long obsessed planners in Paris. The **TGV** was extended to Marseille in 2001, and is due to be extended in turn as far as Nice, following a coastal route via Toulon. Increasing accessibility, however, serves to exacerbate existing transport problems within Provence. An attenuated but densely populated linear conurbation without a proper regional mass transportation system, the Riviera is particularly badly affected. Heavy traffic and gridlocks are the norm on the roads, with the temptation to drive everywhere promoted by the suburban and commercial sprawl that has long since eliminated any clear distinction between individual coastal towns. At least things have somewhat improved in Marseille and Nice, with the opening of new **tramways** and **public bike hire** schemes.

1994	2001	2005	2011
Following extradition from Uruguay, former Nice mayor Jacques Médecin is convicted of corruption.	The high-speed TGV train line reaches Marseille.	Prince Albert II succeeds his father Prince Rainier in Monaco.	Parc National des Calanques created near Marseilles.

Books

In addition to their seminal role in French history and the cultural and artistic life of Europe, Provence and the Côte d'Azur have inspired many modern English, American and French writers, whether indulging in the high life like F. Scott Fitzgerald, slumming it with the bohemians like Anaïs Nin, or trying to regain their health like Katherine Mansfield. The two best-known Provençal writers of the twentieth century, Jean Giono and Marcel Pagnol, chronicled peasant life in inland Provence. Titles marked with the ★ symbol are particularly recommended.

FICTION

★ **Sybille Bedford** *Jigsaw: an Unsentimental Education.* Bedford's own precarious childhood on the Côte d'Azur provides rich source material for her evocative novel, which roams between Germany, France and London and depicts the bohemian life of 1930s Sanary-sur-Mer in delicious detail. Sanary also features in Bedford's autobiographical memoir *Quicksands.*

Alexandre Dumas *The Count of Monte Cristo.* A runaway success when initially serialized during the 1840s, Dumas' long, engrossing tale of the prisoner of the Île d'If, who plots escape and revenge on those who wronged him, has never lost its grip on the public imagination.

Lawrence Durrell *The Avignon Quintet.* Five interlinked novels that offer a creative and romantic vision of a fast-disappearing way of life, both rural and urban, in Provence.

★ **F. Scott Fitzgerald** *Tender is the Night.* Glitter is interwoven with darkness in this dense but beautifully written tale of mental illness among the millionaire smart set, played out against the glamorous backdrop of the Riviera in the interwar years.

★ **Jean Giono** *The Horseman on the Roof.* This gripping and extraordinary novel of one man's odyssey through a Provence ravaged by a nineteenth-century cholera epidemic has a very contemporary, post-apocalyptic feel. Giono's other works, such as *To the Slaughterhouse, Two Riders of the Storm, Blue Boy* and *The Man Who Planted Trees* are also recommended.

Sébastien Japrisot *One Deadly Summer.* Suspenseful modern novel of a girl's revenge; noir to the nth degree.

★ **Marcel Pagnol** *The Water of the Hills: Jean de Florette* and *Manon of the Springs.* This rich evocation of hardship, intrigue and family vengeance in rural Provence in the early twentieth century has a humour, warmth and depth lacking from Claude Berri's admittedly ravishing 1986 films.

Patrick Süskind *Perfume.* Hugely successful story of an orphan born with no smell, who gravitates to Grasse and becomes both a master *parfumier* and a mass murderer.

Émile Zola *The Masterpiece.* Born in Aix-en-Provence, Zola draws on his own life and that of his boyhood friend Paul Cézanne to tell the contrasting stories of a successful novelist and an artist obsessed with the creation of one great canvas. The novel offended Cézanne and ended their friendship.

HISTORY, SOCIETY AND POLITICS

John Ardagh *France in the New Century: Portrait of a Changing Society.* This detailed journalistic survey of modern France tries to provide a comprehensive overlook, but gets rather too drawn into party politics and statistics.

Mary Blume *Côte d'Azur: Inventing the French Riviera.* This 1990s attempt to analyse the myth only reconfirmed it, mainly because all the people interviewed had a stake in maintaining the image of the Côte as a cultured millionaires' dreamland. Great black-and-white photos, though.

Robin Briggs *Early Modern France, 1560–1715.* Readable account of the period when the French state started to assert control over the whole country. Strong perspectives on the provinces, including coverage of the Marseille rebellion of 1658.

James Bromwich *The Roman Remains of Southern France.* A comprehensive guide: detailed, well-illustrated and approachable. In addition to accounts of well-known sites, it will lead you off the map to all sorts of discoveries.

Alfred Cobban *A History of Modern France.* Very complete, three-volume political, social and economic history, from Louis XIV to de Gaulle.

Margaret Crosland *Sade's Wife.* An expert on Provence's most notorious resident examines how Renée-Pélagie de Montreuil coped with being married to the Marquis de Sade.

FX Emmanuelli *Histoire de la Provence*. Huge, well-illustrated tome by a group of French academics, which covers the province in as much detail as anyone could conceivably want.

Lawrence Durrell *Caesar's Vast Ghost*. Durrell long promised to write a huge and all-encompassing book about Provence; this much slimmer volume, published just before his death, is probably an easier read, with entertaining essays on, for example, bulls and Arles.

★ **John Noone** *The Man Behind the Iron Mask*. Fascinating enquiry into the mythical or otherwise prisoner of Ste-Marguerite Fort on the Îles de Lérins, immortalized by Alexander Dumas.

Jim Ring *Riviera: The Rise and Fall of the Côte d'Azur*. Highly readable social history of the French Riviera and of the many nationalities who have shaped the region's history, culture and architecture.

Graham Robb *The Discovery of France*. Captivating study of the evolution and "civilization" of France since the Revolution, which makes a superb antidote to conventional narratives of kings and state affairs.

Simon Schama *Citizens*. A fascinating, accessible treatment of the history of the Revolution, with a fast-moving narrative and a reappraisal of the customary view of a stagnant, unchanging nobility in the years preceding the uprising.

Laurence Wylie *Village in the Vaucluse*. Sociological study of Roussillon, full of interesting insights into Provençal village life in the postwar years.

★ **Theodore Zeldin** *France 1845–1945*. Five thematic volumes on French history.

TRAVEL

Carol Drinkwater *The Olive Farm*. Soft-focus memoir of the joys of expatriate life in rural Provence, written by a well-known British actress.

★ **M.F.K. Fisher** *Two Towns in Provence*. Evocative memoirs of life in Aix-en-Provence and Marseille during the 1950s and 1960s.

William Fotheringham *Put Me Back on My Bike: In Search of Tom Simpson*. An in-depth study of Simpson's life as a cyclist, leading up to his tragic death on Mont Ventoux.

Peter Mayle *A Year in Provence*. Though it's often blamed for contributing to the anglicization of rural Provence, there's really nothing to dislike about this bestselling memoir. A month-by-month account of the charms and frustrations of moving into an old Provençal farmhouse, it entertainingly covers everything from tips for wooing fickle French contractors to handicapping goat races.

ART AND ARTISTS

★ **Martin Bailey (ed)** *Van Gogh: Letters from Provence*. Attractively produced in full colour – very *dippable* and very good value.

Martin Gayford *The Yellow House*. A tense and absorbing account of the nine extraordinary weeks in 1888 when Vincent van Gogh and Paul Gauguin shared a tiny house in Arles.

Françoise Gilot *Matisse & Picasso: A Friendship in Art*. A fascinating subject – two more different men in life and art would be hard to find.

D. and M. Johnson *The Age of Illusion*. Links French art and politics in the interwar years, featuring Provençal works by Le Corbusier, Chagall and Picasso.

Jacques Henri Lartigue *Diary of a Century*. Book of pictures by a great photographer from the day he was given a camera in 1901 through to the 1970s. Contains wonderful scenes of aristocratic leisure and Côte d'Azur beaches.

Sarah Whitfield *Fauvism*. Good introduction to a movement that encompassed Côte d'Azur and Riviera artists Matisse, Dufy and Van Dongen.

FOOD AND DRINK

Alain Ducasse *Flavours of France*. Celebrity cookbook that follows Ducasse from the kitchens of the Louis XV restaurant in Monte Carlo to La Bastide de Moustiers.

Hubrecht Duijker *Touring in Wine Country: Provence*. Guide to the top vineyards and wine cellars of Provence.

Kenneth James *Escoffier: the King of Chefs*. Biography of the famous chef who started his career on the Côte d'Azur.

Richard Olney *Lulu's Provençal Table*. Classic Provençal recipes and interesting commentary from Lulu Peyraud, proprietor of the Domaine Tempier vineyard in Bandol. Great black-and-white photos.

Roger Vergé *Cuisine of the Sun*. The classic cookbook of modern Provençal cuisine, from the legendary chef of the *Moulin de Mougins*.

Patricia Wells *The Provence Cookbook*. More than 200 recipes rooted in the *terroir*, plus vignettes on suppliers and markets, and wine-pairing suggestions.

BOTANY

W. Lippert *Fleurs de Haute Montagne*. Palm-sized guide to flowers of the Haute Montagne, with colour photos and botanical names; available from French bookshops in the trekking areas..

French

French can be a deceptively familiar language because of the number of words and structures it shares with English. Despite this, it's far from easy, though the bare essentials are not difficult to master and can make all the difference. Even just saying "Bonjour, Madame/Monsieur" and then gesticulating will usually get you a smile and helpful service. People working in tourist offices, campsites, hotels and so on almost always speak English and tend to use it if you're struggling to speak French – be grateful, not insulted.

On the Côte d'Azur you can get by without knowing a word of French, with menus printed in at least four languages, and half the people you meet fellow foreigners. In Nice, Sisteron and the Roya Valley a knowledge of Italian would provide a common language with many of the natives. But if you can hold your own in French – however imperfectly – speak away and your audience will warm to you.

Provençal and accents

The one language you don't have to learn – unless you want to understand the meaning of the names of streets, restaurants or cafés – is **Provençal**. Itself a dialect of the *langue d'oc* (Occitan), it evolved into different dialects in Provence, so that the languages spoken in Nice, in the Alps, on the coast and in the Rhône Valley, though mutually comprehensible, were not precisely the same. In the mid-nineteenth century the *Félibrige* movement established a standard literary form in an attempt to revive the language. But by the time Frédéric Mistral won the Nobel Prize in 1904 for his poem *Mirèio*, Provençal had already been superseded by French in ordinary life.

Two hundred years ago everybody spoke Provençal, whether they were counts, shipyard workers or peasants. Today you might (if you're lucky) hear it spoken by the older generation in some of the remoter villages. It just survives as a literary language: it can be studied at school and university and there are columns in Provençal in some newspapers. But unlike Breton or Occitan proper, it has never been the fuel of a separatist movement.

The French that people speak in Provence has, however, a very marked **accent**. It's much less nasal than northern French, words are not run together to quite the same extent, and there's a distinctive sound for the endings – *in*, *-en*, and for *vin*, and so on, that is more like *ung*.

Pronunciation

Consonants are much as in English, except that: "*ch*" is always sh, "*c*" is s, "*h*" is silent, "*th*" is the same as t, "*ll*" is like the y in "yes", "*w*" is v, and "*r*" is growled (or rolled). One easy rule to remember is that consonants at the ends of words are usually silent. *Pas plus tard* (not later) is thus pronounced "pa-plu-tarr". But when the following word begins with a vowel, you run the two together: *pas après* (not after) becomes "pazaprey". **Vowels** are the hardest sounds to get right. Roughly:

a	as in hat	i	as in machine
e	as in get	o	as in hot
é	between get and gate	o, au	as in over
è	between get and gut	ou	as in food
eu	like the u in hurt	u	as in a pursed-lip version of use

More awkward are the **combinations** *in/im, en/em, an/am, on/om, un/um* at the ends of words, or followed by consonants other than norm. Again, roughly:

in/im	like the an in anxious	**on/om**	like the don in Doncaster
an/am, en/em	like the don in Doncaster		said by someone with a
	when said with a nasal		heavy cold
	accent	**un/um**	like the u in understand

LEARNING MATERIALS

French Dictionary Phrasebook (Rough Guides). Mini dictionary-style phrasebook with both English–French and French–English sections, along with cultural tips for tricky situations and a menu reader.

Get By In French (BBC Publications). Phrasebook and cassette. A good stepping stone before tackling a complete course.

Mini French Dictionary (Harrap/Larousse). French–English and English–French, plus a brief grammar and pronunciation guide.

Breakthrough French (Palgrave/McGraw Hill; book and two cassettes). An excellent teach-yourself course.

Pardon My French! Pocket French Slang Dictionary (UK Harrap). The key to understanding everyday French.

A Comprehensive French Grammar (Blackwell). Easy-to-follow reference grammar.

À Vous La France; France Extra; France-Parler (BBC Publications; EMC Paradigm). Comprising a book and two cassettes, these BBC radio courses run from beginner's to fairly advanced French.

Basic words and phrases

French nouns are divided into masculine and feminine. This causes difficulties with adjectives, whose endings have to change to suit the gender of the nouns they qualify. If you know some grammar, you will know what to do. If not, stick to the masculine form, which is the simplest – it's what we have done in this glossary.

ESSENTIALS

today	aujourd'hui	**that one**	cela
yesterday	hier	**open**	ouvert
tomorrow	demain	**closed**	fermé
in the morning	le matin	**big**	grand
in the afternoon	l'après-midi	**small**	petit
in the evening	le soir	**more**	plus
now	maintenant	**less**	moins
later	plus tard	**a little**	un peu
at one o'clock	à une heure	**a lot**	beaucoup
at three o'clock	à trois heures	**cheap**	bon marché
at ten-thirty	à dix heures et demie	**expensive**	cher
at midday	à midi	**good**	bon
man	un homme	**bad**	mauvais
woman	une femme	**hot**	chaud
here	ici	**cold**	froid
there	là	**with**	avec
this one	ceci	**without**	sans

TALKING TO PEOPLE

When addressing people you should always use *Monsieur* for a man, *Madame* for a woman, *Mademoiselle* for a girl. Plain *bonjour* by itself is not enough. This isn't as formal as it seems, and it has its uses when you've forgotten someone's name or want to attract someone's attention.

Excuse me	Pardon	**How do you say it**	Comment ça se dit
Do you speak English?	Vous parlez anglais?	**in French?**	en français?

What's your name?	Comment vous appelez-vous?	please	s'il vous plaît
My name is...	Je m'appelle...	thank you	merci
I'm ...	Je suis	hello	bonjour
...English	anglais[e]	goodbye	au revoir
...Irish	irlandais[e]	good morning/afternoon	bonjour
...Scottish	écossais[e]	good evening	bonsoir
...Welsh	gallois[e]	good night	bonne nuit
...American	américain[e]	How are you?	Comment allez-vous? /Ça va?
...Australian	australien[ne]		
...Canadian	canadien[ne]	Fine, thanks	Très bien, merci
...a New Zealander	néo-zélandais[e]	I don't know	Je ne sais pas
yes	oui	Let's go	Allons-y
no	non	See you tomorrow	À demain
I understand	Je comprends	See you soon	À bientôt
I don't understand	Je ne comprends pas	Sorry	Pardon, Madame /Excusez-moi
Can you speak slower?	S'il vous plaît, parlez moins vite	Leave me alone! (aggressive)	Fichez-moi la paix!
OK/agreed	d'accord	Please help me	Aidez-moi, s'il vous plaît

FINDING THE WAY

bus	autobus/bus/car	on foot	à pied
bus station	gare routière	Where are you going?	Vous allez où?
bus stop	arrêt	I'm going to...	Je vais à...
car	voiture	I want to get off at...	Je voudrais descendre à...
train/taxi/ferry	train/taxi/ferry		
boat	bateau	the road to...	la route pour...
plane	avion	near	près/pas loin
train station	gare (SNCF)	far	loin
platform	quai	left	à gauche
What time does it leave?	Il part à quelle heure?	right	à droite
What time does it arrive?	Il arrive à quelle heure?	straight on	tout droit
a ticket to...	un billet pour...	on the other side of	à l'autre côté de
single ticket	aller simple	on the corner of	à l'angle de
return ticket	aller retour	next to	à côté de
validate your ticket	compostez votre billet	behind	derrière
valid for	valable pour	in front of	devant
ticket office	vente de billets	before	avant
how many kilometres?	combien de kilomètres?	after	après
how many hours?	combien d'heures?	under	sous
hitchhiking	autostop	to cross	traverser
		bridge	pont

QUESTIONS AND REQUESTS

The simplest way of asking a question is to start with *s'il vous plaît* (please), then name the thing you want in an interrogative tone of voice. For example:

Where is there a bakery?	S'il vous plaît, la boulangerie?	We'd like a room for two	S'il vous plaît, une chambre pour deux
Which way is it to the Eiffel Tower?	S'il vous plaît, la route pour la tour Eiffel?	Can I have a kilo of oranges?	S'il vous plaît, un kilo d'oranges?

QUESTION WORDS

where?	où?	when?	quand?
how?	comment?	why?	pourquoi?
how many/ how much?	combien?	at what time?	à quelle heure?
		what is/which is?	quel est?

ACCOMMODATION

a room for one/two people	une chambre pour un/deux personnes	blankets	couvertures
a double bed	un lit double	quiet	calme
a room with a shower	une chambre avec douche	noisy	bruyant
		hot water	eau chaude
a room with a bath	une chambre avec salle de bain	cold water	eau froide
for one/two/three nights	pour un/deux/trois nuits	Is breakfast included?	Est-ce que le petit déjeuner est compris?
Can I see it?	Je peux la voir?	I would like breakfast	Je voudrais prendre le petit déjeuner
a room on the courtyard	une chambre sur la cour		
a room over the street	une chambre sur la rue	I don't want breakfast	Je ne veux pas de petit déjeuner
first floor	premier étage		
second floor	deuxième étage	Can we camp here?	On peut camper ici?
with a view	avec vue	campsite	un camping/terrain de camping
key	clef		
to iron	repasser	tent	une tente
do laundry	faire la lessive	tent space	un emplacement
sheets	draps	youth hostel	auberge de jeunesse

DRIVING

service station	garage	put air in the tyres	gonfler les pneus
service	service	battery	batterie
to park the car	garer la voiture	the battery is dead	la batterie est morte
car park	un parking	plugs	bougies
no parking	défense de stationner/ stationnement interdit	to break down	tomber en panne
		petrol can	bidon
petrol station	station essence/station service	insurance	assurance
		green card	carte verte
fuel	essence	traffic lights	feux
(to) fill it up	faire le plein	red light	feu rouge
oil	huile	green light	feu vert
air line	ligne à air		

HEALTH MATTERS

doctor	médecin	stomach ache	mal à l'estomac
I don't feel well	Je ne me sens pas bien	period	règles
medicines	médicaments	pain	douleur
prescription	ordonnance	it hurts	ça fait mal
I feel sick	Je suis malade	chemist	pharmacie
I have a headache	J'ai mal à la tête	hospital	hôpital

OTHER NEEDS

bakery	boulangerie	camping gas	camping gaz
food shop	alimentation	tobacconist	tabac
supermarket	supermarché	stamps	timbres
to eat	manger	bank	banque
to drink	boire	money	argent

toilets	toilettes	**cinema**	cinéma
police	police	**theatre**	théâtre
telephone	téléphone	**to reserve/book**	réserver

NUMBERS

1	un	**21**	vingt-et-un
2	deux	**22**	vingt-deux
3	trois	**30**	trente
4	quatre	**40**	quarante
5	cinq	**50**	cinquante
6	six	**60**	soixante
7	sept	**70**	soixante-dix
8	huit	**75**	soixante-quinze
9	neuf	**80**	quatre-vingts
10	dix	**90**	quatre-vingt-dix
11	onze	**95**	quatre-vingt-quinze
12	douze	**100**	cent
13	treize	**101**	cent-et-un
14	quatorze	**200**	deux cents
15	quinze	**300**	trois cents
16	seize	**500**	cinq cents
17	dix-sept	**1000**	mille
18	dix-huit	**2000**	deux milles
19	dix-neuf	**5000**	cinq milles
20	vingt	**1,000,000**	un million

DAYS AND DATES

January	janvier	**Monday**	lundi
February	février	**Tuesday**	mardi
March	mars	**Wednesday**	mercredi
April	avril	**Thursday**	jeudi
May	mai	**Friday**	vendredi
June	juin	**Saturday**	samedi
July	juillet	**August 1**	le premier août
August	août	**March 2**	le deux mars
September	septembre	**July 14**	le quatorze juillet
October	octobre	**November 23**	le vingt-trois novembre
November	novembre	**1999**	dix-neuf-cent-quatre-vingt-dix-neuf
December	décembre		
Sunday	dimanche	**2010**	deux-mille-dix

Food and drink terms

When in a restaurant or café always call the waiter or waitress *Monsieur* or *Madame* (*Mademoiselle* if a young woman). Never use *garçon*, no matter what you've been taught at school.

BASIC TERMS

pain	bread	**poivre**	pepper
beurre	butter	**sel**	salt
céréales	cereal	**sucre**	sugar
lait	milk	**vinaigre**	vinegar
huile	oil	**moutarde**	mustard
confiture	jam	**bouteille**	bottle

verre	glass	cuit	cooked
fourchette	fork	cru	raw
couteau	knife	emballé	wrapped
cuillère	spoon	Sur place ou à emporter?	Eat in or take away?
cure-dent	toothpick	à emporter	takeaway
table	table	fumé	smoked
l'addition	bill	falé	salted/spicy
offert/Gratuit	free	fucré	sweet
(re)chauffé	(re)heated		

SNACKS (CASSE-CROÛTE)

un sandwich/une baguette	a sandwich	nature/aux fines herbes	plain/with herbs
...au jambon/fromage	...with ham/cheese	au fromage	with cheese
...au jambon beurre	...with ham & butter	croque-monsieur	grilled cheese and ham sandwich
...fromage beurre	...cheese & butter		
...au pâté (de campagne)	...with pâté (country-style)	croque-madame	grilled cheese, ham or bacon and fried egg sandwich
oeufs...	eggs...		
au plat(s)	fried eggs	pan bagnat	bread roll with egg, olives, salad, tuna, anchovies and olive oil
à la coque	boiled eggs		
durs	hard-boiled eggs		
brouillés	scrambled eggs	tartine	buttered bread or open sandwich
poché	poached eggs		
omelette...	omelette...		

SOUPS (SOUPES) AND STARTERS (HORS D'ŒUVRES)

bisque	shellfish soup	potage	thick vegetable soup
baudroie	fish soup with vegetables, garlic and herbs	rouille	red pepper, garlic and saffron mayonnaise served with fish soup
bouillabaisse	soup with five fish and other bits to dip		
bouillon	broth or stock	velouté	thick soup, usually fish or poultry
bourride	thick fish soup with garlic, onions and tomatoes	assiette anglaise	plate of cold meats
		crudités	raw vegetables with dressings
consommé	clear soup		
pistou	parmesan, basil and garlic paste or cream added to soup	hors d'œuvres variés	combination of the above plus smoked or marinated fish

PASTA (PÂTES), PANCAKES (CRÊPES) AND FLANS (TARTES)

pâtes fraîches	fresh pasta	socca	thin chickpea flour pancake
nouilles	noodles		
raviolis	pasta parcels of meat or chard, a Provençal, not Italian, invention	panisse	thick chickpea flour pancake
		pissaladière	tart of fried onions with anchovies and black olives
crêpe au sucre/aux œufs	pancake with sugar/eggs		

FISH (POISSON), SEAFOOD (FRUITS DE MER) AND SHELLFISH (CRUSTACES OR COQUILLAGES)

aiglefin	small haddock or fresh cod	araignée de mer	spider fish
anchois	anchovies	baudroie	monkfish or anglerfish
amande de mer	small sweet-tasting shellfish	barbue	brill
		bigourneau	periwinkle
anguilles	eels	brème	bream

bulot	whelk	rouget	red mullet
cabillaud	cod	rouquier	Mediterranean eel
calmar	squid	St-Pierre	John Dory
carrelet	plaice	saumon	salmon
chapon de mer	Mediterranean fish (related to Scorpion fish)	sole	sole
		telline	tiny clam
claire	type of oyster	thon	tuna
colin	hake	truite	trout
congre	conger eel	turbot	turbot
coques	cockles	violet	sea squirt
coquilles St-Jacques	scallops		
		FISH TERMS	
crabe	crab	aïoli	garlic mayonnaise/ or the dish when served with salt cod and vegetables
crevettes grises	shrimp		
crevettes roses	prawns		
daurade	sea bream	anchoïade	anchovy paste or sauce
écrevisse	freshwater crayfish	arête	fish bone
éperlan	smelt or whitebait	assiette de pêcheur	assorted fish
escargots	snails	Béarnaise	sauce of egg yolks, white wine, shallots and vinegar
favou(ille)	tiny crab		
flétan	halibut		
friture	assorted fried fish	beignets	fritters
gambas	king prawns	bonne femme	with mushroom, parsley, potato and shallots
girelle	type of crab		
grenouilles (cuisses de)	frogs' (legs)	brandade	crushed cod with olive oil
grondin	red gurnard	colbert	fried in egg with bread crumbs
hareng	herring		
homard	lobster	croûtons	toasted bread, often rubbed with garlic, to dip or drop in fish soups
huîtres	oysters		
langouste	spiny lobster		
langoustines	saltwater crayfish (scampi)	darne	fillet or steak
		en papillote	cooked in foil
limande	lemon sole	estocaficada	stockfish stew with tomatoes, olives, peppers, garlic and onions
lotte de mer	monkfish		
loup de mer	sea bass		
maquereau	mackerel		
merlan	whiting	la douzaine	a dozen
morue	salt cod	frit	fried
moules (marinière)	Mussels (with shallots in white wine sauce)	friture	deep-fried small fish
		fumé	smoked
oursin	sea urchin	fumet	fish stock
pageot	sea bream	gelée	aspic
palourdes	clams	gigot de mer	baked fish pieces, usually monkfish
poissons de roche	fish from shoreline rocks		
poulpe	octopus	goujon	several types of small fish, also deep-fried pieces of larger fish coated in breadcrumbs
poutine	small river fish		
praires	small clams		
paie	skate		
rascasse	scorpion fish		

MEAT (VIANDE) AND POULTRY (VOLAILLE)

Agneau (de pré-salé)	lamb (grazed on salt marshes)	bœuf	beef
		bifteck	steak
andouille, andouillette	tripe sausage	boudin blanc	sausage of white meats

boudin noir	black pudding
caille	quail
canard	duck
caneton	duckling
cervelle	brains
châteaubriand	porterhouse steak
cheval	horse meat
contrefilet	sirloin roast
coquelet	cockerel
dinde, dindon, dindonneau	turkey of different ages and genders
entrecôte	ribsteak
faux filet	sirloin steak
fricadelles	meatballs
foie	liver
foie gras	fattened (duck/goose) liver
gésier	gizzard
magret de canard	duck breast
gibier	game
graisse	fat
jambon	ham
langue	tongue
lapin, lapereau	rabbit, young rabbit
lard, lardons	bacon, diced bacon
lièvre	hare
merguez	spicy, red sausage
mouton	mutton
museau de veau	calf's muzzle
oie	goose
os	bone
pintade	guinea fowl
porc, pieds de porc	pork, pig's trotters
poulet	chicken
poussin	baby chicken
ris	sweetbreads
rognons	kidneys
rognons blancs	testicles
sanglier	wild boar
saucisson	dried sausage
steack	steak
taureau/Toro	bull meat
tête de veau	calf's head (in jelly)
tournedos	thick slices of fillet
travers de porc	spare ribs
tripes	tripe
veau	veal
venaison	venison

MEAT AND POULTRY DISHES

aïado	roast shoulder of lamb, stuffed with garlic and other ingredients
bœuf à la gardane	beef or bull meat stew with carrots, celery, onions, garlic and black olives, served with rice
canard à l'orange	roast duck with an orange-and-wine sauce
canard périgourdin	roast duck with prunes, pâté de foie gras and truffles
cassoulet	a casserole of beans and meat
choucroute	pickled cabbage with peppercorns, sausages, bacon and salami
coq au vin	chicken cooked until it falls off the bone with wine, onions, and mushrooms
gigot (d'agneau)	leg (of lamb)
grillade	grilled meat
hâchis	chopped meat or mince hamburger
pieds et paquets	mutton or pork tripe and trotters
steak au poivre (vert/rouge)	steak in a black (green/red) peppercorn sauce
steak tartare	raw chopped beef, topped with a raw egg yolk

MEAT AND POULTRY TERMS

blanquette, civet, daube, estouffade, hochepôt, navarin and ragoût	types of stew
aile	wing
blanc	breast or white meat
broche	spit-roasted
brochette	kebab
carré	best end of neck, chop or cutlet
civit	game stew
confit	meat preserve
côte	chop, cutlet or rib
cou	neck
cuisse	thigh or leg
èpaule	shoulder
mariné	marinated
médaillon	round piece
pavé	thick slice
en croûte	in pastry
farci	stuffed
au feu de bois	cooked over wood fire

au four	baked	bonne femme	with mushroom, bacon,
garni	with vegetables		potato and onions
grillé	grilled	bordelaise	in a red wine, shallots and
marmite	casserole		bone-marrow sauce
mijoté	stewed	boulangère	baked with potatoes and
rôti	roast		onions
sauté	lightly cooked in butter	bourgeoise	with carrots, onions,
			bacon, celery and
FOR STEAKS			braised lettuce
bleu	almost raw	chasseur	white wine, mushrooms
saignant	rare		and shallots
à point	medium	chatêlaine	with artichoke hearts and
bien cuit	well done		chestnut purée
très bien cuit	very well cooked	diable	strong mustard seasoning
		forestière	with bacon and
GARNISHES AND SAUCES			mushroom
américaine	white wine, Cognac and	fricassée	rich, creamy sauce
	tomato	galantine	cold dish of meat in aspic
arlésienne	with tomatoes, onions,	mornay	cheese sauce
	aubergines, potatoes	pays d'Auge	cream and cider
	and rice	piquante	gherkins or capers,
au porto	in port		vinegar and shallots
auvergnat	with cabbage, sausage	provençale	tomatoes, garlic, olive oil
	and bacon		and herbs
beurre blanc	sauce of white wine and	véronique	grapes, wine and cream
	shallots, with butter		

VEGETABLES (LÉGUMES), HERBS (HERBES) AND SPICES (ÉPICES), ETC

ail	garlic	fenouil	fennel
anis	aniseed	férigoule	thyme (in Provençal)
artichaut	artichoke	fèves	broad beans
asperges	asparagus	flageolets	white beans
avocat	avocado	fleur de courgette	courgette flower
basilic	basil	genièvre	juniper
betterave	beetroot	gingembre	ginger
blette/bette	swiss chard	haricots verts	string (French) beans
cannelle	cinnamon	...rouges	...kidney beans
câpre	caper	...beurres	...butter beans
cardon	cardoon, a beet related to	...blancs	...white beans
	artichoke	laitue	lettuce
carotte	carrot	laurier	bay leaf
céleri	celery	lentilles	lentils
champignons: cèpes,	mushrooms of various	maïs	corn
chanterelles, girolles,	kinds (red) cabbage	marjoline	marjoram
morilles chou (rouge)		menthe	mint
chou-fleur	cauliflower	navet	turnip
ciboulettes	chives	oignon	onion
concombre	cucumber	panais	parsnip
cornichon	gherkin	pélandron	type of string bean
échalotes	shallots	persil	parsley
endive	chicory	petits pois	peas
épinard	spinach	piment	pimento
épis de maïs	corn on the cob	pois chiches	chickpeas
estragon	tarragon	pois mange-tout	snow peas

pignons	pine nuts	ratatouille	mixture of aubergine, courgette, tomatoes and garlic
poireau	leek		
poivron (vert, rouge)	sweet pepper (green, red)	rémoulade	mustard mayonnaise, sometimes with ancho vies and gherkins, also salad of grated celeriac with mayonnaise
pommes de terre	potatoes		
radis	radishes		
raifort	horseradish		
riz	rice		
romarin	rosemary	parmentier	with potatoes
safran	saffron	sauté	lightly fried in butter
sarrasin	buckwheat	à la vapeur	steamed
sauge	sage	Je suis végétarien(ne)	I'm a vegetarian
serpolet	wild thyme	Il y a des plats sans viande?	Are there any non-meat dishes?
thym	thyme		
tomate	tomato	biologique	organic
truffes	truffles	raclette	toasted cheese served with potatoes, gherkins and onions

DISHES AND TERMS

beignet	fritter	salad Niçoise	salad of tomatoes, radishes, cucumber, hard-boiled eggs, anchovies, onion, artichokes, green peppers, beans, basil and garlic (rarely as compre--hensive, even in Nice)
farci	stuffed		
gratiné	browned with cheese or butter		
jardinière	with mixed diced vegetables		
à la parisienne	sautéed in butter (potatoes); with white wine sauce and shallots		
		duxelles	fried mushrooms and shallots with cream
à l'anglaise	boiled		
à la grecque	cooked in oil and lemon	fines herbes	mixture of tarragon, parsley and chives
râpé(e)s	grated or shredded		
pistou	ground basil, olive oil, garlic and parmesan	frisé(e)	curly
		gousse d'ail	clove of garlic
primeurs	spring vegetables	herbes de Provence	mixture of bay leaf, thyme, rosemary and savory
salade verte	lettuce with vinaigrette		
gratin dauphinois	potatoes baked in cream and garlic		
		petits farcis	stuffed tomatoes, aubergines, courgettes, peppers
mesclum	salad combining several different leaves		
pommes château, fondantes	quartered potatoes sautéed in butter	tapenade	olive and caper paste
		tomates à la provençale	tomatoes baked with breadcrumbs, garlic and parsley
pommes lyonnaise	fried onions and potatoes		

FRUITS (FRUITS), NUTS (NOIX) AND HONEY (MIEL)

abricot	apricot	citron vert	lime
amandes	almonds	dattes	dates
ananas	pineapple	figues	figs
banane	banana	fraises (de bois)	strawberries (wild)
brugnon, nectarine	nectarine	framboises	raspberries
cacahouète	peanut	fruit de la passion	passion fruit
cassis	blackcurrants	grenade	pomegranate
cerises	cherries	groseilles	redcurrants
châtaignes	chestnuts	mangue	mango
citron	lemon	marrons	chestnuts

melon	melon	reine-Claude	greengage
miel de lavande	lavender honey		
mirabelles	small yellow plums	**TERMS**	
myrtilles	bilberries	agrumes	citrus fruits
noisette	hazelnut	beignet	fritter
noix	nuts/ walnut	compôte	stewed fruit
noix de cajou	cashew nut	coulis	sauce of puréed fruit
orange	orange	crème de	chestnut purée
pamplemousse	grapefruit	marrons	
pastèque	watermelon	flambé	set aflame in alcohol
pêche (blanche)	(white) peach	fougasse	bread flavoured with
pistache	pistachio		orange flower water or
poire	pear		almonds, can also be
pomme	apple		savoury
prune	plum	frappé	iced
pruneau	prune		
raisins	grapes		

DESSERTS (DESSERTS OR ENTREMETS), PASTRIES (PATISSERIES) AND CONFECTIONERY (CONFISERIE)

bombe	a moulded ice-cream dessert	petit Suisse	a smooth mixture of cream and curds
brioche	sweet, high-yeast breakfast roll	petits fours	bite-sized cakes/pastries
calissons	almond sweets	poires Belle Hélène	pears and ice cream in chocolate sauce
charlotte	custard and fruit in lining of almond fingers	tarte Tropezienne	sponge cake filled with custard cream topped
chichis	doughnuts shaped in sticks		with nuts
clafoutis	heavy custard and fruit tart	tiramisu	layered pudding of mascarpone cheese,
crème Chantilly	vanilla-flavoured and sweetened whipped cream	truffes	alcohol and coffee truffles
crème fraîche	sour cream	yaourt, yogourt	yoghurt
crème pâtissière	thick eggy pastry-filling	**TERMS**	
crêpes suzettes	thin pancakes with orange juice and liqueur	barquette	small, boat-shaped flan
fromage blanc	cream cheese	bavarois	refers to the mould, could be a mousse or custard
gaufre	waffle	biscuit	a kind of cake
glace	ice cream	chausson	pastry turnover
île flottante/ œufs à la neige	soft meringues floating on custard	chocolat amer	unsweetened chocolate
macarons	macaroons	coupe	a serving of ice cream
madeleine	small sponge cake	crêpes	pancakes
marrons	chestnut purée and cream on a Mont Blanc rum-soaked sponge cake	en feuilletage	in puff pastry
		fondant	melting
		galettes	buckwheat pancakes
		gênoise	rich sponge cake
mousse au chocolat	chocolate mousse	pâte	pastry or dough
		sablé	shortbread biscuit
nougat	nougat	savarin	a filled, ring-shaped cake
palmiers	caramelized puff pastries	tarte	tart
parfait	frozen mousse, some times ice cream	tartelette	small tart

CHEESE (FROMAGE)

The cheeses produced in Provence are all either *chèvre* (made from goat's milk) or *brebis* (made from sheep's milk). The most renowned are the *chèvres*, which include Banon, Picodon, Lou Pevre, Pelardon and Poivre d'Ain.

Le plateau de fromages is the cheeseboard, and bread (but not butter) is served with it. Some useful phrases: *une petite tranche de celui-ci* (a small piece of this one); *je peux le goûter?* (may I taste it?).

Glossary of French terms

abbaye abbey

arrondissement district of a city

assemblée nationale the French parliament

AJ (Auberge de Jeunesse) youth hostel

bastide medieval military settlement, constructed on a grid plan

Beaux-Arts fine arts museum (and school)

borie dry-stone wall, or building made with same

calanque steep-sided inlet on coast, similar to Norwegian fjord, but not glacially formed

car bus

chambre d'hôte room for rent in private house

chasse, chasse gardée hunting grounds

château mansion, country house or castle

château fort castle

chemin path

codene French CND

col mountain pass

consigne luggage store

côte coast

cours combination of main square and main street

couvent convent, monastery

defense de... It is forbidden to...

dégustation tasting (wine or food)

departement county – more or less

donjon castle keep

église church

en panne out of order

entrée entrance

faubourg suburb, often abbreviated to fbg in street names

ferme farm

fermeture closing period

fouilles archeological excavations

gare station; **routière** – bus station; **SNCF** – train station

gîte d'étape basic hostel accommodation primarily for walkers

Gobelins famous tapestry manufacturers, based in Paris; its most renowned period was in the reign of Louis XIV (seventeenth century)

GR (grande randonée) long-distance footpath

halles covered market

hôtel a hotel, but also an aristocratic townhouse or mansion

hôtel de ville town hall

jours fériés public holidays

mairie town hall

marché market

mas provinçal farmhouse

place square

porte gateway

presqu'île peninsula

puy peak or summit

quartier district of a town

relais routiers truckstop café-restaurants

RC (Rez-de-Chaussée) ground floor

RN (Route Nationale) main road

santon ornamental figure used especially in Christmas cribs

SI (Syndicat d'Initiative) tourist information office; also known as OT, OTSI and maison du tourisme

SNCF French railways

sortie exit

tabac bar or shop selling stamps, cigarettes, etc

table d'hôte meal served in lodging at the family table

toue tower

transhumance routes followed by shepherds for taking livestock to and from suitable grazing grounds

Vauban seventeenth-century military architect – his fortresses still stand all over France

vieille ville old quarter of town

vieux port old port

village perché hilltop village

zone bleue restricted parking zone

zone pietonné pedestrian precinct

Glossary of architectural terms

ambulatory covered passage around the outer edge of a choir of a church

apse semicircular termination at the east end of a church

Baroque High Renaissance period of art and architecture, distinguished by extreme ornateness

Carolingian dynasty (and art, sculpture, etc) founded by Charlemagne, late eighth to early tenth century

chevet east end of church, consisting of apse and ambulatory, with or without radiating chapels

Classical architectural style incorporating Greek and Roman elements – pillars, domes, colonnades, etc – at its height in France in the seventeenth century and revived in the nineteenth century as Neoclassical

clerestory upper storey of a church, incorporating the windows

Flamboyant florid form of Gothic

fresco wall painting – durable through application to wet plaster

Gallo-Roman period of Roman occupation of Gaul (first to fourth century AD)

Gothic architectural style prevalent from the twelfth century to the sixteenth century, characterized by pointed arches and ribbed vaulting

Merovingian dynasty (and art, etc) ruling France and parts of Germany from the sixth to mid-eighth century

narthex entrance hall of church

nave main body of a church

Renaissance art-architectural style developed in fifteenth-century Italy and imported to France in the early sixteenth century by François I

retable altarpiece

Romanesque early medieval architecture distinguished by squat, rounded forms and naive sculpture

stucco plaster used to embellish ceilings, etc

transept cross arms of a church

tympanum sculpted panel above a church door

voussoir sculpted rings in arch over church door

Small print and index

A ROUGH GUIDE TO ROUGH GUIDES

Published in 1982, the first Rough Guide – to Greece – was a student scheme that became a publishing phenomenon. Mark Ellingham, a recent graduate in English from Bristol University, had been travelling in Greece the previous summer and couldn't find the right guidebook. With a small group of friends he wrote his own guide, combining a highly contemporary, journalistic style with a thoroughly practical approach to travellers' needs.

The immediate success of the book spawned a series that rapidly covered dozens of destinations. And, in addition to impecunious backpackers, Rough Guides soon acquired a much broader readership that relished the guides' wit and inquisitiveness as much as their enthusiastic, critical approach and value-for-money ethos.

These days, Rough Guides include recommendations from budget to luxury and cover more than 200 destinations around the globe, as well as producing an ever-growing range of eBooks and apps.

Visit **roughguides.com** to see our latest publications.

Rough Guide credits

Editor: Claire Saunders
Layout: Ankur Guha
Cartography: Deshpal Dabas
Picture editor: Natascha Sturny
Proofreader: Susanne Hillen
Managing editor: Monica Woods
Assistant editor: Jalpreen Kaur Chhatwal
Production: Charlotte Cade
Cover design: Nicole Newman, Roger Mapp, Ankur Guha

Editorial assistant: Olivia Rawes
Senior pre-press designer: Dan May
Design director: Scott Stickland
Travel publisher: Joanna Kirby
Digital travel publisher: Peter Buckley
Operations coordinator: Helen Blount
Publishing director (Travel): Clare Currie
Commercial manager: Gino Magnotta
Managing director: John Duhigg

Publishing information

This eighth edition published May 2013 by
Rough Guides Ltd,
80 Strand, London WC2R 0RL
11, Community Centre, Panchsheel Park,
New Delhi 110017, India
Distributed by the Penguin Group
Penguin Books Ltd,
80 Strand, London WC2R 0RL
Penguin Group (USA)
375 Hudson Street, NY 10014, USA
Penguin Group (Australia)
250 Camberwell Road, Camberwell,
Victoria 3124, Australia
Penguin Group (NZ)
67 Apollo Drive, Mairangi Bay, Auckland 1310,
New Zealand
Penguin Group (South Africa)
Block D, Rosebank Office Park, 181 Jan Smuts Avenue,
Parktown North, Gauteng, South Africa 2193
Rough Guides is represented in Canada by Tourmaline
Editions Inc. 662 King Street West, Suite 304, Toronto,
Ontario M5V 1M7
Printed in Malaysia by Vivar Printing Sdn Bhd

432pp includes index
A catalogue record for this book is available from the
British Library
ISBN: 978-1-40936-372-9
The publishers and authors have done their best to
ensure the accuracy and currency of all the information in
The Rough Guide to Provence, however, they can accept
no responsibility for any loss, injury, or inconvenience
sustained by any traveller as a result of information or
advice contained in the guide.
1 3 5 7 9 8 6 4 2

MIX
Paper from
responsible sources
FSC™ C018179
www.fsc.org

Help us update

We've gone to a lot of effort to ensure that the eighth
edition of **The Rough Guide to Provence & the Côte
d'Azur** is accurate and up-to-date. However, things change
– places get "discovered", opening hours are notoriously
fickle, restaurants and rooms raise prices or lower standards.
If you feel we've got it wrong or left something out, we'd like
to know, and if you can remember the address, the price,
the hours, the phone number, so much the better.

Please send your comments with the subject line
"Rough Guide Provence & the Côte d'Azur Update" to
🅐 mail@uk.roughguides.com. We'll credit all contributions
and send a copy of the next edition (or any other Rough
Guide if you prefer) for the very best emails.

Find more travel information, connect with fellow
travellers and book your trip on 🅦 roughguides.com

ABOUT THE AUTHORS

Neville Walker has worked on every edition of this book since 2002, and is also the author or co-author of Rough Guides to Gran Canaria, Germany and Austria. A freelance author and feature writer, he reviews London restaurants and has contributed articles on European travel to magazines and newspapers in the UK, Ireland and the USA. He lives in London and Austria.

Greg Ward has written or co-written twenty Rough Guides titles, including Brittany and Normandy, France, Spain, Greece, the USA, Hawaii, Las Vegas, and, in 2012, the Titanic. For more details, visit his website, ⓦgregward.info.

Acknowledgements

Neville Walker would like to thank Stéphane Onno at the Hotel Floride in Nice, Theresa Foley and the team at DFDS Seaways in Dover, Patrick Daly at the Association of British Travel Organisers to France, Mark Silver at Le Mas Candille, Geoff Hinchley and last but not least Claire and Greg for being so pleasant to work with.

Greg Ward would like to thank Claire Saunders for her hugely creative and constructive editing; Carmel, Graham, Ruby & Lulu Ramsay for their wonderful hospitality; Neville for all his hard work and commitment; and Samantha Cook, the perfect companion for the whole big adventure.

Photo credits

All photos © Rough Guides except the following:
(Key: t-top; c-centre; b-bottom; l-left; r-right)

p.1 Corbis: John Miller/Robert Harding World Imagery
p.2 Corbis: Bertrand Gardel/Hemis
p.4 Corbis: Sylvain Sonnet
p.5 Getty Images: Cornelia Doerr
p.8 Getty Images: DeAgostini
p.9 Corbis: Jon Hicks (b). Getty Images: Brian Lawrence/Photographer's Choice (t); Picture Press RM (c)
p.11 Corbis: David Pattyn/Foto Natura/Minden Pictures (c); Louis Laurent Grandadam (b)
p.12 Corbis: Bertrand Gardel/Hemis
p.13 Corbis: Keren Su (c); Theo Allofs (b); Tristan Deschamps/Photononstop RM (t)
p.14 Corbis: Jean-Daniel Sudres/Hemis (b); Walter Rawlings (tr). Getty Images: VALERY HACHE/AFP (tl); Yann Guichaoua/SuperStock RM (c)
p.15 Corbis: Pierre Jacques/Hemis
p.16 Alamy: Hemis (t). Corbis: Pierre Jacques/Hemis (b)
p.17 Getty Images: BORIS HORVAT/AFP (c)
p.18 Alamy: Tibor Bognar (t). Getty Images: DEA PICTURE LIBRARY/DeAgostini (c)
p.19 Corbis: Romain Cintract/Hemis (t). Getty Images: Brian Lawrence (b)
p.20 Alamy: JOHN KELLERMAN (tr). Getty Images: Picture Press RM (tl)
p.42 Getty Images: David C Tomlinson
p.45 Corbis: Chris Hellier
p.65 Corbis: Camille Moirenc/Hemis (t)
p.80 SuperStock: Minden Pictures
p.83 SuperStock: Antonio Moreno
p.99 Alamy: Yadid Levy (bl). Corbis: Camille Moirenc/Hemis (br); Franck Guiziou/Hemis (t)

p.110 Corbis: Pierre Jacques/Hemis
p.113 SuperStock: Peter Schickert
p.141 Corbis: MOIRENC Camille/Hemis (b); Tim De Waele (t)
p.150 Corbis: Franck Guiziou/Hemis
p.153 Alamy: Didier ZYLBERYNG
p.167 Alamy: kpzfoto (br); Maria Grazia Casella (t)
p.196 Corbis: Sergio Pitamitz
p.199 Corbis: Sylvain Sonnet
p.207 Alamy: Travel Pictures (br). Corbis: Camille Moirenc/Hemis (t)
p.231 Corbis: Atlantide Phototravel
p.246 Getty Images: Photononstop RM
p.249 SuperStock: GARDEL Bertrand
p.273 Corbis: Bertrand Gardel/Hemis (t). SuperStock: MOIRENC Camille (b)
p.300 Corbis: Camille Moirenc/Hemis
p.303 Alamy: Ian Dagnall
p.331 Corbis: Laurent Giraudou (br). Getty Images: STEPHANE DANNA/AFP (t)
p.343 Corbis: Construction Photography
p.351 Alamy: LOOK Die Bildagentur der Fotografen GmbH (t). Getty Images: Wendy Connett (b)
p.388 Alamy: Peter Barritt

Front cover Field of sunflowers © SuperStock: Cornelia Doerr
Back cover St-Tropez harbour © Getty/Sylvain Sonnet; Bouches de Rhone ©Corbis: Camille Moirenc

Index

Maps are marked in grey

Map symbols

The symbols below are used on maps throughout the book

⊠ Post office	∴ Ruins/archeological site	〣 Waterfall	〒 Lighthouse
ⓘ Tourist office	⚍ Campsite	⚘ Viewpoint	🐦 Bird/nature sanctuary
🅿 Parking	⌂ Refuge	Cliffs	⛪ Church/chapel
♦ Point of interest	♜ Chateau	▲ Mountain peak	Building
⊙ Statue	♜ Fort	✈ Airport	Stadium
⌣ Bridge	⛪ Monastery	★ Bus stop	Park
● Museum	⛷ Skiing	Ⓜ Metro station	Beach
⌂ Abbey	⚓ Swimming	— Tramway	Cemetery

Listings key

■ Accommodation

● Restaurant/café/bar

■ Club/nightlife/live music

● Shop

MAKE THE MOST OF YOUR CITY BREAK

NEW YORK CITY   HONG KONG & MACAU   BERLIN   MARRAKESH   ROME

FREE PULL OUT MAP WITH EVERY SIGHT AND LISTING FROM THE GUIDE

ESSENTIAL ITINERARIES AND RELIABLE RECOMMENDATIONS